ON KUYPER

ON KUYPER

A COLLECTION OF READINGS ON THE LIFE, WORK & LEGACY OF ABRAHAM KUYPER

Edited by
Steve Bishop and John H. Kok

DORDT COLLEGE PRESS
2013

Cover design by Robert Haan
Cover image: public domain
Layout by Carla Goslinga

Unless otherwise noted quotations from Scripture are taken from the NIV.
Scripture taken from the HOLY BIBLE, NEW INTERNATIONAL VERSION˚. NIV˚. Copyright
© 1973, 1978, 1984 by International Bible Society. Used by permission of Zondervan
Publishing House. All rights reserved.

Printed in the United States of America.

Dordt College Press   www.dordt.edu/dordt_press
498 Fourth Avenue NE
Sioux Center, Iowa 51250
    United States of America

ISBN: 978-0-932914-96-5

Library of Congress Cataloging-in-Publication Data

On Kuyper : a collection of readings on the life, work & legacy of Abraham Kuyper /
Edited by Steve Bishop and John H. Kok.
      pages cm
  Includes bibliographical references.
  ISBN 978-0-932914-96-5 (pbk. : alk. paper. 1. Kuyper, Abraham, 1837-1920. I.
      Bishop, Steve, 1958- II. Kok, John H.
  BX9479.K8O5 2013
  284'.2092--dc23
  [B]
                    2013009715

Table of Contents

PART I

Kuyper, the man and his context

Kuyper the politician

Kuyper the church reformer

Kuyper the theologian

PART II

Kuyper and cultural trends

Kuyper and education

Kuyper and common grace

Kuyper and sphere sovereignty

Acknowledgements

The following articles contain slightly revised versions of the original published forms. All are reprinted with the permission of the authors, editors, and/or publishers.

Our thanks go to the authors for permitting publication in this volume and to David Hanson and Todd Steen for providing copies of papers.

Van Dyke, Harry 1998. "Abraham Kuyper: heir of anti-revolutionary tradition." Paper presented at the international conference "Christianity and Culture: The Heritage of Abraham Kuyper on Different Continents" held on 9–11 June 1998, Free University, Amsterdam.

Kuyper, Catherine M. E. 1960. "Abraham Kuyper: his early life and conversion." *International Reformed Bulletin* 3.

Bratt, James D. 1987. "Raging tumults of soul: the private life of Abraham Kuyper." *The Reformed Journal* 37(11): 9–13.

Henderson, R. D. 1992. "How Abraham Kuyper became a Kuyperian." *Christian Scholar's Review* 22 (1): 22–35.

Van Dyke, Harry 1998. "How Abraham Kuyper became a Christian Democrat." *Calvin Theological Journal* 33(1): 420–435.

Langley, McKendree R. 1979. "The political spirituality of Abraham Kuyper." *International Reformed Bulletin* 76.

McGoldrick, James Edward 1994. "Every inch for Christ: Abraham Kuyper on the reform of the church." *Reformation & Revival Journal* (Fall): 91–99.

Venema, Cornelius, P. 1999. "Abraham Kuyper – his life and legacy. Part 5 of 6." *Outlook* (Jan): 15–19; and Part 6 of 6 *Outlook* (Feb): 17–21.

McGoldrick, James Edward 2008. "Claiming every inch: the worldview of Abraham Kuyper." In *A Christian Worldview*. Taylors, SC: Presbyterian Press.

Bacote, Vincent 1997. "Called back to stewardship: recovering and developing Kuyper's cosmic pneumatology." *Journal for Christian Theological Research* 2(3).

Palmer, Timothy P. 2008. "The two-kingdom doctrine: a comparison study of Martin Luther and Abraham Kuyper." *Pro Rege* 37(3): 13–25

Ericson, Edward E. 1987. "Abraham Kuyper: cultural critic." *Calvin Theological Journal* 22(2): 210–227.

Strauss, D. F. M. 1999. "The viability of Kuyper's idea of Christian scholarship." *Journal for Christian Scholarship* 125–139.

Bacote, Vincent 2008. "Abraham Kuyper's rhetorical public theology with implications for faith and learning." *Christian Scholar's Review* 37(4): 407–425.

Zuidema, S. U. 1972. "Common grace and Christian action in Abraham Kuyper." In *Communication and Confrontation*. Translated by Harry Van Dyke. Toronto: Wedge, 52–105.

Klapwijk, J. 1991. "Antithesis and common grace." In *Bringing Into Captivity Every Thought*, edited by J. Klapwijk, S. Griffioen and G. Groenewoud. Translated by Herbert Donald Morton. Lanham: University Press of America, ch. 8.

McConnel Timothy I. 2002. "Common grace or the antithesis? Toward a consistent understanding of Kuyper's "sphere sovereignty." *Pro Rege* 31(1): 1–13.

Vollenhoven, D. H. Th. 1998. "Sphere sovereignty for Kuyper and for us." Translated by John H. Kok. Originally published as "De souvereiniteit in eigen kring bij Kuyper en ons." *Mededelingen van de Vereniging voor Calvinistische Wijsbegeerte* (December, 1950) 4–7. This translated version was first published in *Philosophy as Responsibility: A Celebration of Hendrik Hart's Contribution to the Discipline*, edited by Roel Kuipers and Janet Catherine Wesselius. Toronto: University Press of America, 2002.

Ratzsch, Del 1992. "Abraham Kuyper's philosophy of science." *Calvin Theological Journal* 27: 277–303.

Menninga. Clarence 1998. "Critical reflections of Abraham Kuyper's *Evolutie* address." *Calvin Theological Journal* 33(2): 435–443.

Heslam, Peter S. 1999. "A theology of the arts: Kuyper's ideas on art and religion." In *Kuyper Reconsidered. Aspects of his life and Work*, edited by Cees van der Kooi and Jan de Bruijn. Amsterdam, VU Uitgeverij.

Covolo, Robert S. 2009. "Re-fashioning faith: the promise of a Kuyperian theology of fashion." *Cultural Encounters* 5(2): 41–62.

Sherratt, Timothy 1999. "Rehabilitating the State in America: Kuyper's overlooked contribution." *Christian Scholar's Review* 29(2): 323–346.

Skillen, James 2004. "*E pluribus unum* and faith-based welfare reform: a Kuyperian moment for the church in God's world." *In Pursuit Of Justice: Christian-Democratic Explorations*. Rowman & Littlefield and Center for Public Justice, ch 4.

Harinck, George 2002. "Abraham Kuyper, South Africa, and apartheid." *The Princeton Seminary Bulletin* 23(2): 184–187.

Van Leeuwen, Mary Stuart 1996. "Abraham Kuyper and the cult of true womanhood: an analysis of *De Eerepositie der Vrouw*." *Calvin Theological Journal* 31(1): 97–124.

Van de Streek, Hillie J. 1998. "Kuyper's legacy and multiculturalism: gender in his conception of democracy and sphere sovereignty." *Pro Rege* 27(1): 16–24. This paper was originally prepared for the Conference on Christianity and Culture: The Heritage of Abraham Kuyper on Different Continents, June 9–11, 1998, Amsterdam, The Netherlands.

The following are published for the first time:

Gousmett, Chris "Abraham Kuyper on creation and miracle."

Wagenman, Michael R. "Abraham Kuyper and the church: from Calvin to the neo-Calvinists."

Dooyeweerd, H. "Kuyper's philosophy of science." Translation by D. F. M. Strauss. The original version was published as "Kuypers wetenschapsleer." *Philosophia Reformata* (1939) 4: 193-232.

Klapwijk, J. "Abraham Kuyper on science, theology, and university." The original version was published as "Abraham Kuyper over wetenschap en universiteit." In *Abraham Kuyper, zijn volksdeel, zijn invloed.* Edited by C. Augustijn, J. H. Prins, and H. E. S. Woldring. Delft: Meinema, 1987. This revised version was translated by Herbert Donald Morton and Gerben Groenewoud.

Abbreviations used throughout this volume:

AK:ACR   *Abraham Kuyper: A Centennial Reader*, edited by James D. Bratt. Grand Rapids/Carlisle: Eerdmans/Paternoster, 1998.

GG   Kuyper, Abraham 1902–05. *De Gemeene Gratie.* 3 vols. Kampen: Kok; 3rd ed. 1931–32. Kuyper, *De Gemeene Gratie*, Vols. I–III. Leiden, 1902–05, Vol. IV. Leiden, 1905; hereafter cited as *GG*, according to the 3rd unaltered (pagination moved up 4) impression. 3 vols.; Kampen, 1931–32.

LC   Kuyper, Abraham [1899] 1931. *Lectures on Calvinism.* Grand Rapids: Eerdmans (various identical reprints over the years).

PP   Kuyper's opening address at the First Christian Social Congress in the Netherlands on 9 November 1891, *Het sociale Vraagstuk en de Christelijke Religie*, Amsterdam: Wormser, 1891, was translated by Dirk Jellema under the title *Christianity and the Class Struggle*, Grand Rapids: Piet Hein, 1950. In 1991 James W. Skillen's "thorough revision" of the Jellema translation appeared under the title *The Problem of Poverty*, Washington DC/Grand Rapids: Center for Public Justice/Baker, 1991. In 2011, Skillen's introduction and translation (plus Roger Henderson's essay "How Abraham Kuyper became a Kuyperian") were republished under the same title: *The Problem of Poverty*, Sioux Center: Dordt College Press, 2011. All page references are to this most recent printing.

PrRege   Kuyper, Abraham 1911–1912. *Pro Rege, of het Koningschap van Christus*, 3 vols. Kampen: Kok.

PST   Kuyper, Abraham *Principles of Sacred Theology* [1898]. Grand Rapids: Baker, 1980. (First published in 1898 by Charles Scribner's Sons, under the title *Encyclopedia of Sacred Theology*.) Kuyper, Abraham 1899. *Encyclopedia of Sacred Theology: Its Principles.* Translated by John Hendrik De Vries. London: Hodder and Stoughton.

WoHS   Kuyper, Abraham 1900. *The Work of the Holy Spirit.* Translated by Henri De Vries. New York: Funk & Wagnalls (reprinted, Grand Rapids: Eerdmans, 1979).

On Kuyper: An Introduction

Steve Bishop

Abraham Kuyper was born in Maassluis in the nineteenth century and he died in The Hague in the twentieth century, but his impact and legacy stretch well into the twenty-first century. In his day Kuyper sought to awake Christians from "a pietistic slumber."[1] Today his work and writings are helping many to see the fullness of God's good creation and to dispel the dualistic daydream that has had many under its spell.

In this volume we have scholars using the Kuyperian framework to critique and develop Christian perspectives on the church, miracles, education, politics, scholarship, fashion, art, science . . . as Kuyper famously declared:

> no single piece of our mental world is to be hermetically sealed off from the rest, and there is not a square inch in the whole domain of our human existence over which Christ, who is Sovereign over *all*, does not cry: "Mine!"[2]

No area of life is exempt from the claims of the risen Christ. This was certainly true for Kuyper; he not only preached it he lived it.

Who was Kuyper?

In a sense it depends on whom you ask. He was a multifaceted and multitalented character. He was born in a liberal Calvinistic home, studied at a modernist university and became a church pastor. He was then converted. He was a newspaper editor; he edited two newspapers *De Heraut* and *De Standaard*. He shaped a new Christian political party, the Anti-Revolutionary Party, became a politician and founded a new church denomination – all while working as a church pastor. He was active in the advancement of Christian schools and education and founded a Christian university. He was a theologian; he was the first professor of theology at the Free University (VU) and wrote an important work on the Holy Spirit. He also found time to become the prime minister of Holland (1901–1905). He certainly took seriously his square inch theology!

It is not surprising that in 1898 B. B. Warfield, who claimed to have learned Dutch so he could read Kuyper, said of him:

> Dr. Kuyper is probably to-day the most considerable figure in both political and ecclesiastical Holland.[3]

Kuyper has been described as a renaissance man, and this renaissance man is certainly undergoing a renaissance. John Vriend, one of Kuyper's translators, maintained that the

---

1 Bratt, James 1997. "The Dutch Schools." In *Reformed Theology in America*, edited by David F. Wells. Grand Rapids: Baker, ch.5, 121.

2 "Sphere Sovereignty." In *AK:ACR* 488.

3 Warfield, B. B. [1898]. "Introductory Note." In *PST* xii.

twenty-first century was the "real Kuyper century."[4] If we look at the number of books, papers, and articles that have recently been published on or about Kuyper, it certainly looks that way.

This reader provides evidence that work on Kuyper and Kuyperianism is alive and well. The bibliography at the end of this book identifies well over 350 works that have been written on or about Kuyper. Unfortunately, only a small selection can be made more accessible in this volume.

Why the Resurgence of Interest?

In an age of individualism and narcissism, Kuyper's transformative message stands in sharp prophetic contrast. The neo-Calvinism of Kuyper provides a clear biblical framework in which to apply Christianity to all areas of life. Many contemporary theologians are looking for a social theology. Kuyper marked out one and implemented it over a century ago! As one biographer writes: "Although Kuyper never preached the social gospel, he did frequently accentuate the social implications of the gospel."[5]

Several key themes have helped shape Kuyper's approach to culture. These include: the sovereignty of God, the cultural mandate, worldview, common grace, the antithesis, and sphere sovereignty many of which come under scrutiny in articles in this volume. These themes provided the theological and theoretical framework for Kuyper's neo-Calvinism.

The Contours of a Kuyperian Neo-Calvinism

The sovereignty of God

If God is sovereign, then his lordship must extend over all of life, and it cannot be restricted to the walls of the church or within the Christian orbit. The non-Christian world has not been handed over to Satan, nor surrendered to fallen humanity, nor consigned to fate. God's sovereignty is great and all-dominating in the life of that unbaptized world as well. Therefore Christ's church on earth and God's child cannot simply retreat from this life. If the believer's God is at work in this world, then in this world the believer's hand must take hold of the plow, and the name of the Lord must be glorified in that activity as well.[6]

These words from the preface to *De Gemeene Gratie* sum up Kuyper's position. It starts and ends with the sovereignty of God. If God is sovereign, and he is, then cultural development is essential: retreating from the world is not an option.

Sphere sovereignty

All things then are subject to the sovereignty of God. This led Kuyper, following Groen van Prinsterer, to develop a theory that became known as sphere sovereignty. There are different independent spheres, but God is sovereign over them all.

This notion provided a corrective to Statism, which maintained that the State makes laws and regulations and is in control over many areas of life. Sphere sovereignty starts from the sovereignty of God rather than the State or any other created thing.

---

4 Cited on John Boer's Social theology website http://www.socialtheology.com/kuyperiana.htm [accessed 16 December 2012].
5 Vanden Berg, Frank 1978. *Abraham Kuyper: A Biography.* St Catherines, Ontario: Paideia Press. (Original edition Eerdmans, 1960.)
6 Kuyper, A. "Preface." *De Gemeene Gratie.*

In his 1880 inaugural address to the VU, he outlined his idea of sphere sovereignty.[7] This provided the justification for, for example, separate schools and universities. The VU, founded by Kuyper was to be a free university, free from state or even church control.

Sphere sovereignty maintains that the only sovereign is God. He has established laws or norms for other areas of society such as the family, the church and so on. Within their own sphere these areas are thus sovereign under God's laws and norms for that aspect of life. No one institution should dominate or dictate to another, there is no hierarchy of institutions. This development and flourishing of every area is an outworking of the cultural mandate.

The cultural mandate

Kuyper's square inch quote, cited above, is an embodiment of the cultural mandate given in Genesis 1:26–28 and Genesis 2:15. This subduing, ruling, tilling and keeping is in part a mandate for the development of culture, for the unfolding of the potentialities within the God-given good creation. It is expressing the kingdom of Christ in all areas of life; no areas are exempt.

Christianity as a Weltanschauung (creation, fall and redemption)

When Kuyper first introduced Christians to the notion of worldview in his 1898 *Lectures on Calvinism* it was fresh, innovative and radical (*LC* 11). Now it is *de rigueur* to talk of a Christian worldview. Kuyper first identified the main Christian worldview in terms of the narrative embedded within creation, fall and redemption – again these ideas have become the starting point for most discussions on cultural issues.

Common grace

One major theme that has been closely associated with neo-Calvinism, and Kuyper and Bavinck in particular, is common grace.[8] Henry Van Til described Kuyper as the "theologian of common grace."[9] Common grace is bestowed on all: Christians and non-Christians.

Kuyper distinguished between particular grace – sometimes called saving grace – and common grace. The first abolishes and undoes sin completely for the saved; the second extends to the whole of human life.[10] For Kuyper there is a close relationship between the

---

7   "Sphere Sovereignty." In *AK:ACR*.

8   Louis Berkhof claims that "Up to the present Kuyper and Bavinck did more than any one else for the development of the doctrine of common grace." *Systematic Theology*. Edinburgh: The Banner of Truth Trust, 1958, 434.

9   Van Til, Henry R. 1972. *The Calvinistic Concept of Culture*. Philadelphia: Presbyterian and Reformed, ch. 8. His chapter on Kuyper is titled: "Abraham Kuyper: Theologian of Common Grace and the Kingship of Christ."

   Kuyper wrote a series of articles over a six-year period on the topic of common grace for *De Heraut*. These were subsequently published in three volumes as *De Gemeene Gratie* (*GG*) in 1902, 1903 and 1904. A major translation project is under way to translate these works into English. Part has been translated as "Common Grace." In *AK:ACR* 165–201. The first fruits of the *GG* project have been published: Kuyper, A. 2011. *Wisdom & Wonder: Common Grace in Science & Art*. Translated by Nelson Kloosterman. Grand Rapids: Christian's Library Press. These chapters didn't appear in the Dutch *GG* because of a publisher's oversight and had to be published separately.

10 "Common Grace." In *AK:ACR* 168. Referenced in what follows as *CG*.

two and separation "must be vigorously opposed" (*CG* 185). He uses the illustration of two branches of a tree that are intertwined but have the same root system (*CG* 186). That root system is Christ, the firstborn of all creation. His position on special and common grace is Christological; Kuyper writes: "There is . . . no doubt whatever that common grace and special grace come most intimately connected from their origin, and this connection lies in Christ" (*CG* 187). Special grace, he asserts, "assumes common grace" (*CG* 169). Common grace is only an emanation of special grace and that all its fruit flows into special grace (*CG* 170). Common grace must have a formative impact on special grace and vice versa (*CG* 185).

Common grace means that the creation ordinance of dominion over nature given in the cultural mandate before the fall can be realized after the fall (*CG* 179).

Common grace has a twofold effect: it tempers and transforms. On the one hand it curbs the effects of sin and restrains fallen humanity. On the other it upholds the ordinances of creation and provides the basis for Christian cultural involvement; common grace provides the foundation for culture. The cultural mandate to develop and fill the earth has not been rescinded. Therefore, cultural withdrawal is not an option for Christians.

It is also important to state what common grace does not imply. It is not a saving grace. It is not a denial of total depravity or of limited atonement – Kuyper was an advocate of both. It does not blur the distinction between the regenerate and the unregenerate, between the kingdom of light and the kingdom of darkness, between the church and the world. It does not mean that all things are permissible. Common grace does not nullify the antithesis – they are both important aspects of Kuyper's thought. Though how he held them together is open to debate. It is important that common grace and the antithesis are seen together.

Incidentally, Kuyper never claimed originality in his development of common grace; rather, he described himself as a copyist of Calvin. Kuyper made explicit what was implicit in Calvin.

The antithesis

Antithesis means opposition. In the nineteenth century Hegel utilized the term; however, in Kuyperian thought it took on a different connotation. It marked a difference between those who held to a Christian starting point and to those who did not; the difference was in worldview. There is an antithesis between those who start with the knowledge of God and those who do not. Hence, we can have two kinds of science: regenerate and unregenerate; each system has different starting points.

This is in part one of the reasons why Kuyper advocated separate institutions for Christians. A Christian political party will have separate starting points from a party based on naturalistic lines. The foundations will be different and so the outworkings will be different. Commitment to Christ can't be accommodated or harmonized with naturalism or any other non-Christian philosophy. There is a cosmic battle: between light and dark, between the kingdom of God and the dominion of Satan. There is a marked contrast between belief and unbelief.

This notion of antithesis is integral to the idea of worldviews.

The aim of this book is to provide an introduction to Kuyper's life and thought through the eyes of others. The breadth and scope of these articles all stand as testimony to

Kuyper's desire to see the lordship of Christ extend to every area of life.

Those unfamiliar with Kuyper would do well to read the two general articles by James McGoldrick and then the more biographical works by Kuyper's daughter Catherine Kuyper, and then those of James Bratt and Roger Henderson. The cultural context that Kuyper was born into is well described and discussed in Harry Van Dyke's article that opens this volume.

I am grateful to all the authors here for allowing publication of their work – each have brought to light important and significant aspects of the life and work of Kuyper.

1

Abraham Kuyper:
Heir of an Anti-Revolutionary Tradition

Harry Van Dyke

Introduction

During the commemoration of Kuyper's Stone Lectures in Princeton last February 1998[1] one might have gained the impression that Abraham Kuyper had been a blazing comet who lit up the sky for a time and then disappeared beyond the horizon; he came from nowhere and then vanished without a trace. Of course we knew better, yet no one so much as mentioned that he had many forerunners and many followers. It is the thesis of this paper that Kuyper rejuvenated Dutch Calvinism – brought it "into rapport with the times" – by building on a movement that was nearly a hundred years old. Kuyper's many followers, who in turn built on him, deserve extensive treatment all their own, something I will not undertake here. As for his forerunners, each made unique contributions to a tradition that he would utilize and turn to political profit. The following notes on these forerunners may help explain the impact Kuyper had in his own day. I would like to introduce you to Bilderdijk, Da Costa, Groen van Prinsterer, Heldring, Wormser, Esser, and Kater.

1. Willem Bilderdijk (1756–1831): Framing a Worldview

Born in the same year as Mozart and dying in the same year as Hegel, Bilderdijk was both an artist (albeit as a poet) and a philosopher (though an amateur one). He straddled the eighteenth and nineteenth centuries and was an incorrigible Romantic who resisted the Enlightenment philosophically but also politically. When in 1795 French and Patriot armies inundated his country and installed a Revolutionary regime, this practicing lawyer refused to swear the new oath of allegiance and was forced into exile. During the Restoration years the now old man earned a modest living as a private lecturer in Leyden. He attracted students of some of the better families in the land, "corrupting the flower of our youth" (as one observer noted anxiously) by means of bitter invectives against the spirit of the age and blistering attacks on the received opinions of the ruling elite. He delivered himself of his highflying harangues in a dazzling display of astonishing erudition. In his forceful way Bilderdijk broke the monopoly of the Regent interpretation of Dutch history,

---

1   Paper read at the international conference "Christianity and Culture: The Heritage of Abraham Kuyper on Different Continents," held on 9–11 June 1998, Free University, Amsterdam. Select portions were used in an essay in honor of Professor John C. Vander Stelt in Kok, John H. ed. 2001. *Marginal Resistance*. Sioux Center: Dordt College Press, 1–23.

a version which (not unlike British Whiggism) attributed the growth of liberty to the republican forefathers of the ruling middle classes, in disregard of the role of the Reformed Church and the House of Orange. Thirteen volumes of his *History of the Fatherland* were published posthumously, as were 16 volumes of his *Collected Poems*.

I want to look with you at one of his poems, a poem that I believe characterizes the Tradition we are here tracing. In his sonnet of 1786, *De Wareld*, Bilderdijk passes in review the great schools of philosophy throughout Western history in order to find an answer to one of the most fundamental questions mankind can pose: What is the world? Can we unlock its secret and know it in its deepest essence? Here is my poor but best approximation of that poem:

The World

What are you, structured frame 'yond mental powers' clasp?
  Chain of effect and cause, to which there is no end,
  Whose possibility the mind can't comprehend,
Whose actuality our reason fails to grasp?

O deep abyss, where can our consciousness then enter?
  What are you? Mere appearance, pressed upon the sense?
  An imprint of the mind, remaining ever dense?
A notion that we forge, like a conceited mentor?

  Or is your being then external to, though near me?
  Do you exist? Is not existence just illusion?
Or of some other being but a mere effusion?

  Thus did I fret myself, until God answered: Hear me!
  All things depend on me; whatever is, is mine:
The whole world is my voice, and summons you to fear me.

In the first quatrain the poet wonders whether the mystery of the universe will yield to human understanding. Line 2: Is the world a universal concatenation of causes – as the Stoics taught? Lines 3 and 4: This the mind can hardly conceive: the world just is – but don't ask how.

The second quatrain gives voice to modern philosophers. Line 6: Is the world mere sense perception – as British empiricism held? Lines 7 and 8: Or a mental impression only, a concept, an idea – as maintained in German idealism?

Thus the octet proceeds, as Danie Strauss points out,[2] from ancient philosophical skepticism to modern philosophical subjectivism which grounds reality in the creative powers of the human mind. The journey has not laid the poet's quest to rest; other schools of thought will now be consulted. This marks the turn in the sestet of the sonnet. Line 9: In the Middle Ages solipsism was avoided by affirming the reality of substance, with objective existence outside of oneself. Line 10: But perhaps "existence" is no more than an illusion? Line 11: Or perhaps an emanation from a higher Being – as Neoplatonists believed?

Still the poet finds no rest in any of these answers. His survey of philosophy has only wearied him. So he goes straight to the source of all Wisdom. Here, at line 12, is the real turn in the sonnet: God himself instructs him how to understand the world: The world is a word, and it says: Fear God and keep his commandments, for this is the whole duty of

---

2 Strauss, D. F. M. n.d. In *Roeping en Riglyne* (undated offprint).

man. That is the conclusion of the matter.

According to the Bilderdijk scholar Jan Bosch, this poem contains Bilderdijk's world-view in a nutshell: "the calling voice of God that resonates in the human heart."[3] Even more importantly, as Bosch also notes, the sonnet marks the "first attempt in Dutch at a Christian totalizing thought oriented to the true Origin of the cosmos."[4] Herman Bavinck has remarked that for Bilderdijk everything that is, is an image or analogy "pointing to a spiritual world which lies behind it and which reveals something of the virtues and perfections of God"; the creature has no existence in and of itself, and must be given its being from moment to moment by the Creator.[5]

To return to the sonnet: its significance lies particularly, I feel, in its attempt to frame a comprehensive approach to the burden of philosophy; one that proceeds unequivocally from the Christian concept of creation and resolutely renounces all notions of the self-sufficiency of the world and of human autonomy – whatever is, depends on God, and is oriented toward Him in a perpetually restless mode of being. Of special appeal is the unabashed confessional stance taken in the heart of a philosophical "dialogue," one that is intensely relevant to the dialogue. In the face of centuries of metaphysical speculation, Bilderdijk reaches directly for a biblical response. We know from history that the personal life of the poet was compromised, but not his life-principle. To be sure, the question has been raised – in the splendid intellectual biography that came out earlier this year – whether the sonnet is a true reflection of the poet's own conception at this time,[6] but this question, however intriguing, is not germane to our inquiry here. What the published sonnet did was adjure contemporaries to resist the temptation to compromise with worldly patterns of thought; it encouraged them not to be timid in the face of the canon of Western philosophy – not to hesitate about the perfect right of Revelation to instruct Reason. Bilderdijk's answer foreshadows Kuyper's emphasis on taking creation as one's starting point also for thought. True, Kuyper may have claimed a bit too much in his commemoration address on the sesquicentennial of Bilderdijk's birth,[7] but he was right in recognizing Bilderdijk as a man of importance not only for the Dutch nation but also for the Calvinist revival of the nineteenth century. Bilderdijk wrote many tracts in defense of the faith of the Reformation, heaping scorn upon its modern detractors. We might not want to go so far as to assert with the author of a popular biography that Bilderdijk carried the old-time religion single-handedly, Noah-like, from the old world of its near total eclipse into the new world of the nineteenth century, where it would flourish once more.[8] Yet we do appreciate Bilderdijk's historical significance in having been a preserving force in a destructive age. The age was killing the faith of the Reformation but Bilderdijk's pen was one of the instruments that helped to keep it alive, thus inaugurating a tradition that would be both aggressive in confronting modern culture and comprehensive in positing its counterclaims.

3 Bosch, J. 1961. "Willem Bilderdijk als wijsgerig historievormer," in *Perspectief; feestbundel van de jongeren bij het 25-jarig bestaan van de Vereniging voor Calvinistische Wijsbegeerte*. Kampen: Kok, 228–40, at 233.

4 Ibid., 229.

5 Bavinck, H. 1906. *Bilderdijk als denker en dichter*. Kampen: Kok, 56.

6 Van Eijnatten, Joris 1998. *Hogere sferen: de ideeënwereld van Willem Bilderdijk*. Hilversum: Verloren, 84.

7 Kuyper, A. 1906. *Bilderdijk in zijne nationale beteekenis; rede gehouden te Amsterdam op 1 Oct. 1906*. Amsterdam and Pretoria: Höveker & Wormser.

8 Van Reest, Rudolf 1940. *'n Onbegriepelijk mensch; het leven van Mr W. Bilderdijk*, 2nd impr. Goes: Oosterbaan & Le Cointre, 259, 270–71.

2. Isaac da Costa (1798–1860): Challenging the Spirit of the Age

The story of this Sephardic Jew from Amsterdam begins with the conversion of him and his cousin and bosom friend Abraham Capadose around 1818 in Leyden, where both were studying law. The two friends would be lifelong members of the *Réveil* in the Netherlands, a movement that kindled evangelical fervor well beyond the middle of the century. The movement was a revival of Christian faith and the Christian life, the resultant of an indigenous revived Calvinism (as represented by Bilderdijk) and important influences from abroad, notably Switzerland. The Réveil became the nursery of resistance to any dechristianization of Dutch society. Ultimately it was to put Reformed people back in the center of public life. Its aim was to rechristianize modern culture using modern means, under the motto, "faith working by love."

The birth cry of the Dutch awakening is generally held to have been Isaac da Costa's notorious broadside of 1823, *Grievances Against the Spirit of the Age*. In rather intemperate language the tract fulminated against the shallow optimism of the time and derided the complacent beliefs in social progress and human perfectibility. It was a declaration of war on the Enlightenment project as this was beginning to make headway in the Netherlands – a pointed repudiation of that project's basic premise: human autonomy, the banning of Christian principles from the seats of learning and from the public arena.

Public opinion was so scandalized by the pamphlet that its author's home for a time was under police protection. The aging Bilderdijk came to the defense of his pupil, but this only added to the ire of "progressive" newspapers like the Arnhem *Courant*, which lampooned Da Costa as "the conceited monkey of the old baboon."[9] Eventually Da Costa saw himself compelled to abandon his legal practice and spend the rest of his days as a man of letters, as a lecturer (by subscription) on historical and religious subjects, and as the host of Sunday *soirées* where he led in Bible study bathed in prayer and song.[10]

By midcentury Isaac da Costa had developed into a forward-looking Christian citizen. He espoused the need to update the tools of orthodox Christians in order to help them stay abreast of their times, not just for self-preservation but also for being a more effective witness. Not only would scientific theology have to be taken vigorously in hand, but a progressive political program would have to be developed in which the eternal principles of the Word of God would be applied to the problems of the day. The Revolution of 1795, and again of 1848, while evil in themselves, had nevertheless afforded ways and means, such as participatory government and disestablishment, of which Christians should avail themselves to contribute to the "unfolding of God's counsel for mankind." We are to be *against* our age, but also *of* our age, he wrote to his friend Groen van Prinsterer.[11] The year before, Da Costa had been instrumental in organizing a voters' association in his riding in Amsterdam and writing a program for it – "in its essence, a fruit of *the* ages; in its form, of *this* age!" – or as he would put it in another one of his occasional poems: We will not be led by the spirit of the age and its errant light, yet we shall always distinguish the *spirit* of

---

9   Cf. Westerhuis, D. J. A. 1925. "De 'Arnhemsche Courant' contra Da Costa ultimo anno 1823." *Stemmen des Tijds* 14(3): 370–77.

10 See Ten Zythoff, Gerrit J. 1987. *Sources of Secession: The Netherlands Hervormde Kerk on the Eve of the Dutch Immigration to the Midwest.* Grand Rapids: Eerdmans, 57–97; cf. Kluit, M. E. 1970. *Het Protestantse Réveil in Nederland en daarbuiten, 1815–1865.* Amsterdam: H. J. Paris, 167.

11 Da Costa to Groen, 18 July 1852; in *Brieven van Mr. Isaac da Costa*, ed. Van Prinsterer, G. Groen 3 vols. (Amsterdam, 1873), 2: 91–93.

the age from the *course* of the age.[12]

There was much common sense in Da Costa's strategy: "The malady of our age must be combated with the means which, by God's all-wise providence, are given in the malady itself. . . . No abolition of constitutions, no formal restoration of a Calvinist state and church can give us back the historical and truly spiritual principle. . . . The enemy must be conquered, at any rate combated, on his own terrain. . . ."[13]

This last statement foreshadowed the realignment of cultural forces that began to show its initial contours in the 1850s under the leadership of Groen van Prinsterer.

3. Guillaume Groen van Prinsterer (1801–76): Opposing Principle with Principle

Like Da Costa, Groen van Prinsterer decided early on that he had to be in fundamental opposition to the whole tenor of his age. Attendance at Bilderdijk's private lectures during his student years at Leyden first sowed the seeds of this nonconformism. Such a stance might have condemned Wim Groen (as he was known) to a lifetime of sterile reaction, were it not for his belief that a third way was possible, a path between revolution and counterrevolution, an approach to problems that would be *anti-revolutionary* – that is, opposed to the "systematic overturning of ideas" whereby truth and justice are founded on human opinion rather than divine ordinance – and simultaneously an approach that would be *Christian-historical* – that is, open to revealed norms for human life, corroborated by the experience of the ages.

Like Edmund Burke, Groen appreciated history as "the known march of the ordinary providence of God." While the Scriptures always had priority for him, he felt it was neither prudent nor godly to fly in the face of past wisdom, particularly where it reflected biblical maxims and gospel mandates.

It was very much Groen's trenchant analysis of the nature of modernity that determined the strategy for a century of distinctive Christian action in his country. Groen formed a bridge between the spontaneous early protestors Bilderdijk and Da Costa against theological liberalism and the secularization of politics, and the systematic antirevolutionary theorists that would come after him, such as Kuyper (1837–1920) and Dooyeweerd (1894–1977). In his lecture series of 1845–46, published the following year under the title *Unbelief and Revolution*,[14] Groen threw down the gauntlet against the leading lights of his day. The root cause of the malaise of the age, he set forth, was unbelief – unbelief as it was first elaborated into a system and then applied in a social experiment. It was the Enlightenment that had dismissed divine Revelation and the Christian tradition as the basis of society and had replaced them with a twofold "philosophy of unbelief," one that recognized no truth beyond human reason and no authority apart from human consent. The lectures traced the outworking of this new philosophy: the supremacy of reason produces atheism in religion and materialism in morality, while the supremacy of the human will leads to popular sovereignty in political theory and anarchy in political practice. These logical

---

12 Da Costa n.d. *Kompleete Dichtwerken*, ed. Hasebroek, 3 vols., 8th impr. Leyden: Sijthoff, 2: 253, 3: 121.

13 Da Costa to Groen, 11 Nov. 1852; in *Brieven van Mr. Isaac da Costa*, 2:105–06. Cf. Rullmann, J. C. 1926. "Da Costa in zijn beteekenis voor de anti-revolutionaire partij," *Anti-Revolutionaire Staatkunde* 2: 165–88, 225–44; Rullmann, J. C. 1928. "Het Réveil en de opkomst der Anti-Revolutionaire Partij," *Anti-Revolutionaire Staatkunde* 4: 461–76.

14 For an abridged translation, see Van Dyke, Harry 1989. *Groen van Prinsterer's Lectures on Unbelief and Revolution*. Jordan Station, Ont.: Wedge, 293–539.

outcomes had been dramatically revealed in the French Revolution and in all subsequent imitations of that great experiment.

According to Groen, therefore, a correct appraisal of the French Revolution and its aftermath must take into account its profoundly religious impulse. By religion he meant man's ultimate commitment either to God or to whatever takes His place. Religion had been the motor of the events that launched the modern world; the Revolution of 1789 was driven by a surrogate religion, namely the ideology of secular liberalism. This ideology was not renounced in the Restoration of 1815. Consequently, the same subversive ideas continued to undermine the foundations of society and to stifle wholesome reform; eventually they would ignite fresh flare-ups of revolutionary violence. Like Tocqueville, Groen came to the disturbing conclusion that the Revolution had become a permanent feature of European civilization. We are living in a condition of permanent revolution, so ended his lectures; revolutions are here to stay and will grow in scope and intensity – unless men can be persuaded to return to the Christian religion and practice the Gospel and its precepts in their full implications for human life and civilized society. Barring such a revival, the future would belong to the most consistent sects of the new secular religion, socialism and communism.[15]

The political spectrum that presented itself to Groen's generation offered no meaningful choice, in his estimation. The radical left was composed of fanatical believers in the "theory of practical atheism"; the liberal center was occupied by warm sympathizers who nevertheless cautioned against excesses and preached moderation in living out the new creed; the conservative right included all who lacked either the wit, the wisdom or the will to repudiate the modern tenets yet who recoiled from the consequences whenever the ideology was implemented in any consistent way. Thus none of the three "nuances" of secular liberalism represented a valid option for Christian citizens. Groen ended his lectures with a compelling invitation to resist "the Revolution" in whatever form it manifested itself and to work for a radical alternative in politics, along anti-revolutionary, Christian-historical lines. *"Resist beginnings"* and *"Principle against principle"* were to be the watchwords.

When the book came out, reactions from Christian friends were most interesting. Aeneas baron Mackay wrote Groen to say that "the Word applied to politics was new to me, and now that I have placed that candle in the darkness I see sorry things, but *I see*."[16] Elout van Soeterwoude wrote some time later to question the implied vision of a Christian state and a Christian society. Would positing an alternative "principle" suffice? And had so-called anti-revolutionary forms ever been more than just Ideal-types, he wondered. "I have always believed," he objected,

> that wherever men feared God they strove after such forms; wherever the Christian religion has lived in men's hearts since the Reformation, such forms have been realized here and there, yet always but in part, and the more these things weakened and vanished, the more did men depart from them and did the revolutionary spirit gain ascendancy. It was therefore always the good that a few people desired and accomplished – in faith, in the fear and power of God. But

---

15 I know of only one British reaction to Groen's book thus far; it appeared after some portions of it were translated into English; see Lloyd-Jones, D. Martyn 1975. "The French Revolution and After." *The Christian and the State in Revolutionary Times.* London: Westminster Conference, 94–99.

16 Mackay to Groen, 26 Aug. 1847; in Groen van Prinsterer, *Schriftelijke Nalatenschap, Briefwisseling,* ed. J. L. van Essen et al., 6 vols. (The Hague, 1925–1992), 3: 810.

it was hardly the principle of the State. Nor will it ever be that. Yet anywhere, at any time, even today, God can raise up leaders who administer affairs for a time in a Christian spirit. Apart from Christ, the principle, even if accepted, is dead. Will the majority ever be Christian? I think not; but [it may] perhaps submit for a time to the power of faith. Therefore your labor is not in vain. . . .[17]

The poet-theologian Nicolaas Beets had found the book so gripping

. . . that I could not put it down until I had read it all and yesterday afternoon closed the book with a prayer on my lips. . . . Your book makes it clear to me: the nations are walking in ways where no return is likely, no halt avails, and progress is the increasing manifestation of the man of sin. Who can arrest, who can deliver but the Lord alone?[18]

Beets' younger colleague J. P. Hasebroek communicated that *Unbelief and Revolution* had greatly clarified for him the relation between gospel and politics. To be sure, he had always believed that the Word of God, as absolute truth, contained the core of all truths, including the basic principles of all genuine political science. But Groen's book provided a yardstick "by which all the new phenomena emerging in the politics and society of our time may be measured and evaluated."[19] When the book was reissued twenty years later, Professor De Geer of Utrecht made a telling remark. After observing that "unbelief is showing itself more brazen all the time," he voiced a concern which was Groen's concern exactly: what are the faithful doing about it? They have no sense, he complained, of what it means to be church. Christian action is paralyzed by internal division and individualism. Unbelief can do what it wants: it finds itself opposed by isolated individuals only.[20]

It would be another four years before Kuyper would raise his *Standaard* to overcome this individualism by means of a Groenian type of isolationism: that is, to break with conservatism and rally the Christian body for developing a collective Christian political mind, and then to orchestrate united Christian action. That mobilization was possible after 1872 thanks to Groen's lifelong "strategy" of retrenchment, namely, to identify the nonnegotiables and stand by one's principles. *"In our isolation lies our strength,"* he insisted to the tiny party of his followers, explaining: We do not mean thereby that we want to be "political hermits" but that we have a "distinctive point of departure." To establish and preserve one's distinctiveness would keep one's identity intact and one's testimony pure: "I would rather end up in the company of only a few, or if necessary all alone, than abandon a starting point without which we would not only lose our influence but cease being a party."[21]

Much of Groen's support lay among the (as yet) disenfranchised "people behind the voters." Among them he knew the presence of the Christian body that held him up in prayer, the same body that would later become Kuyper's dues-paying members. It irked the opposition to hear Groen claim that he did not just represent a fraction of the population but the "core of the nation." The party of the "anti-Revolution" was a national party, Groen insisted, "because it is linked to the faith of our fathers and our historical traditions" and its program "resonates in the Christian conscience of the Dutch people." At the end of his life Groen took comfort from the fact that "as long as I was faithful, the orthodox

---

17 Elout to Groen, 23 June 1849; in *Briefwisseling*, 3, 27–28.

18 Beets to Groen, 8 Sept. 1847; in *Briefwisseling*, 2, 812.

19 Hasebroek to Groen, 22 Sept. 1847; in *Briefwisseling*, 2, 820f.; see also 3: 851.

20 De Geer to Groen, 11 Oct. 1868; in *Briefwisseling*, 4, 261.

21 Van Prinsterer, G. Groen 1866. *Parlementaire Studiën en Schetsen*, 3 vols. The Hague, 2, 336–37.

people were never unfaithful to me."[22]

Central to Groen's career was his defense of freedom of education. He called it "freedom of religion with respect to one's children."[23] In parliament and in the press, he spearheaded the campaign against the common or comprehensive, religiously mixed government schools for primary education. At first, he and his friends fought for the mere right as private citizens to establish alternative schools. As education progressed and became publicly endowed, he objected to the government monopoly on taxes earmarked for schooling. Groen denied the possibility of neutrality in nurture. In his estimation, modernists were using public education in the hope of transcending religious differences through a strictly rational approach and preparing children to become enlightened adults in a unified society. In practice, the so-called neutrality of the common school, Groen observed in 1861, "grows into the most pernicious partiality favoring unbelief and ends in making proselytes for the religion of reason and nature." The schools struggle, which did not end until the pacification bill of 1920, was Groen's most important legacy to his nation, a nation that escaped a monolithic society based on secular liberalism only when liberals at last were forced to concede that in education there ought to be equal rights or a level playing field for all citizens. After the church question, it was the schools struggle that would propel Kuyper onto the national stage.

4. Ottho Gerhard Heldring (1804–76): Calling for United Action

This country pastor was to give the initial impulse for united Christian action in his country. His parish work had brought him face-to-face with the wretched conditions of peasants and day-laborers. Inspired by Ezekiel 34:4, he became involved in land reclamation, the digging of wells, and literacy programs through conducting night classes and composing readers for the young. He pioneered the establishment of homes for orphans and neglected children.[24] Since all this cost a great deal of money, Heldring became a master beggar, via letters and visits in *Réveil* circles, to raise funds for his many philanthropic causes. When the Society for the Utility of the Commonweal, active in promoting public education nationwide, approached him with a lucrative offer for adopting one of his readers, on condition that he suppress certain passages deemed "too sectarian," the pious author was briefly tempted to compromise. In frustration, Heldring tried to arouse interest for a more formal, structured approach to works of *Réveil*. What ought we to do? asked his circular letter of 1845; shall we continue our separate ways, or is united action possible?

This initiative resulted in biannual meetings in Amsterdam of the "Christian Friends." Usually chaired by Groen, these meetings were spent discussing projects, sponsoring activities, and raising funds. The cause of Christian education was also close to the hearts of the Friends. Another meeting was devoted to the question: Should Christians form a political party? We have no choice, was Groen's opinion; our constitutional system requires political alternatives. Those who hold to the same principles should band together and try to achieve their goals by proceeding according to well devised plans to persuade voters and

---

22 Smitskamp, H. 1945. *Wat heeft Groen van Prinsterer ons vandaag te zeggen?* The Hague, 28, 118, 124–28.

23 Van Prinsterer, G. Groen 1840. *Bijdrage tot herziening der Grondwet in Nederlandsche zin.* Leyden, 89.

24 John de Liefde published articles on "Pastor Heldring" in *The Christian Miscellany and Family Visitor*, 1856, 240–43, 272–74; *The British Messenger*, April 1863, 40ff.; and *The Sunday Magazine*, February 1865, 321–25.

influence lawmaking. Christians are members of the Nation and as such have rights in the State, as well as consequent duties, namely to uphold these rights and to fulfill these duties in communion with the brothers.

One result of these meetings was the appearance, from time to time, of antirevolutionary voters' associations in urban ridings. Another was the regular publication, from 1847 to 1875, of *De Vereeniging: Christelijke Stemmen*, a quarterly edited by Heldring, with contributions in theology, history, literature, inner mission, and philanthropy as well as articles of political analysis and debate. After about a decade, however, the meetings in Amsterdam died out because the Christian Friends could not agree on a common stance against the incursion of modernism in the National Church, some favoring a "juridical" approach (use the church courts to discipline, suspend or defrock offenders) with others recommending a "medicinal" approach (preach the full gospel, which alone is able, in time, to overcome its deniers).

5. Johan Adam Wormser (1807–62): Abandoning Establishmentarianism

This court bailiff from Amsterdam had his own approach to the challenge of modernity. In his book of 1853, *De Kinderdoop*, he argued that, factually, almost all Dutch people had received Christian baptism. This meant that the Dutch nation had been sealed into the covenant of grace and thus could lay claim to God's promises. The only thing wanting was that the nation in many respects was either ignorant or negligent of its part of the bargain: to embrace that covenant and dedicate itself in all the ramifications of national life to God. Hence Wormser wrote: "Teach the nation to understand the meaning of its baptism, and church and state are saved."

Wormser agreed with Groen that the worst enemy in the battle for reasserting the Christian character of Dutch society was the world flight and politicophobia of orthodox Christians. For the country was increasingly being brought, unopposed, "under the sway of the Revolution ideas and their destructive effects." This state of affairs must be turned around. After all, "the question is far from settled whether the nation, just as it formerly exchanged its pagan character for the Christian one, is now disposed to trade its Christian character for an atheistic one." And just because, he added defiantly, the revolution principles "have corrupted *much*, they do not have the right to corrupt *all* our institutions."[25]

Clearly Wormser was not yet ready, in the middle of the nineteenth century, to give up on the ideal of a Christian society. In more sober moments, however, Wormser would write to Groen that perhaps the situation had so altered that a radical reorientation was needed. He felt this to be true in particular for the struggle to keep the nation's schools Christian. He was by no means insensitive, he wrote, "to what is called the national church and our national schools, institutions and character. The memory of what God in his grace has done in our land, and of the public institutions which arose as a result of that, always has much that is precious and appealing to me." But the problem was that amid much spiritual awakening and revival of *persons*, the reformation and revival of time-honored *institutions* was proving much more difficult. In the growing conflict over the spiritual direction of Dutch society, the nominal Christian character of many institutions might well be removed by the Lord himself, and through the crisis the members of His Body could

---

25 Wormser, J. A. 1853. *De Kinderdoop, beschouwd met betrekking tot het bijzondere, kerkelijke en maatschappelijke leven* [Infant baptism, considered in relation to personal, church and social life]. Amsterdam, 8–9, 44.

then grow to greater solidity and independence.[26] By 1860, both Wormser and Groen, along with many others, divested themselves of the last remnants of thinking in terms of corporate Christianity and Constantinian establishment, to turn to free schools and a free church in a state that would favor the adherents of neither modernism nor orthodoxy. This was to become the guiding idea of Kuyper's public philosophy.

And so gradually a pattern of separatism became visible that had really characterized the anti-revolutionary movement from the very beginning. The so-called line of antithesis that ran right through the Dutch nation, making division between orthodox believers and all others, was not an invention of Abraham Kuyper. As early as 1841 Elout van Soeterwoude had to explain to an English anti-slavery activist why Holland's evangelical Christians did not want to open their Abolition Society to "all men of good will" (as Wilberforce had been able to do in England) but had to limit membership to confessing Christians only. Time and again it has been our unhappy experience, Elout wrote, that such common undertakings end up banning the Christian basis of the work in favor of a kind of neutrality that lacks the faith that can overcome the world.[27] And a few years later, when no professorial chair was made available for Isaac da Costa in the City University of Amsterdam despite a long list of prominent names endorsing the nomination, Groen had mused: if Christian principles cannot be brought to our public institutions, perhaps we will wake up to see the need for our own institutions.[28] Here lie the historic roots of the Dutch phenomenon of "pillarization," or, as I prefer to call it, *institutionalized worldview pluralism.*[29]

6. Isaac Esser (1818–85): Instructing the Common People

Groen wrote tough, sinewy prose, in highbrow papers. Fortunately, popularizers of the antirevolutionary worldview were not lacking. Of these, Isaac Esser, a soapbox evangelist in The Hague, deserves a brief mention. Esser had distinguished himself as an administrator in the Dutch East Indies, where he had combated corruption, prosecuted slave trade, and actively promoted Christian missions among the natives. Once repatriated, he joined campaigns against modernism in the national church. Unsuccessful in a bid for a seat in parliament in 1864, he threw himself into the renewed struggle for Christian day schools. His activities ranged from handing out tracts at fair grounds during carnival season, to writing a weekly series of articles on a sound colonial policy, translating psalms into the Malay language, setting up a ragged school, and serving on the Board of Governors of the Free University.[30]

The book *Unbelief and Revolution* had meant a great deal to Esser during disturbances in 1848 on Java, so in 1874 he approached the author for permission to quote extensively from it in a primer that he was composing "for the people behind the voters." When Groen

26 Wormser to Groen, 1 April 1844; in *Brieven van J. A. Wormser*, ed. Groen van Prinsterer, 2 vols. (Amsterdam, 1874), 1, 17–18.

27 Elout to Rev. E. Miller, 7 Dec. 1841; in *Briefwisseling [of Groen van Prinsterer]*, 5, 793–95.

28 Groen to Da Costa, 16 Nov. 1844; in *Brieven van Da Costa*, 1, 188–89.

29 See Van Dyke, Harry 1996. "Groen van Prinsterer's Interpretation of the French Revolution and the Rise of 'Pillars' in Dutch Society." In *Presenting the Past: History, Culture, Language, Literature.* Series Crossways, Vol. 3, edited by Jane Fenoulhet and Lesley Gilbert. London: Centre for Low Countries Studies, University College, London, 83–98.

30 Smid, T. D. 1966. "Isaäc Esser," *Woord en Wereld* 3: 205–20, 302–11.

was shown a sample of the text, he advised Esser to abandon the method of using direct quotations and instead turn his "excellent talent for popularization" to good account by saying the same thing in his own words. The upshot was the appearance later that year of Esser's *Anti-revolutionaire Catechismus, ook voor het volk achter de kiezers*. The booklet has been called "a most peculiar publication in anti-revolutionary history."[31] It signaled the conviction among the common people who followed Groen and prayed for him that the anti-revolution in the country would be nothing if not a grassroots movement involving thousands of (as yet nonvoting) "ordinary" believers. Here are a few representative questions and answers from Esser's catechism:

> *Question 1*: What is the infallible touchstone of all that is just and moral, both for nations and private persons? *Answer*: Holy Scripture! Unconditional submission to God's Word. *"It is written"* is the guarantee of dutiful obedience as well as dutiful resistance, of order and freedom.
>
> *Q. 2*: Are there any other tests of justice and morality? *Answer*: Undoubtedly! History and nature are also tests. Throughout the ages history and nature have taught [mankind] to start with God and to consult experience. . . .
>
> *Q. 12*: Do only governments have divine right? *Answer*: By no means! All authorities are God's lieutenants, God's ministers – for your good, writes Paul. We are to obey them for the Lord's sake; they are to obey God. Higher power is a gift of God which is to be used in His service, to the benefit of others and to His honor. The Sovereign bears the image of God on earth, but this is nothing extraordinary or special which he is privileged to have above other people. A father bears the image of God to his child, a judge to the accused, a mistress to her maids. Anybody who is anything or has anything is an image-bearer of God, obligated and called, each according to his gift as a good steward, in the name and according to the example of our Lord, to walk in the good works which He has ordained for us. . . .
>
> *Q. 24*: How does the anti-revolutionary see the French Revolution? *Answer*: As a work of unbelief and revolt, of apostasy from the living God and at the same time as a judgment of God.
>
> *Q. 25*: How can you prove this? *Answer*: From the plain facts of the revolution. The tree is known by its fruit. . . .
>
> *Q. 47*: Is the struggle of our day at bottom a religious struggle? *Answer*: No other. Underneath all the burning questions of our day lies the religious question. It all comes down to this: Who is sovereign, God or man?[32]

7. Klaas Kater (1850–1916): Mobilizing the Workingmen

Canvassing the contributions of leaders of the first and second rank, like Groen and Esser, should remind us that the anti-revolution was also very much a grassroots movement. Many of the orthodox belonged to the common people who in a "census democracy" such as Holland then was often lacked the property or income qualifications to have the right to vote. These "people behind the voters" still awaited their emancipation. Though under the circumstances they were not easily empowered to participate in decision-making for the future, this was not for lack of interest on their part. We hear of a cigar maker's shop in Amsterdam where one of the workmen would read aloud from the writings of Groen

---

31 Van Wehring, J. *Het Maatschappijbeeld van Abraham Kuyper*, 53.
32 Esser, I. 1874. *Antirevolutionaire Catechismus*. The Hague, 3, 7, 18, 48.

while his fellow workers filled his quota during that time.[33] The story of the emancipation of the working classes in the Netherlands includes many names, among which Klaas Kater figures large.[34]

But it all began with another man – with Julien Wolbers (1819–89), the owner of a painting and decorating firm in Haarlem who retired early to devote himself to the promotion of the rising social movement which he wished to influence in a Christian direction. In the summer of 1871 he started a weekly called *De Werkmansvriend*. Despite its patronizing name ("The Workingman's Friend") the weekly was well-received by working-class people who could resonate with the opening editorial, which stated: "The social question is the order of the day. The industrious workman has a right to claim that his wages should be commensurate to his needs and those of his family, and that he ought not to suffer want or be forced to deny himself all physical relaxation and every opportunity to ennoble his mind." But, Wolbers continued, the improvement of the workingmen's lot depends on their own activity: what they need is "a healthy spirit of self-confidence, coupled with reliance on and invocation of higher blessing." The editor placed his hope in honest work, duty, piety, education, vocational training, mutual aid in case of illness, etc., "provided all this is pursued in a sound spirit of moderation and order, and not through violence." The paper would therefore combat that new manifestation of the Revolution in the world, the International, whose principles:

> lead workmen to be discontented with their rank and lot, arouse their resentment against those more generously endowed with temporal goods, and excite them to resistance if not revolt. . . . Under the fine-sounding slogans of seeking to progress, of wanting to champion the rights of the workingman, to emancipate labor, to promote liberty, equality and fraternity, they are liberally sowing the seed which, according to our most sacred convictions, will only bear bitter – and for the workman himself most pernicious – fruits. . . . The revolutionary movement is characterized by apostasy from God and the denial of His love and power. We, by contrast, believe that only a return to God, acknowledging and obeying His Word, sincerely believing in His grace in Jesus Christ, will promote the salvation, including the temporal well-being, of the workman, as of all men.

Against this background the paper announced its intention to be a clearing house for news about "such workingmen's associations which, averse to the criminal agitation of the International, aim to ameliorate the workman's lot in the gradual way of order and law, without violent upheavals." As he thus opposed the Revolution with the Gospel, Wolbers was pitting Groen against Marx.

Predictably, rival papers run by social democrats warned against mixing "theology" with the social question. In reply, Wolbers reassured them that "no theological disputes, no sermons, no catechism" would appear in *De Werkmansvriend*. "Yet we cannot imagine a society without religion. Where religion is lacking society will not thrive. The healing of our sick society and the wellbeing of the workman cannot be attained, we believe, except through a revival of religion and obedience to God's Word." Accordingly, *De Werkmansvriend* intended to deal with the various social issues from a Christian standpoint, "and therefore not without regarding religion as one of the most important factors." In the pres-

---

33 Wormser to Groen, 27 August 1851; in *Brieven van Wormser*, 1: 238.

34 Cf. Hagoort, R. 1927. *Gedenkboek Patrimonium*. Utrecht, 104–35, 164–80; Hagoort, R. n.d. [1956]. *De Christelijk-sociale beweging*. Franeker, 70–84.

ent circumstances the editors may not be silent observers who know in their hearts that "to forsake God and His service and no longer to honor His Word as the highest law" leads a people to the abyss.

One young enthusiastic journalist who joined Wolbers as editor of *De Werkmansvriend* was Willem C. Beeremans (1852–1937). Beeremans was particularly interested in giving guidance to the rising labor movement. Writing in 1873 that what was needed was "a return to a Christian society," he asserted:

> there are no purely social questions. Every one of them, however many there be, must find their solution in Christianity, must be solved according to the demands of God's laws. . . . To be sure, workmen's associations are not religious gatherings . . . but is it just, is it fair, timidly to exclude or eschew all religion when discussing social issues?

Beeremans advocated looking to God's Word rather than "rallying under the red flag." While recognizing the legitimacy of labor unions and the need for social reform, he objected to a purely horizontal approach to these questions, noting in particular that the widespread negation of divine providence encouraged the working classes to attack the very foundations of society and to put all the blame for their present plight on employers and social institutions. We hear a great deal at union meetings about *brotherhood* and *love of neighbor*, he wrote, but no one remembers the first and great commandment: *to love God*.

But how "Christian" can trade unions be? To those who objected that it would be out of the question, for example, to open union meetings with prayer, Beeremans retorted:

> Exactly! Herein lies the unhappy condition of our society. It has slid from the foundation of God's Word, on which it stood steady and firm, to place itself on another soil, in which it must sooner or later sink away. . . . Unions will only be useful to the working class in particular and society in general if, there too, men would push their demands more into the background and ask first of all what God demands.

Another contributor to the weekly, Jacob Witmond (1832–99), a trained evangelist turned journalist, soon joined Beeremans in his endeavor to arouse interest in a novel venture: organizing an avowedly Christian Workingmen's Association. Together they persuaded the Amsterdam labor activist, Klaas Kater, to join them.

This initiative would prove historic. Kater, a largely self-taught man, had written a number of candid contributions in *De Werkmansvriend* exposing poor wages and working conditions in a variety of firms mentioned by name. He had been president of a local bricklayer's union and had begun to play a leading role in the fledgling national federation of labor unions. However, he had felt compelled to resign from the latter when running into firm opposition to his idea of *samenwerking* (cooperation) with owners and management. Other reasons for his withdrawal were profanity, Sabbath desecration, and flirting with the marxist International. For the time being, Kater was at a loss where else to work for labor reform.

Shortly thereafter, he felt vindicated in having left the national federation when, at the urging of Young Liberals on its board, it adopted a change in its constitution by which it came out strongly in support of the "promotion and extension of neutral public primary and secondary education." Kater now agreed, when approached by Beeremans and Witmond, that Christian workmen had no choice but to create an alternative by forming a parallel organization. To remain silent in the face of such "senseless demands," purport-edly made on behalf of "the workingmen of Holland," was tantamount to "denying Christ [and] contributing to the ruin of our people as a Christian nation."

The three men called a meeting on 3 January 1876 where preparations were made for a distinctively Christian social organization embracing employers and employees and taking for its basis, direction and goal "Him who is the center of world history and outside of Whom there is no salvation." Out of this initiative was born the organization named "Patrimonium" – the name being indicative of the members' determination to stand on guard for the national Christian "heritage." In the very month that Groen lay dying – May 1876 – a constitution was drafted and an organization launched that would represent the anti-Revolution in the world of labor.

Kuyper's daily newspaper *De Standaard* at first did not pay much attention to this new development. On several occasions Kater complained to the editor-in-chief of being ignored.[35] Before long, however, Patrimonium was the largest social organization in the Netherlands. Although in later decades it would be eclipsed by separate organizations for workingmen and for employers, nevertheless a pattern was set: for the socio-economic sector, too, Holland's Christians (not the churches or the clergy) ran their own distinct organizations in a bid, along with other-minded, parallel organizations (such as bread-and-butter unions and the social democratic movement) to influence the future conditions of the daily workplace. To this day, consociational democracy in the Netherlands is also reflected in the institutionalized worldview pluralism of its socio-economic structure.[36]

Our interest here lies with a number of distinct expressions and formulations found in Patrimonium's Constitution as well as in the commentary written by Kater, its first president. The founding fathers were very conscious of the fact that they were adding a new branch to the antirevolutionary movement in the land. Article 1 stated that the organization accepted "God's Word and the traditions of our people as the trustworthy foundations of a Christian Society," and Article 2 listed among the means of promoting its aims: propagating its principle, holding meetings, studying history, aiding widows and sick or injured workmen, sponsoring a popular book series, operating a reading room, and establishing trade schools and consumer and housing cooperatives. Curiously, an earlier pamphlet had specified for the reading room that it should have "a collection of books in which, for example, the works of Groen van Prinsterer have a prominent place." This seems rather appropriate for an organization whose president had addressed its member-ship at the start of a meeting as "spiritual sons of the late lamented Groen van Prinsterer."[37]

After Patrimonium received a royal charter in March 1877, Kater was invited to introduce the new organization to the readers of *De Werkmansvriend*. He emphasized that the guiding principle of Patrimonium in the social sector would be *samenwerking*, the harmonious cooperation of all who acknowledged God and His Christ as the supreme ruler and whose aim in life was to glorify His Name, irrespective of the class to which

35 Kater to Kuyper, Dec. 12, 1877; Aug. 8, Aug. 11, Nov. 10, 1879; see letters in Kuyper-archief, Documen-tatiecentrum voor het Nederlands Protestantisme, Free University, Amsterdam.
36 Cf. Fogarty, Michael P. 1957. *Christian Democracy in Western Europe, 1820–1953.* Notre Dame: UNDP, chaps. xv–xviii; Lijphart, Arend 1968. *The Politics of Accommodation: Pluralism and Democracy in the Neth-erlands.* Berkeley: California UP, passim.
37 Hagoort, *De Christelijk-sociale beweging,* 52.

they belonged. We demand recognition as members of society, he explained, as creatures who may not be suppressed or exploited. Class distinctions should be reduced, mutual aid encouraged, and injustices set right. By what means? Not by coercion, but by persuasion:

> We believe that the fate of the world is guided by an Almighty hand, wherefore we are unwilling to stretch forth the hands of violence to seize the property of others: nor do we wish, by resorting to compulsion when circumstances seem favorable to us, to appropriate to ourselves what He has entrusted to others.

No doubt such phrases might have lulled some employers to sleep. But docility was not the intention. Boldly Kater addressed the structural violence embedded in a capitalist society:

> But should the rich of this world wish to administer the goods entrusted to their stewardship exclusively to their own benefit, to use them solely for their own advantage, then we affirm that in this regard the doctrine of Proudhon is altogether true: "Property is theft." Hence we wish, in accordance with the Word of God, to testify against every form of violence that exalts itself against Him, whether it proceeds from workingmen or from whomsoever. Accordingly, we reject all strikes, as fruits of the revolution. But we also condemn every association of money or power entered into for the purpose of securing a monopoly.

Kater had read his Groen well. The latter had been very critical of the new socio-economic developments inspired by liberalism. In a series of pamphlets of 1848 Groen had written:

> Our worst ailment is pauperism. Poverty, no work; ruptured relations between the higher and lower classes; no bond save wages and labor; proletarians and capitalists. Whither will this lead? That is uncertain. But there is no doubt whence it came.
>
> It came from 'Liberty and Equality' as understood by the Revolution. Just one detail. When that slogan was first raised, guilds and corporations too had to go. The desire was for free competition; no restraints on skills and industry; no hateful monopoly exercised by individuals or societies; then the development of private initiative and commerce would guarantee a better future. The future that was envisioned has arrived. Can it be called better? *I am of one voice here with the leading spokesmen of the present-day revolution.* It is this liberty, this unrestricted competition, this removal, as much as possible, of the natural relationship of employer and employee, which tears the social bonds, ends in the dominance of the rich and the rule of the banking houses, robs artisans of regular sustenance, splits society up into two hostile camps, gives rise to a countless host of paupers, prepares for the attack by the have-nots on the well-to-do and would in many people's eyes render such a deed excusable, if not legitimate. It has brought Europe to a state so dreary and somber as to cause many to tremble and cry out: Is there no way to revive, in some altered form, the associations that were so recklessly crushed under the revolutionary ruins?[38]

Kater, as he echoed these sentiments – including his bow to Proudhon – was not merely harking back to a radical outburst by his venerated statesman. His boldness was borne up by deep-seated convictions. His article of April 1877 in *De Werkmansvriend* concluded with these words:

> To this end we await the help of Him who has made the heavens and the earth, and we call out to all, be they rich or poor, of gentle or humble birth, employer and employee: Join us, so

---

38 Van Prinsterer, G. Groen 1848. *Vrijheid, Gelijkheid, Broederschap; toelichting op de spreuk der Revolutie.* The Hague, 83–84 (emph. added).

that our dear fatherland, our cherished royal house, and all inhabitants of these lands so richly blessed of God, may be preserved from the Spirit that is not of God, from the ruinous plans of the revolution.

The new organization attracted many members. Here was a "brotherhood" that did not disregard their Christian loyalties but appealed to them! Also, Patrimonium's initiative in setting up housing cooperatives met a great need. Besides attending to social concerns, members also gave their support to the ARP, hoping for a kinder dispensation some day. Often not voters themselves, they volunteered for election campaigns and helped round up voters on election day.

Understandably, a little over a decade later Patrimonium's leaders expressed grave disappointment at the slow progress in social reforms made by the first Anti-Revolutionary cabinet, the Mackay Ministry of 1888–91. Our own parliamentarians, Kater stated forthrightly in his annual presidential address of November 1890, do not feel our misery because they stem from the aristocracy. He added ominously: if the ARP does not soon field some candidates from the working classes, our members are thinking of starting a Christian Labor Party.[39] At this, Kuyper took alarm. He immediately began to take steps towards organizing a Social Congress to address the social question in solidarity with all the brothers, of whatever class or station in life. There he would, in his opening address, call for "architectonic critique" of existing society (*PP* 44). There he would pray the prayer repeated on many lips afterwards: "They cannot wait, not a day, not an hour."[40]

8. Abraham Kuyper (1837–1920): Seizing the Initiative

And now we come to the heir of all these personalities, voices, publications, to the man who like no other succeeded in turning this rich tradition to political profit. The broad outline of Kuyper's career is familiar enough not to be repeated here, but it may not be entirely superfluous to bring to mind that this towering giant did not *singlehandedly*, between the age of 35 and 49, create a daily newspaper, a political party, a separate university, and a new, free, orthodox Reformed denomination. In each case he was a *co*founder – a leader, inspirer, tireless organizer, to be sure, but always surrounded by a score of peers who acted as his collaborators and assistants, advisers, supporters and critics.

More to the point for us may be to listen to a statement of his deepest motivation. In 1897, looking back over his career thus far, Kuyper, then 60 years old, composed a little poem (adapting one, he admitted, by Da Costa[41]), which he recited at a public reception honoring his 25-year editorship of *De Standaard*. In translation, the poem runs somewhat as follows:

> My life is ruled by but one passion,
> One higher urge drives will and soul.
> My breath may stop before I ever
> allow that sacred urge to fall.
> 'Tis to affirm God's holy statutes
> In church and state, in home and school,

---

39 *Jaarboekje van het Nederlandsch Werkliedenverbond Patrimonium voor 1891* (Amsterdam, 1891), 81–85.

40 Cf. also Van Dyke, Harry 1998. "How Abraham Kuyper Became a Christian Democrat." *Calvin Theological Journal* 33: 420–35. *See infra* Chapter 5.

41 Cf. Da Costa, Isaac *Kompleete Dichtwerken*, 1: 201–02.

Despite the world's strong remonstrations
To bless our people with His rule.
'Tis to engrave God's holy order,
heard in Creation and the Word,
upon the nation's public conscience,
Till God is once again its Lord.[42]

After his two-stage conversion – first when still in university, then as a young pastor – Abraham Kuyper determined that he wanted to master what he decided had been the strength of the core of the nation: historic Calvinism. He would revive the 16th century confession of Calvin and Beza, develop the theology of Voetius and the fathers of Dordt, and update the public philosophy of Hotman, Languet and Marnix. For obtaining works in the latter category he wrote to the best guide available: Groen van Prinsterer. Groen responded by recommending authors whom he regarded as the "founding fathers" of modern Christian-historical constitutional law: Edmund Burke, François Guizot, and Friedrich Julius Stahl. For good measure, he also sent him packages of complementary copies of his own works. Kuyper devoured them and began to spread the word in lectures to a student club in Utrecht, the place of his second charge. After moving to Amsterdam and starting his newspaper, made possible in part by Groen's munificence, there followed an amazing collaboration between the two publicists: in commentary on public affairs they passed the ball to each other, Kuyper in his daily *De Standaard*, Groen in his biweekly *Nederlandse Gedachten*. On one occasion Kuyper wrote: "Thanks for your formulation on p. 203 of your latest installment: it will be the text for my next talk to the students."[43] And thus was born Kuyper's earliest statement in political philosophy: *Calvinism: Source and Safeguard of Our Constitutional Liberties.*[44]

As a theologian by training, a church historian by predilection and an ordained pastor by profession, Kuyper gained national prominence especially as a talented journalist. Friend and foe read the scintillating editorials in *De Standaard*, the paper he launched on 1 April 1872. In late 1873, in a by-election for the Second Chamber in Gouda riding, sympathizers with Groenian politics and subscribers to *De Standaard* nominated – without the

---

42 A different meter may work better in English, as follows:
    As for me, in my life I shall always be striving
     – my mind and my heart be impelled to give all –
    may breathing forsake me, my heart stop its beating,
    before I abandon that most sacred call:
    It is to establish, in home and in schooling,
    in church and in state and on every terrain,
    the laws that our God has ordained for his creatures,
    and thus help our people their bearings to gain.
    And so to impress on the mind of the nation
    the order revealed in Creation and Word
    that the people repent and submit to His statutes –
    again be a nation whose God is the Lord.

43 Kuyper to Groen, 10 Nov. 1873; in *Briefwisseling*, 6: 468, 473. The reference is to *Nederlandsche Gedachten* of 22 Oct. 1873, in which Groen had written: "In the Calvinist Reformation according to Holy Scripture, in the history of their and our martyrs' church, lies the source and safeguard of the blessings of which 1789 gives the treacherous promise and the wretched caricature."

44 *Het Calvinisme, oorsprong en waarborg onzer constitutionaele vrijheden* (Amsterdam, 1873); English translation in *AK:ACR* 281–317.

candidate's prior permission, as was quite customary – as their favorite son: "Dr. Abraham Kuyper, pastor in the Reformed Church of Amsterdam." The first round was inconclusive: 957 votes for the liberal candidate, 767 for Kuyper, and 599 for the candidate supported by Catholics and conservatives. As a show of voter strength, it pleased Kuyper greatly, as it did Groen. And the numbers indicated that the runoff election might actually go Kuyper's way; would he then have to accept and leave the parsonage to enter parliament? Kuyper agonized over the possibility. And sure enough, the results on January 21 were 1252 votes for the Liberal candidate, as against 1504 for the Anti-Revolutionary. Kuyper's soul-searching intensified. His published correspondence with Groen shows that it took him a full three weeks before he accepted.

What held him back? He complained of lack of clarity about a concrete platform to stand on. "One thing would give me courage," he wrote the old man in The Hague; "if I had a set goal and could see a path plotted toward it." Then he continued: "Tomorrow I shall therefore set my thoughts on paper. Then I shall send these to you, to approve or put aside." Two days after came the "loose thoughts," as the writer himself called them. "You will appreciate my purpose," he wrote Groen. "Accepting a seat is to me like accepting a mandate, so I feel the need to know what direction to follow and what to undertake. I cannot take a *leap in the dark*. Therefore I beg indulgence for my sketch. If it is all wrong, tell me freely. But at least give me the assurance . . . that your prudence has gone over the thought of the young man."

The "sketch" consisted of a memorandum of only 1500 words and displayed its author's political instinct, foresight, boldness, and above all, principled pluralism. Here are some lines:

> We should distinguish between what the anti-revolutionaries pursue as a *party* and what they present as a *general* political program to the nation as a whole. Only like-minded men can work for the former; the latter can be promoted by men of all parties. The former could become the latter only if the whole nation were converted to anti-revolutionary principles.
>
> To anticipate the future we ought to take our cue from the present situation, in which the conservatives are dying away, the liberals, drawing no recruits from the younger generation, are destined for one part to revert to conservatism, for the other to vanish into the radical wing, with the result that when the generation now being educated at our secondary schools and universities is ready to take its place in society it will no longer be possible to stop the triumph of revolutionary radicalism unless we at this early stage take position at the head of the movement and seize the initiative in further developing our constitutional forms in a strictly neutral [nonpartisan] sense, in order to avert a development in a positively anti-Christian spirit. Failing this, we shall inevitably be forced by future developments into the corner of reaction, forfeit our influence on public opinion, and in the end find our shameful place between ultramontanists and conservatives.[45]

Apparently, Christian politics in Kuyper's mind was not an endeavor to establish a "Christian society" in some theocratic sense. Neither was it the work of a lay "pressure group" or "special interest group." Rather, as he put it, Christian politics "must offer a *modus vivendi* even to the opponent." The memorandum continued:

---

45 From the "*Memorandum presented to Dr. G. Groen van Prinsterer van Prinsterer by A. Kuyper during the latter's deliberation re accepting a seat in the Second Chamber*," 4 Feb. 1874; published in *Briefwisseling*, 6: 735–38.

Our basic principle may not be an attempt to impose Christianity by force, open or indirect, but rather should be the belief that if Christianity is to regain its free and unhampered place in society it is only in and through the nation's and the individuals' *conscience* that it shall rule and thereby liberate state and society.

For this reason, no demanding any privileges; no ignoring the new phase political life has entered in part due to the Revolution; no attempts at subverting our civil liberties; but an effort to make them good and to graft them onto a better root.

Proceeding from these premises, the fact will have to be recognized that our present constitutional order . . . has not kept pace with the evolution of political life at the grassroots level, that it is a layer of ice underneath which the water has flowed away, and that it lacks even the vitality to catch up to the political evolution the nation is undergoing.

From this it follows that our party (1) must take up position not behind but in front of today's liberalism; and (2) must characterize that liberalism as stationary and conservative, hence ought to choose as its objective a revision of the Constitution, not in a partial but in a general sense. Our party, too, must be *liberal*, but in contrast to revolutionary liberalism it must stand for a *Christian* liberalism, different in this sense that it seeks a liberalism not against or without Christ but a liberalism that returns thanks to Him, a liberalism that is not against or without a historic past but is accepted as the fruit of that past, a liberalism that is not restricted to the confines of our Constitution but in place of that straitjacket offers a garment in which the nation can breathe and grow freely.

To this end the Constitution is to be purged of whatever tends to cause the State, in spite of itself, to favor its own form of religion, one which must necessarily be anti-Christian in essence and character. Purged of whatever separates the State from the life of the nation. Purged of whatever restricts the free course of the Christian religion. Purged, finally, of whatever obstructs the free development of the organic life of the nation.

How would all this be applied concretely? Kuyper devoted a number of paragraphs to each of the major political issues. By way of illustration, this is how his paragraph on education begins:

Education is to be under the direction, regulation and inspection of the State.

For higher education the State is to endow a state university with fixed assets, in order that it may develop as a corporation solely in accordance with the innermost law of science. No appointment of professors by the State, only curators, by the Crown, from nominations.

To the free universities which one may wish to found in addition, the same benefits are to be assured in respect of titles and degrees, not as regards endowment. Only in this way can a Protestant university come into existence at Utrecht and a Roman Catholic one at 's-Hertogenbosch, as the vital centers of the two large elements of the nation. . . .

No one knew if this vision was practicable or just a pipedream, but Kuyper accepted his seat in parliament and embarked on a round of feverish activity. His maiden speech was about the social question, in particular child labor. He supported the Anti-School Law League, helped organize the People's Petition against the Liberal school bill of 1878, and in the following year achieved a national federation of antirevolutionary voters' associations, resulting in the Anti-Revolutionary Party, with which local cells of the League soon merged.

It is still a thrill to read the series of broad ranging, brilliant articles in which he explained the new party's political program.[46] They articulated an inspired vision for the

---

46 As so many of Kuyper's series of articles written for the press, this series too was collected and published in book form; cf. Kuyper, A. 1879. *Ons Program*. Amsterdam. The volume numbered 1307 pages. Starting

public square by a student of Calvinism, a disciple of Groen, and, incidentally, an admirer of Gladstone. The series appeared in *De Standaard* between April 1878 and February 1879 and has been systematically analyzed by McKendree Langley in terms of Christian thought, long-term goals and short-term electoral outcomes.[47]

Conclusion

Our conclusion is clear. Kuyper steeped himself in a tradition that was nearly a century old. He reaped where many others had sown. He mobilized a people already armed, elaborated a worldview and a program of action already sketched, accelerated a movement already in motion. Of course he was more than the sum of his inheritance, the upshot of historical antecedents, a vector of historical forces. He was also unique. But only against the backdrop of his historical context are we able to assess just how unique Abraham Kuyper really was.

---

in 1880, a large number of appendices were removed from reprint editions, reducing the volume to 500 pages.

47   Langley, McKendree R. 1995. "Emancipation and Apologetics: The Formation of Abraham Kuyper's An-ti-Revolutionary Party in the Netherlands, 1872–1880." *PhD Thesis*. Westminster Theological Seminary, Philadelphia.

2

Abraham Kuyper: His Early Life and Conversion

Catherine M. E. Kuyper

Abraham Kuyper was born in 1837 in the little town of Maassluis. His father, Jan Frederik Kuiyper, was a minister in the Established (Nederlands Hervormde) Church. His mother, Henriëtte Huber, daughter of a Swiss officer of the guard, was a lady of great intellect, as mothers of prominent men often are. It was a beautiful autumn Sunday morning when Abraham put in his appearance on this globe. He proved to be what the Dutch call a Sunday child (*Zondagskind*) in many ways in his later life.

He was a peculiar looking little chap with an extraordinarily large head – so big that mother Kuyper had trouble buying suitable hats for him. Often she had them specially made. Sometimes these hats were a bit odd and drew the attention of the boys in the street, who considered him and his hat a source of unusual merriment, and hooting after him cried: "There is steam under that hat! It is inflated with gas!"

As a child his parents were rather anxious about him because he gave the impression of being slow, even a little backward. He could not read as quickly as other children of his age. They were afraid he was a hydrocephalus (baby with a water head) and took him to a specialist who, after examining him closely, exclaimed:

> Nothing serious! In fact, nothing the matter at all! This boy has an unusual supply of gray matter, and if his little body can feed it, and he should live, he will be a great man some day; for his brains are of extraordinary size and will be of tremendous capacity!

Young Kuyper at Middelburg

When the lad was about three-and-a-half, his father accepted a call to Middelburg in the province of Zeeland. Here the Kuyper residence was located near the harbor, at the Punt, where the merchant marine was concentrated. Little Bram would sit for hours at the drawing-room windows, watching the boats entering and leaving port. When he grew older, he could not resist the temptation to walk the gangplank to see the interior of a boat. He wanted to know how ships were built and how the sailors lived. On board these anchored ships he was often surrounded by sailors intensely interested in the little fellow, whose many questions they tried to answer.

As he grew older, he went on regular visits aboard ship, especially on Sundays, when he often delivered a little sermonette to the sailors. He took tracts from his father's study and also, secretly, some of his father's cigars to reward those who had behaved well and had listened attentively to his childlike sermon. Really this young evangelist fascinated those rough boys. They just had to listen to him and, of course, they enjoyed the cigars, too! Little Abram became a real friend to them. But when they used bad language or took the Lord's name in vain, he would give it to them – and a good scolding it was, too! To those who did not behave well, he refused the reward: the coveted cigar!

His mother was very proud of him. She cherished the idea that her Sunday child would one day be a minister like his father. But little Bram had different ambitions. His *idée fixe* at the time was to travel the high seas, ultimately to be captain on a large boat, and to start as soon as possible as an apprentice at a nautical school. But God frustrated his plans. He called him to quite a different future. God was preparing him to be a church reformer, and then afterwards in the distant future, to be a captain indeed, but on the Netherland's ship of state!

A Student at Leiden University

In 1849 his father received a call to Leiden. We know from my aunts that Abraham at this time was given the choice between becoming a sailor or a student. His sisters persuaded him to look forward to entering Leiden University; and so when his father accepted the Leiden pastorate, young Bram began his schooling in the grammar school there. Although then twelve years of age, he had never entered a schoolroom before! He had been previously tutored only by his parents. Among his schoolmates his record was enviable, as he stood consistently at the head of his class. When leaving this grammar school, Abram was chosen to deliver the valedictory, which he did in excellent French.

In 1855, when Abraham was seventeen, he became a student at the historic Leiden University. He enrolled for both Philology and Theology. He had no money for distractions, which proved a blessing for him – no theatre, no drinks – which are the ruin of many a European student. He knew well how to divide his time, for already as a student he worked out a definite daily schedule and stuck to it rigidly. Till the end of his life, the rigid budgeting of his hours was the secret of his great success. He knew how to achieve an incredible amount of work in a given period. He lived by the clock. Work, meals, walks, writing, holidays, visits, interviews: all formed a part of his busy program, and usually he started with a look at his watch. Often we teased him later in life that the great old man had become a slave to the second hand.

During his student life, he got up at ten and worked till late in the night, because he felt he could better concentrate when the family was asleep and the house quiet. Though he was a strenuous worker, he was by no means dry; on the contrary, he was gay, enjoyed a good joke, and was full of fun.

The Leiden manse had a lovely garden, where he received his fellow-students on Saturday afternoons. As he had retained his love for water and boats, he planned at one time a water trip with them. They all embarked in a "*trekschuit*" ("*tow-boat*") decorated with Chinese lanterns and spent several days vacationing, doing their own cooking!

He was very fond of a lively discussion. His father called him "*animal disputax*" (disputatious creature)! He would memorize long portions of poetry and walk through the house reciting them. He thought this belonged to his philological training. He stood at the top of his class and Dr. De Vries said he expected him to be a somebody someday.

Abram also studied the Gothic language. At one time during an examination, Professor De Vries asked him to read a part of the Gospel according to St. John (Ulfilas' translation). He was very nervous because he was not quite sure that he had mastered all of it. When the professor told him to stop and to translate, he was in despair. He asked kindly if he might finish reading the chapter as it belonged to the story. This was granted. His nerves calmed down. As he read on, the text became more familiar and the translation, including the first part, was then clear to him, He passed his BA in the Classics *summa cum laude.* And as Dr. Rullmann writes: "His philological study has been of great influence on his style. His deftness and clarity of expression remind us again and again of the great rhetoricians and historians of the ancient Latin civilization. Just as those, so with Kuyper, the right word follows the thought quite willingly, but his style shows greater vivacity and exuberance, which makes him more a romanticist than a classicist." However, he followed no definite school, for Kuyper created his own Dutch idiom.

The time spent at Leiden University proved a period of fiery trial for his faith. Dr. Scholten's dogmatic courses robbed him of the faith of his youth, although he never became an atheist. His home influence and early training proved a real stronghold spiritually. But through Scholten's influence he went so far astray that when Professor Rauwenhoff openly denied the bodily resurrection of our Lord, Abram assented to it and joined his fellow-students in literally applauding the assertion. Later, after his conversion, he repented of this and as often as the thought came back to him, he felt horror-stricken. Could this man ever become a vessel fit for the Master's use? Yes, for God controlled his life and would bring him back to the faith of his fathers and that in a most wonderful way!

The Prize Essay On à Lasco

In 1858, his tutor and faithful adviser, as Kuyper always considered Dr. Mathijs de Vries, drew his attention to a prize essay contest offered by the University of Groningen on a critical comparison between John Calvin's and (the Polish Reformer) John à Lasco's conception of the church. De Vries urged Kuyper to enter the contest. Abram willingly consented. He started at once, full of enthusiasm, to gather the necessary sources.

Calvin's works were readily available at the Leiden University library, but when he tried to get à Lasco's works, he sought in vain. Even at the world's best libraries in London and St. Petersburg, not one volume was to be found. Facing this paramount difficulty, he went to Prof. De Vries and told him that he had decided to withdraw from the contest. His tutor, however, did not acquiesce but urged him to look around in private libraries. "And, my boy," he concluded, "start in Haarlem at my father's home. He possesses a rich collection of books on Church History."

Abram went to Haarlem to meet this elderly gentleman. But a new disappointment was in store when Dominie De Vries told him that he did not recall a single volume of à Lasco on his shelves. "Come again next week; I'll take a look to make sure," he said in parting. After a week Kuyper returned to Haarlem but without the least hope of finding what he wanted so badly. Imagine his joy as well as surprise when the minister, upon entering the library, showed him a complete collection of à Lasco's writings. These books did not exist anywhere else. The young student was so amazed that he definitely saw in this God's providential finger. This ended his long period of spiritual apathy, and he started again to pray, thanking his God fervently for this happy find, which seemed to him to give a sanctified character to this particular study. For eight months he worked at it steadily and zealously.

But even this study did not mean a spiritual change. He considered it only as an historical problem. His argument in the prize essay was rather a sustained criticism of Calvinism and perhaps an approach to the Irenic-Ethicalist point of view.

As the outcome of the contest, the Groningen Theological Faculty honored Kuyper with the first prize: a gold medal. Laudations and congratulations were showered upon him. No wonder that this young man, just twenty years of age, felt very proud of himself. But the physical and mental strain of the months of arduous toil took its toll, and Kuyper suffered a serious breakdown. His brain seemed exhausted. He could not even recall a book title. The doctor ordered a complete rest for months. But Abram just could not be idle. If his mind were to relax, his hands could be busy. Then and there, his old love for boats was revived. He bought the necessary tools and began to build a miniature ship – a two-masted vessel, such as he had seen so often in his early youth in the harbor at the Punt. When he had finished, a captain told him the replica was perfect; not a single pulley or string was missing. His fiancée dressed the little sailors, made the flags and embroidered her name on the top flag: "Johanna." This little ship later became the pride and joy of his children. It is still to be seen in the Kuyper-House in the room which was once his study.

In the Crucible

He next decided to improve his English by reading some novels with his youngest sister. They started with Miss Yonge's *The Heir of Redclyffe*, a plot which left a deep impression upon his religious life. He writes about this in his *Confidentie*. This story brought him to the first stage of his conversion. The chapter of Guy's death and Philip's remorse revealed to him his own sinful heart. Guy had forgiven Philip tenderly and lovingly for all the wrong he had done in trying to spoil his life. Kuyper saw that in God's sight the haughty and talented Philip was nothing at all, a nobody, but poor Guy was the hero. Abram writes, "And before I knew, I knelt down and wept. What my soul passed through in those minutes, I realized later. From that hour I despised and hated that which I had previously admired, and instead sought for that which I had thus far despised. This masterpiece of Miss Yonge's has been for me the breaking down of my self-sufficient and stubborn heart."

It was in the summer of 1863 that Abraham Kuyper took his Doctor of Theology degree, *summa cum laude*, on the dissertation for which he used his completed and corrected prize essay on à Lasco. That same summer he married Johanna Hendrika Schaay and went with her to the parsonage of Beesd, a small village in Gelderland, where he became pastor of the Nederlands Hervormde Kerk. He started his work in this part of God's vineyard with his usual zeal and enthusiasm. Day after day he ministered to the spiritual needs of this people, never suspecting the tremendous opposition that lay in store for him. As he says in his *Confidentie*: "A congregation was entrusted to me, but I did not come to give of what I possessed – but with a silent prayer that my own empty heart might be fed by the congregation! In the circle which I frequented a strong conservatism with a kind of orthodox hue without any spiritual power prevailed. There was no voice out of the deep, no sound from an historical past." His parishioners were smugly satisfied and complacent with things as they were. They absolutely refused to contribute to Kingdom causes and for Kingdom needs. Among them there was also a sizeable number of malcontents, who had been a headache to every previous pastor. But Kuyper treated them impartially, visiting them all alike in their humble homes.

Pietje Baltus and Abraham Kuyper

On one such visit God brought him in contact with a young woman, Pietje Baltus, daughter of a common laborer, who led him to the feet of the Savior, there to find redemption in His blood. At last his heart was opened. She steadfastly refused to come to church, refused to shake hands with him, for, said she, "You do not give us the true bread of life." Sympathetically she told him just what she believed and how she dissented from the views he held and preached. She showed him the old parchments, which contained the Calvinistic Confession. She was thoroughly familiar with their contents, having read them all. She told Kuyper what Christ had done for her personally. Often he sat in that humble home for hours, just listening. He marveled at the faith as well as the knowledge of this girl. How strong her faith in the absolute sovereignty of God! Gradually she led him to a deeper study of Calvin's *Institutes*, where he found the same truths of which Pietje was trying to convince him. The ideas and ideals of this famous Genevan Reformer had been kept much alive in this peasant hut. Then and there started the tremendous struggle in the soul of Abraham Kuyper. Here he found his Peniel, where God became victor! Here God prepared him for his gigantic task in Church and State. The deepening and propagating of the Calvinistic principles and confession became his highest ambition. To that noble cause he gave his entire life, dedicating all his many talents to the great task for which God Himself had called and equipped him.

Never did Kuyper forget Pietje Baltus, his spiritual mother in Christ. Till the very end of his life her photo stood on his writing desk in front of him as an inspiration and challenge. It is still there in the "Kuyperhuis," where his study is kept intact just as he left it.

He stayed in Beesd until 1867. During this time he prepared and published the *Opera* (Works) of John à Lasco in the original Latin, thereby establishing his reputation in scholarly circles.

To Utrecht and Greater Service

The publication of the *Opera* led to an amusing incident in his later life. In 1903, Mr. Birrel, the English Minister of Education, dined with us. Desirous of paying Dr. Kuyper a compliment, he told him of his admiration for all he had published and added that he wondered how, with all his scientific achievements, he had also found time to publish such a magnificent "opera." We all looked surprised for my father had never been a musician. Still Mr. Birrel stuck to his assertion. "I'm quite sure I'm correct," he said, "for I know it was a Polish opera." Then the truth dawned on us: he had somehow been informed of the editing of the *Opera* of à Lasco!

In 1867, when Kuyper was thirty years of age, he left Beesd and moved to Utrecht, where he began the great struggle to deliver our country from government autocracy, a struggle which lasted till the end of his life. First of all, he started to purify the Church from declension and heresy, striving to bring her back to a sound Calvinistic basis, to ground her anew in her confession in obedience to her King and Savior, Jesus Christ. He stimulated discussions with his colleagues who, though orthodox, had gone astray on different points. It was at that time that he delivered his first and memorable lecture, "Appeal to the People's Conscience." Present at that meeting was Mr. Groen van Prinsterer, then leader of the Anti-Revolutionary Party. This great Calvinistic statesman then stood alone in the breach like a general without an army. He felt at once great affinity for Dr. Kuyper and found in him the man he needed to take the lead, and he became his staunch friend and fatherly adviser.

From this time dates the birth in his breast of the all-consuming ideal to conquer every area of human life and make it consciously subject to Christ, the King: *Pro Rege!* Or, as he formulated it in more concrete language at another time: "Nowhere in all of human life and society is there so much as an inch of space of which Christ does not claim: It is Mine!"

3

Raging Tumults of Soul:
The Private Life of Abraham Kuyper

James D. Bratt

Abraham Kuyper's personality is usually treated as an adjunct of his ideas. This father of an important strand in Dutch Calvinism appears in the typical sketch as a stout-hearted, brilliant, universal man, entirely fit to proclaim the sovereignty of God over every area of life to an unbelieving age. The portrait has the militancy, brilliance, and courage right. But there was more to the character and its development than that. Since Kuyper himself cultivated a close identification between his person and his cause, it is appropriate, in this the 150th anniversary of his birth, to delve behind his received image and consider the private side of the man. It is also appropriate to reverse the angle of vision, to ask what effect Kuyper's character had on his ideas. A good place to begin is with his nervous breakdown That Kuyper suffered a collapse or two is no surprise given his times. Neurasthenia ("prostration" or "weakness of the nerves") was all the rage in the late nineteenth century. No claimant to high bourgeois status could go on long without it – or without the protracted idling at a spa that was its "cure." But since Kuyper insisted that he was not like his age, why did he conform to its image on this score? Why did this man who spoke, like the Master he served, with authority, who was sure he knew the will of God and was quick to declare it on every issue under the sun – why did he collapse so utterly that people worried for his future, and not once but three times? Why did he fall beneath "raging tumults of soul" into a "darkness" and lassitude so profound that he could not read more than two pages of a book or write even a postcard?

Kuyper's family and followers assured each other that the cause was overwork. That serves so far as it goes. Even the universal man can take on too much. But the question then arises, Why the overwork? Why did Kuyper feel compelled to do *everything*, to strain and push himself virtually to death? That query takes us into a darker tangle. Kuyper was a warrior, a combatant every day of his life. But he did not often recognize that his conflict with forces without was mirrored by one within. His breakdowns occurred when the two conjoined to overwhelm him.

Kuyper had no followers at the time of his first collapse, but when they later read his account of it (in *Confidentie*, 1873) they surely applauded. This was the type of fall they expected, a classic Reformed-pietist conversion from pride to humility, liberalism toward orthodoxy, self-seeking to reliance on Christ. Kuyper's account begins in mid-1859. He is twenty-one years old and in the crucial career transition from undergraduate to graduate work. A nationwide essay competition has been announced, and Kuyper is determined to win. But he cannot find the requisite source materials and is near despair when, "as if by a miracle of God," he comes upon them in a private library. And "when the prize was won," Kuyper says, "even my self-righteous heart gave part of the glory" to God (39). What Kuyper does not recount here is the eight months of extraordinary concentration and labor which he put into the project and which left him, prize in hand, in complete exhaustion. He lay around for days with a book on his lap, unable even to tell its title. He built a model ship, but that did not help. A trip up the Rhine, including taking the cure at Baden and Wiesbaden, did.

Back at Leiden, Kuyper's career urges flamed back to life. He finished his doctorate in short order, but then confronted the prospect not of a good academic post but a pastorate in one or another out of the way parish. At that juncture his fiancée sent him *The Heir of Redclyffe*. Therewith began phase two of the crisis.

Charlotte Yonge's sentimental novel is almost unreadable today, but it swept the English-reading world upon its publication in 1853. Cultivated young men were particularly attracted: Oxford undergraduates, British officers in the Crimea, and stalwarts like Kuyper on the continent. Its storyline spoke directly to his recent turmoil, but also to the broader patterns of his youth and the question of his future. The story pits two aristocratic cousins against each other. Philip is suave, arrogant, independent, always a winner; Guy is mild, deferential, and pious. Philip takes special delight in pestering his cousin, but when an accident turns the tables, Guy returns good for evil. That is only the first stroke. The tables turn again (we are in Victorian romance, remember), and Guy on his deathbed shows such nobility of character that Philip is driven to shame, confession, and pardon. Reading these scenes, Kuyper says, his own eyes moistened with Philip's and he knelt with him in profound prayer: ". . . every word of self-condemnation he uttered cut through my soul as a judgment on my own ambition and character. . . . from that moment on I have despised what I earlier admired and sought what I earlier disdained" (42).

Kuyper's identification with Philip was well-earned. Precocious, charming, invincible, he had dominated his family as a youth. He then cut smoothly through a superlative university (Leiden), casting off his parents' piety on the way, and capped it off by conquering all comers nationwide. A Romantic hero was aborning, defining himself by himself, carving out the first step in a career of fame. But God, his body, and his psyche immediately laid him low. At home and at the baths Kuyper had ample leisure to reflect on the drives that had brought him to this pass.

For all his prayerful resolution, however, Kuyper's next fifteen years showed him to have taken only half a turn. He changed his theology but kept his character. Philip's assertiveness would now serve Guy's Lord: surely that made all the difference. Accordingly, Kuyper's new orthodoxy was more stringent than his father's had ever been. Assertiveness needs a firm launch-pad, and if the self no longer sufficed, then God and his Word would. But only if absolutized into a Calvinistic system built from unshakable principles by hard logic into a complete edifice. This construction occupied Kuyper from his recovery in 1860 through the end of his first pastorate in 1867. By then, he said in telling language, he had found a permanent dwelling place "in the cleft of the rock," "built on the rock," "hewn from the rock of thought," enabling him to "laugh in the face of every storm" (47). Enabling him to raise a storm too.

Kuyper opened his national career in 1867 with a tract arguing for the purity and proper control of the church. For the next twenty years, until he and his followers split from the National Church in 1886, the "church question" remained central to his thought. The political and educational enterprises he developed in these years were extensions (and guarantors) of church reform, and such reform was meant to lead to national revitalization. In fact, the nature of the church had been on Kuyper's mind from the start. His prize essay had addressed the church models of Calvin and Jan Laski, and *The Heir of Redclyffe* culminated with Guy's being buried to (as Kuyper quoted the novel)

> "the words of his Mother church – the mother who had guided each step of his orphaned life." There I stopped. Such a church I had never seen and did not know. Oh to have such a church! . . . It became the homesickness, the hunger of my life. (43)

This remarkable language, which Kuyper repeated in later writings, indicates how personal dynamics were bound up in Kuyper's public polemics. So do the epithets he used to describe the church as he had known it in Leiden: "Lies," "hypocrisy," and "carnal routine . . . exhibited themselves there in the most pathetic way . . ." (35). And for Kuyper the closest figure caught up in that syndrome was his own father, pastor of one of the Leiden churches. Kuyper's relations with his father had been formal and proper at best, although even that did not keep them from arguing politics in front of company. The son's church crusade can be seen as an extension of that quarrel by other means. So was his theological tack. Early in their careers both Kuypers faced the perennial choice of their circle: whether to maximize Reformed confessionalism or to moderate doctrine and emphasize ethics and ecumenism instead. Kuyper's father had deliberately opted for the second; young Abraham took the first and had some of his bitterest battles with representatives of the second. One need not be a sworn psychohistorian, therefore, to recognize that Kuyper's church battles involved, among other things, the redemption of a tarnished Mother and the exorcism of his father. In that connection it is worth noting that the line from world literature that Kuyper quoted most often (and in reference to the epochal discovery of the books for his prize essay) was the "To be or not to be" of *Hamlet*.

If one father proves false, another must be had. Kuyper found him in the late 1860s in Groen van Prinsterer. Long the national head of the confessional Reformed party, Groen was impressed by Kuyper's bold defense of their position against the "irenic ethicals" at the conference where the two first met. The young prophet thereafter maneuvered to be publicly bedecked with (in his terms) the old Elijah's mantle. That campaign led to his second breakdown. To qualify as true heir, Kuyper had to read himself up to the level of Groen's considerable learning. But he also had to excel this "general without an army" by showing effective leadership in the trenches of movement organization. So Kuyper shifted to the center of the church battle by taking a congregation in Amsterdam in 1870. Two years later he added the editorship of a daily newspaper. Two years after that he entered Parliament, giving up his pastorate but remaining immersed in the city's church councils. Thus in 1874, at age thirty-seven, Kuyper was occupied with three potentially full-time positions, each involving him in furious study, politicking, and ideological combat. Small wonder he returned to the therapy of the bath, soaking his arms and face in cold water or, more efficiently, holding ice compresses to his head while laboring at his desk into the wee hours, trying to master every question, anticipate all possible retorts, develop his own rebuttals. He alone, he felt, had to uphold the glory of God, the future of the nation, the honor of his party. Not surprisingly, his behavior in Parliament defied all protocol and managed to unite the other parties from left to right in rebuke.

Kuyper needed peace, comfort, and something different, so he took ship in late May 1875 to find it. He alighted in Brighton, England, where Robert Pearsall Smith was holding meetings to encourage the higher life of Christian sanctification. Drawing off the recent Moody-Sankey revivals and leading on to the Keswick holiness movement, the Brighton meetings offered Kuyper a paradigm of Anglo-American evangelical piety. He bit hard and returned home to propagandize the movement in his paper. How wonderful the unity in Christ, he recalled, when he himself broke the communion bread for two French and Prussian officers who had lately been shooting at each other. How soothing the calm of personal consecration, how sweet the service of the Spirit. Kuyper assured his readers that he was not advocating perfectionism or straying from the old Reformed way. But the quickness of their suspicions intimated otherwise. In fact Kuyper *was* considering another path, one reminiscent of the ethical evangelicalism, cultural quiescence, and softer dogmatics of his father (himself set on his clerical career by an English evangelist). Instead of choosing, Kuyper tried to combine the two – without success. Adding mission rallies to his other work hardly brought rest, and chanting "Dare to be a Daniel" on the floor of Parliament did not mollify the opposition. To a Catholic member, the pose of perfect consecration only put a high-gloss sheen on this "whited sepulcher." Spiritually it was a severe temptation to pride. Pearsall Smith showed as much that same summer when he was discovered in holy congress with a female convert. Kuyper suffered his worst collapse a few months later.

Kuyper never talked much about this crisis, perhaps because it could not lead to an exemplary conversion. Yet the record is fairly clear. Frenetic but exhausted, unable to work or to rest, Kuyper left the Netherlands in February 1876 for sixteen months abroad, mostly at Nice and Lake Como. This time he took the walking cure. Four-hour hikes through the Alps gave him the kind of fatigue that led to sleep. What passed through his mind can only be inferred from his actions upon returning home. He gave up elective office "for good." He apologized, a bit obliquely, for his pride. He defended classic Calvinism as more likely than Holiness promises to produce true sanctification. And on that basis he launched three remarkable years of movement organization. By 1880 he had in place permanent national networks to support a Calvinistic political party, university, and elementary school system. In sum, Kuyper had pruned his career options, had settled his theological qualms, and had harnessed his filial dynamics. Since Groen had died during Kuyper's exile, the latter returned to the sole leadership of the neo-Calvinist movement.

Personally, he undertook a new discipline – or in his daughter's words, an "iron regimen" regulated in every part to the minute. Breakfast, alone, at 8:30. Writing and reading, absolutely undisturbed, in his study from 9:00 to 12:30. A quick processing of visitors until 1:00, then lunch and off to the Free University to lecture and consult. Dinner and devotions with the family (their only slot) from 5:30 to 6:30. Then the famous walks, covering the same route and the same two hours every evening, during which he rehearsed his editorials and articles for the next day. Back home, some conversation, a glass of wine, and to bed. As to the annual cycle, a short winter vacation – abroad, often at Cologne – for the first days of the new year. In mid-summer, a longer holiday at the baths – again abroad, often near Dresden – with no family, friends, or work along. Absolute rest was required to regird for absolute work. The labor-breakdown-recovery cycle had been ritualized into every day and year.

Still, he suffered the effects of neurasthenia for six more years, until around 1883, just when the battle for church reform heated up to its climax. Kuyper led the campaign with full ardor, but the results in 1886 were disappointing. Some, but not all, of his followers separated from the National Church, which could therefore never be cleansed and become the vanguard of national revival. Kuyper looked thereafter to politics instead. But that only exacerbated the tension in his own house, now coming out along fraternal rather than filial lines. Kuyper accentuated his democratic-populist themes; A. F. Savornin Lohman, a close and long-standing colleague, argued for a conservative course. As the struggle intensified, Kuyper stood for election again and at age fifty-seven returned to Parliament, to polemics, and to overwork. Summer vacation that year, 1894, ended with him succumbing to a heavy cold that developed into pleurisy and pneumonia. Though the "somatic" causes of this crisis were evident and life-threatening, its "psychological" dimension was apparent enough to Kuyper to put him on a familiar trail: several months' rest in the South. There he wrote a moving meditation on sickness as the individual's share in humanity's sin and evil. On the other hand, as he said, it could work to "make small what was too high; to turn self-trust into trust in God. . . . to quicken pity and compassion, greater love and sympathy for others"; and "above all . . . to glorify the Name . . . [of him] who through the dark clouds of suffering sends the clear and precious beams of his holy mercy" (Rullmann, 146–47). The first lessons of his first crisis were being repeated. But not the fraternal concord of *Redclyffe*. Kuyper took up his parliamentary duties promptly in 1895 and did his part in the battle between the two factions that led to splitting the party and Lohman's dismissal from the Free University faculty.

By all accounts the years that followed saw Kuyper at his peak. Impressive honors came to him, especially an honorary degree at Princeton (1898) and the prime minister's chair at The Hague (1901). But the latter turned out to be the punishment of answered prayer. Only his pride was injured when his cabinet fell in 1905, but Kuyper took the usual remedy – this time a nine-month tour of the Mediterranean that brought him honors in every port and plentiful occasions for world-historical commentary. It also cost him his political future at home, for his party repaid this "desertion" by awarding future plums to its younger leaders. Kuyper never gave their ventures more than tepid support. His prickly independence increased with age on everything from social policy to his summer vacation. As late as 1917, in his 80th year, he insisted on taking the trip into wartime Germany alone. A little later his lung ailments returned, and he began the final descent to his death in 1920. God gave this lion just the kind of death he needed, his daughter said. The slow separation from power left him helpless before the mercy of his Lord but not entirely changed. This man of eighty-three years, a dozen offices, scores of honors, and a 232-title bibliography went to his grave, like Calvin himself, mourning all the work he had left to do.

Such a complex of Calvinism, labor, and iron will was classically described by one of Kuyper's contemporaries, Max Weber. Indeed, Kuyper's regimen might have walked out of Weber's pages. Weber's own habits did. The exacting schedule Weber followed in young manhood as he pursued several degrees and careers simultaneously resembled Kuyper's in every part, religious devotions excepted. Weber too suffered severe breakdowns in his late thirties and late fifties, the first lasting for five years and growing out of a patricide more nearly literal than Kuyper's. A similar collapse put Kuyper's closer contemporary, William James, in limbo from ages twenty-five to thirty-two. James's case is usually ascribed to philosophical causes, but he suffered the same combination of intellectual doubt, career indecision, and hostility for father that afflicted the other two. All three had vacillating, preemptory sires who in the sons' eyes had sold out to corrupt or ineffectual careers, yet blocked their offspring from doing better. The fathers exercised power but no true authority, and the sons had to find or construct such in themselves.

In this way the personal mirrored a cultural problem. As Walter Houghton sketches it in *The Victorian Frame of Mind*, the blessed queen's reign (1837–1901) saw the successive undermining of traditional authorities (aristocratic, ecclesiastical, philosophical) across Europe. For that reason, the era was obsessed with maintaining social and intellectual order. With no bureaucratic specialization as yet developed which was adequate to the task, the duty fell to individual giants – thinkers and movers who could construct the one big system that would put things back in place. The job was so immense, the stakes so high, that anyone who applied was prone to messianism and mortification, to extreme but finally unavailing labor and subsequent collapse. Even on the level of individual identity, romantic self-construction became absurd in a realist, proletarian age. Such were the burdens of Kuyper and company.

The three shared one other trait. Behind their fathers stood stout Calvinistic grandfathers and a tradition the grandsons knew well. Certainly they appraised their heritage differently, but they gave much of their careers to sorting out its import. The question thus arises, To what extent was Kuyper's personal course symptomatic of his tradition as well as his times? Some continuities are unmistakable. The tendencies to rush to judgment, to confuse persons with principles, to be genial in private with opponents (and friends) but to eviscerate them in print, to inflate confidence into self-righteousness and conviction into pomposity – such have appeared not only among succeeding generations in Amsterdam but in Grand Rapids and Toronto, Chestnut Hill and L'Abri. Doubtless the syndrome was amplified by these centers' belief that they were fighting for their spiritual lives against the historical tide. Doubtless one does not wish to settle for false conciliation. Doubtless other traditions, Christian or not, have fostered similar effects; the recent PTL follies have shown what wonderful nastiness can go forward under an evangelical rhetoric of love and forgiveness.

But Kuyper's career surely highlights once more the paradoxes of Calvinism – a system that begins with the inscrutable sovereignty of God and ends in the enforceable clarity of law; that starts out denying and ends up magnifying human agency; that warns of human depravity, yet can feed all ambition. These tensions must end in (self-)destruction or in a self-deprecating humor that echoes the laughter from heaven. As "the tribune of his people," Kuyper did not allow that much in public. But in retirement he could do better. When asked how he knew he had done God's work, Kuyper replied, "When you've done it as long as I have, you can't be sure anymore." To keep trying nonetheless, to press conviction with due caution, is Kuyper's personal legacy to our time.

4

How Abraham Kuyper Became a Kuyperian

R. D. Henderson

In this essay[1] I shall attempt the task of explaining how and why Abraham Kuyper, unlike so many of his fellow students at Leiden University in the late 1850s, did not end up as a "liberal" theologian, a "dead orthodox" minister, or a "culture-fearing" pietist, but instead became the founder of what is rather cryptically known as "Kuyperianism."[2] As a provisional definition let us say that a person is a Kuyperian if he or she, like Kuyper, seeks to act upon the conviction that "there is not a square inch in the whole domain of our human existence over which Christ, who is Sovereign over *all*, does not cry: 'Mine!'"[3]

Although he was considerably more than this, Abraham Kuyper was at least a Christian scholar. Because he lived in one of Europe's smaller countries, it is easy to view his Christian political, scholarly, and journalistic accomplishments as those of a big fish in a small pond. Yet his actions and the great clarity with which he articulated the ideas behind them have caused his influence to spread far beyond the borders of The Netherlands. His example motivated Dutch immigrants in setting up Christian educational institutions in North America and has inspired people in many places. Through his lectures at Princeton University (1898) and published writings (a number of which were translated into English at the time and many more recently) and through the writing of various U.S. evangelicals, his influence has now spread far and wide, offering the idea of "Christ the transformer of culture."[4] His work serves as a significant model of Christian scholarship, thought, and organized activity, and as such is a source of instruction.

I shall place my discussion of how Kuyper became a Kuyperian within the following contexts or scenes. The first of these is Kuyper's family background and the course of

---

1   This essay has benefited considerably from criticisms made by Peter Heslam and Harry Van Dyke. The translations from the Dutch are mine.

2   In the absolute sense this task is impossible on principle. In my view, its impossibility does not arise from a lack of historical source material or the like, but because no combination of explanatory factors (e.g., historical, social, psychological, economic, aesthetic, etc.) can ever fully explain the course of a human life. God alone comprehends the mystery of human history, and yet it is profitable to study praiseworthy persons in order to imitate in our own unique way the good things they did and stood for.

3   This quotation is taken from Kuyper's address given at the opening of the Free University in Amsterdam, *Souvereiniteit in eigen kring* (Sovereignty in [their] own sphere) (1880); translated as "Sphere Sovereignty," in *AK:ACR* 463–490.

4   George Marsden refers in his article, "The State of Evangelical Christian Scholarship" to "The triumph – or nearly so – of what may be loosely called Kuyperian presuppositionalism in the evangelical community." (1987. *The Reformed Journal*, September: 14).

his early life. A second offers a glimpse of his goals and achievements, indicating what Kuyperianism meant in practice. A third sketches the background to Kuyper's "conversion," namely his early university years and his relationship with his fiancée. The last portrays the attitudes and discovery that made him break with "liberalism" (in all of its forms) and convinced him of the necessity of Christian action on many fronts. At the end of the essay I will draw some conclusions and give a brief evaluation of Kuyper's ideas and achievements.

A word about my methods in reading the accounts of Kuyper's early transitional phase, such as the one found in his own autobiographical *Confidentie*[5]: I wondered to what extent they had been stylized to fit a later self-image. With many of his early letters now in print,[6] one is able to check his later statements, at least for self-consistency, with earlier ones, especially since some of the letters were written a matter of days after the events they describe. These sources are supplemented by various other letters, writings, and published early sermons. Hence I have relied primarily, though not exclusively, upon a comparison of statements made by Kuyper himself under a variety of circumstances and at different times.

Biographical Introduction

Abraham Kuyper was born on October 29, 1837 in a small town at the mouth of the river Meuse, near Rotterdam, called Maassluis. His mother, Henrietta Huber (1802–1881), had worked as a governess before becoming a teacher at a girls' boarding school in Amsterdam. Kuyper's father, Jan Frederik (1801–1882), was a pastor in the state-organized church (*Netherlandsch Hervormde Kerk*) but had come from an uneducated family in Amsterdam.[7] In 1841 the Kuyper family moved from the parish of Maassluis to that of Middelburg, the provincial capital of Zeeland. After eight years in Middelburg they moved once again, this time to the university town of Leiden. Here the young Abraham received a good education, learning both ancient and modem languages at school. He proved to be an excellent pupil and gained the highest honors. At the time of his graduation from secondary school, for instance, he was valedictorian and spoke on a topic of his choice. His address displayed his keen interest in (German) literature, history, and theology. The title of his speech in German was *Ulfila: der Bischof der Visi-Gothen und seine Gothische Bibelübersetzung*.[8] In the fall of 1855 Kuyper began studying theology and literature at Leiden University. By 1858 he had finished his first degree, passing exams in literature, philosophy, and classical languages *summa cum laude*.

It was at this time that Abraham first met Johanna Hendrika Schaay (1842–1899)

---

5   1873. *Confidentie: Schrijven aan de Weled*. Heer J. H. van der Linden. Amsterdam: Höveker and Zoon. (Hereafter referred to as *Conf.*) This was a sketch of his early life written in the form of a (long) letter to a friend.

6   Puchinger, G. 1987. *Abraham Kuyper: De jonge Kuyper* (1837–1867). Franeker: Wever. (Hereafter cited as *De jonge . . . .*) See also: Puchinger, G. 1998. *Abraham Kuyper: His Early Journey of Faith*. Amsterdam: VU University Press.

7   Having learned English from foreign sailors, Jan Frederik was enlisted as a young man to translate tracts for an English Methodist missionary, one A. S. Thelwall (1795–1863), who had come to Amsterdam to bring the Gospel to the Jewish people. Appreciating the young man's talents, Thelwall and his Dutch associates arranged for the financing of his further education and training for the ministry.

8   "Ulfilas, Bishop of Visogoths, and His Gothic Translation of the Bible."

to whom he was soon to be engaged. Johanna was sixteen at the time, and Abraham was twenty-one. Johanna, whose father was a stockbroker, lived in Rotterdam. During their five years of engagement (1858 to 1863) Abraham and Johanna corresponded regularly, leaving an extensive record of their thoughts, ideas, and feelings. Their letters are an important source for understanding Kuyper, his character, and the development and changes in his thought during his theological training. In 1863 they were married, shortly before Kuyper became pastor in Beesd.

As a young student at Leiden University in the late 1850s, Kuyper was subject to the growing influence of "modern" German and Dutch theology with its new theories about the nature of religion and Scripture. One of the most important theologians at Leiden was J. H. Scholten (1811–1885). Although he respected Scholten greatly, Kuyper did not feel nearly as close to him as to his literature professor, M. de Vries (1820–1892), an eminent scholar of the Dutch language and its literature. De Vries proved to be an invaluable inspiration to Kuyper and in 1859 suggested that he try to enter a competition announced by the theology department of the University of Groningen for the best essay comparing John Calvin's and John à Lasco's views of the church.[9] Kuyper took up the challenge and worked hard, almost compulsively, for several months in hope of winning the prize. This meant that his time with Johanna in Rotterdam had to be cut even shorter than usual. Finally, in 1860 his labors were rewarded by winning the prize: a gold medal and with it, much honor. Kuyper was left exhausted, and shortly after receiving the prize he began to suffer some kind of head pains, making it almost impossible for him to study. This condition persisted for many months, causing him much grief and worry about the possibility that he might not gain the highest evaluation at his coming final exams. Nevertheless, Kuyper completed his degree in theology (*kandidaats*) in December 1861, *summa cum laude*; by September of 1862 he had turned his prize-winning essay into a doctoral dissertation.

Gezicht op Beesd aan de Linge (view of Beesd by the River Linge)
© Gert-Jan Veenstra used with permission.

---

9 John à Lasco (1499–1560, also known as Jan Laski) was a Polish-born Protestant Reformer, preacher, and theologian. He was a close acquaintance of Erasmus and Cranmer, and debated Menno Simons (of the Mennonites) in 1544. He travelled extensively, holding positions in both Holland and England.

Besides his constant financial worries (Kuyper's family was not well-off), his great fear in life was that of being stuck in a small church parish somewhere in the countryside for the rest of his life. This helped fuel his restlessness, uncompromising study habits. Kuyper's early letters also reveal that he had an untempered will, absolute determination, and relentless desire to succeed. He was often unhappy with himself, ill-at-ease in the university world, and disappointed with his fiancée's slow intellectual development. In 1863, shortly before being called to his first parish of Beesd, a small village between two branches of the Rhine, Kuyper underwent what he calls a "conversion" as a result of reading a novel by Charlotte Yonge entitled *The Heir of Redclyffe* (1853). His four years in Beesd (1863–67) were a period in which he "worked out his salvation with fear and trembling" among the devout, though uneducated, people of this district. It was a time of unlearning some of what he had learned at university, rethinking the essentials of Christianity, and finding the rudiments of Kuyperianism.

Besides this, Kuyper continued his earlier efforts of tracking down the writings and letters of John à Lasco, through correspondence with and occasional trips to the great libraries of Europe. In 1866 he published a two-volume work containing over one thousand pages of writings, hundreds of letters, and an extensive introduction to Lasco's life and work. While the tomes were well received, especially by church historians, they did not bring him nearly as much attention as a small pamphlet he wrote the following year.

The pamphlet Kuyper published in 1867 was titled: *Wat moeten wij doen, het stemrecht aan ons zelve houden of den kerkeraad machtigen? Vraag bij de uitvoering van Art. 23* (What should we do, exercise the vote [in calling pastors] ourselves or authorize the church council? A question about the implementation of Article 23).[10] In thirty-four pages he discussed a topic of great interest at the time: the question as to the basis, defense, and limitations of authority, in and over the church, between the state and the church, as well as between other institutions or entities. Much of the strength of the essay comes from the historical background Kuyper sketches in the process of arguing his points. It combined his learning as a church historian, his skill as an orator, and his strong conviction as a newly orthodox Christian.[11] His words struck a deep chord of resonance in a wide but as yet ununified audience.[12] The tract received many favorable reviews and was probably responsible for his being called later that year to the large parish of Utrecht, an important university town.

One of the reasons Kuyper's treatise had such an impact was the work done previously by the senior statesman G. Groen van Prinsterer. For many years Groen van Prinsterer (1801–1876) had been an activist for church reform and a solitary confessor of Christ in the political arena. In many ways he prepared the way for Kuyper by mobilizing the

---

10 (Culemborg: Blom, 1867). (Hereafter cited as *Wat moeten wij doen. . . .*) This manuscript was rejected by the first publisher to whom Kuyper offered it. Discouraged, he decided to throw the piece away. Only his wife's prodding got him to take it out of the wastebasket and try sending again.

11 This pamphlet is important for the purposes of this essay because it marks Kuyper's transition from "liberal" to "confessional" Christianity and addresses themes that became key elements of Kuyperianism.

12 In reviewing the pamphlet, P. D. Chantepie de la Saussaye mentions that Kuyper, "who was initially an adherent of the Leiden School of theology, now places himself with the orthodox party – which is the fruit of the independent research and personal experience." This was quoted by Groen van Prinsterer in a letter to Kuyper, April 4, 1867. Their correspondence has been published under the title: *Briefwisseling van Mr. G. Groen van Prinsterer*, vol. V (1990).

evangelical wing of the church through his years of writing and struggle in church and parliament. During the first decade of Kuyper's and the last of Groen's public career, they worked together on a variety of projects and committees. An initial brief exchange of letters took place between Kuyper and Groen in 1864, but in 1867 their correspondence began to take off and show signs of a growing interest and affinity with one another. Kuyper probably read some of Groen's writings in the important years 1864–1867.[13] This venerable historian and political writer deeply affected the course of Kuyper's life and thought; his influence began toward the end of Kuyper's transitional phase – the focus of this essay. If there was a single thinker who Kuyper most emulated, it was Groen. He shared Groen's stance on many issues and in countless ways and it was on account of his example that he eventually went into politics. Like Groen, he was both highly romantic and highly rational, passionate and analytical; and yet like Groen he was neither a "Romantic" nor a "Rationalist."[14]

Kuyper's Goals and Achievements

As to the general course of Kuyper's life and thought, I will now summarize some of its main features. Before his death in 1920 at the age of eighty-three, Kuyper had published innumerably many books, scholarly articles, pamphlets, newspaper editorials, and sermon collections, as well as several volumes of parliamentary speeches. His personal correspondence was also extensive, revealing a constant flow of ideas, plans, and projects. He was an aggressive organizer active on many fronts. In 1867 he made his first plans to form an association, the Marnix Vereeniging, for the study of Reformation history in the Netherlands. He was active in The Christian National School Union, which worked for the freedom of confessional education. Recognizing the need for a well-organized political union, in 1879 he set up the country's first formal political party.[15] In 1880 his Association for Reformed Higher Education realized its goal of founding a Christian university, the Free University in Amsterdam. He helped found the *Gereformeerde Kerken* (Reformed Churches), whose membership was formed from the people and congregations who, mournfully, felt forced to leave the state-organized church in 1886. He helped focus attention on the plight of the working classes by publishing on the issue[16] and by arranging a conference devoted to "the social question" in 1891. Some of his other noteworthy areas of activity found him serving as chief editor of a national daily newspaper for five decades, as an influential theologian and educator, as a member of parliament (he quit as a pastor and became an elected MP in the 1870s) and as prime minister (1901–1905). He was

---

13 Groen sent Kuyper a copy of his major work *Ongeloof en Revolutie* in 1867. This work is now available in English with an extensive introduction and commentary by Van Dyke, Harry 1989. *Groen van Prinsterer's Lectures on Unbelief and Revolution.* Jordan Station, Ontario: Wedge Publishing Foundation, see esp. 55, 83, and 267.

14 Over against the exaltation of both reason and feeling, Kuyper sets Christ's gift of renewed and redeemed life. The point he inevitably makes is that people should feed and depend most of all, not on their own minds or emotions, but upon the Maker of their minds and emotions, the Source of Life.

15 In fact that Kuyper re-organized the so-called Anti-revolutionary party along democratic lines. As a movement it had already existed for fifty years under the leadership of G. Groen van Prinsterer.

16   For example, *De Arbeiderskwestie en de Kerk* (The Labor Question and the Church) (1871), and his 1891 lecture "Het sociale vraagstuk en de Christelijke religie," published as *The Problem of Poverty*. Sioux Center: Dordt College Press.

driven from power in 1905 in the aftermath of a railway strike.

Kuyper made significant long-term contributions towards a restructuring of state and society along pluralistic lines, respecting not only individuals and corporations but also communities of faith or persuasions.[17] According to him, these persuasions constituted the basic trends in state or society, such as Protestant, Roman Catholic, socialist, and each was entitled to organize freely and act publicly on a "level playing field." Each persuasion was entitled to have certain institutions of its own, for example, schools and labor associations, which were to receive equal treatment from but were not to be meddled with by the state. No one community could claim to represent the national community as such. Every person belonged first of all to a persuasion contributing to the state. Hence, no group could rightfully claim that its goals and the state's goals were synonymous. While institutions such as church or synagogue should not have control over the state, as persuasions the different communities were fully entitled to receive support from it and exercise their influence upon it. Kuyper believed this would vastly increase everyone's opportunities to express and live out his or her convictions in all the areas of life. The open confrontation of convictions, he thought, would show forth the truth of revealed religion all the more.

In his championing of pluralism, Kuyper's abiding concern was the spiritual revitalization of the church and the re-Christianization of the nation. In many ways he would achieve these goals during his lifetime. However, his overpowering style, uncompromising convictions, and unrelenting mental powers spawned considerable antipathy in the wake of his success. While not everyone in his own country knows his name today and some who do, feel little affinity with this stalwart (with his ideal of Christian action on many fronts), there are those who prize his many contributions, including his devotional writings[18] as a storehouse of wisdom.

The Background to Kuyper's Conversion

As a pastor's child Kuyper knew a lot about Christianity at an early age. From what he says later we gather that he had a strong childhood faith.[19] He respected his father and when the time came to choose his own course of study and profession, he too chose theology and the ministry. At the time Kuyper entered Leiden University its theology department was known for its "progressive" or "liberal" orientation. After two or three years of study, his childhood Christian faith had been replaced by a more enlightened one in which "moralism" and "intellectualism" (neology) largely supplanted traditional Christian dogma.[20] By "intellectualism" I mean the position that sees development of the

---

17 By "persuasions" (*richtingen*) Kuyper meant the major communities to which people belong by virtue of holding to certain basic religious and intellectual tenets.

18 See, e.g., Kuyper, Abraham 2008. *Near Unto God*, adapted by Schaap, J. C. Sioux Center: Dordt College Press.

19 See *De jonge* . . . (191) and Kuyper's sermon *"Een Band Voor God Ontknoopt"* (A Tie Severed Before God) (1867) in the collection: *Predicatien, in de jaren 1867 tot 1873, tijdens zijn Predikantschap in het Nederlandsch Hervormde Kerkgenootschap, gehouden te Beesd, te Utrecht en te Amsterdam* (Sermons given in the years 1867–1873 during his pastorate in the Netherlands Reformed Church, in Beesd, Utrecht, and Amsterdam) (Kampen: Kok, 1913) (Hereafter cited as Predicatien), 241.

20 In Kuyper's own words, "Initiated into the academic world, I stood defenseless and unarmed against the powers of negation, which, before I had suspected anything, robbed me of my inherited faith. This faith had not rooted itself deeply in my unconverted, self-seeking mind or temperament, and thus it dried up when exposed to the burning heat of the skeptical spirit" (*Conf.* . . . 35). In a letter to Groen van Prinsterer,

intellectual life as the highest good. This orientation also took the form of "moralism," which seeks the moral improvement of the person in the apprehension and nurturing of "the divine" in the human. Kuyper's intellectual position, which he assumed at Leiden, allowed him to interpret religion (including Christianity) as providing popular forms in which these goals could be pursued by the common people.

The published correspondence casts a fascinating light on this development. In many of his letters to Johanna we can see that he is trying to initiate her into this new way of thinking about religion, especially at the time she is preparing to make her public confession of faith. He wants her to see its human side and true nature, apart from all the forms and particularities each tradition puts upon it (see *De jonge. . .* 77ff.). While she is doing her best to learn from him, a certain level of resistance is apparent in her attitude towards Kuyper's persistent theologizing. At some points she defers to her own pastor, who was catechizing her, and feels compelled to tell Abraham that she simply disagrees with him and does not want to discuss the matter any further at the moment.

As he embraced this new approach he perceived that it was a whole way of thinking, a comprehensive view which was at stake. Not surprisingly we see in his letters a fairly consistent line of thought manifesting itself in a variety of contexts. We find, for example, that he no longer has room for traditional beliefs in the supernatural, the transcendence of God, the divinity of Christ, the afterlife, the last judgment, or the superhuman authority of Scripture. Jesus, he says, was merely a human being, and although "the divine moral consciousness which is weak and sickly in us was at work in him in full force."[21] On another occasion he tries to make clear to Johanna that God should not really be thought of as out there beyond the stars (transcendent), but as really only manifest in us (immanent).

Realizing the problems that this way of thinking would bring when he became a minister in a local church,[22] he sought new meanings in the old words. Hence, even though God had now become a purely immanent "moral essence" for Kuyper (*De jonge. . .* 147), he still speaks to Johanna about "desiring to live to the Glory of God," to stand in "his service," and to seek constantly "to make one another better and holier" (*De jonge. . .* 78–9). In another letter to Johanna, dated October 18, 1858, he explains that he believes God has created humans with "a divine capacity, i.e., with the capacity to become perfect or divine. By this," he continues, "I understand not rationality but religious ethical feeling . . . the rational and religious feeling in us is God" (*De jonge. . .* 59).

As time went on, the cynical climate of university theology left Kuyper's faith intellectually parched, yet on the emotional level he was still open, even vulnerable, to things spiritual. Besides emphasizing the need to be more conscious and self-aware, he also

---

dated April 5, 1867, Kuyper says that the "modern instruction" at Leiden University caused him "to sink away into complete neologism for four years." Many years later he repeats this: "For years I entertained these illusions of modernism," he says in a speech in parliament *Handelingen der Staten-Generaal. Zitting van 14 Juli, 1902,* Eerste Kramer. This was quoted in Van Der Kroef, J. N. 1948. "Abraham Kuyper and the Rise of Neo-Calvinism in The Netherlands." *Church History* 17(4): 317.

21 *De jonge . . .* 146–7, 59, 79, 108. He goes on to say that Jesus "is a man and nothing but a man and only as such is his existence important to me – the man Jesus was so great and perfect, and I, too, am intended to be thus" (*De jonge . . .* 59).

22 He mentions this problem to Johanna in a letter in 1858 (*De jonge . . .* 60). Abraham also complains to her in a letter of December 7, 1862 that some churches do not want pastors like himself who are not orthodox (*De jonge . . .* 172).

stressed the importance of listening to one's own heart. Doing so seems to have played an important role in Kuyper's conversion.

Kuyper's Conversion (1863)

The story is apparently straightforward. Abraham receives a book from Johanna, a novel by Charlotte M. Yonge, *The Heir of Redclyffe*.[23] He reads it and is struck by the similarity between the temperament of Philip, a character in the novel, and his own temperament. He sees and understands Philip's demise as resulting from pride, in contrast to the weaker character, Guy, who eventually triumphs by humble faith and trust in God. Kuyper is deeply moved, repents of his own selfishness and pride, and is converted.

Determining the precise nature of Kuyper's conversion is difficult. In many ways it appears to have involved a religious "conversion" in the sense in which evangelicals speak of this. The main complication, however, is that he also seems to have had a strong faith as a child. Nevertheless, it is clear from his letters and his own testimony that he had strayed a long way away from the faith of his childhood, at least intellectually, during his university period, and that his "conversion" marked a turning point in his life.

In describing himself prior to his conversion, Kuyper uses the expressions "self-satisfied," "selfish," "striving," "thirst for glory," "hard-hearted," "flippant," and "egotistical."[24] Although it is hard to tell to what extent these evaluations applied to him, his letters do reveal a rather obsessive concern for success and the future, unbridled ambition, and an easily wounded pride. But he was also simply strong-willed and highly-strung. As to misdeeds of a character more specific to himself, Kuyper says that he had constructed his own religion, endorsed false virtue, and wanted to come to God on his own terms. Religion was a subject of study and trifling discussion bereft of any notion of sin, or seriousness of life. It was part of a "cool, rigid philosophy" (*Predicatien* 242). He characterizes his student years as a departure, a detour away from the "simple and pious" faith he once had as a child (*De jonge . . .* 191, *Predicatien* 241). Nevertheless, this childhood faith was not properly adapted as he grew up: it was left "too long without forming a transition to the world and to adolescence – and then came the shock – the childhood faith collapsed . . ." (*De jonge . . .* 192). Later he says,

> My being brought to Christ did not come about as a gentle transition from a childlike piety to a blessed feeling of salvation, but required a complete change in my personality, in heart, will, and understanding. This makes it understandable that the specific life circumstances that worked together to this end made a particularly deep impression on me and with my conversion determined the direction that my spiritual life had to take. (*Conf.* 35–36)

In a letter to Johanna he confesses that he once tried to destroy that same picture of God in her that he himself had possessed during his childhood. "As a man," says Kuyper, "I

---

23 Charlotte M. Yonge (1823–1901) was a Christian novelist brought up under the influence of the Oxford Movement. She spent all her life at Otterbourne near Winchester, England. She received a deep sense of devotion to the church from her father, a close friend of John Keble, a leading figure of the Oxford Movement. Remaining single, she propagated the Christian faith through her countless novels and by teaching Sunday school. It is interesting to note that the Oxford Movement, which flourished in the 1830s and 40s under the leadership of John Keble, J. H. Newman, and E. B. Pusey, was in part a reaction to theological "liberalism." It was a revival of Anglican high church piety inspired by a new Romantic ideal of primitive Christianity.

24 *De jonge . . .* 186, *Predicatien* 241, and *Conf.* 40–41.

found that image again in the good Guy [the character in *The Heir of Redclyffe*]. . . . He taught one how one, also as a grown man, could have a childlike faith" (*De jonge* . . . 192).

Yonge's character Philip spoke deeply to Kuyper's relentless striving for success, to his fear of failure, and to his desire to be better than all his peers. He came to the conclusion that what he was anxious about could never be supplied or satisfied by any of his own efforts. He experienced Philip's defeat in the story as "a judgment upon [Kuyper's] own striving and character" (*Conf.* 41). Somehow Philip showed Kuyper his own spiritual poverty, bringing him to his knees and "crushing his heart" (*Conf.* 41–2).

Abraham speaks to Johanna about Guy as if he were a real person to whom he owed an incalculable debt. The contrast of the two characters struck Kuyper in an extraordinary way, breaking down his pride and "opening up [his] heart" (*De jonge* . . . 186). He gave up his attempts to order things in his own way and found a new openness and peace with God – a God he had not known in his own theological system. He now spoke of a God outside of himself, one who sometimes stood against him, one who spoke, acted, and existed on his own terms.[25]

The recognition that his life had been going in the wrong direction was a humbling experience and Kuyper took it and its consequences very seriously. This meant that he had a lot of intellectual backtracking to do, especially in his thinking about God. The process was difficult and painful and came at a moment when he had to go on speaking and expressing what he believed, namely in his newly assumed work as preacher in the village of Beesd.

One aspect of this conversion is especially noteworthy. Through reflection upon his own experiences, Kuyper came to see an interconnection among the previous ideas or attitudes he had held.[26] He looked back upon himself not merely as a sinner haphazardly ignoring God and violating His law, but as one who had had his own starting point, worldview,[27] and principle of unity. In other words, there was an underlying pattern in his thought that manifested itself in all its elements. Kuyper expresses this in terms of there being a "line" or a "direction" in each person's life and thought.[28] There are "two directions, two paths," he claims, "open to everyone. Each has his own principle and in the systematic development from that principle, the one necessarily flows forth out from the other, which is a constant order of thought whose internal power and coherence really marks it as a life direction . . . starting from a . . . spiritual orientation of the human heart" (*Predicatien* 1867, 239).

---

25 Regarding his theological studies Kuyper says "I did become acquainted with Calvin, I did become acquainted with Lasco, but in reading them it never occurred to me to think, now that this is truth. My heart still resisted. I read and studied them concerning an historical question, a formal matter, and I simply tore their ecclesiastical insights from the root that gave them life." (1873: 46).

26 See "*Wat moeten wij doen* . . . " 28–29, where Kuyper first speaks of "direction," the "coherence of people's ideas," and "of man being a unity and living for his principles."

27 The term "worldview" is taken from his farewell sermon given four years after his conversion, *Predicatien* 238. The term, as we shall see below, became an important and regular item in Kuyper's thought and vocabulary after 1867.

28 In his farewell sermon he publicly acknowledges that when he arrived in Beesd (1863) he did not have very much to give his (first) congregation since he had just come to a turning-point in his own spiritual development.

Rural Calvinism

This process of transition from a liberal to a confessional Christianity was assisted in an unusual way through his congregation in Beesd. There was a group of people there, mostly unlettered farmers, apparently known by some as the "malcontents" (*Conf.* 44), who had a depth of faith and knowledge of Scripture that confounded the young pastor. They were rural Calvinists still living out of the Reformation tradition in this isolated district, nestled between two branches of the Rhine. These people held fast to the faith by insisting upon the use of the Canons of Dort, the Heidelberg Catechism, and the other articles of faith.[29] In their ungroomed speech Kuyper says he recognized the voice of the Genevan Reformer, with whom he had become familiar while writing his prize-winning essay.

In the course of his regular pastoral visits Kuyper came to the house of a young woman, only seven years his senior, who had been staying away from church and was at first unwilling to receive him.[30] When Kuyper enquired as to the reason for her absence, she replied forthrightly that it was because he was not preaching the pure word of God. She went on to show Kuyper, her persevering pastor, what he had missed in Holy Scripture and in the Reformed confessions of faith. Kuyper reports that he had many such "discussions" with her and other members of this group, including the headmaster of the local school. He sensed the presence here of a church that had stood the test of centuries. In these simple folk he encountered a cogent Christian faith, a seriousness of conviction and a "well-ordered worldview" (*Conf.* 45) of the kind he had never met with before. They forced him to choose between "full sovereign grace," as they put it, and the escape hatch of the free thought he had still been keeping open for himself. Says Kuyper: "Their obduracy became a blessing for my heart and the rising of the morning star for my life"; "I had grasped but had not yet found the Word of reconciliation" (*Conf.* 45). The change was crowned and completed by a new and extensive reading of the works of John Calvin and other church reformers.

Kuyper summarizes his conversions in the Preface to an English translation made at the time of his *Encyclopedia of Sacred Theology* (1898); he speaks in the third-person:

> There are primordial principles which are fundamental to Calvinism, and these only he [i.e., Kuyper] defends. He is no Calvinist by birth. Having received his training in a conservative-supernaturalistic spirit, he broke with faith in every form when a student at Leyden, and then cast himself into the arms of the barest radicalism. At a later period, perceiving the poverty of this radicalism, and shivering with the chilling atmosphere which it created in his heart, he felt attracted first to the Determinism of Professor Scholten, and then to the warmth of the Vermittelungs-theologie, as presented by Martensen and his followers. But if this warmed his heart, it provided no rest for his thought. In this Vermittelungs-theologie there is no stability of starting-point, no unity of principle, and no harmonious life-interpretation on which a

---

29 While few specific details are known about these people, they formed one of many Bible-centered house groups (conventicles) that existed in The Netherlands at the time. Their place and influence was increased by the revival that began in Switzerland under the teaching of Robert Haldane in 1817 and spread to The Netherlands in the 1820s, the so-called *Réveil*.

Back in 1834, another congregation in a remote part of the far North of the country had helped its pastor, in a similar way, to turn back to this confessional faith, namely, Hendrik de Cock in Ulrum, Groningen. De Cock became a leader of the Reformed people who seceded from the state-organized church in 1834 (the *Afscheiding*). Many of his followers eventually immigrated to North America.

30 Her name was Pietje Baltus (1830–1914). She followed Kuyper's career with interest throughout the rest of her life, though she did not always agree with his political activism. Cf. *De jonge* . . . 207–211.

world-view, based on coherent principles, can be erected. In this state of mind and of heart he came in contact with those descendants of the ancient Calvinists, who in the Netherlands still honor the traditions of the fathers; and it astonished him to find among these simple people a stability of thought, a unity of comprehensive insight, in fact a world-view based on principles which needed but a scientific treatment and interpretation to give them a place of equal significance over against the dominant views of the age. To put forth an effort in this direction has from that moment on been his determined purpose. . . . (*PST* viii)

Many things are remarkable about this story. First of all, it was people of the rural Netherlands (in the Betuwe region) who taught their future leader some of his most important lessons of life and faith. Secondly, this experience cemented his affinity with them – "the little people," who were to become his most faithful (political) supporters. The bond between them and Kuyper was a source of mutual strength and encouragement, and continued so throughout his long career as preacher, teacher, and national leader. Thirdly, this affinity with the uneducated country folk was not merely an external connection but took root in Kuyper's personality, style, and faith. He was willing to be taught by uneducated people who had conviction born of Scripture and wisdom born of life. They gave him more than the learned theologians of the university had done.[31]

Kuyper's Discovery

Now we come to the final scene in Kuyper's working out of Kuyperianism. While serving as pastor in Beesd, and still in his process of transition, Kuyper read a book just published (1864) by his former professor, J. H. Scholten, entitled *Het Evangelie naar Johannes. Kritisch Historisch Onderzoek* (The Gospel of John: An Historical Critical Investigation).[32] Reading this book gave rise to the insight and courage that he needed to break once and for all with his "modernist" past, freeing him from much of the power of the "liberalism" he had previously imbibed. Kuyper tells us about this some years later, in a footnote to his critical treatise *Het Modernisme, een Fata Morgana op Christelijk Gebied* (Modernism: a Fata Morgana on Christian Ground).[33]

As far as I have been able to reconstruct it, the story goes like this. At the time that Kuyper was studying in Leiden (*circa* 1858) and attending lectures, his professor, Scholten, in spite of his "liberalism," was still teaching the Johannine authorship of the Gospel of John. According to Kuyper, Scholten had given various reasons for holding this view; for example, "so historical were the persons, so internally cogent, so clearly did everything bear the mark of naturalness and authenticity" (*Modernism* . . . 73) that the Fourth Gospel had to have been written by the Apostle John. Given his close acquaintance with Scholten's views and arguments it came as quite a shock to Kuyper to find that in his new book (1864) Scholten had totally changed his position on the authorship of John. Naturally Kuyper was interested in knowing how such a radical and swift change of views had come about.

---

31 His basic orientation remained close to everyday life where God could be glorified through ordinary work. M. R. Langley expresses this for the political realm in his book title: *The Practice of Political Spirituality: Episodes from the Public Career of Abraham Kuyper*, 1879–1918. Jordan Station, Ontario: Paideia Press, 1984.

32 Leijden: Akademische Boekhandel van P. Engels, 1864.

33 Amsterdam: Höveker and Zoon, 1871. (Hereafter cited as *Modernism* . . . .) This booklet was not translated into English until 1998, although it was translated into German as early as 1872: *Die modern Theologie (der Modernismus) eine Fata Morgana auf Christlichem Gebiet*. Zürich: G. Hoehre.

Kuyper's recent experience had taught him firsthand that there was more at stake in one's view of God and Scripture than the results of scholarly study alone. In reading Scholten's new book, Kuyper was struck by this and by something Scholten said in the Foreword. Evidently, Scholten's new position was influenced by a change in his worldview. "Professor Scholten himself acknowledges," Kuyper writes, "that the main reason for his divergent results is the transition he had made in recent years from a Platonic to a more Aristotelian worldview" (*Modernism . . .* 73, note 52). In his Foreword, Scholten says that scholarship in recent years has seen a shift towards the empirical and away from ideal-historical and metaphysical construction. Scholten is now interested in what really happened, interested in the historical Jesus, and not in the stories told about Him. The task of the historian is to examine critically the *reports* of facts. Scholten says that his views on John changed as he came to see that "the worldview of the Fourth Gospel writer, no longer fits into the frame of our contemporary worldview, which rests on an empirical basis" (*Het Evangelie naar Johannes . . .* 1864, iv).

Undoubtedly Kuyper interpreted Scholten's statement in a different way than Scholten had intended, namely, as a basic religious attitude influencing the results of one's academic work. Unlike Kuyper, Scholten was thinking only about the advancement and correctness of the new "empirically" based worldview, which science now rested upon, and not about the systematic implications of his statement. At this point, however, Kuyper seized upon the universal structural significance of what Scholten says, namely, that a worldview is something that influences scholarship and in this case led Scholten to such a basic, rapid and unforeseen change in views. Kuyper states that, "Through the reading of this book, supplemented by my memories of his enthusiastic delivery of lectures, which made such a deep impression on me, the authority of modern criticism was undone for me" (*Modernism . . .* 73). In other words, he came to the conclusion that it was primarily a change in "worldview," occasioned by what Scholten calls the new outlook "of our time" and the understanding that the outlook of the Gospel writer(s) was based on an antiquated worldview, that caused Scholten to see the Fourth Gospel in a new light and to draw a new and contrary conclusion about its authorship. "With this," Kuyper notes, "Scholten recognizes an *a priori* as the guiding star of his criticism" (*Modernism . . .* 73).

Kuyper does not conclude from this, however, that Scholten is a poor scholar doing substandard work. Quite to the contrary, he concludes that Scholten has candidly, if inadvertently, disclosed something of vital importance about every scholar, namely, that he or she is dependent upon a worldview. A worldview influences and helps the scholar to conceive and work out new theories and ideas. This recognition of what he calls the "a priori," the central role that worldviews play in scholarly activity, gave Kuyper the courage he required to disagree with an older, more learned scholar like Scholten. By breaking with him he broke with "modern" theology as such. Kuyper's discovery helped him to resist the powerful influence of the popular intellectual trends of his day.

All of this took place after 1863 and while living in Beesd. Although Groen's name was not often mentioned at the time, Kuyper knew of his Christian orthodoxy, Calvinism and Anti-revolutionary way of thinking and they served as role model to him.

Two biblical terms which become key elements of Kuyperianism are "life" and "heart." Both are widely used and both have definitions packed full of meaning. Life is identified with Christ, and heart with the *dependent* root of human existence, decision and action.

Conclusions

It is now time to return to the question posed at the outset: How did Kuyper become a Kuyperian? Although I do not pretend to be able to answer this question fully, I have tried to show that the main source from which Kuyperianism sprang was Kuyper's discovery that human obedience or disobedience to God expressed itself in terms of a course, a pattern, a *direction* of life. He first noticed such a pattern while reflecting on his own pre-conversion thought and action. During his period of transition from a liberal to a confessional Christianity, while living in Beesd, he started thinking about the derivation of such patterns. Sometime around 1865 he came to the conclusion that they resulted from the influence of worldviews. While he did not define "worldview" at the time,[34] he associated it with a primary *set of attitudes* about God and the world expressed in internally unified answers to basic questions of life. Although not the same, he took religion and worldview to be inseparable.[35] As such, religion necessarily involves a universal vision of reality that cannot ultimately be limited to a private realm but has a key role to play in life – thought and action. This means that there is no wholly neutral ground anywhere in society but that every terrain is occupied by a (religious) principle, Christian or otherwise.

Kuyper's conviction that there is a worldview implicit in each persuasion, as well as an underlying unity within thought and belief, led him to conclude that in order to be faithful to Christ, the sovereign Lord, we should try to work out Christian ideas and plans of action on all fronts. Kuyperianism arose with the recognition of the coherence of things, the inter-coherence of our thinking and believing, and the unity of life and faith. This awareness drove Kuyper in his many-sided attempts to organize Christian scholarship and action, and to develop alternative "Christian" approaches and institutions – all for the greater glory of God.

One important societal implication of the Kuyperian perspective or program has been called "principled" pluralism, the right of each recognized persuasion to organize distinct institutions within the state on the basis of its convictions. This right grows out of the sacredness of conscience (of people's basic convictions) and the recognition that humanity is made up of persuasion**s**. When the persuasions or communities are publicly acknowledged, and acknowledge one another, they can more freely and openly compete on an equal legal footing. Kuyper fought for this type of pluralism because he believed 1) it would allow communities to flourish – in the Christian case, to serve God more fully; 2) it was the fairest system *for all*; and 3) because the Christian principle could win in influence since it was grounded in revealed truth and would show itself to be true and reliable in practice. Whatever level of public funding if any a country decides to give to the schools, the media, the arts, health care, transportation, recreation, etc. is divided among the persuasions.

Critical Musing

While Kuyper's worldview-insight was highly significant, it is liable to some misconceptions; it could seem to suggest that a worldview has an exclusive and unlimited influence upon a person's (or a persuasion's) thought and action. But apparently people do not always act

---

34 He did not really do so until 1898 when he gave his famous Stone lectures at Princeton University, *Calvinism*. Amsterdam: Höveker and Wormser; New York: Revell, 1899. Later published as *LC*.

35 Cf. 1867. "*Wat moeten wij doen . . .* ": 30.

consistently or in accordance with even their own deepest convictions. Still, a framework of belief does not simply become irrelevant or unnecessary because sometimes transgressed.

5

How Abraham Kuyper
Became a Christian Democrat

Harry Van Dyke

In the very year that Pope Leo XIII issued his famous encyclical *De Rerum Novarum* about the social question, Dutch Calvinists met for three and a half days in Amsterdam to discuss a similar set of problems. Billed as a "Social Congress," the conference opened on the evening of 9 November 1891 with a solemn prayer and the singing of "A Mighty Fortress Is Our God," followed by a stirring address by Abraham Kuyper entitled, "The Social Question and the Christian Religion" (*PP*). Thus was launched an intensive three days that were destined to reinforce the political vision of Kuyper and his following, broaden the agenda of the party he led, and further identify the Anti-Revolutionaries as a branch – a deeply rooted and deftly organized branch – of the western European movement toward Christian Democracy.

The Organizing Committee of the Social Congress had put together a richly varied program. Each morning session of the three-day conference began with a "devotional hour" led by local pastors.[1] This was followed from 10 a.m. to 1 p.m. by three different "sections" or parallel workshops. Section one dealt with the religious aspect, section two with the socio-economic aspect, and section three with the political aspect or "the social question." Plenary sessions were held after lunch, from 2 to 4 p.m. Conferees were not idle after supper: one evening they met for an "hour of prayer"; another evening they could choose among three discussion groups: one for Christian employers, one for Christian women, and one for Christian journalists.

The fare was heavy. Who were expected? Attendance was open to men *and women*[2] who could agree with the conference's Statement of Principles and pay the modest fee of two and a half guilders.

The press release announcing the conference was dated October 26 and signed by the Organizing Committee. This committee was composed – predictably, as we shall see below – of three Anti-Revolutionary members of Parliament and three representatives of the board of the Christian Workingmen's League "Patrimonium" (Our Heritage). The

---

1 Specifically, these were W. H. Gispen, minister in a church of the Secession of 1834, and C. G. J. van Hoogstraten and B. van Schelven, both of whom served "Doleantie" churches that had broken with the national church as recently as 1886. The two denominations, adhering to the historic Reformed confessions and a Presbyterian polity, would merge in the following year (1892).

2 Bold type in the original advertisement.

secretary was the local bookseller and Christian activist Johan Adam Wormser Jr., while Dr. Kuyper served as chairman and convener.

Looking back, one can say that the conference, which was the first of its kind in the Netherlands,[3] was of singular significance for the development of Christian – i.e., Calvinist, or better still, neo-Calvinist – social thought and for united social action on the part of modern Dutch orthodox Protestants. At the same time, the history of the events leading up to the conference reveals that its critical importance was due in no small part to the fact that it came almost too late. It is these events, and Kuyper's involvement in them, that form the focus of this article.[4]

The Socio-Economic Context

Sometime during the conference, Kuyper uttered words that were destined to be quoted for years afterward. Speaking of the working classes and their distress, Kuyper exclaimed, *"They cannot wait, not a day, not an hour!"* Although these words may not have captured the mood of everybody at the conference, they were certainly intended to reflect the crisis of the time and to express the same sense of urgency so much in evidence in the papal encyclical of that year. A movement toward Christian democracy was the belated response to a mounting crisis. In general, nineteenth-century Europe had seen the estrangement, from church and the Christian faith, of a disproportionately high number of people from the working classes. More immediately in Kuyper's case, there was the imminent threat of a widespread defection of working-class supporters from the Anti-Revolutionary Party, a party of which Kuyper was the hitherto undisputed leader, mentor, and publicist and which spearheaded united Christian action in the political life of the nation. These factors would move Kuyper at last to becoming a declared Christian democrat.

What was the situation facing the Anti-Revolutionary leader in the year 1891? Holland stood poised on the threshold of industrial takeoff. Traditionally a farming, fishing and trading nation, by 1870 the Dutch had begun to introduce modern machine production in secondary industry. Here as elsewhere, however, industrialism brought with it grave social problems – problems that could not be effectively tackled unless *laissez-faire* liberalism were overcome. A parliamentary inquiry of 1887 had shaken people from their complacency when it reported on deplorable working conditions in mills, workshops and factories, compounded by wretched living conditions in the working-class districts of the industrial towns. But new hope dawned in March 1888, when election results revealed that perhaps the tide was running out for the Liberals: for the third time since the democratic constitution of 1848, they failed to capture the majority of seats in the lower house of Parliament, an outcome that was due in no small part this time to an informal coalition of Calvinists and Catholics instigated by Dr. Kuyper and Monseigneur Herman Schaepman.[5] The victory at the polls prompted the king to invite the Reformed statesman Aeneas baron Mackay to form a government composed of Roman Catholics and Anti-Revolutionaries. Expectations ran high. What would this Christian cabinet, with

---

3   Additional "Christian Social Congresses" were held in the Netherlands in 1919, 1953, and 1991.

4   The present article is an amplified version of my "Het Eerste Christelijk-Sociaal Congres: beter laat dan nooit," *Transparant* 2, no. 3 (1991): 6–10. *Transparant* is the quarterly journal of the Vereniging van Christen-Historici, Utrecht. An English version appeared in *Calvin Theological Journal* 33 (1998): 420–435.

5   Cf. Schaepman's letters to Kuyper during this period, in KA (see note 18 below), nrs. 4081, 4084.

its avowed social conscience, do for the working poor?[6]

Half a year into its mandate, the Mackay Government at last introduced a labor bill. The proposal limited working hours for women and children and provided for a modest beginning of work site inspection. After another six months of parliamentary debate, the bill was finally passed, and once it had received royal assent, it became law in the summer of 1889.

Working-class circles greeted the measure with mixed feelings. On the one hand, they were grateful for state intervention in one of the worst evils of the prevailing system. On the other hand, with the new restrictions on women's and children's labor, how would the loss in family income be compensated? More, much more, was needed. Men felt increasingly frustrated by the slow rate at which reforms were being initiated. For example, there was still no protection for male workers. Already under the previous administration there had been talk of creating Chambers of Labor, bodies through which workmen would have real input into establishing guidelines regarding working conditions and job ranking.

The sitting government announced that perhaps the idea of chambers of labor had merit but needed further study. It struck a Committee of Inquiry to examine the concept as well as look further into labor conditions both in industry and in the agricultural sector languishing in a depression since the 1870s. Such a cautious approach was not the kind of action expected from a cabinet with which the lower classes had thought they could identify even though many of them still did not meet voter qualifications based on one's tax assessment.[7] The delay was interpreted by the disenfranchised as a stalling tactic, a betrayal by a privileged voting class ignorant of the plight of those beneath them or else content to turn a blind eye.

Growing Working-Class Unrest

Evidence was increasing that the traditionally docile workers in farm and factory were prepared to resort to measures of their own. In the spring of 1888, a three-month strike had rocked the textile town of Almelo in the east. That summer, a strike among tugboat personnel was narrowly averted in Rotterdam. In February 1889, some four thousand textile workers went on strike in Enschede, to resume work in May only after mediation by Father Alfons Ariëns. In May of the following year, wildcat strikes broke out among the peat workers around Heerenveen in the northern province of Friesland; this turned into a bitter standoff that ended only when socialist agitators saw their persuasive powers defused by their more peaceable counterparts from Patrimonium. While this split in labor enabled owners and managers to restore order, Frisian workers were of one mind politically: Those who rule over us do not know our dire situation; we must have input in the places of power! A mass rally was held and a resolution demanding universal suffrage was adopted. The rally was organized by social democrats and supported by anarchists, so Christians stayed away. But the Frisian locals of Patrimonium were not unsympathetic. Their leaders, especially

---

6   Schutte, G. J. 1991. "Achtergronden en voorgeschiedenis van 1891," in *Een arbeider is zijn loon waardig.* Schutte, G .J. ed. The Hague: Meinema, 10–32.

7   As recently as 1887 the electorate had doubled in size as the result of an interim measure that gave the vote to all males over age twenty-two who could prove themselves "mentally fit or materially prosperous," qualifications that Kuyper dubbed idolatrous worship of "God Intellect and God Mammon." As it was, the measure still only enfranchised some 14 percent of the adult population, yet enough to tip the scales in favor of the confessional parties.

those in the capital city of Leeuwarden, had reached the conclusion that members of the working classes should be given not only the right to vote but also the chance to run for political office. And one of them, pastor Jan van Andel, publicly voiced the idea that the Christian social movement ought to come out with a well-articulated social program.[8]

In the fall of 1890, there was fresh labor unrest in Friesland, this time in the clay belt along the northern seashore. Farm laborers joined forces in a "brotherhood" for purposes of collectively negotiating wages with their employers. When the farmers refused to sit down with a delegation of the brotherhood, strikes followed over a wide area. Many farmers now hired "scabs" to replace their rebellious farmhands. The strikers responded with a boycott. They circulated lists of specific farms and announced: *"None of us will ever work there again!"* In Patrimonium's weekly, the board member from Friesland, Pieter van Vliet Jr., reported that participants in the boycott "even" included Christian workmen, a shocking fact that he nevertheless considered "understandable." He followed this observation with a series of articles that examined the background causes of the antagonism. The bond between farmer and farm laborer, he explained ruefully, was disappearing: absentee landlords were raising rents to finance a luxurious lifestyle abroad, so their tenants, to offset the difference, were more and more replacing permanent farmhands with day laborers.[9] Earlier, Van Vliet had made an interesting distinction, one that he felt was radical enough yet fully in line with the "anti-revolutionary principles" of Patrimonium. "We are Christian citizens," he declared; "very well, as Christians we know that we must suffer injustice and wait upon the Lord, but as citizens we have a right to request, though not demand, a living income without being passed off as revolutionaries."[10]

A Christian Labor Party?

After voices of this kind, the 1890 annual meeting of Patrimonium was bound to be a rowdy one.[11] It would lead directly, exactly one year later, to the great Social Congress of 1891. On November 10, 1890, eighty-eight delegates, representing some 7,500 members, met in Amsterdam. The membership meeting passed two important resolutions: (1) it appointed a committee for drawing up a social program; (2) it invited the Anti-Revolutionary Party (ARP) to join it in organizing a Social Congress.[12] The first decision seemed to say: we'll have to tackle the problem ourselves; the second: perhaps we can awaken our party from its slothful slumber and prod it to take political action. The public meeting the next day was opened by president Klaas Kater, a self-taught man who had co-founded Patrimonium in 1877 after breaking with his own bricklayers' union that favored confrontation, not cooperation, in labor relations.[13] Kater appears to have decided that the time had come for

---

8   Waringa, G. G. 1987–. "Ds. Jan van Andel (1839–1910); zijn Leeuwarder bloeiperiode." In *Jaarboek voor de geschiedenis van de Gereformeerde kerken in Nederland.* D. Th. Kuiper et al. ed. Kampen: Kok, 2: 97–120, at 109.

9   De Vries, Gabe [pseud. P. van Vliet] 1889–90. "Friesche toestanden." *Patrimonium; orgaan van het Verbond 5; as reprinted in Jaarboekje van het Nederlandsch Werkliedenverbond Patrimonium voor 1891* (Amsterdam, 1891), 100–110.

10 De Vries, in *Jaarboekje voor 1890,* 95.

11 Cf. Langeveld, H. J. "Achtergronden, organisatie en resultaten van het Christelijk-Social Congres van 1891." In *Een arbeider is zijn loon waardig,* 103–41.

12 Jaarboekje voor 1891, 81–85; Hagoort, *Patrimonium,* 313–16.

13 Hagoort, R. 1927. *Patrimonium (Vaderlijk Erfdeel); gedenkboek bij het gouden jubileum.* Utrecht, 120–121;

tougher language and perhaps tougher action, in the hope of waking up the leadership of his kindred political party.

"Our own brothers may be in power today," Kater began, "but their legislative proposals are slow in coming and are far from radical. Accordingly, our relationship to the Anti-Revolutionaries will have to change. They must not think they can rely on us forever as their hewers of wood and drawers of water. Many of us, who have no vote, work hard for them during election campaigns, but afterwards they seem to forget all about us. If things don't improve we may have to break with the ARP and form our own party!"

Kater's words electrified his audience. Tensions rose even higher when he continued, "The lordly gentlemen we help elect talk like antirevolutionaries but act like conservatives." They have no practical knowledge of the social field. True antirevolutionaries just don't believe, he added with nasty innuendo, that "plutocrats and aristocrats know the needs of our back alleys or are willing to help relieve them," and yet the ARP never nominates any of us "little people" to run for Parliament. The Party prefers men from the higher classes, including men who pay their workers starvation wages.[14]

Kater's speech was a tactical maneuver. Present in the audience was long-time sympathizer and friend Dr. Kuyper, who in editorials in his daily *De Standaard* had for almost a year criticized both the government and the Anti-Revolutionary (AR) caucus for its disappointing legislative performance. Might not party leader Kuyper, to whom Kater had given a copy of the speech earlier in the week,[15] be persuaded to take a stand and publicly endorse the novel, democratic idea of delegating working-class people to Parliament to plead their own cause? Certainly the escalating labor unrest in Friesland and elsewhere allowed of no delay.

In the discussion following Kater's provocative speech a great deal of support was heard for the democratic proposal. "Our antirevolutionary leaders have neglected the social question," many complained. "They have done little in the way of studying the problem, and they are doing nothing for our class of people." The delegates from Haarlem tried to capture the mood in an unambiguous motion: the ARP must send one or more workingmen to the Second Chamber.[16] At this, the political leader asked for the floor. Dr. Kuyper expressed his warm sympathy for the issue under discussion. He admitted that much work had been left undone and that the time was pressing. However, he begged to point out that the motion was premature; "after all, had not the meeting last night passed a resolution mandating Patrimonium to invite the Party to help organize a Social Congress? That was the place to talk these matters through, as brothers in the Lord." Then Kuyper sat down. His intervention had effect. The motion was withdrawn.[17]

For the moment, the breach seemed healed. But in the days that followed, Kuyper received several letters from aggrieved members of Parliament who felt deeply insulted by Kater's speech and the widely reported discussion of it.[18]

Hagoort, R. n.d. [1956]. *De Christelijk-sociale beweging*. Franeker, 65.

14 *Jaarboekje voor 1891*, 81–85; Hagoort, Patrimonium, 312–316.

15 Hagoort, *Patrimonium*, 318.

16 I.e., the lower house of Parliament.

17 *Jaarboekje voor 1891*, 92–96.

18 The correspondence of this time makes for fascinating reading. The more than nine thousand letters sent to Kuyper during his lengthy public career are now stored in the Kuyper-archief, Documentatiecentrum

The first plaintiff was Theodore Heemskerk, AR member of Parliament with a law degree from Leiden, son of the former (conservative) prime minister Jan Heemskerk and himself a future prime minister (1908–13). "People are leveling baseless accusations against us," he wrote. "All they need to do is look up the debates published in the Parliamentary Record and see how I and others have pleaded for Chambers of Labor."[19] "And why has editor Kuyper," he added, "paid so little attention in *De Standaard* to the valiant struggle we put up to amend the recent Labor Act along more anti-revolutionary lines? Surely a public rehabilitation is in order."[20]

A second letter came from Kuyper's loyal party activist T. A. J. van Asch van Wijck, a man who in addition to his law degree held the title of *jonkheer* (squire). He was scheduled to give a speech to the Amsterdam local of Patrimonium and he now submitted the text to the one man whose advice he valued in these critical times. "Kater's insults and insinuations need to be gainsaid," Kuyper read in the draft speech, "because far from boasting of our rank or title we champion the causes of the little people, such as private Christian schools and Chambers of Labor." As for forming a separate Christian labor party, such talk betrayed ignorance and ingratitude. Kater should admit that he is wrong and that his standpoint "must necessarily lead to Socialism." This speech was never delivered because Kuyper persuaded the author not to "hold a philippic" against Kater. "All the same," Van Asch van Wijck now wrote Kuyper, "the editor of *De Standaard* should think better of supporting Kater even indirectly," because his radical ideas might influence our working-class people and "will drive our Party, its left as well as its right wing, into the arms of the Conservatives, more dangerous in my opinion than the party of the Anarchists."[21]

Thus warned against the new radicalism within the bosom of his constituency, Kuyper had to reassess his strategy. Would he continue to support the likes of Kater, "even indirectly"? He knew the common people as no other and could justify their cries for improvement. Had he not, at the start of his career, between 1864 and 1874, pastored flocks in the peasant village of Beesd,[22] in a lower-middle class ward of Utrecht,[23] and in the dock-workers district of the Amsterdam church? And had he not, as early as 1869, spoken of the necessity to "steer in the direction of democracy" by broadening the franchise to include more of the "people behind the voters" (i.e., his own warmest supporters, inherited from Groen van Prinsterer)?[24] Did he not devote his maiden speech in parliament to the Child Labor Bill, to which he had given his negative vote only because it did not go far enough?[25] Had he not also argued in that same session for a national labor code?[26] And

voor het Nederlands Protestantisme, VU University of Amsterdam (hereafter referred to as KA).

19 Cf. *Handelingen van de Tweede Kamer der Staten-Generaal*, 21 Nov. 1899, 173–186. The pleas had been forceful indeed, as had the warning that another inquiry would only delay the labor question.

20 Heemskerk to Kuyper, 12 Nov. 1890; KA 4742.

21 Van Asch van Wijck to Kuyper. 29 Nov. 1890; KA 4757; MS of (part of) the intended speech in KA, drawer LE.P2, nr. 5.

22 Details in Henderson, R. D. 1992. "How Abraham Kuyper Became a Kuyperian." *Christian Scholar's Review* 22(1): 22–35, at 31–33. *See infra* Chapter 4.

23 He had been assigned the Lijnmarkt and surrounding streets, which included a red-light district; see Rullmann, J. C. 1928. *Abraham Kuyper; een levensschets*. Kampen: Kok, 40.

24 In an editorial in the Sunday paper *De Heraut*, 5 November 1869.

25 Kuyper, A. 1890. *Eenige kameradviezen uit de jaren 1874 en 1875*. Amsterdam, 139–203; see esp. 183n.

26 Ibid., 191–197.

had he not written an inspired and thorough commentary on the social paragraph of the Party Program?[27] And what about his short monograph on manual labor, published only the year before, in which he had defended the right of the laboring classes to organize themselves to represent their legitimate interests?[28] In short, did not all his antecedents point in the direction of working for an extension of democracy to include that class of people whose plight continued to be largely ignored? Kuyper's mind appears to have been made up. His next move would take him further on the road to what was increasingly becoming known as Christian Democracy.

A Workingman in City Council?
Events followed each other in quick succession. On Friday evening, November 14, 1890, in the same week as the boisterous annual meeting of Patrimonium, the Anti-Revolutionary voters' club of Amsterdam met to nominate candidates for the upcoming municipal elections. Kuyper attended the meeting and spoke eloquently in support of the nomination of Bart Poesiat. This move took many by complete surprise, since Poesiat was "only" a carpenter, a foreman of a maintenance crew at a local brewery, and the recently retired secretary of Patrimonium. Could this decent yet very "common" man run for city councilor? None of his social class had ever been a serious AR candidate in any election. But Kuyper argued that they had to stand on guard for their sacred principles: since Amsterdam's socialists were nominating a workingman, so should they; moreover, Poesiat was devoted to the House of Orange so would be able to counteract the socialists' dangerous republicanism. Kuyper's nomination was supported and the motion carried. To the chairman's consternation, Brother Poesiat accepted on the spot!

Chairing the meeting had been Professor Fabius, himself a city councilor. He felt that the meeting had gotten completely out of hand and that same evening wrote a letter of resignation as president of the club. His aristocratic sensibilities appear to have been rudely violated, for he sent a volley of bristling notes to Kuyper in the days that followed. Could the two not have had a heart-to-heart talk, one wonders, since they must have run into each other almost every day at the fledgling Free University where they both taught? In any case, four notes have been preserved.

To be sure, Fabius conceded in one of his communications, the spinelessness of our caucus in The Hague can give rise to "unhealthy democratic notions"; but this latest step is ludicrous. The notion that only a workingman can best represent the interests of workingmen makes no sense; after all, Fabius noted naively, such a man lacks the opportunity and the education to orient himself adequately in the social field. Sarcastically he went on, "I suppose that if the socialist women's league decide tomorrow that kitchen maids are not represented on council and nominate a kitchen maid, it will be the principled thing to do for our voters' club to likewise nominate a kitchen maid, preferably one who loves the royal family. Then Mr. Hovey can walk to council meetings in the company of

---

27 Cf. Langley, McKendree R. 1995. "Emancipation and Apologetics: The Formation of Abraham Kuyper's Anti-Revolutionary Party in the Netherlands, 1872–1880." *PhD Thesis*. Westminster Theological Seminary, Philadelphia, 135–138.

28 Kuyper, A. 1889. *Handenarbeid*. Amsterdam. Containing seven articles that had appeared in *De Standaard* during February of that year; English translation in *AK:ACR* 231–254.

his hired hand and his kitchen maid."[29]

But who was Mr. Hovy? He was candidate Poesiat's employer. Willem Hovy, the owner of an establishment for the manufacture of beer and vinegar, had been a respected AR city councilor for many years.[30] This wise and gentle man, almost as upset as the professor, penned a mildly worded rebuke to his longtime friend Kuyper. It wasn't right for brother Poesiat not to have consulted me, he explained; he is the supervisor at my plant and if I as his employer give him leave to attend council meetings I would have to take his place in the meantime "since he represents me to his subordinates." This rather sophistic argument was reinforced by a more general objection. The entire episode did not sit well with Hovy. In his opinion it spelled "false democratism." The ARP should not move in this direction: "The Lord is mighty and willing, at our humble petition, to raise up men whom He has also given a heart for the plight of the workingman. The workingman does not need to leave his post for that."[31]

Kuyper was not swayed. Whether Poesiat won or lost [he lost], his nomination was the signal for new marching orders. The general had resolved to push on toward his long-range objective. But would he be able to marshal his officers, those barons and squires, businessmen and professionals? The following spring, in his pre-election speech to the assembled party deputies – men from the higher, middle and lower classes – he laid his cards on the table. Antirevolutionaries should be in the lead in welcoming the inevitable, namely democracy; but of course it had better be a democracy developed along Christian lines: Christian democracy. With Christian practical sense he explained why:

> The politics of Europe is indisputably in search of a new configuration. The oligarchy of the financially and intellectually advantaged classes is finished. The masses are now in a state of ferment. Interest in social concerns has pushed itself to the foreground. . . .
>
> This agitation is not likely to lead on at once to a violent revolution, at least not in our country. Our national character is too phlegmatic for that. But it does push our politics inevitably in the direction of democracy. . . .
>
> Considering this state of affairs and this course of development, what is the Antirevolutionary party to do? Must it just resist what seems to be going too far, or should it put itself in the vanguard to guide the movement into safer channels? That is the leading question that is to determine our national action. And so let it be said here, said with emphasis, that [we] are duty-bound in Christ, come what may, to position ourselves courageously in the breach of this nation and to prepare for a Christian-democratic development of our national government. This can still be done now. But if you squander this God-given moment and let it pass unused, you will be to blame for having thrown away the future of your country and you will soon bend under the iron fist that will strike you in your Christian liberty and, unsparingly, also in your wallets and property.
>
> I repeat: A Christian-democratic shape must be given to our state institutions precisely to

---

29 Fabius to Kuyper, Nov. 14, 17, 22 and 23, 1890; KA 4748, 4749, 4753, 4754.

30 Hovy was a loyal supporter and benefactor of Patrimonium. The Maecenas of the Free University, he helped found it and served as the president of its Board of Governors. Originally Reformed, the beer brewer later joined the Moravian Brethren in Zeist. Cf. Smid, T. D. 1964. "Willem Hovy (1840–1915)," *Antirevolutionaire Staatkunde*: 239–257, 278–296. For Hovy,s company, see Van der Woude, Rolf 2009. *Geloof in de brouwerij; opkomst, bloei en ondergang van bierbrouwerij De Gekroonde Valk*. Amsterdam: Bas Lubberhuizen.

31 Hovy to Kuyper, 16 Nov. 1890; KA 4745.

hold back ochlocracy [mob-rule] along anti-Christian lines. . . .[32]

Kuyper went on to outline what shape, in his view, Christian democracy should have in his country. It would once more place the nation under God and recognize government as a divine institution. It would respect freedom of conscience, particularly by ending discrimination against Christian education. To restore the nation "in its organic relations" it would grant suffrage to all heads of households and install chambers of labor and agriculture. And finally, he concluded with rising passion,

> must not the *spirit of the Compassionate One* be poured out over our whole government administration? We are not a pagan but a Christian nation, a nation that has to take the human heart into consideration also in its heaviness and nameless suffering. . . . That nameless suffering is not lightened but made heavier when the State seeks its strength in a heartless bureaucracy, knows no other power than that of coercion, and follows the model of *Mammon* rather than that of the *Gospel*. The Antirevolutionary party accordingly asks that a *different spirit* might control our public administration; that our legislation might show *a heart* and officialdom some *sympathy* for suffering citizens; that powerless *labor* might be protected from coolly calculating *capital*; and that even the poorest citizen might count on the prospect of swift and sound *justice*.[33]

Organizing the Congress

Meanwhile there was a Social Congress to organize. Once Patrimonium's resolution to have a joint congress had been endorsed by the Central Committee of the ARP, it fell to Kuyper to convene a program committee. He recruited Wormser as secretary, "volunteered" three members of the AR caucus in Parliament, and wrote Kater that he counted on his personal participation as well.

Klaas Kater, however, was feeling more and more depressed. The repercussions to his speech had been explosive. He replied to Kuyper that he contemplated resigning as president of Patrimonium. Kuyper, hard at work at damage control, persuaded him not to do so. Yet the charge, repeated in many circles, that Kater "did not recognize ranks, stations and callings" stung the man. His position was becoming nearly impossible, so he felt he should keep his role to a minimum in the preparation of the Congress. Kuyper must have written him again, for only a few days later Kater informed Kuyper that he would put his shoulder to the wheel after all and serve on the Organizing Committee. But it would be prudent, he cautioned, to invite a Frisian as a second person from Patrimonium: "All my troubles to keep the Frisians in our organization will have been in vain if only Hollanders are chosen for the committee." The name Kater proposed was Van Vliet.[34]

Although this proposal suggests regional (or even ethnic) rivalry, more likely it was a move to co-opt self-styled radicals who were impatient with perceived moderates. Kuyper took the hint but was beginning to run into obstacles of a far more serious nature. The Congress would need contributors of papers, chairmen for the sections, reporters from the workshops. Scores of letters left his home. The response was most discouraging. One had prior engagements and sent his regrets; another considered himself not competent; still

32 Kuyper, A. "Maranatha," *Deputatenredevoering* of 12 May 1891; English translation in *AK:ACR* 205–228, at 221–222.

33 Ibid., 225–226 (italics in Kuyper's original).

34 Kater to Kuyper, 15 and 19 December 1890; KA 4767, 4770.

another declined to work with men such as Kater. Most correspondents complained that the time for preparation was far too short; they were not familiar enough with the whole subject and needed more time for study and reflection.

The time was indeed short. At the outset, the Organizing Committee had planned the Congress for the end of February 1891. To get more volunteers for chairing and reporting, the date was soon moved to June, and finally to October.[35] When it occurred to Kater at the last minute that many lost wages and travel costs could be avoided by scheduling the Congress in the second week of November to coincide with the annual meeting of Patrimonium, it was so decided.[36]

More Social Unrest in the North

All this time, developments on the socio-economic front were not standing still. The winter of 1890–91 was unusually severe and the poor were suffering. Again the northern provinces seemed especially hard hit. Dr. L. H. Wagenaar, pastor of a Doleantie church in Leeuwarden and a graduate of the Free University, wrote a letter of alarm to his former professor about the news that was reaching him from the Frisian countryside. The danger is real, he wrote Kuyper, that "Irish conditions" will come to prevail in our clay belt. The farmers are forbidding the laborers to organize themselves and are trying to provoke violence "so they can shoot into them." Some of our best workmen, he continued, both in the cities and in the country, "the pith and marrow of our party," are near starvation: "Their wretched condition, endured in wondrous silence, defies description." Wagenaar explained that people's diet was limited to potatoes, most of which had frozen so were lacking in any nutritional value: "Dominee van Andel, P. van Vliet and I confer often and are studying Mosaic Socialism."[37] "Our conclusion is the nationalization of all land, with long-lease or copyhold, heritable in the generations."[38] Radical indeed! But the three men were already turning their minds to the next general elections for Parliament. After Van Vliet ran and lost in two by-elections in succession, Wagenaar, in his next letter to the party chairman, strongly recommended Van Vliet for a Frisian district where the ARP had a chance of winning: he deserves a chance, "not as a working-class candidate, but as a very capable and cultured anti-revolutionary who is particularly informed about social conditions." As a clincher Wagenaar used an argument that was sure to catch the Chairman's attention: "If our party does not come to the defense of *our little people* who are perishing under their burdens, it will lose all its influence in Friesland."[39]

Kuyper listened, and gave his blessing to the candidacy of Van Vliet for Parliament, as he had done earlier of Poesiat for city council. That summer of 1891, Van Vliet fought

---

35 I stumbled upon the minutes of the Organizing Committee among the 1891 records of the Amsterdam voters' club, deposited in the Documentatiecentrum mentioned above (note 18). The fact that Wormser served both bodies as secretary at this time may explain this misplacement.

36 Leo xiii's encyclical on the social question is dated March 1891. If the Dutch brethren had stuck to their original date, their congress would have scooped the Vatican. But then, who would have noticed?

37 Not "state socialism," he confided in a letter to a Dutch propagator of the ideas of Henry George, but a system as in ancient Israel, to escape the judgment of Isaiah 5:8, "Woe to you who add house to house and join field to field. . . ." See Langeveld, "Achtergronden," 120.

38 Wagenaar to Kuyper, undated [late 1890]; KA 4783. The prevailing system – leasehold tenure, involving the auctioning of parcels of land to the highest bidder – was indeed one of the structural causes of rural poverty.

39 Wagenaar to Kuyper, undated [early 1891]; KA 4784; emphasis in the original.

a hard campaign in the promising district around Sneek. He lost. But so did many other Coalition candidates throughout the country. The Liberals regained their majority and formed the new government. This reversal dashed the hopes of many for an accelerated program of social reform. Liberals still favored a minimalist government protective of exaggerated property rights. The legal framework within which the lower classes had to live and work seemed more entrenched than ever.

Protest, however, did not die down. A Christian school principal from the village of Middelstum in the north published a pamphlet about social conditions in the Groningen countryside. Its conclusion hit hard: Our laborers are being exploited by the farmers, and our Reformed farmers are no exception! Kuyper's *De Standaard* reviewed the publication favorably, but throughout August the Groningen *Courant* published over thirty letters to the editor protesting the allegation leveled by "Graphoo" (an obvious pseudonym). The Reformed farmers retaliated by spreading the rumor that the pamphleteer was a socialist if not a communist. Thereupon "Graphoo," who as N. Oosterbaan was not unknown to Kuyper, dropped him a hint.[40] Soon after, *De Standaard* ran a short editorial referring once more to all the facts contained in the controversial pamphlet, which was written, it emphasized, "by a spiritual kinsman of ours." The diversion tactic failed; but the breach did not heal.[41]

Conclusion

Finally, November arrived, and with it the long-awaited Social Congress. It was attended by more than 500 people. Kuyper had found his chairmen for the three main sections: for the religious aspect of the social question, Dr. F. L. Rutgers, professor of theology in the Free University; for the socio-economic section, the Rev. Dr. Hendrik Pierson, director and chaplain of a number of philanthropic institutions; and for the political aspect, Dr. A. F. de Savornin Lohman, professor of law in the Free University and Minister of Interior Affairs in the late government. The list of designated reporters from the sections featured such well-known Reformed theologians as Bavinck, Noordtzij, Sikkel, and Van Andel. The franchise question in the narrow sense was not officially on the agenda; the focus would be on the social question in all its broadness.

"They cannot wait, not a day, not an hour!" Kuyper's opening address did penance on behalf of all: "We should feel ashamed that the voice of conscience has not spoken more loudly within us before now, or at least that it did not stir us to earlier action. We should feel humiliated that, in the face of so crying a need, we have not long since been acting in the name of Jesus" (*PP* 21). In the printed version he inserted this footnote: "We must admit, to our shame, that the Roman Catholics are far ahead of us in their study of the social question" (*PP* 18), a remark that is followed by an impressive enumeration (not included in the English translation) of many publications, especially French ones. It is evident that Kuyper wanted to make real progress at this conference. Philanthropy, deeds

---

40 Oosterbaan to Kuyper, 21 Sept. 1891; KA 5005. This teacher was active in the local AR voters' club.

41 Conditions in rural Groningen around 1900 are depicted in a volume of short stories by Keuning, Pieter 1917. *Kinderen in verstand en boosheid* [Children in understanding and in malice] (7th impr. 1975). The title was taken from 1 Corinthians 14:20. After its publication the author was afraid to visit the village of Spyk where he had grown up and which appeared barely camouflaged in his book. A popular saying at the time reflected the power position of the "big" farmers: "I have three men working for me: one in the goul, one in the stoul, and one in the schoul" (in the barn, the pulpit, and the school house).

of neighborly love, will always be necessary, he explained to the assembled Calvinists, since it is obvious that "the poor man cannot wait until the restoration of our social structure has been completed. Almost certainly he will not live long enough to see that happy day. Nevertheless, he still has to live; he must feed his hungry mouth and the mouths of his hungry family" (*PP* 69). But relief measures, public or private, will no longer suffice. What is needed is partial demolition and reconstruction. We will not get anywhere, the speaker held forth, without drastic structural reforms – without "architectonic critique" (*PP* 44) of the whole framework of our society; for if things continue the way they have always gone, "life on earth will become less and less a heaven and more and more a hell" (*PP* 45). The well-to-do in the audience were not spared. Kuyper goaded them in a daring application of pastoral psychology:

> those who are diverted by fear for their money box have no place marching in the ranks with us. This is holy ground, and he who would walk on it must first loosen the sandals of his egotism. The only sound permitted here is the stirring and eloquent voice of the merciful Samaritan whispering in our ears. There is suffering round about you, and those who suffer are your brothers, sharers of your nature, your own flesh and blood. You might have been in their place and they in your more pleasant position. (*PP* 68)

Clearly Kuyper wanted to see action, strategic reform, fundamental change – starting today. But, oddly enough, nowhere in the published Proceedings of the Congress do we find those oft quoted words, "They cannot wait, not a day, not an hour." Half a century later, an aged journalist who had covered the conference solved the mystery. He could recall distinctly how Dr. Kuyper had said those words at the conference *in a prayer*.[42]

The speech and the prayer mark Kuyper's definitive transformation into a Christian Democrat. He never again looked back. The conference kept the left wing within the fold and thus saved the party from breaking apart along class lines. That break, however, did come a few years later, when members disagreed sharply over the suffrage issue.[43] In the aftermath, Kuyper, though he had been unreservedly supportive of a further extension of the franchise, adopted a more moderate tone and sounded warnings against "democratism." "*Democracy* is a great good," he maintained, "in that it allows men of all ranks and classes to sit on representative bodies and participate in legislative activity; but beware lest it imply the ideology of popular sovereignty: then democracy can founder on the shoals of crass materialism, class struggle, vulgarization, or the egotism of interest groups. That is the error to avoid."[44] Yet ever since the memorable year 1891, Kuyper's party was more widely democratic and less class-conscious than any other in the country. Seen in that light, the marriage in 1980 of Kuyperians and the spiritual grandchildren of Leo XIII – the Catholic People's Party – was more than a marriage of convenience. The union that took the name Christian Democratic Appeal, with its strong social conscience, is a political alliance that has still to be reckoned with at every election.

---

42 Personal communication to the author by M. C. Smit, at the time archivist at the Kuyper Institute in The Hague, quoting H. Diemer.

43 In 1894, Alexander de Savornin Lohman, insisting on the unconstitutionally of a franchise bill that Kuyper supported despite such "hairsplitting," led a secession from the party, to found the Free Anti-Revolutionaries, a more conservative-aristocratic group that later joined a more theocratically oriented organization to form the Christian-Historical Union; cf. Stellingwerff, J. 1987. *Dr. Abraham Kuyper en de Vrije Universiteit*. Kampen: Kok, 189–201.

44 Kuyper, A. 1895. *Christus en de Sociale nooden; en Democratische klippen*. Amsterdam, 57, 74–91.

6

The Political Spirituality of Abraham Kuyper

McKendree R. Langley

Introduction

The meaning of the Christian faith in the modern world is a basic question with which generations of believers have struggled. The visible demonstration of faith has been found to be particularly difficult in an age of secularization and practical unbelief. Yet all men live their lives before the face of God. We are commanded to love God and our neighbor. Believers are to live the Christian life. As Francis Schaeffer has so perceptively stated:

> The important thing after being born spiritually is to live. There is a new birth, and then there is the Christian life to be lived. This is the area of sanctification; from the time of the new birth, through this present life, until Jesus comes or until we die."?[1]

Concerning sanctification, Schaeffer added: "Whatever is not an exhibition that God exists misses the whole purpose of the Christian's life now on this earth."[2] While believers generally are concerned with sanctification or spirituality, they usually define it in terms of personal piety and church life. Rarely is this concern for living the Christian life expanded to include public matters in the nation and the world in any clear-cut fashion.

Yet at important points the Bible speaks of the necessity of what can be termed political spirituality. David, after being anointed the future king of Israel, expressed a politically spiritual attitude when King Saul and his army sought to assassinate him for reasons of state. But David had no hatred towards the king. On the contrary, he honored the reigning king, prayed to the Lord for political deliverance, and praised him among the people (Psalm 57 and 1 Samuel 24). King Solomon in Psalm 72 prayed for wisdom to institute social justice and to create a national environment of well-being (1 Kings 3:3–14). The Lord Jesus (Matthew 25:31–46) declared that the inheritance of the kingdom of God is related to helping the poor, the distressed and the stranger. James (1:27) defined true religion in terms of helping widows and orphans and keeping oneself unstained by the world. These scriptural texts suggest the existence of political spirituality as a partial but legitimate expression of the Christian life.

One Christian who exemplified a Reformed political spirituality was Dr. Abraham Kuyper (1837–1920). At key points in the career of this great Reformed theologian-statesman, this political spirituality came to clear expression.

---

1   Schaeffer, Francis 1972. *True Spirituality*. Wheaton: Tyndale House, 5.

2   Ibid., 72.

As a Pastor

It was during the mid-1860s that Kuyper, in his first pastoral charge at the small country church at Beesd in the Netherlands, became acquainted with the Anti-Revolutionary or Christian-Historical worldview as it was expressed by the historian–statesman G. Groen van Prinsterer (1801–1876) in his *Unbelief and Revolution* (1847, 2nd ed. 1868). In reflecting on this important work, Kuyper wrote enthusiastically to Groen on 11 April 1867 that it gave him " . . . . a photograph of your mind."[3] *Unbelief and Revolution* changed Kuyper's outlook in a most fundamental way, for it presented a powerful Calvinistic critique of the secularization of public life in the western world that flowed from the idea of complete human emancipation from God's standards in the French Revolution of 1789. This religion of unbelief had been applied to every area of life, including theology, politics and morality. Kuyper saw that Groen was correct in asserting that the only true alternative to this practical unbelief was the Gospel of Christ. The true norms for humanity come from the sovereign God of the Bible, not from the sovereign will of the people. Thus Kuyper correctly realized that Groen was calling for a Christian alternative to unbelieving secularity in all of life, in order to be faithful to God and to deal justly with one's fellow man.[4]

Kuyper wrote to the author of this book, when the second edition was published in 1868, to express his joy – since *Unbelief and Revolution* contained a critique of the antithesis between belief and unbelief in church and state.[5] This Anti-Revolutionary perspective even influenced Kuyper's preaching at a fundamental level.

On 10 November 1867 the Rev. Abraham Kuyper began his ministry at the Reformed Church in Utrecht with a sermon on John 1:14, "The Incarnation of God as the Fundamental Principle of the Church." The Incarnation of Jesus Christ was affirmed as historical fact, giving the church its *raison d'être*, in distinction from any notion of human religiosity. Both theological modernism and the viewpoint of comparative religion were properly rejected as denials of this divine-human incarnation in time and space. This doctrine of Christ must be adequately expressed as a part of evangelical truth in the confessional standards of a denomination. It should be a factor for true unity in the visible church. But in view of the existence of modernists in the high councils of the Dutch Reformed Church, Kuyper declared that either reform or eventual separation would be necessary to maintain confessional orthodoxy. He emphasized that the basis of such orthodoxy was the preaching of the new birth by personal faith in the incarnate Christ. Only by this gospel can the eyes of men be opened to see the cosmic battle raging between the spirit of the age and the spirit of Christ. The antithesis is between the children of the world and the children of God. By the power of God's Spirit, believers must be made sensitive to this cosmic battle. Kuyper pointed out that Christians have a calling from the Lord to be active in this contest; for there is no aspect of life that should remain untouched by the Christian. There is no important question of life in which the believer should refrain from seeking an answer from the Lord. The Christian family should be the starting

---

3   Kuyper to Groen, 11 April 1867 in Goslinga, A., ed. 1937. *Briefwisseling van Mr G. Groen van Prinsterer met Dr. A. Kuyper: 1864–1876*. The Hague/Kampen: Zuid-Hollandsche Boek- en Handelsdrukkerij/Kok, 8; author's translation.

4   Cf. Van Prinsterer G. Groen, 1973, 1975. *Unbelief and Revolution*, Lectures VIII, IX and XI, ed. and trans. Harry Van Dyke with Donald Morton. Amsterdam: Groen van Prinsterer Fund: 2 vols.

5   Kuyper to Groen, 12 October 1868 in Goslinga, 17.

point for the outworking of Christ's Spirit in every area of life. Christ is the righteous savior of the world.[6] Thus Kuyper, as a young pastor, saw that the new birth and Reformed orthodoxy were the basis of political spirituality.

Several years later, while still a pastor at Utrecht, Dr. Kuyper made his first major political speech on 18 May 1869 at the Congress of the Association for National Christian Education. His address on the necessity of Christian schools was "An Appeal to the Conscience of the People." It was pointed out that there was a struggle going on in the country between the forces of secularism and Reformed Christianity. The focal point of this struggle concerned the control of the schools and thus the influence over the younger generation. Kuyper strongly believed that if the schools continued to be controlled by secularists who were pushing a modernistic "dogma-free" Christianity, then the Reformed people would gradually be forced to compromise their obedience to Christ with disastrous consequences. As goes the school, so goes the nation. It seemed that the secularization process would overwhelm public life unless something were done. Thus the young leader called for the creation of a Christian political movement to work for the acceptance of Calvinist schools along with Catholic, 'secular" and other schools – all financed by public funds in proportion to the number of students and tax payers in each group. The young pastor called for Reformed Christians to compete with other groups in a pluralist context; he appealed to Christian conscience. But the realization of such a noble goal required systematic political action to propound a credible case for this cause. Reform of the school laws had to start on the primary level. Only with the introduction of a truly pluralistic school system would Reformed parents of modest means be able to send their children to educational institutions providing instruction from a Christian perspective.[7]

As a Journalist

As time passed, the young minister's Christian leadership was nationally recognized. In August 1870 he accepted a call from the most important congregation in the Netherlands, the New (Reformed) Church at Amsterdam – the Dutch "Westminster Abbey," where the sovereigns of the House of Orange are crowned. On 1 January 1872 he became the editor of the church weekly, *The Herald.* On 1 April 1872 he assumed the editorship of the Christian political daily newspaper, *De Standaard.* Dr. Kuyper persistently wrote editorials for *De Standaard* from 1872 to 1919 – forty-seven years! His Christian journalism was one of the key factors in the rise of the Reformed political movement, the Anti-Revolutionary Party, which significantly influenced the course of national life.

In his journalistic work, Kuyper emphasized that the believer has a divine mandate to be the servant of Christ in every aspect of life. This concern was expressed in his concept of the "ordinances of God." The Lord is the Creator and sustainer of creation and culture. By the normative Scriptures, his law structures can be properly seen in special revelation and in common grace. An important task of the state is to retard the social manifestations of human sin. The Christian must seek to integrate scriptural norms with the realities of public life. The result must be the articulation of Christian political principles to be applied in a concrete national situation.[8]

---

6   Kuyper, A. 1913. *Predicatien.* Kampen: Kok, 255 –275.
7   Kuyper, A. 1869. *Het Beroep op het Volksgeweten.* Amsterdam: B. H. Blankenberg, Jr.
8   Kuyper, A. 1873. "Ordinantien Gods." *De Standaard*, October 16–November 7. In Kuyper, A. 1879. *Ons*

During March and April 1873, Dr. Kuyper wrote an autobiographical fragment entitled *In Confidence*. In it he explained his struggle with theological modernism, his conversion and the development of his Reformed world-view between about 1859 and 1873. He pointed out that *De Standaard* was begun as a national voice for the Reformed common people. Kuyper had editorial responsibility to write the "leaders" which would articulate the Anti-Revolutionary, Christian-Historical viewpoint in distinction from the ethical normlessness of secularism. *De Standaard* was the means, he declared, to organize the forces of Reformed orthodoxy as an active Christian alternative to modernism, conservatism, liberalism and Catholic ultramontanism. The national and international crisis required the witness of an orthodox confessional stance in the Reformed Church and an Anti-Revolutionary presence in society. In this autobiography Kuyper's heart was broken, humbled and inspired by his faith in the living Christ of the Scriptures.[9]

An excellent early example of this political spirituality was the full-page editorial, "To the Voters," published in *De Standaard* on 9 June 1873, the day before the national parliamentary elections. Although unsigned, internal evidence indicates that this editorial was written by Kuyper himself. This election appeal was made during the initial phase of the organization of the Anti-Revolutionary Party. An organization favoring Christian schools – the Anti-School-Law League – was actually running this campaign in conjunction with local Anti-Revolutionary voters" clubs. A full list of independent Anti-Revolutionary parliamentary candidates was presented to the voters for the first time throughout the nation. But the secularist Liberal Party – the establishment – was forecast to win most of the contests. It was in this context that Kuyper developed the meaning of political spirituality in the election of 1873.

The editorial began by describing the national political crisis caused by the intolerant secularists – both Conservatives and Liberals. It was then asserted that true healing could only come from Christ. It is he who has been given all power in heaven and earth, and thus over the Netherlands. Confession of Christ applies even to political life, because he came to fulfill the law and the prophets even for the citizen. Given the general political-spiritual crisis and the obligation of Christian obedience to the Lord, refusal to vote would be a neglect of the Christian duty to attempt to improve the political situation. The leader-writer then enquired rhetorically: Which party will you vote for? He wondered if the reader had looked at the principles of the various parties and evaluated them from a biblical perspective. In this decision, the Christian must also seek to love the Lord with all his heart, mind and strength (Matthew 22:37). The Conservatives talked about religion but only as a means to maintain law and order. But the editor asked: Can God's name be used for such merely pragmatic purposes? The Liberals as secularists banished God's name from politics. The Socialists doubted the existence of God altogether. The Catholics were skillful in making alliances, first with the Liberals and then with the Conservatives, but never were they satisfactory representatives of orthodox Protestants. The reader was urged to make up his own mind. The "leader" asserted that for the man of Christian principles, voting was as much a confession of faith as worshipping in church on Sunday. The fundamental issue for *De Standaard* was stated as follows: "The question is not if the candidate's heart is favorable to Christianity; but if he has Christ as his starting-point *even for politics*, and will speak

Program. Amsterdam: Höveker & Wormser, 116–129.

9   Kuyper, A. 1873. *Confidentie.* Amsterdam: Höveker.

out for his name!"[10] However, since Anti-Revolutionary candidates could not be elected in most districts, the editor admitted that those looking for victories might just as well stay away from the polls. But he urged all enfranchised Anti-Revolutionaries to vote as part of a national Christian political witness to the validity of Anti-Revolutionary principles. When seen in this light, Anti-Revolutionary candidates running on independent tickets (and not in league with the Conservatives) and Anti-Revolutionary voters supporting them, were a demonstration of the growing Christian political presence in society. Thus *De Standaard* urged, "Confess Christ even in the Election of 10 June 1873!"[11] The Anti-Revolutionary readers were asked what they had done in the campaign during the previous months to articulate the Christian political cause and thus to influence public opinion. The editorial finally inquired if the voters had prayed about the election. The Anti-Revolutionary Party was made up of people who believed in the power of prayer made in the name of Christ, for he is the sovereign Lord over nations and elections. The editorial ended with a strong appeal to awaken the Spirit of Christ in national life.

This election manifesto clearly stated that in national life the fundamental dividing-line was between those who desired to base their politics on the gospel in distinction from all humanism, and those who did not.

As Party Chairman

As chairman of the Anti-Revolutionary Party, Kuyper delivered a famous speech on the centenary of the French Revolution to the party congress of 3 May 1889: "Not the Liberty Tree but the Cross." This speech was a good example of Kuyper's power as a Christian thinker and political orator. Christian reflection on the meaning of a century of secularization of European public life, was the subject of this address. Kuyper developed four major themes on the subject: the true nature of the French Revolution, the gospel versus the Revolution, the Evangelical Awakening of the nineteenth century, and the *raison d'être* for the Anti-Revolutionary Party.

Concerning the French Revolution of 1789, Kuyper declared that it was based on the unbelieving Enlightenment philosophy of Voltaire and Rousseau. The revolutionaries preached a gospel of earthly salvation and political liberation. But the results were the blood bath of Robespierre's reign of terror, war and the imperialism of the two Napoleons. The French Revolutions of 1830 and 1848, as well as the urban proletarian uprising at Paris in 1871, were later manifestations. But in a wider sense the Revolution of 1789 secularized public life in the western world and made humanistic political parties the dominant force, whether liberal, conservative, socialist or communist. In this larger humanistic movement, man seeks to order his world as he sees fit.

Kuyper's fundamental concern was to demonstrate that the gospel was antithetical to this secularity of the Revolution. The struggle of the Anti-Revolutionary Party, he brilliantly declared, was against the *principle* of the Revolution – human autonomy – not just its superficial results. Christ, not Voltaire, is the Lord Messiah over the nations. But true freedom must be grounded in the ethical new birth that only Christ can give to men. He alone can break the dominant power of sin. In distinction from Enlightenment thought, which saw man as basically good, the Christian confesses that man has fallen into sin. It

---

10   "Aan onze Kiezers." *De Standaard*, 9 June 1873, author's translation.

11   Ibid., author's translation.

is the human heart that is in need of conversion. And true political liberation, declared Kuyper, can only come from ethical rebirth by faith in the Messiah. The secularists speak of man's power, but the Bible speaks of God's sovereignty over heaven and earth.

But after the French Revolution, the party chairman continued, came the Evangelical Awakening. Again throughout Europe there was gospel preaching which stressed conversion of the heart to Christ and ethical improvement in the Christian life. Believers saw that liberation from the domination of sin and unbelief could be accomplished by Christ alone. Evangelization was begun; orphanages and homes for wayward girls were established; Bible societies were organized and Christian literature was distributed. But the Evangelical Awakening as a spiritual movement was naïvely unaware of the titanic struggle between belief and unbelieving secularity, as well as unhistoric in its ignorance of its own ties with the Christian past and lacking in theological substance by being too generally evangelical.

The genesis of the Anti-Revolutionary Party began when Groen van Prinsterer saw that political work was needed to develop fully a Reformed alternative to the secularization of public life, to replace the revolutionary spirit of secular idolatry with a Christian spirit in every area of life. Thus Anti-Revolutionaries became involved in seeking to change Dutch law, to allow for a school of Christ to be fully equal to the school of Reason. The baptismal promises of parents concerning their covenant children were seen by Kuyper to require Christian schools to provide for the national survival of a viable Christian community. Further political action was required for the free outworking of the gospel in church, school and Press to allow for an ethical liberation of the citizenry. Kuyper emphasized that Anti-Revolutionaries recognized the sovereignty of God over the nations, while strongly believing in social pluralism. The Anti-Revolutionary Party, he continued, would seek to convince the electorate of the validity of its position but without coercion. Recognition was made of the three equal groupings in the Netherlands whose rights must be respected: rationalists, Catholics and Calvinists. The government must not show spiritual or political favoritism to any one of these groupings. Kuyper also said that his party worked for a widening of the vote, endorsed the right of workers to form labor organizations – including Christian labor unions – and recognized the existence of the social question of urban and rural poverty as well as the need for more adequate policies for defense, diplomacy, trade, and justice in the colonies.

In order for such a Christian-Historical viewpoint to be effective, it was necessary to organize the Anti-Revolutionary Party independently of the secularist Liberal-Conservative dilemma and based on the Calvinist heritage. This party presented an alternative to the prevailing liberal ideas in politics, religion, and scholarship. Such independence from political humanism brought about the first Anti-Revolutionary–Catholic coalition government, the Mackay–Keuchenius Ministry (1888–1891), which Kuyper strongly defended as the only means to overcome the dominance of secularist politics.

Kuyper ended his speech by declaring that, after a century of growth, the liberty tree of the French Revolution was demonstrated to be poisonous while the cross of Christ alone could give true life to men and nations: "As for us and our children, we will no longer kneel before the idol of the French Revolution; for the God of our fathers will again be our God!"[12]

---

12 Kuyper, A. 1951. "Niet de Vrijheidsboom maar het Kruis." In Kuyper, A. et al., *Geen Vergeefs Woord*. Kam-

As Champion of the Poor

But political spirituality for Kuyper was not only a matter of opposing the spirit of the age; it also made him sensitive to the problem of poverty. After his years as a pastor to the urban poor of Amsterdam (1870–1874), his term in Parliament (1874–1875) and his chairmanship of the Anti-Revolutionary Party (from 1879), Kuyper opened the First Christian Social Congress in 1891 with his magnificent address on "Christianity and the Class Struggle" (which has been translated into English!). Kuyper raised the basic question: What should we, as Christ-confessors, do about the social needs of our age? While recognizing that Catholics such as Pope Leo XIII, and Protestants such as Frederick Denison Maurice and Groen van Prinsterer, as well as socialists such as Karl Marx, had been reflecting on poverty for some time, much more reflection by evangelicals was needed. "The social question," Kuyper pointed out, "has become *the* question, the burning *life-question*, of the end of the nineteenth century" (*PP* 47–8). Social justice had rightly become the cry of the socialist movement. Groen was quoted to the effect that in socialism there is a measure of truth mingled with error, which gives it its power; one should also attempt the improvement of *material* conditions, the unjustness of which redoubles the power of the socialist error; socialism finds its source in the French Revolution and thus is conquerable only by Christianity (*PP* 19).

Kuyper then offered several Bible references that indicated a believing social sensitivity: among these texts are Ecclesiastes 4:1 on the injustice of unrelieved oppression, James 5:1–4 on the divine denunciation of the rich who exploit the poor workmen, and 1 Timothy 6:10 on the love of money as a corrupting influence on humanity. It was the bourgeois influence of the French Revolution that finally unleashed the economic individualism of *laissez-faire* capitalism in continental Europe. "Dog eat dog" became the rule. As in the reign of terror, the solution for political or economic anarchy proposed by many was the all-powerful state. Kuyper saw five avenues by which Christians could come to grips with the ghetto of poverty: (1) Confession of God as maker of heaven and *earth – his* ordinances apply to earthly society; (2) recognition of spheres of free initiative in society distinct from the state; (3) acceptance of the Christian teaching that humanity is of one blood – society is interconnected and inter-dependent; (4) recognition that the ownership of property is stewardship of what belongs to God – the socially responsible use of private and public property is a Christian duty; (5) the divine function of government is to promulgate justice – when injustice occurs in society, it is the responsibility of the state to intervene with effective legislation. For Kuyper, material prosperity was not the determinative factor but rather spiritual and material happiness before the Lord. Kuyper concluded: "The question on which the whole social problem really pivots is only whether you recognize in the less fortunate, even in the poorest, not merely a creature, a person in wretched circumstances, but one of your own flesh and blood: for the sake of Christ, *your brother*" (*PP* 67). In calling for Christians to stand with the Anti-Revolutionary Party on the social question, Kuyper added: "For those who are diverted by fear for their money box have no place marching in the ranks with us. This is holy ground, and he who would walk on it must first loosen the sandals of his egotism" (*PP* 68).

pen: Kok: 37–60.

As Prime Minister

A final example of political spirituality comes from the period in which Abraham Kuyper was prime minister of the Netherlands (1901–1905). By 1900 the Socialist parties, labor unions and anarchist agitators had arisen to challenge the existing Christian and secularist parties. Questions of poverty, social improvement of the plight of the lower classes, the nature of democracy and revolution were widely discussed. The Socialist spokesmen sought to appeal to *all* the workers, Christian and non-Christian, with bread-and-butter logic. They were attempting this to lure believing workers away from the Calvinist and Catholic labor unions – Patrimonium and the Roman Catholic People's Union.

On 9 December, 1902, Prime Minister Kuyper took part in the parliamentary debate on this question. His opening remarks concerned the position that a Christian party should take on poverty and socialism. There was an absolute antithesis between the life-views of Marx and Christ: materialism versus divine sovereignty. The Christian parties (including the Anti-Revolutionary and Catholic Parties) had a responsibility to present a political alternative to socialist materialism. The prime minister then pointed out that there were two sets of texts in the Scriptures on the question of property and poverty: one set of texts to which the rich appealed, and another set which the oppressed used to support their quest for economic justice and political change. It was wrong for wealthy Christians to close their eyes to the second set of texts. But it was also wrong for the socialists to lose sight of the first set of texts in order to make Christ into a purely socialist agitator and to woo Christian workers to the Social Democratic Party. Instead, Kuyper emphasized, the Christian must keep both sets of texts in mind when faced with poverty and economic injustice. Because we do not want to deny Christ, he declared, the Kuyper administration would give social reforms a top priority. The prime minister ended by promising that his government would resign if its social reform bills were not passed by Parliament.[13]

Conclusion

Political spirituality is a neglected yet important aspect of Christian sanctification in relation to people, money, government and justice. It is based on personal faith in Jesus Christ as Savior and Lord, as well as on the Reformed orthodoxy flowing from the new birth. This faith is the evangelical core of Kuyper's viewpoint. This politically mature spirituality is related to the confession of the lordship of Christ over culture, the doctrine of common grace, and public stewardship. Both human sin and divine grace are operative in public life.

A positive Christian alternative to all humanist political perspectives is the natural result of political spirituality. Such a view is neither world-flight nor abdication to the standards of the world, but the redeeming of culture to the glory of God. We are not merely to be against what is evil but positively working for the good. This viewpoint provides a spiritual way of evaluating the political process. It is not merely a Christian utilization of humanist categories for public life – such as pragmatism, a candidate's image, appeals to voter selfishness, and avoidance of discussion about basic political perspectives

---

13 Kuyper, A. n.d. *Parlementaire Redevoeringen*, II, *Ministerieele Redevoeringen*, Tweede Kamer, Amsterdam: Van Holkema & Warendorf, 261–267. Some texts the rich would undoubtedly appeal to are Exodus 20:15, 17; John 12:8; and 1 Peter 2:13–1 8. The poor would perhaps appeal to Leviticus 19:13; Ecclesiastes 4:1; Luke 10:7; and James 5:1–6.

on man, government and God. In reading great amounts of Kuyper's journalism in *De Standaard* and elsewhere, I have been impressed with his ability to examine public events spiritually, yet with a sense of the antithesis between the obedience of political well-being and the disobedience of the political manifestation of sin, as seen, for example, in the campaign of 1873 and his "Not the Liberty Tree but the Cross."[14]

Put in contemporary terms, political spirituality is neither liberation theology nor a revitalized theocratic social ethic. Rather, it is firmly based upon the continuing validity of God's moral law – the Ten Commandments – and the gospel of Christ. Christian political principles are the resulting application of scriptural normativity to politics. In another sense, political spirituality implies an attitude of thankfulness to God that the public situation is not as bad as it might be on account of common grace; yet with a conviction of dissatisfaction that the *status quo* falls short of the gospel standard.[15] A category of this political spirituality needs to be included in the public life of the nations of the world, including America. If evangelicals neglect to concern themselves with this political aspect of sanctification, they will increasingly find themselves impotent to bring a healing influence upon American life.

---

14 The idea of Kuyper's politically spiritual attitude has been suggested by Prof. A. Anema, "Dr. Kuyper en het Staatkundig Leven." In Scholten, L. W. G. 1937. et al. *Dr. A. Kuyper: 1837–1937*. Kampen: Kok, 82–6 and Puchinger, G. 1970. "De Jonge Kuyper" Nederlandse Gedachten, The Hague, 5 December 1970. But the term "political spirituality" in relation to Kuyper is my own.

15 For this concept of Christian political thankfulness and dissatisfaction, I am indebted to Willem Aantjes, recent parliamentary leader of the Anti-Revolutionary Party and the Christian Democratic Appeal, for a speech I heard him deliver on "Political Responsibility" to a student group at De Populier Theater in Amsterdam on 13 November 1975.

7

Every Inch for Christ:
Abraham Kuyper on the Reform of the Church

James Edward McGoldrick

When the Free University of Amsterdam opened in 1880, its founder, Abraham Kuyper (1837–1920), declared in his inaugural address: "There is not an inch in the entire domain of our human life of which Christ, who is sovereign of all, does not proclaim 'Mine!'"[1]

In making this assertion, Kuyper committed himself and his colleagues to operate Europe's only truly Christian university on the principle that all truth is God's truth and that every area of human endeavor must submit to Christ, the King of Kings. Kuyper founded the Free University as a major means to promote the reformation of church and society, i.e., to achieve the "restoration of truth and holiness in the place of error and sin."[2] The evils he had in mind had permeated the Netherlands broadly and deeply, hastened by the French Revolution of 1789. The Dutch nation, which had once been a bastion of biblical faith, had largely succumbed to the secular humanism that French intellectuals had generated in the eighteenth century and Napoleon's armies had disseminated in lands they occupied.

By the time the French occupation of the Netherlands ended (1814), the French dictum *ni dieu ni maitre* (neither God nor master) had become a common point of view among the country's academic and intellectual elite which controlled the universities, where ministers of the Dutch Reformed Church obtained their education. A vague supernaturalism existed which was agreeable to the tastes of reason portrayed as an example of love and kindness but ignoring sin, guilt and God's gracious provision to save sinners.

Even before the arrival of the French rulers, some powerful forces had been leading the Dutch Reformed Church away from its historic allegiance to Scripture. Modernists had been attacking the Bible and the traditional confessions of faith derived from it, while *ethical* theologians depreciated supernatural features of Christian belief and stressed moral principles as the essence of faith. Skeptical university professors denounced John Calvin and extolled Renaissance humanists such as Desiderius Erasmus.

In November 1814 William, Prince of Orange, returned to Amsterdam, ending eighteen years in exile. City officials welcomed him jubilantly as "Sovereign Prince of the

---

1 Kuyper, Abraham 1880. *Souvereiniteit in Eigen Kring [Sovereignty in Its Own Sphere].* Translated by Wayne A. Kobes. Amsterdam: J. H. Kruyt, 35. (See also the translation in *AK:ACR* 463–490.)

2 Kuyper, Abraham 1877–1886. *A Pamphlet on the Reformation of the Churches.* Translated by Herman Hanko, collated from *The Standard Bearer*, vols. 54–63 by Randall K. Klynsma, section 51.

Netherlands." The former Dutch republic became a constitutional monarchy by action of the Congress of Vienna (1814–15), which restored legitimate rulers in lands liberated from Napoleonic control.

The new King of the Netherlands was a highly authoritarian leader who styled himself an enlightened monarch and desired a strong central government that included state authority over the Dutch Reformed Church. Since the king endorsed the prevailing liberal theology, he used the agencies of the state to promote a broad church to embrace almost all Protestants without regard to doctrine. A national Synod had final authority over affairs of the Reformed Church, but it was in session only two weeks per year, and the king could veto its decisions. A state Department for Reformed Worship controlled the synod's executive committee.

Protests against the new church government and the defection from orthodox beliefs led to a secession from the National Church in 1834. This occurred at a time of *reveil* (revival) in several parts of Europe. The *reveil* was, for the most part, broadly evangelical rather than Reformed in character, but it had the effect of stimulating a resurgence of Calvinism in the Netherlands. Hendrik de Cock, a former modernist pastor converted through the study of the Bible and Calvin's *Institutes of the Christian Religion*, was a pioneer in the effort to purify the National Church. He incurred severe criticism from pastors and ecclesiastical officials who resented his demand that they uphold the doctrines affirmed in their church's confessions of faith. De Cock and pastors who supported him suffered suspension from the ministry, which convinced several congregations to withdraw from the Dutch Reformed Church. This separation, known in Dutch as the *Afscheiding* (secession), produced a new denomination – the Christian Reformed Church – which held its first synod in 1836.

The Dutch government reacted swiftly to suppress the seceders. It denied that the constitutional guarantee of freedom of religion applied to them, and soldiers appeared in Virum and Appeldorn, where they were billeted in homes of orthodox believers who supported the *Afscheiding*. Law courts almost always ruled against the seceders and imposed heavy fines upon them. Failure to pay led to confiscation of their properties. De Cock spent three months in prison. Leaders of the Dutch Reformed Church encouraged the state to persecute seceders by applying articles 291–294 of the criminal code, which prohibited meetings of more than twenty people without permission from the government. Reformed believers in other lands appealed to King William to end the persecution, but he ignored their pleas. Leaders of the *Afscheiding* offered to return to the National Church, if it would reaffirm the Reformed confessions and return to its historic character, but the progress of modernism within that body made that impossible.

Persecution of orthodox Protestants continued irregularly until the accession of William II in 1844, when the state relaxed repression of dissenters. Meanwhile thousands of Reformed Christians emigrated to the United States and Canada, where they enjoyed full freedom of worship. In 1857 they formed the Christian Reformed Church in America, a body in fellowship with the *Afscheiding*.

During the period of persecution the seceders found a champion in Dr. Guillaume van Prinsterer, a distinguished lawyer and historian and a secretary of state in the king's cabinet. Although Groen disapproved of the secession and remained within the Dutch Reformed Church, he defended the separatists and criticized his own church for departing from its foundations. He blamed indifference toward truth in the National Synod for the schism of 1834, and he strove valiantly to encourage orthodox people within the Dutch Reformed Church to demand its allegiance to biblical doctrine as expressed in the *Belgic Confession*, the *Heidelberg Catechism*, and the *Canons of Dordt*, its official statements of faith. The efforts of Groen and others of his conviction were, in the end, unable to stem the tide of infidelity in their church, so a second secession, much larger than that of 1834, was the consequence. Abraham Kuyper became leader of this movement.

Kuyper obtained his higher education at the University of Leiden, from which he received the Doctor of Theology in 1862. While a student he absorbed many antibiblical ideas that his modernist professors espoused. He related later that he had once joined others in applauding a scholar who denied Christ's bodily resurrection. Reflecting upon his time at Leiden, Kuyper wrote, "In the academic world I had no defense against the powers of theological negation. I was robbed of my childhood faith. I was unconverted, proud, and open to doubting."[3]

Despite doubts about the Bible, Kuyper became a Dutch Reformed pastor at Beesd, a village in Gelderland, where he stayed four years and then moved to the Domkerk, a large congregation in Utrecht. During his residence in Beesd (1863–67), Kuyper ministered to people who had remained loyal to Christ and some of whom had a remarkable knowledge of Scripture and of Reformed theology. Kuyper later said, "When I went there (Beesd) from the university my heart was empty."[4] It did not remain empty, because believers in his congregation prayed for their pastor and sought his conversion. One in particular, Pietje Baltus, a peasant woman in her 30s, was critical of Kuyper's preaching, and her influence altered his life forever.

> Miss Baltus witnessed to her pastor about the grace of God in her life, and she explained how her beliefs differed from his. She presented him with the historic Reformed Confessions and related their doctrines to her learned minister, who allowed a peasant to teach him God's Word. She urged him to read Calvin's *Institutes*. He did so, and his conversion followed. He testified that she and others at Beesd were the agents who led him to embrace the Christ of the Gospels.[5]

In Calvin's *Institutes* Abraham Kuyper found the concept of God as the father of believers and the church as their mother. After his conversion he said, "My life goal was now the restoration of a church that could be our mother."[6] While at Utrecht (1867–1870), Kuyper became chief spokesman for a movement to defend local congregations against authoritarian, intrusive policies of the National Synod. As leader of the orthodox party within the Dutch Reformed Church, he urged congregations to choose only truly Reformed officers, and he advised churches to free themselves from financial dependence upon the state.

---

3   Kuyper, Abraham 1873. *Confidentie: Schrijven aan den Weled. Heer J. H. Van der Linden.* Amsterdam: Höveker & Zoon, 35. (*Confidential Writings to Mr. J H Van der Linden* – translated by McKendree R. Langley.) (See also the translation in *AK:ACR* 46–61.)

4   Ibid., 44.

5   A vivid account of this matter appears in an article by Kuyper's daughter. See Kuyper, Catherine M. E. 1960. "Abraham Kuyper: His Early Life and Conversion." *International Reformed Bulletin*, 5 (April): 19–25. *See supra* Chapter 2.

6   Kuyper, *Confidentie*, 48.

In 1870 Abraham Kuyper moved to Amsterdam to become pastor of the large Nieuwe Kerk. That cosmopolitan city had been a stronghold of modernism, but Kuyper's preaching drew large audiences, especially from the lower and middle classes, who appreciated his orthodoxy. His influence in Amsterdam made it a dynamo in the cause for reformation.

To advance the reform of the church and to prompt believers to accept their religious and social responsibilities, Kuyper in 1871 began editing *De Heraut* (*The Herald*), a weekly Christian newspaper, "The Herald of the Free Church and the Free School in the Free Netherlands," as its masthead proclaimed. In 1872 he founded *De Standaard* (*The Standard*), a daily paper that quickly gained nationwide readership as an organ of Reformed orthodoxy. The influence of this publication led eventually to formation of the Anti-Revolutionary Party, a Christian political movement to assert Christ's lordship over public affairs. Obtaining state recognition of the right of Christians to operate their own schools was the initial objective of the party and perhaps its most enduring success.

As leader of the orthodox party within the National Church, Kuyper declared:

> The church I want is Reformed and democratic, free and independent, as well as fully organized in doctrinal teaching, formal worship, and the pastoral ministry of love.[7]

To accomplish this he summoned believers to adhere to the principle of "continuous purification and development. The Reformed Church is always reforming before God."[8]

Kuyper's specific objective was to abolish the synodal system of church government which, since 1816, had deprived local congregations of much autonomy. He believed that only a church free from state control could reform itself and thereby regain its former character; thus he called for vigorous evangelism to parallel all efforts to win freedom for the congregations. At this time (1873) he was still optimistic about the success of his quest for the reform of the Dutch Reformed Church. In Amsterdam he organized church leaders to combat liberal trends in the National Church and was able to place orthodox believers in some places of influence.[9]

In his efforts to promote internal reform of the National Church, Abraham Kuyper saw that theological education was of utmost importance, and the Free University of Amsterdam was his answer to the modernism that had infected the faculties of the state universities. He formed an Association for Higher Education on a Reformed Basis to collect funds, and many of the most faithful contributors were people of small means who gave sacrificially. When the Free University opened in 1880, Kuyper was its rector, and he remained on the faculty until 1908. Because he believed all truth is God's truth and every inch of creation belongs to Christ, he established not only a school of theology but a university in which the entire curriculum, in all the arts and sciences, was to affirm a biblical worldview.

Much to the regret of Kuyper and his orthodox supporters, efforts to cleanse the Dutch Reformed Church failed. It refused to accept pastors educated at the Free University, and the government would not accredit its degrees unless recipients passed qualifying examinations at state universities. By 1883 Kuyper had become pessimistic about prospects for church reform, although he continued to strive for it. In that year

---

7   Ibid., 63.
8   Ibid., 69.
9   Kuyper, A. 1884. *De Heraut*. 20 April, no. 330.

he published *Tractaat van de Reformatie der Kerken* (*A Pamphlet on the Reformation of the Churches*), which he had been preparing for ten years. His concept of reform featured the belief that defenders of orthodoxy should stress their continuity with the sixteenth-century Reformation and the historic creeds of their church. Secession should be a last resort. Kuyper had criticized the *Afscheiding* because its leaders had not pursued reform of the National Church long enough but had engaged in schism. In Kuyper's view the preaching of the Word and the proper administration of the sacraments are the marks of the true church. Although no Christian body maintains these marks perfectly, false churches discard God's Word, pervert the sacraments, and oppose lovers of truth, as the National Synod had been doing. Separation from such a church is necessary when it prevents its members from obeying God. Believers must refuse to support any ecclesiastical action that involves such disobedience.[10] Kuyper warned, "Satan creates a church for Antichrist by subverting existing Christian churches."[11] When it becomes necessary for believers to leave an apostate church, they must try to persuade others to do the same. Godly pastors especially have this duty, and pastors and laymen must then form a true church, if one does not exist in their area.[12] Christians must not, however, leave a church just because it is imperfect:

> Just because your church is sick or crippled, you may not withhold from her your love. Just because she is sick, she has a greater claim on your compassion. Only when she is dead and has ceased to be your church, and when the poisonous gasses of the false church threaten to kill you, do you flee from her touch and withdraw your love from her.[13]

One may not leave his church unless one is certain it has become a synagogue of Satan.[14]

Although Kuyper estimated that about 500 congregations of the Dutch Reformed Church were still preaching the Word and rightly administering the sacraments, he concluded by 1886 that the National Synod had become incurably corrupt, and separation was necessary. Degeneration in the national Church had begun with laxity about doctrine and proceeded to evil behavior of its members. When officials of that church discarded the requirement that pastors subscribe to the *Belgic Confession*, the *Heidelberg Catechism*, and the *Canons of Dordt* and tried to impose that policy upon orthodox congregations, Kuyper led a protest. The National Synod then removed Kuyper and seventy-four elders in Amsterdam. This convinced affected local churches to join with others that had already seceded. The separatists called themselves the *Doleantie* (grieving ones) because they sorrowed over the necessity for withdrawal.

The Dutch government and the National Synod reacted to their orthodox critics by seizing their church properties, sometimes by force. About 200 congregations of 170,000 members formed *De Doleerende Kerk* (The Sorrowing Church), and many more local churches followed suit. In 1892 most of the congregations of the *Afscheiding* merged with Kuyper's group. By then the new Reformed Church of the Netherlands had about 700 congregations and 300,000 members. Known by its Dutch name *Gereformeerde Kerk*,

---

10   *Pamphlet on Reformation*, section 56.

11   Ibid., section 49.

12   Ibid., section 58

13   Ibid., section 59.

14   Ibid., section 53.

the new body restored traditional church polity and affirmed allegiance to the historic Reformed confessions. Such were the accomplishments of the reformation of 1886–1892, as orthodox believers took the painful but necessary steps to maintain their loyalty to the Savior, who is entitled to rule every inch of His creation and preeminently His church. As Abraham Kuyper declared, "to esteem God as everything and all people as nothing is the Calvinistic *credo*."[15] Orthodox Christians in every land and every era must be constantly vigilant to preserve the purity of Christ's church, for "Satan sets himself over against God and imitates in the desperation of his impotence, all that God does, to see if he is able to succeed in destroying God's kingdom with God's own instruments."[16]

---

15   Kuyper, Souvereiniteit, 38.

16   Kuyper, Pamphlet on Reformation, section 49.

8

Abraham Kuyper –
Answering Criticisms of His Worldview

Cornelis P. Venema

During the period of Abraham Kuyper's reformatory work in the late nineteenth- and early twentieth-centuries, a number of criticisms were raised against features of his world and life view. These criticisms were offered not only within the context of struggles within the Dutch Reformed churches, but also within the context of Kuyper's public witness. Since the time of Kuyper's labors in the Netherlands, several of these criticisms have continued to be raised within the broader Reformed community in North America.

Not only during his lifetime, but also in terms of his influence within the Reformed community subsequent to his death, Kuyper has been a controversial figure. Reactions to his views range from uncritical praise and loyalty to vigorous and general dissent. To some, Kuyper is a heroic figure whose legacy is an unmixed blessing. To others, Kuyper is an ignoble figure whose legacy is a source of unhappy controversy and compromise among the Reformed churches. To still others, Kuyper is a mixed blessing whose legacy is neither wholly beneficial nor detrimental to the challenges facing the Christian community today. Due to the persistence of these criticisms, I believe it is necessary to identify them clearly and to assess their validity.

In my consideration of several common criticisms of Kuyper's worldview, I will not attempt to identify all of Kuyper's critics or give a complete statement of their arguments. Nor will I attempt to provide a complete response to their criticisms of his position. Rather, I will only provide a kind of broad-stroked description of these criticisms together with some preliminary observations regarding their merit or demerit. The fact that I have entitled this chapter, "Abraham Kuyper: answering criticisms of his worldview," should be enough to indicate that my sympathies lie finally more with Kuyper than with his critics.[1]

---

1   I do not intend in what follows to address the kinds of criticisms that were made of Kuyper's life and legacy at a conference held at Princeton Theological Seminary early in 1998. At the conference, Kuyper was de-

---

This chapter was originally written in the form of two essays, which were part of a longer series on Kuyper's life and legacy that I wrote for the *Outlook* to commemorate the 100th anniversary of Kuyper's Stone Lectures, Lectures on Calvinism. See Venema, Cornelis P. 1999. "Abraham Kuyper: His Life and Legacy." Outlook 49 (1): 15–19; and "Abraham Kuyper: His Life and Legacy." *Outlook* 49 (2): 17–21. For a recent study of Kuyper's *LC*, see Heslam, Peter S. 1998. *Creating a Christian Worldview: Abraham Kuyper's Lectures on Calvinism*. Grand Rapids: Eerdmans.

Criticisms of Kuyper's Doctrine of the Church

One feature of Kuyper's worldview that has been the focus of considerable criticism is his doctrine of the church.[2] On each of the key elements of Kuyper's doctrine – the church's freedom from inappropriate hierarchalism and governmental interference in its distinctive area of competence, the distinction between the church as institute and as organism, and the "pluriformity" of the church – critics of Kuyper have raised serious objections. In order to address these criticisms, I will phrase them in the form of questions and then evaluate their validity.

Was Kuyper a Congregationalist?

One of the distinctive features of Kuyper's doctrine of the church was his vigorous opposition to every illegitimate abuse of church authority, particularly on the part of the "broader" assemblies of the church. In Kuyper's understanding of authority and its exercise in the churches of Jesus Christ, a clear demarcation needs to be made between the authority of the state and of the church. The church stands alongside the state as an institution of God with a particular task and calling. Therefore, the state has no right to interfere directly in the affairs of the church or attempt to govern its activities. Within the circle of the church itself, Kuyper was equally insistent upon the *relative autonomy of each local church under the authority of Christ, as this authority is exercised through its office-bearers.* The only universal bishop of Christ's church on earth is Christ Himself. All other office-bearers owe their calling and authority to Christ Himself, who calls them to their respective offices within the local congregation and directly grants them the responsibility to oversee the congregation's life and worship.

In Kuyper's doctrine of the church, therefore, the authority exercised by the broader assemblies (classis and synod) is a *delegated* authority. Whereas the authority of the local church council is original, the authority of the broader assemblies is *delegated to them and is to be exercised according to the requirements and limitations spelled out in the church order to which the churches commonly consent.* The authority of broader assemblies must be carefully circumscribed so that the original authority of the local church council is not compromised. For Kuyper, this understanding of the original authority of the local church councils was enshrined in the confessions of the Reformation and the original church order of the Dutch Reformed churches.[3] It also constituted a necessary hedge against the

---

nounced among other things for his alleged sexism, racism and colonialism. Though there are admittedly elements in Kuyper's thought that could (and have) serve(d) these illegitimate ends, they do not constitute by any measure the most important elements of his thought. Rather than join the chorus of voices in condemning Kuyper for his sins against contemporary standards of "political correctness," I would prefer to focus upon the more enduring and central aspects of Kuyper's legacy. I hasten to add, however, that Kuyper did express views on these subjects that are unacceptable from a biblical point of view. Often, in expressing himself on these subjects, Kuyper betrayed the influence of Romanticism and Hegelianism, especially their ideas of historical development and progress.

2   For an assessment of Kuyper's doctrine of the church, and one that expresses some of these criticisms, see Henry Zwaanstra, Henry 1974. "Abraham Kuyper's Conception of the Church." *Calvin Theological Journal* 9(2): 149–181.

3   For example, the Belgic Confession in Article 31 states that "As for the ministers of God's Word, they have equally the same power and authority wheresoever they are, as they are all ministers of Christ, the only universal Bishop and the only Head of the Church." Similarly, the first Article adopted by the National Synod of the Dutch Reformed churches in 1571 reads, "No church shall lord it over another, no minister

tendency of the church assemblies (and their officers) to exceed their legitimate authority. The only way to preserve the blessing of Christ's rule in His churches over against the tyranny of church hierarchy and unrestrained exercise of authority is to guard carefully the direct rule of Christ over the local congregation.

Now, it has been alleged that this view of the freedom of the local churches from church hierarchy represents a departure from the historic Reformed view of the *connection* between the local churches through the broader assemblies of classis and synod. According to this criticism, Kuyper's stress upon the relative autonomy of the local churches can only lead to a spirit of independentism and congregationalism. The weight of gravity in Kuyper's view of the church shifts inordinately to the local church, so that the mutual responsibility and answerability of the churches to one another is seriously compromised. Kuyper's doctrine of the church does not do justice, then, to the unity and the catholicity of the church, since it permits the local churches under Christ to exercise an authority that is unrestrained by the principles of the connection and inter-relationship of the churches as members of the one church of Christ.

Undoubtedly, a full answer to this objection would require a study of the history of the Reformed churches and their form of church government, including the provisions of the church orders that have been used by them. In my judgment, however, Kuyper's understanding represents a proper adherence to the historic Reformed principle that Christ directly rules over the churches through their office-bearers. Kuyper's view is neither *congregationalist*, where the original authority resides in the congregation's members, nor *hierarchicalist*, where the original authority resides in the broader assemblies and their officers.

Though Kuyper did not concede any original authority to the broader assemblies, he did acknowledge their authority, as delegated and acknowledged by the churches in common, to be a real authority which obligates the churches to be accountable and responsible to each other. What Kuyper opposed was the idea that the broader assemblies could *impose their will upon the local churches and councils* beyond the limits set forth in the church order or irrespective of their adherence to the Scriptures and the confessions. For Kuyper, should a broader assembly abuse its authority by contravening the teaching of the Scriptures or the confessions, or by exceeding the boundaries of its delegated authority as stipulated in the church order, the local church council was not obligated simply to submit to its decisions. Every church remains free under Christ to be subject to His Word alone. Furthermore, should churches join together in a communion of churches (denomination or federation), they should do so on the basis of a commonly held confession and acknowledged church order. Where no such common confession or practice of church government exists, there would be no legitimate basis for the kind of inter-relationship among the churches that properly expresses the unity of the church.

In these emphases, Kuyper did not err or stray from the line of the Reformation. In my judgment, he might better be regarded as a true champion of biblical principles of church polity that require continued emphasis among the Reformed churches today.

---

of the Word, no elder, nor deacon shall lord it over another, but everyone will guard against any suspicion and enticement of lordship." This latter article has been a standard article in all the church orders of the Dutch Reformed churches since the Synod of Dort in 1618–1619.

Did Kuyper belittle the "institutional" church?

Kuyper's distinction between the church as *institute* and as *organism* has often been regarded as slighting or belittling the centrality of the institutional church. Because Kuyper stressed the importance of the believer's calling as a member of the church as organism, it has been argued that he laid the basis for a limited view of the importance of the church as institute. In support of this criticism, some have argued that among "neo-Calvinist" followers of Kuyper the institutional church is viewed as largely subordinate and inferior to the church as organism.[4]

In Kuyper's articulation of this distinction between the church as institute and as organism, he sought to emphasize the calling of Christian believers *beyond the boundaries of the institutional church.* However important and central may be the ministry of the church as institute, the calling of Christian believers is more comprehensive and life-embracing than their calling as members of a local congregation. In marriage, family, education, business, politics, and the like, Christian believers, who do not cease in these areas to be members of Christ and partakers of His anointing, are called to offer themselves as living sacrifices in thankful obedience to Christ. They do not live or fulfill their calling in these spheres under the direct and immediate authority of the institutional church. Though the gospel of the kingdom which the church is called to minister speaks to all of life, it would be an inappropriate overstepping of boundaries on the part of the church as institute to enter directly into these areas of life.

Therefore, Kuyper never intended the distinction between the church as institute and the church as organism to belittle the importance of the institutional church. Rather, the distinction was formulated by Kuyper to maintain the church's *focus* upon the administration of the keys of the kingdom on the one hand, and to encourage Christian believers to take their confession of Christ's lordship into the marketplace of life on the other hand. For example, when the church presumes to have expertise and authority to directly intervene in the affairs of the state, the particular calling of the church to preach the gospel and to nurture her members in the faith is inevitably neglected. The church then becomes a kind of "political force," and the authenticity of the gospel is compromised by its identification with a particular political party, cause or figure. Alternatively, when believers who are members of the church are encouraged to view their calling as Christians as *restricted* to their activity as members of the institutional church, the legitimate labor of Christ's members in a variety of areas of life is called into question. In both of these respects, Kuyper's distinction between the church as institute and as organism is useful, even necessary.

However, perhaps to avoid misunderstanding, it would be preferable to use different language than that used by Kuyper to make this distinction. It has been suggested, for example, that it might be better to restrict the term "church" to its common use in the Bible. In the Scriptures, the most common use for the term "church" is as a reference to the local congregation of Christ's people.[5] This congregation or church is under the care

---

4   For possible illustrations of this tendency, see Olthuis, John A. et al. 1970. *Out of Concern for the Church.* Toronto: Wedge; and Olthuis, James A. et al. 1972. *Will All the King's Men.* Toronto: Wedge.

5   I say "most common" because there are biblical examples of the use of the term "church" to refer more comprehensively to the "universal" church comprised of all believers (e.g., Matthew 16:18; Ephesians 1:22–23) or the church as a broad fellowship or communion of believers (e.g., Ephesians 4:1–16; 5:22ff.;

of Christ Himself, supervised by those office-bearers (ministers, elders, deacons) whom He charges with a distinct calling, and who are responsible to administer the means of grace. This is what the Scriptures most commonly mean when they speak of the "church." It is what Kuyper meant to refer to when he spoke of the church as "institute."

When he spoke of the church as organism, Kuyper meant to refer to the broader and more comprehensive calling of those who, as members of Christ's church, are also *citizens of the kingdom of God*. As citizens of the kingdom of God, believers have a calling in every area of life to serve and honor their King. Believers are to seek the honor of Christ not only in the church but also in all of the areas of life claimed by Christ. Rather than speaking of the church as organism, then, it would be better to speak of the institutional church and the kingdom of God. Though the institutional church plays a foundational role by administering the gospel of the kingdom, those who are members of the church are called as *citizens of the kingdom* to serve Christ in every area of His dominion. The distinction which Kuyper describes between the church as institute and the church as organism might just as well be expressed as a distinction between the *instituted church* on the one hand, as the central embodiment of and instrument for ministering the gospel of the kingdom, and the many facets of *kingdom life* on the other hand.

Should the "pluriformity" of the church be encouraged?

One characteristic emphasis in Kuyper's worldview is his aversion to the uniformity of modern life with its "blurring of the boundaries" between differing kinds of creaturely institutions, spheres of life, and the like. Kuyper was a life-long opponent of the tendency of modern thought toward monism, the worldview that failed to distinguish properly between the Triune God and the creation, and between the diversity of kinds of creatures which God has created. The bland uniformity and commonness of modern life – in its architecture, dress, music, business, politics, education – was something Kuyper viewed with grave suspicion. Nothing was more repugnant to Kuyper in politics and in the church, for example, than a kind of *forced and artificial unity or oneness*.[6]

Something of this emphasis upon diversity came to expression in Kuyper's rather expansive doctrine of the "pluriformity" of the church. Appealing to the diversity of creation, the variety of circumstances within God's providence, and the limitations of human knowledge and understanding, Kuyper articulated a doctrine of church pluriformity that *approved the diversity of churches and denominations*. Rather than being regarded as a sinful deflection from the biblical standard of unity among the churches, Kuyper regarded the diversity and pluriformity of the churches to be a kind a necessary, even inevitable, expression of such factors as the diversity of creation and the variety of God's providence. That the churches are pluriform in confession, in church order, in practice, and in so many other ways, is not something to be viewed with dismay or regret, but with benign approval.

Though there are elements of Kuyper's doctrine of the pluriformity of the church that have a measure of validity, his doctrine tends to lend sanction to or provide illegitimate

---

Colossians 2:19; cf. 1 Corinthians 12).

6 For Kuyper's emphasis upon pluriformity in the face of the bland uniformity of modernism, see Kuyper, Abraham 1998. "Uniformity: The Curse of Modern Life." In *AK:ACR* 19–44; and idem, "The Blurring of the Boundaries." In *AK:ACR* 363–402; and Mouw, Richard J. 2011. *Abraham Kuyper: A Short and Personal Introduction*. Grand Rapids: Eerdmans, 16–22.

cover for the church's sinful diversity or pluriformity. While it is one thing to emphasize the catholicity of the church and to resist the sectarian temptation to restrict the true church only to the purest churches – Kuyper's recognition of the church's pluriformity does achieve these ends – it is quite another thing to endorse the actual pluriformity of the church in the way Kuyper does. By appealing to the motifs of creational diversity, providential circumstances, and the limitations upon any church's grasp of the wholeness of truth, Kuyper grants to the existing (*de facto*) diversity of the church a kind of normalcy (*de jure*). However, the actual pluriformity of the church is more often the product of sinful departure from the standards of God's Word than it is the benign result of the inevitable diversity of human life and organization.

As a result, Kuyper's doctrine of the church's pluriformity glosses over as rather insignificant the real differences of confession and practice that obtain between those churches that claim to be true churches of Jesus Christ. Rather than encouraging a biblical practice of ecumenicity, based upon efforts to reach a *true unity of confession and practice* among the churches, Kuyper's doctrine tends to lend tacit approval to the existence of a multiplicity of different churches with widely varying confessions and practices. It grants normative standing to an actual state of affairs with which believers ought not to be at peace, namely, the sadly divided and fragmented character of the church of Jesus Christ in our day.[7]

Were Kuyper only to have insisted that the church is catholic, comprising a great number of churches, some more pure, some less pure, he would have been on surer ground. Likewise, were he only to have maintained that denominational or federative union among the churches requires genuine unity of confession and practice, not an artificial appearance of unity through organizational conformity, his view could be defended. However, Kuyper meant much more than this in his defense of the pluriformity of the church. To the extent that his doctrine went beyond legitimate emphases such as these, it does not measure up to the Scriptural norm for the unity of the church of Jesus Christ.

Sphere Sovereignty or Sphere Responsibility?
One of the most distinctive and provocative elements of Kuyper's worldview was his articulation of the principle "sphere sovereignty." According to Kuyper, the various spheres of life within God's creation stand under the universal sovereignty of God. God's sovereign authority is administered through a diversity of human instruments and created institutions, each of which has its own peculiar task and authority under God.[8]

Thus, in the development of his political theory, Kuyper insisted that the state is directly instituted of God, granted the authority and power of the sword, to provide for a just ordering of society and the preservation of peace. The state's authority is not under that of church, nor is the authority of the church under that of the state. Each is "sovereign in its own sphere," but subject to the direct sovereignty of God who instituted the state and the church for distinct callings and tasks. Similarly, the other spheres of life – marriage, family, school, business, economics, art – have been instituted by God and given a specific

---

7   For an exposition and critique of Kuyper's doctrine of the pluriformity of the church, see Berkouwer, Gerrit C. 1976. *The Church*. Grand Rapids: Eerdmans, 51–63.

8   See "Sphere Sovereignty." In *AK:ACR* 461–90; McGoldrick, James E. 2000. *Abraham Kuyper: God's Renaissance Man*. Auburn, MA: Evangelical Press, 62–72; Mouw, *Abraham Kuyper*, 23–27.

mandate or task.

When Kuyper used the language of "sovereignty" in this understanding of the diversity of life spheres, it was not his purpose to suggest that these areas of life are autonomous or a law unto themselves. On the contrary, it was his purpose to stress their direct accountability and responsibility to God who called them into existence for a particular task or service within His kingdom. Nor was it Kuyper's intention to suggest that these various spheres of life are to exist in a kind of *isolation* the one from the other, without any kind of mutual interaction or accountability. Kuyper acknowledged a kind of sphere *universality* in which each of the various life spheres was accountable or responsible to the other, *so far as its peculiar task was concerned.* The state, for example, has a responsibility not only to protect the freedom of the church to fulfill her calling, but also to require that the church contribute to the legitimate ordering of human life. If a church building were to flaunt local fire codes or engage directly in political activities, for example, then the state would be obligated, in order to fulfill its divine mandate, to insist upon compliance with those laws that serve the interests of public safety or the distinct calling of the church. The sovereignty of these life spheres only underscored their freedom from interference on the part of other spheres with respect to *their internal affairs and responsibilities.*[9]

One criticism that has often been registered against Kuyper's principle of sphere sovereignty is that it too sharply separates between the various life spheres. By speaking of sphere *sovereignty*, Kuyper lent support to a view of the relation between the spheres of life that is radically pluralistic. The responsibility of the various spheres of life to each other is either minimized or rejected altogether. As a result, the different spheres of life become a kind of "law unto themselves," immune from criticism or responsibility to other legitimate authorities. Sphere sovereignty gives rise, accordingly, to a kind of vision for life that isolates the various spheres of life from each other. Mutual accountability is denied between these spheres of life, and *high walls* are erected between them.

One of the areas where this criticism is most often heard relates to the matter of Christian education and Christian schools. If the Christian school, for example, is a sovereign sphere, neither an organ of the church (non-parochial) nor an extension of the home, then it is no longer accountable in any meaningful way to the authority of the church or of the home. Furthermore, because the calling of the Christian school is quite specific, the constitution that governs its affairs may be neither the confessions of the church nor the aspirations of the parents of the children. The school's constitution is an educational creed, not a church creed. When parents entrust their children to the instruction of teachers in such a school, the expertise and calling of the teachers is such that parents are not to interfere directly in the areas of the school's or the teachers' competence.

For those who express this criticism of Kuyper's doctrine of sphere sovereignty, the common complaint is that the Christian schools and their teachers are encouraged to ignore the concerns of the church – that instruction in the Christian school be distinctively

---

9   There are any number of examples of Kuyper's emphasis here that can be easily understood. For example, in the area of education, one of the most important questions that needs to be addressed is: Whose responsibility is it? Should the state assume the responsibility to educate its citizens? Or should this be the responsibility of the church (a parochial school)? Or should it be the responsibility of parents or an association of parents? No one can avoid addressing these questions. Kuyper's principle of sphere sovereignty represents a principled attempt to address this and many other questions relating to the respective callings of various life spheres.

Reformed, for example, in accord with the confessions of the church – and to treat the concerns of parents as a kind of illegitimate intrusion into the affairs of the school. As a result, Kuyper's view of sphere sovereignty has the practical effect of throwing up barriers between the church and home on the one hand, and the Christian school on the other. To use rather colloquial language, the Christian school is able to "thumb its nose" at the church and home when they express directly their disapproval regarding the policies and practices of the school.

This is a potent criticism of Kuyper's principle of sphere sovereignty, and it certainly should be admitted that in some cases this principle has been used to isolate the various spheres of life from each other. There are no doubt instances where some Christian school administrators and teachers have sought refuge in the principle of sphere sovereignty so as to avoid their accountability to the church and the home. The critical question, however, is whether this kind of practice represents a genuine application of Kuyper's principle.

I would argue that it does not, but rather represents a serious corruption of Kuyper's position. When Kuyper spoke of sphere sovereignty, it was not his purpose to isolate these spheres from each other or refuse any legitimate accountability on the part of one life sphere to another. Certainly, it was not his position that the church's confessions have no authority over the instruction that takes place in a Christian school, least of all a Christian school established by an association of parents who subscribe to such confessions. Nor was it his position that, when parents through an association establish a Christian school, they cease to exercise authority over the functioning of the school. Kuyper was well aware of and advocated the principle of what is called in *loco parentis*, that is, that the Christian school teacher serves "in the place of the parents" as one entrusted with a specific responsibility to teach in accord with the convictions of the parents. He was also keenly aware of the fact that the Reformed confessions must give direction and shape to the formation of a Reformed, Christian school.

Kuyper emphasized the principle of sphere sovereignty in order to maintain that the church, the home and the school, have distinctive tasks under God to whom they are ultimately accountable. The church is not the home, nor is the home the school. Each is different and has its own calling within the kingdom of God. Each is finally *responsible* to God and, for that reason, to the other so far as their respective callings are concerned. For this reason, Kuyper's principle of sphere sovereignty might better be termed a principle of sphere *responsibility*. Though relatively free from inappropriate interference by other spheres, each legitimate sphere of human life is *directly responsible* to God for its calling and authority. Once it is recognized that Kuyper's primary emphasis lies upon each sphere's accountability to God, it should become clear that Kuyper's purpose was not to grant to any sphere of life a kind of radical independence or freedom from responsibility to other legitimate, God-ordained authorities.[10]

Criticisms of Kuyper's View of the Antithesis

Having considered some of the more common criticisms of Kuyper's doctrine of the church and his principle of sphere sovereignty, we now consider those criticisms that relate to Kuyper's understanding of the antithesis and of common grace. Here too Kuyper's

---

10 I owe the language, "sphere responsibility," to my colleague, Mark Vander Hart, who first suggested it to me during conversations about Kuyper's views.

viewpoint has evoked rather different responses. Indeed, something of the complexity of Kuyper's thought is evident in his emphasis upon both the antithesis and common grace. Among those influenced by Kuyper, quite different approaches and viewpoints have been adopted, depending upon the role and prominence of one or another of these principles.[11] Some have enthusiastically embraced Kuyper's insistence upon the antithesis between faith and unbelief as it affects every area of life. As a result, their policy has been to separate vigorously from all illegitimate entanglements with the world in the area of worldly amusements, organizations and institutions, etc. Others have more affinity to Kuyper's view of common grace and have adopted, accordingly, a more affirmative policy toward the world. Each of these policies can easily find support in Kuyper's writings.

One of the keynotes of Kuyper's life was that of the antithesis between faith and unbelief. This antithesis between the truth and the lie, the kingdom of Christ and the kingdom of this world, cuts through all of life and profoundly influences human life at every level and in all of its expressions. There is no neutral place so far as the recognition and service of Christ as King is concerned. Whether it be in marriage, the home and family, the business enterprise, the school or academic institution, the political party, the labor union – in all the areas and spheres of life one either works "*for* the King" (*pro Rege*) or *against* Him.

For this reason, one of the distinctive fruits of Kuyper's reforming activity in the Netherlands was the promotion of distinctively Christian institutions whose formative principles were based upon the Christian worldview. Not only in the Netherlands, but also in North America, those who have followed Kuyper have sought to establish *separate Christian organizations* in various life spheres. Kuyper's influence was far-reaching in the promotion of, for example, Christian schools at every level (from primary school to university), Christian labor unions, and Christian political associations. The consequence of this emphasis is known today in the Netherlands as a process of *verzuiling* ("pillarization") in which the whole of society is structured along ideological lines with different groups (Reformed, Catholic, secularist) developing separate institutions to express their particular principles.[12] Similarly, the conflicts within many Reformed communities regarding the subject of "worldly amusements" and the dangers of world-conformity were the product, at least in part, of a Kuyperian emphasis upon separation from all illegitimate entanglements with the principles and practices of the world.

Kuyper's stress upon the antithesis and its implications for the separate development of Christian institutions has been criticized in several ways. One criticism often voiced is that Kuyper's emphasis encourages a kind of *isolationism* in which the Christian community develops a radically separate form of existence in each sphere of life. By insisting upon the separate development of Christian institutions in every area of life, Kuyper's worldview encourages *pluralism* within human society that unnecessarily and dangerously isolates differing communities from each other. As a consequence, there is little place for any bonds of community or society that bridge the differences between ideological or religious communities. This can lead, say Kuyper's critics, to a kind of isolation from the world on

---

11 The Protestant Reformed churches, for example, have historically embraced Kuyper's insistence upon the antithesis but rejected entirely his development of the doctrine of common grace.

12 See Heslam *Creating a Christian Worldview*, 2–8, for a brief description of this process in Dutch society and its connection with Kuyper's influence.

the part of the Christian community that will be counter-productive to any leavening influence within society. Furthermore, within the academic sphere, Kuyper's stress upon *two kinds of science* can lead to an obscurantism within the community of Christian scholars, one which rejects any accountability to or inter-action with the broader world of scholarship.

A different, though related, criticism of Kuyper's insistence upon the antithetical development of distinctively Christian institutions is the charge that it often produces an *unrealistic*, even *triumphalistic*, social policy.[13] Advocates of Kuyper's vision have often maintained that – no matter how impractical it might prove to be – the Christian community must establish its own organizations in order to be faithful in the service of Christ. Nothing less than a Christian political party or a Christian labor union, for instance, will answer to the need to honor Christ's lordship, respectively, in politics and labor relations. Critics of Kuyper's vision frequently argue that this approach is naïve at best, grandiose at worse. It assumes that Christian believers not only can form such organizations, but also can expect them to make a real difference in society. But it is hardly possible in a country like the United States that a Christian political party could be formed that would have any meaningful impact upon the formation and implementation of public policy. Nor is it likely that – in spite of the brave talk about the *transformation* of this or that dimension of modern life – these efforts will make any appreciable difference in the patterns of western secular society. Often, it is alleged, these efforts result more in *being conformed* to than *transforming* the world.

It is difficult to respond to these criticisms of Kuyper's emphasis upon the antithesis and its implications for Christian practice. Some of them do not so much address Kuyper's position as distortions or one-sided approaches on the part of those who claim to be working "in his line."[14] Others represent a lack of appreciation for the biblical teaching that the believer and the believing community are to be *separated from* the world in

---

13 In recent years, some Reformed theologians have advanced what is termed a "two kingdoms/natural law" alternative to Kuyper's neo-Calvinistic worldview. According to advocates of the "two kingdoms" perspective, Kuyper's neo-Calvinism fosters a triumphalistic view of the Christian's calling in the public square, and needs to be displaced by a more modest perspective that limits Christ's redemptive kingdom to the sphere of the church and advocates a more "common" view of the calling of Christians and non-Christians alike in the broader sphere of human life and culture in the world. For an exposition and defense of the two kingdoms paradigm, the following sources are representative: Van Drunen, David 2010. *Natural Law and the Two Kingdoms: A Study in the Development of Reformed Social Thought*. Grand Rapids: Eerdmans; Van Drunen, David 2010. *Living in God's Two Kingdoms: A Biblical Vision for Christianity and Culture*. Wheaton: Crossway; Van Drunen, David 2006. *A Biblical Case for Natural Law*. Grand Rapids: Acton Institute; Van Drunen, David 2010. "Calvin, Kuyper, and 'Christian Culture.'" In *Always Reformed: Essays in Honor of W. Robert Godfrey*, edited by R. Scott Clark and Joel E. Kim. Escondido: Westminster Seminary California; Van Drunen, David 2012. "The Two Kingdoms and Reformed Christianity: Why Recovering an Old Paradigm is Historically Sound, Biblically Grounded, and Practically Useful." Pro Rege 40(3): 31–38; Horton, Michael 2011. *The Gospel Commission: Recovering God's Strategy for Making Disciples*. Grand Rapids: Baker, esp. chapters 8 & 9, 210–93; and Hart, Daryl G. 2006. *A Secular Faith: Why Christianity Favors the Separation of Church and State*. Chicago: Ivan R. Dee. For a neo-Calvinist response to the "two kingdoms" perspective, see McIlhenny, Ryan C., ed. 2012. *Kingdoms Apart: Engaging the Two Kingdoms Perspective*. Phillipsburg: Presbyterian & Reformed; and Venema, Cornelius P. 2012. "One Kingdom or Two?: An Evaluation of the 'Two Kingdoms' Doctrine as an Alternative to Neo-Calvinism." *Mid-America Journal of Theology* 23: 75–128.

14 For a defense of this claim, see Venema, "One Kingdom or Two?" 90–127.

order to *be consecrated* to the Lord's service. Still others reflect the conviction that the transformation of individual believers is a more appropriate policy than the formation of Christian organizations which often become an obstacle to real transformation.[15]

However, in some cases Kuyper's emphasis may produce the kinds of ill fruit described. Ironically, the separation from the world which Kuyper advocated on the basis of his doctrine of the antithesis can become the occasion for a kind of isolationism which cuts the Christian community off from any meaningful (including evangelistic)[16] engagement with the world. This is ironic in view of Kuyper's emphasis upon separation from the world *for the sake of a distinctively Christian practice in the world*. Kuyper did not intend the formation of Christian institutions to be the means of escape from engagement in legitimate worldly vocations. Rather, he intended these institutions to be the means of expressing and exhibiting Christ's lordship over all of life in the various life spheres. The kind of isolationist practice that characterizes some advocates of Kuyper's principle of the antithesis represents a distorted and one-sided appropriation of Kuyper's insights. This practice often reflects an appreciation for Kuyper's emphasis upon the antithesis, but a rejection of his emphasis upon common grace.

One legitimate aspect of these criticisms of Kuyper's understanding of the antithesis relates to the *different situation* Kuyper faced in the Netherlands at the end of the nineteenth and the beginning of the twentieth century. What Kuyper advocated and encouraged in terms of the separate development of Christian institutions in the Netherlands in this period is often impractical in North America at the end of the twentieth century. This is not a concession to a kind of pragmatism that measures what is proper by what is practical. But it is a recognition that there were unique circumstances and developments in the Netherlands during Kuyper's lifetime that cannot be replicated in North America in our day. Though the principles Kuyper articulated are of continuing significance, the policies that these principles recommend may be somewhat different. Though the formation of separate Christian organizations, where this is feasible and permitted, may be a preferred means to express the lordship of Jesus Christ in different areas of life, alternative means may in some cases have to be found by the Christian community today.[17]

---

15   This last objection to Kuyper's promotion of Christian institutions does not seem very compelling. The failure of an institution to fulfill its promise (e.g., a Christian school) might simply call for renewed effort to improve the institution or form another, similar institution. Though no one should place their trust in such institutions, they are often a helpful means of acknowledging and expressing the lordship of Jesus Christ.

16   In this connection, it is interesting to note that Kuyper does not seem to offer much help in terms of the evangelistic and missionary calling of the church. Kuyper lived in a world very different from the one many of us face in North America at the opening of the twenty-first century. The terms often used to describe the contemporary situation, "post-modern" and "post-Christian," would not describe the situation in which Kuyper worked. Whereas the Christian community today in the West faces a new missionary situation, Kuyper simply assumes the presence of a Reformed community of churches. He does not directly address the question of how the gospel should be communicated to a culture that has turned away from the Christian faith. For illustrations of how Kuyper's worldview can be affirmed in a manner that coheres with the church's missionary identity, see Keller, Tim 2012. *Center Church: Doing Balanced Gospel-Centered Ministry in Your City*. Grand Rapids: Zondervan; and Goheen, Michael W. 2011. *A Light to the Nations: The Missional Church and the Biblical Story*. Grand Rapids: Baker Academic.

17   For example, in some circumstances "home schooling" may be preferable to the Christian school as a means of providing Christian education for the children of Christian parents. These circumstances could include: the absence of a good existing Christian school; inadequate financial resources for tuition; the strength and aptitude of the child's parents for teaching at various levels; the unique circumstances of the

Common Grace and "Positive" Calvinism

It is fitting that I should reserve to the last the doctrine of common grace as Kuyper developed it. No feature of Kuyper's thought has been the subject of more sustained reflection or severe criticism than his understanding of common grace.[18] No feature of Kuyper's thought has provoked greater dissension among his critics. On the one hand, there are those who receive Kuyper's doctrine of common grace as an important "corrective" or antidote to his at times extremist development of the principle of the antithesis. According to these critics, the doctrine of common grace blunts the sharp edges of Kuyper's view of the antithesis, preventing the kind of isolationism and obscurantism of which I spoke in the preceding. On the other hand, there are those who regard Kuyper's development of this theme as a kind of "Trojan horse" within the camp of a Christian worldview. By developing and expanding the doctrine of common grace beyond anything known previously in the Reformed tradition, Kuyper opened the door to the very thing his emphasis upon the antithesis ought to have nailed shut – a policy of *conformity* to the world.

One of the remarkable features of the discussion of Kuyper's doctrine of common grace is the prominent role this doctrine has played within the (Dutch) Reformed community in North America. Students of the history of the Reformed churches in North America are familiar with the debates regarding common grace, for example, that troubled the Christian Reformed Church in the early decades of the twentieth century and led to the formation of the Protestant Reformed Churches.[19] Though I will not enter into the history and course of these debates, these ecclesiastical developments reflect the intense and ongoing debate that Kuyper's doctrine of common grace has evoked.

Among those who appreciate Kuyper's doctrine of common grace, it is generally acknowledged that this doctrine allowed Kuyper to account for the possibility and propriety of engagement with the world in every legitimate human endeavor. Because common grace expressed God's continued goodness toward the creation in upholding, maintaining and directing its life and development, Christians were obligated to continue to serve

---

child; political, cultural or legal obstacles to the establishment of a separate Christian school, etc. It should also be noted that there might be circumstances where the preferred policy for the Christian community is one of withdrawal from involvement in some areas of modern life.

18 For a summary and assessments of Kuyper's doctrine of common grace, see "Common Grace." In *AK:ACR* 165–204; Kuyper, A. "Common Grace in Science." In *AK:ACR* 441–60; Kuyper, A. 2011. *Wisdom & Wonder: Common Grace in Science and Art.* Jordan J. Ballor and Stephen J. Grabill, eds., translated by Nelson D. Kloosterman. Grand Rapids: Christian's Library Press; McGoldrick, *Abraham Kuyper: God's Renaissance Man*, 141–57, Mouw, *Abraham Kuyper*, 64–74; and, *see infra* Chapter 19, Zuidema, S. U. 1971. "Common Grace and Christian Action in Abraham Kuyper, in *Communication and Confrontation.* Toronto: Wedge, 52–105.

19 See Bratt, James D. 1984. *Dutch Calvinism in Modern America.* Grand Rapids: Eerdmans, 37–54, 93–22; and Zwaanstra, Henry 1973. *Reformed Thought and Experience in a New World.* Kampen: Kok, 68–131. Zwaanstra describes in considerable detail the debates within the Reformed churches (especially the Christian Reformed Church) in North America regarding Kuyper's views and the doctrine of common grace. Both of these authors argue that different sectors of the Reformed community tended to emphasize one or another of Kuyper's principles. Those who emphasized the antithesis are termed "antithetical" Calvinists by Bratt and "separatist" Calvinists by Zwaanstra. Those who emphasized the doctrine of common grace are termed "positive" Calvinists by Bratt and "American" Calvinists by Zwaanstra. Though these labels and party designations tend to oversimplify matters, they do help to sort out some of the debates and differences of emphasis that characterized conflicting groups within the Dutch Reformed community of churches in North America.

God within the full range of human life and culture. Because God by His common grace hindered and prevented the full expression of sinful rebellion in human life and culture, much that was good and praiseworthy could be found and appreciated by the Christian community in its use of the products of human culture. According to Kuyper, common grace accounted for the presence of institutions like the state, the progress of science and scholarship, the arts, and the like, which Christian believers are obligated to receive with gratitude and use in the service of Christ. However corrupted or distorted through human perversity and sinfulness, these fruits of God's common grace in the preservation and development of the creation are not to be despised or wholly rejected. Therefore, common grace provided Kuyper with a basis for encouraging Christian activity *in* the world rather than *flight* from the world. This doctrine provided the kind of balance Kuyper needed to prevent his understanding of the antithesis from spinning off in the direction of the kind of isolationism described in the preceding.

Those who have little appreciation for Kuyper's doctrine of common grace view this doctrine in an entirely different light. According to these critics, Kuyper not only failed to show any meaningful *connection* between his understanding of "particular" and "common" grace, but he also provided a basis by means of this doctrine for emasculating the antithesis of its power. By expanding the doctrine of common grace, Kuyper laid the foundation for the kind of *positive* Calvinism that has little eye for the antithesis between faith and unbelief, but a keen eye for all the ways the kingdom of Christ and of the world converge. This positive Calvinism finds much of the culture and scholarship of the world to be congenial to the Christian faith. It looks eagerly for common ground with the world and risks thereby accommodation to the allurements of worldly success and approval. Though it still speaks of the need to "transform" all of life, its practical policy is one of "conformity" to the dictates of contemporary culture and scholarship. Rather than seeking to distance the Christian community from the world's patterns of thought and life, the mind of common grace looks upon the world and its products as benign and non-threatening.

That Kuyper's doctrine of common grace could give rise to such widely divergent responses ought to caution against too simplistic an evaluation of his position. However, it is striking to notice how Kuyper is criticized by some for emphasizing too much the antithesis. This criticism maintains that Kuyper's doctrine of the antithesis can only lead to isolationism and radical separation from all worldly engagements. Others also criticize him for emphasizing too much the doctrine of common grace. This criticism then maintains that Kuyper's doctrine of common grace can only lead to world conformity and accommodation to sinful human culture and scholarship. Two more conflicting sorts of criticism could hardly be imagined.

At the risk of being regarded as too sanguine in my assessment of Kuyper, I would argue that these criticisms of Kuyper represent a kind of one-sided caricature of Kuyper's worldview. Neither of them answers to the complexity and breadth of Kuyper's full position, a position that resists playing off the antithesis against common grace as though these were inherently at odds. No doubt many of Kuyper's followers have embraced one or another aspect of his thought – some emphasizing the Kuyper of the antithesis, others emphasizing the Kuyper of common grace. Kuyper's legacy includes not only those who are sometimes termed "antitheticals," but also those who are sometimes termed "positive" Calvinists. Each of these approaches can appeal to Kuyper against the other. But in so doing they confirm that Kuyper's worldview was more complicated and rich than their own, often one-sided worldview which offers a more simplistic handling of the issues Kuyper aimed to address.

Now this does not mean that Kuyper's doctrine of common grace is wholly satisfactory. There is real ambiguity in Kuyper's doctrine on the question of the relation between particular and common grace. In some of his formulations, Kuyper so emphasizes the working of God's common grace that it seems to have a completely independent significance, unrelated to the purpose and working of God's special grace in the salvation of His people.[20] As a result, Kuyper does not always carefully articulate the significance of common grace as it provides a context for the accomplishment of God's redemptive purposes. Nor does he provide an adequate account of the kind of inter-relation that exists between the principle of the antithesis and the doctrine of common grace. It is not surprising, therefore, that students of Kuyper have been able to take hold of one or another of these emphases while rejecting or depreciating the other.

Conclusion

It has not been my purpose in this chapter to provide a complete account of the value of the controversial features of Kuyper's worldview that I have considered. What I have presented amounts to a rather general and popular response to common criticisms that have frequently been articulated in criticism of Kuyper's reformatory labors and articulation of a Calvinistic world and life view. My primary goal in the evaluation of these criticisms of Kuyper is to affirm the continuing usefulness and value of his worldview for the contemporary practice of Reformed believers.

As the Christian community in North America, especially the Reformed community, confronts the challenges of the present day, Kuyper's writings and ideas represent a rich resource of biblical and Reformed insight. They deserve to be read and pondered, as the challenge of presenting the Christian worldview confronts the forces and currents of contemporary culture. If withdrawal from the world and retreat from the challenge of modern scholarship are not viable options for us – as I believe they are not – then we have a great deal of hard work to do in carefully studying the resources of our tradition and articulating the catholic claims of the biblical worldview in our time.

For this reason, Kuyper's legacy is not so much the ideas or principles he articulated, important and useful as they may continue to be. Nor does Kuyper's legacy reside primarily in the extraordinariness of his life and labors. We do not pay homage to any person. Rather, Kuyper's legacy lies in his *insistence that we bring every thought and work captive to the obedience of Christ*. There can be no rest for the Christian or the Christian community in relentlessly seeking to love the true and living God with all of our soul, mind and strength. This means not only that every thought be brought captive to Christ, but that every deed be tested by the standard of God's kingdom and its righteousness. The Triune Redeemer who is the Creator of all things demands and deserves nothing less than that from us.

---

20 *See infra* Chapter 19, Zuidema, "Common grace and Christian action in Abraham Kuyper" for a thorough evaluation and criticism of Kuyper's doctrine of common grace. Students of Kuyper's doctrine of common grace generally acknowledge that it remains an unfinished item on the agenda of Reformed theology. Cf. Heerema, Edward 1990. *Letter to My Mother: Reflections on the Christian Reformed Church in North America*. Freeman, SD: Pine Hill Press, 5–22. Heerema describes the doctrine of common grace as "unfinished business" so far as the history of the Christian Reformed Church is concerned.

Kuyper's legacy remains best expressed in his well-known words, spoken on the occasion of the founding of the Free University:

> [N]o single piece of our mental world is to be hermetically sealed off from the rest, and there is not a square inch in the whole domain of our human existence over which Christ, who is Sovereign over *all*, does not cry: 'Mine!'"[21]

---

21 "Sphere Sovereignty," in *AK:ACR* 488.

9

Claiming Every Inch:
The Worldview of Abraham Kuyper

James Edward McGoldrick

When in 1880 the Free University of Amsterdam opened for classes, its founder Abraham Kuyper delivered the inaugural address in which he asserted, "there is not an inch in the entire domain of . . . human life of which Christ, who is sovereign of all, does not proclaim 'Mine.'"[1]

Creation of the Free University marked a public commitment of Reformed Christians to implement in education their belief that all truth is God's truth, an assertion they believed made necessary by the growth of secularism as the dominant worldview in Dutch society. The basis of education in the new university was to be: "Faith in God's Word, objectively infallible in Scripture and subjectively offered . . . by the Holy Spirit" (*SS* 486). This was to be a "line of demarcation" distinguishing the Free University from public institutions of higher learning where opposition to historic Christianity prevailed. The Christian university was to be free from state control and, therefore, at liberty to conduct its research and teaching within the framework of a biblical worldview. Kuyper maintained that Christians must have a comprehensive view of all of life from a Scriptural perspective, which is the basis for their choices and informs all their actions. It deals with the most fundamental issues of life: *Where did we come from? Why are we here? Where are we going? How do we get there?*

In opposition to the naturalist-secularist modern worldview, Abraham Kuyper declared humanity and all of creation to be in an *abnormal* condition because of sin. This is particularly evident in the noetic effects of sin which pollute human minds and prevent them from achieving the proper understanding of themselves. As a consequence, they divide life into religious and secular categories, an egregious error caused by their abnormal condition, that is, they are "dead in trespasses and sins" (Ephesians 2:1). In Kuyper's words, lost sinners have "all the properties belonging to a corpse."[2] He maintained there are two kinds of people. "Both are human: but one is inwardly different from the other . . . thus they face the cosmos from different points of view, and are impelled by different impulses. . . . [This means there are] two kinds of human *life* . . . [and] two kinds of *science* [scholarship]" (*PST* 154).

---

1   Kuyper, Abraham 1880. *Souvereiniteit in Eigen Kring [Sovereignty in Its Own Sphere]*. Translated by Wayne A. Kobes. Amsterdam: J. H. Kruyt, 35. (See also the translation in *AK:ACR* 463–490.)

2   Kuyper, A. "Calling and Repentance." (Available at http://the-highway.com/calling-repentance_Kuyper. html). Accessed 15 February 2013.

A biblical worldview is necessarily antithetical to all competing views in every domain of life. Kuyper and his colleagues at the Free University applied this principle of antithesis in education, philosophy, law, science, etc., and concluded there could be no compromise with unbelief.[3]

Kuyper became Holland's most vigorous proponent of Reformed orthodoxy, but he did not begin his labors as a minister with that conviction. A brilliant student from childhood, he followed his father into the ministry of the Dutch Reformed Church, after graduating from the University of Leyden as a Doctor of Theology. While engaged in preparation for his career, Kuyper uncritically accepted the rationalistic approach to theology, which had become the routine method of instruction in all public universities in the Netherlands. Years after his conversion he related that he had begun his pastoral work while yet in an unbelieving state, and he praised God for the witness of parishioners at the village church in Beesd who recognized his plight and prayerfully sought his salvation. Miss Pietje Baltus, for example, challenged her pastor's failure to preach gospel truth and testified to him of the grace of God in her own life. She presented Kuyper with the historic confessions of their church and convinced him to read John Calvin's *Institutes of the Christian Religion*, a work his professors had ridiculed.

Although the learned pastor tried to rebut Miss Balthus and other orthodox critics of his ministry, he soon relented and began listening carefully to their appeals. By the grace of God, the witness of those common people without academic credentials became the human means to bring the skeptical Kuyper to Christ and to transform him into a defender of the faith he once scorned.

At the close of his three-year ministry in Beesd, Kuyper moved to Utrecht to join the pastoral staff at the Domkerk, the leading congregation of the National Church in that city. This church had a reputation for orthodoxy, but its leaders were poorly prepared to confront the challenges from liberal theologians, and some of them timidly avoided controversies. Kuyper, however, soon called for an energetic defense of the historic Reformed faith. As he said, "we cannot be passive and silent toward those who reject God's Word and our holy faith"[4] By taking that position, Kuyper placed himself in an antagonistic relationship to leaders of the Dutch Reformed Church and their political benefactors in the civil government. His aspiration was to cleanse the state church of false teaching and to emancipate it from dependence upon state financial support. He described his aspirations this way: "for my own sake and for others, the restoration of a church that could be our Mother had to be the goal of my life."[5]

The long road to reformation proved to be perilous, and in the end, unsuccessful, and by 1892 separation from the Dutch Reformed Church was the only honorable course remaining for believers of the Bible, a step they took as a last resort and with profound sorrow. Persecutions, which included arrests, fines, expulsions from the ministry, and loss of church properties, were the price they paid for loyalty to God's Word.[6]

---

3   Frame, John M. 1995. *Cornelius Van Til: An Analysis of His Thought*. Phillipsburg: P&R, 22, 188.

4   The details of his conversion and subsequent defense of the Reformed faith are in his essay "Confidentially," in *AK:ACR* 45–61.

5   Ibid., 61.

6   An account of these events appears in McGoldrick, James Edward 2000. *God's Renaissance Man: The Life and of Abraham Kuyper*. Darlington, England: Evangelical Press, 20–45.

In order to assert Christ's lordship over the church that professed to serve his cause, Kuyper and the orthodox party employed journalism, education, and even political action. Two newspapers, *The Standard*, a daily publication, and *The Herald*, a weekly edition, vigorously promoted orthodoxy while calling readers to lives of Christ-likeness and devotion to duty as the Lord's people. These organs were champions of parents' right to provide the education they desired for their children, as they regarded schools as part of the domain Christ claims for himself. On the masthead of *The Herald* was the motto *For a Free Church in a Free Land*. Years of struggle and many defeats on the way did not deter this endeavor.

Because only the national legislature could end the state monopoly over education, Kuyper led the Way in forming the Anti-Revolutionary Party, a Christian political movement to assert Christ's cause in public life. By then Kuyper had become pastor of the *Nieuwe Kerk* in Amsterdam, a city known as a center of liberalism. His fervent preaching and staunch orthodoxy drew large crowds, nevertheless, as he continued in his role as defender of the faith and, as a consequence, faced hostility from officials of the National Synod and their supporters in church and state. Kuyper strove to dissolve the National Synod in order to restore lost autonomy to local congregations, for he believed that was essential for the success of genuine reformation. All through this struggle, Kuyper urged his people to engage in zealous evangelism.

Since he regarded Christian education as indispensable for the success of his projects, Abraham Kuyper in 1874 left his pastoral position to seek a seat in parliament, where he could promote legislation to free Christian families from the burden of taxation to fund public schools. Only education in truth could combat the prevailing humanism, so he sought tax relief and government payments to private schools as chosen by parents. In this endeavor especially he was the champion of the *kleine luyden* (common people) who, until then, had no right to vote and, therefore, little influence in affairs of state. When Kuyper won a seat in parliament, he led efforts to enlarge the electorate, and by 1896 49% of adult males could vote, whereas that figure had been only 12% in 1870.[7] The Anti-Revolutionary Party did not seek a theocracy (or "ecclesiocracy") but a separation of church and state into distinct, but not alien, spheres of authority. Always the party respected the rights of non-Christians. Kuyper knew the Netherlands had become a diverse society, and he sought the same freedom in education for secular humanists and Roman Catholics that he desired for his own Reformed Protestants. A Roman Catholic political party soon formed in response to the Anti-Revolutionary Party, and the two movements shared a common interest in freedom for their schools. Collaboration between them in 1889 led to partial success, when Parliament enacted a law to grant private schools one-third of their expenses from public funds. Full funding did not occur until 1917, but the state monopoly over education ended in 1889.

Concurrent with the effort to obtain equality for private schools, there was comparable movement in higher education. The initial success in this regard came with the creation of the Free University of Amsterdam. Kuyper began advocating freedom for private universities in 1875, when he asked parliament for such recognition. In the face of opposition from the three public universities, he organized the Association for Higher Education on Reformed Principles, which gained the status of a legal corporation in 1879.

---

7   Vlekke, Bernard 1945. *Evolution of the Dutch Nation*. New York: Roy Publishers, 316–321.

Creation of a Christian university became a matter of some urgency when the Dutch Universities Act (1877) removed the teaching of theology from the university curriculum and replaced it with comparative religion. Thereafter all public institutions were to be neutral toward all religions, including Christianity. Kuyper reasoned that formation of a theological seminary would be an inadequate response to this legislation, so he proposed a full-orbed university committed to the Reformed faith. He desired not only sound instruction in theology, but an entire curriculum based on a biblical worldview. The Netherlands then needed a school in which all professors would be informed believers who would teach all disciplines from a Christian point of view.[8] At first the state required graduates of the Free University to pass qualifying examinations at one of its universities to validate their degrees, and the Dutch Reformed Church refused to ordain graduates of the Christian university as ministers.

During his tenure as a professor at the Free University (1880–1901) Abraham Kuyper eventually convinced the civil authorities to recognize degrees from the university he founded, and in 1901, he became Prime Minister of the Netherlands at the head of a coalition government formed in collaboration with the Catholic Party. In that position he obtained legislation which granted equality to private universities and other schools. The Free University was still the only private institution of its kind, but in 1923 the Roman Catholics opened the University of Nijmegen under the provisions of the law Kuyper had introduced in 1903.

Consistent with his worldview, Kuyper argued for a university with a confessional basis where instruction proceeds on subscription to objective truth. He allowed for pluralism in education rather than to deprive secularists of their rights and showed himself thereby to be more tolerant than the liberals who had tried to preserve the state monopoly. He, of course, rejected the humanists' claim to neutrality in learning, because he knew all pursuits of knowledge begin with assumptions of faith that cannot be verified empirically. Christians begin with a commitment to the sovereignty of God; secularists assume the autonomy of man. Both are dogmatists.

Abraham Kuyper and the Anti-Revolutionary Party sought in all areas of life but concentrated on freedom for Christian Schools, humane policy in the Dutch colonies, and protection for industrial workers often subject to exploitation. Kuyper did not want the church to become a political or educational institution, so he did not establish church schools or a church newspaper. He sought parent-controlled schools and a university separate from the church as well as the state. The Anti-Revolutionary Party was not a clerical organization but one which functioned with Christian principles in the political sphere. Through his party and his service in parliament, Kuyper led his beloved *common people* out of political isolation to become involved in public life, there to the rights of Christ in society at large, not only in the church.

Facing The Antithesis

First as a member of Parliament, later as Prime Minister, Abraham Kuyper opposed both liberals and conservatives because those parties espoused a humanist worldview. He adamantly opposed the various socialist factions because of their overt materialism and their

8   See McGoldrick, *God's Renaissance Man*, 52–61 and Kolfhaus, Wilhelm 1930. "The Significance of Abraham Kuyper for Reformed Theology." *Evangelical Quarterly* 2: 302–312.

inclination toward violence to gain their objectives. In his opinion, the conflicts between the Anti-Revolutionary Party and its secular opponents were due not only to incompatible material aspirations. They, on the contrary, reflected the collision of irreconcilable life-principles. For him the manner in which people regard God, themselves, and the universe stands as the crux of the battle between good and evil, a struggle in which the opposing forces have no common ground. The current term culture war would have served Kuyper well. In this engagement it will not do to reply to the enemies' attacks in a piecemeal manner when two antithetical worldviews are locked in mortal combat. "Principle must be arrayed against principle," since a clash of life systems is in progress (*LC* 11–12). Only Calvinism has the means to wage this struggle effectively.

Kuyper supported his concept of antithesis by citing the battle cry of the French Revolution, *No God, No Master*, as evidence that secularists aim to "free" mankind from divine authority. The Reformed faith alone provides a comprehensive system embracing man's relation to God, to other men, and to the world. Calvinism can do this because it does not restrict itself to ecclesiastical and theological matters (*LC* 19–23). It emphasizes both the dignity of man as God's image-bearer and his depravity as a sinner in rebellion against divine authority. In Kuyper's own words, "every man, simply because he is a man, should be recognized, respected, and dealt with as a creature created after the divine likeness" (*LC* 27).

Calvinism, in contrast to the idea of equality popular in the French Revolution, desires to see all humans "on their knees before God, consumed with a common zeal for the glory of his name" (*LC* 28). The only social distinctives Calvinism recognizes are those God has mandated by conferring his gifts and the authority that pertains to offices that people occupy in his providence.

Although God created human beings with the dignity of his own image, the fall has corrupted human nature in all its facets, and that includes the mind, blinded by sin to its own condition. Apart from the regenerating power of the Holy Spirit, a fallen human "does not perceive, and cannot perceive, the real condition of his own being, nor of his reason" (*PST* 384–85). This renders futile efforts to prove God to unregenerate people. That would be like displaying a beautiful jewel before a blind person and expecting him to appreciate it. Likewise, secularists assume the world is in its natural condition because they maintain a worldview that excludes God, so Christians must challenge their basic principles and ask the Holy Spirit to remove their blindness and to make the claims of Scripture convincing. It is a great mercy that God has not left humans to depend upon their depraved reason but has sent his Spirit to regenerate them, thereby to convince and enable them to accept the truth of revelation (*PST* 387–402, 557–561). Were the Holy Scriptures, wrote Kuyper, "to be carried into the world, without the regenerating and illumining activity of the Holy Spirit to precede, accompany, and to follow it, no church would ever be seen among the nations" (*PST* 634).

In assessing the significance of human depravity and the consequent antithesis it has produced between regenerate and unregenerate minds, Kuyper declared:

> we are not dealing with isolated sinful facts but a power of sin that controls sinful life in all its expressions. All sin has a common face, bears the stamp of a common origin, shows a well-ordered coherence in its manifestations and a regular development in its progress. In a word, there is a *history* of sin. . . . Sin puts the stamp of God's image on its own counterfeit

currency and misuses its God-given powers to imitate God's authority. . . . Sin lives solely by plagiarizing the ideas of God.[9]

Kuyper's perception of the human condition led him to reject a rationalistic method of apologetics. He believed unregenerate people do not have the capacity to be objective in assessing the claims of God. Kuyper therefore called Christians to attack the *basis* of anti-Christian worldviews, and he believed the very meaning of life is at stake in this contest. Sin has disposed the mind against God, so it does not operate properly and cannot be neutral toward its Creator. A person's worldview reflects the moral and spiritual condition of one's mind. A worldview then is not an abstract idea but a genuine expression of one's moral state.[10]

The insistence that the defense of Christianity must feature a systematic assertion of principles rather than a rebuttal of specific arguments is a conviction Kuyper developed after reading a work of James Orr (1844–1913), a Scottish Presbyterian theologian and historian. In 1891, Orr delivered lectures later published as *The Christian View of God and the World*. In this impressive book of great erudition, the author maintained Christians must respond to competing worldviews with comprehensive statements of their position, for nothing less could be effective.[11]

Agreeing with Orr, Kuyper affirmed the lordship of Christ over all creation, a truth he presented forcefully in his own *Lectures on Calvinism* in 1898. There he cited modernism/secularism as the archenemy of God's truth, especially modernism as expressed in the ideas that undergirded the French Revolution, Darwinian evolution, and German pantheism. Kuyper contended that traditional defenses of particular doctrines could not avail in this struggle. Only the full-orbed worldview, which Calvinism alone can produce, could be effective.[12] He knew learned modernists presented their views in logical, coherent arguments based on their axiomatic principles, so Christians must do nothing less. In his lecture "Calvinism and the Future," he declared:

> against this deadly danger [modernism], ye, Christians, cannot successfully defend your sanctuary, but by placing, in opposition to all this, *a life- and world-view of your own, founded as firmly on the base of your own principle, wrought out with the same clearness and glittering in an equally logical consistency.* (*LC* 190)

To illustrate the need for a systematic defense, Abraham Kuyper cited conflicts between Christians and secularists in science. Such controversies are not due to the relative quality of scholarship as one camp engages the other. Instead they are results of opposing assumptions about the present state of the universe. Modernists hold the world as it is now is in a normal condition and develops through natural evolution. Christians, however, maintain that the present condition is abnormal because of the cosmic effects of sin and that only divine action can restore it to its original state (*LC* 130–131). Cosmic redemption is then the major feature of the Christian worldview.

---

9   "Uniformity: The Curse of Modern Life." In *AK:ACR* 21–23 (emphasis Kuyper's).

10 A perceptive analysis of Kuyper's contribution on this point and on the whole matter of the mind appears in Naugle, David 2002. *Worldview: The History of a Concept*. Grand Rapids: Eerdmans, 256ff.

11 Ibid., 7–14. Orr, James 1893. *The Christian View of God and the World*. Edinburgh: Andrew Elliot, especially lecture III.

12 *LC* 135–136; for a keen analysis of Kuyper's *LC*, see Heslam, Peter S. 1998. *Creating a Christian Worldview*. Grand Rapids: Eerdmans.

Whether a person accepts the modernist-secularist hypothesis or the opposing Christian belief will be a consequence of his or her religious and philosophical axioms. There is no actual conflict between faith and science, and every scientific investigation begins with an act of faith. All scientists assume their sense perceptions are accurate and their logic correct. The perceived conflict is due to mutually exclusive assumptions about the condition of the universe, which neither camp can verify empirically. Each position has its own Supreme Being "as the point of departure for [its] worldview, and "those starting points are mutually exclusive since, for the secularist man is ultimate, but for the Christian God is supreme" (*LC* 133). Spiritual regeneration or the lack thereof determines where people stand with regard to the claims of God. "He who is not born again," Kuyper contended, "cannot have a substantial knowledge of sin and he who is not converted cannot possess certainty of faith; he who lacks the *testimonium Spiritus Sancti* cannot believe the Holy Scriptures" (*LC* 137).

Common Grace

Although Abraham Kuyper was emphatic about the noetic and cosmic effects of sin and the depravity of fallen nature, he understood that humans can accomplish relative good despite their unregenerate condition. Such attainments he attributed to the operations of common grace, which

> does not kill the core of sin, nor . . . save unto eternal life, but it arrests the complete effectuation of sin, just as human insight arrests the fury of wild beasts. . . . In a similar manner God by His 'common grace' restrains the operation of sin in man, partly by breaking its power, partly by taming his evil spirit, and partly by domesticating his nation or his family." (*LC* 123–124)

Since humans are sinners in rebellion against God, He owes them no favors whatever, but in his kindness he has granted various gifts to the rebels and thereby makes possible a relatively stable and enjoyable life on earth. God has not abandoned his creation but rather intends to restore it to its former glory. Common grace is the means of preservation, a prelude to full restoration. The Holy Spirit makes the work of common grace effective, as he guides history' toward its goal. Along the way he bestows talents and abilities upon both regenerate and unregenerate people so that even the latter make valuable contributions in the nature of civic good. The historic documents of the Reformed faith affirm this teaching, for example, the *Canons of Dort*, III, iv, 4 and the *Belgic Confession*.[13]

As people enjoy the benefits of common grace, they are responsible to be good stewards of creation. The creation mandate (Genesis 1:27–31) requires this, but sin has made them ungrateful and irresponsible. Regeneration changes that attitude radically so that Christians operate in the arena of common grace as servants of God and man, and they respect nature as a gift of grace. Through science, technology, government service, and private enterprise they have the means to maintain their proper relationship to creation.[14] Although common grace brings benefits to everyone, the elect benefit most, because it creates conditions in which they hear the gospel and come to Christ. Jesus is not however, only the redeemer of the elect, but *the* reconciler of the creation to God and the re-creator of the heavens and the earth. One day the whole world will "be his conquest, the trophy

---

13 Bacote, Vincent E. 2005. *The Spirit in Public Theology.* Grand Rapids: Baker Academic, 127.

14 Ibid., 144; Kuyper "Common Grace," in *AK:ACR* 167–71—referred to subsequently as *CG*.

of his glory" (*CG* 171).

While unbelievers will not honor God as the source of their talents, Christians must do exactly that. In the course of their grateful employment of God's gifts, they must be *Christian* in all their pursuits. They must reject any sacred-secular dichotomy and remember every inch of creation belongs to their Savior. Christ has not abandoned the world, so neither may his people. Since God works by both *special* and *common* grace, Christians are not to leave such areas as art, science, technology, and politics to unbelievers. Affirming the kingship of Christ negates a world-denying pietism that assigns priority' to protecting oneself from the evils of society. Although the world is in a corrupted condition, it is not under the rule of Satan, evil humans, or impersonal fate. Christ is king, now and forever! (*CG* 166).

> There is thus no doubt [argued Kuyper, referring to Colossians 1:15–18] . . . that common grace and special grace come most intimately connected from their origin, and this connection lies in Christ. (*CG* 187)

> . . . the church does two things: (1) it works *directly* for the well-being of the elect . . .; but (2) it works *indirectly* for the well-being of the whole of civil society, constraining it to civic virtue. (*CG* 190)

Although the church is an influence for good in society at large, it must not attempt to impose its confession upon the state. It should instead exert moral authority without seeking authoritarian control over society. The city of God and the city of this world are separate; light from the city of God illumines the other city, as believers fulfill their duty to be "the light of the world" (Matthew 5:14) (*CG* 200).

In an 1891 address to a convention of the Anti-Revolutionary Party, Abraham Kuyper forcefully decried Christians who deny or ignore Christ's authority in politics, and he assailed that attitude as capitulation to evil. Kuyper blamed the French Revolution for spreading humanist ideas contrary to divine revelation, and he concluded that humanism had brought the worship of man and had made earth, not heaven, the final point of reference. He accused religious humanists of perverting the church as a way to subvert the Christian faith, and public schools he identified as the primary instruments to further the humanists' agenda. Kuyper was especially pointed in his critique of public universities in which Darwinian professors taught students to regard themselves as animals rather than bearers of God's image.[15] (*CG* 208–12).

Kuyper's opposition to Darwinism was in part because it leads to the belief that material prosperity is the ultimate good. This view and the state policy that promotes it will cause morality to "degenerate into the pursuit of utility until, in the end, even though people do not descend from the animal world, [it] will degrade them into brutes."[16]

Speaking for the community of Reformed believers, Kuyper said, "Calvinists . . . thank God for making it possible for men to dwell together in a well-ordered society and for restraining us personally from horrible sins." For this reason, rather than leave the arts and sciences to unbelievers, Calvinists seek to explore all God's works, and they do so within the respective spheres of activity which God has ordained, for they insist every inch of creation belongs to Christ (*LC* 125–28).

---

15 "Maranatha," in *AK:ACR* 208–212.
16 Ibid., 224.

Conclusion

Abraham Kuyper, it is obvious, was not a mere theorist, but one who sought specific means by which to implement his worldview. The Anti-Revolutionary Party, the Free University of Amsterdam, and his newspapers, all illustrate his activism. While he regarded Christians as pilgrims on the way to heaven, he called them to accept responsibility to perform their duties on earth, which includes exploring the resources of creation while working with them to glorify the Creator. In doing so Christians must remember the antithesis between themselves and unregenerate people who consider the condition of the world as normal! (*LC* 130–32). In the sphere of education this recognition is of crucial importance, so believers must not be content to pursue theology while leaving the other academic disciplines to non-Christians. To do that is to employ "the tactics of the ostrich," and thereby to ignore Christ's claim to every inch (*LC* 139). "Wherever man may stand," argued Kuyper, "whatever he may do, . . . in agriculture, in commerce, and in industry, or his mind, in the world of art, and science, he is . . . constantly standing before the face of his God, . . . he has strictly to obey his God, and above all, he has to aim at the glory of his God" (*LC* 53)

Kuyper, of course, knew the present sinful state of humanity causes even regenerate people to misunderstand their proper relationship to the various spheres of life. There is always a temptation to regard the practice of one's faith as an emotional experience and an escape from the problems of earthly existence. Consistently pursued, this leads to ignoring public life as though it were unrelated to faith. True Christianity, however, is not confined to feelings, since "God has fully ordained . . . laws . . . for all of life, . . . the Calvinist demands that all of life be consecrated to His service. . ." (*LC* 53).

The overriding principle of Calvinism is *cosmological*, that is, the affirmation of divine sovereignty over all of creation, so "the Calvinist cannot shut himself up in his church and abandon the world to its fate" (*LC* 73) He will, to the contrary, proclaim a worldview that addresses the fundamental issues most pertinent to human needs. This will necessarily produce a conflict between Christians and the secular culture around them, as regenerate and unregenerate minds interpret reality differently. The diversity of worldviews is due to the noetic effects of sin and to the activity of evil forces, since "our struggle is not against flesh and blood, but against . . . the powers of this dark world and against spiritual forces of evil in the heavenly realms" (Ephesians 6:12). Since God has intervened into history from the outside, his revelation makes it possible to have an accurate worldview. He has already revealed the meaning of creation, so humans are not free to assign their own meanings to it. Creatures must not try to supplant their Creator, which is exactly what rigorous humanists seek to do. God's law is the standard of judgment, so moral values are not mere sentiments or conventions. The biblical worldview presents "an absolutist perspective on life that is real, true, and good."[17] Humans form their worldviews in terms of their acceptance of God or as a consequence of their idolatry. Those who presume they are autonomous engage in rebellion against God, and such people cannot understand the world or themselves correctly. They participate in the war of good against evil on the side of evil, contesting Christ's claim to every inch of the *cosmos*.[18]

---

17 Naugle, *Worldview*, 266. Chapter nine of this work is an insightful analysis, one on which I have drawn extensively.

18 Ibid., 275–283.

Worldviews are important because they show how people and societies perceive reality, and they affect how people answer the deepest questions of life and its significance.[19] Modern secularists deny the reality of sin and so blame social structures and institutions for the unhappiness and misery' humans must endure. Rather than admit the need for regeneration, they justify revolution as the means to change such structures. As Kuyper expressed this matter, humanists fail to "comprehend the true context, the proper coherence, and the systematic unity of all things."[20] Because of the noetic effects of sin, unbelievers do not see the connection of creatures to their Creator. Like animals that see objects but do not understand their structure or purpose, unregenerate minds do not see created beings and objects as parts of God's panorama.

They view the universe without appreciation for its Architect (*CGiS* 450). The antithesis between *natural* and *spiritual* man (1 Corinthians 2:11–15) does not stop with their conflicting assessments of either general or special revelation. It extends to all of life, as only recipients of regenerating grace achieve "a view of the world that is in harmony with the truth and the essence of things" (*CGiS* 458).

Abraham Kuyper knew the development of social structures through common grace would not produce perfection, something that would occur only at the return of Christ. He was a *neo-Calvinist* in that he adapted the principles of the Reformed faith to the needs of his own era because he believed improving the human condition is a Christian responsibility. He never promoted social-cultural development as his ultimate concern; for he understood mankind's greatest need is forgiveness for its sins to be obtained only through faith in Christ. While he rejoiced that common grace enables even unbelievers to make useful contributions, Kuyper remembered their sinful refusal to glorify God for his gifts. Therefore he urged Christians to seek the salvation of the lost, that they too would acclaim Christ's dominion over every inch.

---

19   Ibid., 345.
20   Kuyper, A. "Common Grace in Science," in *AK:ACR* 449 – referenced further as *CGiS*.

10

Called Back to Stewardship: Recovering and Developing Abraham Kuyper's Cosmic Pneumatology

Vincent Bacote

Abraham Kuyper's cosmic pneumatology provides a highly significant contribution to the further systematic development of the doctrine of the Holy Spirit. It merits further examination in the present for two reasons. First, the cosmic work of the Spirit has tended to be neglected in Western systematic treatments of pneumatology; and second, modern approaches to cosmic pneumatology are incomplete. How so? A somewhat hyperbolic statement to this effect comes from Hendrikus Berkhof, who, in his 1964 volume on the Holy Spirit,[1] noted that the relation between the Holy Spirit and creation was in need of development, and that he only knew Calvin and Kuyper to have written on it. In the intervening three decades, this aspect of pneumatology has received increased attention by theologians. Jürgen Moltmann, in *God in Creation*[2] and *The Spirit of Life*,[3] calls for a holistic doctrine of the Spirit, and adopts a panentheistic understanding of this relation, thereby hoping to engender greater respect for the created order. Colin Gunton highlights the Spirit's work as perfecter of creation so that the renewed creation will give praise to God.[4] The World Council of Churches' Seventh Assembly in Canberra focused on the theme "Come, Holy Spirit, Renew The Whole Creation," and led to several *Ecumenical Review* articles reflecting on aspects of the theme, though none focused on the further development of the Spirit's role in creation. Ken Gnanakan's missiological response to Canberra focuses on the Spirit's role in re-creation, and also emphasizes the ecological concern that stems from this focus, as a corrective to misinterpretations of the stewardship paradigm.[5] Michael Welker looks at the characteristic traits of God's reality and power in the structural patterns of life.[6] Mark Wallace calls for an ecological pneumatology,

---

1   Berkhof, Hendrikus 1964. *The Doctrine of the Holy Spirit*. Richmond: John Knox Press.

2   Moltmann, Jürgen 1985. *God in Creation: An Ecological Doctrine of Creation*. The Gifford Lectures 1984–1985. London: SCM.

3   Moltmann, Jürgen 1992. *The Spirit of Life: A Universal Affirmation*. Trans. Margaret Kohl. Minneapolis: Fortress.

4   Gunton, Colin E. 1992. *Christ and Creation*. Grand Rapids: Eerdmans.

5   Gnanakan, Ken R. "*The Holy Spirit, Creation and New Creation*." Evangelical Review of Theology 15 (April): 101–110.

6   Welker, Michael 1994. *God the Spirit*. Trans. John Hoffmeyer. Minneapolis: Fortress.

revisioning the Spirit as a life-giving force rather than as a metaphysical entity.[7] Geiko Müller-Fahrenholz expresses the Spirit as "the core-energy of creation itself," and as the divine means to connect the cosmic, personal, and social elements of life.[8] Catharina J. M. Halkes[9] and Rosemary Radford Ruether[10] are among feminist approaches to the question. These have all contributed to the discussion, but, in my opinion, have not adequately or properly developed the ecological, cultural, and sociopolitical implications of the Spirit's role in creation.

What do I mean when I say that these recent contributions have not adequately or properly developed the ecological, cultural, and sociopolitical implications of cosmic pneumatology? I mean that it is my view that these works are either incomplete in some sense (such as in scope), or that the proposals for expressing and applying the implications of cosmic pneumatology are not within the limits of orthodoxy. What follows are brief statements concerning what may be missing in these works. In the case of Moltmann, his concerns for the health of creation are valid, and I appreciate his desire to redirect our focus to God's immanence in creation (while maintaining an emphasis on divine transcendence). But I resist expressing the Spirit-world relation in a panentheistic manner, as I believe this unnecessarily blurs the creator/creature distinction.[11] I have a question in this regard. Is it necessary to imply a kind of interdependence between God and the creation in order to engender a better ecological theology? Moltmann also desires that the creation be allowed a sabbath rest, in contrast to being perversely "developed" (i.e., devastated) under the guise of stewardship. It may be true that much creation stewardship has been a lightly-masked domination of creation (while masquerading as dominion), but is this sufficient reason to move away from stewardship properly performed? Instead of abandoning the concept, should we not strive to do it right instead? Colin Gunton's work is focused on Christ but does a great job of demonstrating a Trinitarian approach to the created order. What is lacking is an emphasis on the sociopolitical and cultural implications of the Spirit's cosmic work as it moves creation toward its goal, and that is probably because it is beyond the scope of that particular work.

As mentioned above, though the WCC Assembly in Canberra focused on the Spirit in creation, it did not result in the production of any works (within the bounds of orthodoxy) that developed the various implications of the Spirit's role in creation. Gnanakan's article is impressive, but the article simply offered some suggestions for corrections in perspective regarding the ecological implications of stewardship of the created order. In that he offered suggestions, his article did not focus on developing the implications of the Spirit's cosmic work. Welker's work is focused on discovering the Spirit's reality in divergent and even contradictory structures of life experience. The aspects of his work which focus on

---

7   Wallace, Mark. I. 1996. *Fragments of the Spirit: Nature, Violence, and the Renewal of Creation*. New York: Continuum.

8   Müller-Fahrenholz, Geiko 1995. *God's Spirit: Transforming a World in Crisis*. Geneva: WCC Publications.

9   Halkes, Catharina J. M. 1991. *New Creation: Christian Feminism and the Renewal of the Earth*. London: SPCK.

10 Reuther, Rosemary Radford 1992. *Gaia and God: An Ecofeminist Theology of Earth Healing*. San Francisco: Harper Collins.

11 For an in-depth engagement with Moltmann, see Bouma-Prediger, Steven 1995. *The Greening of Theology: The Ecological Models of Rosemary Radford Ruether, Joseph Sittler, and Jürgen Moltmann*. Oxford: Oxford University Press.

the Spirit's activity in creation are more focused on renewal and redemption than on preservation, so there is a difference in focus between Welker and Kuyper. There is not a particular emphasis on the stewardship of creation as a result of the Spirit's preserving work. While it might be improper to label his work as inadequate or incomplete, it might best be said that Welker's pneumatology arrives at its sociopolitical implications through a different means than Kuyper's. Wallace's work is very honest and intriguing, and it attempts to be a postmodern approach to the question of the Spirit's cosmic work, with a central focus on ecology. While I admire his concerns, I disagree with his view that all biotic forms are on the same level, as his work intentionally contends against the notion of human stewardship over creation. Indeed, there is interdependence among life-forms on this planet, yet is it not also true that humans are unique as bearers of the *imago Dei*, and is there not a mandate for stewardly dominion over creation? Further, I find Wallace's conception of the Spirit in creation to be too pantheistic (he admits that this may be the case in chapter five of *Fragments of the Spirit*). Fahrenholz's case is similar, in that his efforts to express the Spirit's presence in creation also blur the creator/creature distinction. Though he admits that they are metaphors, the concepts of "womb" as a primeval space in God for creation and "respiration" as the manner in which God sustains the creation are too pantheistic. I understand what Fahrenholz wishes to convey, but his metaphors make the divine-creation relationship too close. I also disagree with his use of the category of myth as a means for expressing an understanding of ultimate reality. His use of this category leads me to ask what he views as "real" in the history of creation, and what he views as "mythic creations" designed to provide categories of understanding for our life in a particular place and time. Halkes and Reuther share a concern regarding the patriarchal theological and sociocultural perspectives which allow and encourage the abuse and domination of both women and nature. Neither author develops her alternative approaches to such patriarchal abuse from an explicitly pneumatological standpoint, though the Spirit is acknowledged as being active in creation. A further problem with Reuther is her positive appropriation of non-Christian perspectives as part of her development of an ecotheology, the most obvious example of which is in the book's title, the concept of "Gaia," the earth as a divine living organism. This is the most explicitly pantheistic approach of all of the authors, and, as stated above, pantheism obliterates the creator/creature distinction. Another noteworthy point of disagreement is that both Halkes and Reuther desire an end to the stewardship of creation (which they, like many of the other authors, view as domination and violence to creation).

I propose to demonstrate the contemporary relevance of Abraham Kuyper's cosmic pneumatology. This aspect of Kuyper's pneumatology calls us to approach creation with respect, to recognize that we are stewards of the earth, particularly because the Spirit is involved in creation in the form of "common grace."

For Kuyper, there are three aspects of the Spirit's activity in creation. First, the Spirit performs a perfecting function in the creative act. As the Father spoke and produced the material of creation, and the Son formed and ordered creation, so the Spirit's role is that of bringing the potentialities of creation to their most complete end. Kuyper writes:

> . . . [O]ur creation will be complete only when we have become what God designed. . . . Thus to lead the creature to its destiny, to cause it to develop according to its nature, to make it perfect, is the proper work of the Holy Spirit. (*WoHS* 21)

What is the end of this perfection for Kuyper? It is "the glory of God" (*WoHS* 22).

A central purpose of the Spirit's cosmic work is to be immanent in creation and to promote the progress and development of the created order toward its proper *telos*.

Second, Kuyper views the Spirit as the animating principle of all life. He says:

> How intangible are the forces of nature, how full of majesty the forces of magnetism! But life underlies all. Even through the apparently dead trunk sighs an imperceptible breath. From the unfathomable depths of all an inward, hidden principle works upward and outward. It shows in nature, much more in man and angel. And what is this quickening and animating principle but the Holy Spirit?
>
> . . . This inward, invisible something is God's direct touch. There is in us and in every creature a point where the living God touches us to uphold us; for nothing exists without being *upheld* by Almighty God from moment to moment. . . . And as the Holy Spirit is the Person in the Holy Trinity whose office it is to effect this direct touch and fellowship with the creature in his inmost being, it is He who *dwells* in the hearts of the elect; who *animates* every rational being; who sustains the *principle of life* in every creature. (*WoHS* 25–26)

No life can be sustained apart from the Spirit's involvement, apart from divine "vitalization." The third aspect of the Spirit's role in creation is the restraint of sin. The Spirit constantly opposes sin and prevents creation from falling into chaos. This is a vital function as the Spirit moves creation to its end of glorifying God (*WoHS* 24).

In Kuyper's theology, the cosmic activities of the Spirit are implicitly linked to common grace. In describing the role of common grace in creation, Kuyper's comments are inextricably related to his statements concerning the Spirit's role in creation. Speaking of common grace in the Stone Lectures on Calvinism, Kuyper says:

> . . . Calvinism has wrought an entire change in the world of thoughts and conceptions. In this also, placing itself before the face of God, it has not only honored *man* for the sake of his likeness to the Divine image, but also *the world* as a Divine creation, and has at once placed to the front the great principle that there is a *particular grace* which works Salvation, and also a *common grace* by which God, maintaining the life of the world, relaxes the curse which rests upon it, arrests its process of corruption, and thus allows the untrammeled development of our life in which to glorify Himself as Creator. (*LC* 29–30)

As described earlier, Kuyper understands the cosmic work of the Spirit as that which seeks God's glory in a perfected *telos*, upholds and maintains the world, and resists the sinful curse on creation so that creation may develop and move toward its intended end. He also says:

> . . . there is no sun, moon, nor star, no material, plant, or animal, and, in much higher sense, no man, skill, gift, or talent unless God touch and support them all.
>
> It is this act of coming into immediate contact with every creature, animate or inanimate, organic or inorganic, rational or irrational, that, according to the profound conception of the Word of God, is performed not by the Father, nor by the Son, but by the Holy Spirit. (*WoHS* 44)

From these statements it is clear that the Spirit can be understood as the agent of, or the one who provides the context for, common grace. The Spirit's life-giving and life-sustaining touch is the "engine" of common grace.

For Kuyper, it is this common grace that serves as the impetus for political involvement, social action, and cultural development. Regarding this, S. U. Zuidema says:

Common grace supplies the believer with the material for fulfilling his calling to be culturally formative and to fight the battle of the Lord in the world of culture. The sphere of common grace . . . is the area where Christian scholarship, Christian politics, Christian social action and individual Christian activity are to be developed. Common grace provides the platform, as it were, on which these cultural tasks are to be acted out. Common grace is *the presupposition of the possibility* of Christian cultural activity.[12]

Further, Kuyper understands common grace as compelling us to responsibly attend to and develop creation, saying:

. . . for our relation *to the world*: the recognition that in the whole world the curse is restrained by grace, that the life of the world is to be honored in its independence, and that we must, in every domain, discover the treasures and develop the potencies hidden by God in nature and in human life. (*LC* 31)

As stated above, the Spirit's cosmic activity is the source of common grace. These last two statements lead to the conclusion that the Spirit as provider of common grace is the driving force behind a total engagement with the world, and further that the Spirit's cosmic work in common grace calls for responsible stewardship of the created order. Common grace calls for fervent involvement in creation, but with a fervor tempered by a great respect for creation.

How does this pneumatologically derived approach to creation-stewardship relate to the contemporary situation? In an interesting reversal of a wide-spread consensus, many consider stewardship to be a patronizing approach which permits humanity to act destructively in relationship to the environment. James Nash expresses the dilemma well:

Though the ethical concept of stewardship justifiably has positive connotations to many Christians, implying love and service, it has negative ones for substantial numbers of environmentalists (including many Christians). Stewardship conveys to them, because of historical associations with Gifford Pinchot and others in this century, the notion of anthropocentric and instrumental management of the biosphere as humanly owned "property" and "resources."[13]

Nash, thus, is ambivalent toward the use of the term, and understandably so.[14] Nevertheless, the perceived misappropriation and abuse of the stewardship paradigm does not therefore call for lexical or conceptual alternatives, but for an alternative which is instead the proper application of stewardship, and which provides a counterbalance to the caricatured representations of the paradigm in many circles.

Kuyper's cosmic pneumatology sounds a prophetic call for "responsible" stewardship, by virtue of the Spirit's intimate involvement in and with creation. Because of the Spirit's role in common grace, all persons are called to greater responsibility as stewards of creation. It is true that the recipients of particular grace are understood as having a greater motive

---

12 Zuidema, S. U. 1972. "*Common Grace and Christian Action in Abraham Kuyper.*" In *Communication and Confrontation.* Edited by Gerben Groenewoud. Translated by Harry Van Dyke. Toronto: Wedge, 56–57. *See infra* Chapter 19, page 251.

13 Nash, James A. 1991. *Loving Nature: Ecological Integrity and Christian Responsibility.* Nashville: Abingdon, 107.

14 This in spite of the fact that Thomas Derr has recently challenged this "naturalistic" view as contrary to the scientific evidence as well as to the theological tradition. See Derr, T., Nash, J., and Neuhaus, T. 1996. *Environmental Ethics and Christian Humanism.* Edited by M. L. Stackhouse. Nashville: Abingdon.

for heeding the call to responsible stewardship, but it is also true for Kuyper that common grace provides even those who are not partakers of particular grace with some capacity for developing the creation to the glory of God.[15]

How is it that Kuyper's cosmic pneumatology leads to a level of responsible stewardship where nature is respected and not viewed as the object of simple anthropocentric domination? While Kuyper holds a view of "dominion" where the world is subject to humanity, this subjection is understood as a serving, "holy duty," to be performed under God in all the world in all parts of life (*LC* 57). In the performance of this duty, "Christian action in the domain of common grace must minister to the structures of creation and the structures of common grace (which for all intents and purposes coincide) – instead of overturning them! . . . Its results can only be a 'higher development' of 'nature' and the 'natural,' i.e., of the creature."[16] Nature is lifted and respected on its own terms in Kuyper's approach to common grace. This leads to an urge toward cooperation with the Spirit in helping creation reach its potential. Creation is affirmed as good and worthy of full, responsible engagement. Further, due to common grace, "No Christian has a legitimate reason for withdrawing from the world of God's creating. That holds for the whole of creation, to its farthest reaches; that holds for 'all areas'; that holds in principle for the whole world of culture, politics included."[17] There is no room for a sectarian apoliticism in Kuyper's pneumatology, nor for an anti-creational opposition between technology and theology. Rather, science and politics become means of respecting creation as we transform it in a stewardly fashion to the glory of God.

This pneumatologically derived approach to stewardship leads to a positive environmental perspective, and to well-considered approaches to the environment without needing to resort to alternative proposals. Conceptually, it is not necessary to conceive of the God/world or Spirit/world relation in pantheistic or panentheistic forms in order to produce or encourage sound ecological theology and public policy. The many ideological avenues which emphasize God's immanence in order to raise or create ecological consciousness run the risk of attributing the negative as well as positive aspects of the world to God, including evil and injustice. Also, these conceptual paradigms, when taken to the extreme, put God at risk by connecting the destiny of creation with divine destiny. While Scripture affirms that God responds to human action in creation, and even that God grieves over sin, it does not portray a "God at risk" who is somehow at the mercy of human decision. Is it not more accurate to the deepest levels of analysis as well as biblical to conceive of God as Kuyper does, as a transcendent Trinitarian God who relates to creation in an intimate manner through the sustaining presence of the Spirit?

Practically speaking, responsible stewardship may manifest itself in an environmental concern which may lead to various forms of social action. There is no place for callous disregard of the environment because of an other-worldly focus. Indeed, there has been much Christian neglect of the environment, and the time is now at hand to develop an orthopraxis which reflects the high ideals of responsible stewardship. To do nothing would be to resist the Spirit and misuse common grace.

While it is easy to see how Kuyper's view of the Spirit's work in creation leads to

---

15 Zuidema (65), *see infra* page 258.

16 Zuidema (72), *see infra* page 263-64.

17 Zuidema (72), *see infra* page 263.

responsible ecological stewardship, how is it that the Spirit's involvement in creation leads to "responsible" cultural development and political involvement? A good way to understand this relation is to inquire about the function of culture and politics. If we understand both politics and culture as activities in which we "work with" the material of creation, or if we view these activities as our acting "upon" creation, then it follows that both areas require responsible stewardship. As with the environment, it is important that we properly apply these approaches to the created order. We must not understand stewardship and dominion to be license for domination. At this juncture it is important to remember the earlier quote that all activity in creation, the realm of common grace, must minister to the structures of creation. Culturally speaking, the objective is to develop human potencies and sociocultural structures toward a God-glorifying end. Politically, Zuidema puts it best:

> Christian political action will have to be more than lobbying for legislation to preserve the "Christian heritage" of Sunday observance: it will have to be the expression of a political philosophy and program that touches upon every aspect of political life.[18]

Kuyper's objective in common grace is not for Christians to be a certain breed of citizen, but simply to be citizens *par excellence* who embody the best in public and private life.[19]

As stated earlier, it is primarily Christians who Kuyper has in mind, as it is those who are being sanctified who will be most concerned to be good stewards of common grace. However, this does not mean that non-Christians are unable to develop the creation; rather, that they will be less inclined toward cultivating the potencies in common grace for the purposes of God's glory.

This discussion of the Spirit as the ultimate driving force behind ecological, political, and cultural responsibility eventually leads to the question of appearances. What forms will ecological plans, political philosophies, or cultural norms and values take if there is cooperation with the Spirit's enabling, sustaining, and developing power? What should this cooperation look like? Should it look like Calvin's Geneva mediated through Kuyper's Amsterdam? Probably not; but it means that we, like they, need to discern where the works of responsible stewardship lie in the natural and cultural cities of our day. Is it necessary that one ally oneself with Kuyper's political and cultural program, in which he called for separate Christian organizations? Possibly, but one cannot make hard and fast assertions concerning many ancillary particulars, since these may vary between societies and cultures. One answer to the first question could be that, while one might not rigidly call for one type of ecology, politics, and culture, there should be certain common characteristics among all attempts to be responsible stewards of creation. What are these characteristics? At the very least, there should be a climate of service and nurture, a climate of justice, an attitude of humility, and a zeal for creative development – characteristics which are encouraged by common grace. Regarding the latter two questions, it is certainly not necessary to become Kuyperian clones. For example, while in some cases it is indeed necessary that Christians form separate organizations, and while some social structures may even call for the manifestation of the church militant, all societies are not the same, and the requirements

---

18 Zuidema (73), *see infra* page 264.
19 Zuidema (73), *see infra* page 264.

of responsible stewardship will vary, even to the inclusion of situations in which Christians work with non-Christians. In fact, it is practically impossible to effectively participate in a modern democracy without some alliance with those of different beliefs. Moreover, although I am arguing for the value of Kuyper's paradigm, I am not necessarily arguing for his application of that paradigm. Some may disagree with Kuyper's political and cultural views,[20] yet one need not adopt his positions in order to appreciate, utilize, and develop his work.

Some might argue that Kuyper's doctrines of cosmic pneumatology and common grace are only sufficient for certain cultures or certain epochs. While it is true that one might not find all of Kuyper's approach to be valuable, my argument is that Kuyper's cosmic pneumatology is generally useful for all, and will prove to be indispensable as we seek to develop approaches to pneumatology for the future. We may need to reconfigure or restate aspects of his pneumatology as we understand more about the Spirit and creation, but we cannot ignore his contribution. While there is a growing number of theologians who have written about cosmic pneumatology, this increase has hardly made Kuyper irrelevant or useless. There is fertile ground in Kuyper for further development, particularly as we seek to understand how the Spirit is related to all aspects of a public theology.

Pneumatologically derived responsible stewardship provides us with an impetus and rationale for engagement with the myriad, complex issues which impact society. It is important to recover a proper understanding and application of the stewardship paradigm, and Kuyper's approach is quite helpful. As we seek to systematically complete the picture of the Spirit's role in creation and the vital implications which follow, we do well to incorporate the essence of Kuyper's approach. The Spirit's sustaining and developing power rouses us from our neglect of the environment and our lack of substantive progress in political and cultural development. If this "call of the Spirit" is heeded, then the stage may be set for significant, transformative contributions to the issues of the day.

---

20 Some may also view Kuyper as a cultural imperialist and latent racist, but the debates regarding these issues are not in themselves germane to the argument of this paper. They may play a role in discussions of Kuyper's applications of the paradigm at issue here, but arguments in favor of such applications are not being espoused in this essay.

11

Abraham Kuyper on Creation and Miracle

Chris Gousmett

Introduction

It has been the confession of the Church since its earliest days that God created all things and constantly maintains them in existence. This continuing relationship of God to his creation includes the mighty acts of power performed on behalf of his people, bringing healing and deliverance and providing for many needs. These mighty acts aroused wonder and reverent awe in those who witnessed their unusual power and appropriateness. The people of Israel, and the believers in the early church, had no difficulty in acknowledging the ability and the willingness of God to perform such acts on their behalf, and this is reflected throughout the Scriptures.

However, the Church eventually came into contact with the heritage of Greek thought, which emphasized the analysis of things and events in the world. The biblical perspective was concerned with the ultimate meaning and significance of the creation, and did not give analytical descriptions of things and events in the manner of Greek thought. So when the Church Fathers attempted to define more closely the biblical understanding of the relationship between God and the creation, they borrowed concepts from Greek philosophy to do so.

Since the Greek concept of reality was incompatible with the biblical perspective, the blend of these two approaches produced problematic formulations. The principal problem was the concept of substance. Substance or matter was the basic material from which everything was made. It was formless and had to receive its shape and individuality through the imposition of the activity of non-material forms. Since this matter was eternal and self-sufficient in its own right, it was independent of God (although some held that God had created matter). The forms which gave shape to matter had a similar independent character, and were used by God in creation but were not themselves created by him. Thus the early church Fathers' view of God's relationship to the creation unavoidably distorted the biblical message by using these unbiblical themes.[1]

The way in which the relationship between God and the creation is expressed has a profound influence on the formulation of the concept of miracle. If God is to work

---

1   For a study of how this synthetic approach affected the church fathers in the field of anthropology and eschatology, see Gousmett, Chris 1993. "Shall the Body Strive and not be Crowned? Unitary and instrumentalist anthropological models as keys to interpreting the structure of Patristic eschatology." *PhD Thesis*, University of Otago. Available online at http://www.earlychurch.org.uk/book_gousmett.php; accessed 15 February 2013.

miracles in a creation which has an independent character, self-sufficient over against God and functioning according to natural law (i.e., a law intrinsic to nature and not established, or at least not sustained continually by God) then God must break into this independent nature. A miracle can then take place only by abolishing or suspending a natural law so that a miracle, assumed on this basis to be contrary to natural law, can occur.

Thus instead of the biblical view of God's intimate and constant relationship with the world, God is exiled from his own creation. This is the fruit of autonomous thought which sets itself over against God and conceives itself and all of reality to be independent of God.

Here I will examine principal themes in the doctrine of creation and miracle as developed by Abraham Kuyper, one of the leading figures, together with Herman Bavinck, in the renewal of Calvinism in nineteenth-century Holland. I will focus especially on the influence of scholastic philosophy on his thought, as well as the insights he gained into the biblical confession of creation and miracle.

Kuyper's Doctrine of Creation

The concept of creation as matter which received its form through the rational activity of God was not wholly avoided in the early neo-Calvinist movement. Kuyper and Bavinck both used the terminology and concepts of neo-Thomistic scholastic thought in this respect, although they also held to a biblically reforming position, which is in conflict with this scholastic view. It is to their credit that they saw the unbiblical nature of scholastic thought; but, lacking a truly biblical philosophical system, there was little they could do to avoid it.

The doctrine of creation is foundational to Kuyper's theology. Thus he attacked the theological error of pantheism on the one hand, and the philosophical and scientific error of evolutionism on the other. Both errors were an assault on the integrity of Revelation and the coherence of the Christian view of reality. Bavinck had also attacked pantheism, and Kuyper's attack followed similar lines. Both saw the obliteration of boundaries and distinctions as its fundamental error, beginning with the fundamental boundary between God and the cosmos:

> The most distinctly marked boundary line lies between God and the world; and with the taking away of this line all other boundaries are blurred into mere shadows. . . . God created the boundaries. He is Himself the chief boundary for all his creatures and the effacement of the boundaries is virtually identical with the obliteration of the idea of God.[2]

Kuyper saw pantheism's abolition of the God/cosmos distinction as having disastrous consequences not only in theology, but equally in the social and political realm. His doctrine of sphere sovereignty is rooted in the concept of the God/cosmos distinction and would be impossible without it.[3] For Kuyper the boundary between God and the cosmos is absolute. There are no transitional beings between God and the cosmos; in fact, there is nothing at all between God and the cosmos. Any neo-Platonic emanation theory is cut off here.[4]

---

2   Kuyper, A. 1892. *Pantheism's Destruction of Boundaries*. Translated by J. Hendrik de Vries. Published in the *Methodist Review* (July and September, 1893): 520–35, 762–78.

3   Bolt, John 1982. "The imitation of Christ theme in Bavinck's cultural-ethical ideal." *PhD Thesis*. University of St Michael's College, Toronto, 146–147.

4   Kuyper, A. 1892. "Between a creature and the creator lies nothing. There are no transitional beings. . . .

Creation is not a generation from God, but a divine calling-into-being, and it is other than God (*E Voto* I:195–196). Along with the calling into being of creation, God established the laws for creation as a whole, and for each individual creature (*E Voto* I:190). Kuyper contends that it is unthinkable that God could call a single creature into being without also specifying the law for its existence. For God is sovereign over all things, governs all things, determines all things and controls all things through his Law:

> It is completely unthinkable that God the Lord should call a single creature in life without as well specifying also the life-law for this creature in and through the creation of it. Is this now thus that God the Lord, because he is our Creator, also of itself has given in the creation the law for the existence of all creatures, and that no *creation* of a single creature is thinkable without that of its accompanying life's-law, then it lies in the foundation of the cause, that the Lord our God, who governs everything, has determined everything, and controls everything through his law, is also the lawgiver for the higher existence of mankind. (*E Voto* III:463)

Therefore nothing can exist without the law by which it is determined and controlled by God. By these laws God established and maintains the order of creation (*E Voto* I:236). These laws are his servants (*E Voto* I:238); they do not act independently of God once they have been established. Such a deistic idea was as repugnant to Kuyper as was pantheism. These laws are themselves subject to God's will and dependent on him:

> . . . nature and each of its powers and each of its laws do not exist in themselves, but from moment to moment are only what they are through the command which proceeds from the mouth of God.[5]

And subject to the laws, which are God's servants, are the creatures which have been called into being. By these laws the creatures function; they cannot be separated from the law which governs them. Were they to be separated, creation would be divided in two, and nature would be denied its dependence on God (*E Voto* I:191). Neither the creation nor God's law for it are to be separated from God. While the boundaries are maintained, there is an unbroken relationship between God and his creation:

> His law rests on his eternal wisdom and thus is perfect; and, once given being as perfect, they rest in the sovereignty of his sacrosanct and supreme will. God the Lord and His Law are not to be separated. (*E Voto* I:59)

Nature does not stand over against God with its powers and laws; instead it is subject to God (*E Voto* I:238). All creatures are determined by the sovereignty of God. He has determined for all creatures what they are and will be and do. God has established a law for all creatures (*E Voto* I:189–190). This law or laws for the creation is the will of God, as it is expressed in his eternal counsel:

> The law of existence for the creation, in so far as God has bound himself to his creation, we must now take to be this command, as this was determined in his counsel. (*E Voto* I:192)

It is the will of God which is the law that governs all things. In God's eternal plan, all things find their unity, including creation and redemption:

The boundary between creature and creator is absolute." *E Voto Dordraceno*. Kampen: Kok. Vol. I, 97. Cf. Kuyper, A. 1929. *Dictaten Dogmatiek*. Kampen: Kok. Vol. II. *Locus de Creatione*, p. 42. All translations from Dutch are by the present author unless otherwise indicated.

5   *E Voto* I:239. Cf. *Dictaten Dogmatiek*, Vol. III, *Locus de Providentia*, p. 76.

Thus one needs merely to return to the counsel of God, which lies back of creation and recreation, and embraces both in unity, in order once for all to escape from the mechanical representation of a Divine interference in an independently existing nature. Sin and misery will, without doubt, continue to bear the character of a disturbance, and consequently all re-creation the character of providence and restoration, but both creation and re-creation flow forth from the selfsame counsel of God. (*PST* 427)

This is developed in an almost neo-Platonic fashion by Kuyper.[6] The ideas in the mind of God are expressed in the coming into being of each of His creatures.

That there is no thing created apart from the Word, gives us to understand that in each creature an idea of God expresses itself, that in each creature an idea of God is at work and embodies itself in that, since in the eternal word is the fullness and glory of the ideas of God, nothing can be created except through the Word and by the Father.[7]

Through this emphasis on God's plan, we see how each of the persons of the Trinity is involved in the creation, since Kuyper is strongly Trinitarian on this point. Everything was planned by God the Father, which plan He then spoke forth by the Word, the Son; and after all things have been called into being through the Word, the Spirit leads them to their goal.[8]

This concept of the work of the Spirit in developing created reality is associated with Kuyper's emphasis on the organic character of creation, which he saw as an organism containing the seeds of all things in potency and in an undifferentiated state.[9]

Genesis 1:2 reveals first the creation of matter and its germs, then their quickening. . . . [By] the brooding [of the Holy Spirit] in Genesis 1:2, by which the formless took form, the hidden life emerged and the things created were led to their destiny. (*WoHS* 30)

These seeds develop and give form to matter, thus giving rise to individual creatures. This individuality of each creature is governed by its logos, which is the form into which the organism develops matter. The logos or form is the creaturely expression and embodiment of the idea of God for each creature, and is developed according to the counsel of the Father, by the Son through the works of the Spirit. The work of the Spirit uses the seeds in creation, since it is "the manifestation of a potency in creation leading to the completion and restoration of creation according to God's purpose."[10]

Kuyper sees each living creature as a combination of an organism and the matter that is given form by the organism.

Among creatures there are three kinds. There are those that are merely material, others that are simply spiritual, and there are those that exist both spiritually and have a material presence. A

---

6   Steen. P. 1983. *The Structure of Herman Dooyeweerd's Thought*. Toronto: Wedge, 40–41. See the discussion of this theme in Herman Bavinck in Gousmett Chris 1984. "Bavinck and Kuyper on Creation and Miracle." *Anakainosis* 7 (1–2): 5.

7   Kuyper, *GG* II:210.

8   *E Voto* I:207. Cf. *WoHS* 21. See the discussion of this theme in Herman Bavinck in Gousmett, Chris 1984. "Bavinck and Kuyper on Creation and Miracle." *Anakainosis* 7(1–2): 3.

9   Steen. op. cit., p. 90.

10 Kuyper, A. 1891. *Dictaten Dogmatiek*, Vol. III, *Locus de Providentia*: 48. For further details of the logos speculation, ultimately deriving from Stoic philosophy, and how this was introduced into the concept of miracle by Augustine, see Gousmett, Chris 1988. "Creation order and miracle according to Augustine." *Evangelical Quarterly* 60 (3): 217–240. Available online at: http://www.allofliferedeemed.co.uk/gousmett.htm.

drop of water is solely material, an angel solely spiritual, and human beings are both spiritual and material at the same time. (E Voto III:550–51)

This matter is not eternal, but neither can it be a purely created substance.

Here Kuyper's thought is burdened by the scholastic distinction between form and matter, and this distinction is the source of a fundamental dialectical tension in Kuyper's thought, manifest in the contrast of internal/external, tangible/spiritual, and visible/ invisible. This contrast is parallel to the duality of God's Being and God's Name, and leads to the duality of God and creation. As the life-principle takes on outward reality in matter, so God's Name is manifest in reality. This contrast of internal/external leads to the duality of phenomenon and noumenon in Kuyper's epistemology, although, as Dooyeweerd points out, he gives the subjective critical epistemology of Kant an objective idea-realistic twist through the use of his metaphysical Logos.[11]

The connection within each contrasting pair is organic. There is also an organic bond between the life-principle or organism and matter, and between God and creation. Since all things are created by the Word, the creation can be called an organic whole. There is also a gradation in creation; it ascends in degrees and thereby the Word reveals itself in increasing richness and fullness. This organic connection within creation and between creation and God is seen by Kuyper as the source of life for the creation. There is an implied analogy of being between God and man as is evident from his epistemology. Thus Kuyper is unable to maintain his emphasis on the absolute character of the distinction between God and the creation.[12]

The Logos-speculation evident in this part of Kuyper's theology is derived from Augustinian neo-Platonist idea-realism combined with the ancient logos-speculation of Aristotle and the Stoics.[13] Logos-speculation emphasizes the idea that the world finds its origin in God as the highest intellect, the absolute Logos. The world came into being, in this conception, because this divine Logos had conceived the idea of it, and possessed the power to bring these ideas into objective existence. The ideas are the product of the divine thinking subject, and all things depend on the reality of the universal ideas. By this means the world was logicized, and the creaturely order is tied in to logical universals.[14]

Creation-Order and Miracle

Miracles for Kuyper are in no way supernatural interventions by God in the usual course of nature. Rather, they are tied directly to the creation order in Kuyper's thought. The laws for both nature and miracles are the products of God's will, His sovereign command over the creation. The only difference between the ordinary events of nature and miracles is that while God wills both, and thus both are dependent on God, He mostly wills the usual course of nature, and only rarely wills a miracle to happen (*E Voto* I:241).

The idea that God must break into the course of nature from outside to perform a miracle is based on the notion that nature is independent of God, having its own powers and laws. Kuyper rejected both of these ideas. Nature is what it is by the constant command

---

11 Dooyeweerd, Herman 1939. "Kuyper's wetenschapsleer." *Philosophia Reformata* 4: 223. For the English translation, *see infra* Chapter 14, page 172.

12 Velema. W. H. 1957. *De Leer van de Heilige Geest bij Abraham Kuyper.* 's Gravenhage: Van Keulin: 70–78.

13 See Gousmett. "Creation order and miracle according to Augustine," 217–240.

14 Klapwijk, J. 1980. *Honderd jaar filosofie aan de Vrije Universiteit.* Kampen: Kok, 534–535.

of God:[15]

> There is thus no mention of an intervention in the course of things, for nothing happens by a power outside of God, but everything happens solely as it does through God's will, and as soon as he for one moment ceases to will it so, it happens no more; or if he wills it otherwise, it happens otherwise. (*E Voto* I:240)

Kuyper accepted the idea of supernaturalism only in so far as it meant that God transcends nature. He thus spoke of the supernatural in the sense that the acts of Christ, in that they involved the power of God in confounding sin and evil, possess a supernatural character. A miracle then is not a purely supernatural event, but the supernatural power of God is seen at work in restoring creation, working alongside of the powers of nature. Because of sin,

> . . . miracles are now necessary, since a miracle is nothing else than the entrance of a new order in the disturbed higher order, and where once the miracle must intervene, and of itself, it indicates that the completion of the great work can come into being through nothing other than a miraculous, unexpected event intervening from outside.[16]

Thus a miracle is not the introduction of something new into creation, but the removal of the dislocations in the order of the cosmos introduced by sin and the curse.[17] There are two reasons why Kuyper rejects the idea that a miracle introduces something new. First, the creation itself is complete and cannot increase, and secondly the introduction of something new would destroy the organic nature of creation, since that new thing could not be intrinsic to creation, which would then itself no longer be a single organism.[18]

> . . . *grace* never creates one single new reality. This does not take place even in miracles. In no miracle does anything originate which is to be added as a new element to the existing cosmos. The very possibility of this is inconceivable and would destroy the organic character of the cosmos. (*PST* 373)

> [God] indeed works all miracles from the deeper lying powers, which were fundamental to the creation itself, without at a single point placing a second creation by the side of the first. Wherever the Scripture speaks of a *renewal*, it is never meant that a new *power* should originate, or a new *state of being* should arise, but simply that a new shoot springs from the root of creation itself, that of this new shoot a graft is entered upon the old tree, and that in this way the entire plant is renewed and completed. . . . The miracle, therefore, in its concrete form is not from nature, but from the root from which nature sprang. It is not mechanically added to nature, but is organically united to it. (*PST* 428)

Miracles in Scripture form a whole with creation and find in that their organic connection. They break through sin in proportion to the extent of the influence of sin; they do not work against nature but against the sin that disorders nature.

> Are we now justified in saying that miracle antagonizes nature, violates natural law, or transcends nature? We take it, that all these representations are deistic and take no account of the ethical element. If you take the cosmos as a product wrought by God, which henceforth stands outside of Him, has become disordered, and now is being restored by Him from without,

---

15   Berkouwer, G. C. 1952. *The Providence of God.* Grand Rapids: Eerdmans, 195–196.

16   Kuyper, A. 1929. *Van de Voleinding.* Kampen: Kok. Vol. II, 54.

17   Kuyper, A. 1897. *Dictaten Dogmatiek*, Vol. III, *Locus de Providentia*, 47.

18   Ibid., 221.

with such a mechanical-deistical representation you must make mention of something that is *against* or *above* nature; but at the penalty of never understanding miracle. (*PST* 425)

However, Kuyper points out that a miracle, even when worked by Christ, is always the power of God. The creation has no power in itself to work miracles; neither has Christ, since he performed these miracles not as God, but as a man whose prayers were answered by God.[19]

This power of God is present continually, but in a miracle it comes to the fore.[20] In a miracle we see the power which spirit possesses over matter restored.[21] Thus a miracle is in no sense an interference in the lawful course of natural events. It happens solely through the will of God, as do all events. But in a miracle we see God willing something other than his usual will. Thus the miraculous lies in our awareness, and our surprise when what we are used to is replaced by the unusual. It is something which seizes our attention and it is therefore a sign from God (*E Voto* I:240–41).

> But apart from that which is surprising and unusual for us, a miracle is precisely the same as a usual working of nature for they are both a command coming from the mouth of God and it is his servants, the elements and the powers of nature, which also bring them about. (*E Voto* I:241)

Even the miracles of the redemptive acts of God are recognized only in faith. They are not self-evident, a compelling testimony to God apart from faith.

> This is the miracle. Even when others see nothing at all poured out from heaven, the eye of faith observes the manna for the soul raining down from on high, scattered abroad by Jesus for his whole church. Just as Jesus once saw Satan fall from heaven like a bolt of lightning, while others saw nothing, so also those who have been quickened by the Spirit see a constant rain of grace falling down from the clouds of heaven upon parched souls.[22]

For Kuyper, miracles are above all evidences to mankind of the continuing providence of God for his creation. Since the fall we are unable to discern correctly the dominion of God over nature, and we have lost sight of our forfeited place exercising dominion as God's stewards. Fallen mankind is in awe of the power of nature and is inclined to worship it, since it so directly influences him and he is subject to its capriciousness.

> Miracles find their significance in the struggle of mankind, weakened by sin, in a nature strengthened against him by the curse. Without miracles nature rapidly assumes an impression of greater strength, and superior being and higher status than the spirit. This leads to an apostate worship of nature. (*PrRege* I:143)

---

19 Kuyper, A. 1897. *Dictaten Dogmatiek*, Vol. II, *Locus de Creatione*, 53–4. For details of Kuyper's pneumatic Christology, see Gousmett, Chris. "The Christ of the Spirit: The relationship of the Holy Spirit to the Incarnate Christ in Athanasius and Kuyper." Unpublished paper available at http://www.allofliferedeemed.co.uk/gousmett.htm

20 *PrRege* I:475. "... also in the period of the completion, the acts of Christ possessed a partly spiritual, partly material, partly social and partly anti-demonic character, and that also then the acts would be above all of a supernatural character. Rather, it must be established, that the acts of the King in the Kingdom of God possess a preponderantly supernatural character; that the miracle is inseparable from this; and that both the body and the soul, and the powers of the spiritual world just as much as the powers of nature, were ruled by supernatural acts. For what we call a miracle, comes not by this but it rises to the fore."

21 *PrRege* I:185. "Jesus restored human power over nature by the miracle."

22 Kuyper, A. 1888. *Dagen van Goede Boodschap – Op den Pinksterdag (Met Hemelvaart)*. Amsterdam, J.A. Wormser. Unpublished translation by Jack van Meggelen, 2008. Used by permission.

Since mankind is subject to the power of nature and appears helpless against it, faith that God has nature under control rapidly dwindles. Instead worship and faith are directed towards evil spirits supposed to be in control of natural forces.[23] The need for miracles arises from this, for only by means of a miracle can the power of God and his control over nature, a nature strengthened against man by the curse, be demonstrated to humankind.

> Hence the need for miracles; to affirm this truth of God's almighty power and control of a nature strengthened by the curse so it rules over man. . . . The fear that God is not supreme over nature drives away faith; this can be restored only through God's miracle power and signs, worked before our eyes. (*PrRege* I:149)

Kuyper uses this argument to demonstrate the significance and indispensability of the creation. If God goes to such trouble to demonstrate his power over nature, then it is worth striving for its renewal. Else it would be simpler to do away with nature and begin again with a new creation. But the curse on creation can be countered only by a miracle, which in effect reverses the power of sin. Kuyper describes the "signs" as a demonstration that there is a power able to check every result of sin in the material world. Thus their meaning was not merely to provide relief for those who immediately benefited, but as an assurance to all those who hear of them in later generations as a permanent foundation of hope (*PST* 422–23). Thus their character as a sign is more crucial than the immediate benefit for the participants which was of short-term duration.

> For this purpose they could not create a *new* reality (Lazarus indeed dies again), but tended merely to prove the possibility of redemption in facts; and this they had to do under two conditions: (1) that successively they should overcome every effect of sin in our human misery; and (2) that they should be a model, a proof, a σημεῖον, and therefore be limited to one period of time and to one circle. Otherwise it would have become a real palingenesis, and they would have forfeited their character as *signs*. . . . Thus only does *hope* receive its indispensable support. (*PST* 423)

Kuyper says that miracles cannot be understood apart from their relationship to sin and the curse.[24] For here we see the ordinances of God for the creation, in that God is working in creation and directing it to a higher goal, and in so doing is countering the effects of the fall. Thus the rage of nature against mankind is controlled by the miracles of God (*E Voto* I:152). Kuyper calls all miracles the "spiritual and material acts of recreation" (*E Voto* I:420).

The second important point made by Kuyper is that in miracles we see the original power of mankind over nature restored through Christ (*E Voto* I:185). Matter was intended to be subject to spirit; through restoration of the human spirit, its power over matter is likewise restored. In a miracle we see matter directly subject to spirit, while in culture we see it indirectly subject to spirit.[25]

---

23 *PrRege* I:148. "Since nature appears so strong and dominant over man, then they doubt that God is also more powerful than nature, and its ruler."

24 *E Voto* I: 144. "This worship of nature or evil spirits supposed to be in nature can be countered only by God's miracle-working power; i.e. his divine power over all the power of nature. Only in this light is the significance and indispensability of nature obvious. Miracle is not to be understood without this connection with sin and curse."

25 *E Voto* I: 186. "The spirit has dominion directly over matter in a miracle, while the same spirit at present has dominion over matter through means of the development of the human spirit."

The Logos-speculation that logicizes Kuyper's theories is evident in his contention that the miracle power of Jesus is a consequence of the superior knowledge or science which he possessed, as well as a consequence of his possession of superior power. His dominion over evil spirits was possible because of his knowledge of the spiritual world.[26] Likewise the wise men of Egypt (Exodus 7–8) possessed a secret knowledge of nature which gave them power over nature. However, these wise men were deceitful in that they portrayed their power as the result of sorcery and not simply as natural knowledge (which others did not possess and which, according to Kuyper, has since been lost). This knowledge operated under the common grace of God, since it contributed to the raising of the level of culture, but when it was used against Moses and Aaron it was exposed as vanity compared to the miracle power of God.[27]

The miracles worked by Moses used natural powers. They did not introduce anything new into creation; there was no divine intervention. The plagues are simply the working of nature on a higher plane. The magicians recognized this higher power but did not abandon their unbelief.

They were indirect miracles, because they used natural powers, executing judgment on the pride of Pharaoh. The plagues can be explained by the working of nature on a higher plane. However, this power was so much higher and applied in such a manner as to be recognizably so to the Egyptians. However having recognized this they sank back into their unbelief. The death of the firstborn and the passage through the Red Sea all demonstrate the power of God over all powers of nature, as the Israelites saw (*E Voto* I:151).

And so in a miracle we see the power of God working in nature and directing it to a higher goal than the one to which we are accustomed. There is nothing peculiar or supernatural in a miracle; it is simply the creation coming under the direction of the Spirit.

> Miracle has rescued for the human race faith in the Living God. . . . The significance of miracles is lost if we depart from the ordinances of God for mankind. Man stands powerless and helpless against the rage of nature which has broken out, but by a miracle he sees that God is Lord and master of nature. This can only be shown by miracles. By this means he learns of a power higher than that of nature but working in nature and directing it to a higher goal. (*E Voto* I:152)

Conclusion

Kuyper was led by the Scriptures to a biblically reforming insight into the work of God, but was hindered in giving this insight full and consistent expression because of his dependence on scholastic philosophy. His views influenced members of the reformational movement

---

26 *E Voto* I: 356. "The miracle works which Jesus performed, are not only a revelation of power, but plead as much for a knowledge, a science, which Jesus possessed of created things, which was far above our knowledge. Jesus' dominion over the "evil spirits" from which the victims beseeched him to save them, presupposed that this spiritual world was not an unknown territory for Jesus."

27 *E Voto* I: 150. "The wise men of Egypt had inherited an instinctive knowledge of nature and were familiar with mysteries, which gave them a certain power over nature. This instinctive knowledge has since been lost. The magicians of Egypt portrayed this power over nature as the result of sorcery and not of traditional natural knowledge. This knowledge had its good side in that it raised the level of culture, but when it was used against Moses and Aaron, who had access to the miracle power of God, which exposed the mysteries of Egypt as vanity. This miracle power brought judgment."

in the 1930s, most notably J. H. Diemer.[28] It is noticeable that neither Vollenhoven nor Dooyeweerd appear to have made any extensive comments on the nature of miracles.[29] The most significant comment by Dooyeweerd that I am aware of is this:

> The miracles which were described in the Holy Scripture are not magical, purely subjective phenomena. They are not in conflict, but rather in full agreement with God's creation order, meaning that they are not *counternatural* but *natural*. However, sin has deformed human nature on its subject side. The grace of faith is the restoration and perfecting of this nature, on its historical analogy, but it is not in a scholastic sense *supra*-natural.[30]

There remains therefore a task for the spiritual heirs of Kuyper is to continue his work, diligently uncovering the influences of unbiblical thought in his exposition of the faith, and finding more satisfactory ways of expressing the rich insights which he has gained for us. A more biblically attuned theory of miracles is one area where much work still remains to be done. I have tried to outline the direction in which this could perhaps fruitfully be pursued in the concluding chapter of my thesis on Diemer.[31]

---

28 J. H. Diemer held to many of the same concepts as Kuyper. See Gousmett, Chris 1985. "The Miracle of Nature and the Nature of Miracle: A Study of the Thought of J. H. Diemer Concerning Creation and Miracle." M. Phil F. Thesis, Institute for Christian Studies, Toronto, 1985. Available online at: http://www.allofliferedeemed.co.uk/gousmett.htm.

29 See the brief comments on Vollenhoven by Kok, John 1992. *Vollenhoven: His Early Development*. Sioux Center: Dordt College Press, 248 and 247.

30 Dooyeweerd, H. 1958. 'De verhouding tussen wijsbegeerte en theologie en de Strijd der Faculteiten." *Philosophia Reformata* 23: 65. This is the only reference to miracles by Dooyeweerd that I have been able to find, apart from a passing comment that miracles were rejected by the Enlightenment. (*A New Critique*, II, 352.)

31 Any explorations in this area should take careful account of the work of Kallas, James 1961. *The Significance of the Synoptic Miracles*. London: SPCK. Janse also seems to follow a different path while remaining within the Kuyperian tradition. Janse, A. 1982. *Inleiding tot de Calvinistische Filosofie*. Amsterdam: Buijten & Schipperheijn, and Maarssen: Stichting voor Reformatorische Wijsbegeerte. This is a reprint of articles from the 1930s. See Chapter 31, pages 59–62, on "Miracles."

12

Abraham Kuyper and the Church:
From Calvin to the Neo-Calvinists

Michael R. Wagenman

During the mid-nineteenth century, sparked by the momentous advance of Enlightenment ideas and values, European Christendom was under siege and burning fast. Large swaths of society – previously considered ordained by God and unmovable – were shifting as their Christian foundations were battered to a pulp. As a result (and as one example of Christianity's response to Modernism's deadly influence), a reformulation of Dutch Reformed Calvinism was beginning to take place in northern Europe.

Drawing on the insights and work of antirevolutionary predecessors such as Guillaume Groen Van Prinsterer (1801–1876), Abraham Kuyper (1837–1920) launched the most organized, formidable, popular as well as academic counterattack to the Enlightenment in Holland. His insights found their clearest articulation in his 1898 Stone Lectures at Princeton Theological Seminary wherein Kuyper presented his reformulated Calvinism as the only viable world encompassing system of thought able to contend with the extensive reach and influence of the Enlightenment.

Kuyper's insights comprised an interdisciplinary approach, blending philosophy and theology, in which "sphere sovereignty," "common grace," "antithesis," and "worldview" became not only "buzz words" for the theological movement but also storehouses for future scholars from which to draw rich and extensive potential for future reflection.

Kuyper's legacy then passed to the Dutch Reformed theologian Herman Bavinck (1854–1921) who is credited with giving a thoroughgoing theological shape to Kuyper's contributions which were more occasional and rhetorical (what you would expect from a journalist and statesman). Bavinck, from the Free University in Amsterdam, translated Kuyper to the next generation as well as to the Reformed churches of the Netherlands who would carry this Kuyperian world and life view around the world in the mid twentieth century, postwar emigration (focused in South Africa, Brazil, and North America – United States and Canada).

For the Reformed/Evangelical branch of Western Protestant Christianity, the theological legacy of Kuyperianism has been profound, sweeping, and as yet inexhaustible. This former Prime Minister of the Netherlands and founder and first Chair of Systematic Theology of the Free University of Amsterdam today stands at the head of a worldwide ecumenical movement within global Christianity.

The influence of Kuyper's theological insights and contributions have helped the twentieth century church recover its mission to proclaim and embody the gospel in every aspect of life and in all institutions of culture, not only those directly ecclesial. These themes have influenced the work of successive Dutch theologians such as Hendrikus Berkhof and G. C. Berkhouwer, British figures such as the late John Stott and N. T. Wright, and North American theologians Louis Berkhof, Albert Wolters, and Gordon Spykman. The list of prominent names related to this movement – from the twentieth century alone – could go on for pages.

The mid-twentieth century Dutch diaspora exported this reformational Christianity far and wide. In North America, it is this Kuyperian tradition that fuelled the widespread cultural enterprises of the Dutch immigrants to Canada following the Second World War. Bringing this world engaging mind-set to gospel inspired institution building, the Canadian wing of the Christian Reformed Church, for example, was instrumental in forming hundreds of congregations across the country, a coast-to-coast network of private Christian elementary and secondary schools, Christian postsecondary colleges and universities (the Institute of Christian Studies, University of Toronto, 1967; the King's University College, Edmonton, Alberta, 1979; and Redeemer University College, Ancaster, Ontario, 1982), a Christian labor union (Christian Labour Association of Canada, 1952 numbering about 30,000 members), a Christian political party (Christian Heritage Party, 1986), an international relief and development organization, etc. Kuyperianism is a movement that propels the church out into the entire world.

In light of this history, this chapter seeks to briefly examine the Calvinist ecclesiology that Kuyper sought to renew for his own time and place. Second, I would like to turn to a focused examination of Kuyper's ecclesiological contributions, summarized under the four headings of Creation, Unity and Diversity, Covenant, and Institute/Organism. In closing and by way of summary, I will attempt to chart the on-going relevance of Kuyper's project for the church today.

Pre-Kuyperian Calvinist Ecclesiology

Kuyper's doctrine of the church did not emerge from a vacuum. Kuyper's context was the growing influence of Enlightenment ideals and the growing inability of the Dutch Calvinism of Kuyper's day to comprehensively respond to and address these tidal waves of cultural shift. In the period following John Calvin (1509–1564) and the Post-Reformation confessional tradition, the understanding of the church in which Kuyper was trained for ministry had a roughly identifiable shape.

The church (the *ekklesia*) was understood to be the result of God's sovereign electing grace by which God gathered (or "called out") from the whole mass of humanity those who would profess Christian faith, be marked by baptism, and become members of God's eternal covenant in and through Jesus Christ. That is to say, the church was the result of God's work of grace in the rebellious world of sinful humanity. Apart from God's redemptive selection of individuals to have faith, humanity would be lost. But God is faithful and the remnant of those responsive to God's covenantal love are those who comprise the church. For Calvin and the later Reformers, this elect group in the mind of God comprised the Body of Christ, the one trans-historical community of the church.

This understanding of the church as the Body of Christ, biblical language to be sure, meant that the church found its redemption and on-going sanctification through its union with Christ, the Head of the church. That is, through the mysterious work of the Holy Spirit, the elect are truly united to the risen, ascended, and ruling Jesus Christ. And this union means that every spiritual blessing in Christ flows to the believer for their salvation, edification, preservation, and resurrection. God elects humanity, incorporates them into a Body, and unites them to the Head, Jesus Christ – a living, vital relationship that can never be severed. It is this union with Christ which gives the individual believer and the church as a whole its life-force and energy (temporal and eternal).

But not only is the church a supra-temporal Body, existing only in the mind of God, but the church also takes on historical and temporal shape in space and time. The Body spans the dividing line between what appears to humanity as life and death. That part of the single organic community of the church which exists at any given point in time is spread throughout the world. It is not located in one particular place, among one select group of people. There is no preferred language or culture. In this sense, the church in the world is catholic – in the sense of spread across the breadth and diversity of humanity. But the church is also catholic in the sense that it is found in every generation and will continue to the end of time. There is never a point in space or time where the church disappears, though changes in culture, governmental policies, or Christian faithfulness may bring greater or lesser presence of the church in varying locales.

In any given temporal or geographic community, the elect gather together in local congregational institutions. These local congregations are known by the three-fold marks of the true church: the pure preaching of God's Word, the proper administration of the sacraments, and faithful exercise of church discipline. The purpose of these ecclesial activities is the calling of unconverted humanity to faith and loyalty to Jesus Christ and the building up of believers' faith and obedience of lifestyle which distinguish them from the unrepentant.

Finally, during the period between the Post-Reformation era and the mid-nineteenth century in Holland, the church was not only believed to be a vertically-oriented theological community but also a horizontally-bound sociological community. The local congregations of the church were marked by internal love, submission, encouragement, and service. It should also be noted that this horizontal, temporal existence of the church was not purely introspective – the church maintained cooperative political and social bonds with other institutions, particularly the civil authorities.

Kuyper's Neo-Calvinist Re-Visioning of the Church

Abraham Kuyper (1837–1920) is credited with the translation of a renewed Calvinist theology to the modernist world of late-nineteenth and early-twentieth century Holland. Through his prodigious publications and widespread public speaking, Kuyper is often seen as the founder of the neo-Calvinist (or Kuyperian) branch within the Reformed tradition, a unique form of Christianity marked by world-engagement and vibrant (almost mystical) piety. This world-engaging vision of Christian faith sparked a tremendous shift in the posture of the church to the culture. This adjusted self-understanding of the church has contributed, from Kuyper's day to the present, to push the church into the world missionally.

While it is Kuyper's name which is attached to this modern renewal of Calvinism, to be fair to Kuyper's historical predecessors, he did stand on the shoulders of some significant others. Groen van Prinsterer, for one, was significant is laying the "anti-Revolutionary" foundation upon which Kuyper would later build. This Dutch "anti-Revolutionary" spirit was in direct conflict with Enlightenment ideals which were spreading through northern Europe during this period, resulting in drastic and violent upheavals in society, a trail of blood and tears in the wake of revolutions for the sake of "equality, fraternity, and liberty." Kuyper eventually served as the Prime Minister of Holland, the Anti-Revolutionary Party gaining the political upper hand. Besides this political success, Kuyper disseminated his theology through journalism, the founding of the Free University of Amsterdam, and volumes of theological and devotional works which continue to be read with joy and fruitful instruction.

Under Kuyper's profound influence and insightful theological mind, a number of key theological contributions were made to Reformed-Calvinist ecclesiology. These contributions to Calvin's and the Post-Reformation period's ecclesiology can be summarized under four main headings which we will explore presently: creation, unity and diversity, covenant, and institute/organism. It is the combination of these four main insights of Kuyper's which gives the church a deep theologically-rooted basis from which to engage the whole of society with the redemptive message of the Gospel.

Creation

We look, first, at the way in which Kuyper, more emphatically than Calvin, rooted the church in God's creational order. Kuyper believed that it was the nature of God's creation that human society is comprised of multiple realms or "spheres" of life (the family, the state, the school, the arts, etc.). And each of these spheres had its own sovereign authority, delegated in pluralist fashion to it by the world's creator, redeemer, and sustainer, Jesus Christ. Each sphere, therefore, had a measure of independent, relativized sovereignty or authority over its domain of creational life. All together, these various spheres make up the richness of cultural human life.

> That perfect and absolute Sovereignty of the sinless Messiah at the same time contains the direct denial and challenge of all absolute Sovereignty on earth in sinful man; because of the division of life into spheres, each with its own Sovereignty. . . . Thus there is a domain of nature . . . also a domain of the personal, of the domestic, of the scientific, of the social, and of the ecclesiastical life; each of which obeys its own law of life, and each subject to its own head. . . . Now in all these spheres or circles the cogwheels engage one another, and it is precisely because of the mutual interaction of these spheres that there is an emergence of that rich, many-sided, multi-formed human life.[1]

The church, Kuyper is saying, is rooted in the creation order; it's not merely a voluntary human construction that may or may not fit depending on the changing winds of cultural mood.

Kuyper used these words in his speech at the founding of the Free University, an institution whose curriculum would be "free" from state or church control – an educational institution in which research into God's world could happen free from the influence of other "spheres." In order to argue for such an institution (in a day when the reigning ideologies placed hegemonic straight-jackets on social institutions), Kuyper had to argue

---

1   Kuyper, Abraham 1880. "Sphere Sovereignty." A Public Address Delivered at the Inauguration of the Free University of Amsterdam. Translated George Kamps (the Free University of Amsterdam, 1880), 5.

that the world has an inherent pluriformity – in Kuyper's case this came about through pluralism. Vincent Bacote calls this the struggle for "structural pluralism" and "worldview pluralism":

> Kuyper's objective is to argue for a form of pluralism in society rooted in God's sovereignty and the structures of creation itself . . . . Kuyper made the case for sphere sovereignty with two objectives in mind. First, he wanted to make the argument, in terms of *structural* pluralism, that education had the right to operate free of government intervention. Second, in this speech he also contended for *worldview* pluralism, in which he asserts that Christians have the right to operate their own confessionally based institutions in a context that had grown hostile to the Reformed faith throughout the nineteenth century.[2]

Richard Mouw's understanding of Kuyper is that this pluriformity in both society (the "spheres") and the church (an extension of the idea that various churches work in harmony but independently within a variety of traditions) is a natural consequence of the entire Calvinist enterprise, recognizing that the pluriformity of churches does not in any way obliterate the unity of the church in Christ (contra Lutherans and Roman Catholics) but is rather a result of divine intentions for diversity in Creation.

> Kuyper's views about the role of the church in culture were grounded in his conviction that the real problem in the long-standing Christendom arrangement was not simply that the church was too closely allied with the state; the real problem was with the underlying ecclesiology that informed that alliance. . . . For all the problems caused by a divided Christianity, he argued, it was necessary, for the vitality of religious life in particular and society in general, for a variety of churches to conduct their respective ministries.[3]

Kuyper's argument is based on the conviction that God has instituted a plurality of creational institutions in society among various social, civic, and cultural arenas: government, family, church, and business being the foundational ones. And each of these arenas has its own mandate and authority to pursue its mandate from the creator God who has delegated this authority to each sphere. And while this authority may border upon other arenas and inform other spheres of life, each sphere is independently accountable to the divine sovereignty of God in Christ.

The church, consequently, has its own ontological reality apart from the permission or authority granted (or not) by any other sphere. The church is not required to justify its existence or its ministry or mission in the world before the bar of judgment operative within another sphere – say, the government. It is a given part of human cultural reality with an integrity of its own. In its own sphere, it has been delegated a certain sovereignty that may not be infringed upon by any other sphere. We should note that Kuyper does ultimately allow for the State to have a certain kind of overarching sovereignty among the various spheres of creational life. Kuyper argues that this is ordered by God so that the State can exercise its proper adjudicatory function in society, ensuring the free and unhindered exercise within each sphere of its divinely delegated mandate.

The church, then, for Kuyper is rooted in the potentials of creation but unfolding historically in time under God's Providence. The church is not merely a human organization,

---

2   Bacote, Vincent 2008. "Abraham Kuyper's Rhetorical Public Theology with Implications for Faith and Learning." *Christian Scholar's Review* 37(4): 413–414, italics original. *See infra* Chapter 17, page 211.

3   Mouw, Richard J. 2007. "Culture, Church, and Civil Society: Kuyper for a New Century." *The Princeton Seminary Bulletin* 28(1): 60.

bendable to changing human whims and aims, but bears an ontologically divine mark of authority in the world. The church is not dispensable but a given reality of human life for a particular purpose (what Kuyper calls a "confessional" purpose). And not only is the church's place in the world a result of divine decree but the confessional authority of the church to carry out its own particular mandate comes with divine sanction as well. To invoke a term from the philosophical side of the neo-Calvinist tradition, the church has its own "creational norm" or blueprint or law for how it is to function in the world. And what we begin to discern here is that while the mandate or function of the ecclesial sphere is focused on the confessional aspect of human life, this is not an aspect of human life sequestered off to the private margins of cultural life. Rather the church has an open and constructive posture toward the other domains of cultural life. The church, while having a unique role, is nonetheless a part of the public square, alongside a pluriformity of other cultural institutions.

This is a significant development from Calvin in that the church is not merely a post-Fall religious institution for the redemption of human persons. The church, for Kuyper, is also a divinely ordained creational "sphere" in the midst of society which has an independent sovereignty while simultaneously being interconnected with other creational-cultural "spheres." God in Christ is interested in more than the conversion of individuals; God is also concerned with the redemption of communities and human culture as a whole as well. Thus, Kuyper's contributions enable us to begin our ecclesial reflections in Genesis 1 and the account of the world's theological creation rather than holding off until Genesis 3 and God's decision to intervene following human rebellion. For Kuyper, the church is a part of creation.

Unity and Diversity

A second development Kuyper makes to Calvinist ecclesiology is the idea that the church has an inherent unity within rich diversity (or diversity within unity). This follows from the church's rootedness in Christ as well as its temporal existence in creation. The creedal attribute of the church's unity results from the church's radical Christocentricity and is confessed together with its pluriform temporal expression of multiple denominations and congregations. Kuyper's contributions here provide a dynamic theological framework within which to understand ecclesial confessions which appear to be disjointed to everyday experience.

We begin with unity. To describe Kuyper's insight on this point, we must begin with his 1900 publication, *The Work of the Holy Spirit*. Kuyper's theology of the church, developed further in this text, can be outlined as follows: The church, like other created realities, has a unity of being made up of a spiritual essence and a physical form. In its spiritual essence, the church is one in its unity and holy. In its temporal, physical, formal manifestations, the church is localized in various "fragments" and engaged in a war against its spiritual defilement which it "war[s] against" (*WoHS* 196). But this is not to say that there are two churches – one united and holy and another fragmented and embroiled in a battle against sin (or one supra-temporal and one temporal). Rather, these are two ways of viewing or speaking of a single thing. There is "one Church, invisible in the spiritual and visible in the material world" (*WoHS* 197). And Kuyper argues that it is the work of the Holy Spirit to bridge these two aspects of the church, by opening the imagination of the human viewer to apprehend and appreciate the presence of the Spirit in the temporal.

> The spiritual eye of the believer must therefore be reopened for the work of the Holy Spirit in the churches. The unspiritual man has no eye for it. A consistory, classis, or synod is to him merely a body of men convened to transact business according to their own light, the same as a meeting of the directors of a board of trade, or some other secular organization. . . . But to the child of God, with an eye for the work of the Holy Spirit, these church assemblies assume an entirely different aspect. He acknowledges that this consistory is no consistory, this classis no classis, this synod only apparently so, except the Holy Spirit preside and decide matters together with the members. . . . For without Him no ecclesiastical meeting is complete. (*WoHS* 198)

Kuyper's ecclesial argument on this point, which he also developed in his Lectures on Calvinism that he delivered at Princeton Theological Seminary in 1898 and published shortly thereafter, is that the church is ultimately rooted in the ascended Christ and in him alone. Similar to the way in which he asserts elsewhere that the earth is the theological center of Creation, so with the church, Christ its head is the ecclesiastical center. And since Christ is ascended to Heaven, beyond Creation, the primary locus of the church is there as well, rather than within Creation where sin dominates and rebellion abounds. By rooting the church in the person of the ascended Christ, Kuyper is fixing the church ontologically beyond Creation and beyond the temporal with its devastating power of sin, where moth and rust destroy (Matthew 6:20). This appears to be what Kuyper means by saying that the church has, "at present its center and the starting-point for its action, not upon earth, but in heaven" and that the church has its "new root in Christ" (*LC* 59). This is, for Kuyper, what Calvin's "Body of Christ" language means theologically and more fully unfolded: that the church is that community, rooted in the sovereign rule of Christ, the world's true Lord, and that centered in him in his resurrected, ascended, and reigning heavenly ministry the church is intimately bound to Christ in the New Creation of God's eschatological future. This is the Reformed emphasis on the "already but not yet" of the church relative to God's Kingdom. In Christ, the eschatological Kingdom of God has already come into the temporal present. But, in the temporal manifestation of that Kingdom, its fullness has not yet arrived. But since Christ is the Head of the church, his Body, the church in its temporal location even now begins to experience the "shadows" of this heavenly grace from its heavenly root.

A second reason why Kuyper roots the essence of the church in Christ's Heavenly reign is because he believes this is what the creedal catholicity of the church means in its fullest and widest understanding. Because the church's ontological center lies outside of Creation, it can simultaneously incorporate all believers of the past, present, and future as well as earthly geographic breadth. Kuyper notes that "all regenerate human life forms one organic body, of which Christ is the Head, and whose members are bound together by their mystical union with Him" (*LC* 59). Or elsewhere, anticipating the problems of divergent views, Kuyper observes that "the reality and fullness of the Church of Christ cannot exist on earth [because h]ere is found, at most, one generation of believers at a time . . ." (*LC* 61). Kuyper recognizes that if the church were to have its root within Creation, in the church's temporal manifestation, it could only be the church of today – of the present. But by positing the root of the church in Christ in Heaven, outside of the shackles of space and time, the church can be that living mystical body which, because of its union in

Christ, is united together in one undivided, truly catholic community, free from spot or blemish or fracture. It is in this way that Christ's Headship of the church functions: "that Christ in human form, in our flesh, has entered into the invisible, behind the curtain; and that, with Him, around Him, and in Him, our Head, is the real Church, the real and essential sanctuary of our salvation" (*LC* 62). This is the "one, holy, catholic, and apostolic Church" of the Creed, in its essence.

For Kuyper, the church's ontological essence, then, is twofold: First, it is radically and thoroughly Christocentric, rooted only and ultimately in the person of Christ, the tangible gift of love from God the Father for the world's redemption. Therefore, the church is a place of radical and gracious love – the love of God revealed through the love of Christ in his salvific mission. And second, the church gains its being, its identity, and its divine energy from its root in God's eschatological (already but not yet) renewed creation through Christ's ascended state of glory. This means that the church is a place of sweeping and compassionate hope – hope that through faith God's cosmic promises of redemption and renewal will faithfully come to pass, sweeping creation up out of sin into its glorious inheritance to the praise and glory of God.

This ontological unity is only one side of the matter though. The church also is phenomenologically diverse, a fact every observer readily understands. The church is not simply a supernatural community with no concrete connection to the created world and its other creational structures or institutions. Neither does the church form a kind of "second layer" to created life, producing a kind of supernatural aura around the natural. Rather, the church operates within and in harmony with the already-existing structures and institutions of creation. Kuyper emphasizes that "the waters of the Church do not flow outside the natural stream of human life, but cause the life of the Church to proceed hand in hand with the natural" world (*LC* 65). There is a unity between God's work of grace in the entire world and God's work of grace in the domain of the church such that they coincide and are related to each other, not disjointed and at odds with each other. In other words, there is a deeper unity between common and special grace than typically allowed for. Traditional treatments of this distinction often conclude that common and special grace are two different things. But Kuyper's reflections on the matter lead us back to a deeper unity between them, a unity found in the being of God himself, the author of grace entirely. This presumes that grace restores nature rather than grace and nature being in a dialectical struggle against each other. God's grace at work in the church is a restorative, healing grace that does not obliterate the natural Creation but rather addresses it in its rebellion and lovingly turns it back to its original intention. This is Kuyper's understanding of grace and Creation joined "hand in hand." But there is also incredible diversity within Creation, a diversity the church participates in as well.

This understanding of the relationship between the grace of God at work in the church and the work of God in Creation is brought to bear on the ecclesiological question of why there are so many different versions of Calvinism in the world, not to mention the multiplicity of denominations and styles of Christian worship across all the traditions of Christianity. Kuyper is readily aware of the natural wide variety and diversity within human life. Nationality, personality, temperament, and culture all form a rich tapestry of human communities which bear the mark of the Creator in all their richness. Because God's redeeming grace works "hand in hand" with the created natural world, churches will by natural result bear a similar diversity of expression – sometimes even in theology and worship. He says, "the differences of climate and of nation, of historical past, and of disposition of mind come in to exercise a widely variegating influence, and multiformity in ecclesiastical matters must be the result" (*LC* 63–64). This diversity may in fact result in "differing degrees of purity" – whether in doctrine or liturgy – but all this diversity does not result in a hierarchy of churches in terms of their faithfulness to Scripture or Christ.[4] For, Kuyper asserts, the diversity of churches "places them all side by side" in "equal rank and as manifestations of one and the same body" before God and "annihilates the absolute character of every visible Church" such that no church is perfect or the norm for all times and places (*LC* 64). The church doesn't just float on top of natural, created human life. The church is deeply embedded in the natural creational design of God and doesn't obliterate nature with grace.

To summarize Kuyper in this second area of further development beyond Calvin, the temporal manifestation(s) of the church in the world is deeply embedded in the nature of Creation. As such, there will be a natural (and good) diversity of ecclesial expressions – resulting from the natural diversity of peoples, cultures, and times. And yet this diversity is not the final word that can be said about the church for the church's root reaches so deeply down into Creation that it comes to be anchored in the risen and exalted Christ who is not only the Creator but who has also ascended to the place of cosmic power and authority above all of Creation. And here the church – in all its diversity – finds its true and enduring unity. As a result of this, churches are radically dependent upon Christ as their Lord and source of direction in ministry, a direction that is given through God's revelation in Scripture. Kuyper is trying to communicate that creational diversity can only be theologically explained if there is a unity to all the diversity in God, the world's Creator.

Covenant

Third, Kuyper expands upon Calvin's ecclesiological tradition by arguing that the union with Christ which Christian believers mutually share within the church makes the church a specifically covenantal community. This covenantal nature of the church's being is mediated by the Holy Spirit who binds Christians to Christ as well as binding Christian believers to each other – locally as well as catholically. This is accomplished, according to Kuyper, through the mediating power of God's Word revealed in and addressed to the church. In this way, Kuyper, therefore, propels ecclesiology beyond mere sociology.

A question could be posed about this covenantal union with Christ in the church: in this relationship between God and humanity or between Christ (the Head) and the church (the Body), how does this vital union occur? Does either party have primacy or take the initiative? For there is an inherent struggle when the question is framed as a binary polarity between two active parties. Depending on whether one puts the emphasis on the divine or the human side of the question, the ecclesiological result varies. For example, if the accent falls on the divine side, then the Holy Spirit's work in the church supersedes and supplants

---

4   *LC* 64. While Kuyper does skirt the idea of a hierarchical gradation of churches according to the "purity" of their doctrine, his statement or two in this vein are not addressing this point. Rather, the point Kuyper is arguing for is that this diversity of churches parallels the diversity of Creation and that this all points to the sovereignty of Christ which each local congregation must have the "liberty" (78) to work out the implications of freely, without interference from neighboring congregations, the State, or authoritarian ministers.

the human actions taking place with their divine intent. The will of God for the church, effected through the working of the Holy Spirit, overrules human actions and directs decisions and circumstances apart from human agency to the possible contrary – with the result being a kind of divine determinism. If, on the other hand, the accent falls on the human side, then human agency overrules and possibly cancels out God's providential sovereignty. It seems either way one goes, a very unsatisfactory understanding results – either God cancels out humanity in achieving the divine will or human agency is elevated to a place above or prior to God's sovereignty.

Kuyper offers an insight here that attempts to put the entire question on a different footing, possibly opening up a new conclusion to the question. First of all, Kuyper does not appear to conceive of the question as a dilemma – as two (equal or not) opposing actors facing off against each other where one wins and by implication the other loses. This binary understanding may quite possibly be where the problems start. Rather, for Kuyper, God's Word plays a mediating role between God and humanity. This tripartite understanding is a significant shift. As God (in the person of the Holy Spirit here) reaches out to humanity (creation), God achieves this relation through his Word, the Word of his self-revelation. God's Word becomes the agency through which the Holy Spirit interacts with God's creation (here, the church). And similarly, it is God's Word that humanity is called to respond to – either in dependence and faithfulness or in rebellion. Bavinck will later say that "The Word and the Word alone is truly the soul of the church."[5]

This can be seen in the way Kuyper quotes at length from the liturgical prayers of the church of his day, specifically the prayers of illumination and guidance before and after ecclesiastical assemblies. For example, he quotes the opening prayer in which the Holy Spirit is invoked "that Thou wilt be pleased to be present with Thy Spirit according to Thy promise, in the midst of our present assembly, to guide us in all truth" (*WoHS* 199). It is quite clear that for Kuyper, God's "promise" and the "truth" are synonymous with God's Word, where the promises of God and the truth of God's self-revelation are found for humanity.

Kuyper does at this point, when quoting the concluding prayer for church assemblies, appear to fall into the binary understanding of the relation. It is in this prayer, after thanksgiving is offered to God for being present with the assembly by his Spirit, that acknowledgement is offered and request is made that the Holy Spirit "direct . . . our determinations according to Thy will" (*WoHS* 199). Yet, the full meaning of this request is revealed when the prayer immediately thereafter asks that this same Spirit would "bless our intended labor and effectually to execute Thy begun work" (*WoHS* 199). There is something much more nuanced and subtle going on in Kuyper's mind than a simple binary logjam between these two parties. While there is human dependence upon God's work in and through the Holy Spirit, there is simultaneously an acknowledgement that human agency has real weight, status, and effect in this divine-human encounter.

What is possibly open to misunderstanding here is clarified by Kuyper as he outlines his understanding of these prayers. Kuyper's understanding of this relationship between God and the church via God's Word, effected through the Holy Spirit, could be called Kuyper's theology of church government (or polity) as that is how he phrases the introduction to

---

5   Bavinck, Herman 2003. *Reformed Dogmatics*. Edited by John Bolt. Translated by John Vriend. Grand Rapids: Baker Academic. Volume 4, 275.

this explanatory section that follows the quotation of the two church assembly prayers.

First, the lordship of Christ in the church is affirmed. And for Kuyper, this "lordship" is not an abstract, purely theological claim. It is a concrete assertion about the temporal results of Christ's Lordship exercised in history. He says emphatically that "King Jesus institutes" both "the offices" of the Church and as well "appoints the incumbents" (*WoHS* 199). Second, God and the church are related to each other as "the churches submit themselves unconditionally to the fundamental law of His Word" (*WoHS* 199). And, thirdly, the link between God and the church is effected through the Holy Spirit who "come[s] in the assembly to direct the deliberations" (*WoHS* 199). And, this presence of the Holy Spirit is further explained by Kuyper when he says that it is "not whether *better men* come in power, but whether the *Holy Spirit preside* in the assembly . . . He can not do [this] except the Word of God be the only rule and authority" (*WoHS* 199).

So, here we have Kuyper's clearly stated understanding of this relationship between the triune God and the ecclesiastical institution: it is a tripartite relationship with God's Word in a mediating position between two covenant partners – God and humanity (or the church). It is not as though we just need better leaders in the church (what Kuyper calls "better men"), leaders who are more attentive (due to natural inclination or supernatural insight) to the mysterious leadings of the Holy Spirit. Rather, as God faithfully reveals himself by his Word in the power of the Holy Spirit, so the church is called to be dependent and obedient, faithfully responding to God's Word. And it is this divine faithfulness met with human obedience which is what Kuyper understands the presence and working of the Holy Spirit in the church to mean. Kuyper, elsewhere, points to the theological virtue of love as the divinely-initiated and humanly-responsive bond between two persons and between God and the Church (*WoHS* 575–79). Love is that which covenantally unites two parties into a new unity without sacrificing their individual identities (what Kuyper refers to as "truth"). This is, again, a tripartite way of understanding the relations. It is this love, Kuyper argues, which "lies in the Church" (*WoHS* 575).

Thus, we have a key development in Kuyper's ecclesiology here: not only is the church a divine creation in the midst of society but it is the place where divine-human connection happens through the work of the Holy Spirit and the mediating presence of God's Word of address to humanity (and to which humanity is called to give faithful allegiance and dependence). It is the presence and work of the Holy Spirit to bridge God and the church: the church as it exists holy and unified on God's side and defiled and fractured on the creational side. Thus, when the church is assembled for worship or ecclesiastical government, the Holy Spirit produces a bridge such that a real encounter with God is made possible through faith in his Word. This is an ecclesiology which pushes one to recognize that there's more to the church than "meets the eye."

Covenant, a hallmark theological theme among Reformed Christians, for Kuyper becomes that which establishes a mediating position that identifies the nature of the church's temporal manifestation in the world. The church is not coterminous with the natural world. But neither is it coterminous with divine being. The church straddles these two dimensions of the realm of the Creator outside of the space-time universe and the realm of Creation.

Thus, the church as an institution is not the mediator of salvation but God through his Word remains the sovereign mediator. As such, all of life is lived *coram Deo*, not just when one is "at church." "Calvinism," Kuyper argues, "vindicates for religion its full universal character, and its complete universal application" (*LC* 52). This is an apprehension of the full import of the Christian faith – where all things exist for the sake of glorifying God, the natural as well as the human aspects of the world. "A religion confined to feeling or will is therefore unthinkable to the Calvinist" (*LC* 52). The demand of biblical Christianity is that one's "whole being, including all his abilities and powers, must be pervaded by the *sensus divinitatis* . . . [from] the very center of his consciousness" to the farthest edge, "reach[ing] down to his beard and to the hem of his garment" (*LC* 52). The same holds true for the social realm of life – there is no private, spiritual or religious sphere which faith must be relegated to:

> A religion confined to the closet, the cell, or the church, therefore, Calvin abhors . . . [for] God is present in all life . . . and no sphere of human life is conceivable in which religion does not maintain its demands that God shall be praised, that God's ordinances shall be observed, and that every *labora* shall be permeated with its *ora* in fervent and ceaseless prayer. (*LC* 53)

Church as Institute and Organism

Prayer and work, both performed before the presence of God is what the church seeks to create in the world: persons who respond faithfully to God's Word in the totality of their covenantal life with God. The institutional church is that institution within society which aims to officially foster within humanity the ability to respond to God in faith always and everywhere. The church as organism is the whole of the people of God sent into the wideness of the world to work and pray faithfully as God's representative ambassadors. Kuyper's rhetorical power is evident here as the themes of sphere sovereignty and the Calvinist conception of all of life being religious hits its highest notes:

> Wherever man may stand, whatever he may do, to whatever he may apply his hand, in agriculture, in commerce, and in industry, or his mind, in the world of art, and science, he is, in whatsoever it may be, constantly standing before the face of his God, he is employed in the service of his God, he has strictly to obey his God, and above all, he has to aim at the glory of his God. Consequently, it is impossible for a Calvinist to confine religion to a single group, or to some circles among men. Religion concerns the whole of our human race. This race is the product of God's creation. It is His wonderful workmanship, His absolute possession. Therefore the whole of mankind must be imbued with the fear of God, – old as well as young, – low as well as high, – not only those who have become initiated into His mysteries, but also those who still stand afar off. For not only did God create all men, not only is He all for all men, but His grace also extends itself, not only as a special grace, to the elect, but also as a common grace . . . to all mankind. (*LC* 53)

There is an inherent dynamic here between these two modes of the church's being in the world. Kuyper captures this dynamic when he writes,

> To be sure, there is a concentration of religious light and life in the Church, but then in the walls of this church, there are wide open windows, and through these spacious windows the light of the Eternal has to radiate over the whole world. Here is a city, set upon a hill, which every man can see afar off. Here is a holy salt that penetrates in every direction, checking all corruption. (*LC* 53)

An important observation can be made at this point regarding Kuyper's more fully developed understanding of the covenantal relationship between human religious freedom and the nature and role of the church in her two primary modes of being. It is this: that in the way Kuyper phrases these two sections quoted above, it is not the bricks and mortar of the Church building in the midst of society which effect God's gracious influence in the world. Instead, it is the believing and worshipping community assembled in the church building for worship. And it's not this in the sense that the passer-by on the sidewalk outside on a Sunday morning would hear the singing of a hymn of praise to God or hear a sentence or two of the sermon rooted in Scripture as the preacher's voice carries out the window. Rather what Kuyper seems to have in mind here is the way in which the assembled congregation, believing, worshipping, being discipled, is then blessed and sent into the world where they will organically spread throughout the whole of humanity to accomplish this influencing work. This appears to be what Kuyper is getting at when he uses the word "concentration" when speaking "of religious light and life in the Church." This light is concentrated in corporate worship and dispersed and refracted during the rest of life, in the whole of life, through the various callings and occupations of each Christian as they go about their regular weekly routines. Thus, it is this gathering and sending dynamic which Kuyper seems then to apply to the "city, set upon a hill" whose light radiates throughout the world or the "salt that penetrates in every direction."

Kuyper is picking up on the dynamics inherent within both biblical metaphors – that of a concentration being spread throughout a larger space, penetrating the whole from the center. The light of the city shines in the darkness to the very remotest distance. And the arresting power of the salt once spread through the entirety of the meat, does its "checking" work against "all corruption." This is a dynamic that breaks down if either action becomes the focus – either the gathering or sending. If the light remains hidden within the city walls or if the salt remains in the shaker, they are of no effect. Likewise, if the source of the light is extinguished, its rays may travel but will soon fade away; if the storehouse of salt runs empty, the salt which has been used up will lose its saltiness and no longer perform its necessary function. Therefore, both concentration and extension must take place in a living, dynamic rhythm for the image to work and the meaning to remain intact.

There is a tension here, though, between Kuyper and Calvin. Whereas Calvin's ecclesiology was based on revealed doctrine, privileged the church as institute, and still retained a "top-down" hierarchy as in the Roman Catholic church (though not embodied in a priestly hierarchy), Kuyper will go on to have a long-standing emphasis on the church as organism, the spread of the church's influence through the whole of society. Zwaanstra notes:

> In the introduction of his [Kuyper's] doctoral dissertation . . . Kuyper, after indicating his dependence on Hegel, Strauss and Rothe, predicted the formulation of a new, living and powerful Protestant conception of the church. This new conception would break fundamentally with the dualism of the Reformers and be based on divine immanence, the presence and operation of God in the world.[6]

Therefore, for Kuyper, the gathered, institutional church community is the other corresponding pole to the organic and independent life of faith which each believer lives before God in this dynamic, covenantal relationship of Christian faith. While it may appear at first to be somewhat counter-intuitive, without the church, the independent

---

6   Zwaanstra, Henry 1974. "Abraham Kuyper's Conception of the Church." *Calvin Theological Journal* 9: 153.

life of each believing Christian would expire in the end. The reason for this, according to Kuyper, is because human life in its present state is one of being "fallen" into sin. Human life presently is not "normal" but rather "abnormal" and in need of God's saving grace in Jesus Christ. Whatever affinities Kuyper's thought may have with a kind of incipient Hegelianism (Protestantism as the highest human development of religion and the like), this is where Kuyper is seen as not tied ideologically to a kind of theoretical process theology. He emphasizes the Fall as a "lamentable degeneration" which is only able to be corrected by a "restorative soteriology" such that "[e]very attempt to explain sin as an incomplete stage on the way to perfection . . . [is] an insult to the majesty of God" (*LC* 55).

This is Kuyper's understanding of the church as an observable institution in society versus the church as an organism spread through all the various elements of a culture. The church is that concentration (assembled for corporate worship) and extension (apostolically sent into the whole of the world) of God's grace, through which "God regenerates us – that is to say he rekindles in our heart the lamp sin had blown out." Primarily, Kuyper argues, God does this through the reading, preaching, and proclamation of his Word in Scripture. Scripture reveals a theocentric world to us, a theocentric world that "stands in direct opposition" to the self-centered world of our fallen imagination. And it is when God works his special, specific, saving grace into a person's life through his Word in Scripture, and that person begins to wrestle with the inherent religious conflict between the world displayed to them in Scripture and the self-centered world of their own imagination, that this "regenerate" person begins to understand "both the inanity of the world around him, and the divine reality of the world of the Scriptures." This experience which becomes a "certainty" in the human consciousness is what is understood by Kuyper as "the testimony of the Holy Spirit" – the process by which a person begins to not look around themselves for confirmation in their dependent earthly existence but "upward, through the prism of the Scriptures" to God, the source and center of all of reality (*LC* 58). This "prism"-function is what is understood as the doctrine of the sufficiently of Holy Scripture, covenantally binding God and his Creation for redemption.

Kuyperian Ecclesiology in Summary

Kuyper's ecclesiology is a fascinating study of theology responding creatively and theologically to the needs of his immediate context. The value of Kuyper's reflections on the church is seen not only in its rootedness in Scripture or the tremendous cultural impact of his successors but in the ability of his concepts to equip the church even today to seek greater faithfulness to Christ. In conclusion, Kuyper's ecclesiological insights can be crystallized in the following five ways, each of them rich with potential for helping the church of any age rediscover its mandate, discern the spirits of its age, and engage the whole of the culture for Christ.

(1) For Kuyper, the church is ontologically a creational given. It is one of many cultural "spheres" of human life, created by God, which has its own delegated sovereignty from Christ alongside others and exists in a cooperative relationship with them for the richness of human society.

(2) The church is a single, unified community of the redeemed, existing as a mystical body in God's electing mind and united in Christ its Head. Simultaneously, the church as a temporal manifestation exists in creaturely diversity, according to

the varieties of human time, culture, geography, temperament, understanding, and conviction.

(3) The church exists in a covenantal relationship with God, with God's Word playing a revelatory and mediating role between God and his creation. God graciously reaches out to the church by his Word; the church faithfully responds to God through obedience to that same Word. As such, the church is neither coterminous with the world nor God.

(4) The church is an epistemological context, a concrete formative community within which we can come to inhabit a particular time, place, and historical tradition which shapes our understanding of the content and consequences of faith, which guides our interpretation of scripture, and which forms us for particular ways of interacting with the world.

(5) The church is the result of the fullness of God's electing grace in Jesus Christ, the elect One, who in turn shares the fullness of his redemptive mission with those existing in union with him. This is the gift of fullness given to the church. But this fullness also has a mandate aspect to it: the church is that vanguard/cutting-edge place where the fullness of the world's redemption is being worked out in history.

13

The Two-Kingdom Doctrine:
A Comparative Study of Martin Luther
and Abraham Kuyper

Timothy P. Palmer

There is confusion in the Reformed world about the two-kingdom doctrine. A series of articles by a Westminster Seminary professor is arguing for a "Reformed two-kingdom doctrine;" and the *Calvin Theological Journal* is printing his articles without a reformational response. In a recent publication, this professor claims that even Abraham Kuyper holds to the two-kingdom doctrine.[1]

The two-kingdom doctrine is the belief that the kingdom of God is coextensive with the institutional church and that life outside of the church does not really belong to God's kingdom. I have already argued in these pages that such a designation is not the most appropriate term for John Calvin's theology;[2] but to suggest that Abraham Kuyper holds to the two-kingdom doctrine borders on the absurd.

This essay will first consider the original statement of the two-kingdom doctrine in Martin Luther's theology. We will then ask whether Abraham Kuyper holds to this teaching. We will argue that Kuyper's doctrine of the kingship of Christ excludes a two-kingdom teaching.

Luther's Two-Kingdom Doctrine

The two-kingdom doctrine began with Martin Luther. It was developed because of confusion in his day about the roles of church and state. Both the Catholic church and the Anabaptist movement were confusing this distinction.

In the Catholic church of Luther's day some theologians were insisting that the Roman church had temporal powers, while some political leaders were assuming ecclesiastical responsibilities. The separation between church and state was very blurred.

In particular, Duke George of Saxony forbade the printing and reading of Luther's works in his territory of ducal Saxony, and a few other German princes were taking the same line.[3] This was a clear infringement on the rights of the church and the Christian believer.

---

1   Cf. Van Drunen, David 2005. "The Two Kingdoms: A Reassessment of the Transformationist Calvin." *Calvin Theological Journal* 40 (Nov); Van Drunen, David 2007. "Abraham Kuyper and the Reformed Natural Law and Two Kingdoms Traditions." *Calvin Theological Journal* 42 (Nov): 283–307.

2   Palmer, Timothy 2007. "Calvin the Transformationist and the Kingship of Christ." *Pro Rege* 35: 32–39.

3   Ozment, Steven 1991. *Protestants: The Birth of a Revolution.* New York: Doubleday, 122–24.

Meanwhile, some of the Anabaptists were trying to set up a temporal kingdom on earth, while others were completely rejecting the temporal government, teaching that the only legitimate government in the world was that of the church.[4]

It is in this context that Luther developed the two-kingdom doctrine. Much ink has been used to describe and comment on this teaching.[5] Although there will be a continued debate about the nuances of his teaching, the main ideas are clear. By way of summary, we will focus especially on two of Luther's works.

This teaching is set out first in some detail in 1523 in Luther's "Temporal Authority: To What Extent It Should Be Obeyed."[6] The German title is "Von welltlicher Uberkeytt."

Luther's starting point is the recognition of two classes of people: "we must divide the children of Adam and all mankind into two classes, the first belonging to the kingdom of God, the second to the kingdom of the world" (*LW45* 88). Corresponding to these two kingdoms are two types of government:

> For this reason God has ordained two governments: the spiritual, by which the Holy Spirit produces Christians and righteous people under Christ; and the temporal, which restrains the un-Christian and wicked so that . . . they are obliged to keep still and to maintain an outward peace. (*LW45* 91)

The kingdom of God is thus the church. Its members are the true believers, and its king is Jesus Christ. Jesus rules by his Word, not by the sword. He rules by the Gospel, not by the law. The Sermon on the Mount typifies the ethics of this kingdom. Love and non-violence characterize this kingdom. Luther writes: "Christ is King and Lord in the kingdom of God." And, "he is king over Christians and rules by his Holy Spirit alone, without law" (*LW45* 88, 93).

But the kingdom of the world or the temporal government is different. Since unbelievers will not listen to the Gospel or the Holy Spirit, God ordained another government, the temporal government. "All who are not Christians belong to the kingdom of the world and are under the law" (*LW45* 90). The Scriptural justification for the temporal government is Romans 13 and related passages. While the kingdom of God is ruled by the Word of God, the kingdom of the world is ruled by the sword. While the kingdom of God is ruled by the Gospel, the kingdom of the world is ruled by the law.

From the above it is clear that the kingdom of the world is not the same as the kingdom of Satan. The kingdom of the world is a third kingdom between the kingdom of Christ and the kingdom of Satan. It has an ambiguous status between these two kingdoms. The kingdom of the world consists of unbelievers, but its government is ordained by God and comes from God.

So who is the king over this kingdom of the world? For Luther, "Christ is King and Lord in the kingdom of God"; but *"Christ's government does not extend over all men."* (*LW45* 88, 92; emphasis added). As we shall see more clearly later, in Luther's theology

---

4   Ibid., 126–127.

5   For summaries and bibliographies, see: Althaus, Paul 1972. *The Ethics of Martin Luther.* Translated by R. Schultz. Philadelphia: Fortress; and Lohse, Bernhard 1999. *Martin Luther's Theology.* Translated by R. Harrisville. Minneapolis: Fortress.

6   Luther, Martin 1962. "Temporal Authority: To What Extent It Should Be Obeyed." Translated by J. Schindel and W. Brandt. In *Luther's Works* 45. Philadelphia: Fortress, 81–129—referenced further as *LW45*.

Christ is not lord over the temporal world: instead, it is the prince or the emperor who is lord in this sphere.

Where does the Christian belong in this scheme? Of course, the Christian is part of the kingdom of God. The Christian person is ruled by the Gospel and the Holy Spirit. And yet the Christian is also part of this world. He or she is subject to the temporal government. Luther writes: "at one and the same time you satisfy God's kingdom inwardly and the kingdom of the world outwardly" (*LW45* 96).

Here we have the beginnings of the doctrine of the two persons within a Christian: the Christian person is the one who inwardly is subject to Jesus Christ; the secular or worldly person is the one who externally functions in society and is subject to the earthly king. Two persons exist within a believer: the Christian person and the worldly or secular person.

These thoughts from Luther's 1523 document are expanded upon nine years later. In 1532 the mature Luther published his commentary on the Sermon on the Mount.[7] At issue is the question as to how to apply Jesus' teaching in this sermon. For example, should a soldier or a policeman turn the other cheek while on duty? Should the government not resist an evil person, as Matthew 5:39 might suggest?

In response to these issues, Luther said that it is essential to distinguish the "secular and the divine realm" (*LW21* 5). So, when Jesus says that the poor in spirit are blessed, this refers to the spiritual realm, not the secular or worldly realm. The spiritual realm relates to "how to live before God, and above and beyond the external." But, "having money, property, honor, power, land and servants belongs to the secular realm" (*LW21* 12).

Again, when Jesus says that the meek will inherit the earth, he is not speaking about a governmental officer, who "must be sharp and strict . . . and get angry and punish"; rather, he is dealing with a Christian in his private relations. Thus, "we have two different persons in one man" – the Christian person and the secular person (*LW21* 23).

The command to remove an offending eye or hand again applies to the spiritual realm, not the secular one. Likewise, denying one's self and hating one's soul "have nothing to do with the secular affairs or the imperial government." Instead, all this is said in relation to spiritual life and spiritual affairs" (*LW21* 90).

In the context of these last sayings, Luther makes some incredible statements *excluding* Jesus Christ from the secular realm. Luther says:

> Therefore we must not drag [Christ's] words into the law books or into the secular government. . . . *With the secular area [Christ] has nothing to do.* (*LW21* 90; emphasis added)

On the issue of oaths, Luther again says that "Christ has no intention here of interfering with the secular realm, nor of depriving the government of anything. All he is preaching about is how individual Christians should behave in their everyday life" (*LW21* 99).

In respect to Jesus' instruction not to resist evil, Luther says that "Christ is not tampering with the responsibility and authority of the government, but he is teaching his individual Christians how to live personally, apart from their official position and authority" (*LW21* 106). On the same passage, Luther writes:

> Do you want to know what your duty is as a prince or a judge or a lord or a lady, with people

---

7   Luther, Martin, 1956. "Sermon on the Mount." Translated by J. Pelikan. In *Luther's Works* 21. St. Louis: Concordia: 1–294—referenced further as *LW21*.

under you? You do not have to ask Christ about your duty. Ask the imperial or the territorial law. (*LW21* 110)

Finally, on not laying up treasures on earth, Luther says that:

> Christ is giving instructions to the individual or the Christian man and that a sharp distinction must be made between the Christian and the man of the world, between a Christian person and a secular person.

He continues:

> Of course, a prince can be a Christian, *but he must not rule as a Christian*; and insofar as he does rule, his name is not 'Christian' but 'prince.' The person is indeed a Christian, but *his office or his princedom does not involve his Christianity.* (*LW21* 170; emphasis added)

In the same passage, Luther explains his distinction between the Christian person and the secular person. A Christian prince should say:

> My status as a Christian is something between God and myself. . . . But above and beyond this I have another status or office in the world: I am a prince. The relation here is not one between God and this person, but between me and my land and people. (*LW21* 170)

However, this theory has obvious difficulties. Is not Jesus Christ lord over the entire world, and not just the church? If all of societal life outside of the church is not under the lordship of Christ, then who is king in this "secular" realm? Does not the two-kingdom doctrine give considerable autonomy to "secular" life, putting it outside of the rule of Jesus?

This danger has been noted by a number of significant theologians. Helmut Thielicke said that the two-kingdom doctrine of Luther "makes it dangerously easy for the world to be dissociated from the Gospel."[8] Jürgen Moltmann says that "the two kingdoms doctrine gives no criteria for a specific Christian ethics."[9] Moltmann prefers the idea of the lordship of Jesus Christ over the two-kingdom doctrine.

Karl Barth said that since the two-kingdom doctrine excluded Jesus Christ from the realm of the state, the German Lutherans were more apt to support Hitler's Nazi state.[10] Whether this theory is true or not, it is interesting to note that the Resistance in Calvinist Holland was stronger than in Lutheran Scandinavia. When the state is removed from the lordship of Jesus Christ – as in the two-kingdom doctrine – then the possibility of a Christian approach to politics is reduced.

There is thus a broad consensus as to the nature of Luther's two-kingdom doctrine which stands in contrast to the Reformed view of the Lordship of Jesus Christ over all of life. The two-kingdom doctrine creates a huge autonomous area of life that is not under the lordship of Christ.

A Dualist View of Abraham Kuyper

When one comes to Abraham Kuyper, it is astonishing to find that David Van Drunen puts Kuyper in the two-kingdom camp. For Kuyper there is no square inch of reality which is not under the lordship of Christ. How in the world can Kuyper then be in the

---

8   Thielicke, Helmut 1966. *Theological Ethics*, vol. 1. Foundations, edited by Wm. Lazareth. Philadelphia: Fortress, 369.

9   Moltmann, Jürgen 1984. *On Human Dignity*. Translated by M. D. Meeks. London: SCM, 76.

10 See Thielicke, 368–369.

two-kingdom camp?

Van Drunen attempts a definition of the two-kingdom doctrine in his article on Kuyper. There he says that the two kingdoms are the spiritual kingdom, which finds "institutional expression in the present age only in the church"; and the civil kingdom, which encompasses "the various non-ecclesiastical cultural endeavors, particularly the work of the state." God rules the spiritual kingdom through Christ the redeemer and the civil kingdom through Christ its creator and sustainer.[11] This two-kingdom doctrine, to which Kuyper allegedly holds, stands in contrast to "neo-Calvinism or transformationism, in which all spheres of life are seen as subject to redemption and the claims of the redemptive kingdom of Christ in the present age" (284). In the following pages, we will show the absurdity of suggesting that Kuyper holds to the two-kingdom doctrine. Is not Abraham Kuyper himself the one who taught us that all of life is subject to the kingship of Jesus Christ?

David Van Drunen is a crusader of the nature-grace dualism. In Kuyper, he assumes that the civil kingdom is grounded in Christ's work as creator and the spiritual kingdom is rooted in Christ's work as redeemer. The former is the realm of common grace and natural law; the latter the realm of special grace. Van Drunen assumes that for Kuyper there is a "clear distinction between the church and the rest of life, and, for both doctrines, the chief distinction lies in that the former is the place where salvation is ministered and the latter a place where it is not" (300). The following pages will demonstrate that Kuyper does not fit into this nature-grace straightjacket.

It is curious that this crusader of the two-kingdom doctrine when writing of Kuyper seldom speaks of the kingdom of God and never speaks of the kingship of Christ.

It would seem that talk of kingdoms would involve talk of Jesus Christ the king, who dominates Kuyper's thinking. So what is the kingdom of God for Kuyper?

Kuyper Rejects the Two-Kingdom Doctrine

An essential source in respect to Kuyper's view of the kingdom of God is his magisterial *Pro Rege*, which means "for the King." It is noteworthy that Van Drunen's study of Kuyper's view of the kingdom of God omits this vital source. From 6 January 1907 to 8 January 1911, Kuyper wrote a series of articles in *De Heraut* under the rubric of "Pro Rege" (For the King).[12] These were published in 1911 and 1912 in the three-volume *Pro Rege*.[13] The basic structure of this work already shows how foreign a two-kingdom doctrine is to Abraham Kuyper. In broad strokes Kuyper develops the kingship of Christ over seven areas of life: Christ's subjects, the church, the family, society, the state, science and art. All of life falls under the kingship of Christ. There is no neutral ground for him.

In his introduction to the three-volume *Pro Rege*, Kuyper combats the two-kingdom doctrine. The very first sentence reads: "*Pro Rege* intends to remove the division that exists in our minds . . . between our *church* life and our life *outside* the church" (*PrRege* I:v). Dualists focus primarily on the area of the church where Christ is seen as a Savior who removes our sins. But Christ is more than this. Christ is king over all of life. The realization of this

---

11 Van Drunen, "Abraham Kuyper and the Reformed Natural Law and Two Kingdoms Tradition," 283–84.

12 Rullmann, J. C. 1940. *Kuyper-Bibliografie*, vol. 3. Kampen: Kok, 378.

13 Kuyper, A. 1911–1912. *Pro Rege of het Koningschap van Christus*, 3 vols. Kampen: Kok. Quotations from this work are my own translation—referenced further as *PrRege*.

has led to the formation of "our Christian press, our Christian science, our Christian art, our Christian literature, our Christian philanthropy, our Christian politics, our Christian trade unions, and the like" (*PrRege* I:vi–vii). The rest of this massive work develops this basic principle.

In his big work on Common Grace, Kuyper makes the same point. Some dualistic Christians maintain that Christ is exclusively the Expiator of sin. (This is the two-kingdom doctrine.) But Kuyper forcefully rejects this view: "The idea that Christ has no significance but as the Lamb of God who died for our sin cannot be maintained by those who read Scripture seriously." We cannot hold that Christ was given to us only for our justification and sanctification; we should rather follow Paul who says that Christ is our "full *redemption*."[14] He continues:

> To put it in a nutshell, shall we imagine that all we need is a Reconciler of our soul or continue to confess that the Christ of God is the Savior of both soul and *body* and is the Re-creator not only of things in the invisible world but also of things that are visible and before our eyes? Does Christ have significance only for the *spiritual* realm or also for the *natural and visible* domain? (*CG* 171)

Kuyper calls it "one-sidedness" to "think exclusively of the blood shed in the atonement and refuse to take account of the significance of Christ for the body, for the visible world, and for the outcome of world history." Such a posture runs "the danger of isolating Christ for your soul" (*CG* 172).

> Then the word "Christian" seems appropriate to you only when it concerns certain matters of faith or things directly connected with the faith – your church, your school, missions and the like – but all the remaining spheres of life fall for you *outside the Christ*. (*CG* 172)

Kuyper warns *against* the doctrine of two kingdoms or "two distinct circles of thought: in the very circumscribed circle of your soul's salvation on the one hand, and in the spacious, life-encompassing sphere of the world on the other." Such people claim that "Christ is at home in the former but not in the latter" (*CG* 172).

For Kuyper, then, Christ is the redeemer of all of life, contrary to the two-kingdom doctrine and Van Drunen's perception of this. Christ is our "full *redemption* . . . the Savior of both soul and body" (*CG* 171).

One can hardly make the point more clearly. There is no autonomous area of life. There is no independent kingdom existing between Christ's kingdom and Satan's kingdom. Kuyper speaks of just two kingdoms: the kingdom of Christ and the kingdom of Satan. "Just as God rules over spirits and humans, over spirit and matter, including all of creation, so also Satan desires to establish his kingdom over against God" (*PrRege* I:505). The two kingdoms are those of God and Satan: "Kingdom against kingdom, prince against prince, chief against chief, king against king!" (*PrRege* I:508). There are only two kingdoms, Christ's and Satan's, and both lay claim on all of life. There is no intermediate kingdom.

Nature-Grace Dualism?
Since there is no two-kingdom doctrine in Kuyper, one wonders whether Kuyper subscribes to a nature-grace dualism. When Van Drunen speaks of "a two kingdoms-like dualism" in

---

14 "Common Grace." In *AK:ACR* 171—referenced further as *CG*.

Kuyper, presumably he is referring to a nature-grace dualism.[15] He adduces distinctions such as Christ's offices of creator and redeemer, and the contrast between common grace and special grace to support his view. He thinks that the realm of grace has redemptive significance while the realm of nature does not.

Although Kuyper does at times use nature-grace terminology, it should be put on record that he vigorously opposes such a dualistic scheme. In his work on common grace, after rejecting the two-kingdom doctrine, he then rejects the nature-grace dualism. He says:

> For if grace exclusively concerned atonement for sin and salvation of souls, one could view grace as something located and operating outside of nature. . . . But if it is true that Christ our Savior has to do not only with our soul but also with our body . . . then of course everything is different. We see immediately that *grace* is inseparably connected with *nature*, that grace and nature belong together. (*CG* 173)

He continues:

> For if we set *nature* and *grace* against each other as two mutually exclusive concepts, we get the impression that nature now persists *apart from* all grace and that grace is and has been extended exclusively to God's elect. This inference is *absolutely untenable*. (*CG* 173)

Kuyper rejects "the inaccurate antithesis between *nature* and *grace* that has come down to us from medieval theology" in favor of a more "Reformed principle" (*CG* 174).

In the same work, Kuyper writes:

> Therefore, common grace must have a formative impact on special grace and vice versa. All separation of the two must be vigorously opposed. Temporal and eternal life, our life in the world and our life in the church, religion and civil life, church and state, and so much more must go hand in hand. They may not be separated. (*CG* 185–86)

In the following pages, we will see that Christ the redeemer renews and redeems that which he created. Christ's redemption is not restricted to the soul but includes the physical world. Nature and grace are not two separate realms; rather, Christ's grace transforms the natural world. Of course there is a distinction between the physical and spiritual side of a person, but this is not a "dualism" as Van Drunen asserts, but rather a "*distinction*," as Kuyper calls it (*CG* 186).[16]

Instead of a nature-grace dualism, I suggest that a redemptive-historical scheme is more faithful to Kuyper. The structure of Kuyper's theology is built around a creation-fall-redemption scheme. It was the eternal Son of God who created the world and mankind. It was the same Son who redeemed his creation.

The Kingship of Christ Over All of Life

For Kuyper the kingdom or kingship of Christ is derived from the sovereignty of the Triune God. The original power and sovereignty rest in the Triune God (*PrRege* I:307).

Kuyper emphasizes the fact that the kingdom of God includes all of reality: "This kingdom of God embraces all things, visible and invisible." This king – God – has power over people, the land and nature. "In short, *everything* is his. *His kingdom is over everything.*

15 Van Drunen, "Abraham Kuyper and the Reformed Natural Law and Two Kingdoms Tradition," 303.
16 Ibid.

. . . His kingdom is a kingdom of all ages, of all spheres, of all creatures."[17]

For Kuyper there are three stages of the kingdom of God.

> The kingdom of heaven is a tangible reality which was present on earth in paradise, which was banished from this earth through sin and the curse, and which, returning with Christ from heaven and begun at his manger and the cross, has actually come to power again on earth. (*E Voto* IV:470)

In the period of the Old Testament Jehovah was reigning. But the Old Testament constantly looked forward to the reign of the Messiah. The kingdom of heaven in a real sense began with the first coming of Jesus. It was John the Baptist who said, "Repent, for the kingdom of heaven is near" (Matthew 3:2).[18] The kingdom of Christ, according to Kuyper, began with the first coming of Christ.

Kuyper says of this kingdom: "it can never be said that this kingdom bears a purely *spiritual* character" (*PrRege* I:412). This is evident from the three years of Jesus' ministry. "In the few years that the king of the kingdom of God stayed on earth, he revealed the majesty of this kingdom of his in every area of human life" (*PrRege* I:471). Jesus brought regeneration to the soul and physical healing to the body; he impacted all dimensions of society, including the family, the workplace, the government and the poor; and he confronted the evil spirits (*PrRege* I:472–74). Kuyper stated: "The idea that the action of Jesus in his kingdom was exclusively *spiritual* in nature seems . . . ever more untenable" (*PrRege* I:475). There is no nature-grace dualism here.

In his three-volume *Pro Rege*, Kuyper lists seven representative areas of Christ's kingly rule. The first area is the lives of individual believers.

The heart of Christ's kingdom is the true believers. The believers are those who respond willingly to the reign of Christ. Using language from earthly kingdoms, Kuyper calls the believers Christ's "subjects" (*PrRege* II:1). He enumerates various duties of these subjects: they are to confess their king, be witnesses to their king, take up their cross, be soldiers for their king and deny themselves for their king (*PrRege* II:22–74). It is Christ's subjects who will serve their king in the world.

These subjects form the mystical body of Christ. There is a bond of love that binds Christ to his subjects. Not only is there a master-servant relationship but also a relationship of friendship. We are Christ's friends (*PrRege* II:12–21).

Kuyper says that Christians are not are not "new people" who are newly created but rather people from the created world who are "renewed." Christians are new people only in the sense that they are renewed. That is the meaning of "rebirth" (*PrRege* II:126). For Kuyper there is continuity between creation and redemption in the life of a believer.

The second area of Christ's rule is the church. Although the mystical body of Christ is the invisible church, "Christ also desired and established here on earth an external, visible, perceptible manifestation of that body, and in this manifestation the body of Christ entered into the world as *the church of Christ*" (*PrRege* II:131). This is what is often called the visible church.

This church was established by Christ when he called the apostles and gave them the keys of the kingdom. Christ established the structure of this church by ordaining

---

17 Kuyper, A. 1895. *E Voto Dordraceno. Toelichting op den Heidelbergschen Catechismus*, vol. 4. Kampen: Kok: 465–66. Quotations from this work are my own translation—referenced further as *E Voto*.

18 See *PrRege* I:384–91, 405–408.

its sacraments, offices and discipline. The preaching of the Word is a central part of this church (*PrRege* II:139–234).

Although Jesus' kingdom is found in all of life,

> the congregation (*Gemeente*) . . . forms the living center of that kingdom, through which Christ allows the power of the Spirit to go out among the children of men in all the world and in all of history. The congregation forms the essential chief ingredient of his kingdom, and it is only in the congregation that his royal honor and majesty not only work but are also recognized and honored. (*PrRege* I:340)

The third area of Christ's rule is the family. A Christian family is one that is rooted in creation. It conforms to the creational norms. But sin interfered. Therefore, "Christ is redeemer also for the family life" (*PrRege* II:362; see also 369). A Christian family will "not lose its original ordinances but rather will be brought back to the purity of these original ordinances." This is "not the bringing in of something new but the restoration of the old which was spoiled" (*PrRege* II:356). There is thus no nature-grace dualism here. Christ is the creator *and* the redeemer of the family.

The Christian family is guided by creational norms. But how do we know what these norms are? Kuyper finds them in Scripture. The fifth commandment of the Law of Moses tells children how to behave. Paul expanded upon this command in Ephesians. In 1 Corinthians 11 Paul explained the creational hierarchy.[19] Thus there is no conflict between creational and scriptural norms. Both govern the Christian family; both come from Christ the creator and redeemer.

Finally, a Christian family will have a family altar. Kuyper says that "a family is not Christian only because a family altar is established, but a Christian family is not conceivable where the family altar is absent" (*PrRege* II:465).

The fourth area of Christ's rule is society. Society is a separate sphere between the family and the state. Kuyper begins this section by describing the cosmic struggle between the spirit of Christ and the spirit of the world. The "spirit of the world restlessly renews its attack on the kingdom of Christ," and "this will persist until the spirit of the world has exhausted its last strength." In the end, the power of Christ our king will defeat the spirit of the world. "But if this is the nature of Christ's kingship, how is it possible for this kingship to be restricted to his church, the family and the state and not to society?" Kuyper reminds the reader that the statements of Scripture about Christ's kingship are all-embracing. "To him is given *all power* on earth and in heaven. *All things* are subject to him. Nothing is excluded." So how can one neglect "this broad terrain of our social life" (*PrRege* II:8–9)?

Many Christians feel the claim of Christ over their personal lives but not "over the broad terrain of life where the scepter of Jesus' kingship extends." The result is "that the kingship of Christ does not *live* for them." For them Christ is there exclusively for the salvation of their souls but not for the life outside of the church (*PrRege* II:10–11).

These pietistic Christians are like house sparrows. "The big society with its richly developed life does not exist for them. And even if they do read a newspaper, they are only attracted to the obituaries and the advertisements. The rest does not interest them." But, even house sparrows fly around on occasion, while these people do not! (*PrRege* II:26). Such provincial Christians are practical examples of the two-kingdom doctrine.

---

19 *PrRege* II:379–85, 437–44.

Societal life is grounded in creation. In the Garden of Eden, there was a social relation between Adam and Eve. Sin distorted this relationship, but Christ came to restore society and establish a Christian society (*PrRege* III:15–23). "Christian" here "does not mean a new discovery and a new creation but a return to the original creation." In the Christian society, the original creational ordinances are honored (*PrRege* III:23). Thus, "the royal rule of Christ over societal life is bound to these ordinances" (*PrRege* III:22).

In Kuyper there is no conflict between creational ordinances and the Word of God. Both express the will of God. Kuyper writes: "For on almost every point in the social question, God's Word gives us the most positive direction" (*PP* 61). Kuyper lists the family, marriage, colonialization, work and state intervention as areas which God's Word addresses.

So how does Christ rule in society? Kuyper identifies at least four means of Christ's rule: the Christian church, the Christian school, the Christian organization and the Christian press (public opinion) (*PrRege* III:164–204). Again, Kuyper rejects the two-kingdom doctrine: "The inaccurate and superficial idea that Christ is only our savior and redeemer and not also our king and judge is completely rejected precisely through the Christian school" (*PrRege* III:183).

The need for Christian organizations is partly grounded in Paul's complaint about Christians taking brothers to court before unbelievers. But the rationale is deeper. There is a danger when Christians participate in a mixed organization. For then, "unconsciously they will exchange the principle of the Christian life for the impure principle of the worldly society" (*PrRege* III:189). Therefore, Kuyper recommends separate Christian organizations.

The fifth area of Christ's kingship is the state or the political arena. The state was not present in creation; instead, the state is a product of God's common grace that was revealed in the history of mankind especially after the flood and the tower of Babel. Here too the reign of Christ extends.

Kuyper identifies three main ways in which Christ rules the state. First, Christ influences and directs political leaders, both pagan and Christian. Examples of the former are Joseph's Pharaoh, Cyrus and Nebuchadnezzar. But Christ also governs Christian rulers like Constantine, Charlemagne and the house of Orange. Some of these rulers applied Christian principles in their kingdoms (*PrRege* III:272–82).

Christ also rules the state through the law. Kuyper speaks of a "mystical law" which is valid for all peoples and all lands. This divine law can be found both in our conscience and in Scripture. There is no opposition between the two since both came from Christ the creator and redeemer. There is only one law of God. Of course, we cannot apply the Mosaic law directly to our contemporary life. But the Mosaic law, like the New Testament, contains principles that are relevant for our contemporary nations. A Christian government should bring its laws into conformity with the principles of Christ (*PrRege* III:282–93).

Christ also rules the state through Christian political parties. In the Europe of Kuyper's day, there were parties that were advocating anti-Christian principles. The Christian forces must fight against such principles. This is why Groen van Prinsterer advocated "the party of the living God" to combat such ideas. Christians who for many years have honored Christ as the savior of his church must now begin to honor Christ as the king over the state (*PrRege* III:302, 304).

The sixth area of Christ's reign is the realm of science or scholarship (*wetenschap*).

"Kingship is power," says Kuyper, opening this section. When we talk of Jesus' power, we are talking of Jesus as king. Scripture has at least ten references to the power of Christ over all things. But the church of Christ has often put his kingship in the shadow, despite the testimony of Scripture "that *all things*, except God the Father, have been given to him and placed under his feet. How then can science . . . be removed from the power of Christ?" (*PrRege* III:354–55). Science too must be brought under the lordship of Christ.

Jesus Christ is the truth: "True science, both of visible and invisible things, in the end boils down to a science of Christ, because in him are hidden all treasures of knowledge and wisdom" (*PrRege* III:464). Christ's majesty requires one to research visible things, to understand the science that is in Christ, and "to bring the knowledge of the visible and the invisible things together in the harmony of one's faith consciousness." We cannot separate the knowledge of the visible and invisible things. Nature is the greatest theater of God's glory (*PrRege* III:466–67).

The final area of Christ's kingship in this study is the area of art. Art (*kunst*) is an ability (*kunnen*) from God. It is a gift from God which can be used properly or misused. Art is both an instrument and an inspiration. As an instrument or means of influence, art is completely neutral. But the spirit of art determines whether the art is Christian or not. If the spirit of the art is godly, then the art will point us to God; but if the spirit of art is demonic, then the art too will point us away from God (*PrRege* III:531–33).

Around 1910 Kuyper was negative towards modern painting and music. He felt that there was a real danger of idolatry. The artist and his or her art were often idolized, and the art itself easily became self-autonomous (*PrRege* III:526–29). Huge crowds would go to the art galleries and the artist would be worshiped, but the art was bad: "If it is more naked, it is better; if it is more filthy and coarse, it is more expensive." Modern music was not much better. Kuyper feared that modern art and music were becoming another Sodom and Gomorrah (*PrRege* III:530).

For Kuyper a "special relation exists between art and Christ." This is easily missed by those two-kingdom people who see Christ only as the savior of our souls. The question must be asked "whether art itself as such lies within the government of the king of God's kingdom" (*PrRege* III:534–35). The answer is positive since Christ's creation also belongs to his kingdom. There is continuity between his creation and redemption. The new earth of Revelation 21 will not be a "newly created world, but a *recreated* one; it will not be a different world, but the same one" (*PrRege* III:537).

Kuyper says:

> Of course the Redeemer and Savior has significance for the world of beauty since sin and the curse brought disturbance, desecration and corruption also in this world of beauty." Sin is "a deviation from the original state of affairs," and thus "the reconciliation [*Verzoening*] brings about nothing else than purification in the world of this distorted beauty. (*PrRege* III:544–45)

Art belongs both to the world of creation and redemption. "Not only *Christian* art, but art *in itself*, no matter how misused and polluted, belongs to Christ's kingly territory. . . . The only proper appreciation of the world of beauty depends on a confession of the divinity of Christ" (*PrRege* III:545).

The kingship of Christ over all of life is powerfully stated in Kuyper's three-volume *Pro Rege*. But Kuyper laments the fact that this kingship of Christ is constantly rejected in his day. In 1910 he put Islam at the top of the list. Islam does not recognize the kingship of Christ. But in "Christian" Europe there is also a "darkening" of Christ's kingship. Scientific and technological developments reduce our dependence on God. Modernism as seen in the world cities, the growth of capital and modern art glorify man instead of Christ (*PrRege* I:1–112).

But within the church there is also an undermining of Christ's kingship. When Christ's kingship is limited to the visible church – in the two-kingdom dualistic fashion – then his royal power is limited. Bad theology leads to an undermining of Christ's kingship. Kuyper criticizes the "sentimental longing for heaven" of the pietists and other dualists. When they pray "Thy kingdom come," they are only thinking about escape from this world and a personal flight of their souls to heaven. "In the realm of sentimentality there is an enthusiasm for a sort of spirit life, a desire to have it good for oneself and to spend eternity with other passionate souls" (*E Voto* IV:476). This theology is essentially selfish.

The Reformed longing for heaven is totally different. It is focused on God's glory and God's kingdom, and it has to do with all of life. Your God is "not a holy, heavenly emergency help who only exists to pour out his blessings on this earthly kingdom, and then to disappear out of your thoughts. Your God is in heaven as the one and only center who draws everything to himself" (*E Voto* IV:477–78).

This pietistic dualism also exists within the Reformed churches. In Islam, religion relates "to every area of life." But Kuyper laments "how seldom in Christendom the broad scope of the kingship of Christ is felt" (*PrRege* III:580). Even our Heidelberg Catechism is weak on this point. The answer to question 31 about the kingship of Christ speaks about personal salvation "but is silent about the broader significance, and precisely this silence has led to a one-sided view of the kingship over the believers" (*PrRege* III:583).

Conclusion

Since Abraham Kuyper has such a strong belief in the kingship of Christ over all of life, it is clear that it is inappropriate to speak of a two-kingdom doctrine in Kuyper. The kingdom of God in his theology is not the institutional church but is found in all of life. As he put it, "the Kingdom of God is not in the least limited to the institutional church but rules our entire world-and-life view."[20]

Since Kuyper does not hold to a two-kingdom doctrine, this calls into question the persistent and ill-advised use of "Reformed two-kingdom doctrine" by Van Drunen. Our dualist delights in pointing to an alleged two-kingdom doctrine throughout the Reformed tradition. But if Kuyper does not teach a two-kingdom doctrine, then it is questionable to what extent other Reformed theologians hold to this same teaching.

The theology of Kuyper in the tradition of Calvin stresses the lordship of Christ over all of life. This is a radical difference from Luther's two-kingdom doctrine. If indeed "there is not a square inch in the whole domain of our human existence over which Christ, who is Sovereign over *all*, does not cry: 'Mine!'"[21] then Christ's kingdom is broader than the institutional church. His kingdom impacts all of life.

---

20 "Common Grace in Science." In *AK:ACR* 458.
21 "Sphere Sovereignty." In *AK:ACR* 488.

14

Kuyper's Philosophy of Science

Herman Dooyeweerd

Introduction

It did take some time before I was able to decide to publish the paper that I presented at the Annual Meeting of the Association for Calvinistic Philosophy on *Kuyper's Philosophy of Science*. I hesitated because I had found myself compelled to lay the finger on certain lines of thought in the writings of Kuyper, Woltjer, and Bavinck that are in no way compatible with the *reformational basic conception* as it was developed particularly by Kuyper. The critique that I came to formulate in respect of these Calvinistic thinkers was not something "pleasant" for me. They were my tutors and I have great respect and love for them, as well as for the pioneering work that they accomplished in a time when being at the Free University was still seen as a sign of abdicating from a scientific conscience.

In addition, continuing with the positive elaboration of the *Philosophy of the Cosmonomic Idea* on the foundations that they laid seemed more fruitful an endeavor, insofar as these are indeed rooted in their reformational basic conception, than to criticize specific components of their labor that can hardly be reconciled with this conception.

But when the *Philosophy of the Cosmonomic Idea* was accused from a certain corner of "undermining" the work of Kuyper, Bavinck, and Woltjer and when conceptions of the latter two were repeatedly raised against this philosophy, it became clear to me that it was no longer possible to escape from *rendering an account* of the critical screening to which the *Philosophy of the Cosmonomic Idea* indeed subjected their philosophical views. Every misunderstanding in this regard could have in the long run led to disastrous consequences and possibly generated the false impression that the adherents of this philosophy had something to hide regarding their attitude towards the "reformed tradition in philosophical thought."

For that is certainly *not* the case! It is not a lack of piety or respect for the pioneers of the previous generation that occupied the forefront in this critical sifting work. Rather the latter is actually completely in line with their *reformational orientation*. A lack of *true* piety towards their pioneering work would be at play if, *contrary to one's own best judgment*, attempts were made to maintain some of their philosophical conceptions as *reformed* when it can be demonstrated that they cannot be tolerated by the scriptural-biblical religious basic conception of the Reformation because they clearly originate from a pagan or a

---

Translated by D. F. M. Strauss; edited by John H. Kok.

humanistic point of departure. Not even a tradition of centuries is able to eradicate the original mistake present in such views.

When Jan Woltjer Sr.'s philosophy of science, in connection with that of Kuyper, is subjected in what follows to serious critique, this may not be interpreted as us giving Woltjer the boot. The issue merely concerns the philosophical conceptions of Woltjer that are currently circulating within the differences of opinion and used as weapons against the *Philosophy of the Cosmonomic Idea*.

To highlight another side of Woltjer's philosophical ideas here, those that had a sound effect on the *Philosophy of the Cosmonomic Idea*, would not be difficult. Woltjer, however, compared to Kuyper, did not publish very much, and it is undeniably the case that epistemological views found in some of his published addresses, against which the *Philosophy of the Cosmonomic Idea* would raise its most serious objections, have decisively influenced many in the circle of reformed scholars. He worked these views out in such a complete and consistent fashion that one is inclined to either fully *accept* or *reject* them. This clearly speaks to Woltjer's critical philosophical spirit, who in his epistemological views did not allow for any divergence – once a basic idea is accepted he pursues it with an inflexible logic. But it also in a much sharper way highlights the discrepancy between Woltjer's theory of science and his reformational religious basic conception.

The critique that follows of certain of his views does not mean to lay *blame* on a thinker who took the lead in arguing the warrant of reformed scholarship. Doing so would evidence a serious form of ingratitude for a thinker who lived in a period in which, according to Kuyper himself, reformed scholarship was still a sprig, unable to deliver straightaway a sound theory of research and scholarship [*wetenschap*] in which the religious basic conception of Calvinism – defended by him with so much force – had reached complete fruition. Reproach is only then in place if it is attempted to hold on to these views during the next period after it has been demonstrated extensively and with sound arguments that these conceptions are not any longer useful within a reformed context.

If it then still happens that the "tradition" is used against the *Philosophy of the Cosmonomic Idea* without taking into account the to-the-point reasons which led to the abandonment of those traditional philosophical views, while at the same time ignoring the *positive* contribution of the *Philosophy of the Cosmonomic Idea* to the construction of a reformational philosophy, then such an attitude rightfully deserves the reproach that it does not pursue the reformational line of the triumvirate of Kuyper, Bavinck, and Woltjer. It has been said so many times that repeating it almost becomes boring: The *Philosophy of the Cosmonomic Idea* does not pretend infallibility either in respect of its positive philosophical conceptions or with regard to its critique on traditional philosophy.

But it is justified that its adherents demand that their work will be taken seriously both by kindred spirits and those who in principle oppose it and that a serious consideration will be dedicated to it.

This also applies to what follows as a discussion of Kuyper's philosophy of science.[1] I will be pleased to receive a critical appraisal of the views presented in my exposition if it is focused on the real issues and if it – in the case of like-minded people – rests on grounds

---

1   For this purpose the paper read at the last Annual Meeting of the Association for Calvinistic Philosophy has been expanded considerably. These elaborations will mainly be found in those text portions that are indented on both the left and the right.

derived from the biblical-reformational starting point.

Indeed then such an exchange of ideas must bear fruit.

* * *

In the issue of *Reformation* commemorating Kuyper I have contributed an article with the title: "What the *Philosophy of the Cosmonomic Idea* owes to Dr. Kuyper." It was at once meant to serve as a defense against the continued accusation coming from a certain corner that the *Philosophy of the Cosmonomic Idea* signified a negative twist to the lines drawn by Kuyper as an expression of the reformed tradition of Calvinistic thought. As far as I know no attempt has been made to invalidate this fundamental defense. But of course it stands to reason that this as yet did not win the plea in front of these like-minded opponents.

The crux of the matter is that Calvinistic thought in the recent time arrived at a crossroad and that both diverging approaches merged in Kuyper's scholarly work. It is possible to argue that this situation flows from the many-sidedness of Kuyper and that it is only the reprehensible one-sidedness of his followers that ought to receive the blame for the current differences of opinion. But this representation of the issue would be too simplistic to be true. The only condition upon which it could have been acceptable is that within Kuyper's thought the said divergence indeed acquired an inner reconciliation.

But this is not the case.

The truth is that it can be shown that both trends of thought in Kuyper's scientific work are in conflict with each other and that an inner reconciliation is precluded by the fact that they proceed from mutually exclusive starting points.

It is remarkable that this divergence mainly restricts itself to Kuyper's systematic scientific labor where he frequently attempts to find a point of connection in traditional philosophical conceptions. But in those contexts where he remained fully true to himself and developed his majestic understanding of the Calvinistic life and world view, he indeed built upon the reformational religious basic principle, which enabled him to produce work with an unparalleled principled clarity and sharpness, work from "one piece." His famous "Stone" lectures, *Het Calvinisme*, is probably the best example in this regard, although one has to be critical about its historical constructions.

As soon as Kuyper attempts to pursue this religious basic conception of Calvinism in his systematic scholarly work it appears to be the case that its powerful scope is hampered and that the solid direction is lost. Undoubtedly the reformational basic principle is maintained and wherever Kuyper clings to this line also his scientific grasp may indeed be called reformational while accomplishing foundational work for Christian thought as a whole. Yet it was not possible for this principle to work itself out freely. A second direction of thought manifested itself, namely, the traditional attempt to establish a synthesis between the Christian starting point and that of immanence philosophy. That then leads to a reception of a considerable amount of traditional philosophical ideas which are not compatible with the religious choice made by Kuyper. This philosophical legacy is partially from a scholastic origin and partially stems from modern epistemology.

The scholastic line mainly expresses itself in the view of soul and body, the theory of the *logos*, and in the idea-realism, while the modern influence manifests itself in the various subdivisions of Kuyper's philosophy of science, which bears the stamp of critical realism.

One may be tempted once again to add a remark that makes a plea for the many-sidedness of Kuyper and that points at his willingness to follow the line of historical continuity causing him not to throw overboard without any piety those traditional philosophical conceptions which reformed thinkers from the beginning took over from scholastic philosophy. This remark will also allude to his openness for the philosophical needs of the modern era in that he did not hesitate in his philosophy of science to learn from modern epistemology.

But unfortunately the issue is not that simple. I shall consider the second point later, but regarding the first one the following needs to be said. The argument about the necessity of honoring the historical continuity in Calvinistic philosophy loses its effect in the face of the undeniable fact that according to all those who are well-informed about the issue, a truly Calvinistic tradition of philosophical thought does not exist. The Reformation never succeeded in developing its own philosophy on the basis of its reformational Christian basic conception.[2] What is derived from the philosophical ideas of the traditional school philosophy has no claim to be acknowledged as belonging to a *Christian* philosophical tradition if it may turn out to be the case that it unbreakably coheres with a philosophical starting point that is at odds with the religious basic principle of the Reformation.

This lack of a truly Christian philosophy becomes even more important in the light of the fact that within Scholastic philosophy the large majority of thinkers in principle rejects the idea of a Christian philosophy.

From the perspective of Roman Catholicism this view is justified because it completely matches the traditional Roman view of the relation between nature and grace. Nature is after all seen as the autonomous portal to the sphere of grace, and philosophy, belonging to the realm of nature within this mind-set, only remains philosophy as long as it follows the light of "natural reason" apart from the Divine Word revelation in Christ. Even though natural reason (*naturalis ratio*) may harbor an inner longing for knowledge exceeding the limits of its own disposition, the fulfillment of this desire cannot be obtained within the domain of philosophy itself. This higher knowledge lies outside the sphere of philosophy. It resides within the grace-domain of the church.

The scholastic theory about soul and body, which – as a traditional thomistic-aristotelian understanding – was largely taken over by reformed thinkers, is therefore not entitled to lay claim to the qualification that it is a Christian philosophic conception.

> According to this theory, soul and body are two incomplete substances (*substantiae incompleta*), while the 'immortal soul" as "anima rationalis" (rational soul) is designated as the *"substantial form"* of the body. In the well-known difference of opinion between Voetius and his Cartesian colleague Leroy (Regius) the former explicitly defended this view of the "school philosophy."[3] Traces of this view are clearly seen in the terminology of the *Westminster Confession*. When

---

2   Compare also the statement of Hepp in his *Testimonium Spiritus Sancti* (p.57): "that Christendom never produced a philosophy true to its root." His subsequent exposition shows that he sincerely regrets this state of affairs.

3   Cf. Voetius, G. *Dispp. Selectae* t. I:870–881, in particular the exposition *De rerum naturis et formis substantialibus*. In particular he here defends the logic, metaphysics, and physics of school philosophy ("nominatim logicam, metaphysicam et physicam" – op. cit. pp.871–872). Regarding his synthesis point of view, compare his *De errore et haeresi* (*Dispp.* t. V:74): "Est ergo Philosophia (scl. Peripatetica) accomodanda ad Theologiam Christianam, non contra."

my honored colleague Hepp therefore calls upon this confession (in the second brochure of the series *Dreigende Deformatie* [Threatening Deformation], it only demonstrates how careful one has to be with citations when an attempt is made to see the battle against the aristotelian-scholastic view of the soul as a deviation from the confessions, while at the same time it is denied that the *philosophical* conception of scholastic psychology is protected.

For binding an ecclesiastical confession to the Scholastic-Aristotelian philosophy would be more than a threatening deformation. Such a binding would only take place as the *result* of a process of deformation and therefore it should not be attributed to anyone in the current differences of opinion. Even such a convinced adherent to scholastic philosophy as Voetius definitely refused – in his struggle against the Cartesians regarding the soul – to bring the whole issue to an ecclesiastical forum in spite of the fact that the Cartesian soul conception indeed threatened the church dogma.[4]

In itself this of course does not show yet that this theory would not be useful in a Calvinistic philosophy.

The *Philosophy of the Cosmonomic Idea* never defended the view that a philosophy springing from a non-Christian root cannot contain important elements of truth.[5]

To my mind the impossibility to accept traditional views such as these within a reformational philosophy is demonstrated when it can be shown that they are not to be reconciled with the religious basic conception of the Calvinistic reformation.

I have extensively demonstrated the latter in respect of the traditional view of the soul as a substance centered in reason. This view definitely clashes with the reformational understanding of the radical fallenness of human nature, but it does harmoniously fit the Roman Catholic view of nature and grace. Rome indeed constantly rejected the doctrine of radical depravity.

Since the Scholastic soul-body conception forbids it *per se* to acknowledge the heart in its biblical sense as the center of human nature, it must lead to anthropological results that can never be incorporated in a Calvinistic philosophy.

> It should always be kept in mind that the Aristotelian conception of the soul as *anima rationalis* is intrinsically connected to Aristotle's metaphysical theological idea of God as "pure" or "absolute Reason."
>
> Self-knowledge after all unbreakably coheres with the knowledge of God.
>
> If "reason" indeed is to be seen as the essential core of human nature, as it is alleged in the Scholastic-Aristotelian theory regarding the "soul" as "substantial form," then no room is left for the *radical* depravity of human nature as an effect of the fall. For that matter, no one ever located the *root* of sin in "natural reason."
>
> The Scholastic theory therefore referred sin to the lower "faculty of desire" as

---

4   Regius defends the thesis that the union of body and soul does not produce an entity "per se" but only "per accidens." Voetius saw in this theory – undoubtedly rightly so – a threat to the dogma regarding the incarnation of the Word.

5   It also never denied the *scientific* character of a philosophical theory merely on the basis that such a theory is rooted in the immanence standpoint. To the contrary, by virtue of its Christian starting point the *Philosophy of the Cosmonomic Idea* strongly made a plea for *scholarly tolerance* – which in fact is seriously endangered through the dogma of the autonomy of thought.

its source. It conceived "faith" as a "donum superadditum," as a supra-natural gift of grace to the *intellect*.[6] Through sin this gift was lost. But "natural reason" is not corrupted through this loss, since at most it is "wounded" by it. As such it remains the *good* essential core of human nature.

Aristotle taught – undoubtedly in line with Plato – that only the *nous*, the rational soul-part, is immortal. It is not certain that he also accepted *individual* immortality, since he found the principle of individuation (*principium individuationis*) in "matter." Aristotle assumed that generated as an animal, that is to say, merely endowed with an animal essential form, the sensitive soul (*anima sensitiva*), the human being would have its "immortal reason" implanted "from the outside." It was not possible for Thomas Aquinas to take over this theory unaltered, because in this form it would clash with the entire church tradition. He did accept the Aristotelian view that the human being receives from its parents only the "anima sensitiva et vegetative" (animal soul and plant soul),[7] while the "anima rationalis" is implanted from the outside through a separate act of creation by God (this is the so-called psycho-creationistic conception).[8] But he accommodated this Aristotelian conception to the church tradition in the sense that he proceeded from the *simplicity* and *unity* of the human soul and ascribed individual immortality to the entire soul with all its natural "abilities." However, this conception could only be carried through if it is accepted – while still continuing the Aristotelian legacy – that the rational soul as "substantia incompleta" (incomplete substance) at its entry into the human body disrupts (currumpit) the already present "anima sensitiva et nutritiva (vegetativa)" in its animal nature. Out of itself it now develops these "lower" soul-functions in a *typically human* way that is, within this conception, essentially *rational*.[9]

The above-mentioned psycho-creationistic view is once again in harmony with the Roman Catholic understanding of human nature. However, the reception of this theory by reformed theologians naturally had to lead to the same irreconcilable conflicts with the reformational basic conception regarding the radical corruption that we have noticed in connection with the view of the soul as "anima rationalis."

Reformed theology now faced a dilemma: *either* one has to accept that in the separate creation of the "anima rationalis" God created a "corrupted soul," which is unacceptable, *or* sin must have its origin in the *anima sensitiva* and the body, which had to contradict the doctrine of the radical fall.[10] It is not possible for

---

6   Cf. Aquinas, Thomas *Summa Theologica*, II, II q. IV art. II jᵒ q. VII

7   *Summa Theologica*, 1 q. 77 a 7c: ". . . imperfectiores potentiae sunt priores in via generationis, prius enim animal generatur quam homo."

8   *Summa Theologica*, q. XCVIII a. II: "Ed ideo haereticum est dicere, quod anima intellectiva traducatur cum simine."

9   Thomas Aquinas did not acquire clarity about the union of this dual generation (namely, the natural abilities resulting "from below" and those flowing from "above" from the essential form of being human). This tension is treated in a striking way by Gustav Siewerth in his work: *Die Metaphysik der Erkenntnis nach Thomas von Aquin* (Munich and Berlin, 1933, pp. 22ff.).

10   Whoever knows the *Philosophy of the Cosmonomic Idea* will understand that the rejection of the psycho-creationistic view in its traditional sense does not entail the acceptance of the traditional position of traducianism, which for that matter does not question the Scholastic conception of body and soul.

me to discuss the supposed "solutions" to this antinomy. The semi-romanticizing view that since the fall God would have created the rational soul without *justitia originalis* in the sense of a "higher faculty" though without sin, because sin merely occurs when this faculty is employed in a certain direction, can neither be reconciled with the doctrine of original sin [*erfzonde*] nor with the doctrine of the radical fall as a *condition*. This antinomy turns out to be even worse when it is attempted to combine the traditional conception with the Scriptural view of the *religious* character of the center of human nature.

What is naturally more important for a Calvinistic philosophy than a purely theological investigation of these "solutions" is the search for the *origin* of the antinomy evinced in this attempted synthesis of two soul conceptions that radically exclude each other: that of Aristotelian Scholasticism regarding the *anima rationalis* and that of the Biblical view about the religious *root* of human existence – corrupted by sin but reborn in Christ.

The entire ecclesiastical doctrine about the "simplicity" only fits the *heart* in the sense of the *religious center* of human nature, in which we indeed transcend the temporal diversity of functions and where our entire existence is concentrated in its religious *root-unity*.

On the standpoint of immanence-philosophy – which gave birth to the theory of the *anima rationalis* as substantial form – this "simplicity" cannot be maintained without inner contradictions.[11]

The religious root of human existence, as unity of our self-awareness and consciousness of God, is indeed "simple." And as such transcends theoretical concept-formation. But the "anima rationalis" is a theoretical abstraction from the temporal human body and as such remains caught in a theoretical diversity of "functions" or "capacities" (according to the Scholastic psychology).

Stating the "simplicity" of the soul necessarily contradicts the view that the "intellect" is its essence and that the "body" is its "matter."[12] For the intellect after all is within this conception not the *entire* soul.

In the Aristotelian-Platonic theory of immortality this clearly comes to expression. Here immortality is only reserved for the *nous* – viewed as the intellect purified from all sensitive functions (the rational part of the soul in Plato).

An after-effect of the Scholastic theory regarding the supposed "simplicity" of the rational soul (*anima rationalis*) is found in Kant's epistemology where he proclaims – in the criticistic sense of a "transcendental unity of apperception" – that the I-ness is the logical form-unity of all theoretical synthesis. This "logical form-unity of the I-ness," which is supposed also to transcend the diversity of

---

11 Thomas Aquinas discusses this issue in his *Summa Theologica* (1 q. LXXVII a. VI and attempts in vain to solve it with the Scholastic distinction between *forma substantialis* and *accidentalis*.)

12 Much to the point is the remark of Siewerth (op. cit., pp.27–28): "What mounts at this point is the question about the possibility of a real, vital, substantial union of a uniform, spiritual actual form – which does not perform any act in itself – with a purely passive substrate. It is the problem of the abilities and activities of what is composite and unified. This uncertainty and lack of clarity in an encompassing and founding manner remains the ground of the fate of a Thomistic theory of the soul in all its parts where on the whole the analogue of the metaphysical composition of the secondary form and matter is encountered."

thought categories,[13] must serve as a transcendental-logical unity ABOVE the logical diversity. But this is the embodied self-contradiction, which can only be explained as an after-effect of the Metaphysical-Scholastic conception of the simplicity and indivisibility of the "*anima rationalis*" in Kant's epistemology.

In a *logical* sense there is only a modal logical unity *within* a logical diversity, but no unity that *transcends* this diversity. In his "Paralogisms of rational Psychology" Kant rejected the metaphysical twist Scholasticism gave to this theory. What he did not realize is that its *epistemological turn*[14] must terminate in the same antinomies!

What also properly belongs to the traditional Scholastic conception of the soul is the question what kind of activity is still found in the "immortal soul" *after* its separation from the body. This entire problem flows from a soul conception that views the "soul" as a theoretical abstraction from the full temporal existence of the human being.

Once this path of abstraction is chosen the question becomes unavoidable what there is that remains for the separated rational soul when it is *conceived* in isolation from its pre-psychical functions.

The *Philosophy of the Cosmonomic Idea*, which had demonstrated the *unbreakable* temporal-cosmic coherence of *all* modal functions, answers to this question: nothing remains![15] At the moment of natural death the entire temporal existence – and not a mere *abstraction* from it – is left behind.

The traditional substance-concept in the final analysis rests on nothing else but an internally antinomic reification of a given functional complex which by virtue of the order of creation is in self-insufficiency connected to all other functions.

For this reason the *Philosophy of the Cosmonomic Idea* does not account for the Scriptural dichotomy of soul and body in terms of what is temporal, but in terms of the bi-unity of the supra-temporal religious center or root (the "heart" or "soul") and the entire temporal functional garb (the "body").

The "religious center" is not a theoretical abstraction from temporal existence, but the full, concrete unity of self-consciousness and the awareness of what is divine, the *self-hood* of the human being or the "inner person" in the Scriptural sense of the term.

For this reason the question about which functions or capacities are left for the "anima separata" (separated soul) does not have any meaning from this point of view. The "simplicity" of the religious center of existence lies in its religious nature

---

13 *Critique of Pure Reason*, Transcendental Logic, Second Part, paragraphs 15 & 16.

14 See the *Critique of Pure Reason*, General Remark concerning the transition from rational psychology to cosmology (Edition Groszherzog Wilhelm Ernst, pp. 322–323: "Thought, considered as such, is merely the logical function and therefore pure spontaneity in the combination of the multiplicity of a merely possible intuition. . . . Through it I conceive myself neither as I am, nor as I appear, but I solely think of myself as any object as such, from which kind of intuition I perform an abstraction."

15 This statement should not be misinterpreted. The answer "nothing" only refers to an abstraction from the temporal function-complex of the soul, an abstraction which was elevated by Scholastic psychology to a "substance." The "soul" certainly is not a theoretical abstraction. It is a concrete unity. This not in the least entails a rejection of the confession of the "resurrection of the flesh" and the fundamental identity of the functional garb [*functiemantel*] after resurrection.

as concentrated root-unity of existence, which as such also forms the center of the entire *conscious* life.

By contrast, this question indeed constitutes the crux of the "philosophical psychology" of the Scholastic natural theology.

When one seriously reads the expositions of Thomas Aquinas in the first part of his *Summa Theologica* in this regard, the artificial and internally antinomic nature of the traditional soul conception is striking.

Thomas Aquinas holds that in the soul as separated from the body (*anima separata a corpore* – see *Summa Theologica*, Pars I, Questio LXXVII, Art.VIII) abilities such as the intellect and the will (according to him the *appetitus intellectivus*) are found and that these *pure* capabilities of the soul *necessarily* continue to be present in the soul after the demolition of the body. By contrast the sensitive and the vegetative functions belong together to body and soul as substances. Therefore when the body is demolished these functions do not continue in an *actual* way, since they merely *potentially* continue to reside in the soul (*sicut in principio aut radice*– see *Summa Theologica*, I, q. LXXVII, a. VIII). These functions indeed require for their activities a *bodily organ*. At this point a new difficulty arises, namely how the "separated soul" can still know anything. After all, although according to the Aristotelian-Thomistic epistemology the human intellect can operate independent of the brain as bodily organ, it nonetheless is a *tabula rasa* (a clean lay). Concepts are only abstracted by thought from the sensory *phantasmata* and in order to absorb the latter sense-organs are required. In *questio* LXXXIX, art. I Thomas extensively discussed this issue. The many "difficulties and counter-arguments" discussed here already demonstrates to what an extent this issue caused an embarrassment for him. He cannot find a solution other than holding that the "separated soul" could neither know through inborn concepts nor through "abstracted species," and also not through the recollection of species, but only through species that are communicated through an "in-flowing of the light from the divine intellect." Whereas this divine illumination would be the "natural knowing mode" of the angels, and therefore amongst them would lead to a perfectly clear knowledge, with the human being it is "*praeter rationem suae naturae*" since the natural knowledge here entails the connection between body and soul and therefore merely yields a general and confused cognition (*cognitio confusa et communis*).

This solution, however, immediately generated a new problem. Does this knowledge still belong to human nature (see *Summa Theologica* LXXXIX a. I)? This is indeed a crucial issue for the traditional Scholastic conception regarding the "immortal soul" for according to this view the "soul" is the "substantial form," the *ontic form* of the human being.

If the knowledge of the "anima rationalis separata" (the separate rational soul) is no longer "natural," then the theory regarding the unchanged persistence of this "part" of human nature is seriously challenged. Thomas Aquinas solves this difficulty with a short statement: "*Nec tamen propter hoc cognitio vel potentia non est naturalis: quia Deus est auctor non solum influentiae gratuiti luminus, sed etiam naturalis.*"

But this "solution" does not touch the cardinal question. Indeed the question was not whether – in terms of the thomistic scheme of nature and grace – the intended knowledge belongs to the sphere of "grace," but if it can still be counted as part of *human* nature. In an earlier context Thomas Aquinas denied the latter when he remarked that this knowledge falls "*praeter rationem naturae suae (scl. Humane)*," even though he accepts within all intellectual substances ("*substantiae intellectivae*") a divine illumination.

Moreover, an *actual* knowledge purely derived from the influence of divine illumination is according to Thomas exclusively belonging to the essential nature of the angels. What he attempts to argue, nonetheless, is that the "*praeter rationem naturae*" is not yet the same as the *extra or supra naturam* and that the combination with the body only concerns the "*modus essendi animae raitonalis*," from which it follows that sense-based knowledge is merely the intellectual *mode* naturally belonging to the bond between body and soul. With this a comparison is made with those entities that are "light by nature," whose nature, according to the Aristotelian physics, does not alter when they find themselves outside their "natural place" (*Summa Theologica*, q. LXXXIX a. I). But this comparison derailed since in qu. LXXXIV (art. III) it was extensively argued that the human soul, in contrast to that of the angels, by nature can acquire *actual* knowledge *only through the mediation of the senses*. This is pertinently done with an appeal to the same comparison with the "natural upward movement of light bodies." In the case of the "light bodies" the "*esse levum*" is still "*solum in potentia*."

Similarly human knowledge exclusively consisting in species concepts would be purely potential in nature. It can only become *actual*, that is active, through the mediation of the "*phantasmata*" in sensory perception. But can this knowledge suddenly, *without* this mediation, become *actual* after the separation from the body? Within the argumentation of Thomas Aquinas this constitutes an inner antinomy.

Equally artificial is his answer to the question whether or not the separated human soul can still experience sadness and joy: "*tristitia et gaudium sunt in anima separata, non secundum appetitum sensitivum, sed secundum appetitum intellectivum; sicut etiam in angelis*" (*Summa Theologica* 1 q. LXXVII a. VIII).

But what kind of knowledge is it then that this speculative metaphysics about the continued existence of the soul intends to furnish? It is a speculative construction on the basis of empty concepts. Given its purely antichristian origin they can be maintained neither in a Christian theology nor in a Christian philosophy.

The same applies to the so-called idea-realism insofar as it would, in connection with the metaphysical *logos* theory, attempt to construct the temporal world order via the theory of the so-called *analogia entis* (analogy of being) out of human reason. The dilemma nominalism-realism is unacceptable on the Christian transcendence standpoint.

A truly Calvinistic philosophy that observes both trends of thought, namely the reformational and the scholastic, as being operative within the tradition of reformed thinking therefore cannot accept *either* of them.

The first insight necessary for the erection of such a philosophy is precisely *that in the past such an ambiguous attitude indeed caused the ineffectiveness of Calvinism within the domain of philosophy.* And exactly the same applies to attempts to accommodate the modern humanistic epistemology with its typical problems and method to the reformational basic conception.

Also here the irreconcilability of starting points in principle obstructs every synthesis attempt.

It is my intention to elaborate these theses more extensively through a critical assessment of Kuyper's philosophy of science

*   *   *

As is known, Kuyper developed his philosophy of science in the second volume of his "Encyclopedia of Sacred Theology" (*Encyclopaedie der Heilige Godsgeleerdheid*). It is important to note that the first impression of this work appeared in 1894, that is, three years after prof Woltjer senior presented his well-known oration on: "The Scholarly Knowledge of the Logos" (*De Wetenschap van den Logos*). This is of importance because the conceptions of Woltjer did influence Kuyper in a demonstrable way.

Two years after the appearance of the second part of Kuyper's *Encyclopedia* Woltjer published his oration: "Ideal and Real" (*Ideëel and Reëel*) in which he more fully develops his epistemological ideas. For the next generation it is highly intriguing to see how Woltjer, as rigorous logical thinker, in these two orations pursues a uniform line of argumentation up to its final destination, whereas in the thought of Kuyper, by contrast, owing to a dual line of argumentation, one observes a persistent inner divergence and contradiction. Though Woltjer presented us with explanations which are from a formal philosophical point of view on a higher level, this advantage was bought at the cost of almost completely relegating the religious basic conception, which Kuyper summarized in such powerful perspectives, to the background. But please do not misunderstand me. I do not contemplate for a moment to assert that Woltjer would not whole-heartedly have accepted this conception. I am convinced that he would have done that. But in Woltjer's *philosophy of science* the all-determining basic ideas of this conception did not come to expression because Woltjer consistently constructed his view on the basis of his *logos* theory. In the thought of Kuyper the latter only acquired a secondary importance. Intimately cohering with this we find an appreciation of science and scholarship in the thought of these two eminent Calvinistic thinkers that differs in principle.

Proceeding from his *logos* theory Woltjer allows himself to be tempted to come to an appraisal of science (in his *Ideëel and Reëel*) that borders upon an *overestimation* of science.

He writes that "science, according to the idea enclosed within it as it is enclosed within everything and the relationship of the things, constitutes a treasure, more precious than anything else." He traces the everything-surpassing value of science to the creation of the human being in God's image: The divine *Logos* expressed itself within the human logos: "The human spirit proceeds from God and knows within the created things its Creator and flourishes therefore in this knowledge."[16]

In a totally different way Kuyper expresses himself in his well-known views on "Twofold Science" in the second volume of his *Encyclopedia.* Here he states that:

---

16 *Verzamelde Opstellen*, p.219.

the palingenesis in the first place does not motivate scholarly labor. For that purpose it is too elevated, it is too noble in origin. One should be sober and awake from the intoxication which absorbed so many who became drunken from the wine of science. . . . Merely mention the one name of Christ Jesus and you feel soon how one should let go of the entire scientific concern, with its demand that it should occupy the first place. . . . There is a human development and expression of life that does not operate on the level of science and still occupies a much higher position. There is a worship and self-denial in front of God, there is a love and self-denial for the neighbor, there is a flourishing in what is pure and courageous and character building that transcends all beauty of science by far.

Also consider the following remarkable passage:

Whether science, bound as it is to the *forms of consciousness of our existence*, will be able to present something to our *eternal* existence, is highly questionable; but this we know, that, as certain as there glows a spark of sacred love in our heart, this spark can never be extinguished since it will once with the breath of eternity light up in its full glow. Experience now teaches that this new life, originating in palingenesis, is more inclined to move in a more noble direction than to be thirsty for science. This may turn into a shortcoming, and often degenerated into an aversion or disparagement of science.[17]

This difference in the appreciation of science between Kuyper and Woltjer is remarkable and is hardly reducible to a mere difference in *accentuation*.

For even though Woltjer pays thorough attention to sin and recreation, nowhere does this Christian line of thought lead him to a depreciation of the central position which his *logos* theory occupies in his assessment of science and scholarship.

Moreover, nowhere in Woltjer's philosophical conception of the human soul do we find any room for the "heart" in the sense of the religious root of human existence. Rather he continues the traditional theory about the two capacities of the soul: the intellect and the will. Once again, in line with this tradition, he assigns the primacy to the former. Although he acknowledges that the *logos* is actually merely a function, namely the highest function of our cognizing capacity, he believes that as such it should absorb all prior functions within itself and that it has to govern the will as a separate function.[18] He gives prominence to the *unity* of the soul and it is remarkable that he calls it the *I*. However, it cannot be denied that according to this conception the center is located in the *logos* as the unity of thought and the expression of words.

One also finds this conception of the soul and the *logos* as its center in Kuyper's *Encyclopedia*. Just like Woltjer, Kuyper explicitly mentions that this view represents the traditional reformed understanding, defended in particular by Calvin.

But where Woltjer in his two mentioned publications without any impediment further develops this trend of thought, this is not at all the case with Kuyper, and, for that matter, also not with Calvin.

In order to understand these diverging lines of thought in Kuyper's philosophy of science properly it is necessary first of all to highlight the religious basic conception which served as the foundation for his Calvinistic world and life view.

As is known, four years after the appearance of the second volume of his *Encyclopedia*,

---

17 *Encyclopedie* II, pp.112–113 – the italics are mine: HD.

18 *De Wetenschap van den Logos, Verzamelde Opstellen*, p.23. The generation also of the "lower" functions from the *logical* essential center of the *anima rationalis*, as we have noted earlier, is completely in harmony with the Thomistic concept of substance.

he presented his Stone Lectures (in 1898) in Princeton. The religious basic conception essentially found in the *Stone Lectures* is already present in the *Encyclopedia*.

In the first Stone lecture Kuyper explains that Calvinism indeed entails its own life and world view. In general he states that such a life and world view has to find its point of departure in a specific view regarding our relation to *God*.

Then an important passage follows – a passage apparently currently forgotten but actually worth memorizing:

> If such an action will impregnate our entire life then it has to proceed from that point in our consciousness where life is still undivided and brought together in its unity, not in the differentiated branches but in the root from whence all these ties stem. And that point cannot only be found in the opposition between everything *finite* in human life and the *infinite* found behind it. Only *there* do we find the common source from where the various streams of human life emerge and differentiate.
>
> Personally we constantly experience how this is the deepest layer of our awareness, the point where the heart discloses itself for the Eternal, where all rays of our life coincide as if in one focal point, and only there regain the harmony so frequently and painfully lost in life.

Where Kuyper comes to a closer development of the religious starting point of Calvinism he writes:

> Just as the entire creation culminates in the human being, also the glorification can only find its consummation in the human being, created after the image of God; not because humankind searches for this, but because God implanted through creation the only genuine religious expression through the *semen religionis*. God *made* humankind religious through an awareness of divinity (*sensus divinitatis*), allowed by God to play on the strings of the human *heart*.

Without any doubt Kuyper here has in mind the heart in the sense of the religious root of the entire life of a person. Elsewhere he expresses it as follows: "the heart, certainly not understood as sense-organ, but as that place within you where God works and from whence He also affects your head and brain."[19]

It was only Kuyper who accomplished here the tremendous grasp which, with one stroke, radically turned around in a Scriptural sense the anthropological perspective. Neither in the mentioned writings of Woltjer nor in Bavinck's *Beginselen der Psychologie* (*Principles of Psychology*) is this conception found. Both remained fully captured by the scholastic theory of the abilities of the soul with the intellect as the central leading part of the soul.

In the discussion of the statement that the heart is the wellspring of life (Proverbs 4:23) Bavinck, in his mentioned work, explicitly identifies the heart with the seat of the affects or with the inborn drives as arranged under "desire."

And how does Woltjer explain the word of *Ecclesiastes* that eternity was set in the human heart?[20] He interprets this completely in the sense of the Scholastic soul conception

---

19 *Honig uit rotssteen* (*Honey from Rock*), II, Amsterdam 1883, p.35.

20 *Translator's note*: The translation of Ecclesiastes 3:11 generated different interpretations, such as that the phrase translated with "set eternity in the heart(s) . . ." ought to be translated with the word "history," implying an awareness of past, present, and future [see J.M. Spier: *Tijd en Eeuwigheid* (*Time and Eternity*), Kampen 1953, pp. 141ff.]. Dooyeweerd's rebuttal to similar examples of an alternative "theological exegesis" is found in his article on "Creation and Evolution" ("Schepping en Evolutie." *Philosophia Reformata*, 1959: 116–117, note 3). Here he argues that the central religious meaning of the term "heart" is at stake

as well as his *logos* theory and *idea realism*: "The idea of the infinite is laid in our spirit," so he writes in his *Ideëel en Reëel* (*Ideal and Real*), "through it our *thought* transcends *finite matter*."

It does not require any further argument to realize that there is an abyss between Kuyper's reformational and Scriptural conception of the heart on the one hand and the Scholastic view of Bavinck and Woltjer on the other.

Behind all our temporal functions, including thinking, Kuyper assumes a central religious root, the *heart* as concentration point and deeper unity of our entire existence. From this at once all forms of an over- or under-estimation of scholarship are precluded. Woltjer, by contrast, interprets "heart" in this text, where it certainly means "center of consciousness," simply as "thought," as "logos." Also purely in line with the Scholastic dichotomy between "spiritual form" and "matter," located within the boundaries of the temporal cosmic order, he interprets the word of Ecclesiastes in the sense of an intellectual concept of the infinite, within the human thought-function, which would through that exceed "finite matter." Through all of this Woltjer arrives at a completely different view of science and scholarship than Kuyper and to a totally different view of reality compared to what Kuyper presented in his Stone Lectures.

First of all I remark that Woltjer, where he speaks about the word "idea" in his work *Ideëel en Reëel* (*Ideal and Real*), with a provisional small restriction, understands "idea" in a Kantian sense: "We do not discern any objection," so he remarks, "to employ the word in a Kantian sense, though while provisionally leaving aside the concept of *necessity*, which for Kant is a priori." At another place he remarks: "in the form of a totality the idea is a concept of reason, insofar as through it the range of the many as well as the mutual place of the parts are determined in an a priori way." "We intend therefore with [the word] idea a concept of reason in the form of a whole, that is to say such that the relationship of the parts to the whole is completely determined."[21] In deviation from Kant's view Woltjer then assigns to these ideas an objective reality. This view is then further elaborated in the Augustinian and Thomistic sense of the *universalia ante rem in mente divina* (pre-existing ideas within the Divine Mind) and the *universalia in re* (the universal forms within things). Entirely in a similar sense this view is found in Bavinck's *Christelijke Wereldbeschouwing* (*Christian Worldview*). This idea-realism in the case of Woltjer leads to a peculiar view of reality with a strong Augustinian and neo-Platonic orientation.

Moreover, Woltjer accepts different *degrees of reality*. He asks:

> To what do you attribute more reality? To that which in itself is a plurality or to that which in itself is a unity? Is it not to the latter? Well, then you have to acknowledge that your own spiritual existence, which you recognize in opposition to the multiplicity of things outside yourself as an enduring identical unity, possesses more reality than the material things. And is it not the case that that which is free, because it enjoys through its freedom more independence, is therefore more real than that which is bound within itself and through that dependent? If yes, then from this point of view you must also acknowledge the higher degree

---

if the term "eeuw" (or: "eeuwigheid") is rendered as "the times" or "history," because in that case one can just as well pull the heart up to the modal level, totally losing sight of its central (supramodal) nature. Dooyeweerd writes: "For 'history' in its temporal sense must find in the human heart its concentration on God's eternal providential plan."

21 *Ideëel en Reëel* (*Ideal and Real*), Collected Essays, 1881.

of reality of the spiritual above the material world.[22]

For this reason he also accepts *degrees of individuality*:

> The individual is constituted by moments that are accidental in respect of the idea. To the effect that the species stands on a higher level the individual acquires more significance. Within the inorganic world, where, for that matter, the concept *species* in its proper meaning does not find an application, it does not exist. It is found in the realm of plants, and it becomes more manifest to the extent in which the multiplicity of relations embedded in the idea of a species becomes more numerous.[23]

Woltjer does give a remarkable articulation to this gradual view of reality, for example with legal theory:

> Every expression of law becomes more real insofar as it approximates the idea of justice more closely. When a law is made as an expression of the legal consciousness of a people, thus largely replacing ignorance and restricting egoism, then that code of law in reality has a higher ranking than the legal consciousness of individuals because it more closely approximates what is *just*. (op. cit., p.227)

On the other hand a totally different view of reality has to flow from Kuyper's religious basic conception of Calvinism where the heart is conceived as the religious root and concentration point of the entire existence of a person.

Moreover, to this religious basic conception belongs the pregnant confession of the sovereignty of God in the sense of the absolute sovereignty of the Creator, expressed in the well-known Calvinian adage: *Deus legibus solutus, sed non exlex* (although God is above the law He is not arbitrary). And this confession gives a totally different orientation to one's view of reality.

Although I am convinced that Woltjer whole-heartedly accepted this religious basic conception it did not sufficiently work itself out in his view of reality. It was obstructed by his metaphysical *logos* theory and his doctrine of the reality of the concepts of reason within the Divine *logos*.

In the history of Christian thought the idea-realism intimately coheres with the speculative *logos* theory.

The Aristotelian-Scholastic trend in this *logos* theory accepts the intellect as the "essence" of God,[24] just as it discovers the image of God only within the human "intellect."[25] Through all of this it resulted in a complete denaturation of the Scriptural doctrine of God's creational sovereignty. The Aristotelian idea of God, according to which God as first unmoved mover is pure "Reason" (not infected by matter) in the sense of pure form-activity, is irreconcilable with the Christian idea of creation.

---

22 Op.cit., 208. That this view of reality intimately coheres with the neo-Platonic theory of ideas cannot be contested. The Philosophy of the Cosmonomic Idea has shown that it is not consistent with the Biblical idea of creation, since the Scriptures nowhere provide a foundation for the view that material things are less *real* than the human being, not even to mention the construction about an "anima rationalis."

23 To my mind, this conception regarding degrees of individuality cannot be explained in terms of the idealism in its Augustinian and Thomistic understanding. Much rather it points in the direction of neo-Kantian or Romantic influences suggesting an *irrationalistic* leaning. In the traditional idea-realism, matter indeed remains the *principium individuationis* (the *principle of individuation*). It is also impossible to relate the position taken by Woltjer with the conceptions of John the Scott.

24 See Thomas Aquinas, *Summa Theologica*, q. XIV a. IV.

25 See Thomas Aquinas, *Summa Theologica*, q. III, art. 1.

Already Thomas formulated the thesis that the good is not good because God has ordained it, for God had to give effect to the good because it is *good*, i.e., because it is consistent with the rational nature of the human being and with God's reason. Only the "compulsory effect" of the natural moral law is traced back to God's will. The Augustinian and neo-Platonic line in the *logos* theory, as it is followed by Woltjer, by contrast attempts to reconcile the realism of ideas with the full Sovereignty of God's creational will. The Augustinian doctrine of the "*lex aeterna*" (eternal law) with its higher and lower degrees of reality essentially attempts to accept God's creational will as the origin of the neo-Platonic idea of the world order.[26]

Yet it once again concerns two lines of thought that are irreconcilable in their religious root.

The late Scholastic nominalism of William of Ockham realized this. It is remarkable to observe how this trend, with the rejection of the speculative *logos* theory, at once also affected the idea-realism. In his theory of the *potestas dei absoluta* Ockham attempted to maintain the sovereignty of God's creational will, which does not allow for subsuming God's work of creation under the law of reason ideas.

Yet it was not at all the case that Ockham wanted to bring to expression the Biblical doctrine of creation. In essence he presented a voluntaristic construction through which the Christian view is actually denatured to an extent exceeding that of the speculative *logos* theory. Ockham after all understood the creational sovereignty of God in the sense of despotic arbitrariness without realizing that the concept of arbitrariness only makes sense under the yardstick of the law, leaving open room to play for the possibilities of arbitrariness.

The Calvinistic conception of God as sovereign Creator in principle broke with this entire dilemma of *realism* or *nominalism* because this dilemma in the final analysis measures God's sovereign will with human norms. Here the starting point is not chosen in reason or in the so-called faculty of the will. Rather it is found in the transcendent religious sphere. Calvin precludes radically the realistic speculation which believes that through rational argumentation it can penetrate to the essence of God *per se*. He points out to the reader that God's law is the final yardstick for good and evil. Human thought can never move beyond the law as boundary. But Calvin equally fulminates against nominalistic voluntarism since it is also an assault on God's holiness.

All of this also coheres with a remarkable difference in view regarding the object of theology in the thought of Kuyper and Woltjer. Kuyper, in his *Encyclopedia*, explicitly rejects the view that God could be the object of theology because human reason is limited to the temporal cosmos. But since the Revelation of God is given within the boundaries of the cosmos it can be the object of theology. Woltjer, by contrast, often designates God Himself as object of this discipline. The *logos* theory of Woltjer does not accept the law-boundary for human thought, something that is essential for Kuyper. It is striking that Kuyper, when he remains faithful to this religious line of thought, with great

---

26 See also Otto Schilling, *Naturrecht und Staat nach der Lehre der alten Kirche* (1914), pp. 174–175: "In a completely unforced and natural way this eternal law, with the natural moral law flowing from it, is thus absorbed within Christian thought. Augustine achieved this by modifying this concept, derived from classical philosophy, in a Christian sense, insofar as he traces this true, eternal law that corresponds with nature back to the personal will of the omniscient God."

clarity articulates a cosmonomic idea which in all its basic features matches the basic idea accepted by the *Philosophy of the Cosmonomic Idea* and which indeed provides a basis for a truly Christian view of reality.

It is in the second Stone Lecture, where Kuyper accounts for the relationship between Calvinism and religion, that we find the confession of God's sovereignty as Creator expressed in the theory of the distinct law-spheres or spheres of ordinances. He writes: "Nothing is created without a corresponding ordinance for its existence. It is the fullness of ordinances of God for *all* of life, demanding all of life to be dedicated to God." The metaphysical *logos* theory is here completely eliminated. The cosmonomic idea is conceived in a religiously pure way. Just look at the manner in which Kuyper elaborates this idea more explicitly:

> What now is for the Calvinist *God's ordinances*? Nothing else but the firm conviction rooted in the heart [take note: not in "reason" – HD], namely that all of life is first contemplated by God and only afterwards was it realized, and that therefore there is a God-given law for all created life. There is no life outside you in nature without ordinances, currently designated as laws of nature, an expression that we can accept on condition that it does not intend to speak about laws *of* nature, but about laws *for* nature. Similarly there are ordinances for the heavens and the firmament above, as well as ordinances for the earth below, through which the earth continues to exist, because, as the Psalmist says, these ordinances are *the servants of God*. Therefore there are also Divine ordinances for my body, for the blood flowing through my veins, and for the breathing of the lungs. And furthermore there are Divine ordinances for my thinking in logic, Divine ordinances for my imaginitivity within the aesthetic domain, and also orderings, ordinances of God, for the domain of morality. (*Het Calvinisme*, pp. 61–62)

Everyone who has even the slightest acquaintance with the theory of law-spheres of the *Philosophy of the Cosmonomic Idea* will have to concede that in the scientific investigation of the structure of reality it is nothing but thinking through and elaborating this religious understanding of law found in the thought of Kuyper.

Nonetheless it has been contested that the idea of sphere-sovereignty developed within this theory, in the sense of the modal irreducibility of law-spheres, has any connection to the view of Kuyper.

Rather we once again give the word to Kuyper himself. In his lecture on "Calvinism and Art" we find the following remarkable passage:

> Hegel's attempt to explain art in terms of ideas and thought essentially contradicts the nature of art. Our intellectual, ethical, and religious [meant is faith – HD] life as well as our aesthetic life each disposes over its own sphere. These spheres are running parallel and therefore one should not attempt to deduce the one from the other. It is one and the same movement, one and the same urge, the same excitement in the mystic root of our existence, that sought outward expression in this fourfold branching off. . . . However, when the question is asked how a conceptual unity can emerge within each one of these four terrains, then it repeatedly turns out that this unity within the finite is only to be found in that one point where our lives rise from the source of the Infinite. There is no unity in your thought but through an interconnected philosophical system. And there is no notable system of philosophy that does not rise up to the well-spring of the Infinite. Similarly, there is no unity in your moral existence but through an inner bondage to the *moral world order* and there is no moral world order conceivable but under the impression of an Infinite power who has set the order within this moral world. Finally also within your aesthetic expression there is no unity possible but under the artistic inspiration of an Eternal Beauty, who flows towards us from the source of

the Infinite and rises towards the Infinite. (Ibid., p.144)

What is striking in these statements in the first place is the prominent positing of the religious unity of God's law in its Origin and central fullness of meaning. Here the cosmonomic idea completely runs parallel with understanding of the heart as religious concentration point of all temporal functions of reality. From this the mutual sphere sovereignty naturally follows, the mutual irreducibility of the respective law-spheres explicitly mentioned here by Kuyper.

The metaphysical logos-theory, ultimately reducing all laws to ideas within the divine Logos, is here cut off at the religious root, as will appear more clearly below.

Within this conception it is not possible to allude to lower and higher degrees of reality depending upon the proximity or distance from the idea. Kuyper's view of reality here simply stands in direct opposition to that of Woltjer.

* * *

After unfolding Kuyper's religious basic conception as compared to Woltjer's logos theory, I come to a further analysis of both lines of thought in Kuyper's *theory of science*.

The first train of thought builds on Kuyper's religious basic conception, which I outlined above. It gets worked out in what he has to say about the religious antithesis in science and culminates in the rejection of current philosophy and the call for a Christian philosophy,[27] in the aforementioned assessment of science, and in the very important teaching about the role of *pistis* or implanted faith function, in coming to know.

The second line is one that arises from a metaphysical logos theory. It moves Kuyper, in the first place, given its connections to modern criticism, to a so-called critical-realist epistemology and, secondly, to an encyclopedic system of the sciences, within the context of five faculties, that literally loses all connection with the religious basic conception and is, almost without question, infused by logos speculation. In this same line also lies a logos-theory influenced approach to the dichotomy of soul and body, which Woltjer had earlier applied to the relationship of logic and the study of language.

At the moment I want to pursue the second train of thought in order to show that it runs into an irreconcilable conflict with the former.

In the Senate of the Free University the Lohman conflict generated the well-known theses regarding the precise significance of the reformed principles as foundation for the practice of scholarship. These theses pointed at the necessity to subject the epistemological questions raised by Kant to an assessment from the perspective of the reformed principles, because they were unknown to those who lived in the sixteenth century, Calvin included. But already two years earlier Kuyper, in his *Encyclopedia*, undertook his well-known attempt to do this without reaching any unity owing to his ambiguous starting point.

Kuyper proceeds from the usual opposition of the subject and object of science and he took the subject in the sense of the general consciousness of humanity, understood as

---

27 See a response to the critique of Dr. Daubanton in *De Heraut* of 9 February 1896: "If someone says, '*The Encyclopedia of Sacred Theology* is *in no way* theological' and they adhere to a philosophy that knows no other principle than what Hegel held dear, then we pronounce that this way of seeing things is beside the truth and leads to the nullification of all bone fide theology. The situation is completely different when one, as Dr. Kuyper does in the *Encyclopedia*, rejects current philosophy and puts a *Christian* philosophy in its place."

a supra-individual communal consciousness in which the individual consciousness of the researcher participates. The object then is the entire cosmos as object of our knowledge

It should be observed that this traditional subject-object schema already contradicts Kuyper's religious basic conception in which he explicitly acknowledged the intellectual sphere as *one of the (law-)spheres of the temporal cosmos itself*. Indeed, within this conception the *entire cosmos* can never be the "object"[28] of theoretical thought, for then theoretical thought itself would have to *transcend* the temporal cosmos. This is indeed, as I have argued more than once in this journal, what is assumed by the critical transcendental philosophy of Kant. And this conception, manifesting itself in the theory regarding the "transcendental thought-subject," was indeed the last apparent possibility for immanence philosophy to maintain the autonomy of theoretical thought within the domain of philosophy, in the context of critical self-reflection. However, this theory necessarily led to the identification of the "cosmos" with a theoretical abstraction from reality in its fullness which afterwards indeed functioned as "Gegenstand" of the epistemological subject. This, in turn, then once again led to a theoretization of reality that sets aside what is "given" within naive experience.

As soon as one acknowledges – with Kuyper – that the intellectual sphere is *completely* fitted *within* the boundaries of the temporal cosmos – where it can only function as one amongst many spheres, this epistemological subject-object schema cannot be maintained any longer. In his view regarding the knowing *subject* Kuyper already completely moved away from the position of Kantian epistemology. Yet, in his conception regarding the relationship between subject and object he continues to be captured by the problem setting of immanence philosophy.

According to Kuyper there must exist an organic connection between subject and object ensuring the possibility of knowledge.

He proceeds from the customary epistemological view of humanism, particularly articulated by Kant, according to which all knowledge is acquired through two functions only, namely perception and logical thinking. These two functions are captured in the concept *intelligere*, designating the ability to know, and alongside it, as a second (pure) capacity of the soul, only the will is acknowledged. This necessarily generates the problem how the so-called epistemic object can enter subjective consciousness.

The solution which Kuyper provided for this problem is known. Completely on a par with Woltjer he distinguishes within the epistemic object *moments* or simple ingredients and the relations between these moments. In their ideal unity these moments constitute the object as a composite whole.

These *moments* then arrive through our receptive awareness (affection) in our consciousness and they are *non-logical* in nature. Within our physical experience they display a purely *sensory* character and within spiritual experience a purely spiritual nature. The relations, by contrast, are in their lawfulness *logical* in nature; indeed *objective-logical* and contained in the ideas which the divine Logos laid within all creatures.

---

28 What is meant is the theoretical "Gegenstand." It is unfortunate that Kuyper here also accepts the common theoretization of reality in identifying "object" and "Gegenstand."

But this entire distinction between moments and relations as such derives from modern epistemology since Locke. The latter sharply distinguished between the simple "elements" (ideas) of the object known, given to us only as impressions of "sensation" ("äuszeren Sinn" in Kant), and as the spiritual impressions of "reflection" ("inneren Sinn"). It is only through the combining activity of the "reflection," that is the logical relations arising from our thought-function, that a mutual connection between them is established. Locke was satisfied to settle for an irreconcilable dualism between the apriori knowledge of necessary relations and empirical knowledge derived from elementary impressions. The Scottish philosopher David Hume, in his major epistemological work, developed a radical psychologistic epistemology in which he tore apart the sharp divide of Locke between *sensation* and *reflection*, between *objective* and *subjective* sensitive-psychic experience. Hume developed a radical psychologistic epistemology in which the "natural relations"[29] are robbed of their objective valid character and traced back to the operation of psychical laws of association applicable to the awareness of natural relations. This led to the skeptical outcome that scientific knowledge – in particular the causality laws and the substantial unity of natural entities – is purely subjective in nature, lacking every objective foundation.

At this point Kant intervened in the epistemological debate. He posed the critical question concerning the necessary conditions making possible universally valid knowledge. He continues the view of Locke and Hume that our experience of the "outer world" is only given to us in sensory impressions of objects that are in themselves unconnected. Kuyper called these elements "moments." But these impressions would then be ordered through so-called aprioristic forms of intuiting and thinking necessarily lying at the foundation of experience. The things we can experience in the world are constituted through a synthesis between thought and the matter of sensory experience.

To Kant every *determination* of the object bears a *transcendental-logical* character. The lawful relations between sensory moments of experience are therefore not, as Hume taught, explicable by means of psychical association, since they have a subjective-logical, aprioristic origin.

In this way autonomous thinking is indeed elevated to the *law-giver* of empirical reality.

Kuyper and Woltjer gave to this subjective idealistic critical line of thought an objective, idea-realistic twist. They clearly realized that the idea that the origin of the lawful relations within what is known ought to be found in the spontaneous activity of our *thought-function* blatantly would contradict the biblical conception of creation.

Instead of considering a different foundation for the problem of knowledge, by proceeding from the religious basic conception of Calvinism, where self-consciousness and the structure of human experience would have acquired a totally different understanding, both of them took refuge to the metaphysical logos theory in order to escape from the Kantian subjectivism.

> Dissolving empirical reality epistemologically into "moments" and "relations" finds its foundation in a psychologistic atomization of what is *given* in our experience. As it is extensively demonstrated by the *Philosophy of the Cosmonomic Idea*, this assumption is fundamentally in conflict with our experience. It rests

---

29 These relations combine *successive* psychical impressions. See Hume, *A Treatise of Human Nature*, I, Part I, Section vi.

on the *isolation* of the epistemological problem, which cannot be reconciled with the nature of this problem. It originates in the increasing subjectivism of modern humanistic philosophy and, in a deeper sense, in a starting point which irreconcilably contradicts the religious basic conception of Christianity.

This isolation proceeds from a dogmatic prejudice entailing that the epistemological problem from the beginning is formulated on an internally contradictory basis, namely in terms of the deeply rooted and inherited scholastic view of the "soul" as "substantia rationalis" (*rational substance*). I have already referred to the influence of this latter conception on Kant's theory of the transcendental thought-subject.

The intended prejudice posits the restriction of the sources of our experiential knowledge to the functions of sensory perception and logical thinking, which, as a closed complex, is opposed to a reality "in itself." The origin of this isolation of the epistemological problem lies in the Cartesian understanding of "soul" and "body" as two in themselves *closed*, and therefore merely accidentally connected, "substances."

Aristotelian scholasticism escaped from this isolation because it conceived body and soul not as "closed" substances but merely as incomplete substances, brought to a unity through the metaphysical form-matter schema. Thus it considered not the epistemological problem but metaphysics to be the primary issue. In a philosophical sense this approach indeed penetrated much deeper than epistemological subjectivism in that it did not present its metaphysical prejudices as *dogma* but rather exhibited a critical awareness for its own ontological pre-suppositions.

The *Philosophy of the Cosmonomic Idea* indeed placed the epistemological problem in a radically different setting than what was possible in scholasticism and the modern humanistic epistemology. In line with the Scriptural reformational approach it no longer sought the *center* of consciousness in *theoretical thought* but in the *transcendent religious root* of the entire human existence. In the theory of law-spheres it demonstrated the temporal meaning-coherence of all modal functions of reality. These new insights made it impossible to restrict the structure of human experience to an abstract complex of *functions*. Only at this point was it possible to understand the identity of the horizon of experience and the cosmic horizon of reality without falling prey to idealistic or criticistic misconceptions.

This radical reappraisal of the epistemological problem, however, only became possible through an equally radical rejection of the view, still thoroughly operative within modern epistemology, that soul and body are two substances enclosed within the horizon of time.

Rejecting the substance-concept turned out to be the primary condition also for the reformational articulation of the problem of knowledge. In this the *Philosophy of the Cosmonomic Idea* simply constructively proceeded on the basis of the Scriptural biblical basic conception of Kuyper's anthropology, which acknowledged the religious root of human existence.

Yet Kuyper and Woltjer did not question the assumed *logical* character of all lawful relationships without distinction. As a substitute for the *human* logos they elevated the *divine* Logos, the divine Reason, to the level of Origin. This was done in their exploration of the realistic theory of ideas to which we have referred above. The relations within the knowable things are therefore not merely *subjective*, but *objective*-logical in nature and therefore, as logical relations, they can only be grasped through our *logical thinking*.

In a relative sense one can appreciate this attempt to escape from Kantian subjectivism in epistemology with an appeal to the "rational" divine plan of creation.

But who does not realize that this entire logicistic-idealistic orientation regarding the lawful relations in the cosmos flagrantly clashes with Kuyper's religious *Cosmonomic Idea*, in which he confessed so sharply and clearly the *mutual irreducibility* of the modal law-spheres!

What is here observed is how the logos theory leads to an inner "logification" of the law-spheres, while the religious understanding of God's Sovereignty as Creator alternatively has to lead to the theory of the sovereignty within the own sphere of the temporal law-spheres of reality.

Undoubtedly also in Kuyper's and Woltjer's logos theory the *diversity* of the objective ideas as they are implanted through creation in the things is maintained – but it is a diversity *within* the *Logos, within* the *objective concepts of reason*. In other words, it is a diversity which can solely be *logical* in nature.

But only in the thought of Kuyper, and not in that of Woltjer, is this highlighted dualism to be noted. Moreover, Woltjer constructs his philosophy of science completely on the basis of the speculative *logos* theory, whereas in the case of Kuyper the latter is simply a side-line adjacent to the main line of his religious basic conception.

The time has come that, within the confusing sphere of the contest that arose within our circle around the *Philosophy of the Cosmonomic Idea*, it should be realized clearly what the issues are and that one cannot any longer accept a kind of *harmonia praestabilita* between Kuyper's Calvinism and his logos theory – which in reality appears not to exist.

One can follow the diverging line stemming from the logos theory and the scholastic view of soul and body within Kuyper's encyclopedic system of sciences. Distorted as it is by the fully historically determined schema of five faculties, this view can hardly claim any scientific merit.

Just consider the rich perspectives for a truly philosophical encyclopedia provided by the basic idea of a divine world order present in Kuyper's basic conception – where every sphere of ordinances, amidst its temporal coherence with all the others, bears its own irreducibility, while every sphere has its own place and order within the whole. This view, alongside the theory of individuality-structures of reality as it is developed by the *Philosophy of the Cosmonomic Idea*, could have made a contribution to erect the idea of an encyclopedia on a truly reformational basis.

As an alternative we now find a quasi-Hegelian schema for the classification of the disciplines in five faculties. On the one hand it is oriented to the trilogy: God, the human being, nature, and on the other to the dichotomy of soul and body in its traditional scholastic sense.

Kuyper writes:

> If one asks about the distinctions determining the factual division of scholarly labor (namely in five faculties), then it soon turns out that the thinking spirit directed its attention distinctly at the *human being* and at the surrounding *nature*. Regarding its own essence,

the human being is respectively concerned with its psychical and social existence. But even before separately directing its attention at these four groups of disciplines, the human being in particular directed itself towards the *knowledge of God*. The correctness of this division arising from practice is apparent. The principle of division is the subject of science, that is the *anthropos*. This now leads to the coordination of the human being itself with nature, which it controls, and with God, by Whom humanity feels itself controlled. And it is this trilogy, intersected by another threefold division, pertaining to the human being *qua talis*, namely the distinction between the *one* human being and the many humans and, adjacent to it, the opposition between the *somatic* and the *psychical* existence of the human being. Thus the subject started to investigate the knowledge of God in the *theological faculty*, and in the *faculty of the natural sciences* the knowledge of nature. Furthermore, the somatic existence of humanity is investigated in the *medical* faculty and the psychical existence in the *philological* faculty. Finally, in the *juridical* faculty all studies are combined in its focus on the relationship between human beings. Although the boundary lines between these provinces of knowledge are nowhere fixed, and although between any two of them a more or less contested domain exists, it cannot be different because the divisions of the object of science organically cohere, and likewise the reflection of this object also exhibits within the consciousness of the subject an organic character.[30]

It is therefore not strange that within this schema, in the footsteps of Woltjer, philosophy, in close connected to linguistics and history as disciplines, is simply coordinated with those special sciences outside the philological faculty.

As a consequence the truth that philosophy equally has to provide to all the disciplines necessarily their *theoretical* foundations was not apprehended, and in particular the relationship between theology and Christian philosophy was not elucidated at all.

Within this line of argumentation Kuyper took philosophy to be that discipline which has the "psychic existence of the human being as object." The same object applies to the other philological sciences: history and linguistics.

Later on Kuyper developed a more precise idea of philosophy, namely as the totality of human knowledge. Yet he does not even attempt to arrive at a view that is consistent in this regard. Is it therefore surprising that Kuyper here fears the development of sociology as theory of human society, which threatens to break apart the artificial schema of the juridical faculty?

But fortunately we are here only on an unfruitful and dead ended *side-track* of Kuyper's argumentation. What temporarily has made impossible a meaningful elaboration of the rich soil of Kuyper's Calvinistic basic conception is the speculative logos theory and the traditional scholastic views regarding the dichotomy of soul and body.

The matter-spirit dichotomy, in its linkage with the speculative logos theory, made it impossible for Kuyper to develop the idea of sphere-sovereignty in an organic sense in a theory of law-spheres.

Where Kuyper by contrast succeeded in liberating himself from this strange schematism, totally foreign to his basic conception, he managed to lay the foundations for Calvinistic thought, upon which one can constructively build with gratitude and peace of mind.

To this belongs, in addition to his penetrating theory regarding the religious presuppositions of science and in connection with in the all-determining idea of the

---

30 *Encyclopedie*, II, 139–140.

antithesis, his equally important theory of the *pistis* (faith-function) in the process of knowing.

When Kuyper's philosophy of science is explained this important *pistis* theory indeed receives attention but unfortunately when its significance for philosophy is highlighted it is normally interrupted at that crucial point where the actual coherence of this *pistis* theory with the deep religious basic conception of Calvinism clearly comes to light.

In Part I, Chapter II, § 11 of the second volume of his *Encyclopedia*, Kuyper commences with an extensive explanation of the so-called *formal* function of the *pistis* in the process of knowing and he gives the following definition: "this function of our psyche, through which it, without providing any discursive proof, straightforwardly and immediately acquires certainty." However, this provisional circumscription as yet does not touch what is essential to the *pistis*. It practically coincides with the accepted understanding of intuitive evidence and apparently as such allows for a combination with the logos theory. But it is Kuyper himself who emphatically protests against this identification of *pistis* with intuitive evidence. The actual crux of his *pistis*-conception does not really function within his epistemology. This theme is explored anew when he investigates the correlation of faith and revelation in theology.

Kuyper therefore penetrates much deeper than what is normally suggested and the entire flow of his argumentation makes it incorrect to view his initial "definition" as the completion and final stance of his epistemological *pistis* theory. It is only in Section 2, Chapter 1 (§ 25, pp.218/3) that Kuyper brings to expression his religious basic conception within the context of his epistemology. There we read:

> The pistis in fact is within human consciousness the ultimate basic law of all distinguishing. Only through it all the higher 'differentiation' within our consciousness comes into being. It is the daring of breaking apart our unity into a duality; the positing of an other I over against our own I; and this separation is attempted because our own I only finds in that other I its point of support and its final rest. This general better knowledge of faith is the reason why on each terrain there is mention of faith; but at the same time faith in a primordial sense originates because our I positions God, as the eternal, infinite Being, in front of us, and dares to take this on because through this it finds its eternal point of support. Since we did not construct this faith from within and because God created it as part of our human nature, is it nothing else but opening the human spiritual eye and a discerning of another Being exceeding us in everything which appears within our own being. Therefore it does not originate in a Cartesian way from an imprinted idea of God but through God's appearance in our own being in front of that spiritual eye which has been created in such a way that when it opens it discerns Him and in awe is connected to Him.

What is clearly and explicitly stated here is that the so-called formal function of the *pistis* in the process of knowing is entirely controlled by the contents in which faith and revelation are unbreakable correlates. Faith is here recognized as transcendental boundary-function of our entire temporal existence.

Kuyper's theory of the *pistis* adapts itself epistemologically solely in this sense to his doctrine of the necessary religious presuppositions of scholarship, to the radical antithesis in the starting point of scholarship, the view of the heart as the religious concentration-point of human existence, the confession of the creational sovereignty of God in its pregnant biblical sense, and the rich idea of law as it is conceived by Kuyper.

But it is equally clear that this *pistis* theory, that proceeds from Kuyper's religious basic conception and that belongs to the dominant trend in his thought, runs into an irreconcilable conflict with the metaphysical *logos* theory, the scholastic conception of the soul with its abilities and the idea-realism.

In the scholastic psychology there is no room for the function of faith as part of the created human nature. Faith here belongs to the sphere of grace as a *donum superadditum* to the intellect. And it is striking that also in the dualistic antithetical understanding of nature and grace, such as it is found in dialectical theology, the most fulminating protest was raised against Kuyper's conception of the *pistis* as boundary function of human nature. To Barth faith is the totally different, incapable of finding any point of connection in nature.

It is precisely the acceptance of the faith function as boundary function of temporal reality, if it is worked out consistently, that will lead to a proper demarcation of theology and philosophy.[31]

Christian theology may indeed be accepted as a special science with its field of investigation, similar to the other disciplines, being delimited by a modal aspect of reality, even though it maintains an exceptional character owing to the unique nature of this field of investigation and through the circumstance that the Divine Word revelation occupies a central position within it.

In all subdivisions of theology – scholarly Bible research, ecclesiology, dogmatology, and the practical subjects – it remains the view-point of faith that provides a special scientific delimitation to the field of investigation. Therefore all the truly *theological* concepts actually are *boundary concepts* in the pregnant sense of the term. Their contents point beyond the boundary line of time to the religious fulfillment of faith and revelation in the Word incarnate and to the triune God who revealed Himself in it.[32]

Philosophy, by contrast, has the task to unite in its theoretical totality view all the aspects of reality and thus all the fields of investigation of the special sciences, to understand them in their meaning-coherence. Moreover, viewed from a Christian standpoint, philosophy and theology have the same supra-theoretical religious presuppositions. Only where these *presuppositions* of philosophy and theology are different in principle would it be possible to speak of an *a priori* conflict. In his *Encyclopedia* Kuyper understood this with great clarity.

This brings me to the end of what I wanted to say about Kuyper's philosophy of science.

At the beginning I have remarked that it seems as if Calvinism arrived at a cross-road. I have highlighted this thesis through an extensive analysis of the diverging trends of thought present in Kuyper's intellectual endeavors.

At this point I need to add with great emphasis and a deep sense of seriousness that the focus of the present difference of opinions will eventually confront everyone called to collaborate in the development of Calvinistic scholarship to make a choice. For there is

---

31 Compare in this regard my presentation to the theological conference in Zürich on "The natural legal consciousness and the knowing of the revealed Divine law" (*Antirevolutionaire Staatkunde*, 1939, pp. 167ff.).

32 This radically distinguishes biblical theology from all speculative theology. The latter operates with *speculative* concepts which cannot furnish true knowledge since they are nothing but a "construction of reason," guided by an apostate faith in the autonomy of "natural reason."

"periculum in mora"!

Since his death, the spiritual heritage of Kuyper remained undivided. But it was striking to note that gradually a development in Calvinistic thought manifested itself in which the second trend of thought was explored almost exclusively. By contrast everyone was able to see that the legacy of Kuyper's basic conception was left aside without profiting from it. Doctrines such as the antithesis in scholarship, the heart as the religious concentration-point of existence, the *pistis* theory in its material significance, and the sphere-sovereignty of the law-spheres were steadily weakened and less well understood – at least outside the domain of theology. Partially these doctrines were degraded into propagandistic slogans without any tangible content.

When the *Philosophy of the Cosmonomic Idea* emerged and developed in the line of Kuyper's religious basic conception, it was accused of deviating from the reformed tradition, undermining the work of Kuyper, Bavinck, and Woltjer, deviation from the confessions, and so on.

We may find comfort in the fact that after the publication of his *Encyclopedia* Kuyper experienced a similar situation. It was the church council of Bedum who handed over to the Deputants a petition of protest [*bezwaarschrift*] against the restorer of Calvinism aimed at upholding contact between the Reformed Churches and the Theological Faculty at the Free University. The accusation was: deviation from the reformed confessions exactly in those points where Kuyper's religious basic orientation is at stake.

Can it be said that the *Philosophy of the Cosmonomic Idea*, while elaborating this religious basic conception of Kuyper and radically cuts off lines of thought foreign to Calvinism, is guilty of undermining Kuyper's work? Much rather, the opposite is the case. Proceeding in this way indeed does justice to the restorer of Calvinism in the highest sense of the term.

Just as little as in 1896 does it now concern a deviation from the reformed confessions – which are indeed whole-heartedly accepted by all adherents of the *Philosophy of the Cosmonomic Idea*. In the light of the religious and scriptural basic conception of the Reformation the distinction between soul and body acquired a more sound formulation than in the traditional dichotomistic theory of substance, which left only room for the soul as a unity centered in the intellect. On this basis also nominalism is rejected more sharply than is possible on the basis of the idea-realism. No, much rather it concerns an urgent and necessary process laid upon us by virtue of our reformational calling to come to a critical choice between the principles of the Reformation and the traditional philosophical ideas that sprung from an entirely different root.

Therefore the current contest is just as little as in 1896 a sign of inner decay, but rather a joyous sign of a spiritual revival that may richly bear fruits under God's blessing.

15

Abraham Kuyper: Cultural Critic

Edward E. Ericson, Jr.

It is hard to find a post-Renaissance man as multifaceted and as productive as Abraham Kuyper. That this major figure in Dutch Calvinism is so little known in the modern world stems, I am quite sure, from the fact that he did not write in one of the major languages of Europe. Kuyper was a statesman, a politician, an educator, a preacher, a churchman, a theologian, a philosopher. He established a nationwide political party, developed a new denomination, founded a university, became his nation's prime minister, and wrote seminal books.

Yet, if one were to try to summarize in a brief term the central contribution of Kuyper, if one were to try to locate the heart of the man and his life, no one of the above categories would suffice. My own choice for such a summary term would be *cultural critic*. In a slightly more roundabout way, I would call him a participant in the cultural conversation of his time.

One of the truly remarkable things about Abraham Kuyper is how well read and widely (and deeply) learned this public man was. I consider his cultural criticism to be the best of his writing. Could I have chosen for him one of our current fields of academic specialization (the very term is too restricting), I would have chosen the history of ideas.

In Kuyper we have a man who knew that ideas have consequences; for all his activism, he never acted in a vacuum of ideas. Also, he knew which ideas were the consequential ones. And, of all the ideas swirling through his own time of the late nineteenth and early twentieth centuries, the one he saw as both having the greatest appeal and carrying the greatest danger for Western civilization was the idea which imbued the French Revolution. The idea was by Kuyper's time a century old, and in practical political terms it had met its Waterloo. But the idea itself lived on with great power.

I could have spoken of a constellation of ideas instead of just *an* idea – because Kuyper saw the French Revolution as a direct outgrowth of the Enlightenment, and one can say more than one thing about what characterizes the Enlightenment. One can note the idea that man is a rational being. Or the idea that man is perfectible. Or the idea that he is ineluctably progressing toward perfection. Or the Deist notion that the relationship between the terrestrial and the supraterrestrial is a mechanical one, God being the perfect clockmaker who made the perfect clock which never needs repair (no providential divine intervention in the affairs of men).

But I say *idea* rather than a constellation of ideas with a purpose. For all of the above items, as well as many others that might be added in, can be subsumed under a single point: that man is king of the universe, that he can get along quite well, thank you, without any reference to God. This idea of human autonomy was new with the Enlightenment; in general, the Renaissance went never nearly so far. And this single idea, with all its ramifications, has come to dominate the intellectual life of Western civilization for the past two centuries. Virtually all of the modern *isms*, including the political ones of anarchism and the many variants of socialism, exemplify the theme.

Yet, in the ebb and flow of human intellectual history, there is always reaction to actions, rethinking of thoughts. And so, in the early nineteenth century there arose a movement in reaction to certain salient features of Enlightenment thinking. The movement bears the label of *Romantic*. Ever since this movement arose, critics have debated the term and its meaning. It has proven to be such an elusive term that consensus about its meaning will not be achieved until our progeny are as far away from it as we are from the Middle Ages, about which we now have a (surely false) clarity.

Any student of Romanticism finds it *de rigueur* to mention about here A. O. Lovejoy's famous article of 1924 entitled "On the Discrimination of Romanticisms."[1] Still, we can rehearse certain widely accepted generalizations about the term. First, Romanticism, in reaction to the Enlightenment's elevation of dry reason, emphasizes imagination, intuition, and emotion as ways of knowing – of knowing the really important things about human beings. The subjective becomes at least as important as the objective, usually more so – especially as an object for studious investigation. The extreme of this tendency we can call irrationalism.

Second, Romanticism, again in reaction to the Enlightenment, takes great delight in the distinctive, the individual, the unique. It eschews the search for general principles and larger patterns.

Whereas one of classical temper might say that he understands others by understanding himself (think of Samuel Johnson), one of Romantic temper would say that there has never been anyone quite like himself (think of Rousseau). In the extreme this attitude can lead to adoration of the self; it can also lead to hero worship, including a sometimes uncompromising "great men" view of history. Another manifestation of this emphasis is the love for the exotic, the strange, the bizarre (frequently including the long ago and the far away). Romantic literature offers multitudinous examples.

Third, Romanticism features the notion for which we might use the term *organicism*. It is fascinated with process. It emphasizes becoming rather than being, the dynamic rather than the static. When it shows up in a view of history, to take an instance, its emphasis is on change, on flux, rather than on stasis or continuity.

Organicism, of course, refers to more than process. It also offers an image of how things are related to one another. And the image is that of a living entity. Yet again we see a reaction to the Enlightenment thought of the eighteenth century, which the Romantics considered mechanistic: stiff, wooden, stultifying. No imagery of perfect clock and perfect clockmaker for the Romantics! Rather, throbbing life! Everything is related, intimately related, to everything. The world is alive with the sound of pulsing. The organism – what an image!

So it is not surprising that the Romantic would show a bent toward synthesizing rather

1   Lovejoy, A. O. 1924. "On the Discrimination of Romanticisms." *PMLA 39* (June): 22–53.

than distinguishing, toward bringing together rather than separating out. Classifying, systematizing, drawing boundary lines – these activities were not for him. The extreme of this urge is happy mush. I shall have more to say about such items as organicism and the drawing of boundaries later, of necessity.

Of all the entities to be merged, the most important to the Romantics were nature and man. No poet is more eloquent on this subject than Wordsworth. Man was a part of Nature (properly capitalized when Wordsworth is in mind). Further, man could learn from nature – could learn even moral truths from it. The extreme of this tendency is pantheism – about which, again, more later. Though Wordsworth does not quite reach this extreme, he comes close to it.

Compared to the above point of synthesis, the following one is quite minor, showing up primarily among those Germans of the nineteenth century who are now referred to as the Historical School. These writers like to invoke the concept of the *volk*, which featured the belief that there was a natural (organic) unity among a given people, that those who shared blood, language, culture, and state were not merely separate integers but had a communal purpose toward which the flux of history drove them. The extreme of this tendency turned out in fact to be Nazism.

Of these nineteenth-century ideas Abraham Kuyper was fully aware. The question is how he responded to them. We know that he was in thorough opposition to the French Revolution – and to the Enlightenment which gave rise to it. But what did he think of the ideas of that cultural movement of Romanticism which arose in large part as a reaction against the Enlightenment?

I raise this question – and devote the rest of this essay to it – because I have heard two distinguished lecturers on Kuyper, both of whom consider themselves his direct inheritors, say that he was much influenced by the Romantic movement. I doubt that assertion, even though it reflects the received opinion about Kuyper.

What is at stake here is not a small matter that is of interest merely to historians of ideas. What is first of all at stake here is how those who denominate themselves as Kuyperians, as many Dutch and Dutch-Americans Calvinists do, will apply Kuyper's thoughts to issues of the late twentieth century. Before one cites Kuyper as an authority in support of his preferred social and cultural programs, he must know what his master really believed, where he stood.

The term *Romanticism* is not a regular part of Kuyper's working vocabulary. However, many elements that other critics treat under that umbrella term are ones that Kuyper does address. Kuyper's concerns are little with literature, music, and art; they are much more with philosophy, theology, and (especially) the general history of ideas. What I am calling Romanticism would, in his mind, include the German Historical School and the German Idealists in philosophy, as well as a theologian such as Schleiermacher, in addition to those elements of culture for which the term *Romanticism* is more readily used. I do not insist upon the term itself; I use it only as a convenient shorthand. My concern is with early nineteenth-century culture in general. And the focus is inevitably upon German culture – first, since Germans dominated this period and were influential on other Europeans and, second, since Kuyper, as a Netherlander, looked especially to neighboring Germany as a cultural pacesetter.

Although Kuyper seldom used the term *Romantic*, he does use it on occasion. In

"The Evolution of the Use of the Bible in Europe," he refers to "the dangerous Romantic period" and then says, "We may thank God that, this Romantic period having passed sooner than many had expected, the mysticism that as a natural reaction followed was in a quarter of a century obliged to retire to small private circles of no importance for the life of the Church."[2] Whatever else this passage may mean, one thing is clear: Kuyper had a negative opinion of the Romantic period.

Before we consider the specifics of Kuyper's attitude toward Romanticism, we might, in order to provide a context, sketch in broad brush strokes the relationship between the Enlightenment and Romanticism as, it seems, Kuyper saw it. Far from seeing Romanticism as *primarily* a movement in opposition to the Enlightenment, Kuyper apparently saw it as one (not the only) natural, logical outgrowth of its predecessor. For all of the differences between the two, some major ones of which we have summarized above, Romanticism as a whole did not break from that one basic idea of Enlightenment – namely, that man is king of the universe, that he is not beholden to a Supreme Complete Entity (a term which Solzhenitsyn uses when treating the Enlightenment's break from historical Christianity).[3] Romantics are long on wonder and awe. But they do not normally direct those attitudes toward a personal god who is above them and is other than they. They diverge from Enlightenment rationalists on the matter of epistemological predilections, but on this basic ontological issue they do not diverge. So, at least, Kuyper saw the big picture. Thus, my thesis in this essay can be stated negatively: Kuyper rejects Romanticism. Or it can be stated positively: Kuyper saw Romantic and Enlightenment thought as allied, the one issuing from the other. In either case, the resultant picture is that of a Christian, specifically Calvinist, thinker standing athwart the drift of modern thought.

If that assessment is correct, how could any student of Kuyper, especially a self-designated Kuyperian, imagine their man to be under the influence of the Romantics? By far the main reason can be evoked by a single word: *organic*. Romantics often used the concept, sometimes even the word; Kuyper used the word and its cognates almost *ad nauseum*. A minor (it turns out, very minor) reason is his invoking of the notion of the *volk;* he loved his Dutch folk.

Beyond this there is no reason for considering Kuyper as under the influence of Romanticism. In no way does he follow the epistemological lead of the Romantics in elevating imagination and intuition, and he virtually luxuriates in the use of his deductive reasoning ability, as is manifest in his ponderous *Principles of Sacred Theology* (*PST*). Nor is there in Kuyper any taste for the distinctive, the individual, the unique – to say nothing of the exotic, the strange, the bizarre. (There are some hints of the "great man" theory of history, but this notion is valued by some non-Romantics.) Further, one misses entirely in Kuyper an appreciation of nature as some sort of moral teacher. Finally, as for a synthesizing mentality, one should remember that Kuyper over and over employs the term *antithesis*. Surely Kuyper was not unaware of the burden of this term in an age following that of Hegel. And anyone who reads his *Principles of Sacred Theology* (other pieces, too, for that matter) must be aware of how readily this man's mind ran to the tasks of classifying and systematizing. He was much concerned with drawing boundary lines;

2   Kuyper, A. 1916. *Evolution of the Use of the Bible in Europe.* New York: Academic Bible Society, 7.

3   See Solzhenitsyn, Aleksandr I. 1978. *A World Split Apart: Commencement address delivered at Harvard University, June 8, 1978.* New York: Harper & Row, 57.

indeed, that is virtually the whole thrust of a major essay of his on pantheism.

Jacques Barzun is one who has written at some length about the two major uses of the term *Romantic*. He distinguishes between a perennial habit of mind that appears in all generations and the historical period in which notions of such minds gained ascendancy in the culture of the West – to wit, the first half of the nineteenth century.[4] Morse Peckham, a literary critic, following up on Barzun, contends that the mindset of the nineteenth-century Romantics remains dominant down to the present moment.[5] Regardless, Kuyper was not of this mindset. A persuasive case could be made, I am convinced, that Kuyper was of a classical temper, not a Romantic one. But, because the terms, by being big, are exceedingly elusive and because scholars love to haggle over definitions of big terms, I shall restrict myself to trying to show that Kuyper thought and wrote in reaction to those major new currents of thought that surfaced in the early nineteenth century – much as he did those currents of thought that his century inherited from the prior one (the latter rejection being one that none of his students can doubt).

The single most significant work by Kuyper for purposes of this essay is "Pantheism's Destruction of Boundaries," published in two parts in (of all places) the *Methodist Review* in 1893.[6] It does not address all of the issues that we must consider. Specifically, we must look elsewhere to discuss the matter of Kuyper's use of the term *organic*. But even on this point there is a stunning piece of negative information. In thirty-one packed pages of treatment of nineteenth-century pantheism, never once does Kuyper use *organic* or any of its variants. Though others who write about European culture of the early nineteenth century speak of pantheism and organicism in the same breath, Kuyper does not do so. This datum suggests that, when he does use *organic*, he has in mind something different from what is in the minds of those who apply the term to Romanticism. What that something is we shall consider in due course.

The "Pantheism" essay opens with a contrast between deism and pantheism, which terms Kuyper uses as rough synonyms for eighteenth-century Enlightenment thought and nineteenth-century Romantic thought. Were he forced to choose between "a melting pantheism" and "an icy deism," he would opt, he tells us, for the warm one *(BB* 369). Never does he have a good word for anything associated with the French Revolution. But of course he is not forced to make that choice.

What does he prefer? He prefers the eighteen centuries that preceded the French Revolution, not the century that follows it. By the end of the article he is saying,

> In Scripture we confront a cedar tree of spiritual authority that for eighteen centuries has pushed its roots into the soil of our human consciousness; in its shadow the religious and moral life of humanity has immeasurably increased in dignity and worth. Now chop that cedar down. For a little while some green shoots will still bud out from its trunk, but who will give us another tree, who will provide future generations with a shade like this? *(BB* 399–400)

---

4   See Barzun, Jaques, 1961. *Classic, Romantic, and Modern.* Garden City: Doubleday, 1–17.

5   See Peckham, Morse, 1970. *The Triumph of Romanticism.* Columbia: University of South Carolina Press, 35.

6   Kuyper, A. 1893. "Pantheism's Destruction of Boundaries." *Methodist Review* 53 (July and September): 520–535, 726–778. Subsequent references to this essay (retitled "The Blurring of the Boundaries" in *AK:ACR*) will be made using the abbreviation *BB* – and *MR* in those cases where the text was not included in *AK:ACR*.

Not the pantheist. Kuyper here places himself firmly in the line of the West's Great Tradition, the main thread of which is Christianity.

Nineteenth-century pantheism deviates from this line just as surely as does eighteenth-century deism – and for the same basic reason. Speaking to those who cast "yourselves as 'the enlightened' and 'civilized,'" he declares, "You deny the fall into sin; for us that fall is real" (*BB* 398). He refers here not to eighteenth-century deists but to those contemporaries of his who "*cannot* acknowledge a boundary established by the entrance of grace" (*BB* 398). These are under the influence of pantheism. It is pantheism that destroys boundaries. Indeed, he says, "the dominant tone of our age is pantheistic" (*BB* 377). And it is with pantheism that he must, in his time, do battle. If, as he suggests, "philosophic pantheism lies vanquished at the desk," still "practically it works its after effects with no less power, both in special studies and real life" (*MR* 523).

The main evil of pantheism is that it breaks down boundaries; boundaries that the proponent of sphere sovereignty believes are inescapably and inviolately part of the law of creation. It is pantheism that "blurs all distinctions, obscures all boundary lines, and shows a tendency to wash out all contrasts" (*BB* 373). The fact, he asserts, is that these "boundaries that exist independently of our thought in real life do not yield to our attempts to change them" (*BB* 380).

The main boundary, the one from which all others flow, is the one between God and man. This is the "primordial difference" (*BB* 374). He expands: "Faith in the living God stands or falls with the maintenance or elimination of boundaries. It is He who created the boundaries. He himself is the ultimate boundary for all his creation, and to erase boundaries is virtually the same as erasing the idea of God" (*BB* 378). When this boundary goes, we no longer have an adequate object of worship (*BB* 387). When it goes, also "the boundary between good and evil collapses" (*BB* 386).

It is exactly that most important of boundaries that pantheism is set upon obliterating. It is emphatically not the case that Kuyper thinks that if one mundane boundary is broken down – say the one between church and university – eventually the process will end in the erasure of the biggest one. He would not suggest, for example, that because Calvin College, my home institution, is owned by the Christian Reformed Church and thus is in violation of his principle of sphere sovereignty, which would keep church and school separate, the persons involved will therefore ultimately reject the antithesis between God and man. That would be to work from the bottom up, as it were. (Nor does he always approve of boundaries, such as Rome's "line between the consecrated and the profane sides of life" – *LC* 51.) No, the danger is the opposite: to work from the top down. And that is what the pantheistic mentality threatens to do. That point explains why it must be opposed vigorously. That issue is the burden of this essay. Once that mentality is set in motion, amalgamation – synthesis – will be the order of the day. The effect of obliterating the line between God and man will be the obliterating of the line dividing good and evil, guilt and innocence, law and lawlessness, *meum* and *tuum*, church and state, even male and female (see *LC* 27). Pantheism, in other words, has a *tendency*. Not only pantheism *per se* but its tendency as well must be resisted.

In Kuyper's mind the most significant historical manifestation of that tendency is the development of the theory of evolution. Hegel's philosophical synthesizing is bad enough; Kuyper scolds it more than once. Darwin's inventions are worse. "What else is the Evolution-theory," he asks in the "Pantheism" article, "but the application of the pantheistic process to the empirical investigation of the phenomena?" (*BB* 374). He calls "evolution doctrine" the "legitimate daughter" of "the pantheistic tendency of our age" (*MR* 762). Citing an atheist in support, he declares that Darwin's theory is "purely atheistic" (*BB* 377). In case one doubts that he means what he says, he asserts further that "the entire pantheistic stream has left behind on its shores a toxic slime, and it is precisely in Darwin's theory of evolution that this deposit manifests its power" (*MR* 530). One can see what pantheism can lead to!

If it is nineteenth-century rather than eighteenth-century thought that Kuyper feels it urgent to rebut, he nevertheless sees the link between the two ages. Those who emphasize the Enlightenment's notion of human autonomy sometimes use the term *anthropocentrism*. Here is what Kuyper says about the next period, his own (nineteenth) century. He finds that it has three motives that simultaneously impel it: "its enormous *sense of power*, its inflated sense of *human worth*, and its penetration into the riches *of nature*" (*BB* 370). It would seem that all three of these characterize Romanticism (and not just the pantheistic extreme of it) and link it back to the Enlightenment.

Kuyper has his own terms for this notion of human autonomy that he sees as all too alive and well in the nineteenth century. They could not be sterner: *anthropotheism* and *Ego-theism*.

> In its mind man is the alpha and omega. An anthropotheism, as some have dubbed it; a veneration first of the ideal human being; then of the human self, however deep that ego may have sunk into the subhuman. An Ego-theism down to its most revolting implications. (*BB* 370)

The term *pantheism* itself means that all is God – and that God is all. Why, then, does Kuyper substitute the term *anthropotheism* and *Ego-theism*? It is true that pantheism lifts man up into God, lifts him up to the level of God. But it does the same with animals, plants, and inanimate objects. This point could of course be said the opposite way: man is lowered to the level of animals and other things. Well, the whole notion was thought up not by cows and anteaters, not by rhododendrons and rocks, but by humans. Kuyper sees that the declaration that all is God really means that man is God:

> That man then, with his superior power and overstimulated sense of self. Has thrust himself upon a defenseless nature – and *has* mastered it, has led it in a victory procession behind the chariot of his science and sensibility. (*BB* 370)

It is easy enough, then, to see why Kuyper thinks that a declaration for pantheism inevitably leads the culture to agnosticism and ultimately to atheism. And this process is all a legacy of the Enlightenment. So he continues, "These three motives . . . account entirely for the pantheistic cast of our century" (*BB* 370–71).

There is yet more that links Romanticism with the Enlightenment. After referring to the Enlightenment's well-documented enthusiastic "worship of *Progress*," Kuyper notes "the genetic connection between this fevered *Progress* with our pantheists' *process*" (*BB* 372). (Incidentally, the next sentence, replete with Greek, scorns the Romantic notion that "everything is in the process of becoming, but nothing is.") Indeed, when one thinks about it, it is easy to see the congruence ("genetical coherence") between the Enlightenment idea of progress and the Romantic emphasis on process. And what, in terms of Western cultural history, particularly links them? Is it not the denial of the biblical teaching about the fall of man into sin? Sin forecloses the possibility of Utopia. The nineteenth century is at least as eager as the eighteenth to keep that possibility open. I conclude my treatment of the "Pantheism" article with an extended quotation from it:

> . . . how did pantheism, how did evolution acquire such unprecedented power? Certainly not because of Kant or Hegel, Darwin or Haeckel, as if one man could ever transform the mind of his time without being himself a child of that time. No: toward the end of the last century the general outlook, the psychic tone, the set of the human heart, *all of life* down to its innermost promptings had risen up in rebellion against the boundaries God has appointed. Pantheism was in the air people breathed. Hegel and Darwin as children of their age only fostered the birth of the monster that our age had long carried in its womb. . . . So powerful a *life*-movement can be successfully countered only by the movement of an antithetical *life*. (*BB* 396–97)

The essay on pantheism is not the only place where Kuyper explicates his view of the relationship between the French Revolution and Romanticism. The *Lectures on Calvinism*, though less directly on the subject, contain many related passages. Again, just a few citations suffice to display Kuyper's hostility toward the French Revolution. He flatly asserts, "The French Revolution ignores God. It opposes God" (*LC* 87). With it, "the first article of the confession of the most absolute infidelity is – *ni Dieu ni maître* – with the result that "all power, all authority proceeds from man" (*LC* 87). The function of this Revolution was "setting God aside and . . . placing man on the throne of God's Omnipotence" (*LC* 99). For all its rhetoric about progress and the rosy future, its real importance is in its denial of the (wisdom of the) past, in its break with the Great Tradition. Henceforth, "man as such, each individual . . . , was to be his own lord and master, guided by his own free will and good pleasure" (*LC* 176). The French Revolution was much larger than a narrowly political or even national event. It ushered in a watershed change in Western man's view of himself.

The Stone Lectures also reiterate the relationship perceived by Kuyper between the French Revolution and the leading motifs of nineteenth-century European culture. Remarking that pantheism was "born from the new German philosophy," he proceeds in the next sentence to link eighteenth-century France and nineteenth-century Germany: "The leading thoughts that had their rise in the French Revolution at the close of the last, and in German philosophy in the course of the present century, form together a life-system which is diametrically opposed to that of our fathers" (*LC* 18–19). In the realm of politics, he sets the Calvinist's maintenance of "the Sovereignty of God, as the source of all authority among men" directly "in opposition both to the atheistic popular-sovereignty of the Encyclopedians, and the pantheistic state-sovereignty of German philosophers" (*LC* 90). In his discussion of Normalists and Abnormalists, he conjoins pantheism and deism in the Normalist camp, since all Normalists "refuse to reckon with other than natural data" (*LC* 132). (Christians are Abnormalists because they believe that subsequent to the Creation "a disturbance has been brought about by sin" – *PST* 92.)

In his final Stone lecture, after scoring Enlightenment France for its "spirit of dissolution," its "passion for wild emancipation," and its "infamously obscene literature," Kuyper devotes a major extended passage to the German response:

> Then nobler minds, particularly in Germany, perceiving what depth of wickedness had been reached in France, made the bold attempt of realizing this enticing and reducing idea of

"emancipation from God" in a higher form while yet retaining its essence. . . . For a moment this attempt seemed to have a fair chance of success; for, instead of atheistically banishing God from their system, these philosophers sought refuge in Pantheism, and this made it feasible to found the social structure, not as the French, on a state of nature or on the atomistic will of the individual, but on the processes of history and the collective will of the race, unconsciously tending towards the highest goal. (*LC* 177–78)

Note, first, the great distance that Kuyper in this last sentence sets between himself and that group of thinkers called the German Historical School. Note the apparent repudiation of the notion of the *volk*. This sentence should be kept in mind when I later treat briefly that notion. But more important to note is the lineage that Kuyper traces from the Enlightenment to Romanticism. On the big point, the desire for emancipation from God, a common impulse persists.

Kuyper's *Principles of Sacred Theology* has scattered passages on our preceding subject (e.g., *PST* 92), but they are so few and fleeting that we shall save that work for our next subject: Kuyper's use of the term *organic* and its variants. On this point it is impossible to be precise, because he uses the term so loosely. Certainly he does not use it with technical exactness, as some literary critics whom I have read do; I think that he never defines it. He uses it in its everyday, unscientific sense. And sometimes it seems as if his use of it is designed to gain the acquiescence of his favorably disposed reader; if Kuyper uses the term so often, I guess that whenever I read it I am supposed to nod in agreement at whatever point this good word is describing.

But why is *organic* a good word for Kuyper? Simply, it seems, because it is the opposite (antithesis!) of *mechanistic*. And why is *mechanistic* a bad word? Simply, it seems, because it is associated with that cultural milieu that spewed forth the calamitous, even venomous French Revolution. Had not Kuyper spoken directly and emphatically about that Romantic age in Europe following the Revolution, the one to which commentators frequently apply the concept of organicism, one might imagine from his use of this term that he was much indebted to the writers of that age for his *ideas*. Since he *has* spoken directly and emphatically about the errors of their thoughts, all that I think can be correctly said is that he borrowed a *term* from them and applied it in his own ways to his own subjects. In short, his use of their term does not make him one of them. Indeed, his use of *organic* is most frequent when he is discussing the concept of *Encyclopedia*, a term he self-avowedly borrowed from the French Encyclopedists (see *PST* 23), one of whom he certainly is not.

Here is an inexhaustive list of the subjects to which Kuyper applies the term *organic*: the organic unity of humanity, the organic unity of the Body of Christ, the organic unity of the cosmos, the organic character of Encyclopedia, the organicism of science, the organicism of theology, theology as an independent(!) organ, the organic division(!) of scientific study. And here are two statements about organicism from Morse Peckham in his *Triumph of Romanticism*:

Now the first quality of an organism is that it is not something made, it is something *being* made or growing. We have a philosophy of becoming, not a philosophy of being.

Strictly speaking, organicism includes dynamism, for an organism must grow or change qualitatively, but I prefer to use the term "dynamic organicism" in order to emphasize the importance of imperfection and change.[7]

Can anyone believe that Kuyper the Calvinist, with his emphasis on the structures of law in creation, thinks that the cosmos is imperfect and must move (change) toward something better? Or that the Body of Christ must "grow or change *qualitatively*"? Does not his notion of the organic unity of humanity refer to something fixed in the creation order? As for Encyclopedia, science, and theology, is not the whole thrust of *Principles of Sacred Theology* that our task is to discover what is there in creation, rather than to invent something new?

One who reads the Stone Lectures cannot fail to see this point. Kuyper's understanding is that Calvinism has gotten the Bible essentially right. We need not leave our fathers behind. Of course, we need to apply their wisdom to new and different cultural contexts. But he issues no call for a qualitative change from them. Just the opposite: he shows the abiding relevance of their teachings. It is difficult to imagine a less Romantic (organicist) exercise than these lectures.

Kuyper's loose use of the term *organic* is so profuse in *Principles* that a few examples must suffice. But no more are needed to make the point. Speaking of the effects of the Fall upon man, Kuyper says, "What once existed organically, exists now consequently as foreign to each other, and this *estrangement* from the object of our knowledge is the greatest obstacle in the way of our knowledge of it" (*PST* 111). Peckham, fan of all things Romantic, would not recognize this use of the term. In another context Kuyper talks about "Scripture as the document of the central Revelation [which] is therefore organically connected with that Revelation itself" (*PST* 362). On the same page he talks about the content and form of Holy Scripture as being "most intimately and organically connected."

For Kuyper, in these and other examples, the notion of the organic seems to mean coherence, fittingness. All things fit together coherently. And the reason that things are inextricably intertwined in an overall unity is that God has placed an order in his creation. Always lurking behind Kuyper's idea of the organic is his Calvinist understanding of the doctrine of creation with all the original perfection of creation. This view is quite the contrary of the Romantic organicist's starting point in imperfection. For Kuyper, the imperfection, which comes with the Fall, is a breaking of creation's organic unity. All of his uses of the term *organic* derive from this meaning of the term. For instance, science is to be considered an organism because it explores the structures of the created order.

The same point can be seen when Kuyper uses the term *organic* to refer to both the Body of Christ and humanity as a whole. And notice how he merges the two. "There is no organism in hell, but an aggregate. In the realm of glory, on the other hand, there is no aggregate but the 'body of Christ,' and hence an organic whole. This organic whole is no new 'body,' but the original organism of humanity, as it was created under Adam as its central unity" (*PST* 298; see also p. 284 for a parallel passage).

Whereas the following passage does not use the term *organic*, it defines – and in the most traditional Christian way – what Kuyper means by the organic unity of the Body of Christ: "This fellowship of believers, carefully distinguished from instituted Churches, exhibits its universal human character in the fact that it continues its life in successive generations and extends itself to all peoples and nations" (*PST* 393). There is no new

---

7   Peckham, *The Triumph of Romanticism*, 10, 12.

nineteenth-century current of thought in this conception.

When Kuyper uses the term *organic* to talk about humanity, he is always eager to rebut the viewpoint that we may label individualism; his emphasis is always on communion. He insists that "we do not exist atomically, but are bound together with others organically" (*PST* 389). On the matter of inspiration of the Scriptures, he rejects "the individual-mystical conception of inspiration" and advocates what he labels "the organically general one" (*PST* 361). A few pages earlier he calls the first of these views "mystic-atomistic" (*PST* 355). And on the subject of science, he says that "the subject of science is not the individual, but the general subject of human nature" (*PST* 150).

The favorite image of organicism is that of the tree. Peckham and others write about its use. It is used for everything that is considered to be organic, including the unfolding process of history and the human family. Kuyper used it too. Again, though, his usage was casual and imprecise. And one of his uses of it, in a passage too long to quote in full, is quite revealing for the distance it puts between him and the organicists. As he discusses the relationship between natural theology and special theology (i.e., the special revelation of the Bible), he suggests that Calvin's image of the Bible as a pair of spectacles is somewhat insufficient, and he offers an alternative: a tree onto which different wood is grafted. "He who grafts, plants no new tree, but applies himself to one that exists" (*PST* 375). Special revelation is grafted onto natural revelation. "The wild tree is the sinner, in whose nature works the *natural* principium of the knowledge of God as an inborn impelling power" (*PST* 375). Natural revelation leaves sinful man with incomplete knowledge, "while the ingrafted new principium brings it to pass, that this impelling power is changed and produces the fruit of *true* knowledge" (*PST* 375). This business of grafting (to say nothing of the context of natural and special revelation as herein differentiated) violates the organicist's use of the tree image.

Therefore, we may conclude that however many times Kuyper uses the term *organic* (as often as eleven times on a single page, *PST* page 183 being the unofficial winner in a field of stiff competition), the mere use of the term does not make him a Romantic – or even in any significant way a fellow traveler. The firmness of his rejection of Romanticism is roughly on a par with his rejection of the Enlightenment and the French Revolution.

Only a couple of odds and ends are left to be cleaned up: Kuyper's concept of the *volk* and the "great man" view of history.

The concept of the *volk* has to do with the historic mission and destiny of a given people. The people, distinct from all other peoples, are, in some mystical way, the source and repository of wisdom. The force of history impels them, if only they and their leaders divine the signs correctly, toward the fulfillment of their mission.

The most radical and rabid invoking of the concept of the *volk* came in Germany and culminated with Hitler. The most disastrous element in this concept was the matter of blood – specifically, racial purity. In Hitler's words, "It is never by war that nations are ruined, but by the loss of their power and resistance, that power being exclusively a property of pure blood.[8]

Did Kuyper subscribe to the concept of the *volk?* I find no evidence that he did. He does speak approvingly of "the sovereignty of the people," but he does so in the context of denouncing "the Sovereignty of the State," which notion he finds to be "a product of

---

8   Hitler, quoted in *Collier's Encyclopedia*. Crowell-Collier, 1964, 17, 206.

German philosophical pantheism" (*LC* 88). Surely Hitler ended up with sovereignty of the state – with a "State-apotheosis," to use a term from Kuyper. It is true, of course, that Kuyper loved his Dutch people and especially praised the little people. But one should not confuse patriotism and nationalism. It is true, also, that Kuyper did himself no honor by siding with those closest to him in blood and culture, the Germans, in World War I. It is true, further, that he saw some people as having experienced higher development than others. But here it was not blood that counted but something else. Even in that notoriously racist-sounding passage in the Stone Lectures about the Dark Continent, what he lauds the Dutch for bringing to South Africa is not their blood but their Calvinism (*LC* 40). And one might keep in mind that it is particularly difficult for a member of a small nation to have exalted notions of the historic destiny of his *volk*.

On the matter of blood and racial purity, what Kuyper has to say stands Hitler on his head. Even allowing for his being on his best behavior for his American hosts in his Stone Lectures, it is beyond doubt that he is genuine when he praises the United States for its progressiveness and assigns a noteworthy part of the credit to its mixing of bloods of various peoples. He explicitly says that "the history of our race does not aim at the improvement of any single tribe, but at the development of *mankind* taken as a whole, and therefore needs this commingling of blood in order to attain its end" (*LC* 36). If Kuyper's comments on race, blood, and tribes strikes late-twentieth-century readers as anachronistic, he nevertheless speaks a language very different from that of racial or national chauvinism.

No, the concept of the *volk*, as it is developed in Germany in the nineteenth and early twentieth centuries, had little impact upon Kuyper. Here again the main emphasis must be on how thoroughly he withstood the temper of his times.

The matter of Kuyper's possibly being influenced by the nineteenth-century infatuation with the "great men" view of history needs only brief mention. Although the individualism of Romanticism could lead some, like Carlyle and Emerson, to praise great men, the organicism of Romanticism could as well lead others to praise the large, impersonal forces of historical unfolding. But Kuyper broaches this matter so seldom and so briefly that it can in no way be considered an important element of his thought.

This point is underlined when we examine a couple of those rare passages in which he does touch upon the matter. In one, even as he observes the advances that have been made in recent times, he laments that we "miss the forceful personalities, the great men, the stars of the first order. . . . When Gladstone dies, who will succeed him?" (*BB* 389). As if to make clear that he does not place his trust in great men to guide the course of history ever onward and upward – and, indeed, showing how contemptible he considers the modern age to be – he continues,

> If you consider how this century began by putting man on ever so high a pedestal and ends by leaving him in a state of utter weariness, then does it not strike you as a soap bubble which, though strikingly beautiful for a second or two, soon proved to be no more than a cloudy drop? (*BB* 389)

In another passage, Kuyper writes, "Genius is a *sovereign* power," and he speaks of "the sovereign power of personality." Thus far he may sound Romantic, but he immediately adds that "There is no equality of persons" and then says that "Dominion is exercised everywhere; but it is a dominion which works organically; not by virtue of State-investiture, but from life's sovereignty itself" (*LC* 95). And, taking these passages together with others about the development of some people being higher than that of others, we realize what a simple, common-sense statement he is making. He is saying that human beings are different from one another, that there is no equality among them as regards their achievements, that no external mediation can make them equal. Whenever he does praise great men, Kuyper is primarily making an anti-egalitarian statement. Throughout history people have expressed the same sentiment. Calvin would have said the same. Kuyper here is saying nothing new with the nineteenth century, not even in emphasis.

We may sum up this study by declaring that Father Abraham was as thoroughly disposed against the prevailing winds of nineteenth-century thought as he was against the eighteenth-century ideas circulating mainly in France and culminating in the French Revolution. It is wrong to consider him as in any significant way under the spell of the Romantic movement. His allegiance was always to those preceding centuries of the Western tradition when Christianity held sway over the culture and formed a broad cultural consensus – a consensus that broke up in the eighteenth century and that continued to disintegrate thereafter. That he was more emphatic and extended in his denunciation of the eighteenth century than of the nineteenth indicates only that he took aim at the root of the trouble of modernity, that he went to the source.

Abraham Kuyper was not a modern man. He was a traditionalist. He was steeped in the Great Tradition and ever loyal to it. This Calvinist saw Calvin as a part – for him, the best part – of it. He never placed Calvin in a vacuum, apart from this tradition. His cultural criticism demonstrates at every turn this rootedness of his. And his own words rule out his availability to those who go by such self-selected labels as "Kuyperian" and "neo-Calvinist" when they invoke his name in support of their allegiance to post-Enlightenment ideologies against which he sternly set his face.

16

The Viability of Kuyper's Idea of Christian Scholarship

Daniël F. M. Strauss

1. Stating the Problem

The idea of Christian Scholarship crucially depends upon a correct understanding of human thought in its integrality. The decisive issue is whether one proceeds from first juxtaposing "faith" and "reason." When this is done an unbridgeable gulf is introduced – and it seems very difficult if not impossible to come to an integral and radical understanding of the possibility of Christian Scholarship. By looking at the shortcomings still present in Kuyper's conceptions in this regard it will be required to give an indication of the way in which an alternative approach opens up a new understanding of the viability if the idea of Christian Scholarship.

2. Scholastic Influences

The initial position of classical scholasticism was dualistic: human reason, not radically affected by sin but merely "wounded" by it, served as the natural light illuminating humankind's life in all "worldly" affairs. This domain, guided by natural reason, formed the relatively autonomous substructure for the domain of supra-natural grace where the church and the Bible were located. The state, as the highest natural form of life, should accomplish the establishment of the premier natural goal in life, namely goodness, whereas the church, as hierarchical supra-natural institute of grace, should bring humankind to its supra-natural perfection, i.e., his eternal well-being. In *Quadragesimo Anno*, the Papal encyclical of May 15, 1931, this perspective is formulated as follows:

> Surely the church does not have the task to bring man to a merely transient and defective happiness, since it has to take him to eternal well-being.[1]

3. Reformed Scholasticism

Reformed scholasticism tried to re-establish the bond between these two "domains" – without obeying the reformational acknowledgement of Christ's rule over all of life consistently. Dooyeweerd phrases it as follows:

> In Reformed Scholasticism, nature can never be conceived of as the antipode of grace or as its

---

1   Schnatz, H., ed. 1973. *Päpstliche Verlautbarungen zu Staat und Gesellschaft, Originaldokumente mit Deutscher Übersetzung*, Darmstadt, 403.

relatively autonomous substructure. For, in conformity to Augustine, Reformed Scholasticism always binds the natural light of reason to the light of Scripture. In so doing, moreover, it falls into the same misconception regarding the relationship of theology and philosophy that I pointed out earlier in connection with the great church father. Theology is supposed to take the non-Reformed philosophy of the schools under its wing, in order to accommodate it to orthodox Reformed doctrine and to keep its latent dangerous tendencies under control. It will be very suspicious of a Reformed philosophy that does not bind itself to theology, for it is theology, as the "queen of the sciences" (*regina scientiarum*), that is supposed to come up with the Scriptural principles to which the other sciences must conform.[2]

With Kuyper this reformed scholastic position developed into a twofold dualism. On the one hand Kuyper continued the liberating perspective of the reformation, given in his frequently quoted proclamation of Christ's kingship over all spheres of life: "There is no thumb-width within the entire domain of human life of which Christ, the Sovereign of all, does not claim: 'Mine.'"[3] On the other hand he maintained crucial elements of the tradition of reformed scholasticism. The second dualism alluded to manifests itself within this second line of thought. It concerns Kuyper's distinction between common grace and particular grace.

Kuyper eliminates Christ from the domain of "common grace." Christ, as Head of particular grace (and the "church"), cannot exert a direct but only a "sideways" (*zijdelingse*) influence on the sphere of common grace.

> Notwithstanding burning only within the walls of the institutional church, the Christian religion spreads its light through the windows of the church widely outside it, illuminating all differentiations and ties of life, expressing themselves in diverse manifestations of human activity. (*GG* II:272)

For this reason the congregation of Christ, with its "influence on state and civil society," aims at nothing more "than a moral triumph," not applying confessional ties nor exercising authoritarian rule (*GG* II:270). Through its "side-ways" operation the church-institute aims at "carrying human life to a higher level, to enrich and purify it, and to allow it to mature in its fullness" (*GG* II:49). This position is faithful to the position defended by Thomas Aquinas (1225–1274), the supreme medieval champion of Roman Catholic thought. Thomas Aquinas advocates that the conviction that "grace" does not abolish "nature," but perfects it – *gratia naturam non tollit, sed perficit*.

That Kuyper in this line of his thought de-formed the radical and integral meaning of God's creation into two opposite realms/domains, could also be seen from the way in which he distinguished between state and church: "The point of departure of the State is contained in the given nature, that of the church, on the contrary, is supra-natural" (*GG* II:110). And further on the same page: "The opposition is and remain thus that the starting-point of the state is to be found in creation, in nature and in common grace, whereas the starting-point of the church lies in the recreation, in the miracle and in particular grace."

In the testimony of the Reformed Ecumenical Synod about human rights from the year 1983 we read the following correction to dualist worldviews:

---

2 Dooyeweerd, H. 1949. *Reformatie en Scholastiek in de Wijsbegeerte*, Franeker, 62. Dooyeweerd, H. 2012. *Reformation and Scholasticism in Philosophy: Volume 1 The Greek Period*. Collected Works Series A, Volume 5(1). Grand Rapids: Paideia Press, 38.

3 Quoted by Veenhof, C. 1939. *In Kuypers Lijn*, Goes: Oosterbaan, 28. See *AK:ACR* 488.

Dualist world-views always misconstrue the biblical idea of antithesis. The antithesis gets defined, not in terms of a spiritual warfare which is being waged in every sector of life, but along structural lines. It places one set of societal structures off against another – for example, church against state, a mission station against a political party. Christians then end up fighting the wrong battles.[4]

The genuine reformation of human thought means a radical "metanoia," "turn-around," of the human heart: the heart which, being reborn in Christ, would re-direct one's life in its entirety into obedience to God. To explore the image used by Kuyper: Scholasticism confined the "light of Scripture" within the walls of the church institute; reformed scholasticism, according to Kuyper, opened the "windows," enabling the "lamp of the Christian religion" to illuminate human life outside the church; a truly reformational and therefore radically Christian attitude must penetrate to the light of God's Word which, through the life-giving Spirit of God, enlightens the root of human existence renewed by the redemptive work of Christ such that the Christian can blossom in all walks of life – active in serving and honoring God whether you eat or drink. This alternative formulation, that shows full continuity with Kuyper's emphasis on Christ's rule over all of life, provides us with an encompassing starting point in the assessment of Christian scholarship and the ideal of a Christian University.

4. "Twofold Scholarship" ("*Tweeërlei Wetenschap*"): Anticipating modern philosophy of science

In the second volume of his *Encyclopaedie der Heilige Godgeleerdheid* (1894) Kuyper advances his idea of "twofold scholarship."[5] He relates it to two kinds of people – people who differ because their lives depart from diverging starting points manifested in opposing directions, also within the domain of the intellectual enterprise.

Kuyper emphasizes, alluding to regeneration, that this difference finds its origin outside the human consciousness.[6] It does not mean that Christians and non-Christians live in different worlds – their scholarly activities are directed towards penetrating into a cosmic order.[7] As a consequence he does not want to claim a twofold truth because there is no room for two representations of reality that differ in principle. What is considered to be mutual by both kinds of science and scholarship is the concern for a common business, namely that of practicing science, as well as the disposal over a similar sensory apparatus and a shared logic serving the assessment of arguments and demonstrations.[8]

Although we may want to formulate what is shared and what is distinct differently, it is clear that Kuyper did have a clear understanding of the distinctiveness of *structure* and *direction*. This insight indeed captures the core understanding of the biblical revelation because it entails the ultimate rejection of every approach dividing creation into two realms – one that is good and another one that is evil.

The Bible does not localize evil in a terrain, but in the apostate direction of humankind's

---

4   *RES 1983 Testimony on Human Rights*. Grand Rapids: The Reformed Ecumenical Synod, 76.

5   "Tweeërlei wetenschap."

6   Kuyper, A. 1894. *Encyclopaedie der Heilige Godgeleerdheid*. Amsterdam, 98.

7   Ibid., 11.

8   Ibid., 102ff. Less than two decades after this edition of the *Encyclopaedie* appeared intuitionistic math-ematics started to question the universal validity of the logical principle of the excluded middle.

heart, while salvation equally is a directional matter (seek the kingdom of God – on every terrain). If we look at philosophy and the various academic disciplines from the depth perspective of worldview, the most remarkable given is that we are constantly confronted by what we could call a surrogate salvific appeal. In other words, in the multiplicity of non-Christian approaches to scholarship we are invited to a way of liberation, we are requested to move away from one terrain of creation to the "kingdom of freedom/virtue/self-perfection/goodness/autonomy" etc. That means that the directional contrast between good and evil is understood in structural terms, i.e., is identified with specific opposed terrains. For Greek philosophers, for example, evil is found in the material world; for the existentialist philosopher of the twentieth century, it is found in societal structures which threaten the freedom of the individual; for the neo-Marxist and the social conflict theorist (cf. Hegel, Simmel, and Dahrendorf) it is found in the authority structure of social collectivities as such (super- and subordination); for other thinkers in the supposed inevitability of natural causality, and for still others in the emergence of freedom which an individual is supposed to possess. This apostate style of practicing science – in philosophy and in special sciences – constantly indicates the way to the good, to the meaning of life and to freedom.

Each of these ways to salvation rests on a wrong evaluation of a well-created part of creation which, with an inner inevitability, leads to a depreciation of something or some facet within creation (a fundamental characteristic already of the ancient heresy of gnosticism), while at the same time it leads to the idolization (absolutizing) of something else within creation – a point of departure of all idolatrous service which brings honor, meant for the Creator, to a creature.

The acknowledgement of the directing role of faith in scholarly, so-called "rational," activities more than half a century later surfaced anew in the emergence of the modern philosophy of science where Popper advanced the penetrating critical insight that faith in the rationality of reason is not itself rational – he speaks about "an irrational faith in reason."[9] A similar position is advocated by Stegmüller when he states: "A self-assurance of human thought is excluded, wherever one may consider it. One can never reach a positive result without pre-suppositions. One has to believe in something in order to justify something else."[10] In reaction to Kant's famous thesis, expressed in the foreword to the second edition of his *Critique of Pure Reason*, namely that one has to set aside knowledge in order to make room for faith.[11] Stegmüller adds: "A person does not have to set aside knowledge in order to make room for faith. Much rather one already has to believe something if that person wants to speak of knowing and science at all."[12] He furthermore asserts that an ultimate certainty is required, for without it would be impossible even to start: "Some form of an absolute knowledge must exist; without it we would not have been able to begin"; "We must already "possess" absolute evidence, that is we must already

---

9   Popper, K. 1966. *The Open Society and its Enemies*, Vol. II, London, 231.

10 Stegmüller, W. 1969. *Metaphysik, Skepsis, Wissenschaft*, 2n. ed. New York, 314.

11 Kant, Immanuel 1787. *Critique of Pure Reason*, xxx.

12 Stegmüller, W. 1969. "Man muss nicht das Wissen beseitigen, um den Glauben Platz zu machen. Vielmehr muss mann bereits etwas glauben, um überhaupt von Wissen und Wissenschaft reden zu können" (1969: 33 – *Neue Einleitung*).

believe in it."[13] Finally, and perhaps his most remarkable formulation in this regard reads: in science one believes, in religion one knows (or: one claims to know)![14]

In addition to this we have to refer to the notion of a paradigm in the work of Kuhn,[15] later on designated as the disciplinary matrix. In more general terms one can say that modern philosophy of science realized that no single intellectual discipline can operate without (implicitly or explicitly) proceeding from an underlying theoretical frame of reference, from a theoretical view of reality.

In order to appreciate the contribution already made by Kuyper in this regard we must recognize the intermediate position of Dooyeweerd. Throughout the history of philosophy theoretical thought struggled with ontological questions, such as that regarding the relationship between unity and diversity, universality and individuality, constancy and dynamics, knowledge of what could be grasped conceptually and knowledge transcending the grasp of concept formation (idea-knowledge), and so on. Dooyeweerd claims that all theoretical thinking is in the grip of a basic (transcendental) idea in which one finds an idea of the mutually cohering diversity within reality, an idea about the totality of this diversity and an idea concerning the origin of the former. The key elements in Dooyeweerd's account derive from basic biblical perspectives articulated in Kuyper's legacy. The biblical starting point of Christian academic reflection in the Kuyper-Dooyeweerd tradition entails:

1. Accepting God's Law for Creation;[16]
2. Acknowledging the interrelatedness and dependence of created reality;
3. Confessing the rule of Christ over all domains of creation;
4. Subjecting oneself to the key to knowledge: the biblical basic motive of Creation, Fall, and Redemption;
5. Knowing Christ as the fullness of creation (Colossians 1:15–20);
6. Upholding the distinctiveness of "structure" and "direction"[17]
7. Avoiding any absolutization of something within creation.

This many-sided but integral and coherent biblical starting point motivates and underlies the reformational philosophical tradition that guides our remarks below (Calvin, Kuyper, Dooyeweerd).

5. The Viability of the Idea of Christian Scholarship

The themes and distinctions discussed below are meant to illuminate the presence of inevitable issues confronting not only philosophy but also the special sciences. The

---

13 "Irgendein absolutes Wissen muß es geben; ohne dieses könnten wir überhaupt nicht beginnen"; "Absolute Evidenz müssen wir schon "haben", d.h. wir müssen an sie bereits glauben, . . ." (1969, 194).

14 ". . . in der Wissenschaft wird geglaubt, in der Religion weiß man (oder: behauptet man, zu wissen)" (1969, 212).

15 Kuhn, T. 1970. *The Structure of Scientific Revolutions*. 2nd rev. ed. Chicago.

16 Kuyper correctly emphasizes that mere observation does not yield scholarly endeavors as such – the various disciplines emerge only when what is observed is related to a general law – and philosophy finally has to combine what is unveiled in this way in one encompassing grasp (Kuyper, A. 1959. *Het Calvinisme*, 3rd impression Kampen: Kok, 91).

17 This distinction, already alluded to earlier, needs a qualification. The structure of creation is not "directionless" and the direction is not "structure-less." Therefore, we should distinguish between God's direction-giving structure for creation and the structured direction manifest in the God-obedient or God-disobedient response of humankind.

elaboration of Kuyper's thought in Dooyeweerd's philosophy has demonstrated that the answers given to these perennial questions are determined by a theoretical view of reality (a transcendental ground-idea) which, in turn, is in the grip of an ultimate commitment (in Dooyeweerd: "religious ground motive").

We start our brief reflection in this context by looking at the problem of unity and diversity.

Unity and diversity

Kuyper first introduced the principle of sphere sovereignty in order to account theoretically for the diversity within creation.[18] Dooyeweerd explored and deepened this insight by enriching it in two directions:

(i) the interrelationship between the different (sphere-sovereign) modal aspects of reality is accounted for in terms of the principle of *sphere universality* (modal analogies/anti and retrocipations) as developed by Dooyeweerd. In doing so Dooyeweerd widened the scope of the principle of sphere sovereignty beyond distinct societal zones to the fundamental dimensions of created reality (modal aspects and entities);

(ii) interlacements within the domain of concrete things, events and societal relationships – where the internal sphere sovereignty of interwoven structures are kept intact – are called *enkaptic*.

These insights in principle free us from the one-sidedness of monistic isms and also from the reductionistic opposition of atomism and holism.

Universality and individuality

Universality characterizes God's law for creation. It also constitutes a side of whatever is subjected to God's law in creation. In its lawfulness/orderliness/law-conformity every individual entity, event or societal collectivity, in a universal way, shows that it is subjected to a correlating God-given law. The being human of this person, and the being alive of this plant are instances of the mentioned universal orderliness.[19] The humanistic ideal of autonomy, i.e., that the human being is a law unto himself or herself, proceeds from the antinomical assumption that the conditions for being human and the human being meeting these conditions coincide!

Coherence of irreducibles

Perhaps it can be claimed that one of the most basic philosophical problems confronting the various academic disciplines concerns the "coherence of irreducibles." All

---

18 Initially Johannes Althusius (1557–1638) pointed out that the diverse societal collectivities distinct from the state ought not to be seen as parts of the state since each of them has its own laws proper to it. Althusius writes: "It can be said that individual citizens, families, and collegia are not members of a realm [i.e., the state – DFMS]. . . . On the other hand, cities, urban communities, and provinces are members of a realm" (*Politica Methodice Digesta* [1603, 3rd ed. 1614], trans. by Carney, F. S. 1965. *The Politics of Johannes Althusius*, London, 16). Concerning societal life forms distinct from the state Althusius declares: "Proper laws (*leges propriae*) are those enactments by which particular associations are ruled. They differ in each specie of association according as the nature of each requires" (16).

19 In other words, in being human (universal side) every individual human being, in a universal way, exhibits its subjectedness to the (equally universal) God-established law for the existence of human beings.

monistic approaches in philosophy and the special sciences are implicitly answering this question in the negative. Panpsychism – for example the orientation of de Chardin – attempts to reduce every phenomenon to a psychical perspective. In a similar way, the classical mechanistic approach in physics, following Galileo's discovery of the kinematical law of inertia, has tried, at least in its main trend, to view all physical bodies exclusively in terms of mechanical movement.[20] However, Planck's discovery of the quantum and the establishment of the second main law of thermodynamics, i.e., the law of non-decreasing entropy (indicating the irreversibility of physical processes), revealed the untenability of this monistic mechanistic approach in modern physics.

What is normally referred to as "primitives" in logic and foundational studies, indeed pertain to the "irreducibles" mentioned above. These primitives also reflect the inherent limitations of concept-formation and definition – in the final analysis every definition can only define something in indefinable terms. Whenever one tries to define a truly primitive notion, the inevitable result is (antinomic) reduction.

Constancy and dynamics

Heraclitus' concern for the dialectical opposition of constancy and change inspired his famous statement: we cannot step into the same river twice, for fresh and ever fresh waters are constantly pouring into it. Cratylus, a pupil of Heraclitus, confronted Plato with this problem of constancy and change, as can clearly be seen from Plato's dialogue with that name. In this dialogue, Plato had to account for the nature of knowledge in terms of something more fundamental than change. He found it in what he termed to be the essential form of what is known.

Eventually Galileo grasped the fact that uniform motion (constant motion) is a primitive notion and therefore not in need of a physical cause. The physical meaning of a cause always implies certain effects, i.e., dynamic changes. What needs a cause is not motion, but a change of motion[21]– for instance acceleration or deceleration. This implies that the phoronomic (kinematic) facet of reality is indeed a (foundational) condition for energy-operation (with its implied causes and effects). Physical changes pre-suppose some form of continuation (persistence, constancy), for only on the basis of something persistent is it meaningful to point towards changes. This insight paves the way for an understanding of the impasse of historicism. According to historicism everything – law, morality, art, faith, language, and so on – is taken up in the flow of historical change and is everywhere only comprehensible as elements of a historical process. Contrary to this claim we are accustomed to speak of legal history, art history, economic history, and so on. But if law, art, and economics are nothing but history, we in fact must deal with the contradiction of a historical history. Whatever is history, cannot have a history; and whatever has a history, cannot itself be history. The irony is that historicism, reducing every facet of reality to the historical mode, thus has eliminated the very meaning of history – if everything is history,

---

20 The most comprehensive, but perhaps last attempt to reduce all physical phenomena to kinematical movement, is found in the mechanics of H. Hertz – he was the first to broadcast and receive radio waves and established that light and heat are electromagnetic waves.

21 Cf. the analysis of Stafleu, M.D. 1980. *Time and Again: An Analysis of the Foundation of Physics.* Toronto/ Bloemfontein, 80.

there is nothing that can have a history![22] We may expand this analysis by demonstrating that uniqueness (diversity) is correlated with coherence – but it will take us too far. We rather conclude our discussion by briefly reflecting upon the implication of the principle of sphere sovereignty on the choice and meaning of the basic concepts employed by the various disciplines. Indirectly this entire analysis depends on the ontological exploration of Kuyper's basic insight by Dooyeweerd.

6. Inevitable Choices Underlying the Special Sciences – Basic Concepts of Disciplines

Every single scientific discipline uses concepts of function (they differentiate into elementary basic concepts and compound basic concepts) as well as type concepts.

Some examples: The concepts *entropy, volume, mass, acceleration,* and *uniform motion* are all physical *concepts of function* (elementary basic concepts), whereas the concepts of elementary *particle, atom, molecule, macro-system,* and *galaxy* are *type concepts* (thing concepts); the concepts *birth, growth, differentiation, integration, adaptation, maturation, ageing,* and *dying* are biological *concepts of function* while the systematic classification of the plant and animal kingdom concern *concepts of types* (*phyla, classes, orders, families, genera,* and *species*); the concepts *social order, social stratification, social constancy* and *dynamics, social differentiation* and *integration, social solidarity, social conflict* and *consensus, social control* and *power, social significance* and *interpretation* are all (elementary) basic concepts of sociology – they differ from the typical totality concepts referring to societal collectivities such as the *state,* the *firm,* the *school,* the *church,* and so on; the concepts *legal object, jural subject, subjective right, legal norm,* and so on are all (compound) basic concepts of legal science, to be distinguished from the structural (typical) differences between diverse *spheres of law* in a differentiated society, such as the domain of *public law* (encompassing *criminal law, constitutional law, administrative law,* and *international public law/law of nations*), *civil* (or: *common*) *law* (protecting the *personal freedom* of the individual within the legal intercourse of a differentiated society), and *non-civil private law* (the irreducible spheres of competence unique to non-state societal entities).

Analogical basic concepts

What we have called the elementary basic concepts of scientific disciplines actually reveal the inescapable inter-modal coherence existing between the different sphere-sovereign aspects within creation. Because it accounts for the coherence between different aspects of creation, any special scientific discipline delimited by one modal aspect only, inevitably has to use analogical (modal) concepts which are also used by other disciplines, be it that the latter use them in a manner colored by their respective (modal) points of view. A few examples may elucidate this point sufficiently.

---

22 It should be noted that the inter-modal nature of every antinomy does imply a logical contradiction (which is intra-modal), but not vice versa. Descartes' definition (i.e., reduction!) of movement as a "change of place" implies the following logical contradiction: if body is its place, and if movement is a change of place, then a body can only move if it changes "essentially" – implying that it cannot move (or, succinctly: a body can move if and only if it cannot move). The illogical concept of a "square circle," however, does not pre-suppose any (inter-modal) antinomy, since it only concerns the (intra-modal) logical error of not correctly identifying and distinguishing between the two spatial figures concerned. This distinction between antinomy and contradiction is overlooked in Hart's 1984 work: *Understanding Our World.* Lanham: University Press of America, 132, 133.

Wholeness/totality

The concepts whole, coherence and totality appeal to the original irreducible meaning of the spatial aspect. Something continuous (such as a one-dimensional line) evinces an uninterrupted connectedness, i.e., all its parts cohere. But if all the parts are present, then the whole/totality is given! The apparently "purely arithmetical" definitions of Weierstrass, Dedekind, and Cantor deal with the idea of sets of numbers as infinite totalities, implying that the unique character of the spatial aspect is essential in their attempt to reduce space to number – an obviously circular argument! Regarding the totality character of continuity, Paul Bernays (the well-known co-editor of *Die Grundlagen der Mathematik* – in collaboration with David Hilbert) remarks: "(it) undeniably belongs to the geometric idea of the continuum. And it is this characteristic of the continuum which would resist perfect arithmetization."[23]

To this one should add his final assessment of arithmeticism in mathematics:

> The arithmetizing monism in mathematics is an arbitrary thesis. The claim that the field of investigation of mathematics purely emerges from the representation of number is not at all shown. Much rather, it is presumably the case that concepts such as a continuous curve and an area, and in particular the concepts used in topology, are not reducible to representations of number [*Zahlvorstellungen*].[24]

Most variations of holism use some or other non-spatial modal perspective and then explore within that context the (analogical) meaning of the original spatial whole-parts relationship. In every non-spatial aspect the whole-parts relation is differently qualified. Certain developments in the modern concept of matter illustrate this point amply. The very nature of spatial continuity initially suggested that physical space shares the spatial feature of being infinitely divisible. It eventually turned out not to be the case. In a commemorative article dedicated to Carl Weierstrass (1825–1884), the famous mathematician David Hilbert points out that those maintaining that matter is continuous and therefore infinitely divisible, are mistaken. Contrary to the popular conception that "nature does not make leaps," continued empirical research and systematic reflection[25] confirms that "nature indeed makes jumps."[26]

Whereas the original meaning of space (with the implied whole-parts relation) entails both its continuity and infinite divisibility, physical space, on the contrary, is neither continuous nor infinite(ly divisible)! The interrelation between the physical and spatial aspects clearly implies that there are both similarities and differences: physical space and original space are extended – their similarity, but only the latter is continuous and infinitely divisible, distinct from the former which is discontinuous and finite – their difference. In a similar way it can be shown that the true meaning of every other aspect of creation can only be understood when it is analyzed in its unbreakable coherence with all

---

23   Bernays, Paul. 1976. *Abhandlungen zur Philosophie der Mathematik*. Darmstadt, 74.

24   Ibid., 188 (cf. Sketch 5 – p.13).

25   The "Wirkungsquatum *h*" by Planck (1900) and the formulation of Einstein's theory of relativity (1905, 1916).

26   Hilbert, David. 1925. *Über das Unendliche, Mathematische Annalen*, 81–82. Hilbert also points out that the conception of reality as being infinite depends upon Euclidean geometry. By employing non-Euclidean geometry (such as it was done in Einstein's theory of relativity), it was shown that the unlimitedness of physical space does not warrant the inference of its supposed infinity (1925: 83).

those modes of reality differing from the one under consideration. When this coherence is viewed in its concentric relatedness to the central commandment of love we may discern a differentiated multiplicity of articulations, depending upon the modal aspect chosen as point of entry. For example, from the perspective of the economic aspect we meet the meaning of the central commandment of love in the call to stewardship; from the point of entry of the jural mode me discover the meaning of the central commandment of love in the call to justice; and so on.

7. Some Implications for the Current Postmodernism Debate

Against the fore-going background is should not be difficult to appreciate the following assessment: four modal points of entry played a dominant role in the intellectual history of the West, namely atomism (the numerical point of entry); holism (exploring the spatial whole parts relationship); organicism (using the biotic aspect) and the quest for meaning (accentuating the sign-mode of reality – this approach recently received a new impetus through postmodernism).

Without degrading the liberating consequences of thinking through the implications of the principle of sphere-sovereignty in a cosmological perspective, it must be noted that Kuyper consistently followed the organic mode of thought – a mode of thinking that may be seen as the dominant orientation of the nineteenth century. It almost provided a subtle but all-encompassing framework giving shelter to trends of thought that are radically diverging in other respects (just compare Darwinism with Kuyper's basic ideas). In the state, for example, Kuyper saw an ethical organism and even advocated the idea of an organic right to vote (ascribed to the head of the household only!). Interestingly Dooyeweerd initially also consistently used the term organic in order to bring to expression his understanding of the coherence present in creation. This mode of thinking is abundantly present in his Inaugural Address and in his 1931 work on *The Crisis in Humanist Political Theory*,[27] but only a few remnants are to be found in his magnum opus of 1935–1936 *De Wijsbegeerte der Wetsidee*. Long before postmodernism explored the notion of meaning (by emphasizing ambiguity and the grand all-claim – metanarrative(!) – that everything is interpretation, Dooyeweerd sensed the significance of the hermeneutic turn by the end of the nineteenth century and therefore switched from the organic mode to the meaning mode: "Meaning is the mode of being of all that has been created." The meaning-idea started to function in such an encompassing way in his thought that the term meaning was merged into every core insight he developed within his systematic philosophy: just look at phrases like meaning-nucleus, meaning-kernel, meaning-structure, meaning-moment, inter-modal synthesis of meaning, the process of meaning-disclosure, the meaning-character of reality, the fullness and totality of meaning, the origin of all meaning, refraction of meaning (his well-known image of the cosmic time as a prism), and so on. Whereas Kuyper (and Dooyeweerd) anticipated the philosophy of science that developed since the fifties and sixties, Dooyeweerd anticipated the rise of postmodernism! However, an assessment of these issues will lead to problems that require a separate treatment.[28] The reformational

---

27 *Collected Works of Herman Dooyeweerd*. 2010. Series B, Volume 7. Grand Rapids: Paidiea Press.

28 Compare Strauss, D. F. M. 1996. Rationalism, historicism, and pan-"interpretationism." Proceedings of the 1992 Conference on Faith and Science – Pascal Centre: *Facets of Faith and Science, Volume 2: The Role of Beliefs in Mathematics and the Natural Sciences*. Jitse M. van der Meer, ed. Toronto: University Press of

tradition, from Calvin and Kuyper up to Dooyeweerd remained sensitive to the spirit of the age throughout. At the same time we have to realize that to some extent they (and we!) were (are) all victims of implicit and overarching modes of thought successively capturing an entire epoch in the intellectual history of the world. Christians ought to be humbled by this insight, because it liberates us from the sinful and tempting hubris manifested in an overestimation of provisional and fallible human work. However, the presence of God, through His Spirit and through the upholding of the order of creation in Christ, ultimately testifies to a reliable and trustworthy anchorage transcending the relativity of our unique historical situation and transcending our meaning-bound and meaning-variant existence. The dynamics of our on-going calling to be sensitive to the spirit of the age in a changing world, does not ever manage to eliminate the constancy of God's creation order, since the dynamic disclosure of creation cannot take place at the cost of this order but only on its basis.

America: 99–122.

17

Abraham Kuyper's Rhetorical Public Theology with Implications for Faith and Learning

Vincent Bacote

Why Abraham Kuyper?

My interest in Abraham Kuyper emerged in the early 1990s as I was pursuing a greater understanding of theology and culture. While I had been introduced to his doctrine of revelation by Kenneth Kantzer, I did not know much else of Kuyper's thought until I read his Stone Lectures on Calvinism. Before the first chapter had ended, I found myself captivated. I was captivated because until that point I had been exposed only to the views of Christians who argued that the primary purpose for Christians to be involved in areas such as politics and art was "witness." This view of a Christian presence in society leads ultimately to conceptions of public engagement that function as strategies for evangelism. While acknowledging the validity of such approaches, it had often struck me that there seemed to be more that Christians could say about engagement with the public. My initial encounter with Kuyper was my first major exposure to a theological rationale for and approach to Christian public engagement that exceeded a strictly evangelistic emphasis.

Since that initial exposure to Kuyper, I have sought to arrive at a greater understanding of his world and work, and my own work as a scholar and churchman has aimed centrally to develop and perpetuate the best aspects of his work. This article will present my understanding of his public theology as set against the discussion of public theology that has developed in the twentieth century. In reading many scholars on Kuyper, one of the most confusing things about his theology of public engagement is that he can seem to hold contradictory positions: on the one hand, when Kuyper emphasizes the doctrine of common grace strongly, his focus on "commonness" can give the impression that not only should Christians be involved in public life, but they should be willing and able to participate in the public with others who are not Christian. When using the concept of antithesis, on the other hand, often Kuyper uses language that suggests strongly that Christian engagement in public life must take place within institutions created by and for the Christian community. This article intends to demonstrate that Kuyper's approach to public engagement (his public theology) actually bridges both of these concerns and that the unifying factor can be seen in Kuyper's aim to function as a rhetorical public theologian who utilizes many concepts to motivate and mobilize his Christian constituency to public involvement. We begin with a discussion of public theology.

Public Theology

In this paper, the theological provision of a rationale for and practice of rigorous, active involvement in the public sphere, ranging from politics to education to science to art, can be understood as public theology. Specifically, public theology in this sense is not only a theological articulation of the rationale for such public engagement, nor only the attempt to argue that religious convictions play a role in the structure and function of society. It is also the consideration of the claim that some theological matters may be at least comprehensible and at most necessary in public discourse among believers and non-believers alike.

Considered historically, the Christian faith has always had some semblance of a public stance, whether as a movement antithetical to the prevailing powers of the day as in the early centuries of the church, or as a potentially conflicted "advisor" with a complex relationship to the political structure of the day post-Constantine. With the advent of the Enlightenment (beginning with Descartes), the manner in which Christian faith related to public concerns became more tenuous, as the "triumph" of secular reason and post-Darwinian science pushed faith-related discourse to the margins of the public sphere, if not altogether into the closet of individual private lives. While a faith with public implications has always had advocates, the influence of faith on the public sphere dwindled (particularly in Western Europe and the United States) to a significant degree by the late nineteenth and early twentieth centuries, not only among most of the populace but especially among the elites who had the genuine capacity to shape and direct culture and society. If the Christian faith had played an array of advisory roles since Constantine, the result of the post-Enlightenment triumph was the equivalent of a pink slip; the services of the faith were obsolete, no longer required.

The current discussion of public theology can be seen as a response to the privatization of Christian faith after the Enlightenment. For those who sought to advocate some public role for the faith, the pivotal issues in the subsequent debates concerning public theology have related directly to the tension between "common ground" and confessional particularity as seen in Kuyper above. As those in the church and academy have considered this issue, primarily there have been two approaches to public theology that pertain to this paper. Some identify the two approaches as a contrast between the University of Chicago, where "public" refers to the exploration and articulation of common human religious impulses and a view associated with Yale Divinity School that emphasizes describing the distinctive beliefs and practices of Christianity as it takes its place in the public square. The first approach is apologetic and is best represented here by Max Stackhouse,[1] who goes beyond emphasizing religious impulses to placing an emphasis on the possibility of making a public case for theological concepts.[2] The second approach is confessional, as

---

1   There are other authors who take an apologetic approach, though they do differ on many issues. See Tracy, David 1981. *The Analogical Imagination: Christian Theology and the Culture of Pluralism*. New York: Crossroad; Benne, Robert 1995. *The Paradoxical Vision: A Public Theology for the Twenty-First Century*. Minneapolis: Fortress Press; and Tinder, Glenn 1989. *The Political Meaning of Christianity: An Interpretation*. Baton Rouge: Louisiana State University Press.

2   The term "apologetic" here refers strictly to the idea that theological ideas and concepts can be intellectually accessible outside the community of faith, though it does not imply that there is no need for the difficult task of translation in public discourse. This approach does not imply only one method of persuasion, nor does it require a philosophical commitment to foundationalism or non-foundationalism.

represented by Ronald Thiemann.[3]

Stackhouse defines public theology as follows:

> First, . . . that which we as Christians believe we have to offer the world for its salvation is not esoteric, privileged, irrational, or inaccessible. It is something that we believe to be both comprehensible and indispensable for all, something that we can reasonably discuss with Hindus and Buddhists, Jews and Muslims, Humanists and Marxists. Second, such a theology will give guidance to the structures and policies of public life. It is ethical in nature. The truth for which we argue must imply a viable element of justice, and its adequacy can be tested on that basis.[4]

Stackhouse observes a crisis in contemporary society that is rooted in part (if not wholly) in a societal amnesia regarding the place of the deep influences of religion in entire fabric of public life, from family to church to corporate and economic life. He suggests that we need to recover a metaphysical-moral vision that will give guidance to the structures of society and provide meaning and value to the various sectors comprising civil society. Stackhouse argues that this kind of theology is not merely confessional, but "engages philosophy and science, ethics and the analysis of social life, to find out which kinds of faith enhance life. . . ."[5] For Stackhouse, the interaction between religious insight, philosophical wisdom, and social analysis is a key factor in the development of a public theology.[6]

Certain key theological themes emerge in Stackhouse's approach to public theology. The doctrine of creation points us to a reality beyond ourselves to whom we are accountable and who serves as the ultimate reference point for how we are to structure our lives together. Liberation emphasizes social change that is reflected by a response to a just God who governs history and eventually will rectify patterns of oppression. Vocation examines how we should order our life together as a community and society. Covenant focuses on how we are to live out our vocations responsibly and leads to accountability in social relationships. It is the community-ordering side of vocation. Moral law attempts to answer the question "Is there right and wrong?" and asserts that there are universally valid moral laws rooted in God. Sin is the recognition of the human tendency for betrayal of ourselves, our neighbors, our world, and God. Freedom answers the question of how such sinful distortion is possible under a sovereign God, and also serves as recognition of humanity's dual capacity for being genuinely human and genuinely licentious and traitorous. Ecclesiology focuses on the free exercise and critique of religion, and the

---

3   Among other confessional theologians, most of whom can be loosely identified as "post-liberals," see Placher, William 1989. *Unapologetic Theology: A Christian Voice in a Pluralistic Conversation*. Louisville: Westminster/John Knox Press; Lindbeck, George 1984. T*he Nature of Doctrine: Religion and Theology in a Postliberal Age*. Philadelphia: Westminster Press; Hauerwas, Stanley 1993. T*he Peaceable Kingdom: A Primer in Christian Ethics*. Notre Dame: University of Notre Dame Press; and Yoder, John Howard 1997. *For the Nations: Essays Public and Political*. Grand Rapids: Eerdmans. Thiemann's work sets forth this approach to public theology more than adequately. He does have differences from the others, particularly Hauerwas and Lindbeck, but they all share certain core similarities.

4   Stackhouse, Max L. 1987. *Public Theology and Political Economy: Christian Stewardship in Modern Society*. Grand Rapids: Eerdmans, xi.

5   Stackhouse, Max L. 1997. "Public Theology and Ethical Judgment." *Theology Today* 54 (July): 168.

6   For example, see Ibid. and Stackhouse, Max L., Berger, Peter L., McCann, Dennis P. and Meeks, M. Douglas 1995. *Christian Social Ethics in a Global Era*. Nashville: Abingdon Press.

recognition of the rights of other religious groups to propagate their views of sin and salvation in private and public affairs to the people. This is rooted in the "free-church" tradition, and encourages religious institutions to set forth and clarify the metaphysical moral meanings that give purpose and structure to life beyond particular group loyalties. A confidence in "persuasion" is implicit here, confidence in the ability to persuade others regarding the merits of a particular confessional stance in a reasonable way. The final theme is the Trinity, which leads to a conception of reality in terms of a coherent, integrated diversity. It encourages pluralism but under a greater and final unity.[7] The Trinitarian theme points toward a radical appreciation of both transcendence and humanity, viewing both as true but reducing neither to each other.[8] For Stackhouse, these themes clarify and communicate the justice of God in a public context and have components of thought that connect to contemporary human affairs and issues of concern. He hopes that modern adaptations of these themes may provide certain clues for constructing a public theology in this postindustrial, global age. To determine the validity of theological positions, Stackhouse proposes the use of the Wesleyan quadrilateral of Scripture, Tradition, Reason, and Experience. Stackhouse uses these four "touchstones of authority" but modifies them from an ecumenical viewpoint. This approach is clearly apologetic in its assumption that there cannot only be public discussion but also significant understanding of theological ideas and agreement concerning the relevance (even necessity) of Christian faith to the structure and direction of society.

In *Constructing a Public Theology: The Church in a Pluralistic Culture*, Thiemann defines public theology as "faith seeking to understand the relation between Christian convictions and the broader social and cultural context within which the Christian community lives."[9] Drawing on the work of Clifford Geertz,[10] Thiemann desires to set forth a "thick description" of the Christian community and the contemporary context. This descriptive approach is intended to show how a theology shaped by biblical narratives and grounded in the practices and institutional life of the Christian community can provide resources to enable people of faith to regain a public voice in our pluralistic culture. The key challenge is to develop a public theology that remains based in the particularities of the Christian faith while addressing issues of public significance in a genuine fashion. This descriptive approach seeks to identify particular places where Christian convictions intersect with practices that characterize contemporary public life. This is not something that can be known in advance, and the relevance of Christian convictions to public policy issues must be discovered through a process of rigorous inquiry in which faith risks genuine engagement with the forces of public life in pluralistic society. In this element of risk, faith may have to be reshaped and some convictions may be jettisoned after prolonged critical inquiry and engagement with public life.[11] As implied above, Thiemann's theology

7   For a specific example of this theme, see Stackhouse, Max L. 1991. "The Trinity as Public Theology: Its Truth and Justice for Free-Church, Noncredal Communities." In *Faith to Creed*. Heim, S. Mark, ed. Grand Rapids: Eerdmans.

8   All themes taken from Stackhouse, *Public Theology and Political Economy*, 18–34.

9   Thiemann, Ronald F. 1991. *Constructing a Public Theology: The Church in a Pluralistic Culture*. Louisville: Westminster/John Knox Press, 21.

10 See Geertz, Clifford 1973. "Thick Description: Toward an Interpretive Theory of Culture." In *The Interpretation of Cultures*. New York: Basic Books, 10.

11 Thiemann, *Constructing A Public Theology*, 22–23.

is explicitly non-foundational, eschewing general explanatory schemes and seeking to provide a justification of Christian belief specific to the faith community, an attempt to re-describe the internal logic of the Christian faith.

What characterizes Thiemann's approach? First, he calls for a recognition of moral and cultural pluralism. Since there is no longer a common morality or culture, Thiemann seeks a path between moral relativism and cultural/religious imperialism and encourages the practice of a positive religious pluralism. The reaffirmation of the role of religion in public life is vital, and while not apologetic in approach, Thiemann seeks to debunk the notion of religion's absence from public life and to demonstrate that questions of conviction, value, and faith are to be a part of public discourse. As part of this task, confessional public theology seeks a reversal of liberalism's accommodation to culture. While there is a desire to have religious convictions and theological analyses impact the structure of public life and policy, Thiemann does not believe that there is one solution to this intersection of faith and public life simply as a correlate to maintaining confessional integrity. As a goal, he wants to address the challenge of influencing the development of public policy without seeking to construct a new Christendom or lapsing into a benign moral relativism.[12] Much space lies between these alternatives.

Two final characteristics are noteworthy. First there is the acknowledgment that the Biblical narratives demonstrate a way of life and reveal the pattern of discipleship, the way of the cross.[13] Last is the belief that worship helps shape public responsibility. An aspect of public theology is rediscovering the link between worship and education, and recognizing that the church can model an approach to life in a pluralistic society. It is also vital to remember that the church's most important service is to be a community of hope.[14]

As stated above, this approach is associated with Yale, particularly the post-liberalism that is, using George Lindbeck's categories, "cultural linguistic." This is an anthropological, community-specific approach that Thiemann uses to provide his "thick description." He and his fellow post-liberals attempt to articulate a public theology which retains the identity of the church in pluralistic context and which tries to argue from an explicitly confessional stance.[15]

Both Stackhouse and Thiemann exemplify the desire to see the public impact of theology, though they differ fundamentally on the public value of a purely confessional stance. Resisting the post-Enlightenment banishment of theology to the private realm, both approaches to public theology have designs on shaping history as it moves forward by bringing Christianity into the various areas of public life. For the purposes of this article, the central question that remains is "Where does the approach of Abraham Kuyper fit?" "How did Kuyper contend with the post-Enlightenment 'triumph'"? "Was his approach to public engagement primarily apologetic with an emphasis on the theological realities that lie deep within social architecture of society, or was it a theology which required the strict maintenance of a distinctive Christian identity, belief, and practice as one engages the public square?" "Is there any 'common' area of discourse and interaction between

---

12 Characteristics 1–5 summarized from ibid., 38–43.

13 Ibid., 63–71.

14 Ibid., 112–125

15 A specific example of Thiemann's (1996) approach to public theology is his *Religion in Public Life: A Dilemma for Democracy*. Washington, DC: Georgetown University Press.

Christians and others in the public realm, or does Kuyper violate the distinction between these positions?"

Abraham Kuyper and His Public Theology[16]

Abraham Kuyper was a minister, professor, journalist, and politician (ultimately Prime Minister of the Netherlands 1901–05), often at the same time. His approach to public engagement was framed by the problems raised by the movements and thinkers of the modern era as he sought to represent the *kleine luyden*, the confessionally orthodox Christians who were at the margins of society. His public theology had to address the ideas and events of his context, so he could bring the influence of Reformed thought into the public of his era creatively and even improvisationally.

As a living expression of public theology, Kuyper sought to engage the challenges of the modern era and was unique in that he was an intellectual who led a popular movement.[17] His public theology is expressed clearly in the Stone Lectures at Princeton (1898), but one earlier public event is a pivotal precursor.

Kuyper's public theology in summary

In 1880, Abraham Kuyper gave the inaugural speech for the Free University of Amsterdam (Vrije Universiteit),[18] a school intended to be an institution of higher education that not only taught theology, but also science, philosophy, literature, and medicine. The objective of this institution was to provide an approach to higher education rooted in a Reformed worldview.[19] This public address is significant because it advocates the existence of a distinctly Christian institution in the public realm. The heart of the address lies in its title, *Souvereiniteit in Eigen Kring* (translated as "Sovereignty in the Distinct Spheres of Human Life," or more commonly, "Sphere Sovereignty"). Kuyper's objective is to argue for a form of pluralism in society rooted in God's sovereignty and the structure of creation itself. Kuyper argues, in contrast to those who would view the state as possessing unlimited rule, that only God and the Messiah possess such ultimate sovereignty. Then comes Kuyper's step toward pluralism:

> But here is the glorious principle of Freedom! This perfect Sovereignty of the *sinless* Messiah at the same time directly denies and challenges all absolute sovereignty among *sinful* men on earth, and does so by dividing all of life into *separate spheres*, each with its own sovereignty.[20]

For Kuyper, there is a sovereignty derivative of God in the great complexity that comprises human existence. In the realms of politics, art, and education (to name a few), there exist

---

16 Puchinger, George 1998. *Abraham Kuyper: His Early Journey of Faith*, edited by George Harinck. Trans. Simone Kennedy. Amsterdam: VU University Press, 27–28. The implication of Kuyper's vision of public theology is one which is not satisfied with confessionalism alone. For him it is of paramount importance that religious convictions move outside of the confessional enclave and into public life.

17 Bratt, James D., "Abraham Kuyper: His world and work." In *AK:ACR* 2.

18 For a detailed approach to the origin of the Free University of Amsterdam, see Kobes, Wayne A. 1993. "Sphere Sovereignty and the University: Theological Foundations of Abraham Kuyper's View of the University and its Role in Society." *PhD Diss.* The Florida State University.

19 Praamsma, Louis 1985. *Let Christ Be King: Reflections on the Life and Times of Abraham Kuyper*. Jordan Station, Ontario: Paideia Press, 73–76.

20 "Sphere Sovereignty." In *AK:ACR* 467—referenced below as *SS*.

laws of life specific to the particular area.[21] Further, because each sphere "comprises its own domain, each has its own Sovereign within its bounds" (*SS* 467). As noted above, this view of pluralism makes it possible to argue that government, church, and education should all operate under their own authority.

Kuyper made the case for sphere sovereignty with two objectives in mind. First, he wanted to make the argument, in terms of *structural* pluralism, that education had the right to operate free of government intervention. Second, in this speech he also contended for *worldview* pluralism, in which he asserts that Christians have the right to operate their own confessionally based institutions in a context that had grown hostile to the Reformed faith throughout the nineteenth century. Regarding worldview pluralism, Kuyper says,

> Shall we pretend to grow from the self-same root that which, according to the express pronouncement of Jesus' divine self-consciousness, is rooted entirely differently? We shall *not* risk it, ladies and gentleman! Rather, considering that something begins from principle and that a distinct entity takes rise from a distinct principle, we shall maintain a distinct sovereignty for our own principle and for that of our opponents across the whole sphere of thought. That is to say, as from their principle and by a method appropriate to it they erect a house of knowledge that glitters but does not entice us, so we too from our principle and by its corresponding method will let our own trunk shoot up whose branches, leaves, and blossoms are nourished with its own sap. (*SS* 484–85)

Notice that Kuyper's proposal makes room for institutions that represent a variety of worldviews, not just the Reformed perspective.

Importantly, Kuyper's structural pluralism is not the same as subsidiarity, a Catholic view of social order. As Skillen and McCarthy note,

> Kuyper's argument is different from that of "subsidiarity" which stresses a natural, *vertical* hierarchy of responsibilities in social life along with the rightful autonomy of the various parts within the societal "whole" which the state governs. In the subsidiarity argument the state is charged with the protection and promotion of the common good of the whole society, whereas Kuyper is suggesting a more *horizontal* concept of social spheres, among which the state has less encompassing responsibility.[22]

Kuyper's approach places God above everything, and below him the various social spheres are on the same level, interacting with each other like cogwheels and yielding "the rich, multifaceted multi-formity of human life" (*SS* 468). Given his principal thinking, sphere sovereignty is an idea that provides Kuyper and his followers the opportunity and encouragement to engage the public realm. It inspires Christians to be good stewards of society, while keeping ecclesiastical authority from dictating public policy. For Kuyper there is no way that Christians can stay out of public life, as his most famous quote from the speech propounds.

> Oh, no single piece of our mental world is to be hermetically sealed off from the rest, and there is not a square inch in the whole domain of our human existence over which Christ, who is Sovereign over *all*, does not cry: "Mine!" (*SS* 488)

This rhetorical flourish yields the unmistakable conclusion that if the entire creation is

---

21 *SS* 467. Kuyper does not give a number of spheres, saying, "The name or image is unimportant, so long as we recognize that there are in life as many spheres as there are constellations in the sky."

22 Kuyper, A. 1991. "The Antirevolutionary Program." *In Political Order and the Plural Structure of Society*, edited by James W. Skillen and Rockne M., McCarthy. Atlanta: Scholars Press, 241.

God's domain, then Christians are compelled to engage the public square, in this case the creation of a university. Equally significant for the central question of this paper is that Kuyper's argument emphasizes a belief that the various spheres of society have a theological basis while emphasizing Christian distinctiveness as well. The structural and worldview pluralisms articulated demonstrate the tension between an apologetic and confessional approach to public theology.

The Stone Lectures

In 1898, Abraham Kuyper gave the L. P. Stone Lectures at Princeton Theological Seminary. The six lectures given to this American audience present the most comprehensive articulation of Kuyper's thought. Central emphases of Kuyper's "public theological mission" in the Netherlands are on display here. Of particular interest for understanding his public theology are the theological rationale for engaging public life, sphere sovereignty, and the tension between the antithesis and common grace.

Kuyper's objective in the lectures was to set forth Calvinism as a comprehensive life-system that provided a Christian perspective and approach to every area of life. He claimed that Calvinism embodied the ideal of Christianity most accurately (over against Roman Catholicism and Lutheranism) and stood in contrast to major worldviews such Paganism and Islam (LC 20–21). This approach to Calvinism is not strictly a religious system, but "an all-embracing system of principles (LC 19) that provides an approach to every facet of life, including public engagement.

What is Kuyper's theological rationale for public engagement in these lectures? The doctrine of common grace is foundational. Kuyper argues that Calvinism emphasizes not only a particular grace of election but "also a *common grace* by which God, maintaining the life of the world, relaxes the curse which rests upon it, arrests its process of corruption, and thus allows the untrammeled development of our life in which to glorify Himself as Creator" (LC 30). He argues that God's beneficence to the entire creation compels Christians to serve God in every facet of life. For Kuyper, this non-redemptive grace is given so believers honor the world and "in every domain, discover the treasures and develop the potencies hidden by God in nature and in human life" (LC 31). Public engagement is a responsibility of Christians, not an option. As they embrace this responsibility, Christians will discover and develop systems for and approaches to domestic, social, and political life that provide alternatives to other worldviews.

In his lecture on "Calvinism and Politics," Kuyper revisits the idea of sphere sovereignty. Kuyper's purpose in 1880 was to make a place in society for a Christian university (and for institutions representative of other worldviews, even if non-Christian). His purpose in 1898 was to demonstrate the broader idea that Calvinism led to a particular kind of political conception.[23]

In this instance, Kuyper argues for three distinct spheres in the public realm: state, society, and church. As Kuyper stated eighteen years earlier, the root principle of Calvinism was the sovereignty of God over the entire cosmos, and the three spheres derive from God's primordial sovereignty (LC 79). Each of these spheres possesses its own authority within

---

23 As in his speech on sphere sovereignty in 1880, Kuyper sets his approach to the socio-political world in contrast to the radical democracy of the French Revolution and the all-embracing State rooted in Hegel's philosophy. LC 85–90.

itself. In the state, Kuyper argues that as a result of sin, God instituted ruling authorities for the purpose of governance. He suggests further that Calvinism leads to a form of government structured as a republic, and that this was Calvin's preference.[24]

Though he argues that ultimately God provides this form of public rule, he is adamant that it is not a theocracy:

> A theocracy was only found in Israel, because in Israel, God intervened immediately. For both by *Urim and Thummim* and by *Prophecy*, both by His saving miracles, and by His chastising judgments, He held in His own hand the jurisdiction and the leadership of His people. But the Calvinistic confession of the sovereignty of God holds good for *all* the world, is true for all nations, and is of force in all authority, which man exercises over man; even in the authority which parents possess over their children. (*LC* 85)

God's sovereignty is mediated through human authority, including government, and therefore is not the direct rule characteristic of a theocracy. Moreover, while this chapter makes clear that Kuyper desired government according to divine ordinances, it should also be clear that he had no desire to structure society according to the exact dictates of Mosaic law.

In society, Kuyper argues that God has given sovereignty in the individual social spheres "in order that it may be sharply and decidedly expressed that these different developments of social life *have nothing above themselves but God*, and that the State cannot intrude here, and has nothing to command in their domain" (*LC* 91). The individual social spheres (such as business, family, educational institutions, and guilds) have the liberty to function on their own according to divine ordinances that God has established for each one. This does not mean that the government can never intervene, but only becomes involved when differing spheres clash, when there is an abuse of weaker individuals within spheres, or to coerce all of the spheres to contribute to the maintenance of the state's natural unity (*LC* 97). Above all, the state should protect the liberty of the various social spheres, allowing them to flourish.

The church has sovereignty within the state, but not in a Constantinian fashion where the church takes on the role of the most influential advisor.[25] Kuyper contends that Calvinism allows the government to rule apart from the direct influence of the church. While the magistrates are to rule according to God's divine ordinances, they have independence from the church, and God's word rules through the conscience of those invested with governmental authority (*LC* 103–06). Additionally, the church allows liberty of conscience, speech, and worship in society, though individuals within local churches are subject to the judgment of the clergy.[26]

Kuyper's expression of sphere sovereignty in the Stone Lectures sets forth a view of

---

24 Peter Heslam argues that Kuyper is disingenuous on this point and states that Calvin in his *Institutes* IV. XX. 8 showed a distinct preference for aristocracy. See Heslam, Peter S. 1998. *Creating a Christian Worldview: Abraham Kuyper's Lectures on Calvinism*. Grand Rapids: Eerdmans, 144.

25 (*LC* 99–100); Kuyper wishes to distance himself from Calvin's role in the death of Servetus, and he contends that the principle which led to this unfortunate incident lies in Constantinianism, not in the essential principles of Calvinism.

26 (*LC* 107–09; elsewhere, Kuyper argues that it was the "Calvinistic Netherlands." Kuyper's term that promoted freedom of thought and expression throughout society, even if there was a state church. He says, "Whosoever was elsewhere straightened, could first enjoy the liberty of ideas and the liberty of press, on Calvinistic ground" (*LC* 109).

a pluralistic society in which God's sovereignty is differentiated throughout three major spheres (though there are many smaller individual spheres in society) which respect each others' boundaries. In this view, the Calvinistic principle yields a non-theocratic, republican society which promotes the development of the created order when the spheres operate as God intended.

Where do the antithesis and common grace come into tension?[27] Kuyper's lectures on science and art reveal this tension without adequate resolution, but the lectures continue to suggest avenues of public engagement for Christians. In the lecture "Calvinism and Science," initially Kuyper argues that common grace leads to a love for science and that it gives science its own academic domain, but then he makes a stark contrast between two kinds of science (*LC* 130–141). There are those he calls Normalists, who only look at natural data, and there are Abnormalists, who look at the natural realm but find their ideal norm in the Triune God. The ultimate difference between these two is "*two kinds of human consciousness:* that of the regenerate and the unregenerate" (*LC* 137). In effect, this means that Christians and non-Christians have different *kinds* of minds, and the result is that they perceive the entire universe differently and develop approaches to science that reflect their perspectives. Kuyper does not argue that only one group should do science, but that each should be allowed to pursue the discipline in its own circles (*LC* 138). In this lecture the antithesis is set forth as fact to be acknowledged by Christians and others in the society.

In the lecture "Calvinism and Art" Kuyper argues that common grace enables the production of art and inspires Christians and non-Christians alike (*LC* 161). Rather than contending for a particularly Christian conception of art, Kuyper asserts, "Calvinism, on the contrary, has taught us that all liberal arts are gifts which God imparts promiscuously to believers and unbelievers, yea, that, as history shows, these gifts have flourished even in a larger measure outside the holy circle" (*LC* 160). Art is truly "commonly" produced. In addition to arguing that God gives artistic abilities to all kinds of people, Kuyper has another objective. While a part of Kuyper's objective in this lecture is to argue that Calvinism has emancipated art from the church (particularly the Roman Church), he wishes also to assert and promote the view that the world of art (painting, music, and poetry) should develop to its fullest in its expression of all of life (*LC* 163–64). This development can occur by Christians or non-Christians. The important point is that the realm of art, whether it is related to the church or not, should enjoy the support of Christians.

Kuyper's argument for art is in direct contrast to his perspective on science, as Peter Heslam observes:

> That Kuyper was able to display a positive approach to the arts was largely due to his doctrine of common grace, which in this lecture, in contrast to his lecture on science, is emphasized at the expense of his doctrine of the antithesis, which plays no significant role. This discrepancy is one of the clearest indications of what is perhaps the central tension in Kuyper's thought between the antithesis and corresponding isolation on the one hand, and common grace and corresponding engagement and accommodation on the other.[28]

---

27 For a study on antithesis and common grace in the Dutch Calvinist tradition, see Klapwijk, Jacob 1991. "Antithesis and Common Grace." In J. Klapwijk, S. Griffioen, and G. Groenewoud, eds. *Bringing Into Captivity Every Thought: Capita Selecta in the History of Christian Evaluations of Non-Christian Philosophy.* Lanham: University Press of America, 169–190. *See infra* Chapter 20.

28 Heslam, *Creating a Christian Worldview*, 222.

In the Stone Lectures, Kuyper leaves this tension unresolved, but he does achieve his objective of finding ways to encourage Christian engagement of the sciences and patronage of the arts.

Kuyper's lectures at Princeton display the basis for his public theology (common grace), an approach to society under God's sovereignty, and the central tension in his thought between antithesis and common grace. His version of Calvinism not only promotes, but also prompts Christian public engagement in all areas of life. It is true that in certain arenas this engagement is in a Christian circle, while in others it is in the midst of society in general. Either way, there is a call to the responsibility for discovering God's ordinances and developing the potentialities of creation. This reveals Kuyper as neither fully apologetic nor exclusively confessional. How should this tension be understood, or even resolved?

Conclusion: Abraham Kuyper's Rhetorical Public Theology

It is notable that a portrait of Abraham Kuyper's public theology emerges from the context of public address. Though he was a prolific author, it is in his public addresses that Kuyper sets forth his public theology in the best way. In the public forum, Kuyper presents a public theology that contains elements of confessional and apologetic public theology, but he achieves his intended effect primarily through rhetorical power. Labeling Kuyper's approach as rhetorical emphasizes his position as a public figure who used the tools of journalism and public address considerably. The power of his words, as well as their content, were important. Often his arguments are carried in rhetoric that moved his audience to action, though the Stone Lectures was before an American audience that experienced a display of Kuyper as more of an academic than political statesman. Before making the case for Kuyper as the rhetorical public theologian, it is important to address specifically the relation to the approaches to public theology presented above.

Kuyper's affinities to Stackhouse and Thiemann are very significant. By his focus on common grace, recognition of pluralism in civil society, and his emphasis on the search for the ordinances of creation, Kuyper has certain elements in common with Stackhouse. More specifically, there is overlap with Stackhouse's themes, though Kuyper does not use identical language. A good example would be Stackhouse's theme of liberation, which uses language that speaks of social change especially in terms of rectifying patterns of oppression. As the above articulation of his mission reveals, Kuyper's entire public project can be construed in part as a liberation mission for the *kleine luyden* who were relegated to the margins of society. Another good example is that Stackhouse's theme of moral law bears resemblance to Kuyper's search for divine ordinances, and the theme of ecclesiology fits Kuyper's desire for worldview pluralism in society. Kuyper does not make reference to any quadrilateral, but an overview of his work will reveal that he utilizes Scripture, Tradition and Reason variously, though not in identical ways to Stackhouse. With his focus on antithesis, Kuyper, like Thiemann, desires to find a way to maintain the integrity of Christian confession while participating in public life. Thiemann's characteristics that reaffirm the public role of religion and the desire to have religious convictions and theological analysis affect the structure of public life and policy find resonance in Kuyper's emphasis on sphere sovereignty (particularly its initial articulation in 1880 and the emphasis on worldview pluralism) and the Stone Lecture on Science. A final comparison is noteworthy. While Kuyper was very creative in crafting neo-Calvinism in a way that served his public aims (a view shared by scholars sympathetic and critical), it must be said that, unlike Thiemann, he would not suggest potentially radical alteration of the tradition as a possible result of the search for effective public engagement (though Kuyper's theologically conservative critics in the Netherlands feared this very thing). While these apologetic and confessional aspects are significant elements, Kuyper does not land decisively or exclusively in either camp. Perhaps Kuyper's public theology can best be characterized by what yielded its greatest influence: through rhetoric.

John Bolt suggests that it might be best to perceive Kuyper as a poet. By focusing on his rhetorical and mythopoetic perspective rather than strictly his theological and philosophical ideas, one arrives at a view of Kuyper's public theology that helps explain his public effectiveness.[29] Bolt argues:

> To understand Kuyper's success as a *movement* leader, emancipating and prodding into action the marginalized Dutch orthodox *Gereformeerde kleine luyden*, we must see him reviving and using a Dutch, Christian-historical imagination through powerful rhetoric, well-chosen biblical images and national mythology. That is what I mean by Kuyper as "poet," a man of *rhetoric* and *mythos* more than a man of *logos* and *wetenschap*. Here we find a unity to Kuyper's multifaceted career as churchman, theologian, journalist, politician. Kuyper knew triumphant political technique was not enough, politics alone cannot save the world. What then? Few have stated it better in our era than Alexander Solzhenitsyn who learned it from Dostoyevsky: "Beauty will save the world." That is, it is art, the historical mythology imaginatively captured in a peoples" literature, paintings and festivals, the iconographic emblems; it is these that stir hearts and mobilize hands to change the world. Good art nourishes our capacity for self-transcendence, and is our only access to other people's experience, including that past. Literature is "the living memory of a nation . . . [that], together with language, preserves and protects a nation's soul."[30]

In what way does Kuyper the artist stir hearts and mobilize hands? One way that he did this was by invoking the names of Willem Bilderdijk and Isaac da Costa in a speech entitled "Maranatha."[31] By reference to these two figures, Kuyper invoked the national spirit in his people. Further, Kuyper tied biblical images into national history, as when he launched the weekly newspaper *De Standaard* and invoked a day of Dutch liberation.[32]

Bolt also notes Herman Bavinck's comparison between Bilderdijk and da Costa in an 1897 celebration of the twenty-five years for *De Standaard*, where the literary edge is given to Kuyper. Additionally, Bolt points to James Bratt's comparison of Kuyper with Martin Luther King. This comparison reveals, significantly, that both King and Kuyper were authors but are regarded best as orators, and that both men utilized the imagery from national history to rouse their constituency and advance their cause.[33] This should

---

29 For a detailed view of this, see Bolt, John 2001. *A Free Church, A Holy Nation: Abraham Kuyper's American Public Theology*. Grand Rapids: Eerdmans, 3–79. An abbreviated summary of this chapter can be found in Bolt, John 1999. "Abraham Kuyper as Poet: Another Look at Kuyper's Critique of the Enlightenment." In C. van der Kooi and J. de Bruijn, eds. *Kuyper Reconsidered: Aspects of His Life and Work*. VU Studies on Protestant History. Amsterdam: VU Uitgeverij, 30–41.

30 Bolt, "Abraham Kuyper as Poet," 34–35.

31 "Maranatha," in *AK:ACR* 215–216

32 Bolt, "Abraham Kuyper as Poet," 38.

33 Ibid., 40.

not diminish Kuyper as a theological force, but place emphasis on the role of public oral expression as central to his mission.[34]

Kuyper's rhetorical approach is also found in Jan de Bruijn's article "Abraham Kuyper as a Romantic." In this article, there are two aspects of romanticism worthy of note. First, there is the tendency to think in terms of opposites. Kuyper often used this approach when articulating the validity of the Christian position over against another worldview or political system, from Pantheism to Socialism to the French Revolution. This tendency is also evident in the manner that Kuyper often opposed his Calvinist principles against other systems of thought and practice. A second key aspect of Kuyper's romanticism is the "predilection for the dramatic moment, for poses and theatricality . . . used like brilliant actors."[35] While harder to perceive in the Stone Lectures, this element can be seen clearly in a survey of some of Kuyper's speeches, such as the closing words of "Sphere Sovereignty," "Maranatha," or "The Blurring of the Boundaries." The use of the dramatic moment served Kuyper's rhetoric well, winning over his audience. In the following description of Kuyper, de Bruijn reveals the potency of Kuyper as a romantic rhetorician:

> Kuyper was a man of many qualities. His personality was masterful, his knowledge exceptionally wide-ranging; he was a skillful teacher and polemicist; his energy was tireless and he was a brilliant organizer and a tactical genius. Last but not least, with his baroque eloquence with which he repeatedly urged his followers on, he turned the middle classes into a political force, thus radically altering the political balance of power in Holland. It is no wonder that his supporters revered him as a prophet, as a leader sent by God, as the "Lord's anointed" who like a second Moses had led them to the Promised Land. Kuyper, too, saw himself in this light and as a romantic he could make good use of historical and biblical imagery, symbols and myths to emphasize the special and sacred nature of his struggle and leadership.[36]

Of all the qualities listed, it is Kuyper's eloquence and rhetorical use of imagery that made him such a forceful public influence. Like Bolt, de Bruijn suggests that Kuyper's use of artistry provided the greatest force in mobilizing the *kleine luyden*. If Kuyper understood himself as the one sovereignly appointed by God to serve as the Moses of his people, it required such artistry combined with skillful language. The presentation of his views that Christians should be involved in every area of life came clothed in the words of a leader who wanted people to be not only theologically orthodox but also energetically engaged in the tasks of liberation and social change.

Labeling Kuyper's public theology as rhetorical does not mean that Kuyper did not have convictions that lay beneath his exceptional public artistry. An idea such as sphere sovereignty, for example, was not a mere instrument employed in the service of Kuyper's ambition. Rather, Kuyper utilized his mythopoetic imagination as the means for persuading his public of his theological or philosophical positions and for motivating them to action. Furthermore, it is important to recall that Kuyper maintained that there were divine ordinances which could be discovered and set forth as a guide for society, and that his goal was not to merely amaze audiences with poetic language, but to prompt

---

34 It is also noteworthy that Bavinck is seen as the summit of neo-Calvinist dogmatic theology, which makes sense given his greater academic theological output. The bulk of Kuyper's writing reflected his great intellect but was in the form of editorials and speeches.

35 Bruijn, Jan 1999. "Abraham Kuyper as a Romantic," in *Kuyper Reconsidered*, 43.

36 Ibid., 50.

them to public engagement, a goal that he accomplished. Additionally, one cannot neglect Kuyper's emphasis on common grace and antithesis[37] as the chief rationales for forms of participation in public life; and in articulating these opposing tendencies, Kuyper does not abandon argument as much as creatively use rhetoric (as seen in the Stone Lectures).

Abraham Kuyper is not presented often as a theologian who utilized rhetorical genius as a primary means for motivating and mobilizing his audiences, yet he is regarded often as one who did not neatly resolve the tensions in his theological rationales for public engagement. If one places rhetoric at the front, it helps to explain why he does not resolve, in a final, tidy fashion, the greatest tension, between common grace and antithesis. Putting rhetoric at the fore emphasizes Kuyper's ultimate goal: the mobilization of Christians for public engagement and greater public influence in the Netherlands. Depending upon the circumstance, Kuyper would emphasize either commonness for the purpose of "going public" in non-church realms, or antithesis when the necessity of distinctive Christian public engagement was the objective. Much of Kuyper's public theology addressed particular situations. His public life demanded an episodic approach to theological issues, in turn producing moments of great emphasis on commonness or great articulations of Christian distinctiveness. To label Kuyper a rhetorical public theologian is not a refusal to deal with tension, but an embrace of the complexity of Kuyper's public theological task.

Is Kuyper's approach a way forward for the ongoing discussion of public theology? Yes and no. In the sense that his approach brings to the fore the significance of using a skillful rhetorical imagination while one aims for prompting Christians toward public engagement, Kuyper's approach sheds light on an area that is not often addressed in the realm of public theology. The emphasis on rhetoric is not helpful in resolving the issues of commonness and distinctiveness between Christians and non-Christians because it does not focus on the epistemological questions regarding the noetic effects of sin and the subsequent comprehensibility of Christian theological language and concepts. Perhaps the best conclusion of the matter is to note that in spite of the less than tidy resolution of a vital question, Kuyper himself was not deterred from charging into the public square that had been declared off-limits to Christian faith. Even if one emphasizes the confessional over the apologetic, the very least that we must do is follow Kuyper and others into the public arena and sort out the issues as we bring faith to bear on society.

What then does Kuyper's public theology mean for an institution that strives to integrate faith and learning? Kuyper's approach is vital for a number of reasons. The first is due to one of the strongest currents that runs throughout the Kuyperian paradigm: a potent creation emphasis. Kuyper's approach carries with it the view that the entirety of creation belongs to God, that though the world is fallen it remains the creation that

37 Interestingly, de Bruijn notes that Kuyper was a divided personality, which could help explain why common grace and antithesis are never resolved fully. He says, "For like every romantic, Kuyper was not a unified personality; he was no simple one-dimensional figure, but possessed an extremely complex character structure, composed of different layers and often contradictory tendencies, wishes and emotions. In many respects he was a divided and tormented person whose life was not easy and who suffered periods of deep depression. However, he survived because of a faith that expressed itself on the one hand in mystical longings, and on the other in an unremitting, almost compulsive activity and struggle to realize his religious ideals." "Kuyper as a Romantic" in *Kuyper Reconsidered*, 45. An interesting question is: Was Kuyper's primary concern the practical achievement of his goals rather than the precise articulation of a theological construct to undergird his mission?

was declared "very good" in Genesis 1:31. When I teach the doctrine of creation, I emphasize this point heavily because many students approach their Christian lives as an act of escape from the sinking ship that is creation. A Kuyperian approach corrects this improper emphasis. When students understand that the biblical warnings about loving the world really refer to the "world system" that opposes God's desire for human practice upon the terrain of creation and that it does not condemn the creation itself, they begin to move toward a view of Christian life that includes stewardship of the created order. This approach to stewardship brings together faith and learning because the emphases in other disciplines are now validated. For example, God can be glorified in the scientist's laboratory, in the exploration of human longing expressed by poets and novelists, on the artist's canvas, and in the historian's examination of influential persons, societies and ideas. These and other disciplines are not sideshows when set against "spiritual" matters, but instead are vitally important human activities that have the potential to enhance human lives. A Kuyperian creation emphasis also keeps the doctrine of creation itself from being hijacked by discussions on the origins of humans and the cosmos. The Kuyperian approach recognizes origins as a small part of a doctrine that has profound implications for the way that we live. To put it differently, the discussion of origins focuses on the beginning of things, but what about the rest of human activity beyond its origin? There is at least as great a need to emphasize the thoroughgoing nature of our stewardship as there is to argue about origins. It is the recognition of our stewardship of the creation that leads to the integration of faith and learning. In fact, a Kuyperian approach unifies faith and learning by rendering the academic disciplines valid.

A second significant benefit of Kuyper's approach comes from the tension between common grace and antithesis. While the tension was never resolved by Kuyper, these two emphases work well together for thinking about how to approach faith and learning, which is in actuality a public exercise (we teach and model before students how faith intersects with all of reality). A good example of how this works was expressed by one student in my political theology class. He pointed out the example of how a confessionally Christian education (at any educational level) can actually provide training that produces better "public" citizens. Though their education is rooted in a particular worldview (emphasizing antithesis), they are not prepared for life in an enclave but for a life of stewardship of the creation as stated above (public engagement is prompted by common grace). It is true that these citizens are not people who would enter the public square with any illusions of neutrality (as if such a position exists), but they would function in every area of life as people who seek the common good. In a similar manner, a Kuyperian perspective can inform one's approach to a Christian education. Where I teach, we are not aiming to produce graduates who are concerned exclusively with vitality of the Christian community. In the best cases, we are helping to produce young adults who function as thoughtful and involved citizens of the church and larger society. Common grace and antithesis work together to encourage distinctive Christian public engagement. In faith and learning terms, that means a confessionally-based education that yields graduates who serve everyone. The aim is to have graduates who understand that their service throughout society will be refracted through a Christian worldview that informs their understanding and practice in business, education, science, art, and other vocations. Hopefully, most students will become people who see that their faith has great significance for the life within the church and without.

A third benefit comes from the idea of sphere sovereignty. This is associated with Kuyper's famous "one square inch" quote (*SS* 468), and the question of its value is important because of its potential impact on a Christian approach to politics and society. The concept of sovereignty in each sphere is beneficial for helping students move toward thinking about a principled pluralism in society. Rather than having a conception of society as strictly under the control of the state or understanding the state as the only significant social structure, sphere sovereignty recognizes that the family, education, business, the church, and the state (and other spheres) all have an integrity of their own. The resultant pluralism is one which acknowledges God's sovereignty over the various domains of life and which recognizes that there is a divine concern for the different areas of life. Put differently, sphere sovereignty helps students consider the manner in which God's authority is mediated in society. Applied more directly to the realm of politics, sphere sovereignty provides a means of thinking about the best ways to be obedient to the divine commands to love others and do justice in the public realm. By promoting a respect for the various spheres, Kuyper's concept raises, at the very least, the question of how Christians can best promote a just society so that life flourishes in all of its dimensions. Sphere sovereignty does not necessitate a particular political stance on the conservative, libertarian, liberal or socialist spectrum, but does help Christians think about how to create a civil society that allows for the healthy debate among various views, particularly when one considers the worldview pluralism emphasis in Kuyper's 1880 speech. Does sphere sovereignty promote or require the advent of Christian political parties and institutions? Not necessarily, though Kuyper's example demonstrates one manner in which a case is made for confessionally-based public associations and institutions.

A final vital emphasis is the emphasis on rhetoric itself. As stated above, the value of Kuyper's rhetorical approach is that it leads to an emphasis on the verbal stewardship of ideas. The choice of metaphors, historical references, and biblical images should not be done haphazardly. Kuyper's example reveals the good that can result from creative, imaginative use of language when conveying ideas in the public realm. If students studied some of Kuyper's speeches, at the very least they would find inspiration for thoughtful, creative, and distinctively Christian public discourse. In a culture where a casual approach to language often prevails, Kuyper's rhetorical example illuminates the importance being a steward of our language, especially when we are addressing public concerns from the standpoint of our faith.

As much as I would like all of my students to become as Kuyperian as myself, more realistically I hope that the example of Kuyper's public theology will permeate my own approach to education so that I can communicate effectively one option that unifies faith and learning. I believe it comes through with clarity, but the refinement process continues.

18

Abraham Kuyper
on Science, Theology, and University

Jacob Klapwijk

Abstract. This article analyzes Kuyper's theory of science in the light of his neo-Calvinist worldview. First we discuss his thesis that there is an inner connection between faith and science. Tensions become visible between a reformational and a scholastic line of thought (1–4). The next part deals with the humanities and theology. Kuyper turns out to have been influenced by the scholastic Logos theory, yet in theology he also defends the idea of a correlation between faith and revelation (5–7). The third part focuses on the self-organization of the sciences in the university. It shows how Kuyper's doctrine of sphere sovereignty leads to "Free Universities" independent of church and state (8–10) The final part is a critical evaluation pointing up four challenges in Kuyper's theory of science. They concern the mediating role of worldviews, the need for a transcendental hermeneutics, the concept of transformation in science and the importance of a correlative theology based on creation (11–14).

Whoever "speaks" of Kuyper speaks of Calvinism. And whoever speaks of Calvinism risks falling directly into error. In our day and age we are easily inclined to associate Calvinism with a certain type of church organization, church confession or theology. We think for instance of the Reformed-Presbyterian church order, of the Westminster Confession of Faith, or of the theological doctrine of predestination. For Abraham Kuyper (1837–1920) these were all a part of Calvinism, to be sure. Yet for him the scope of the label extended much further. He presented Calvinism as a comprehensive vision, even as a renewed shaping of Christianity derived from biblical revelation. And it was to his mind the sixteenth-century reformers, Calvin in particular, that put this global vision front and center.

An earlier version of this article was published as "Abraham Kuyper over wetenschap en universiteit." In C. Augustijn, J. H. Prins, and H. E. S. Woldring (eds) 1987. *Abraham Kuyper: zijn volksdeel, zijn invloed*, Meinema, Delft, 61–94, 238–241. The present version is shorter, puts more emphasis on the position of theology, and has a critical evaluation added to it. The main text has been translated by my late friend Herbert Donald Morton with the support of a donation from the Stichting Dr. Abraham Kuyperfonds. Gerben Groenewoud translated the final discussion. I gratefully acknowledge the valuable suggestions provided by Harry Cook and Harry Van Dyke.

1. Revolutionary and Romantic Calvinism

In his *Lectures on Calvinism* Kuyper describes Calvinism as a "life-system," a life- and worldview comparable to Paganism, Islamism, Romanism and Modernism (*LC*). Central in this worldview according to Kuyper are three things: the absolute sovereignty of God, the equality in principle of all people, and the worldwide calling of the Christian. God's sovereignty entails that He has set his "ordinances" or laws for the entire creation but that He is not subject to these laws Himself. The equality of all people means that God makes no distinction between some people and other people, and particularly not between so-called clergymen and laymen. And the worldwide calling of the Christian implies that every believer is called from whatever position he or she occupies in this world to the service of God, the reformation of the church, and the transformation of society (*LC* 19–32).

Thus by "Calvinism" Kuyper means to express not just a theological position, a confessional stance or a special type of ecclesiastical polity, but a dynamic vision that already in the days of the Reformation brought about all kinds of transformations in society, first of all in Calvin's Geneva and subsequently also among the Huguenots in France, the Reformed in Holland, and the Puritans and Presbyterians in England and Scotland. It is a view that the Pilgrim Fathers took to the New World and that led, even there, to political, cultural and societal renewals. In short, Calvinism can be described as "world-formative Christianity."[1]

It is this revolutionary Calvinism that Kuyper sought to appropriate over a hundred years ago. He wanted to fan smoldering fire, to shine the light of historic Calvinism on modern nineteenth-century culture. This culture was a secularized or de-christianized one in which a smug and pedantic science was leading the world down a primrose path of confusion and unbelief. Kuyper accordingly considered it to be one of his foremost tasks to make the implications of Calvinism transparent for modern science. How he did so, then, is the subject of this article.

Was Kuyper really concerned with Calvinism, with the views of Calvin and his followers? At many points he surely was. Yet there is also reason to speak of "neo-Calvinism." First, in his analysis of Calvinism, Kuyper employed a remarkable hermeneutical guiding principle, namely, that the special character of a system is not to be sought in what it shares with previous systems but in the features whereby it breaks with the past. Thus he was fascinated by those notions of Calvin that carried him as a reformer beyond medieval scholasticism.[2] Furthermore, Kuyper put Calvinism to his own uses by rendering it applicable to the situation in his own day, bringing it "into rapport" with human consciousness as it had developed by the end of the nineteenth century.[3] And finally Kuyper frequently interpreted Calvinism in the organismic and historicizing manner of German romanticism as he had gotten to know it in a more or less Christianized form in Schelling, F. J. Stahl, and Groen van Prinsterer.

---

1 This is a term of Wolterstorff's. Wolterstorff, N. 1983. *Until Justice and Peace Embrace: The Kuyper Lectures for 1981*, Grand Rapids: Eerdmans, ch. 1. See further *LC* 12–19.

2 Kuyper writes: "I advance the rule – that a system is not known in what it has in common with other preceding systems; but that it is distinguished by that in which it differs from those preceding systems" (*LC* 100).

3 Kuyper, Abraham 1894. *Encyclopaedie der Heilige Godgeleerdheid*, 3 vols. Kampen: Kok, vol. 1, vi.

This romantic interpretation shows up in the emphasis he places on the historical, the organic and the principled in Calvinism. In the first place, Calvinism is for Kuyper more than the personal worldview of Calvin himself. Calvinism is primarily "historical Calvinism," that is, the entire complex of historical phenomena in the fields of church, statecraft, morality, society, science, etc. in which Christendom unfolded itself in Western Europe from the sixteenth century onward. Calvinism is also what lies hidden beneath the surface of history, to wit, an "organic system of ideas," of often barely conscious motifs that "embodied" themselves in "historical Calvinism" and gave it, in former times, an enormous vitality. Yet even with that, not everything has been said. The inspiring notions of Calvinism go back ultimately to spiritual points of departure: the core of the Calvinist life and worldview. These core ideas are generally called "the Reformed principles." Thus Kuyper's neo-Calvinism is not something he takes in a simple way from Scripture or Calvin's *Institutes*. He derives it from a kind of intuitive plumbing of what was going on *at bottom* in the entire history of the Reformation, particularly amongst the Calvinist communities.

Kuyper's neo-Calvinism is as authentic as the views of Calvin himself. But it includes anti-scholastic, romantic and contemporary traits. The present study explores this *reformational basic conviction*, that is, Kuyper's vision of historical Calvinism *and* the way it should be reshaped in modern times. It explores in particular how, given this basic conviction, Kuyper developed, in opposition to the predominant theories of science, a distinctive concept of science, of theology, and of the university. It was this concept to which he proceeded to give organizational shape in the Free University of Amsterdam that he established in 1880.

There is a serious complication. Kuyper's concepts are far from always consistent, even with respect to science, theology, and the university. Kuyper was a journalist; he worked under pressure. His reformational basic conviction did not prevent him from constantly borrowing from modern humanist epistemology and then again from traditional scholastic metaphysics, however much he may have warned against such "accommodations." Thus we need a critical analysis of Kuyper. Let us employ the same guidelines that Kuyper used in analyzing sixteenth- and seventeenth-century Calvinism. Confronted with inconsistencies, let us focus on those visionary elements in Kuyper's thought whereby he, as a reformer, distanced himself both from humanistic and scholastic influences. Also with respect to science!

2. The Pseudo-conflict of Faith and Science

In this section let me begin with a reminder. For Kuyper science (Dutch: "*wetenschap*") is more than natural science. Science embraces not only the physical disciplines but also the life sciences, the humanities and liberal arts, and even theology. In other words, for Kuyper science is an inclusive term. It represents the whole world of academic scholarship.

Kuyper invariably connects science with faith. One of his most striking pronouncements in his *Lectures on Calvinism* is the assertion that the so frequently cited conflict between faith and science does not exist: "Every science in a certain degree starts *from faith*" (*LC* 131). In other words, the so-called conflict is a pseudo-conflict, since on the one side the faith position of Christians leads compellingly to scientific reflection, while on the other side the speculative systems of non-Christian scholars, too, proceed from religious root positions of their own. In short, all science is religiously conditioned.

Nevertheless, science is beset by a fundamental conflict. That conflict is not one between faith and science. It is a conflict between two scientific directions of thought that are diametrically opposed to each other because *both* take their departure from religious ground positions. There is a Christian and a non-Christian view of science, and they collide. The customary suggestion that as soon as a Christian perspective is introduced into the discussion objective science is pitted against subjective belief muddies the real issue, according to Kuyper. Science is opposed to science and, in the background, faith is opposed to faith.

This fundamental conflict at the heart of all science is ruled by what Kuyper has called the "antithesis of principles" (*PST* 641; *LC* 139). Since these principles are of a religious nature, we can also speak of a "religious antithesis." Kuyper means by that the struggle between the kingdom of God and the kingdom of the evil one that began in paradise, that reached its climax on the cross, and that will be fought out until the end of the ages. The religious antithesis is a struggle for the preservation or destruction of the whole of God's creation. Kuyper sees all people as involved in this struggle lock, stock, and barrel, with their entire being. When people turn away from God, they at the same time disturb their inter-human and inner-worldly relations. In contrast, when people turn to Him in belief, they contribute at the same time to the restoration of earthly existence in the direction of the coming kingdom. This kingdom is God's kingdom; it is neither a human attainment nor a Christian achievement.

This is not the place to go into this doctrine of the religious antithesis, let alone its theological backgrounds in the thought of Augustine and Calvin or its organizational expansion by Kuyper.[4] I do however want to mention three implications that Kuyper draws from his Calvinian perspective in the direction of our topic, the relation of faith and science. First, according to Calvinism religion encompasses and permeates the whole of created reality. All that is creaturely is claimed by God and must be consecrated to Him. Religion, in other words, is not just a component but has a "completely universal character." Next, Calvinism sees the whole of life, in particular human nature, as radically disrupted and deranged by sin. Therefore the Christian religion is not just another expression of a normal situation: it is directed towards salvation from sin and the power of the evil one; it is "soteriological." Finally, human thought is not a neutral terrain in human nature, and science is not a value-free zone. On the contrary, blindness and lies have the tendency to distort the results of science on the one hand, while the Christian message implies liberation and renewal on the other. In short, science does not exist outside the religious antithesis. It needs to be based, says Kuyper, on rebirth, on the new life in Christ. Science cannot do without the light of God's Word and Spirit (*LC* 49–59).

To render the meaning of the religious antithesis more discussable for science, Kuyper operates with the distinction between "normalists" and "abnormalists." *Normalists* are the scientists who presume (this is their faith!) that the existing cosmos is normal, who in their view of science accept the facts not only in nature but also in culture and society uncritically as data that are the self-evident point of departure for their theory, who regard

---

4   See Klapwijk, Jacob 1991. "Antithesis and Common Grace." In J. Klapwijk, S. Griffioen, and G. Groene-woud (eds.). *Bringing into Captivity every Thought*. Lanham, MD: University Press of America, 169–190. *See infra* Chapter 20.

human rationality as fully autonomous, and axiomatically waive any explanation featuring help from the outside.

Over against them Kuyper places the *Abnormalists*, that is, those who regard the world in its present outlook as abnormal, derailed and corrupted by sin, and dependent on salvation to attain its intended end. Thus abnormalists proceed from the cosmos as God's good creation and the human person as the bearer of God's image, but also from the mystery of sin as apostasy from God whereby human nature has been corrupted and the world dislocated. Finally, they proceed also from the wonder in born-again people, of the re-creation, the new beginning in Christ, issuing in a reborn cosmos (*LC* 130–141). Abnormalists, yes – for these people seek their point of support ultimately not in the *de facto* nature of reality or in the rational nature of man – even science is "impaired by sin" – but orient themselves to God's revealed purposes, his salvation of and ordinances for created reality.[5]

Kuyper comes to a rather militant conclusion. It is not the so-called conflict between science and faith but the perspectives of the normalists and abnormalists that mark "the principal antithesis, which separates the thinking minds in the domain of Science into two opposite battle-arrays." And this opposition is at bottom religious in character because it arises from "two kinds of human consciousness: that of the regenerate and the unregenerate; and these two cannot be identical."[6]

Kuyper's sketch is clear. So also its consequences? One might want to ask Kuyper if he does not go too far and overshoot his target. Is the religious antithesis really susceptible to division into groups of people? Does it allow itself to be organized into two battle orders of scientists? Or is it a conflict that arises also in the heart of believing persons? "For what I do is not the good I want to do; no, the evil I do not want to do – this I keep on doing," according to the apostolic admonition in Romans 7.

Antithesis in science? How far does the antithetical conflict in science go? Does it entail a total break in scientific communication, a complete demolition of opposing standpoints? Often it seems so:

> . . . these two scientific systems of the Normalists and the Abnormalists are not relative opponent. . . . but they are both in earnest, disputing with one another *the whole domain of life*, and they cannot desist from the constant endeavor to pull down to the ground *the entire edifice* of their respective controverted assertions, all the supports included, upon which their assertions rest. (*LC* 133)

Happily, soup is not always eaten as hot as it is served. More mildly, he explains a little later: ". . . in this domain also it will be seen that only a peaceful separation of the adherents of antithetic principles warrants progress, – honest progress, – and mutual understanding" (*LC* 140).

Matters become tense when Kuyper goes beyond peaceableness to appreciation, yes

---

5   *PST* §43. These two antithetical perspectives on science have been worked out by Dooyeweerd 1997. *A New Critique of Theoretical Thought*. 4 volumes. New York: Edwin Mellen. Vol. 1, 123, 522–524. Against the "immanence standpoint" in scientific theories Dooyeweerd posits the Christian "transcendence standpoint," for in the light of God's revelation a Christian transcends the immanent boundaries of human experience that characterize the nature of non-Christian thought. Instructive is also Dooyeweerd's 1939 article "Kuypers wetenschapsleer" *Philosophia Reformata* 4: 193–232. *See supra* Chapter 14.

6   *LC* 132, 137. See also *PST* §48–49, on "Two Kinds of People" and "Two Kinds of Science."

admiration of others who are of a different mind. Somewhere he calls Plato, Aristotle, Kant and even Darwin "stars of the first magnitude, geniuses of the highest degree."[7] He even recognizes possibilities for cooperation and a common treasury of scientific thought: ". . . it is in the interest of science at large, that mutual benefit be derived by both circles from what is contributed to the general stock of science" (*PST* 159).

The question of course is, to what extent, if at all, such appreciation and cooperation can be legitimated, given Kuyper's antithesis claim. When Kuyper declares, "The formal process of thought has *not* been attacked by sin," and "in almost every department there is some task that is common to all," then appreciation and cooperation are rescued, but the impression also arises that human understanding is made partly immune to the antithesis (*PST* 159, 161). Here Kuyper suggests that the natural sciences and the subordinate labor of the spiritual sciences (philological studies, etc.) "have a very broad field in common," a field that exists outside this religious conflict. The fundamental difference of Christian and not-Christian thinking is not denied, but the gist is that it just extends "across the entire domain of the *higher* sciences," that is theology, philosophy, the humanities etc. (*PST* 600, 679).

The question arises whether this position still comports with Kuyper's reformational basic conviction. The dichotomy in scientific knowledge whereby only the higher part is dependent on the divine truth of faith while the lower part is dependent on the universal validity of reason is sooner scholastic than reformational in character. It presupposes two levels of knowledge. The lower level is broadly human and relatively autonomous; it stands in the light of reason that enlightens every human being. The higher knowledge pertains to a spiritual world and faith in divine revelation; it can be seen as exclusively Christian. This dichotomy can lead at best to a series of accommodations but never to a principled reformation of science.

Must a reformational initiative always lead, then, to a conflict of opinions or an isolated Christian position? Is it only scholastic accommodation that can lead to openness, communication and scientific cooperation, be it on a lower level? A far from attractive and also far from realistic dilemma! Here and there Kuyper tries to break through this dilemma. He presents an innovative solution:

> . . . every faculty, and in these faculties every single science, is more or less connected with the antithesis of principles, and should consequently be permeated by it. . . . Everything astronomers or geologists, . . . historians or archeologists bring to light has to be recorded, – detached of course from the hypothesis they have slipped behind it and from the conclusions they have drawn from it, – but every fact has to be recorded by you, also, as a fact, and as a fact that is to be incorporated as well in your science as in theirs. (*LC* 139)

Kuyper wishes *neither* to regard the lower sciences as totally independent of religious beliefs nor, on the other hand, to drive the Christian researcher into a complete isolation. Rather, he suggests that factual observations and insights from whatever side in the realm of learning should be cut loose from a possibly non-Christian or pseudo-religious "hypothesis or presupposition" and be framed in an alternative, Christian perspective. At the end of this paper I will return to this suggestion.

---

7   "Common Grace in Science." In *AK:ACR* 441–460. This is a partial translation of "De Gemeene Gratie in wetenschap en kunst" (included in the separately paginated *De Gemeene Gratie*, vol. 3), 448–449.

3. Problems in Kuyper's Critical Realism

In his *Encyclopedia of Sacred Theology* Kuyper explains his theory of science in greater detail. Time and again his principled reformational basic conviction shines through, but at first sight the opposite appears to be the case. In part Kuyper joins the modern theory of so-called critical realism, in part he orients himself to the medieval doctrine of the divine Logos.

Kuyper's starting point is the so-called subject-object split, that is, the modern division between the thinking subject and the world as the object of thought, introduced into philosophy by René Descartes. Descartes presented the human person as a self-contained, autonomous subject, set opposite a world of things that the subject wants to understand and control. Kuyper seems to have no difficulty with this Cartesian dualism. He presents the subject in terms of human consciousness in general. The object is the world of corporeal things including the human body to the extent that this body too can be objectified for the sake of scientific analysis (*PST* § 38). He does not pose the question whether this dualism agrees with the unique religious nature of the human person as the bearer of God's image.

In the first instance Kuyper works out the problem of knowledge in the empiricist vein of John Locke. The subject, which is to say human consciousness, is a receptive capacity. It is a susceptibility to "empirical impressions" of physical and even mental things. It is a capacity to absorb into consciousness various moments or "elements" of the object (color and scent, for example) by means of perception and sensory observation and to convert the perceptions into a mental representation of the object (*PST* §39, 42).

The object, the world of perceivable things, is more than a confused pile of all the elements perceived by the subject. For things display system and regularity; they are arranged in an orderly way. The subject is aware that the elements found in the object are connected, just as the subject is aware of a connection between the different objects and between object and subject. Therefore human consciousness must be considered capable not only of forming a representation of the elements in objective reality but also of reflecting on the mutual "relations" between them. The subject does not just observe the world; it endeavors to understand and control the world in its regular coherence and orderly course (*PST* §39).

There are passages in Kuyper's *Encyclopedia* in which he suggests that this critical arranging of sensitive impressions and this mutual relating of elements in a logical understanding of the real world arises from the human mind in the vein of Kant's *critical idealism*. Is the world perhaps a construct of the mind instead of a God-given fact of life? In that case, Kuyper, under Kant's influence, can call human reason not a passive but an "active power," active because "the setting for them [these relations] is present in our own consciousness." Then he calls these relations "the objectification of our thinking" (*PST* 76f.).

For all that, the influence of Kant's critical idealism is limited. It conflicts too much with Kuyper's reformational basic conviction that we live in a real world and that God is the creator of it. And Kant's provocative thesis that the human subject encounters nature as its "lawgiver" clashes with Kuyper's sense that the world owes its causal relationships not to the ordering capacities of reason but to the ordinances of God: they are objectively present in the world. To the extent that the human subject in his scientific analyses likewise "orders," he is really doing nothing other than bringing his subjective representations into agreement with the objective, God-given world. For this reason, one could speak here of *critical realism*, a theory of knowledge the foundations for which were laid in the nineteenth century by the German philosopher Eduard von Hartmann. Von Hartmann's critical realism fits better than Kant's critical idealism with Kuyper's belief in a divine creator.

Yet there is something puzzling about this alleged harmony of the subjective order of thought and the objective order of the cosmos, and thus in critical realism. Is the split of subject and object in modern philosophy an indisputable truth? This post-Cartesian split, is it not a corollary of faith, of a humanistic faith in the autonomy of the human subject that has to objectify and control the world by reason? And if we take the split of subject and object to be an original given in our philosophy, then how to account for the alleged affinity and agreement between subject and object that critical realists so easily claim? How is it possible that human thought is totally equipped to see through the things at hand right on down to their most fundamental causal relationships? Kuyper's romantically tinted answer is that our world is like a living organism. Everything in it is organically connected with everything else in it; there is thus also an "organic relation between subject and object" (*PST* 67). This suggestion marks his position but does not solve his problem.

4. Logos Doctrine and the Human Sciences

One can imagine that Kuyper, embarrassed by questions like these, turned to another theory of knowledge, the medieval doctrine of the Logos. In this doctrine the human subject and the world of objects are indeed affinitive because they are both considered to be creatures of God, fabrications of the divine Spirit, the Logos. After all, not only in the subject but also in the object logical traits can be found. The cosmos is well thought out. In its logical relationships the cosmos is the creaturely expression or objective deposit of the thoughts that inspired God as Logos at the creation of the world. To the human subject, who is the little logos that is created in the image of the divine Logos, the object therefore does not need to come across as something strange and eccentric. The subject recognizes in it something of his or her own transparency as logical subject. Conversely, the germ of the logical thoughts that are hidden in the cosmos the subject finds in his or her own mind; he or she undertakes to articulate these thoughts in science and technology. Just as an artist's apprentice is capable of reconstructing the original concept of the master from a work of art, so humans are capable of thinking the thoughts of God after him, as it were, that is, of retracing the thoughts of God whereby He created the world. Therein lies the meaning of science and technology (*PST* §39).

This doctrine of the Logos, developed in the ancient Stoa, adopted by the Church Father Augustine and incorporated into medieval scholasticism, Kuyper borrowed from his Free University colleague Jan Woltjer.[8] And like Woltjer, Kuyper ties this Logos doctrine to a neo-Platonic realism of ideas. Universal regularities in the cosmos – and that is what Kuyper's "relations" are all about – are traceable to *ideas* (as in Plato), yes to ideas *in the*

---

8   *PST* 194, appeals to Woltjer's rectorial oration at the VU in 1891, "De wetenschap van de Logos." In Woltjer, Jan 1931. *Verzamelde redevoeringen en verhandelingen*, vol. 1. Amsterdam: Standaard, 1–46. The Stoic doctrine of *logoi spermatikoi* or "logical seminal ideas" that would have been implanted in the world fits wonderfully well with the organic metaphors of romanticism.

mind of God (as in neo-Platonism). The cosmos is a real, objective embodiment of the ideas whereby God once created the world. That is why the human mind as the image-bearer of God is logically moored to the objective world. Thus one can say that Kuyper's critical realism, which we described earlier, seeks its foundation in a Platonic and scholastic "realism of ideas." And with that, the Cartesian split between subject and object seems to be superseded!

Kuyper works this perspective out for the human sciences. The world is partly visible and partly invisible, that is, partly somatic or bodily, partly psychic or spiritual. The human sciences focus on the latter. In the human sciences too the issue is to appropriate elements and relations. Here the method of the natural sciences can sometimes prove useful, as in the comparative study of religious *behaviors*. Nevertheless, the human sciences have their own methodology. After all, when it comes to spiritual matters, sensory observation is inadequate to observe the diverse elements and law-like relations that can be distinguished here.

The method of the human sciences must for this reason build knowledge in another way, from the mental subject as such, the latter still construed as general human consciousness. Kuyper's example is jurisprudence. People discover what is just not because they apprehend justice via the senses or with the aid of mental representations. No, its influence is "direct," for justice is a mental or spiritual power that grips people directly and engenders a subjective affection in their consciousness. Such affection leads to a permanent sense of justice or to a sudden inspiration of what is just. Here too, at the spiritual level, people display a twofold receptivity: openness for the moment that presents itself, for instance in the notion of justice, and susceptibility to the relationships that are involved, in this case the legal order.

For Kuyper the natural sciences and the human sciences are no more than extreme poles. Much is to be found between these poles. On the one side, Kuyper mentions mixed human sciences, including linguistics and historical science. The ideal motives of shapers of history acquire material form, as in battles. On the other hand, Kuyper regards the natural sciences as often not strictly empirical-factual but also as hypothetical-constructive, as for example the biological theory of descent (*PST* §42).

It is striking that Kuyper does not always associate the human sciences with the Logos doctrine or the realism of ideas. There was apparently little inducement to do so. The problem of how there can be agreement between subject and object seems more easily resolved for mental than for natural objects of knowledge, assuming that at the mental level an object may impress its stamp directly on an inquiring subject.

In any case, any overly bold support for the Logos doctrine in the human sciences would expose its weak side. That *natural* things would be metaphysically traceable to divine thoughts – "things are thinks," Woltjer[9] used to say with George Berkeley – already means a far-reaching "logification" of created reality. But that in its deepest being all *spiritual* phenomena, too, should be seen as divine thoughts constitutes an intellectualism carried to an extreme. This intellectualism seems to conflict with Kuyper's reformational conviction that God as Sovereign has created everything according to its own character with *different* ordinances, that is to say, ordinances for the physical cosmos and for the organic world, and in the same way not only for the domain of logical thought but also for the fields of

---

9   Woltjer, *Verzamelde redevoeringen*, 217.

aesthetics, ethics and religion.

Yet time and again this intellectualism affects Kuyper's understanding of the human world. Then he presents a human being as a "logos" on a micro-scale. The life of the human consciousness, Kuyper states, "recapitulates itself in the logos, taken as *thought*" (*PST* 194). Does this profile of the human individual as a logical being not conflict with Kuyper's argument about the *religious* identity of the human person? Does it not ignore the Reformed confession of God's sovereignty over all and lead to metaphysical speculations about the alleged affinity of the divine and the human logos? Can earthly creatures rethink the thoughts of the heavenly creator? And does the Logos doctrine not contradict Calvin's confession of the radical depths of sin? How can sin lead to a total dislocation if it arises merely from a deficiency of the intellect?[10]

5. The Architect Gone Mad

We are confronted again with Kuyper the Calvinist. Sin arises not from an intellectual deficiency but from religious apostasy. It permeates all intellectual work, even science. How? Kuyper does not accept any neutrality postulate of science: "In every theory of knowledge which is not to deceive itself, the fact of sin must henceforth claim a more serious consideration." Sin is more than human failing or self-deception. It is essentially the breaking of the bond of love in the direction of God and of the surrounding world. For the problem of knowledge, this implies that the loving, sympathetic apprehension of things from the inside has been lost. Sin in science is a fundamental "*estrangement* from the object of our knowledge." Because of sin it is only superficially and in bits and pieces that we remain able to form a picture of reality (*PST* 106–107, 111).

Because of sin we lack insight into the coherence of the world as well as into its origin and destination.[11] We are without a real overview. There would have to be an Archimedean point, a final point of support *outside* created reality. Sin however shuts creatures up *within* the cosmos.[12] As a result, human knowledge is one-sided, limited, and fragmentary. The human individual is an architect who has gone mad and sits locked in his cell staring out through his window at one of his own constructions. He stares fixedly at the walls and spires but the sense of the whole eludes him since he can no longer grasp the building's purpose.[13]

Thus sin leads to a disintegration and distortion of knowledge. The sciences do offer an enormous heap accumulation of knowledge in detail, but they leave the whence, why and wherefore unanswered. In the world of science this must lead to complete skepticism.

---

10 I have in mind here Calvin's doctrine of sin as a *corruptio totalis*. According to the scholastic philosophy of Thomas Aquinas, sin did not arise from the intellect but from the will as a lower capacity of the human soul, the "capacity to desire," which abandoned the guidance of reason and thus went off the track. Reason, conceived as the essential center of human nature, was only "wounded" as a result, not totally corrupted. It is this view that sin is at bottom only a partial or oblique impairment of human nature that Calvin sharply opposes (*Institutes*, 2.1.9).

11 The view that sin affects science via the central notions of "the origin, coherence, and destiny of things" is fundamental for Kuyper "Common Grace in Science"; cf. *LC* 113f.; *PST* §43. This view reappears in Dooyeweerd's thesis (*New Critique*, vol. 1, 68–99) that religious ground-motives influence science via a set of central notions, the so-called cosmonomic idea.

12 On Kuyper's notion of an "archimedean point," be it outside or inside the cosmos (*PST* 113, 84), Dooyeweerd expands systematically (*New Critique*, vol. 1, 8–21).

13 "Common Grace in Science," 449–450.

That it has not done so is thanks to God's goodness for humankind – in Kuyper's terminology God's "common grace"[14] – because He still blesses people everywhere on earth with common sense, practical wisdom and the intuitive certainties of faith. That is the reason why all science proceeds from faith, faith in our own self-consciousness, in the trustworthiness of the senses, in the correctness of the laws of thought, in the presence of the universal and regular in particular phenomena, in axioms and general principles of a research program, and in the ties that bind us with our fellow man (*LC* 131; *PST* §46). It is these intuitive and practical certainties by which non-Christians too recognize something of the God-given coherence of life, and science is preserved from total dislocation. Yet, it is only in life restored by Christ and in the light of God's revelation that science can really blossom and regain a view of life's origin, intimate coherence and goal.

6. Theology between Critical Realism and Logos Doctrine

We have to turn now to theology. In his *Encyclopedia of Sacred Theology* Kuyper wanted to make his theory of the sciences fruitful especially for the science of theology. But he had a great deal of difficulty in doing so, given the disparity in the *Encyclopedia* between a modern and a scholastic line of thought.

Let us look first at the modern line of thought. Applied to theology, Cartesianism and the critical realism that arose from it turned out to be untenable for Kuyper. How can the *cogito* grasp a sovereign power that transcends the cosmos? God can never become the mere object of a knowing subject or the outcome of a rational proof:

> The object of religion is not only placed outside of this object-subject, but the subject as well as the object, and the relation of both, must find their ground and explanation in this central power. . . . This extra-cosmic and hyper-cosmic character, however, of every central power . . . is the very reason that neither observation nor demonstration are of the least avail in establishing the tie between our subject and this central power. . . . (*PST* 147)

In other words, the modern duality of knowing subject and object of knowledge can never be applied to God if all created reality, thus subject and object, are dependent on a creator that transcends them. The "dependent character of theology" (*PST* §59) excludes the Cartesian split of subject and object. To know God is only possible to the extent that the Transcendent gives itself to human knowledge. How? Through revelation!

More attractive for Kuyper, therefore, was the scholastic line of thought. In this view there is not an opposition but an affinity between subject and object. Particularly in the human sciences we are confronted with mental or spiritual realities that fall beyond the reach of the sensory perception. Spiritual realities are intimate. They press directly on the human mind without any strictly conceptual apprehension. They generate a permanent awareness or a sudden inspiration that connects with the spiritual world.

This argument seems tailored to fit Kuyper's view of theology. For theology is not "science of religion." In the positivist climate of his age, "science of religion" had become a popular formula amongst theologians for saving the academic respectability of theology. Kuyper did not need such a free-floating life buoy. Theology is a *"geesteswetenschap,"* a science of mental or spiritual phenomena. It does not investigate religious rituals but spiritual realities; in the final analysis it deals with God. In the human sciences spiritual

---

14 *LC* 121–126; Klapwijk, "Antithesis and Common Grace."

forces urge themselves on the subject, but in theology we meet God as the "central power" *in* and *above* the cosmos. Proceeding from God as the central power and from His addressing man directly in terms of revelation, theology is able to grasp both the origin of religious consciousness and the phenomena of religious inspiration and its codification in Holy Scripture (*PST* §47).

How then to define theology? Theology has to be taken literally as a "logy" of the divine ("*Godskennisse*"), a science of God, even in a very intimate sense of the word. For if human knowledge in general is already, as we saw, a kind of rethinking of the thoughts of God, then theology certainly is. It is not only knowledge *about* God but in a sense also knowledge *of* God. It is dependent on divine revelation in the sense that revelation "flows from the auto-Theology in God Himself and has Theology, i.e. knowledge of God in man, for its result." Theology is a full-fledged human science but simultaneously a rethinking or reflection of divine self-knowledge (*PST* 263).

This theory had ensconced itself in Reformed theology in the previous centuries through the work of Bernardinus de Moor and others.[15] These men were not burdened with the split between subject and object. They presented theology as a science of God's *revelation*. But they did so in a very special way! They proceeded from the thought that theology is concerned with knowledge of God but that knowledge of God in the absolute sense is reserved for the divine Logos. Thus they concluded that this original or "archetypal" self-knowledge of God falls to the human person, created in God's image, in an inferred or "ectypal" way. True theology is a mirroring of God's self-knowledge. Therefore its object is not God as such but God as He has revealed Himself. *Theologia ectypa* thus seems to be a modest theology. Modern epistemology's ambition to prove or construct everything – if need be, even God or the phenomenon of religion – is foreign to it. Ectypal theology does not seek to ascend to God or to transcend the boundary of creation. It desires to be humble and dependent on the self-knowledge of God: "ectypal theology reveals to us the self-knowledge of God according to our *human capacity*" (*PST* 256).

Yes indeed, De Moor's ectypal theology depends on revelation. But this theology is not to be understood as being simply based on faith in biblical revelation. Revelation is considered to be the channel through which God's absolute and archetypal logical self-knowledge reaches us in terms of an ectypal logical reflection. Kuyper continues to speak the language of the Logos theory when he asserts that human theology is intended to be a strict reflection of archetypal theology based "on logical action." Theology is "*zich indenken in*," that is, "thinking our way into" divine self-knowledge. It is with the help of his *logos* that a theologian is meant to appropriate and process the "knowledge of God" that is made available to him:

> He [man] is not only to appropriate that which has been revealed, but he is himself a link in that revelation. This is exhibited most strongly in his logos, since by his logos he appropriates revelation to himself, and in his logos reflectively (*abbildlich*) reveals something of the eternal logos. (*PST* 264; cf. 268–269, 299)

This line of thought ends up in a kind of Reformed scholasticism. Within the framework of the Logos doctrine, theology becomes an accommodation to neo-Platonic

---

15 Kuyper knew about the distinction between archetypal and ectypal theology from the work of the orthodox Reformed theologians of the seventeenth and eighteenth centuries. He was familiar in particular with the eight-volume *Commentary on Joh. à Marck* of Bernardinus de Moor (*PST* 238, 256).

speculations about the intellectual affinity of God and man: theology presents itself as a copy ("*Abbild*") of divine auto-theology. And this intellectualism, as amongst the ancient Greek "*theologoi*," is strongly elitist: theology is a special entrance to God. Kuyper would certainly not go so far as to say theology is an exclusive entrance to know God, but it surely has a privileged position: "Among the different assimilations of this knowledge of God, Theology as a *science* occupies a place of its own, which is defined by its nature" (*PST* 299).

7. Theology and the Innate, Created Nature of Faith

However, there are intervals in Kuyper's exposition where he calls himself to order. No wonder! His initial modernist interpretation of science implied distance: a logical control of the objects to be investigated. His later scholastic interpretation of science implies affinity: a logical penetration of the objects to be investigated. But can there be any such logical penetration where God is concerned? Does God as the sovereign creator not stand outside and above all subjects and objects? And is He not knowable only through faith? And is this faith a logical activity? Calvin's emphasis on the sovereignty of God and Luther's emphasis on *sola fide* make it rather difficult for Kuyper to chart theology either according to the modern subject-object split or according to the affinities of the Logos doctrine.

Thus at crucial moments Kuyper abandons not only critical realism but also the Logos theory of the earlier Reformed theologians. He develops reservations about the distinction between archetypal and ectypal theology. They hinge on the cardinal question of the character of faith within human consciousness, because the distinction between archetypal and ectypal knowledge of God obscures the reformational insight that the human person can know God only through faith. To Luther *fides* meant saving faith in Christ, indispensable for humans in a state of sin. Kuyper suppose, more in general, that humans have a religious sensitivity in terms of faith. Even the ultimate commitments of non-Christians go back to a fiduciary function that is inherent in human nature. Faith is not a super-natural or super-creaturely gift *added* to human nature once for all at baptism, as the scholastic tradition teaches. "Grace never creates a new reality" (*PST* 238). On the contrary, the principle of Calvinism "constantly urges us to go back from the Cross to Creation" (*LC* 118). Every concrete act of belief or unbelief goes back to faith as it is implanted by the creator in human nature (*PST* 263–269).

The doctrine of faith disrupts Kuyper's adhesion to the Logos doctrine. Previously we noticed that Kuyper saw faith as connected with science. Given the examples he used – faith in the reliability of the senses, in one's own ego, in the validity of the laws of logic – it may have looked for a while as if faith is just an intuitive certainty that guides scientific research. But Kuyper's *Encyclopedia* makes it clear that "faith obtains its absolute significance only in religion" (*PST* 149). Faith is in the final analysis *pistis*, an immediate certainty in the heart that flows from a religious choice and gives direction to life. The deepest essence of faith is the innate, primeval experience of human creatures whereby they discover themselves in distinction from *and* in connection with God who has revealed himself to them as their deepest Origin. In its core, faith correlates with divine revelation. All other evidences of faith are dependent on this primeval intuition.

> Faith indeed is in our human consciousness the deepest fundamental law that governs every form of distinction, by which alone all higher "Differentiation" becomes established in our consciousness. . . . This general better knowledge of faith renders it possible to speak of

faith in every domain; and also shows that faith originates primordially from the fact that our ego places God over against itself as the eternal and infinite Being, and that it dares to do this, because in this only it finds its eternal point of support. Since . . . God created it in our human nature, this faith is but the opening of our spiritual eye and the consequent perception of another Being, excelling us in everything, that *manifests itself in our own being.* (*PST* 266–267)

Because faith is dependent on an appearance of the divine, it is not an inborn concept in the knowing subject, no *idea innata* in the sense of Descartes. Because it has been derailed by sin, it is even less a self-evident human characteristic. Faith has become obscured and darkened! God, however, has revealed himself, also to humanity fallen in sin, and has awakened faith to a new life, in Israel and the church. Therefore in the present dispensation faith has a double face; one must always qualify it with a negative or positive sign: "Christendom and Paganism stand to each other as the *plus* and *minus* forms of the same series" (*PST* 302). It is a matter on the one hand of unbelief, resistance or idolatry, belief in pseudo-revelations. It is a matter on the other hand of rebirth, saving faith, belief in salvation thanks to God's revelation. Only through faith can the subject appropriate divine self-revelation:

> This entire gold-mine of religion lies in the self-revelation of this central power to the subject, and the subject has no other means than *faith* by which to appropriate to itself the gold from this mine. (*PST* 149)

This reciprocal relationship of faith and revelation breaks through the scholastic speculations on the logical affinity of the human and the eternal logos that had impregnated the medieval as well as the old Reformed theology. The human person, created in the image of God, stands in an open relationship to God, and this relationship is in its deepest core not of a logical but of a religious nature. Kuyper likes to appeal to Calvin's *Institutes* (I.3.1) in this matter. In human nature a religious seed has been laid (*semen religionis*) insofar as humans were created with a sense of the divine (*divinitatis sensus*). And where this spiritual eye opens and discerns God's appearance, there faith begins to work (*PST* 263–75; *LC* 45–46).

This Calvin-oriented view of the innate, created nature of faith is fraught with implications for Kuyper's view of science. If all humans have a sense of the divine, it becomes clear why faith and science cannot be uncoupled. Faith is a necessary or (in philosophical language) a transcendental *precondition* for all knowledge, even for scientific knowledge, because an original awareness of God is inherent in every person, even when he or she is the performing subject of science. This conception of faith has a very particular consequence for the status of theological science. Faith belongs not only to its transcendental precondition; it belongs at the same time to its actual theme. I mean the following. The subject matter of theology is not the phenomenon of religion, nor is it God himself. And yet, theology is focused on God. How then? Two activities are implied: logical reflection and faith. On the one side theology is a logical reflection upon the correlation of faith and revelation, that is, upon the way God revealed and reveals Himself in Scripture to those who believe in Him. On the other side this logical reflection is never autonomous; it proceeds from an a priori faith in divine revelation: "The perception of a mightier Ego, which is above and distinct from our own ego, is therefore the starting-point of all religion and of all knowledge of God" (*PST* 267).

This correlation concept[16] – Kuyper did not work it out systematically – implies a redefinition of theology, an alternative for a theology based on Logos speculation. To put it in a nutshell, theology is a study of biblical revelation, not as a religious document in itself, but *as understood in the faith community of the church*. It can only lead to a logical clarification of the revelation of God that the church cherishes in faith. "Theology as science . . . can only lead to a clearer insight into the revealed knowledge of God" (*PST* 292).

> This entirely intellectualistic way excludes, meanwhile, the spiritual experience of the Church in its entirety, as well as of individual believers. . . . This, however, is inconceivable, since theology is born of the Church, and not the Church of theology. Reflection does not create life, but *suo iure* life is first, after which reflection speaks its word concerning it. (*PST* 327)

What is widely recognized today, in particular in phenomenological and hermeneutical philosophies, namely that science is rooted in the pre-theoretical daily life experiences of a community, Kuyper discovered for theology. Theology reflects and refines the faith experiences of the church community. Theology is "bound to its object such as this shows itself in its own circle in life; i.e. *in casu* the Church" (*PST* 51). Thus for Kuyper theology should bear an ecclesiastical signature.[17]

8. Universities as Private Corporations

We return to our general theme, Kuyper's conception of science. Attention needs to be given to the societal organization of science. How did Kuyper want to turn his fundamental view of science into institutional practice? His solution is well known: the free university!

The popular conception is that Kuyper had in mind an academic institution that would practice the sciences in the spirit of Calvinism and that he therefore wanted a "free" university. Even more popular is the view that Kuyper wanted to give "his" university in Amsterdam a confessional hallmark and that he therefore wanted to break the connection with the state. But these notions gloss over Kuyper's argument that *all* scientific investigations should be free, that no thinker should be bound in conscience, and that academic institutions too must be allowed to develop in freedom without disguised subservience to other institutions.[18]

Kuyper was a champion of the emancipation of culture. Societal groups should be able to set themselves up as private communities so that all the spiritual energies of a folk

---

16 Kuyper occasionally defines theology as a theoretical reflection upon the *correlation* of faith and revelation. More often, in his Logos doctrine, he postulates a *continuity* between faith knowledge and theology, as we saw above. The result is an intellectualizing of both faith and revelation. I do not deny that a certain kind of knowledge is inherent in faith. But faith knowledge has an *analogous* character; it does not represent logical but religious insights. Take confessions, psalms and prayers. In contrast to the statements of systematic theology, such expressions cannot be subjected to the logical rules that hold in theoretical arguments.

17 In *PST* Kuyper develops a broad view of the systematic coherence of all the sciences and especially of theology and its subdivisions. For a discussion of his encyclopedia of the sciences and his encyclopedia of theology, see Klapwijk, J. 1987. "Abraham Kuyper over wetenschap en universiteit." In C. Augustijn, J. H. Prins and H. E. S. Woldring (eds) *Abraham Kuyper: zijn volksdeel, zijn invloed*. Delft: Meinema, 82–86. *See supra* Chapter 18 for a revised and translated version of the original article.

18 Kuyper applied this even to theology: "The persistent heretic must be banished from the Church; a professor whose presence is a menace to the highest interests of a school must be dismissed; but from the field of theology no one can disappear, unless he leaves it of his own free will" (*PST* 596).

might be unleashed. Thus he chose decidedly for a "free university," apart from his personal sympathies for Calvinism. He was also fundamentally opposed to any linkage of science to an ecclesiastical confession, even with respect to the Free University of Amsterdam, nowadays known as the VU University Amsterdam. Only theology, as we saw earlier, could for reasons of substance not do without an ecclesiastical setting.[19]

A free university is to Kuyper a university that is free from both state and church. Neither ecclesiastical nor political authorities should interfere in the formulating of problems or in the self-organization of the sciences. In the Middle Ages and also at the beginning of modern times, ecclesiastical supervision had hindered the self-development of science. A symptom of this was the case leveled against Galileo. Later, guardianship arose from the side of the state. A symptom of this for Kuyper was the Dutch Higher Education Act of 1876, which converted theology into some kind of science of religion. Theology was linked by law to historical, exegetical and philosophical disciplines, and dogmatic (systematic) theology was thrown out of Dutch universities. For Kuyper this directly occasioned the founding of the Free University (*PST* §96). But the basic error of his times as he saw it was not the misapprehension of theology but ignoring the insight that science can develop itself under the supervision of the state just as little as it can under the curatorship of the church.

Kuyper elaborated his conception of a free university on historical grounds, for systematic reasons, and on principle. Concerning the first, Kuyper recalled how the original medieval universities, those of Paris, Bologna, etc., were founded as private corporations. State universities were unknown. Science and the university formed a *respublica litterarum*, a world of its own of lettered and educated people alongside the worlds of the church and the state. Yet the church rather quickly found ways to be admitted into the academic world. The church was apprehensive about heretics; the universities were apprehensive about ecclesiastical privileges. In the eighteenth century the universities fell more and more under the influence of the national state. In part they were set up as government institutions; in part they were bent in their direction. Science was hired as a servant of the state. Kuyper could make the most of this "self-demeaning prostitution" of science.[20]

In Kuyper's day the state seemed as a rule to restrict itself to financing the state universities. Yet Kuyper writes with great foresight: "It cannot be said often enough, money creates power *for* the one who gives *over* the one who receives" (*SS* 478). In this connection he calls attention to contrary developments in the direction of the original model of "free corporations." He refers to a selection of private universities in the United States, but also to the Belgian Leuven, the Swiss Freiburg, the (then still) British Dublin, and not to forget, the Free University of Amsterdam (*LC* 140; *PST* §96). From a historical standpoint the model of the state university is in fact an obstacle standing in the way of the entire process of the emancipation of culture.

---

19 At the Free University a reservation was made with respect to theology. Kuyper did not want theology as an academic discipline to be tied to ecclesiastical supervision. But he emphasized that theology should not free itself from the *object* of its study, that is, God's revelation as this is experienced in the faith community of a church. He compared this practical link with the connection between medical science and hospital health care, and between jurisprudence and the administration of law in a given country (*Encyclopaedie der Heilige Godgeleerdheid*, vol. 1, 521). In that sense a binding of theology to the creeds of a church could be defended.

20 "Sphere Sovereignty." In: *AK:ACR* 477—referenced below as *SS*.

9. Universities as a Sovereign Sphere

Kuyper's systematic argumentation in favor of free universities is another story. It is based on the doctrine of sphere sovereignty. *Souvereiniteit in eigen kring* or *Sphere sovereignty* was the title of Kuyper's address at the dedication of the Free University in 1880. The main idea Kuyper summarized in the winged statement: "there is not a square inch in the whole domain of our human existence over which Christ, who is Sovereign over *all*, does not cry: 'Mine!'" (*SS* 488).

The doctrine of sphere sovereignty may be regarded as an elaboration by Kuyper of Calvin's basic idea of the absolute sovereignty of God. God holds all power on earth – power over the realm of nature, over the peoples and nations, over the course and destiny of history, and over culture and society. Even though the earth is bent under the burden of injustice and evil, God does not abandon his creation. He exercises in particular authority over the diverse communities in society, which Kuyper calls "spheres." These communities exist by virtue of the will of God, who has given each sphere its own inner law of life. Through these "ordinances" the life of society is subjected to God's almighty power.

Since Christ's resurrection this power is in his hands: "All authority in heaven and on earth has been given to me" (Matthew 28:18). God's sovereignty resides since Easter in the sign of Jesus' messianic kingship (*SS* 467). Nowhere in the world do we come directly upon God's exercise of power in Christ, but *indirectly* Christ proves his authority to the utmost, namely through people who in one way or another have received a mission, an office, a function: political rulers, church authorities, parents, nurturers, employers, and so forth. Everywhere that people have been placed over other people in the distinct spheres of society, authority is exercised "by the grace of God" or, more precisely, by authorization of the *messiah incognito*.

Is not all exercise and misuse of power sanctioned beforehand in this way? Quite the contrary! The purport of sphere sovereignty is in the first place that all earthly authority is a *derived* authority. It is not an autonomous human power but always a mandate subjected to the rule of God and to messianic criticism. Authority exercised by people must be accounted for.

The purport of sphere sovereignty is, secondly, that earthly authority is *distributed* authority. In order to prevent the misuse of power, God has entrusted the fullness of his power to no single person or circle in society; no potentate can claim it as a "divine right." Human societies have always been divided into spheres: kings, priests, magicians, heads of family have always functioned alongside each other, having their own competency. Usurpation of power, by a royal dynasty for example, remains possible, but sooner or later it evokes resistance from adjoining spheres (*SS* 467f.). And that will occur all the more strongly in a modern society where the spheres have been emancipated.

Sphere sovereignty is, thirdly, a *creational structure*. "It lay in the order of creation," Kuyper says (*SS* 469). This view was developed by the German Calvinist and political philosopher Johannes Althusius and formulated as a doctrine for society by the Dutch statesman Groen van Prinsterer, who delimited the church and the state from each other as "sovereign spheres." For Kuyper sphere sovereignty had become a crucial matter in modern times, since this period also witnesses the rise of two alternative doctrines, the doctrines of absolute state authority and absolute popular sovereignty. Both doctrines flew in the face of Kuyper's conviction that all authority in society to be ultimately anchored in the sovereign will of the creator.

Sphere sovereignty is in the fourth place a *pluralist* notion. Alongside the church, economics, family life, science and art, Kuyper wanted to honor the state as a sphere of its own with its own rules: the administration of law and justice (*GG* III:71f.; *SS* 467–68). But he rejected the glorification of the state or of the so-called sovereign will of the people. His doctrine of sphere sovereignty can be seen as a pluralist vision against the monolithic doctrines of state sovereignty and popular sovereignty.[21]

Kuyper grants the state a special position vis-à-vis the other spheres. The state is called to keep the different communities "within just limits," that is, within the bounds of law. Public justice implies that the state is meant not only to offer the protection of law to individual citizens. It is also meant to do justice to the other communities, for communities can also be threatened in their existence. The state must create public conditions that allow non-state communities to flourish. In that sense the state is the "sphere of spheres" and can even be described as the "master planner."[22] Even with respect to science!

This brings us back to the academic world. The universities and the sciences practiced there constitute for Kuyper a sovereign sphere. Here we find the systematic reason why universities ought to be free institutions. But the state cannot completely withdraw from the scene. As soon as science forms a visible organism, it is up to the state "to define its sphere of justice" (*SS* 477). The state must create public conditions for the free development of science but can have no say on the terrain of science itself. Not even when it comes to appointments! The state has no "spiritual criterion," no mental yardstick by which to judge academic decisions. Any interventions of government are as intolerable an anomaly for the freedom of science today as interference from the side of the church was in the past).[23]

10. Universities as Worldview Oriented

Kuyper considers the concept of free universities *historically* defensible, given the origin of Europe's universities. He considers it *systematically* defensible in terms of sphere sovereignty. He also considers it defensible *as a matter of principle*, given the inner-connectedness of faith and science. To be truly free, science must be able to develop itself consistently, also in a university setting, on the basis of a faith perspective or worldview orientation. With that, we return to the starting point of this article.

Even this principled line of thought in favor of a free university is as such not aimed at claiming an exclusive place for a Calvinist university. The intention is that every academic institution should profile itself according to the life principle that drives it, whether that be Catholic, humanist, evolutionist or whatever. The life-view tie must be strengthened and

---

21 *LC* 85–90; *GG* III: 80–82. In Kuyper's doctrine of sphere sovereignty, pluralist and romantic motifs are tangled together. The spheres are described as independent, created after their own ordinances, but by the same token as "organic parts" of society as a whole (*LC* 90–91). This romantic approach leads to a holistic theory of society that Kuyper then proceeds to limit by posing the state as mechanical *opposite* society as organic.

22 *SS* 468, 472, 477. Because of this asymmetry Kuyper sometimes associates sphere sovereignty only with communities *within* human society. The sovereignty of the state and, eventually, that of the church are then juxtaposed to society (*LC* 90–91, 79).

23 *SS* 478. Kuyper does not carry his systematic argumentation to the limit. In some cases he admits the need for financial support by the state, provided "that it works only for the liberation that would have scholarship again seize 'sovereignty in its own sphere'" (*SS* 478).

"unnatural bonds" should be cast off, beginning with the tie to the state (*LC* 140).

But then also the tie to institutional churches! The existence of Catholic, Lutheran or Calvinist next to public universities and colleges does not necessarily imply formal ties to a church denomination or confession. Kuyper meant only to say that principles are such that they have an all-round power over people. They can drive people not only towards their own type of church but also towards a unique type of statecraft, of science, etc. But Kuyper rejects any lateral linking of church and science just as firmly as he rejects any lateral linking of state and science or of church and state. Kuyper desires a "secularization" of science, not in terms of religious neutrality or absence of ideology but in terms of separation from ecclesiastical supervision. The responsibility of scientists has to be distinguished from and separated from the responsibility of church authorities. In some circumstances theology may be a case apart.[24]

This third, principled line of thought is characteristic for Kuyper's *Lectures on Calvinism*. The universities that set themselves up as free institutions because of their historical origin and systematic view are presented here as having a favorite position to organize research and education in keeping with their own intellectual-spiritual motivation. In contrast it is in the state universities that the academic staff may feel hindered in thinking through the implications of their principles and in working with kindred spirits, and where the illusion is cherished of a fully objective, neutral or principle-free science.

I must add that in the closing part of his "Sphere Sovereignty" Kuyper amalgamates the systematic and principled lines of thought that he distinguishes elsewhere. He does so when, in defense of the Free University in Amsterdam, he wants to "ask for the sovereignty of our own principle in our own scholarly sphere." This argument is confusing. Kuyper may have had good reasons to emphasize the legitimacy of his VU as an institution based on Calvinist principles. But can this intellectual-spiritual position be defended by an appeal to sphere sovereignty? Can we speak of "the royal right of each principle to 'sovereignty in its own sphere'"?)[25]

Sphere sovereignty can set boundaries between different terrains of life (state, church, business, family life, university, etc.). But it cannot demarcate different spiritual principles (Paganism, Humanism, Calvinism, etc.) in the same way. The different terrains are "sovereign" in the sense that they have laws of their own that may go back to creation ordinances. But the worldview differences between paganism, humanism, nihilism, Calvinism, etc. are anything but sovereign positions, for they do not result from creation

---

24 I quote: "A strong confessional church, but no confessional civil society, no confessional state. This secularization of state and society originated, in its deepest ground, from Calvinism" (*GG* II: 175). Only for theology did the VU University specify a confessional tie for practical reasons, that is, in connection with the training for the ministry in a specific denomination. See VU 1895. *Publicatie van den Senaat der Vrije Universiteit in zake het onderzoek ter bepaling van den weg die tot de kennis der gereformeerde beginselen leidt.* Amsterdam, thesis 1.

25 *SS* 481. Kuyper is not always consistent. In some cases he attributes sovereignty not only to communities as wholes like the state and the church but also to the component parts as townships and villages or dioceses and parishes (*LC* 96). However, in the latter the matter is one not of heterogeneous spheres but of homogeneous groups, that is, of comparable parts of the same whole. Amongst homogeneous groups a practical division of tasks is required, not a fundamental delimiting of competences, an appeal to relative autonomy rather than to sphere sovereignty. Sometimes Kuyper even goes further and individualizes the notion of sphere sovereignty referring to the "liberty of conscience" or the "sovereignty of the individual personality" (*LC* 108).

ordinances but from human choices and decisions. They penetrate *into* the spheres of life, giving the institutions there a spiritual (or ideological) direction. These directions are not self-evident at all. They are controversial, giving rise to differences of opinion and theoretical disputes. For the VU, or for any academic institution with a religious or worldview background, this implies that its spiritual identity is vulnerable, open to criticism, not to be legitimized by an easy appeal to sphere sovereignty or creational orderings.

In a certain sense one could say that Kuyper was born a century too soon. Our times have developed a much more critical attitude towards the so-called objectivity thesis or neutrality postulate of the sciences than Kuyper encountered in the positivist climate of thought of the nineteenth century. And even though in our secularized world we often speak about our deeper motivations with less self-assurance than former generations did, it remains a pressing question whether our thinking is not based on similar root convictions, whether for example the present-day debates on fair trade or a sustainable planet are not guided by comparable worldview paradigms, and whether the sophisticated research programs of our universities should have to suffer under the yoke of bureaucratic state planning or merciless marketing strategies. Those are some of the critical questions that have surfaced in our age, and Kuyper would have recognized himself in them!

Critical Evaluation of Kuyper's Theory of Science: Four Challenges

Kuyper presents the human person to us as a fundamentally religious creature that God has set on this earth to be the bearer of His image. Culture and society, even the world of science, in his view ought to reflect this ultimate commitment to God. At the same time Kuyper acknowledges that this bond with God has been thoroughly disrupted. Hence his diligent efforts for the Christianizing of culture and his struggle against the secular humanism of the Modern age.

Is this view still practical in our postmodern era, which not only has declared God dead, but which has also dethroned humanity, and in which indeed nihilism and materialism rule the roost? Anyone who picks up on Kuyper's message and wants to pursue it will have to disengage it from the form that its author chose. Kuyper did not limit his program to the re-Christianizing of the private spheres of family, church and school. On the contrary, he wanted to carry it through in all the terrains of life. He did so by establishing separate Christian organizations. He expanded Groen van Prinsterer's motto, "In our isolation lies our strength," in the nineteenth century to a militant neo-Calvinism over against the revitalization of Catholicism, an upcoming socialism, and the conservative civil order of the so-called Liberal bourgeoisie. In the Netherlands this striving led to "pillarization," that is to say, a splitting up of society on the basis of worldview features, in which the divided segments of the population established their own schools, political parties, labor unions, radio and television stations, daily newspapers, hospitals and the like. This pillarization, so aptly characterized by Harry Van Dyke as "institutionalized worldview pluralism," began to crumble only after the Second World War.

In our century of digital networks, expansive market economies and worldwide ecological crises, we can hardly even imagine the ordered vision of society that Kuyper aimed to achieve. His vision also raises objections. After all, he often extended the idea of a religious antithesis into an organizational antithesis, into a division that aimed to separate the Christian part of the people from the rest of the nation. How biblical is this? Christ does indeed speak of a struggle between the Kingdom of God and the power of the Evil One, a struggle in which we human beings are involved lock, stock, and barrel. However, is it not above all a spiritual struggle? Is it not a struggle that believing persons must first of all pinpoint within themselves, in the rebellion against God that they encounter in their own heart or life?

Nevertheless, Kuyper continues to fascinate with his dream to call the whole people back to the service of God and to even place the world of scientific learning in the perspective of the coming Kingdom of God. Is this message still relevant for us today? Which challenges lie hidden in his theory of science for our times? I will name four. They focus successively on worldviews, transcendental hermeneutics, transformation in science and correlative theology.

11. Worldviews Function as Mediators

Kuyper confronts us in his *Lectures on Calvinism* with the question: what is the basis of our religious view of reality? Is the Christian religion in a general sense our starting point? Or do we seek to join a concrete existing worldview, a life-system that has its roots in the Christian faith and simultaneously renders this faith operative in a given historical situation? Kuyper leaves no doubt about his choice for the latter. He chooses for Calvinism, the worldview that in the age of the Reformation not only restored the relation with God but also took up the challenges of modernity and so ushered in a prominent new era in history.

Kuyper's question entails a prime challenge for Christian philosophizing. Do we begin from a religious starting point in general, for instance the Christian ground-motive in the spirit of Dooyeweerd, or the Holy Scripture in the spirit of Vollenhoven? Or do we, along with Kuyper, place a more specific relation between philosophy and religion? Must we not position ourselves in the religious tradition of Christianity and look there for those worldview conceptions that can help us along in the spiritual struggle with the problems of our own time?

Kuyper and Dooyeweerd clash here. Kuyper wants to take into account the impact of worldviews on philosophical reflection. Dooyeweerd wants to keep worldview and philosophy separated for, although both are religiously determined, they nevertheless are of a different nature and have a distinct task. Worldview is pre-theoretical; it offers practical orientation in our lives. Philosophy is theoretical; it offers scientific reflection.[26] Kuyper would not deny this last point, but he emphasizes nevertheless:

(a) All philosophy has a starting point in a religion or pseudo-religion.
(b) Religions and pseudo-religions become concrete in worldview (or ideological) conceptions.
(c) These worldviews function as mediators between religion and philosophy.

What do these three theses mean for us? Christian philosophy, also in the mode of reformational philosophy, rests on basic concepts that have been formed in history as an expression of a worldview. Are these basic concepts exclusively Christian or reformational? Not necessarily, because in our time, frames of reference are often broader and worldviews opener than in previous centuries. As a matter of fact, in Kuyper's Calvinism we already

---

26 *New Critique*, vol. 1, 128, 156–168.

detected all kinds of novel ideas. Be that as it may, we are at present surrounded by a whole universe of worldview key concepts, such as stewardship, durable lifestyle, ideological critique, personal integrity, the preservation of creation, universal human rights, etc., that have been historically mediated and that can still be acknowledged to be authentically Christian.

Philosophia Reformata offers a good example of this shift towards worldview. In many articles an explicit appeal to a religious ground-motive or to Scripture is simply absent. However, authors do struggle with all kinds of central values that the reader recognizes to be worldview applications of the Biblical message. Looking back we even find this worldview orientation in the philosophy of Vollenhoven and Dooyeweerd themselves! Dooyeweerd's religious ground-motives of the West are replicas of the life-systems in Kuyper's *Lectures on Calvinism*. Moreover, the theory of both thinkers of the modal spheres is a philosophical elaboration of the idea of sphere sovereignty in Groen and Kuyper.

12. From Transcendental Critique to Transcendental Hermeneutics

Along with worldviews we get saddled with philosophical pluralism. After all, every worldview presupposes a viewer who has an outlook on the world from a specific point of view. In other words, worldviews are by definition bound to place and time, and therefore also subject to a change in perspective. Where there are shifting worldviews, there pluralism in philosophy will arise.

Even Kuyper struggled with philosophical pluralism. He sought affiliation with the *Weltanschauung* of the Reformers of the sixteenth century, but it was not enough for him. He did not want to define his Calvinism strictly in terms of the small city state of Calvin's Geneva. Instead he wanted "to connect it with the human consciousness, such as it had developed itself at the end of the nineteenth century."[27] That is why it is correct to speak of "neo-Calvinism."

What Kuyper wanted also affects us. Must Christian philosophy issue into a worldwide theory, applicable *urbi et orbi*? Or should it be timely and topical by constantly anticipating new developments in thought and new relevant problems? Must the Christian colleagues in the Far East, Africa or Latin America articulate their philosophy in exactly the same way as we in the Western world? Is Christian philosophy in principle not a philosophy *in loco*, anchored in the Biblical message but with a local elaboration?[28]

Inherent in philosophical pluralism is the threat of relativism. A counterweight is needed. Let us therefore esteem philosophy in the spirit of Dooyeweerd as a theoretical reflection that distinguishes itself as a "transcendental critique." I mean that philosophy needs to give critical account of the fundamental presuppositions that guide theoretical thought, not only in the form of religious ground-motives, but also of worldview convictions. For even though worldviews do not belong to the field of theorizing, when they have an effect on theories they need to be accounted for philosophically.

How do worldviews operate in theoretical discourse? They throw a certain light on the discussion. They offer a paradigmatic frame of reference within which arguments are critically weighed. More precisely, they form the hermeneutical or interpretative horizon

---

27 *Encyclopaedie der Heilige Godgeleerdheid*, vol. 1, vi.

28 Klapwijk, J. 1987. "Reformational Philosophy on the Boundary of the Past and the Future." *Philosophia Reformata* 52: 126–131.

within which a theory needs to prove itself. Take the theory of evolution. The discussion on this issue between creationists, naturalists and others is often very unsatisfying. Why? Because the opponents are preoccupied with the facts, but hardly ever give critical account of the hermeneutical horizon within which they bring up these facts for discussion.

Kuyper is different. He is aware of the hermeneutical impact of worldviews and life-systems and indeed puts his cards on the table as far as his Calvinism is concerned. He challenges us, in fact, to broaden the transcendental assignment. This implies that we must seek to bring to light in the philosophical discussion not only the religious motives (Dooyeweerd), but also the worldview presuppositions that often form the proper cause of the difference of opinion between us and our opponents. In short, the time has come to make the transition from a transcendental critique to a transcendental hermeneutics of theoretical thought. This last may also be called a "depth hermeneutics."[29]

13. From Synthesis and Antithesis to Transformation in Science

Kuyper takes his starting point in the reformational basic conviction that each person has at depth a religious character and that, in the center of his conscious life, there is an open window to eternity. Thus he breaks with the Scholastic thesis that the human person has a rational nature, a nature that on the one side can develop freely, and on the other side has an inclination to the grace of God as its supernatural perfection. In other words, in Scholasticism scientific reason is autonomous, with a proviso. Whenever reason clashes with faith – which is the openness of the intellect to a higher, supernatural enlightenment – reason must submit to the latter, to the faith of the Church.

Kuyper rejects this relative autonomy of reason that leads to a dual or synthetic view of science and faith. Thus he also rejects the intellectual character of faith as a receptivity of reason for the divine gift of grace. Faith is not a supra-natural orientation; on the contrary it belongs to the creational or natural equipment of humanity. In all circumstances faith gives direction to human activities, also to the project of science. People can turn away from God, but this choice too is religiously determined. For this reason, Kuyper sees in world history the manifestation of a religious division between the reign of God and the forces of evil, an "antithesis of principles" that pervades culture and science.

The big question now is: does this religious antithesis end up in a scientific antithesis? Does it necessarily lead to an organized split between worldly and believing science, a struggle of life and death between the "normalists" and the "abnormalists"? This is indeed at first sight the import of Kuyper's argument.

Upon reflection Kuyper recoils from this radical position. At that point he does not conceal his admiration for Plato, Aristotle, Kant and Darwin and makes an appeal for cooperation between Christians and dissenters. He then seems to fall back into the scholastic dualism of nature and grace, reason and faith. The sciences, at least the lower sciences, are supposed to be secular and free from religious beliefs.

However, there is a third option, as I have argued in this article. At a crucial moment Kuyper asks the question whether the religious antithesis must necessarily lead to a scientific split and hence the establishment of a separate science. Then follows the challenging

---

29 Klapwijk, Jacob 2008. *Purpose in the Living World? Creation and Emergent Evolution.* Translated and edited by Harry Cook. Cambridge: Cambridge University Press, 191–210; Klapwijk "Reformational Philosophy," 115–126.

proposition: Christians can offer space for the factual insights of people of another mind by critical appropriation. How? They can appropriate the factual insights by disengaging them from the religious "hypothesis" on which they are built and by incorporating them in the body of their own science. For factual knowledge is no neutral information; it always functions in a greater meaningful context. In short, being a Christian in science demands an active effort of those involved, namely to frame the facts in a new hermeneutical context, that of faith. In Kuyper's last proposal the Christian religion does not change the facts, but it puts them in a new light. Faith does not present itself as a supernatural counterbalance for science. Nor does it involve a scientific split, an antithetical alternative for mainstream science. But it does lead, time and again, to transformation, that is to a reinterpretation and revaluation of the subjects that are raised in scientific discussions. For a more detailed elaboration of this proposal.[30]

14. Towards a Correlative Theology Based on Creation

No science was nearer to Kuyper's heart than theology. If theology is, as the word itself suggests, the study of God, does it issue into knowledge *about* God or is it perhaps even knowledge *of* God? Put even stronger: does it have to do with divine self-knowledge in the sense that the divine Logos mirrors itself in a special manner in the human logos, more precisely in the logical consciousness of the theologian?

We have to realize that the Logos doctrine has an affinity with the Scholastic position discussed above. Does the key role of the human logos imply that we have an intellectual access to God? Does theology imply that we can think and speak about the Supreme Being without believing? At once the question arises: how does theo-*logical* thinking relate to faith?

At crucial moments Kuyper looks for an alternative to the Scholastic approach. In such a case he primarily appeals to Luther. He points to the Reformer's *sola fide* and *sola Scriptura*. We can only have knowledge of God through believing in God's revelation in Christ and in Scripture; God has revealed Himself through the ages to his people in *faith*. Knowledge of God is therefore a reciprocal relation, for faith is by its very nature oriented towards revelation and revelation by its very nature is intended to solicit faith. To say, as Scholastics do, that theology is a *logical* reflex of the divine Logos is implicitly to deny this correlation. (I prefer to use the term "correlation," which can be found as early as the *Apology* of Luther's colleague Melanchthon, even though the word is not typical of Kuyper.[31]) So, what about theology as an academic discipline? It can be defined as the subsequent logical reflection on the intimate bond between revelation and faith. It is a logical and methodological application of this very correlation.

Kuyper distances himself even farther from Scholasticism by appealing to Calvin. Faith in God does not result from grace as an additional reality, a super-natural gift of divine grace infused in human nature in baptism. In Calvin's view faith has its basis in

---

30 See Klapwijk, Jacob 1986. "Antithesis, Synthesis, and the Idea of Transformational Philosophy," *Philosophia Reformata* 51: 138–154 and "Epilogue: The Idea of Transformational Philosophy." In J. Klapwijk, S. Griffioen, and G. Groenewoud (eds). *Bringing into Captivity Every Thought*. Lanham: University Press of America, 241–266.

31 Melanchthon: "the promise and faith stand in a reciprocal relation" and "the promised mercy correlatively requires faith"; in Latin: "*promissionem et fidem correlativa esse*" and "*promissam misericordiam correlative requirere fidem*" (*The Apology of the Augsburg Confession* [1531]. Tredition Classics 2011, Part 9).

creation itself. The human person has been created so that he or she has by nature a "sense of deity," even though this capacity has been disrupted through sin and needs to be restored by grace, that is, by God's benevolence towards those who repent.

Here I see the relevance of Kuyper's analysis for present-day theology. His view of the connection between faith and revelation is different from Rudolf Bultmann, Paul Tillich and many others. In their method of correlation the relation between subject and object of modern theory of science holds center stage. Bultmann wants to attune the meaning of the gospel to the concrete life situation of the modern subject. Tillich seeks to interpret the symbols of Biblical revelation as answers to the existential questions of the finite human person. Both approaches imply a restriction of the Word by deriving the standard for the Word's meaning from the subject.

Kuyper's conception comes much closer to the method of correlation in Gerrit C. Berkouwer. Berkouwer, too, criticized the polarity of subject and object in Modern theology from the start.[32] Nevertheless, Kuyper surpasses also Berkouwer on a very basic point. Berkouwer's conception of correlation is ambivalent in so far as it emphasizes that faith comes from hearing of the Word, the message of Christ's redemption. However, precisely in this redemptive historical meaning of the word there cannot be any strict correlation between faith and revelation. After all, it is the preaching of the cross that brings about faith in Christ as the redeemer!

However, is faith merely the fruit of the cross? Is it not also the fulfillment of the creaturely destiny of humankind? Kuyper's position is so challenging because along with Calvin he constantly wants to return from the cross to the creation (*LC* 118). Dooyeweerd writes correctly: "Abraham Kuyper was . . . the first to regain for theology the scriptural insight that faith is a unique function of our inner life implanted in human nature at creation."[33] Well then, in this creaturely deepened sense of the word Kuyper displays for us the correlation of faith and revelation as the indispensable link, a source of energy never to be relinquished even in a strictly methodical pursuit of theology.

The gains of this methodological position seem to be quite evident when one takes into consideration that the theology of the twenty-first century will have to prove its mettle on a global stage, that is to say, over against the major world religions and Western secularism. Its message will have to sound as a message of redemption and salvation in the spirit of Berkouwer. However, this message can only take hold when it appeals to something that slumbers in all humankind, a sensitivity for the divine that, however much distorted and suppressed, is created and grafted in human nature right from the beginning and must therefore also be capable of evoking recognition amongst people today.

---

32 Moor, Johannes C. de 1980. *Towards a Biblically Theo-logical Method: A Structural Analysis of Dr. G.C. Berkouwer's Hermeneutical-Dogmatic Method*. Kampen: Kok , 67.

33 Dooyeweerd, H. 1979. *Roots of Western Culture: Pagan, Secular, and Christian Options*. Edited by Mark Vander Vennen and Bernard Zylstra, translated by John Kraay. Toronto: Wedge Publishing Foundation, 91.

19

Common Grace and Christian Action
in Abraham Kuyper

S. U. Zuidema

Introduction

Abraham Kuyper's standard work on common grace, entitled *De Gemeene Gratie*, which first appeared in a series of weekly articles, could not fail to arrest the attention of his followers and contemporaries. In fact it captivated them, touching them in the depths of their minds and hearts. For this work, compelling in its broad sweep and irresistible in its central thrust, delivered them from an "Anabaptist isolationism"[1] by providing them with their eagerly awaited religious justification of Christian involvement, not only individually but also organizationally, "in all areas of life"; of Christian involvement not only in the affairs of the church but also "in state and society, in art and scholarship." It both justified such involvement and encouraged it. And even though it is true that the Anti-Revolutionary Party had been in existence for more than ten years already, henceforward it would certainly also be from this three-volume work that the independent party formation by Dutch Calvinists in the sphere of politics would draw its inspiration and vision. If the Anti-Revolutionary Party does not stand or fall with the doctrine of common grace, its history cannot be written without a proper understanding of the great significance this doctrine has had – and still has – for its adherents.

Kuyper, of course, was not the first to write about common grace and to demand attention for it. He had been preceded in this effort by Herman Bavinck, who in 1894 delivered a rectorial address at the Theological School in Kampen under the title *De Algemeene Genade*. But Kampen as little as Amsterdam could boast that here for the first time in the history of the Christian church 'common grace' was thought about and discussed. Neither Bavinck nor Kuyper considered himself original in this regard. Quite rightly they saw themselves also on this point as pupils of John Calvin, as "copyists" (to

---

1 Cf. *GG* II:52, 349, et passim.

"*Gemeene gratie* en *Pro Rege* bij Dr Abraham Kuyper," *Anti-Revolutionaire Staatkunde* 24 (1954), 1–19, 49–73. Cf. A. Kuyper, *De Gemeene Gratie*, Vols. I–III (Leiden, 1902–05), Vol. IV (Leiden, 1905); hereafter cited as *GG*, according to the 3rd unaltered (pagination moved up 4) impression (3 vols.; Kampen, 1931–32). The translation is by Harry Van Dyke, who wishes to record his indebtedness to Donald Morton for numerous small and invaluable improvements to the final draft.

use Kuyper's own term). In his doctoral dissertation, *Calvin on Common Grace*, Herman Kuiper has presented a well-documented case for the view that Calvin's theology at least implies the doctrine of common grace and that anyone who rejects common grace thereby attacks an essential point in the Christian thought not only of Kuyper and Bavinck but also of Calvin.[2] On this issue no wedge can be driven between Amsterdam and Kampen and Geneva.

Common Grace and *Pro Rege*

Any attempt, meanwhile, to isolate what Calvin, Bavinck and Kuyper taught concerning common grace – the one more systematically than the other – from what they taught concerning God's saving grace by which He in Christ elects, reconciles, and calls sinners unto eternal life would definitely militate against their deepest beliefs. To be sure, Kuyper – from this point on I shall confine myself to his views – repeatedly taught that God's common grace has an independent purpose.[3] By this he meant to say that common grace has a purpose of its own, next to and even over against God's special, saving grace (*GG* II:685). In other words, common grace has a purpose that as such cannot be placed in subservience to God's reconciling, redeeming and electing work in His covenant of grace. In this connection, however, three points should not be overlooked.

First, the only reason why Kuyper was constrained as if by inner necessity to posit this independent purpose of common grace was that he himself had begun by defining too narrowly the purpose of particular grace and the scope of its operation. This narrow definition could have driven him into Gnostic and Anabaptistic waters if he had not also posited the pole of common grace next to the pole of particular grace. The independent goal ascribed to common grace is only "relatively" independent. Kuyper sought to keep his conception in balance by positing the no less "independent" purpose of particular grace, namely: the election unto eternal salvation. It would be in conflict with the deepest religious motives, convictions and inner experiences of Kuyper and his brethren, indeed with this whole type of man, to assume even for a moment that he would want to base his position, or even his activity in the world, on this one pole of common grace with its independent purpose. Ever since Kuyper's conversion experience, the humanist in him could only live on as the tempter to be resisted, as the seducer to be cast out with prayer. A synthesis of Christianity and humanism is the last thing that Kuyper could have intended with his doctrine of common grace. I concur with A. A. van Ruler that Kuyper neither said nor implied anything of the sort.[4] If this doctrine could be used to justify some sort of accommodation to humanism in "the broad domain of common grace" – which it can't – Kuyper would undoubtedly have counted the whole thing but dung for the excellency of the (saving) knowledge of Christ Jesus our Lord. When later he came to write his *Pro Rege*, therefore, the intention was certainly not to offer a fundamental correction of his doctrine of common grace, least of all to quietly vitiate or retract it. To Kuyper's mind, the one did not clash with the other. The doctrine of common grace is anti-Anabaptist, but it cannot possibly be grasped if it is also taken to be anti-soteriological, that is, as diluting the Christian confession of the saving grace of our Lord Jesus Christ. In fact, this doctrine

2   Kuiper, Herman 1928. *Calvin on Common Grace*. (Diss. Vrije Univ.) Goes: Oosterbaan & Le Cointre.
3   *GG* I:254; II:632ff.; III:124.
4   Van Ruler, A. A. no date [1940]. *Kuypers idee eener Christelijke cultuur*. Nijkerk: Callenbach, 12f.

cannot be grasped even if "common grace" is interpreted merely as a kind of Libertine-humanist addition to life, as a domain of life where the Christian for once need not live out of God's grace in Christ but can go his own "natural" way.

That brings me to my second point. What Kuyper intended with his doctrine of common grace was not at all to pave the way for some sort of "neutral" appreciation of the cultural activity and achievements of the unbelievers. Much rather he wanted to blaze a trail for God's believing people to engage in their own distinctive way in the "domain of common grace" – an activity having its origin in and deriving its impulse from particular grace. Kuyper showed a way in which to be active *pro Rege* in the domain of common grace. Van Ruler, who precisely for this reason rejects Kuyper's doctrine, shows thereby that he has at least understood Kuyper correctly.[5]

But there is a third point that should be considered here. S. J. Ridderbos for one has pointed to contradictions in Kuyper's doctrine of common grace.[6] In that he is right. But for just that reason his conclusion on the last page of his book is only a half-truth. He writes there:

> If contemporary Calvinism wishes to avoid becoming stagnant on account of one-sidedness, it should not push to the foreground certain emphases in Kuyper's heritage at the expense of others. One is only true to Kuyper if one refuses to replace the complexity of his thought with an oversimplification that ultimately impoverishes it.[7]

This conclusion is itself an oversimplification and an impoverishment – of Ridderbos' own method of dealing with Kuyper. For we see Ridderbos himself trying to resolve some of the contradictions in Kuyper's doctrine; and we see his effort resulting, too, in the weeding out of a good many needless complexities. In this effort, however, I think he is being true to Kuyper. For Kuyper certainly was not out to produce contradictions; rather, he rejected internal contradiction as error. Thus, one cannot be charged with oversimplifying matters if he is merely resolving contradictions. The resolution of contradictions does not immediately entail the oversimplification and impoverishment of Kuyper's thought; and Ridderbos' warning must therefore be taken cautiously lest, as a half-truth, it preclude a proper understanding of the import and application of Kuyper's doctrine of common grace.

Take the following inner contradiction in Kuyper's argument. Kuyper explicitly both combats the idea of an independent purpose of common grace and teaches it approvingly. He combats the idea when he asserts that also with respect to the divine order for the *present* dispensation it must be said that "the order of *particular grace obtains*":

> To be sure, there is nothing wrong with saying that all things occur for the sake of Christ, that therefore the *Body of Christ* constitutes the dominant element in history, and that this validates the confession that the Church of Christ is the pivot around which in fact the life of mankind turns. He who ignores or denies this can never discover unity in the course of history. For such a person, century follows upon century, and therein growth upon recession, and again progress upon regression, but the stream of life goes nowhere, it is without purpose [!]. This life lacks a center; it has no axis. If this condition has to continue world without end,

---

5   Van Ruler, *Kuypers idee*, 78ff., 136f.

6   Ridderbos, Simon Jan 1947. *De Theologische Cultuurbeschouwing van Abraham Kuyper.* (Diss. Vrije Univ.) Kampen: Kok, 86f.

7   Ridderbos, *Cultuurbeschouwing*, 328.

life will end up being boredom without end; and if it has to break off at some point because the elements of fire or water become too powerful for our earth, then such a break will be totally arbitrary and no purpose will have been served [!]. Nothing will have been gained! The Reformed confession, which maintains that all things, also in this world, aim at the *Christ*, that his *Body* is the chief element and that in this sense one can say that the Church of Christ constitutes the center of world history – this confession offers a principle for a philosophy of history that towers high above the common view of history. We will think twice, therefore, before detracting from this confession in any way whatsoever. Not common grace but the order of *particular* grace *obtains*? (*GG* I:223f.)

Here the doctrine of the independent purpose of common grace is denied in so many words, and history, which in the present dispensation takes place "in the domain of common grace," is conceived of Christocentrically and soteriologically. Here *Pro Rege* sounds the dominant note, or to put it more correctly: here Christ is confessed also as the "King of common grace" and common grace is denied a purpose of its own independent of particular grace.

But this is not the whole of it. Not only in the center of history but also at its end does Kuyper distinguish two lines. For he explains, not just once but over and over again, that common grace is limited to the present dispensation and realizes its purpose in our present "life in time" (*GG* I:497; II:277, 679). This in fact is one of the marks that in Kuyper's view distinguishes common grace from particular grace. Yet at the same time he teaches that the fruits of common grace shall be brought into the Kingdom of glory in the hereafter (*GG* I:458ff.). The reason he gives for this view is that the actual existence of the visible things – the domain of common grace – has as purpose(!)

> . . . to become the possession of particular grace. . . . There will come a time when the present course of things will reach a turning point and then the re-creative power of particular grace will appropriate to itself also the whole domain of common grace. . . . [Hence] the contrast between the domain of particular grace and that of common grace is only temporary. (*GG* II:684f.)

Once more it turns out that particular grace triumphs as it were over common grace. This is far removed from the notion that either at present or in the end common grace will annex particular grace to itself. (Kuyper is no Christian humanist!) It is equally far removed from the notion that common grace has an independent goal and purpose in this life and in the present dispensation. On the contrary, common grace is pictured as flowing into the hereafter, and in such a way that Christ will then finally be "King of common grace." Thus the "independent" purpose of common grace turns out to be quite relative, in truth only appears to be independent. Even its temporary character is but relative and is posited by Kuyper with the one hand only to be retracted with the other.

From all this it is unmistakably clear that particular grace remained closest to Kuyper's heart, together with the Kingship of Christ as the Mediator of Redemption. This is true even when he holds to a relatively independent purpose for common grace and carves out a relatively autonomous domain for common grace. Anyone who would use Kuyper's doctrine of common grace to justify a view of culture and an involvement in culture existing as it were *alongside* faith in God's particular grace, would be misusing it. The only thing Kuyper's doctrine of common grace can justify is the acceptance of a dialectic, polar relationship between the domain of common grace and the domain of particular grace. But even in that case the independence of common grace is never without its opposite pole: common grace cannot be accepted without at the same time accepting the antithesis and the call to Christian action, action *pro Rege*, for Christ the King, action born of the grace of regeneration. Moreover, even as Kuyper maintains this polarity, at heart he remains the pious mystic and the longing pilgrim. This is the heart of Kuyper, this is where it all starts, and this is what he always comes back to. The fact and the fruits of particular grace, as he defined it – these are what finally weighs the most with Kuyper.

Besides, all this refers only to the one Kuyper, a Kuyper reduced to a minimum. The same Kuyper in the same breath speaks of common grace as the grace that comes with Christ as the Mediator of Redemption not only at the end of history, for the life hereafter, but also here and now, in the very midst of human history.[8] To appeal to this Kuyper is as justified as to appeal to the reduced Kuyper. Meanwhile, to press both "Kuypers" to one's bosom is to embrace internal contradiction. This can be acceptable only to followers who are in truth but "followers," men unwilling to disentangle and remove the inconsistency. Such recalcitrance is unworthy of true followers of Kuyper. They who wish to follow Kuyper will have to make a choice here.

Common Grace Makes Christian Action Possible
It has been correctly pointed out by Van Ruler that the whole import of Kuyper's doctrine of common grace, both as to its objective content and as to its author's subjective intention, is to stimulate, as well as to justify, truly Christian action by God's people from out of the particular grace of regeneration by the light of Holy Scripture. Common grace supplies the believer with the material for fulfilling his calling to be culturally formative and to fight the battle of the Lord in the world of culture.

The sphere of common grace is the sphere of action for people who are blessed with particular grace and now seek to administer the blessings of particular grace.[9] It is the area where Christian scholarship, Christian politics, Christian social action and individual Christian activity are to be developed. Common grace provides the platform, as it were, on which all these cultural tasks are to be acted out. Common grace is *the presupposition of the possibility of* Christian cultural activity. Common grace makes this activity born of particular grace possible. Common grace makes the antithesis, makes *Pro Rege* action possible.

Once more it should be stated at the outset that this doctrine in no wise suggests or implies the existence of anything like an area of life where the Christian can operate autonomously, i.e., independently of God's Word and detached from the grace of regeneration. Wherever "common grace" functions as a blank check for a non-Christian walk of life and a non-Christian mind, there the doctrine is brutally violated. With his doctrine of common grace Kuyper aimed precisely at clearing the way for the privilege and obligation of cultural involvement rooted in the communion with Christ, the new Head of redeemed mankind; involvement rooted in the mystic Body of Christ; in the grace of God that regenerates man, redirecting and renewing his "innermost pivot," his "center," his "core."[10] Common grace is here for the sake of Christian action; it justifies and makes

---

8   *GG* II:341, 348, 355; III:515f., 523.

9   Van Ruler, *Kuypers idee*, passim.

10 For these expressions, see *GG* II:212—binnenste spil, middelpunt, kern.

possible the antithesis.

To be sure, Kuyper stressed this much more in his later studies entitled *Pro Rege*. But in doing that he in no wise departed from the plan, the tenor and the contents of his work *De Gemeene Gratie*. To suggest that *Pro Rege* shows traces of self-correction as regards *De Gemeene Gratie* is to suggest too much. Kuyper could do without correction, and so could *De Gemeene Gratie*.

Meanwhile we have hit upon one of the most important concepts in this whole doctrine of common grace as expounded by Kuyper. I am referring to the idea of common grace as "the ground for the possibility of" particular grace, and then especially of the activity born of particular grace. Curiously, a similar idea of "possibility" crops up today in the *Kirchliche Dogmatik* of Karl Barth. For Barth, "nature" is the possibility of "grace." Of course I am aware that Barth also has a second way of talking about "possibility"; namely, that God's grace carries its own possibility with it, in fact *is* its own possibility, makes itself possible, creates along with itself its own "point of connection." Barth's position, consequently, is summed up this way: "nature" or creation is the "external possibility" of grace, whereas grace is its own internal possibility.[11]

I point out this parallel in Barth in order, among other things, to demonstrate that the idea of an "external possibility" has nothing to do with Pelagianism, semi-Pelagianism or Arminianism in one's doctrine of the *ordo salutis*. Kuyper, too, very consciously has particular grace rest in itself: he insists that when we are born again and come to believe, this is due solely to the work of the Holy Spirit. Kuyper's doctrine of the *gratia communis*, therefore, has only the name in common with the Arminian doctrine of the *gratia communis*.[12] With the Arminians, "common grace" plays its own decisive and autonomous role; it is an "*internal*" ground for the possibility of regeneration and conversion of the man who is dead in trespasses and sin. Now this is the very last thing that Kuyper had in mind. His doctrine of election and of the covenant of grace, which he worked out extensively before he had set down on paper so much as one letter about common grace, is free from all Arminian taints. Klaas Schilder is therefore fighting windmills when he uses the term and the concept of Arminianism's *gratia communis* against Kuyper and proceeds on that account to label the term "common grace" unacceptable;[13] he also ignores the fact that the term and the idea of *gratia communis* occur also in Calvin – in a perfectly acceptable sense.

In addition it should be noted that Kuyper, though holding common grace to be indeed the "external" possibility of particular grace, in most cases – with one exception[14] – explicitly calls the Spirit's working of God's regenerating grace "immediate,"[15] hence independent of all "preparatory grace" contained in common grace (*GG* II:207–217). True, Kuyper does teach that to be born again is "possible" only for those who are born, and that it is only owing to God's common grace that after the Fall "to be born" is "possible" at all.[16] But surely this line of argument is not going to tempt anyone to think that Kuyper

11 Cf. Barth, Karl *Kirchliche Dogmatik*, II:l, 255f.

12 Cf. *GG* II:117, 216f.

13 Schilder, K. 1947. *Is de term "Algemeene Genade" wetenschappelijk verantwoord?* Kampen: Zalsman, 14ff.

14 Cf. Kuyper, A. 1893–1894. *Encyclopaedie der Heilige Godgeleerdheid*. 3 vols. Amsterdam; II (2nd rev. ed. Kampen, 1909), 232.

15 *GG* II:207ff., 241, et passim.

16 *GG* I:95, 212ff., 222, 254, 263; II:293, 338, 354, 684; III:423.

thereby meant to somehow maim or weaken the confession that God's grace is particular or to detract from the sovereignty of God's *free* grace?

But enough has been adduced to prove my thesis: Kuyper's doctrine of common grace is there for the sake of his doctrine of particular grace; and first and foremost for the sake of his doctrine that particular grace gives birth to Christian action that is as broad as life and that is not only not impossible and not forbidden, but possible and even mandatory. With this doctrine he summoned God's people, "the church organism," to distinctive Christian activity, to activity *pro Rege*, to "antithetical" activity especially, not in the last place in the form of separate organizations.

1. Particular Grace and Common Grace

Meanwhile, whether Kuyper's doctrine of particular grace allows of Christian action and whether the companion doctrine of common grace does indeed encourage Christian action, remains to be seen. Can common grace indeed render such Christian action possible; can particular grace indeed come to express itself in action along this route?

What is Particular Grace?

What is God's special grace – or, as Kuyper was wont to call it, God's particular grace? It is God's merciful disposition towards sinners with whom He has reconciled Himself for the sake of Christ's meritorious work on the cross and to whom He now freely grants, through His Holy Spirit, out of pure, unmerited, forfeited and gratuitous favor, according to His eternal plan of salvation, Christ and all His benefits.[17] God's particular grace issues in the work of Christ as our Mediator of Redemption, who took upon Himself our flesh and blood, our human nature, and who gave Himself for us as a remission of all our sins, in the "Covenant of Grace and Reconciliation" (*GG* I:296). It issues no less in the work of the Spirit of Christ, who makes us Christ's possession, who dwells in us and works in us, and who brings about in our hearts, in the core and center of our being, that regeneration without which no one can see the Kingdom of God.[18] In short, just read the Canons of Dordt and you will know what Kuyper understood by particular grace.

Particular grace issues in the "Body of Christ," the "corpus Christi mysticum" of Ephesians 1.[19] Van Ruler is quite wrong in seeing in Kuyper an overemphasis of the doctrine of the Holy Spirit at the expense of Christocracy.[20] For Kuyper is quite explicit in stating that regeneration – the work of the Holy Spirit – means that a person is implanted in the "Body of Christ," and that thereby he "personally belongs to Christ" (*GG* II:672). As 2 Corinthians 3:17 says, "Now the Lord is the Spirit. . . ." But Van Ruler has seen quite correctly that the "subjective grace"[21] of God, according to Kuyper – but no less according to the Canons of Dort and no less according to Calvin – begins with regeneration.[22] Consequently, when Kuyper attacks the problem of truly Christian action in the world, there is no question in his mind that this action must arise from the "new man," who is

17　Cf. Kuyper, A. 1892–1895. *E Voto Dordraceno.* 4 vols. Amsterdam: Wormser, II:537.
18　*GG* II:137, 614, et passim.
19　*GG* II:614, et passim.
20　*GG* II:672; *PrRege* II:130f.
21　For this term, see Ridderbos, *Cultuurbeschouwing*, 92.
22　*GG* I:255; II:52, 207ff.

"born again," and that this is in full harmony not only with the rule of Christ but also with the rule of the Spirit. If now Van Ruler wants to call this "spiritualistic,"[23] I will not demur; it is in very truth: acknowledging the work of the Holy Spirit, the Spirit of Christ, "who dwells and works in our hearts"; this is biblical; this echoes John 3. But if Van Ruler wants to posit over against this: "time has come to a standstill, as it were, in eternity,"[24] then I think he is distorting the biblical revelation about regeneration and particular grace and the work of the Holy Spirit. For it is certainly in conflict with the biblical revelation to teach that eternity robs our life-in-time of any significance of its own.

Regeneration is where Kuyper takes his point of departure. And he calls this regeneration "spiritual" in nature (*GG* II:219). One may object to this term and wish to replace it with a better one – provided one does not object to the matter so designated and seek to remove it, and provided one would not have us believe that the salvation in Christ touches our bodies as closely (or, as remotely) as our souls.[25] The whole Bible bears out the meaning of "heart" as the controlling center of man. And this heart is something other than our functioning and something other than our feelings; it is to be distinguished from the issues of life, including the psychical issues of life. Kuyper stands on the basis of the Bible when he has particular grace take its start with the "spiritual" renewal and reversal of the "pivot" of our selfhood and therein with the re-creation of ourselves into "new men." In this, he also stands on the basis of the Reformed creeds.

This point of departure is for Kuyper also the connecting point, the point of invasion and inception, for the re-creation – or for the Kingdom of Heaven (cf. *GG* II:10f., 639). The Kingdom of Heaven is the kingdom of particular grace, in which all participate who are "in Christ," who belong to Him, who are engrafted into Him, and who thus belong to the (invisible) Church of Christ, His "mystic" Body.[26]

It deserves mention at this point that in Kuyper's theology the thesis that grace is *particular* does not mean that it is *individualistic*, i.e., of benefit only to the individual person. This is the conclusion Van Ruler mistakenly draws.[27] When Kuyper calls this grace of God "particular," he does so because he does not consider it bound to any societal structure belonging to this temporal life, be it the family, the church institution, the state, or any social group. While holding this view, however, Kuyper has not been swept into the dangerous waters of individualism, of particularism. He is fully conscious of the Body of Christ into which we are in-grafted through regeneration, and this Body is something else than the sum total of individuals, even of born-again individuals. It is in fact for Kuyper, as it was for Bavinck and Calvin, no less than the re-born, re-created human race, the New Humanity that finds its unity no longer in Adam but "in Christ."[28] The renewed human race has a "spiritual" unity, a "mystical" unity, the unity of "children" of God who have been adopted as sons "in Christ" by the "God and Father of our Lord Jesus Christ." Born-

---

23 Van Ruler, *Kuypers idee*, e.g., 7.

24 Van Ruler, *Kuypers idee*, 137; cf. 126: "Christianly speaking, after all, the significance of things lies in eternity."

25 So Van Ruler, *Kuypers idee*, 146: "If our salvation is hid in heaven, there is on principle no difference between the body's communion with salvation and the soul's. . . . The Spirit does not have a greater kinship with, and therefore hold on, the soul than with and on the body."

26 Cf. *Heidelberg Catechism*, Lord's Day VII.

27 Van Ruler, *Kuypers idee*, e.g., 7.

28 Cf. Ridderbos, *Cultuurbeschouwing*, 133.

again Christians are sons of one Father; they are brothers and sisters in Christ; they belong to the same "household of faith"; they believe that the Son of God leads the "Church of God" and that they "are, and forever shall remain, living members thereof."[29]

For Kuyper, this Scriptural doctrine of the Church chosen unto everlasting life leads to the "mysticism"[30] of the communion with God, of God's "nearness," of God's being near-unto-us and our being near-unto-God, of the intimacy of "being in Christ." This he emphasizes throughout. In his view, this precedes any and all Christian action. In fact, this is the indispensable prerequisite for Christian action.

But having emphasized this, Kuyper goes on to explain, in the second place, that this particular grace is not intended to come fully into its own in this life, but rather in the life to come. Particular grace is directed toward the hereafter (*GG* II:639, 654). In its deepest essence particular grace operates apart from this temporal life (*GG* II:341). Viewed by itself, it can, if need be, operate entirely apart from this earthly life.[31] It saves only unto eternal life, and accordingly is bestowed only on the elect (*GG* II:613). It is not "common" but "particular." It is founded on the election unto salvation and finds its destination in the eternal blessedness of the afterlife.

From this it follows that particular grace is not really directed toward activity in the sphere of our temporal life, in the world of visible things. This explains the tremendous tension so often inserted by Kuyper in the very union he seeks to establish. For how can activity in the domain of the temporal and the visible arise out of particular grace? How can such activity be truly Christian activity? Will this activity in the world, this being busy with things secular and profane, not rather be worldly, secular, profane? It will take us – this is certain, on Kuyper's own view – beyond the sphere of the invisible and the "spiritual," beyond the zone of regeneration in the central core of our being. Particular grace must choose for the theater of its activity an area to which it is by nature foreign: looking to the hereafter for its end and purpose, particular grace has to look to the here and now for its area of operations. How can this be? How can particular grace impel the elect to be active in this temporal life – "*alongside*" their life of the soul and "*apart from*" their being saved? (*GG* III:307).

It will no longer surprise us to find Kuyper explaining somewhere that the early Christians did not engage in any cultivation of the sciences, not even in a Christian cultivation of them, *because* such activity was really beneath their standing.[32] Grace, after all, directs our minds, our hearts, toward the hereafter, hence away from this temporal world and all its pursuits, including the pursuits of science. Particular grace converts a man into a pilgrim who sets his face toward the eternal future beyond the grave.

And, thirdly, to complicate matters still further, particular grace re-creates. It entails no less than re-creation.[33] Now this re-creation means first of all that the destructive effects of sin and curse are brought to naught. But it entails more than that. It does not simply restore the condition of Paradise; it does not take us back to the original state, to what Kuyper calls the "natural" life. It brings something more and something else. It can in fact

---

29 Cf. *Heidelberg Catechism*, Lord's Day XXI.

30 "Mystiek"; cf. *PrRege* II:189ff.

31 *GG* II:654. (The reference is to the high incidence of infant mortality.)

32 *Encyclopaedie* II:112f.

33 *GG* II:613; III:110ff.

be called "supernatural" – not only because it does not arise from our nature, for in this sense Kuyper can call common grace "supernatural" too (*GG* II:67), and rightly so, but also because it brings something other than the original nature. It brings something new, something not even Paradise had known. For – so runs the reasoning – particular grace begins where Adam would have ended had historical development gone on uninterrupted. That is to say, it begins with eternal life; it begins where the covenant of works with Adam was to have ended;[34] it begins with Christ's fulfillment of all the requirements of the covenant of works, hence with the reward for Christ's work as Mediator: namely, eternal life.[35]

This re-creation, to be sure, is a re-creating of the natural; it is not a second creation foreign to the first. The regenerated man is the selfsame man before and after his regeneration.[36] Yet as the same man he is, in Christ, a new creature, for whom the old things have passed away and all things have become new. He "has" eternal life. Death has no more dominion over him. Adam could fall into sin, but one who is born of God does not commit sin; the divine seed remains in him.[37] A change of state such as was possible in Paradise – from sinless to sinful, from righteous to ungodly – is no longer possible for regenerate man; for him a change of state has become an impossibility (*GG* II:210).

Thus the "natural" man has become a "spiritual" man. This is re-creation – the work of particular grace, the all-controlling benefit of Christ whereby the regenerate man becomes one plant with Christ so that he can sin no more (cf. Romans 6). Hence, in contradistinction to the "natural" state of Adam in Paradise, Kuyper calls this new state of the regenerate man "supernatural" (*GG* II:243; III:110).

This last concept should not be misunderstood. Kuyper does not fill the distinction "natural-supernatural" with Thomistic content. To be sure, he indeed has this distinction in common with Thomism. And again, to be sure, as in Thomism so in Kuyper the distinction is usually a polar one. But whereas the Thomist distinguishes already in the state of rectitude a supernatural grace and a supernatural life of grace,[38] not so Kuyper. According to the latter, the man of Paradise was a natural man through and through. But, the Fall having taken place, the man who is redeemed by Christ and endowed with His Spirit is a re-created man, and as a re-created man he is more than – and in some respect different from – the man as he was originally created. Moreover, in Kuyper "supernatural" does not mean what it has come to mean in Thomism, to wit: a partaking of the Divine nature, a divinization of man.[39] To the extent that Kuyper deals with it in connection with the re-creation, the supernatural too is not divine in essence. "Nature," of course, in the sense of the kingdoms of minerals, plants and animals cannot participate, certainly in the present dispensation, in this work of re-creation, subject as it remains to corruption.[40] But

---

34 Correctly observed by V. Hepp; see his 1937 *Dreigende Deformatie, IV: De algemeene Genade*. Kok: Kampen, 73, 78, 87.

35 Ibid., p. 78

36 *GG* I:216, 244; II:193, 214, 294.

37 1 John 3:9; cf. 1 Peter l:23ff.; *GG* II:303.

38 Cf. Smit, M. C. 1950. *De Verhouding van Christendom en Historie in de Huidige Rooms Katholieke Geschied-beschouwing*. (Diss. Vrije Univ.) Kampen: Kok, 27–49. See also *GG* I:131ff.; II:44ff.

39 Smit, *Christendom en Historie*, 36, 37.

40 Cf. Ridderbos, *Cultuurbeschouwing*, 156; and, e.g., *GG* III:21

neither can the whole of man's "visible life in time" partake of the "supernaturalness" of the re-creation. This life was and ever shall remain "natural" – at least for the duration of "the present dispensation."[41]

Thus for Kuyper particular grace means the grace by which we are granted now in the present dispensation, on the basis of Christ's reconciliation and through the operation of His Spirit, the "re-creation" of regeneration in the core of our being, in the pivot of our human selfhood; a grace that will not until hereafter, however, at the "rebirth of heaven and earth," translate the whole of created reality into a supernatural re-creation (*GG* II:685, 689). Wherefore in the present dispensation regenerate man is a pilgrim directed toward the coming day of our Lord Jesus Christ, a stranger for whom the curse-ridden nature, but also the Paradise nature, is a foreign land. The born-again Christian, according to Kuyper, lives in an "alien" world – and in a "lower" world, a world lower in rank than the regenerate man himself who is chosen unto everlasting life and equipped by particular grace with the supernatural "powers of the age to come." Small wonder that the goal and end of regeneration is to be sought in the life hereafter.

What Is Common Grace?

Now it is certain for Kuyper – and it also follows from the above – that where particular grace has done its work of re-creating, there no work, hence no working area, remains for common grace. The sphere of action of particular grace cannot possibly be at the same time a sphere of action for common grace.

Conversely, however, Kuyper is also certain that wherever in the present dispensation particular grace has not yet entered, there common grace finds its own proper and true domain. That is where common grace rules. That at least is where it *can* rule. That is where particular grace has not in advance rendered common grace superfluous, impossible and unthinkable. In this manner then, on the basis of a polar dualism like this, Kuyper is led to locate the "domain" of common grace outside of the regenerated heart, in the temporal and visible, and in the "natural."[42]

Likewise the *nature* of common grace is indirectly predetermined by the nature of particular grace. Common grace cannot be "spiritual," i.e., regenerative; it cannot find its goal and end in the hereafter but only within the present dispensation, i.e., in the temporal; it is never "supernatural," i.e., re-creative; and finally, common grace cannot be saving grace.[43]

The outermost limit to the operation of common grace is that it restores the original condition of Paradise and, without re-creating, reduces the Fall and its results to a minimum (*GG* II:613f.). Here we have that unmistakable "cultural optimism" streak in Kuyper's doctrine of common grace.[44] Common grace checks the operation of sin and the curse on sin, and in principle makes possible again the unfolding of creation's potentialities and the development of the creature. It fosters this unfolding, nourishes it, strengthens it. It makes for a "grace-endowed nature" (*GG* II:613); nature remains nature – the re-creation

---

41 Cf. *GG* II:341, 665, 685, 688; III:341.

42 *GG* I:291; III:109, 331, et passim.

43 *GG* I:86, 296; II :507–511; III:107–110, 146, et passim.

44 So Van Ruler, *Kuypers idee*, 39ff., 44ff.; so likewise, but shilly-shally, Ridderbos, *Cultuurbeschouwing*, 125, 322; so Schilder, "*Algemeene Genade*," 69, 76.

is not shared in by nature – but common grace curbs the destructive operation of sin and postpones the curse on nature; in fact, in the realm of the temporal and the visible (i.e., quite apart from men's hearts) it even enables people to do the good, the moral good, the civic good, opening up the possibility of progress in the life of creation. Thus, next to the stemming of sin and curse, common grace in Kuyper's view also operates for "progress": it serves and promotes cultural development and progress, and makes these possible.[45]

Thus the need for confessing God's common grace follows for Kuyper, among other things, from the manner in which he has defined the domain and the operation of particular grace. Van Ruler, too, notes, in part correctly, that Kuyper's doctrine of common grace is governed by how he conceived God's particular grace – which is granted to His elect unto eternal life – as it relates to the present dispensation.[46] Outside the regenerative operation of particular grace, converting man in his root, there lies the domain of the temporal and the visible world of the present dispensation. But this natural, creaturely domain – for Kuyper there is no contrast between "nature" and "creation," between "natural" and "creaturely"![47] – has since the Fall been subjected to the curse and to the power of sin, and man after the Fall is also in this domain incapable of doing any good and inclined to all evil. Yet likewise for this domain God had announced death as the punishment for sin (*GG* I:213, 220ff.). If God did not deal "graciously" here; if with respect to this temporal and natural life, which is not immediately translated by His particular grace into the glory of the re-creation, He were not "gracious" and long-suffering in some way other than in particular grace, this domain without fail would immediately after the Fall have sunk into nothingness, swallowed up by the curse: there would no longer have been a temporal and natural life. The grounds for the possibility of the prolongation of this domain must be sought in some such divine long-suffering, which indeed does not lead to salvation and supernatural grace but which does at least bridle, arrest, restrain and resist the powers of corruption and death, of Satan, sin and curse. Where particular grace does not rule, there in some way or other – if hell is not to break loose – God's goodness and mercy, God's grace must be operative.[48] This grace can then not work save in a "natural" way only. If this were not the case, it would be equal to God's particular grace and the whole problem would be solved by having been dissolved. It must therefore be limited to a mode of operation that maintains and develops the creature within the bounds of the original creaturely state as had obtained in Paradise; it may not carry things beyond the confines of creatureliness (*GG* III:107ff.); otherwise it would not be common grace but particular grace. In sum, common grace is to particular grace as creation is to re-creation.[49]

This conception differs fundamentally from the Thomistic theme of grace and nature. For Rome on principle uses this theme in the domain of man as he was in Paradise and already there distinguishes between "nature" and "grace" or "supernature." Not so with Kuyper. He distinguishes nothing of the sort in Paradise. There, only creatureliness was present – "nature," if you like. Not until after the Fall is there a saving, redeeming grace

---

45 *GG* II:606, 626, et passim.
46 Van Ruler, *Kuypers idee*, 12.
47 Cf. *GG* II:192, 246, 496, 613ff.; II:47, 65–67, et passim.
48 *GG* I:243; II:611.
49 *GG* II:613f.; III:110.

of God that leads to "re-creation," to the "supernatural" or "gracious" quality proper of a creation that is elevated above its original status and that as such may even be called a "new creation." Kuyper is well aware of this specific distinction. Though he does use the terms "grace" and "nature" repeatedly to distinguish respectively the domains of particular grace and common grace and sometimes even their respective operations, he ultimately and advisedly has the distinction between the two rest in the distinction between re-creation and creation, avowing a preference for this distinction over that of grace and nature (*GG* II:613f.).

Connected with this preference, of a certainty, is the circumstance that Kuyper – in spite of the fact that like the Gnostics he usually limits particular grace, at least insofar as it concerns the present dispensation, to the saving of men's souls unto eternal life – does not follow the Gnostics when they logically go on to accept an antithetical relation between the saved soul and the order of this temporal life. Precisely because he confesses common grace, Kuyper takes great distance from such antithetical dualism in the conceiving of the relation between grace and nature, even of the relation between grace and sin-effected nature. In this connection the specter of the Anabaptistic worldview always looms up before his mind: a worldview that inevitably leads to world-flight – the saved soul shuns all contact with the "world"[50] – or else leads to the error of the radical Anabaptists, who from out of the grace of regeneration seek to erect the Kingdom of God visibly even in the here and now, in order thus to translate the "world," by "Christian" force so to speak, into a world of the re-creation. This revolutionary Christianity Kuyper rejects.[51] He rejects it because it does violence to nature, which has been endowed with common grace; and because it pursues a premature triumph: what God is keeping for the hereafter – the new heaven and the new earth – let no man try to realize in this age! In both types of Anabaptism the controlling assumption is that the born-again soul and the temporal-visible world are *mutually exclusive opposites*, and this is the very thing Kuyper is fighting.

Therefore, Ridderbos, following his teacher Hepp, is quite justified in rejecting the idea that Kuyper's doctrine of common grace is dualistic.[52] For this would make it Anabaptistic or Gnostic, whereas in reality this doctrine, both in tenor and scope, is anti-Gnostic to the core. This is true even as regards the creation after the Fall – let alone therefore the creation as it came forth out of God's hand in the beginning. In consequence, it is not to be wondered at that this doctrine must offend every thinker whose own doctrine of creation is not free from Gnostic stains. For this common grace doctrine places Kuyper outside of and over against the tradition that stretches from Marcion through Occam right up to modern times – to Karl Barth in particular. The latter's "creation docetism," according to which the creature is so intrinsically alien to God that even as created reality it cannot possibly remind one of its Maker, is grounded in nothing less than a dual-antithetical relation between creation and grace, between creation and Revelation. A "grace-endowed nature," such as Kuyper could hold to, would to proponents of this type of Gnosticizing thought spell the end of the "pure gospel," i.e., of an antithetical contrast between nature and supernatural revelation and reality.[53]

---

50 *GG* II:69ff.; III:18, 19.

51 *GG* III:27, 30, 31, 32, 423, 424.

52 Ridderbos, *Cultuurbeschouwing*, 322; cf. 18, 131f., 156.

53 For this, see Berkouwer, G. C. 1936. *Karl Barth*. Kampen: Kok, passim; and Kempff, Dionysius 1949. *Die*

Meanwhile, more needs to be said about this aspect of Kuyper's thought. Hepp as well as his pupil Ridderbos make a mistake, I believe, when they stop here. They judge that since Kuyper is a sworn enemy of this type of antithetical dualism he must be, and in fact is, averse to each and every form of dualism.[54] I submit, however, that this is not the case. For it so happens that Kuyper's "nature" (also the nature endowed with common grace) and Kuyper's "grace" (particular grace and its domain of the "spiritual") do in fact function in his thought as *polar opposites*. Though he wishes to avoid a dualism of two absolute *antitheses* that mutually *exclude* each other, like light and darkness, good and evil, truth and falsehood, nonetheless his exposition rides on a dualism of two contrasting *poles* that at once *attract and repel* each other. When giving a more exact description of the relation between the two domains of common grace and particular grace, Kuyper talks in terms of an opposition: he does not scruple to state that common grace is *in contrast with* particular grace (*GG* II:685). Thus the two appear to be mutually exclusive after all. It becomes a matter of either/or: either particular grace or common grace; both at once is out of the question. Hence his two "domains," which never overlap and never merge. Now the domain of the visible and the temporal is the domain of common grace; this is where the structures of common grace obtain, that is to say, this is where the original creation structures and creation ordinances hold. They hold – though sometimes slightly modified, as in the case of the sword-wielding authority of civil government or the breaking up of the human race into nations and different nation-states;[55] yet even these modifications are only possible within the original creation structures and only serve to realize the original goal and purpose of the world in the present dispensation.[56]

It is precisely under the compulsion of this polar contrast that Kuyper in most places considers the origin of common grace to be different from that of particular grace: common grace rests in Christ the Son of God as the Mediator of Creation; particular grace is rooted in Christ as the Incarnate Word, the Mediator of Redemption.[57] This also explains why he has difficulty in seeing the exalted Christ as the King of common grace.[58] For this would on principle break down his polar contrast. And if this were to break down, Kuyper fears a revival of the Anabaptistic peril: erecting a Kingdom of Heaven on earth by means of a "Christian" revolution with all its attendant evils.[59] Without this polar contrast he fears no less an ecclesiasticizing of life: if the temporal-visible world, too, belongs to the domain of particular grace, then one is only a step removed from the ecclesiastico-political dogma of a Church state – be it Roman Catholic or Calvinist – and from the "establishment" in such a Church state of a State church.[60] For, it must be admitted, precisely the polar contrast between the domain of particular grace – the spiritual and mystical realms – and the domain of common grace – the world of the temporal, visible things and of culture and cultural formation – enables Kuyper powerfully to champion the emancipation of culture

---

Skeppingsleer van Karl Barth. (Diss. Vrije Univ.) Amsterdam and Capetown: J. H. de Bussy.

54 Thus, e.g., Ridderbos, *Cultuurbeschouwing*, 137, 322.
55 For a survey, see Ridderbos, *Cultuurbeschouwing*, 122f., 157f.
56 *GG* II:85ff.; Ill, 109, 110.
57 *GG* I:225ff.; II:637, 646; III:123f., et passim.
58 For this, see Ridderbos, *Cultuurbeschouwing*, 72ff., 87, 294.
59 Cf. Ridderbos, *Cultuurbeschouwing*, 23ff.
60 Cf. Ridderbos, *Cultuurbeschouwing*, 26ff.

and societal relationships – of family, state and society, of science, labor and art – from the tutelage of the institutional church. He has no scruples about introducing a word here that can hardly be said to appeal to many Christians, namely: "*secularisatie.*"[61] The terrain of the world, of common grace, is not the domain of the Kingdom of Heaven (*GG* II:10, 11). The domain of the Kingdom of Heaven is rather the mystic realm of the "spiritual," of the "inner soul," and, further, of the new Jerusalem that will not be revealed until after the present dispensation has passed away. The domain of common grace, by contrast, is by its very nature not "Christian," it does not bear a "Christological" stamp,[62] it does not share in the power of Christ's resurrection nor does it participate in the supernatural gift of grace. At the same time it may not be made subservient in the sense that it might be lorded over by the institution of particular grace, the church.[63] Rather it has an independent, secular, worldly goal.[64] By its inner nature it aims, and under God's providential rule it is aimed, at its own creaturely end, which as such has no real connection with the hereafter and no real connection with the mystic life of the souls that are saved.

Common grace only operates by linking up with the creation and always relates things back to the creation. The creation, to be sure, is in constant development. But this dynamic unfolding is itself creaturely, is embedded in the creation. This means that culture can only be a secular affair.[65] "Christian culture" is hardly something that speaks for itself. For example, a Christian architect is basically an architect, working *qua* architect in the sphere of common grace, with the tools of common grace; like any other architect, Christian or no Christian, he draws on nature, not Scripture, and designs according to the laws of architecture, which are common to all men. When an architect is also a Christian, that is something additional, an added consideration (cf. *GG* III:143f.). Kuyper's polar contrast between particular grace and common grace, between re-creation and creation, allows of no other viewpoint. Architecture arises out of the creation, not the re-creation.

On the extreme "left" the ultimate consequence of this polar dualism appears in Kuyper's inability to view the church institution – in his theory the fruit of particular grace – as having arisen organically from the common-grace-endowed creation, with the result that he must see her as *foreign* to creation and nature, that is, as something "*mechanisch.*"[66] From the viewpoint of creation, there is no room for an institution like the church. It does not fit in a normal way in the temporal, visible world. It is abnormal, when looked at from the perspective of common grace. It is as abnormal as the Cross of Christ. In fact, it is contrary to nature (*GG* I:166).

On the extreme "right," however, the ultimate consequence of this polar dualism appears in those passages where Kuyper regards the contrast between creation and re-creation, between common grace and particular grace, as the grounds on which common grace can even come to stand *antithetically* opposed to particular grace. In those passages it is even so much as called a threat to particular grace.[67] There this evil fruit of the sphere

---

61 *GG* II:279, et al.; cf. Ridderbos, *Cultuurbeschouwing*, 210ff.
62 For Kuyper's opposition to a "pan-Christism," see Ridderbos, *Cultuurbeschouwing*, 86f.
63 *GG* II:635; III:302.
64 *GG* I:307; II:118, 626, 632; III:302.
65 Cf. the expression "het ongekerstende burgerleven" (the unchristianized life in society), *GG* III:425.
66 *GG* I:166; III:103f.; *PrRege* II:349, 350ff.
67 Cf. *GG* I:276f., 447ff., 456; II:630; see also *PrRege* I:43ff.

of common grace is even necessary and desirable, in order to demonstrate that particular grace is absolutely essential.[68] But even in this most extreme case, which according to Kuyper may well be imminent and which will usher in the end of time[69] – please note the limits to Kuyper's cultural optimism and his faith in the unfolding of culture – even then it is not really common grace that will endanger particular grace and threaten it with extinction but it will be the *abuse* of common grace, the unbelievers' misuse of the richly developed creation potentials, that will pit the treasures of common grace and creation against the realm of particular grace and the Kingdom of Heaven.[70]

Yet this last point, in spite of itself, only underscores the polar dualism in Kuyper's conception of common grace. For *common* grace apparently can be used awry, can be used against God and His kingdom – but never so *particular* grace. In the sphere of particular grace one cannot but choose for God and His Christ, whereas in the sphere of common grace one can still choose between two directions. As a matter of fact, common grace can even become common "disgrace" (*GG* II:224).

With respect to this point one can speak of a difference in emphasis between the works *De Gemeene Gratie* and *Pro Rege*. It is no more than a difference in emphasis, to be sure, but the difference is there. Throughout the latter work Kuyper dwells extensively on precisely this dangerous and problematic character of common grace. There he gives it much more attention. Small wonder, therefore, that in *Pro Rege* he argues much more emphatically for the necessity of the organizational antithesis in the domain of common grace, for the need, in other words, of separate Christian organizations (*PrRege* III:184ff.). Thus this form of the antithesis becomes – to adopt Van Ruler's convenient distinction for a moment[71] – less and less a merely practical necessity and more and more a matter of principle.

From the above also emerges, however, that in spite of the enthusiasm with which Kuyper sings the praises of the wonderful fruits that are "yet" allowed to ripen and that may "yet" be gathered on the terrain of this temporal, visible world,[72] he always has a reservation. It is the reservation of every Christian man. It is the reservation of the man Christian, of the mystic, longing for Jesus, of the pilgrim traveling to a better country (*GG* I:489). For all his "worldly" career, the man Kuyper never became this-worldly. Nor was he ever swept off his feet by the this-worldliness of even a *Christian* culture. Common grace, after all, is "only" common grace; some day it will end (*GG* I:105). There is something higher than common grace: there is particular grace. That is the grace that counts. That is the one thing needful. And in the hereafter that Is the one and only thing that remains (*GG* I:220, 224).

Not an Anabaptistic Way of Putting the Problem

The problem that Kuyper wrestled with in his doctrine of common grace will not be appreciated in its real depth and inner tension if this postulated and rather persistent polarly dualistic nature of the fundamental relation between particular grace and common

---

68 Cf. *GG* I:457f.; II:121.

69 *GG* I:451ff.; *PrRege* III:191, 225, 341, 352.

70 *GG* I:452; II:517.

71 Van Ruler, *Kuypers idee*, 123.

72 See, for example, *GG* II:121, 607f., 610, 623, 630f., et passim.

grace, between re-creation and creation, is not at every turn taken into account. For Kuyper's intention, after all, was precisely to show how particular grace and common grace cohere and cooperate, how they influence and condition each other, and what the true nature of these relationships is.[73] His basic questions are: (1) How is it *possible* that common grace can be of significance for particular grace?[74] and (2) How is it *possible* that particular grace can be of significance for common grace?[75] hence (3) Of what significance can they be for each other in the present dispensation?

Indeed, how can a grace-endowed nature serve supernature, and how can Christian action in the natural domain arise from the spiritual, mystical center of the regenerated hearts of the elect and develop into truly Christian activity that ministers to this domain, fructifying and blessing it?

I would like to point out with some emphasis that this is anything but a Gnostic or Anabaptistic manner of dealing with the problem of the relation of the Christian and the world. For, whatever else it may mean, in Kuyper common grace means at least this, that the Christian who is active in the sphere of common grace is not necessarily dirtying his hands or his soul. It was this spirit that could make Bavinck write, "Politics is a holy affair!" And Kuyper agreed. Quite different, that, from modern-day personalism, which assumes that every man who allows himself to get involved (*s'engager*) in the affairs of this temporal world will of necessity involve himself in dirty business: only internally self-contradictory arguments of the "nevertheless" type can then be resorted to as a way out of the self-imposed predicament.[76]

From such dilemmas Kuyper has freed himself. Common grace has at least this value for the spiritually redeemed man, that he is not necessarily sinning when he gets involved in the world of creation and common grace. The structure of creation even after the Fall is not anti-divine; it does not stand antithetically opposed to piety and to love of God from a pure heart. This is really the first point that is gained by Kuyper's doctrine of common grace. Gnostic culturophobia has been exorcised. This clears the air for Kuyper to call for cultural interest, concern, activity. He can do this responsibly, Christianly. Common grace in this sense makes Christian action "in all areas of life" *possible*, legitimate, and justified. No Christian has a legitimate reason for withdrawing from the world of God's creating.[77] That holds for the whole of creation, to its farthest reaches; that holds for "all areas"; that holds in principle for the whole world of culture, politics included.

The second gain that Kuyper's approach makes on the Anabaptist or Gnostic attitude is the thesis that Christian action in the domain of common grace must acknowledge the structures of this domain, must minister to the structures of creation and the structures of common grace (which for all intents and purposes coincide) – instead of overturning them! Christian action is never revolutionary action. Just as common grace maintains and develops the creation, so all Christian action will be obliged to attach and submit to this order of

---

73 Cf. *GG* I:250; II:631f., 639f.

74 Cf. *GG* I:321; II:680ff., 684.

75 *GG* I:293; II:147, 275–283, 634, 673–8.

76 Cf. Mounier, E. 1947. *Qu'est-ce-que le Personnalisme?* Paris: Editions du Seuil, esp. chap. II, "Les Personnalisme de l'Engagement."

77 For examples of Kuyper's railing against "Doperse mijdinghe" (Anabaptistic separation), see *GG* I:468; II:69–76; II:424; et al.

common grace. Its results can only be a "higher development" of "nature" and the "natural," i.e., of the creature.[78] For this reason it will never bring "the Kingdom of Heaven" on earth (*GG* I:432), and for the same reason it aims at something quite different from a kind of Christian culture that as such would anticipate the hereafter in the form of a "supra-natural nature" and a "supra-creaturely" culture. Looked at from the perspective of the creation and the common grace that sustains it, Christian action in the domain of the preserved creation is not something abnormal, odd, exceptional, absurd, antinomian, comical, queer and out-of-this-world, something typical of a "Christian ghetto" (thus Van Ruler), but normal, ordinary, reasonable, logical, in accordance with the law of creatureliness, inconspicuous, something typical of man as man. It is not at all a "Christian specialty." At most it makes of Christians the "best" of citizens in the public life of the nation, the "best" members of the State and the "best" subjects of the Magistrate (*GG* II:341). But it certainly does not make of them a separate breed of citizens; nor revolutionary citizens or anti-bourgeois citizens; nor yet conservative citizens; but simply – citizens!

Such is the fundamental significance of common grace for the activity of the Christ-believers in the domain of the visible and temporal. This is the basic theme that Kuyper is to hammer away at, without pulling any punches, throughout his teachings concerning Christian action and the Christian life style in the temporal, visible world. A Christian marriage is an ordinary marriage, a Christian society is an ordinary society, a Christian family is an ordinary family, a Christian state is an ordinary state, a Christian association is an *ordinary* association – according to the *ordinances* that obtain for marriage, family, society, state and associations.[79] The Christian family is no miniature church; the Christian church is not also a state; the Christian state is not a Christian church; a Christian marriage is no supernatural cloister but simply a conventional marriage; and even a Christian political party is just that – an ordinary party! Christian action is the opposite of overturning the Divine structural principles that are normative for this temporal, visible life. To mention just one more example: Christian political action will have to be more than lobbying for legislation to preserve the "Christian heritage" of Sunday observance: it will have to be the expression of a political philosophy and program that touches upon every aspect of political life.

2. Common Grace as Means for Particular Grace

First among the basic questions to be dealt with in Kuyper's doctrine of common grace must therefore be: How can common grace serve particular grace?

The *fact* that it does indeed serve particular grace is something that Kuyper does not doubt for a moment. Only, he does not regard the factuality as proof of its possibility. What he searches for and wrestles with is an *explanation* of this "fact." Our first task will be, therefore, to ask ourselves which facts Kuyper noted in this connection, after which we shall examine what explanation he gave of them.

The Idea of the Prolongation

Particular grace, as will be remembered, is by its nature – at least in the present dispensation

---

78 *GG* II:276, et passim.
79 *GG* III:passim; cf. *PrRege* II:354ff.

– the grace that saves the souls of the elect for eternity and that essentially accomplishes this salvation by regenerating them, engrafting them into Christ, implanting them as members into the mystical Body of Christ, and translating them into the Kingdom of Heaven. Now in the abstract Kuyper does not consider it impossible that these souls would be created even without the generation of the human race out of Adam and Eve (*GG* II:661). But in reality he takes the position that this may not be assumed. In this temporal life human beings come to be, and the human race continues to be, via generation.[80] But for generation out of our forebears, there could be no regeneration by God's Spirit. But for the continuation of the world after the Fall, there could be no regeneration.[81] If Adam and Eve had suffered death immediately after their fall into sin, not only would there have been no possibility for a human race to be generated out of them, but there would also have been no possibility for the bestowal of the grace of regeneration and election unto everlasting life. There first have to be human beings born, generated, procreated, before such beings can receive the grace of regeneration.[82]

Now the postponement of the sentence of doom, "In the day that thou eatest thereof thou shalt surely die"! [KJV], and with this postponement the prolongation of this temporal world, constitutes the indispensable prerequisite for particular grace. The prolongation itself is not particular grace: it does not regenerate and does not lead to the blessedness of eternal life in the hereafter (*GG* II:685, 689). But grace it is: it is the postponement of curse and punishment. To be sure, Kuyper is of the opinion that God really owed it to Himself to allow Adam and Eve to continue to exist after the Fall; otherwise Satan would have succeeded in his aim to drag God's creation into nothingness and thus defeat God's Self-glorification in His work of creation (*GG* II:611f.) – that is why common grace can be called "natural" (*GG* III:107ff.); still, this does not alter the fact that common grace is an act of God's mercy, of His longsuffering, of His unmerited kindness and forfeited favor.

Again, to be sure, this prolongation is also terrifying (*GG* I:215f.). For just think: were it not for this prolongation, the birth of all those offspring of Adam and Eve who are not elect, and who will therefore be given over to the eternal judgment of punishment in hell, would not have taken place either! Breathtaking is the prolongation of the human race, and thus also the common grace that results in this prolongation: it makes possible not only heaven for the elect but also hell for the damned. Common grace is therefore at the same time "common dis-grace" (*GG* II:224), and common judgment. Nevertheless – and this is where Kuyper differs fundamentally from Schilder[83] – common grace should be called after its first quality. For with Kuyper, election and reprobation are not, as to their worth and end, on the same level. He does not believe in a *gemina praedestinatio*, a double predestination that attaches equal weight and value to election or (and) reprobation. On this point Kuyper, like Calvin, differs not only from Gottschalk[84] but also from Schilder.[85]

---

80 *GG* I:218,220; II:662.

81 *GG* I:222, 254, 263.

82 See note 16.

83 Schilder, "*Algemeene Genade*," passim.

84 Cf. Denzinger, H. 1854. *Enchiridion Symbolarum*, 316–318; Bakhuizen van den Brink J. N. and Lindeboom, J. 1942. *Handboek der Kerkgeschiedenis*, I. Daaman, 209.

85 Schilder, "*Algemeene Genade*," 43f., 57, 59, 62, 64, 73f.; as a result, Matthew 5:45 is hardly done justice on p. 69.

Christ did not come into the world to condemn the world (John 3:17), yet it is precisely His coming that increases the condemnation of the unbelievers since they give no heed to so great a salvation (John 3:18, 19; John 16:22); still, one may not draw the conclusion that Christ came *in order that* redemption and damnation could be equally realized. In the same way, then, one may not draw the conclusion that the covenant of grace of which Christ is the Head and the Mediator, and the particular grace of God, which comes to us in the Word Incarnate and in all the facts of the history of salvation, are equally a "covenant of *curse*," particular *dis*grace, and facts in a history of *damnation*. Here logical thought breaks to pieces on pious adoration. Here Scripture calls a holy halt. And so in the same way Kuyper makes sure not to put common grace on a level with common dis-grace and to call the continuation of the human race equally and simultaneously a blessing and a curse, a benefit and a disaster. The lament of the rich man, "I am tormented in this flame," is far outweighed by the song of the redeemed before God's throne. In my opinion Kuyper rightly calls common grace, as the prolongation of the human race after Adam's fall into sin, common grace, and not at the same time common dis-grace.

The first significance of common grace for particular grace has now emerged: by protecting and sustaining the generation of mankind from Adam's loins, it makes the regeneration of men possible. As such it is no less than the pre-condition for particular grace (*GG* I:222, 254).

What is happening here? In the first place Kuyper is here warding off the temptation to insert a Gnostic notion into the doctrine of particular grace: namely, the assumption that it is not impossible that the "souls" of the elect can come into being quite apart from the procreation of the human race through birth out of the "created" forefathers. Thus he denies the very thing that Van Ruler has termed particularistic and spiritualistic about his doctrine – thereby criticizing, even before his death as it were, Van Ruler's analysis of his doctrine. The thesis that birth is indispensable for rebirth sounds the death knell for all Gnostic dualism, just as it hardly favors the view of psycho-creationism.

In the second place, however, it must be observed that Kuyper himself effects in this connection a mere improvement of the Gnostic notion. This appears precisely when he appeals to "common grace" to account for the prolongation of the human race. His own remark that the prolonged existence of Adam and Eve was certain even after the Fall by reason of the fact that their sin could never destroy God's Counsel according to which He willed to create a human race via procreation out of our first parents, should have brought him to the realization that his exegesis of Genesis 2 ("in the day that thou eatest thereof thou shalt surely die") really agrees with Gnosticism but not with the book of creation, with Genesis itself. In my opinion, Schilder,[86] along with S. J. Popma[87] and also L. A. Diepenhorst,[88] are in the right when, in contrast to Kuyper, they refuse to talk of common grace at this point. To use Kuyper's own words: God owed it to Himself to continue the human race and thus prolong this temporal life. That Kuyper appeals to common grace in this connection can only be explained from a Gnostic remnant in his thinking. To this extent the point can be conceded to Van Ruler that Kuyper's doctrine is not free from "spiritualism."

---

86 Schilder, "*Algemeene Genade*," passim.

87 Popma, S. J. *Hedendaagsche Vragen aangaande de Algemeene Genade*. NDDD, 19.

88 Diepenhorst, L. A. 1947. *Algemeene Genade en Antithese*. Kampen: Kok, 26.

Common Grace as Foothold for the Institutional Church

But there is yet another, quite different way in which Kuyper speaks of common grace as the basis, the groundwork, the possibility of particular grace.[89] This occurs especially in his doctrines of the church as an institution, of the Incarnation of the Word, and of the "special" Revelation that resulted in Holy Scripture.[90]

(I can hardly resist comparing Kuyper with Karl Barth on this point. Already from a strictly theological point of view it is highly interesting to discover that it is once again Gnosticism that separates Kuyper from Barth. In contrast to Barth's Gnosticizing thought, Kuyper's is anti-Gnostic. Consequently, Kuyper's theology is anti-nihilistic, hence far removed from modern existentialist thought, whereas Barth's theology works with Gnostic themes in the doctrine of creation and therefore borders on nihilism and is of a kind with twentieth-century existentialism.[91] It is unfortunate that to date no comparative study has appeared of the theologies of Kierkegaard and Barth on the one hand and Kuyper on the other as regards the doctrine of the means of grace, including the doctrine concerning the person and work of Christ and the doctrine of the Holy Spirit. Such a study might prove worthwhile! In the present context, however, we have to limit ourselves to the views of Kuyper.)

So far I have done no more than point out that according to Kuyper the "domain" of particular grace must be located in the "spiritual," in the "center" of man's being, and in the life hereafter. That is where the heart, the nucleus of particular grace is to be found. If now particular grace is also to "radiate out" from this nucleus,[92] this radiation will still have to proceed from out of this same nucleus and will still have to be regarded as no less than an anticipation of the "powers of the age to come" (*GG* II:243).

Now one such anticipation Kuyper sees in the Incarnation of the Word. And who could possibly disagree with him there? Certainly after His exaltation Christ is no longer a "natural man" even according to His human nature but has become a "spiritual man," having been raised by the "Spirit of holiness" (Romans 1:4); according to His human nature, He is a "new creature," re-created, sharing in eternal life and incorruption, elevated from the creaturely, natural state to the supernatural, glorified state. But Kuyper knows further anticipations of the age to come. Not only the exalted Christ but also the means of grace, the administration of which Christ has entrusted to His church and which do not fall outside the plane of the temporal and the visible, are by their very essence more than and other than mere creaturely phenomena: Holy Scripture is more than a creaturely word; baptism and the Lord's supper are more than "visible signs"; and preaching, the administration of God's Word, is more than a creaturely, natural event.[93] In Kuyper's system, the church institution, i.e., the church of the means of grace, must be a new creation of God's particular grace (*GG* II:253ff.). That is to say, the church institution does not grow out of creation, nor does she stem from common grace. When Kuyper wants to

---

89 Cf. *GG* I:90; III:124: een plek voor het hol van haar voet (a foot-hold); I:278: mogelijkheid (possibility); II:98: voetstuk (groundwork).

90 *GG* II:120, 125–191, 683f.

91 See my "Theologie en wijsbegeerte in de *Kirchliche Dogmatik* van Karl Barth." *Philosophia Reformata* 18 (1953): 77–138.

92 *GG* I:220; II:268ff., et al.

93 *GG* II:253ff., 665, 680; III:104.

emphasize this, he even goes so far as to talk of her in terms of a *Fremdkörper* in creation, calling her a "mechanical" insertion (*GG* II:253; III:103).

This church institution, however, does not form part of the "spiritual" and inner life of the regenerate (*GG* II:254). She is, rather, particular grace's visible instrument (*PrRege* II:210) and also its temporal manifestation and demonstration (*GG* II:254) in the visible, temporal domain of common grace.[94] In this temporal, visible world she is an "appearance," a "form," a "*gestalte*" (*GG* II:254; remarkable: the same word that is used by Barth and the existentialists, but with an entirely different content!) of the Kingdom of Heaven, of the "invisible" church and "invisible" particular grace.

Here now is where Kuyper's views on the significance of common grace for particular grace make their start. In this domain of common grace, to which also Holy Scripture and the church institution in her visible-temporal "form" belong, particular grace seeks a "foothold" (*GG* III:124). This means that if something goes wrong with this domain, the means of grace will share in the chaos: something will go wrong with them too. Preaching and missions, both of them Christian activities in the sense of being activities that arise out of particular grace and that are instruments of particular grace because they serve as means of (particular) grace, need "the broad base" (*GG* II:98, 116f.) of common grace in order to realize themselves as to their "temporal-visible" side. The Christian church so conceived cannot do without the assistance of common grace. For example, she requires political conditions that do not make life impossible for her; further, she calls for a political order and a society in which all things are done in good order, to the end "that we may lead a tranquil and quiet life" precisely while being busy in the work of missions (1 Timothy 2:2 may not be torn loose from 1 Timothy 2:3–6), precisely as Christian propagandists of saving grace.

All of a sudden here, common grace loses its independent purpose. It becomes a *means* to an end that lies above and beyond its competence as well as above and beyond its strength. Common grace is to lay the groundwork for the pulpit.[95]

This is where "Christian" politics comes in. Yes, already here we can talk of Christian politics, but then in the sense of a politics that is not as such Christian in itself but that may be called Christian insofar as and inasmuch as it enables the institutional church to carry out its mission. This is reason enough for Christians to enter the political arena. Very often, as a matter of fact, it is the reason why they enter there independently, with their own party formation. The Christian body is then active in the domain of common grace for ulterior reasons – for reasons of particular grace, for reasons of church rather than reasons of state. And this Body will have to close ranks and form a separate Christian political party, a separate party for Christian politics, if it becomes apparent that powers are gaining the upper hand in this domain that are bent on taking away from the Christian church this possibility, this "base of operations" (cf. *GG* I:449); if anti-Christian powers are in fact exploiting common grace to turn it – from the perspective of particular grace – into dis-grace, and into an antithetical force against the Kingdom of Heaven.[96]

In this indirect way common grace must serve particular grace. And, of course, what

---

94 *GG* II:254, to be read in connection with II:277: "particular grace always works unto eternal life, but what works here is wholly absorbed in time, hence falls under common grace." See also *GG* III:34–40.

95 Cf. Ridderbos, *Cultuurbeschouwing*, 129.

96 Cf. *GG* I:452; II:517; III:149, 153; *PrRege* III:191, 225, 341, 352.

has been said here in respect of the state can be said to hold *mutatis mutandis* for family life, for marriage, for society, in fact for all the areas of common grace. In this indirect sense one can speak of a Christian family and a Christian marriage, of a Christian society, a Christian economy, a Christian state, of a Christian university and Christian scholarship, of Christian literature and Christian art. These do not at all need to stem from regeneration and regenerated hearts. And still they may be called "Christian" insofar as, and inasmuch as, they lend a hand to particular grace, to the church institution, and to the way of salvation along which God leads His elect-for-eternity through this world of time.

This then is the *dependent purpose* of common grace (cf. *GG* II:626), whereby it finds its *raison d'être* outside of itself in particular grace and furnishes this grace with a "foothold" in the face of the forces of chaos, nihilism, and Antichrist. Such is common grace as a means to something else, to an end that lies beyond itself.

State and Church

This broadening of the domain of particular grace, whereby it now also includes the visible and temporal church institution, has as result that for Kuyper the problem of the relation between nature and grace, creation and re-creation, common and particular grace returns once more, this time as the problem of Church and State. The church in his view is more Christian than the state, the clergyman more spiritual than the alderman, the theologian holier than the philosopher. Finding one's life's task wholly within the domain of common grace means occupying a "lower" station in life than if one is busy in this very same domain creating the indispensable conditions for the functioning of the institutional church.

This form of discrimination, however, Kuyper can again relativize. For the Christian character of the church institution is itself a relative thing. She is not *solely* an anticipation of the hereafter in this life.[97] Rather, for all her other-worldly orientation she remains temporal and visible and as such indistinguishable from that which belongs to the domain of common grace. Kuyper will certainly advance this argument against Rome, and for that matter against every view that identifies the *means* of grace with particular grace itself. Against all such views Kuyper will vigorously defend the view that regeneration on principle is not dependent on the administration of the means of grace but rather is an *immediate* work of the Spirit (*GG* II:207ff.). He will oppose any binding of the work of the Spirit to the means of grace. This is where he will introduce the distinction between "being" and "consciousness," holding forth that being born-again is independent of consciousness but that consciousness interacts with the use of the means of grace and requires the Bible and the church.[98] But then the pressing question becomes: Does this consciousness also still fall under particular grace, or is it perhaps, as visible (discernible) activity, already part of the domain of common grace? Indeed, is consciousness not already creaturely, "natural"? The problem remains. Each time it comes back in a different form. The church institution belongs to the domain of common grace, however much she may be a means of particular grace.

The problem becomes even more involved when in his anthropology Kuyper does not follow Rome in her definition of "nature" and "super-nature," whereby man's faith-life as such is a supernatural addition, a *donum superadditum* tacked on to the lower, natural

---

97 She arises from a miracle: *GG* III:110.

98 Cf. *GG* II:212f; *Encyclopaedie* II:195, 196.

life. On the contrary, Kuyper attributes to Adam in the state of rectitude a "creaturely" function of believing.[99] This function, though distorted by the Fall inasmuch as Adam directed his faith away from God to the creature, nevertheless does not need to be created all over again when at "re-creation" it is once more re-directed to the true God and His Revelation. The *direction* and the *content* of this activity of believing may then be different again, but that does not alter the fact that the act of *believing* as such is nothing new. At re-creation, the believing activity of the heart is brought back to order again through the re-creative power of grace, and it will henceforward have to feed again on the means of grace; but in this conversion particular grace in fact restores to a true faith that same function that had turned into unbelief.[100] Kuyper will therefore refuse to attribute faith, as Rome does, entirely to supernatural grace. But no less will he refuse to attribute this reversion-of-unbelief-to-faith to the natural powers of man or else to common grace, as do Arminians and Pelagians and semi-Pelagians. When all is said and done, however, it remains an open question whether Kuyper regards belief-in-Christ as being purely of the re-creation, a purely "mechanical" intervention in the original creatureliness, at bottom something odd, something out-of-this-world that does not go with man. Sooner than say that, he will instead probably fall back on regarding belief-in-Christ as the fulfillment of a general "predisposition" that even apostate man never lost entirely – in that measure obliging himself to resort again, however, to the nature-grace scheme of Roman Catholicism. Undoubtedly there are problems here that Kuyper did not succeed in clarifying. Thus the problems of the coherence and the co-operation of particular grace and common grace, so decisive for Kuyper especially in the problem of Church and State, wholly depend upon the conception he had of the church institution. And this conception, in which he refused to capitulate to Rome's scheme of nature and supernature, is for all that a conception in which he still did not manage to extricate himself entirely from this scheme, unable as he was to separate "the spiritual life" from the actuality of the means of grace in such a radical way as to be able to dispense as it were with these means as far as the living operation of the spiritual life is concerned. Hence we see Kuyper moving from position to position. Sometimes common grace is indispensable for particular grace (i.e., for the institutional church); at other times this independence is relativized again. This relativization is possible because for Kuyper the church institution is not in the strict sense indispensable for the "spiritual" gift of particular grace, allowing him in the final analysis to retreat back into the church as the mystic Body of Christ (*GG* I:337), to which the institutional church *qua* institution does not belong.

Earlier we already came upon Kuyper's first use of the connection between common grace and particular grace, and with that of the concept and idea of a Christian culture. We saw there that its Christian character consisted only in the *indirect* service that the powers and means of common grace can render the institutional church. This service can arise unintentionally from the life in the domain of common grace. As such it can therefore be rendered to the church also by non-believers. Meanwhile, however, this service can also be rendered deliberately from the regenerated heart, out of love for Christ and His cause. It can be inspired by love for His gospel and His church. Such love will inspire Christians in

---

99 *GG* I:162; cf. *Encyclopaedie* II:228ff.
100 *Encyclopaedie* II:228ff.

this common, general domain – which as such is not geared to particular grace nor does it stem from it – to all kinds of activity that does not so much aim at developing this domain toward its own end, but that seizes and exploits the opportunities this domain affords, to be the means to an entirely different sort of end. The impelling motive behind such indirectly Christian activity is then already the notion of working *pro Rege*.

Thus the term "Christian" culture ("Christian" politics, etc.), can in general refer to *Pro Rege* activity – but not necessarily. This ambiguity in the use of the term reveals with irrevocable and inescapable logic the dialectic, the polarly dualistic contrast, between nature and grace. Meanwhile the common grace domain is drawn as close as possible to particular grace – without losing its own character and therefore its polar contrast with the domain of particular grace – when it is regarded and labeled as the domain of "preparatory grace," preparing as it does for the possibility of the means of grace, and with that for the possibility of the working of the Spirit by means of the church institution.[101] Still, the sovereignty of God, which He shows in His particular grace, remains totally independent of this preparatory grace. As such it is anything but inconceivable that preparatory grace did in certain instances prepare for, yet failed to prepare, grace; or rather, that it failed as such to become efficacious because no grace had been prepared by God that leads to regeneration and eternal life. Thus common grace as "preparatory grace" determines nothing in advance with respect to particular grace.[102] The same could be said, for that matter, of the very means of grace themselves.[103]

We should be extremely cautious here in our criticism. Kuyper is wrestling with a problem that every son of the Reformation has in the end to wrestle with. Christ did not come that the world might be condemned. But neither did He come *so that* the world is now automatically saved. He did not institute His church and the offices of the church in order that the world might be condemned. But neither did he institute them so that through them the world is automatically saved, *per opus operatum*, simply by virtue of the work they perform. These considerations led Calvin to speak of the very covenant of grace as a "*medium quiddam*," something intermediate, something in between the reprobation of the human race and the election of the small number of the elect;[104] for which reason Calvin too, exactly like Kuyper later, is ultimately forced to withdraw back into the church as the mystic Body of Christ, into which the members are engrafted through the work of the Spirit. But it also kept Calvin from reducing the institutional church to an "ordinary" institution of common grace and from not reckoning the means of grace, however "creaturely" and "natural" these means "in themselves" may be (Luther is reputed to have said once that the water of baptism is the same water cows drink), among the gifts of God's

---

101 *GG* II:199ff., 207ff.

102 *GG* II:194. One should just compare this passage, as well as Encyclopaedie II:232 and *GG* II:199–207, with Schilder, "*Algemeene Genade*," passim.

103 Cf. *GG* II:238, 660, et al.

104 *Institutio*, III, xxi, 7: ". . . *cum quibus paciscitur Deus, non protinus eos donat Spiritu regenerationis, cuius virtute usque in finem in foedere perseverent: sed externa mutatio absque interiore gratiae efficacia, quae ad eos retinendos valida esset, medium quiddam est inter abjectionem humani generis et electionem exiguipiorum numeri.*" (". . . to those with whom God makes His covenant He does not at once grant the Spirit of regeneration by virtue of Whom they would endure in the covenant unto the end; rather, the external change, without the working of internal grace which would have the power to keep them there, is something intermediate between the reprobation of the human race and the election of a small number of the godly.")

particular grace.[105] An objectivistic doctrine that simply assumes an objective salvation contained in the means of grace and entrusted to the church[106] rules out this complex of problems, but does violence to the revelation of Scripture. The objective fact of a pulpit or a communion table, precisely as "objective fact," is yet without salvation, without grace, and therefore, as far as the problem of Christian culture is concerned, of no earthly use. A pulpit, a baptismal font, a communion table, a Bible represent, when taken by themselves, mentally torn from the God of the Word and of grace, neither God's salvation nor God's grace. Kuyper's problem is indeed a Reformation-inspired problem.

3. The Significance of Particular Grace for Common Grace

Meanwhile, what is beyond dispute is that the doctrine of common grace as the pre-condition for particular grace was considered by Kuyper to be the less important aspect of his doctrine of common grace as a whole. For Kuyper's deepest sympathy and abiding interest lay with "secularization" – this term to be understood in the special sense in which Kuyper used it in this connection! – with the secularization of culture, with the emancipation of life from the servitude of the institutional church, with what he regarded as the "independent" function of common grace. A return to or even a longing for a medieval structure of society like the *Corpus Christianum* was the farthest thing from his mind. Here too he was an antirevolutionary, not a counterrevolutionary. Furthermore, the lines of his thought all focus on the sovereignty of God. Kuyper's mind was of an entirely different cast from the mind that is accustomed to placing the church institution first, let alone from the type of mind that is oriented to the supremacy of the church offices.

With that we have come to the second basic question that engrossed this man's mighty intellect. How does particular grace affect the domain of common grace? Of what significance is particular grace for this domain? Note that this time there is the tacit assumption that the common grace domain is not to be viewed as the pre-condition for particular grace, as a means to a loftier end, but rather as independent, with a purpose of its own.[107] To be sure, the object of both particular grace and common grace is the glory of God, His Self-glorification.[108] But each achieves this in its own proper way and along its own proper path. Particular grace glorifies God in the salvation of sinners, an eternal source of praise unto Him that sitteth upon the throne and unto the Lamb that was slain (*GG* II:610). But common grace is to proclaim the glory of God in its own way. This it does in its temporal, visible domain precisely by bringing the creation to its destination, to its full unfolding and flowering, and by preserving it against the rule of the Devil. It does this by dressing the creation and keeping it, and by fostering and stimulating culture.[109]

To what extent now can particular grace serve this purpose, this end peculiar to the visible, temporal, creaturely realm? Once again we shall first note what Kuyper considered "factual" here, and then in what manner he "explained" these facts.

---

105 *Institutio*, IV.

106 As found with Van Ruler, *Kuypers idee*, 124.

107 *GG* II:275, 278; cf. Ridderbos, *Cultuurbeschouwing*, 156.

108 *GG* II:610–612; III:383

109 *GG* I:90, 247; II:507, 509; III:124.

Indirect Significance

In the first place, then, Kuyper distinguished an "indirect" influence of particular grace on the domain of common grace.[110] He tried to demonstrate, especially from history, how wherever Christianity took root, the visible-temporal life also began to flourish. There the preserving and especially the stimulating forces of common grace were promoted, incited, strengthened, enhanced, heightened; there culture was set in motion toward the fulfillment of the original plan of creation.[111]

To begin with, Holy Scripture, Christ's walk on earth, and the institutional church with her administration of the means of grace unmistakably have this leavening effect, which powerfully strengthens, enhances, ennobles and heightens common grace.[112] All these things permeate the broad domain of common grace, for example in the area of civic virtue, even when their true effect, the saving unto everlasting life, does not take place (*GG* II:242). This holds especially for the development of history in the direction of a universal history of mankind. Precisely owing to the influence of the Christian church, history is becoming increasingly a universal history.[113] Wherever particular grace begins to take effect, there the domain of common grace witnesses the powerful development of the potentials that from the beginning have lain hidden in the creation, including the creation that is man. There common grace works itself out in a more refined and a more efficient manner. There dynamic development, growth, progress will ensue[114] – which would not be forthcoming in the absence of particular grace (*GG* II:664). From this promotion of culture in all areas of life not only the Christ-believer but also the unbeliever residing within the sphere of influence of particular grace reaps the richest benefits. The fact that European-American civilization has arisen as a universally human culture (*GG* II:670f.), and the fact that the nations who did not live under the influence of particular grace have to acknowledge the preponderance of these European-American peoples while they as colonial nations in turn indirectly share again in the benefits of particular grace for the domain of common grace, are among the facts that constitute solid evidence, according to Kuyper, of the salutary effect of particular grace.[115]

Accordingly, everything that is under this influence, even if it does not itself live out of the roots of particular grace, can be called, albeit in an improper sense of the word, *Christian* (*GG* II:671–73, et al.). There is a Christian European-American civilization that really fills the whole world with its blessings. At the heart of this civilization is found the Christian (*GG* II:341), who, precisely because he lives by particular grace, makes for the best citizen (*GG* II:341). In this way particular grace is a blessing for the realm of common grace. In the center of the common grace realm thus blessed, in the midst of this "world," is found the church, like a city set on a hill (*GG* II:275ff.). The indirect fruits, the by-products of particular grace, are the elevation of art and science, the ennoblement of political, social and economic life, the enrichment, in fact, of the whole of public civic life in all its facets. Particular grace as it were "baptizes" common grace, immersing it in its

---

110 Cf. Ridderbos, *Cultuurbeschouwing*, 136, 192ff.
111 *GG* II:246, 260ff., 275ff.; III:144.
112 *GG* I:279; II:242, 273.
113 *GG* I:504; II:184, 246, 671.
114 *GG* II:248, 610; III:437, et passim.
115 *GG* II:177ff., 668ff.; cf. *PrRege* III:311, 316.

blessings. It "christianizes" common grace (*GG* II:672, 674). And it does this in a way that nothing else can.[116] To be "Christian" is not to be opposed to progress, for

> also in Christian circles men will begin to realize that to be co-laborers in the advancement of the national culture is a calling that comes to us from God for the sole reason that only if this advancement is rooted in the Christian religion can it lead to true culture. (*GG* III:405)

Kuyper returns to this theme time and time again. To be sure, nothing but the creaturely, "natural," original life of creation, the domain of common grace, is stimulated by this permeation with particular grace. Nor does this permeation bring about any internal changes in this domain's own peculiar natural character. Yet on the other hand the impact of particular grace on the domain of common grace is of inestimable value because it and it alone can bring about this heightened, enhanced, enriched development of the domain. Common grace, when left to itself, cannot accomplish this. Witness the life of the nations in whose midst the church-like-a-city-set-on-a-hill is wanting. There we find backwardness. There common grace languishes feeble and destitute. There it leads to meager results. Only Christian faith truly sets free the forces of common grace. Take, for example, the world of science. Set free by the Spirit of Christ from the bonds of sin and the devil, one is also set free from the enslavement to nature.[117] Only this setting free enables one to be internally free to adopt a stance over against nature – the pre-condition for any development of the science of nature and the conquest of nature. This makes it understandable why the natural sciences flourish only in those countries where common grace was christianized, baptized.

Even though it is not the actual purpose of particular grace to be serviceable to common grace in *its* domain and for *its* benefit, it cannot be denied that wherever particular grace has entered the hearts of men and wherever the light of God's Word shines forth, there culture thrives. This fruit is not to be spurned. It is of immense benefit to all mankind – to mankind in general, not just to the new humanity. It benefits culture, which is shared in by all. It raises state and society, science and art, marriage and family life to a higher level. Even though it does not lead to a real and true Christian state, society, science, etc., it cannot be denied that that quality of political life, married life, etc., could not exist if an indirect influence of particular grace were not operative.[118] For that reason Kuyper does not scruple to attach to the common grace life that is thus "impregnated with the Gospel" (*GG* III:672) the epithet "Christian": our Christian Europe, a Christian marriage, a Christian state, etc. Common grace then draws strength, as it were, from particular grace, to attain its own proper end in its own visible-temporal domain.

If we concentrate on this particular concept of a "Christian state," it becomes apparent that this concept has something else in view than the concept of a Christian state that we came across earlier. For here the state is not called Christian because it serves the institutional church, serving as a means to an end that transcends that state and is foreign to the state. No, the state here is called Christian because its level of development is due to the leavening effect of the powers of particular grace – even though the state as such has nothing to do with this particular grace and remains what it always was: an institution in

---

116 *GG* II:437: "precisely only the Christians . . ." II:246, 278.

117 *GG* II:275; *PrRege* III:457ff.

118 See the many references in Ridderbos, *Cultuurbeschouwing*, 200ff.

the domain of common grace, a creational institution by origin and nature, the norms for whose conduct are found in the creation ordinances and nowhere else.[119]

Or perhaps also in the Bible? Here Kuyper hesitates. But he thinks he has solved the difficulty by explaining that the Bible also reveals many things that are not really related to particular grace but belong to the domain of the "natural life."[120] A political program that takes these biblical data into account pays heed to the creation ordinances, or to the guidelines of common grace – but certainly not to the commandments and gifts of particular grace. Such a political program is free also to take the Bible as guide, to the extent that the Bible throws "natural" light on political problems and makes us wise unto common grace. This use of the Bible is not by its nature Christian. It is "universally human"; that is, it can be engaged in by all men. It arises from common grace and leads back to common grace.

But is this state of affairs not by the same token a clear proof of the significance of particular grace for common grace? Scripture carries real weight, after all, only with those who belong to the Christ of particular grace. Only where Scripture owing to the Spirit's particular grace gets a grip on people's consciences, does it acquire authority. And only in such surroundings is it to be expected that what it teaches concerning the "natural" life will carry weight also with people who do not acknowledge its supernatural significance for things eternal and spiritual. This common authority of Scripture then is an indirect fruit of the particular authority that Scripture has in the church and in the hearts of the regenerate. All to the good of the people, the nation, the state!

Kuyper's Apologetics

Here, if anywhere, Kuyper acts as the apologist of the Christian religion. World history proves the usefulness, the value of the Christian religion. Where this religion does not flourish, there also culture flags.[121] But where this religion comes to manifestation, there the marvelous phenomenon appears that so many sectors of life begin to blossom forth that in themselves have no intrinsic relation with this religion of regeneration. There the common life of mankind is ennobled and unfolded, there human life becomes dynamic and acquires splendor. There enterprising activity leads to progress in moral and civic life and in control over nature. There science and art flourish. There culture is raised to levels never before attained.

Surely these indirect benefits of Christianity for this temporal life are worthy of some note! Surely they must speak to men's imagination! Surely they vindicate this religion's validity even in the eyes of those who may be skeptical about an afterlife and therefore doubt its "eternal" value – vindicate it on the strength of its irreplaceable and inestimable value for this temporal life! Also for the unbeliever, to live in "Christian" countries like these is much to be preferred to living in a non-Christian world. As far as that goes, also for the unbeliever America has a thing or two up on Tibet.

The Immediate Significance of Particular Grace for the Domain of Common Grace

Apart from this indirect effect of particular grace on the domain of common grace, Kuyper

---

119 *GG* III:41, 52, 62, 289.
120 *GG* II:133–135; III:154, 394.
121 *GG* III:105; cf. I:457.

credits particular grace with yet another, quite different influence: a direct, immediate, and deliberate one. Here at last we can speak of "Christian" activity in the real and proper sense of the word. And here especially emerges Kuyper's doctrine of the *church as an organism*.

It is in this context that Kuyper ascribes to particular grace an inner dynamism: particular grace cannot be contained; it must out; it must *radiate out* into the very realm of the visible and temporal.[122] The structure of the latter terrain remains what it was, creaturely, preserved and in some parts modified by common grace. But the terrain itself now becomes the arena for particular grace. Granted that this particular grace, by origin and at heart, is directed toward the center, the core of man's being and does not arrive at its true and original destination until the hereafter, this does not mean that in this age it would not also direct itself to the whole of human life and move out from its "spiritual" center toward the periphery (*GG* II:684). Whereas Kuyper initially expounded the view that only after the Noachic Covenant (of common grace) had come to an end would the Kingdom of Heaven set in (*GG* I:432), he now drops this spiritualistic and eschatological position in the sense that he makes room for the idea that the Kingdom of Heaven is to be revealed already in the present age, in the realm of common grace – in the form of visible, concrete, tangible manifestations (*GG* II:672). And this now will be the task of the church *organism*.

Without entering more fully now into Kuyper's notion of the church as an organism, suffice it to establish at this point that Kuyper used this notion, among other purposes, for typifying the free and voluntary activity, incited by the impulse of regenerative grace, hence arising from the mystic communion of the Body of Christ, of Christ-believers in the domain of the visible-temporal world of common grace.[123] The term is applied especially in reference to activity not undertaken under the direct leadership of the institutional church and the ecclesiastical offices and not directly related to the church institution as such. This activity, in the second place, can be both organized or not organized: this makes no essential difference for defining what is to be understood by the church organism. What is essential, however, is that Kuyper is not here propounding an individualistic concept of the church as an organism, for he regards all this "out-going" activity as taking its origin in the church as the Body of Christ, in the "mystic" church of Our Lord (*GG* II:253f.). On the one hand, there is no regenerate man who is not engrafted into this Body, who is not a liberated member of this mystic Body. On the other hand, there is in society no visible-temporal structure, be it a free association or a more institutionary body, that has any direct authority over that which has its origin and source in this mystic Body of Christ. For Kuyper, "the freedom of the Christian man" is at stake here. A Christian is "free" from all societal bonds in this visible-temporal world; he is called to the freedom of a discerning faith that can keep at a distance even the institutional church! But never the Word of Holy Scripture, nor the Incarnate Word of God! This is Kuyper's position, and it is in harmony with the creeds of the Reformed churches, to be more exact: with Article VII of the Belgic Confession.[124]

---

122 *GG* II:350, 644, 684.

123 *GG* II:253f., 689; III:425, et al.

124 Belgic Confession, Article VII: "We believe that those Holy Scriptures fully contain the will of God, and that whatsoever man ought to believe unto salvation is sufficiently taught therein. For since the whole manner of worship which God requires of us is written in them at large, it is unlawful for any one, though an apostle,

In its own distinctive way the meaning of Kuyper's battle for "secularization" once more comes into view here. He resists every form of domination by the institutional church over the domain of common grace. He resists no less the idea of "church-sponsored" Christian action in this domain.[125] The Christian stands and must stand fast in the liberty of the children of God and shall live and work as a child of God also in the domain of common grace, also in the church organism.

Now this activity of the Christians, or of the church organism, is regarded by Kuyper, furthermore, as the natural *out-come*, the *coming to light* of what God's Spirit has wrought in the "spiritual" core of the regenerate.[126] Christian action, in other words, is a revelation of the miracle of particular grace in the hearts of the elect and thus a revelation, a concrete manifestation, of the Kingdom of Heaven. And, seeing that Kuyper always immediately relates this "spiritual" realm of particular grace to its eternal destination and to its full implementation in the "age to come," it will no longer seem strange that he also sees Christian action as faith's anticipating of the kingdom that is to come and as faith's working from out of "the powers of the age to come" (*GG* II:689).

Not until Kuyper has worked out this view is he in a position to define the function of *Pro Rege* in the domain of common grace. Not until now is he able to speak of real "Christian action" and of "Christian culture" in the proper sense of the word.[127] Not until now is he able to describe in the "broad" area of the temporal-visible life the working out of that radical antithesis between the kingdom of Christ and the kingdom of this world, an antithesis that originates in the fundamental antithesis between the Mystic Body of Christ and the race of Adam, which in its spiritual root has fallen away from God.[128]

Looked at in a positive way, this Christian activity, which directs itself from out of the spiritual center of particular grace into this temporal life, working itself out there, extending its influence, making the most of the treasures of common grace (and thus of creation and its many possibilities) as raw material for a truly "Christian" culture, means a new and unique way of pressing the domain of common grace into the service of the realm of particular grace.[129] All this activity, with all its many possibilities of expression, Kuyper concentrates in the single (Christian) parole: *Pro Rege*, for King Jesus.

"For King Jesus" – that means here: for the Christ Who as Mediator of Redemption and as exalted Messiah "has been given all power in heaven and on earth."[130] Looked at from the positive side, the most intimate and fruitful co-operation between common grace and particular grace is being carried on here: common grace preserves and develops the structures of creation, and on the basis of this preparatory work particular grace leads culture to a higher, richer and nobler development – to the praise and glory of Christ.[131] That is how the two co-operate – not in the first place for the sake of that development

to teach otherwise . . . nor ought we to consider custom, or the great multitude, or antiquity, or succession of times and persons, or councils, decrees or statutes, as of equal value with the truth of God, . . . for all men are of themselves liars, and more vain than vanity itself. . . ."

125 *GG* II:279, 287ff., 350, 665ff.
126 Cf. *GG* II:337, 644, 654ff.; III:330, 338.
127 Cf. Ridderbos, *Cultuurbeschouwing*, 127n6, 160ff.
128 Cf. *GG* III:527f., 569.
129 *GG* III:149, 570f.
130 *GG* III:281; but especially in *PrRege* I:370, 526, 567; III:582, et al.
131 This is the prevailing tenor of the whole of *Pro Rege*; but it is also present in *GG*, e.g., II:348.

itself, but first and foremost to reveal thereby what the (particular) grace in Christ can do in the (common) domain of human culture.[132]

Once again, unlike the battle cry of the Anabaptist revolutionaries this *Pro Rege* does not call for the tearing down of the creation structures in order to establish an "otherworldly" kingdom in this world. Rather, it actually harmonizes with the highest development of the potentials and tasks that lie enclosed in creation. This slogan is a spur for such development. Hence we are at last dealing here with things like "Christian culture" this time *properly so called*, with Christian politics, Christian family life, Christian scholarship, etc., etc., in the true and unadulterated sense of the word.[133] Cultural activity *pro Rege* arises from regeneration[134] but abides by the ordinances for the life of the creature, by the creation ordinances as maintained and developed by common grace. The purpose of the visible and the temporal, its intrinsic "cultural" goal, its natural, creaturely end, has here become coterminous with the purpose of particular grace: the honor and glory of the exalted Christ and in Him of the Triune God of salvation. The twin goals merge: Christian cultural activity finally ends in exalting the Kingly glory of Jesus Christ, the Savior of the world.

Here Kuyper has dropped his exclusively spiritualistic characterization of particular grace; here also particular grace has lost all traces of an exclusively eschatological end – let alone of any individualistic character it may originally have had. Much rather, we here see particular grace radiating out from its center – even while not forgetting for a single moment to look to the hereafter for the full revelation and realization of its glory – into the life and labor of the domain of common grace. Here Christian culture is not at odds with the expectation of the new earth; here the Christian's sense of calling in this temporal-visible reality is never without the Christian's pilgrim song (*PrRege* II:96ff.); here the spiritual center of particular grace is not weakened for the sake of "broad" cultural pursuits on the surface of life, but neither is that center made averse to or disdainful of (Christian) cultural activity.

Here Kuyper has achieved what he had in mind from the outset: while retaining the mysticism of particular grace and the eschatology of future expectation, he has found a spur for Christian action in the domain of common grace. This was his answer to the question, To be and not to be: To be in the world, yet not be of the world.

4. *Pro Rege* and the Antithesis

As had been indicated, with his *Pro Rege* password Kuyper expresses the *positive* aspect to his idea of a Christian culture properly so called. Next to that, however, he also has a *negative* way of expressing this same basic conviction. This we find in his doctrine of the antithesis. And we find it especially in his views concerning the organizational antithesis in the visible, temporal world.

That this antithesis is a fundamental and undeniable fact in the domain of "the spiritual" is something that Kuyper is never in doubt about. With Augustine he recognizes the deep-seated antithesis between the Kingdom of grace and the kingdom of this world,

---

132 *GG* II:341, 355.
133 *GG* II:672, et al.
134 Cf. esp. Kuyper's idea of a Christian science, in *Encyclopaedie* II:97ff.

between this (invisible) church and the humanity that is included in Adam and his fall, between the "new humanity" and the humanity that has been given up to death, judgment and enmity against God.[135]

But that this antithesis manifests itself also in the domain of common grace and can even make itself felt so strongly there that the kingdom of this world makes capital of the treasures of common grace for the very purpose of driving the kingdom of Christ, the *Pro Rege* army, from its last foothold – that is a conviction that grew on Kuyper more and more.[136] More and more will the antithesis come knocking at our door, precisely in the domain of common grace. The positive work from the *Pro Rege* motive will encounter more and more opposition and increasingly face an organization of the powers and treasures of common grace that is bent on thwarting this positive work.

Kuyper creates room for this conviction by dividing the domain of common grace into two areas: on the one hand there is the area of rational and technical culture, on the other there is the area of moral Culture. The progressive rational-technical conquest of inorganic and organic nature will go hand in hand with a decline in moral-civil society. It will mean a decline of the "higher values" of humanity.[137] And therefore it will mean a conscious antithesis against the kingdom of Christ, precisely because Christian culture upholds, fosters and pursues these higher values. Moreover, the enmity against Christ Himself will constantly increase. As a result, common grace will be misused, will be turned against the Name of Christ and against His followers (*GG* I:452).

All this summons the Christian to posit the antithesis, or rather to open his eyes to the reality of the antithesis. This is what makes *Pro Rege* a battle cry and gives *Pro Rege* action its war-like character. The more the hostility against Christ and against the preservative influence of Christianity comes out into the open in the area of "higher" culture, the more will Christians come to recognize their calling to set up their own distinctive organizations in the public sector of life and the sooner will they rally under the *Pro Rege* banner.[138]

In this context Kuyper will sometimes venture statements that skirt the limits of propriety. For example, for the sake of greater solidarity among the Christians in the cause of *Pro Rege* science and scholarship he considers it "fortunate" (*GG* III:528) that the godless character of the "misuse" of common grace is showing up more brazenly all the time; for the fact that it does so will of course undermine the temptation to blend Christianity and humanism.

But however strongly Christians may be steeled in this antithetical posture, this does not mean that their *Pro Rege* activity is not at the same time a struggle to preserve the highest values of common grace for the benefit of all the people and the entire nation, in fact for all mankind in the present dispensation. Self-interest is not a motive here.[139] The honor of Christ in this age is always a blessing for the whole of humanity – for unbelievers no less than for believers. Yes, in this very antithesis a battle is being waged for "the whole Dutch people," as Kuyper would repeatedly aver; it is a battle in the interest of culture, waged for the sake of strengthening, enhancing and developing common grace in the

---

135 Cf. e.g., *Encyclopaedie* II:97ff.; *GG* II:23.
136 *PrRege* III:225, et al.
137 *GG* I:415ff., 431f., 447–450, 455f.
138 Thus, esp. *PrRege* III:184ff.
139 *GG* II:246, 277; III:405.

common domain and for the "common" people. This concern was never so much as a moment from Kuyper's mind and heart, even when he was most afire for the *Pro Rege* campaign and for the call to take up the antithesis.[140]

> *Here, at this "Pro Rege," this antithesis in the visible-temporal domain of common grace, here we hear the heartbeat of Kuyper and of his doctrine of common grace. In comparison with the use of the gift of common grace for Christian action, all those other things that follow in his doctrine of common grace and that may further be deduced from it are for Kuyper but side-issues.*

That Christian action has priority in Kuyper is evident, among other ways, from the way he reacts when this Christian culture (Christian politics, etc.), properly so called, is endangered by having brought in against it the earlier so-called Christian culture, that common grace culture which indirectly enjoys the fruits of particular grace but which has not directly come forth out of regeneration. This is done, for example, when the public school passes for a "Christian" school – in that second, improper sense. Obviously Kuyper can thus be fought with Kuyper. The Kuyper of the antithesis is then fought off with the Kuyper of common grace. Then the Christian school is combated with the "Christian public" school of a "Christian" nation.[141] When this threatens, when this use of (part of) his doctrine of common grace threatens to frustrate his choice for Christian education and to wound his love for the Christian school, Kuyper is not afraid to retract and even attack his earlier conception of a "Christian" school, a "Christian" culture, a "Christian" country, as being both invalid and misleading.[142] There cannot be the least doubt about it that this second sense of "Christian" was never intended by Kuyper to make the Christian school superfluous. As far as this point is concerned, this is how I would summarize Kuyper's deepest convictions as well as his actual practice: you may not mobilize his idea of a christianized common grace against his idea of a full-blooded and genuinely Christian culture that arises from the living fountains of particular grace, because in so doing you would clearly be making an unbelieving, anti-Christian use, and therefore a misuse, of what Kuyper understood by christianized common grace; therefore, to preclude any misunderstanding, it is better once for all to deny it the epithet Christian, which had been applied to it in an improper sense in the first place. This should clear up the real state of affairs, sharpen the awareness that the antithesis is gathering strength, and quicken the hearts to *Pro Rege* action.

5. The Critical Question

Meanwhile we should not let slip the critical question whether Kuyper, next to enumerating these two, mutually quite distinct, ways in which particular grace in his view operates upon the domain of common grace, also proved able adequately to *explain* these operations by means of his doctrine of common grace and his *Pro Rege* emphasis.

This is a question that was dealt with neither by Hepp nor by Ridderbos, but that had been raised, many years before they ever wrote about common grace, by Van Ruler – who

---

140 Not even in the three volumes on *Pro Rege*.
141 Cf. Ridderbos, *Cultuurbeschouwing*, 160ff.
142 Ridderbos, *Cultuurbeschouwing*, 163.

had answered it in the negative. Neither of our two authors appear to have had a ready answer for Van Ruler; at least, they chose to pass over the point in silence. This neglect is probably due to the fact that once they had determined that Kuyper did not teach an "Anabaptistic" dualism they had no eye for the fact that throughout Kuyper's view of the relation between common grace and particular grace a *polar* dualism is habitually at work. This oversight is to be deplored if only for this reason, that the question raised by Van Ruler concerns the heart of the matter and has occasioned, also in the more immediate circles of Kuyper's spiritual kin, differences of opinion and even of standpoint.

Van Ruler formulates his problem as follows:

> Still, the question that was raised already in our third chapter presses itself upon us with greater urgency than ever: What does the impact of the supernatural powers of particular grace on the natural powers of common grace consist in? (*Kuypers idee*, 97)

He continues:

> Now at last we have to be told, not why a Christian culture is so desirable, but what is to be understood by "Christian culture"! And the answer given to this question suffers from all the inner tensions contained in the principles undergirding the entire conception. Particular grace has been cast too much in terms of eternity for it to be able to make a clearly visible appearance in the world of time. Common grace has been riveted too tightly to the creation for it to be able to bear the insertion of a real hard quantity of particular grace without the break not always remaining visible. (98)

Wherefore he concludes:

> On the one hand Kuyper began by hiding the essence of particular grace too much in the mystic life of the soul to be able later to bring it out again as a culturally formative factor in history. And on the other hand Kuyper equally – and consistently – began by proclaiming common grace too positively as the explanation of God's regiment over life outside the church to be able later to eliminate it or even relegate it to the second place. His insertion of particular grace into Christian culture is never fully successful; his elimination of common grace from Christian culture is never quite complete. (115)

What are we to make of this, and what can we reply to this?

When we consider the two ways in which Kuyper describes the influence and significance of particular grace for the domain of common grace, we cannot deny that he has had to do some adjusting to his view on particular grace, exclusively spiritualistic and eschatological as it had been initially; so much adjusting, in fact, that thanks to it he can henceforth speak of a "fully developed particular grace" – fully developed because it is then no longer limited to the spiritual life of the inner soul and to the life of the hereafter but has "radiated out" into the domain of common grace, choosing this ordinary life for its instrument and making it serve the particular grace of *Pro Rege*. Of course, it goes without saying that once having committed himself to *this* position Kuyper must teach about the domain of common grace that the exalted Christ is also King of common grace and may rightfully demand that it be thus pressed into the service of His Royal rule (cf. *PrRege* III:25). The doctrine that common grace rests in Christ as the Son of God and as the Mediator of Creation will now no longer suffice for Kuyper. He is forced to correct himself on this point. And, however sparingly, he does exactly that. Even Ridderbos cannot get around this self-consistency in Kuyper and is forced to introduce into his study the position to which Kuyper's doctrine finally brought him[143] – despite his admonition to take Kuyper as he comes, in the full complexity of his thought.[144]

What Van Ruler ignores, however, is that Kuyper himself had already made this correction; that in fact the happy hour arrived that he set forth that Christ as the Mediator of Redemption not only may lay claim to the central, spiritual core of man, but also is in principle the new Root of all of created reality and the Head, the new Head, of the "human race" (cf. *GG* II:183). With that, Kuyper had broken with his own polarly dualistic contrast between particular grace and common grace. That is why he could state more forcefully in his writings on *Pro Rege* than in those on *Gemeene Gratie* that we are in the service of Christ throughout the entire domain of common grace (*PrRege* II:527).

Kuyper vacillated between the two positions. He once said that any efforts to bring greater clarity in this problem would be more than welcome (*GG* III:280). He is rather to be admired, therefore, for correcting and replacing the basic conception with which he had begun – a polarly dualistic one – whenever it became clear to him that its inner logic was preventing him from being able to speak of truly Christian action in the domain of common grace. In those instances he did not brook being dictated to even by himself and his own world of ideas, but broke through these harmful constructions of his own, opening the floodgates for the work of the Spirit in His particular grace to pour out over the fields of life in the temporal-visible world as well.

By not taking this self-correction of Kuyper into account, Van Ruler in his conclusions does not do justice to Kuyper. No doubt he is right in saying that Kuyper never succeeds fully in inserting particular grace and never manages completely to eliminate common grace. However, the reason for this is that Kuyper had designedly tied particular grace too closely to the "supernatural" and the new. Also he had paid too little attention to the fact that if and when particular grace changes the *direction* of a man's heart, this re-direction has immediate consequences for his "natural" life, for the whole of his activity in the domain of common grace: life in the domain of common grace once again becomes true religion and is once more experienced and intended as service of God in God's covenant of grace. To be sure, Kuyper does indeed talk of "mediated religion" here (*PrRege* I:193), but because he failed to bring this element sufficiently to the foreground the door was left open to an "abstract" kind of common grace that as such does not lead to true religion but only to a cultivation of the creation potentials. Thus, by his rigid, often philosophical distinction between particular grace's essence as supernatural and really belonging to the realm of glory – the new heaven and new earth – and common grace as never transcending the "essence" of creatureliness, Kuyper gives just cause for the criticism that "his insertion of particular grace is never fully successful." But this is not – and this is the point I want to emphasize above all else – this is not the only Kuyper. *A full picture of Kuyper is not given unless it is also shown that he did not halt before his self-imposed problem, but broke through to the confession that truly Christian action is possible also in the domain of common grace. The fear of the Lord, not distinguishable from the confession and the experiencing of Jesus Christ as our Lord and King, is totalitarian in that it embraces not only the mystic life of the inner soul and not only the life of the hereafter but embraces no less our life "in all areas of life" in the present dispensation. This fundamentally Reformed confession never left him; rather, when*

---

143 Ridderbos, *Cultuurbeschouwing*, 97ff.

144 Ridderbos, *Cultuurbeschouwing*, 328.

in a predicament it saw him over the barricade thrown up by his polarly dualistic view of the relation between the two domains of particular grace and common grace.[145]

This escape, meanwhile, was never such that he needed really to eliminate common grace from the new life in the creation. It is not correct to say baldly that his "elimination of common grace is never quite complete." That the elimination was never quite complete is due to the fact that Kuyper never quite tried or intended it. Kuyper was quite on guard against that "Christian ghetto" into which Van Ruler would like to force him and his followers. He knew better than to admit and accredit the Anabaptistic and Gnostic notion that the "Christian life" is a revolutionary way of life running counter to creation. He had more sense than to identify the Christian activity of the church organism with doing things odd and out-of-this-world, and with outdoing simple, ordinary(!) obedience to the creation ordinances. His *Pro Rege* call and his doctrine of the antithesis were always intrinsically connected with the acceptance and recognition of the creation ordinances and the creation structures and never with an imaginary, would-be "Christian" world. This was the only way Kuyper knew of that avoided a contradiction between creation and redemption, between common grace and particular grace. Creation was to be anything but "eliminated," redemption was to be anything but "perpendicular" to God's work of creation.

While therefore Kuyper is never for a moment willing to disown the Christian Body's longing for the end of its pilgrimage and for the kingdom of glory, he can indeed be seduced more than once into seeing particular grace as the grace that would bring us, as it were, *quite apart from this life* (*GG* III:307), into the realm of glory; yet even this temptation does not prevent him in due time from expressing the opposite view, from teaching that the journey to the Jerusalem that is above takes us right through this life and straight through this temporal reality, and that this pilgrimage demands the labor of the service of God in a religion of thankfulness that devotes itself with all its energies to this life and its God-given structures and ordinances.[146]

Kuyper's Gemeene Gratie *as well as his* Pro Rege *testify to his religious desire to escape a culturally irrelevant and ineffectual Christianity and to pave the way for the Body of Christ, in his days still too much trammeled by an unwarranted renunciation of life and a false contempt for the world, to be once again the salt of the earth and to be once again the leaven of the world – or at least to learn to see that this is what Christianity means.*[147]

At the same time, when Kuyper, with due modesty and a healthy realism yet also in conformity with Scripture and the confessions, teaches that we may expect no more than "the beginnings of a break-through of the powers of particular grace in the visible things of this present life" (*GG* II:689), then he serves as an apt warning for all those pedagogues of Christian action who frightfully overestimate the quantitative (not the qualitative) importance of Christian action in the world. That does not alter the fact, however, that Kuyper is not afraid, having once sounded this caution, to retract as it were his doctrine of the independent purpose of common grace and to write: "Apart from particular grace, common grace would have been without a goal" (*GG* I:449). Nor is he afraid to write: "Not *common* grace but the order of *particular* grace *obtains*;" and to conclude the passage

---

145 *GG* I:468; cf. II:657f., 679; III:19.

146 *GG* III:308; cf. also Ridderbos, *Cultuurbeschouwing*, 264.

147 Cf. *GG* I:468; III:19.

in question, in which he is evidently struggling not to impair altogether his stake in the independent purpose of common grace and yet to acknowledge the Son of God, as Mediator of Redemption, to be also the King of common grace, without pandering to a Christian individualism that makes man and his salvation the center of interest: "In this sense it ought to be recognized therefore that common grace is only a radiation from particular grace and that all its fruits flow back into particular grace" (*GG* I:224). Similarly: "Let no one forget, however, that particular grace always remains supreme, the core and center around which common grace turns" (*GG* I:220). Or again: "That this silencing of God's wrath is possible through common grace finds its explanation exclusively in particular grace. It all turns on and ends in Christ" (*GG* II:420). That is why common grace is said to work *together* with particular grace "in order to enable the powers of the Kingdom to penetrate into the world" (*GG* I:490; cf. I:496); and that is why Kuyper can even write that in common grace "the harbingers" of the Kingdom are already visible (*GG* I:490).

Kuyper himself desires more than once to be freed from the dualism between nature and grace, and then he sees no other way of acquiring this freedom than in the recognition that through particular grace the world that God once made "is restored in the nerve center of its life and purged of the cancer in its root" (*GG* II:183). This insight enables him in this connection to speak already of "the same old world of Adam, fashioned by God and despoiled by us, which [is] saved in Christ" (*GG* II:183).

Furthermore, to give just one more citation, those polarly dualistic thought patterns that predominated as he structurated and elaborated his doctrine and that pursued him every step of the way, Kuyper also, after all, revolts against. He wants to be rid of them and to be set at liberty. Ultimately what he wants to show is

> that *grace* and *nature* belong together and that you cannot see the richness of *grace* if you do not see how its root fibers everywhere penetrate into the joints and rifts in the life of *nature*. Now this connection you *cannot* see if "grace" makes you think first of the salvation of your soul and not first and foremost of the *Christ of God*. It is for this very reason that Scripture constantly reminds us that the *Savior* of the world is at the same time the *Creator* of the world; in fact, that He could only become its Savior because He was its Creator. Of course, it was not the *Son of Man*, the *Incarnate* Word, that created. Also in the Mediator all that was human was itself created, creaturely, as it is in us. Yet Scripture also points out repeatedly that this firstborn from the dead is also the firstborn of every creature and that the *Incarnate* Word always was and remained that same *eternal* Word that was with God and that was God and of Whom it is written that without that Word not any thing was made that was made. Thus we can see how Christ connects with *nature*, inasmuch as He is its Creator; and with grace, inasmuch as He has re-creatively revealed in that nature the richness of grace. (*GG* I:228)

No wonder that precisely in this connection Kuyper vigorously and cogently attacks the notion that our life in the world and for the world is something that is carried on "*alongside* our Christian religion" (*GG* I:226), and over against this view posits the confession that "Christ our Savior has to do not only with our *souls* but also with our *bodies*; that everything in the world belongs to Christ and is claimed by Him" (*GG* I:228).

But, in addition, Van Ruler has not sufficiently, or rather not at all, taken into account the Kuyper who in principle overcomes and removes the polar tension between particular grace and common grace – precisely in his doctrine of particular grace. I am referring to the Kuyper who teaches – as he does in *De Gemeene Gratie* (II:298) – that particular grace does not, in regeneration, work a "conversion of being," a "change in essence," but rather a deeply religious reversal of the "innermost pivot" of I our being, whereby what had *turned into its opposite* through sin is once more *set straight*. For it is not now a polarly dialectical approach to the problem when next he asks how this *reversal* of the "invisibly small yet all-controlling central point" in man can possibly become effective on the *periphery*, that is to say, how a truly Christian life can blossom forth from such a regeneration that does not bring about a different "kind" of life or a change in being or essence. This time there simply is no inner tension for Kuyper to overcome when he continues:

> Now this distinction [between center and periphery] enables us to picture to ourselves how it is possible that a change can take place in that matrix, in that single point from which all activity proceeds, without any change being discernible as yet in the broad periphery. But gradually that change in the center is completed; accordingly it gains in strength and begins to manifest itself also in the "issues of life;" and so at last the change or renewal becomes noticeable throughout the whole periphery. (*GG* II:299; cf. II:59, 65, 68)

Here, precisely in his doctrine of regeneration and particular grace, Kuyper radically rises above that haunting dilemma brought on by the polarly dialectical relation that he usually construed between re-creation and creation.

Conclusion

In summary I conclude that Kuyper gave Van Ruler cause for writing what he did. But no less do I conclude that Kuyper more than once should have given Van Ruler pause in writing what he did. Many a passage in Kuyper, such as I have referred to or quoted above, should have suggested to Van Ruler that perhaps he was presenting only half a Kuyper and that there may also be another Kuyper, a Kuyper who in principle rises above the polar dualism in his view of the relation between re-creation and creation – especially where he writes that particular grace "restores the creation in its root" (*GG* II:183). In that case the Kuyper of Van Ruler, the Kuyper of the particularistic, eschatological and spiritualistic doctrine of particular grace, is a misrepresentation of the true, in any case of the whole, Kuyper. Kuyper himself struggled to reconcile the two lines in his thought, a struggle that became very conscious when he had to deal with the place and significance of the exalted Mediator for the domain of common grace (*GG* III:280). Contradictory statements, as we have seen, were the result.

No true follower of Kuyper can make a halt before these contradictory statements.[148] He will have to choose. As for me, I do not want to make a secret of my position, which is that if there is to be a restoration of Kuyper's doctrine of common grace in which these contradictions no longer occur, it should be undertaken in no other way than in the way of a full-fledged elaboration of the things Kuyper wrote concerning the Christ and concerning particular grace that "restores the creation in its root." In such a restoration, common grace should never again be made to find its purpose in itself. It should never again be placed, even if only as to its origin, outside of particular grace (cf. *GG* II:420).

---

148 Cf. Hepp. op. cit., p. 70: "Are we then denying the possibility of inconsistencies in Kuyper? Of course not. But we ought to have enough respect for men of his stature not to start tinkering with them. If Kuyper has inconsistencies, then that too is the real Dr. Kuyper – inconsistencies and all." My question is: What if he has internal contradictions? All I can say is that I find this a bigoted Kuyper worship, which is untrue to the real Kuyper and which enthrones a false Kuyperianism.

Rather, common grace should then be confessed as a work of God whereby He upholds His creation, maintains His creation ordinances, and thus opens the way for the militant as well as suffering church to fight her warfare *Pro Rege*, throughout this age, with the weapons God in His common grace has provided her – weapons that are forged, in spite of the impulse that is not of God, also by unbelievers, who no less than the believers are fitted by God's common grace with gifts and talents for their tasks, tasks that they perform, whatever they intend and whatsoever they will, in the service of particular grace.

And this will go on until Christ's second coming coincides with the end of the age, when the present dispensation will come to its appointed end (cf. Matthew 24:3). To the glory of Him that sitteth upon the throne. To the glory of the Lamb that bought us, soul and body, to be His own possession, in body as well as in soul.

20

Antithesis and Common Grace

Jacob Klapwijk

Elsewhere I have examined Calvin's views on philosophy.[1] Calvin urged openness to the Word and Spirit of God. The basis of such philosophy ought to be "humility." True to this view of philosophizing Christianly, Calvin reflected on non-Christian thought, openly and critically. Open in the sense that he understood non-Christian thought as possible only by God's sovereign and gracious involvement in the lives and reflections of people; critical, because in Calvin's judgment non-Christian thought was based on what moderns would call self-sufficiency or autonomy. In this chapter I present an account of the *on-going discussion of "antithesis" in Dutch neo-Calvinism since Abraham Kuyper* (1837–1920).[2]

1. Introduction

The question of how to assess non-Christian philosophy arose again in the reformational tradition, be it in a much broader framework of reference, when in the second half of the nineteenth century there was a revival of Calvinism, both in the Netherlands and abroad. One of the most inspiring leaders of this neo-Calvinism was Abraham Kuyper. Following his conversion, Kuyper sought to reassess the importance of the Calvinist Reformation for modern times and modern culture. Kuyper established the Anti-Revolutionary Party, a Christian political party, in 1879. In 1880 he founded the Free University in Amsterdam, based on "the Reformed principles," and became Professor of Systematic Theology at that institution. From 1901 to 1905 Kuyper was Prime Minister of the Netherlands.

Kuyper challenged adherents of the Reformed tradition not only to reflect on the need for Christian statecraft but also to develop a Christian or, more precisely, a Calvinist view of culture and science. He pondered what might be the value of present-day, secularized science for Christians. Must it be accepted gratefully as a gift from

---

1   Klapwijk, Jacob 1991. "John Calvin (1509–1564)." In Jacob Klapwijk, Sander Griffioen, and Gerben Groenewoud, eds. *Bringing Into Captivity Every Thought: Capita Selecta in the History of Christian Evaluations of Non-Christian Philosophy.* Lanham: University Press of America.

2   The following abbreviations are used:
    GG = Kuyper, Abraham 1902–05. *De Gemeene Gratie.* 3 vols. Kampen: Kok; 3rd ed. 1931–32.
    GD = Bavinck, Herman 1895–1901. *Gereformeerde Dogmatiek.* 4 vols. Kampen: Kok; 5th ed. 1967.
    RB = Bavinck, Johan H. 1949. *Religieus Besef en Christelijk Geloof.* Kampen: Kok.
    PR = *Philosophia Reformata.*

God's hand, its apostate features notwithstanding? Or should its apostate direction be unmasked and opposed in the light of the Christian cultural mandate? Is it a sign of God's common grace? Or is it sooner an expression of a universal antithesis between belief and unbelief?

The plan of this study is as follows. First, I devote several sections to a sketch of Kuyper's position on the topic, noting the tensions inherent in his thought. Next, I compare Kuyper's views with those of two other Free University theologians, Herman Bavinck (1854–1921) and Johan H. Bavinck (1895–1964). After that, I discuss the more recent contributions of two philosophers at the Free University, Herman Dooyeweerd (1894–1977) and Cornelis A. van Peursen (1920–1996). In the closing remarks I evaluate the ideas of these thinkers and add some personal conclusions.

2. Abraham Kuyper

Between 1902 and 1905 Abraham Kuyper published one of his most characteristic standard works, *De Gemeene Gratie*, in three volumes. The title itself indicates the framework within which Kuyper sought to answer the question concerning the value of non-Christian culture, science, and philosophy: the doctrine of general or common grace. In the systematic section of this work (vol. II), Kuyper introduces the problem by observing that the church often disappoints one's expectations and the world often exceeds them:

> One is struck by . . . the remarkable fact that, weighed against the doctrine of our depravity through sin, the unconverted world exceeds our expectations; and the church, weighed against the doctrine of the re-birth, disappoints our expectations. (*GG* II:29)

Evidently, Kuyper would expect more from the church and less from "the world." This inclination can be understood to a certain extent as a product of his Calvinist background. On the one side, Kuyper starts from the Reformed doctrine of the total corruption of human nature by sin. This doctrine is expressed in the *Heidelberg Catechism* (the confession of faith which so strongly influenced the preaching, faith life, and theology of Dutch Calvinism and Kuyper's thinking): the natural man is "wholly incapable of doing any good, and inclined to all evil."[3] On the other side, Kuyper adheres to the Reformed confession of all-encompassing salvation through Jesus Christ, through whom the believer is freed from sin and reborn to new life. It is this deep-rooted twofold conviction of humankind's total depravity and of Christ's universal salvation that explains Kuyper's saying that the church turns out to be worse and the world better than one would expect.

To demonstrate that the "unconverted world" exceeds our expectations, Kuyper likes to point to the fruits of philosophy and science which that world has brought forth in such abundance. In view of the seriousness of sin, the explanation for this phenomenon, according to Kuyper, cannot be found in some residue of (partial) goodness in human nature. Kuyper can offer only one explanation for it: the goodness of God. God's goodness toward all people, i.e., God's common grace, explains why persons such as Plato, Aristotle, Kant, and Darwin (!) have shone as "stars of the first magnitude" (*GG* III:498). Not humanity's excellence but God's grace is the cause. Again I quote Kuyper:

---

3   *Heidelberg Catechism*, Lord's Day III, 8.

The doctrine of "common grace" . . . did not arise from philosophical speculation but from the confession of the deadly nature of sin. . . . Apparently, this [confession] did not accord with reality. There was so much that was beautiful, respectable, so much to be envied in that sinful world, also outside the church. This placed one before the choice either to reject all this good against one's better judgment and to go astray with the Anabaptists, or to present fallen man as not so deeply fallen after all and thus to go astray in the Arminian heresy. . . . The solution of this apparent contradiction, however, is . . . that grace is operative outside the church, too, among the heathen, in the midst of the world, not eternal or saving grace, but temporal grace, which restrains the depravity inherent in sin. (*GG* I:11; cf. *LC* 121ff.)

3. Particular and Common Grace

In support of this doctrine of common grace, Kuyper appeals to Calvin. Rightly so, insofar as Calvin, too, had set non-Christian philosophy against the background of the depravity and powerlessness of sinners and God's gracious dealing with the world. Yet, Kuyper's position is not identical to Calvin's. Kuyper is the one who systematized the doctrine of common grace by making a sharp distinction between God's common grace to all people and his "particular grace" to believers. Common grace has a different content, scope, purpose, and ground than can be ascribed to particular grace.

1. *Common grace has a different content.* The content of particular grace is deliverance from sin and the gift of eternal salvation. Common grace, in contrast, "contains of itself not a single grain of saving grace and is, consequently, of a totally different nature" (*GG* I:9). The content of common grace is temporal blessing for humanity and creation. Kuyper explains this as follows. God has said in paradise that if man sinned, he would surely die (Genesis 2:17). Now, grace is sometimes extended to people who are under sentence of death. Similarly, according to Kuyper, God has extended grace to fallen humanity: grace in the sense that punishment (eternal death) has been postponed until the last day; that room has been made for the prolonged history of mankind; that the deadly poison of sin has been restrained – indeed, restrained not only in humans but in the whole of creation (*GG* II:243ff., 265ff.).

2. It follows that *common grace is also broader in scope than particular grace.* Common grace is universal, applying to the whole world and the whole of humanity. Everyone, not just believers, benefits from God's maintaining the order of creation. That art and culture, philosophy and science, and so on, remain possible in this world in spite of sin is to the advantage of all people everywhere.

3. *The purpose of common grace differs from that of particular grace.* To Kuyper, particular grace is the mysterious reality of God's intervention in the human heart whereby a person receives new life and becomes a citizen of the kingdom of heaven. Rebirth is of a supernatural order: not simply given with the creation, it is in fact an eschatological reality, inasmuch as the believer is enabled here on earth to have a foretaste of the powers of the world to come (Hebrews 6:15). In comparison with the original creation the re-creation is not something totally new; still, it cannot be explained in terms of the old. Particular grace and its fruits (new life and, finally, the new heaven and the new earth) transcend the natural creation-order upheld by common grace (*GG* I:243ff.; II:613ff.). Particular grace means, therefore, that God makes a new beginning.

The purpose of particular grace is to anticipate the new heaven and the new earth. Common grace, in contrast, means that God perpetuates the old. The purpose of common grace is to restrain sin and preserve the creature, or, put more positively, to make possible the disclosure of the potentialities inherent in the creation through the actualization, in the course of world history, of all the splendidly diverse fruits of culture (*GG* II:616–23).

4. *Even the ground of common grace is different from that of particular grace.* Kuyper teaches that salvation history and the church, in short, the terrain of particular grace, is borne by Jesus Christ, the crucified Lord: he is the mediator of *salvation*. The creation-order, however, unfolding in the broad stream of history and culture, is the area of God's common grace, founded in the eternal Son of God, the second Person of the divine Being: he is the Mediator of *creation* (*GG* II:635, 647; III:123).

How is one to assess this position? It appears to me that serious difficulties attend Kuyper's contrast between common grace and particular grace, between earth and heaven, creation and re-creation, between cultural activity and salvation of the soul, as if God had different grounds for being merciful to humans. In all of this lurks the threat of a spiritualizing dualism, a kind of mysticism that expresses itself in a bifurcated orientation to the hereafter and to the present. Only rarely does Kuyper manage to integrate the two spheres from a central point of view. Yet, at times he senses that the purpose of particular grace converges with the purpose of common grace: God wants the salvation of the soul to be included in the redemption of the created world. And this full salvation is attributable to the reconciling sacrifice of Christ. In other words, the ground for personal grace is the same as the ground for common grace: namely, the cross of Jesus Christ. The cross of Jesus bears the future but also the present; it bears the church but also the world. To Jesus Christ is given all power in heaven and on earth (Matthew 28:18). At such moments Kuyper honors Christ as the king also in the sphere of common grace. It is then that he proclaims: "There is not a square inch in the whole of our human existence of which Christ, who is sovereign over all, does not say: 'Mine!'"[4]

Mostly, however, the tensions in Kuyper's theology of culture remain, as they do in his personal life. In part, his work echoes the mystery of the born-again heart, the sigh of the weary pilgrim who yearns for his eternal home. In part, he is driven to work with extraordinary vigor at the unfolding of God's creation in state, society, and science. And even here his ideas seem sometimes at odds with each other. At times he regards the creation mandate as a common human task in which Christians and non-Christians struggle side by side. At such times it seems as if the terrain of common grace is equivalent to the realm of nature in medieval Scholasticism. At other times Kuyper is sure that the great cultural mandate leaves no room for cooperation with

---

4   Kuyper, Abraham 1880. *Souvereiniteit in eigen kring: Rede ter inwijding van de Vrije Universiteit den 20sten October 1880.* Kampen: Kok; 3rd ed. 1930; reprint 1980, 32. See also Zuidema, Sytse U. 1972. "Common Grace and Christian Action in Abraham Kuyper." In *Communication and Confrontation. A Philosophical Appraisal and Critique of Modern Society and Contemporary Thought.* Assen: Van Gorcum; Kampen: Kok; Toronto: Wedge Publishing Foundation, 95; *see supra,* page 282. Kuyper encountered great difficulties in seeking to articulate a radically christocentric view of culture, for while he was whole-heartedly devoted to emancipating culture (regarded as the fruit of common grace) from the control of the church (regarded as the institution of particular grace), he feared that an exclusively christocentric view of culture might lead to renewed domination of political and social life by the church.

the non-Christian; he is sure that this mandate proclaims the Lordship of Jesus Christ over the whole world and that it must therefore be translated into a program of organized Christian action in all areas of life, including science and philosophy.[5]

4. Common Grace and the Antithesis

This brings me back again to my main theme. Like everything else in creation, according to Kuyper, thought, science, and philosophy depend upon divine ordinances; they are grounded in "God's own creation" (*GG* III:495). Hence, science, too, is to be regarded as a fruit of common grace. Because sin has darkened the understanding, it follows that all science would end in deceit and self-deception if there were no common grace. Common grace makes science possible. Kuyper is also convinced that science is seriously affected by sin. In fact, Kuyper's opposition to non-Christian science is much stronger than his appreciation of it, despite his theory of *common grace*.[6]

In *De Gemeene Gratie* Kuyper is inconclusive. He finds that there are differences between the sciences. In the natural sciences, he thinks, general validity and common acceptance are possible to a large extent, because in these sciences a great deal depends on exact, objective observation. In history, philosophy, and the other human sciences, however, the subjectivity of the researcher often is a decisive factor, because here questions arise concerning the origin, coherence and purpose of things – questions that cannot be answered through observation alone (*GG* III:508, 512). With respect to the natural sciences, Kuyper seeks to avoid positing an opposition between what is Christian and what is not. Matters are different, however, where theology and the other human sciences (including philosophy of nature) are concerned. Two kinds of science are possible here, regenerate and unregenerate, so that a truly Christian science is obviously required. The distinctive character of such science would entail the consideration of scriptural data, but most importantly it would require the mind of a born-again Christian (*GG* III:514, 521).[7]

Thus Kuyper's position on non-Christian thought is ambivalent. Sometimes he stresses the gifts which God in his goodness grants humanity. At such times he can speak with admiration of Plato, Kant, and others. More often, however, he stresses the theme that only the regenerate can compare "spiritual things with spiritual" (1

---

5 One can find a condensation of this program in Kuyper, Abraham 1911–12. *Pro Rege, of het Koningschap van Christus*. 3 vols. Kampen: Kok.

6 Kuyper states his grounds for maintaining that science is affected by sin. What does it mean, he asks, to say that our knowledge is darkened by sin? Certainly it does not mean that we can no longer observe with our senses or think logically with our minds. No, it means that we no longer see things in their coherence and divine origin. The human mind can still perceive various parts of creation, but it is no longer capable of understanding the unity, origin, and purpose of things. Thus, to Kuyper the darkening of the understanding means not only the end of natural theology and its philosophical ascent to God but also the impossibility of attaining true knowledge of creation. Cf. *GG* III:499ff.

7 That the born-again person would take Scripture, too, into account is to Kuyper an indispensable yet incidental difference, distinguishing regenerate from unregenerate science. It is an indispensable difference because the Bible sheds a bright light on the great questions of the origin, government, and purpose of things. Yet it is incidental, first because a person must be reborn to understand the Scriptures, and secondly because Scripture is primarily concerned with particular grace and with effecting the salvation of the elect. When the Scriptures shed light on creation too, then this is a welcome and indispensable reinforcement of the dim light of common grace. Cf. *GG* III:515.

Corinthians 2:13). That is, he stresses the necessity of specifically Christian human sciences and philosophy. Then he takes sides and pits "the science of the new birth" against the "science outside the influence of the new birth" (*GG* III:515). The idea of common grace now ceases to function as the basis for appreciating non-Christian conceptions and instead becomes the basis for antithetical action; Kuyper uses it to justify taking Christian initiatives and attacking non-Christian endeavors in science. He advocates an "organizational antithesis" in the sciences – the building of a separate Christian scholarly movement within the world of learning.

Kuyper emphasizes the antithesis even more strongly in his renowned *Lectures on Calvinism*, which were presented as the Stone Lectures at Princeton University in 1898. In the chapter "Calvinism and Science" a few words of admiration are devoted to the "treasures of philosophic light" found in ancient Greece and Rome; for those treasures we are indebted to common grace (*LC* 121, 125). But Kuyper goes on straightway to present a program of Christian scientific activity that is even more universal and radical than the one articulated in *De Gemeene Gratie*. It is more universal because Christian and non-Christian activity "both claim the whole domain of human knowledge. . . . [They dispute] with one another the whole domain of life." Kuyper no longer acknowledges a common task even with respect to the "lower," natural sciences. This program is also more radical because, throughout, he speaks in terms of two types of people. Involved are "two kinds of human consciousness: that of the regenerate and the unregenerate." They are not the same, nor can they be made to "agree" (*LC* 133, 137–38).[8]

To Kuyper the difference is striking. The unregenerate mind believes the cosmos to be "normal" as it is. The regenerate mind knows that because of the intrusion of sin, the world is "abnormal" and unable to reach its goal except through regeneration. Thus the antithesis in science is between the "Normalists" and the Abnormalists," there are "two absolutely differing starting points, which have nothing in common in their origin." The Normalists and the Abnormalists "cannot desist from the constant endeavor to pull down to the ground the entire edifice of their respective controverted assertions, all the supports included, upon which their assertions rest" (*LC* 130–34).[9]

---

8   It should perhaps be said that these terms need to be understood in the context of Kuyper's conviction that regeneration – together with the means to regeneration, namely, the incarnate Christ and the holy Scriptures – is "abnormal." See *LC* 134. They connote a supernatural order and anticipate the new creation.

9   Remarkably, Kuyper stresses common grace again in his lecture on art, which is placed after the one on science. It is common grace that makes it possible for Christians to enjoy the art of unbelievers, he says; and (appealing to Calvin) he goes on to reject any linking of art and regeneration. He does so, he says, because art does not belong to believers alone and because art must be more than ecclesiastical art. In short, art is not a product of particular grace but one of the natural gifts (cf. *LC* 161). Kuyper argues that Calvinism could not develop its own Christian art style and at the same time be true to its principle and its calling (149). Yet he is rather unconvincing. Kuyper does not succeed in making clear why regenerate aesthetic consciousness and regenerate scientific thought must part company and go their separate ways. One cannot escape the impression that Kuyper was advancing *ad hoc* apologetic arguments here; and we recall that his movement in the Netherlands produced a free Christian university but not a Christian academy of art. Nevertheless, Kuyper had touched upon this problem years before in *De Gemeene Gratie*. There he speaks of artistic expressions "inspired by the spirit of the abyss" and of others "inspired by the spirit of rebirth." In connection with the latter he alludes, significantly, to a "gap in the life of Christianity" (*GG* III:570f.).

5. Three diverging lines

It can be said that there are a good many ambiguities, tensions, and contradictions in Kuyper's position. More precisely, one can distinguish at least three lines in Kuyper's doctrine of common grace. In the first place, there is a more or less mystical line, when Kuyper relegates common grace and particular grace to two separate areas in such a way that the regenerate heart, saved by God's particular grace, transcends the natural order of existence, the terrain of common grace. Kuyper suggests that in virtue of rebirth (*palingenesis*) a new principle of life is implanted, a principle that is never fully explicable in terms of the natural order of creation. It puts humanity on the way of a higher, spiritual world, to the eternal house of the Father, where all will see God face to face.

It is clear that in this context "common" and "particular" grace are little more than different names for what Kuyper himself sometimes calls the "natural" and the "supernatural" (*GG* II:243). This line of thought, which testifies to a moderate mysticism, has a long tradition in the history of the Christian church – one encounters it in Bonaventure, for example. And wherever this line is found, the value of philosophy and culture, be they of Christian or non-Christian provenance, is relativized in a large measure, as in Kuyper, if not disesteemed altogether. For after all, the heart of the Christian is elsewhere, in the pilgrimage toward the kingdom of glory and in the participation in the eschatological reality of that kingdom where God will be all in all. This first, semi-mystical line is not to be regarded as Kuyper's most original contribution.[10]

In a second train of thought Kuyper elaborates the doctrine of common and particular grace in terms of a theory of two realms as well, but in such a way that a Christian fully accepts his calling in both. The first terrain is now viewed as a common human area where the Christian is called to far-reaching cooperation with those of other persuasions; an example would be the cooperation in the field of the ("lower") natural sciences where the standpoint of faith supposedly plays a negligible role only. Matters are entirely different on the second terrain. On the level of theology, philosophy, and the ("higher") human sciences in general, believers are assigned their own, exclusively Christian task.

This way of thinking may also be called "supernaturalistic," although oriented less to the tradition of mysticism than reminiscent of the synthesizing approach of Thomistic philosophy.[11] This second line in Kuyper's thought can also be said to be not particularly

---

10 Cf. Vander Stelt, John C. 1973. "Kuyper's Semi-Mystical Conception." In Kornelis A. Bril, Hendrik Hart, and Jacob Klapwijk, eds. *The Idea of a Christian Philosophy. Essays in Honor of D. H. Th. Vollenhoven* Toronto: Wedge Publishing Foundation; reprinted from PR 38: 178–190. In Kuyper's case one must, indeed, speak of a semi- or moderated mysticism, as Vander Stelt, following Dirk H. Th. Vollenhoven, does. In the "*palingenesis*," on Kuyper's view, the germ of supernatural life is implanted in the natural life of the believer; and that supernatural life transcends the natural order of creation in principle – and with Christ's second coming transcends it altogether. "Then the re-creating power of Particular grace demands even the terrain of Common grace for itself, including both our bodies and the whole of the world" (*GG* II:685). Certainly there is an impulse in the direction of a higher, supernatural life, but "supernatural" does not mean "divine" in the scholastic vein.

11 Sytse U. Zuidema has noted that one can speak of "Thomism" in Kuyper to a certain degree only. It must be remembered that in Kuyper (a) the distinction between nature and the supernatural is not given with the creation but first appears in connection with God's saving work after the fall; (b) the supernatural transcends the natural forces of creation, yet not in such a way that man participates in the divine being (see preceding note); (c) the dualism of nature and the supernatural is only temporary, because in the rebirth of heaven and earth the whole of created reality will be transformed into a supernatural creation. Cf.

original. Under the names of common and particular grace, a supernaturalistic dualism is reintroduced without the question being answered whether this dualism is in harmony with the exclusivity of the reformational *sola gratia.*

The third line in Kuyper's thought is one in which the distinction between God's common grace to all and his particular grace to believers is not worked out dualistically into a doctrine of two separate terrains of life; the attempt is made, rather, to view all of created reality as an undivided whole, as such damaged by sin but at the same time placed in the light of God's gracious acts in Jesus Christ. Throughout human society, in church, state, and community, the believer is called *pro Rege*, that is, he is called to follow King Jesus. *Pro Rege* means mobilizing Christian forces for the battle against idolatrous and anti-Christian powers at work in culture. To build science on Christian principles is part of that calling. The other side of the coin is that every form of science based on, say, humanistic principles is to be opposed; demanded is a thoroughgoing antithetical attitude toward non-Christian thought.[12]

It is here, I think, that we find Kuyper's most characteristic understanding. Following Calvin and the later Augustine, he takes the blinding power of sin seriously. His view here mirrors the suspicions harbored by believers of the first centuries toward all "wisdom of the world." Since the days of the ancient Church Father Tertullian, no one, perhaps, has placed such emphasis on the contradiction between Christian belief and non-Christian thought. In the final analysis, according to Kuyper, the conflict is not between belief and science but between two beliefs (Christian and non-Christian), demanding two sciences (Christian and non-Christian):

> Not faith and science therefore, but two scientific systems or if you choose, two scientific elaborations, are opposed to each other, each having its own faith. Nor may it be said that it is here science which opposes theology, for we have to do with two absolute forms of science, both of which claim the whole domain of human knowledge. . . . [They dispute] with one another the whole domain of life. . . . (*LC* 133)

Kuyper advanced this third, antithetical line as a Calvinistic view. And so it is, as we have seen, at least to a certain degree. Remarkably though, it seems a Calvinism set to a different key. Kuyper adapts Calvin's criticism of non-Christian thought, but less so his openness toward it. The background of this divergence is probably a difference in starting point. Perhaps one could say that "the foundation of humility" on which Calvin sought to take his stand inclined him to seek out traces of God's presence even in non-Christian thought. This position of humility seems at times to have been supplanted by a position of self-confidence in Kuyper. I mean: a position in which the inclination exists to monopolize God's presence for Christian communities and Christian organizations and to interpret the world of culture and science, to the extent that it is estranged from God, exclusively in terms of human apostasy and unbelief. The doctrine of God's general grace is still defended, but mainly in this sense, that the world of philosophy and culture as such is infused with it and the faithful thus relieved of the obligation

---

Zuidema, "Common Grace and Christian Action in Abraham Kuyper," 63–64; *see supra* pages 256-57.

12 For the tendencies and tensions in Kuyper's view, see again the important article of S. U. Zuidema. See also Klapwijk, Jacob 1987. "Abraham Kuyper over wetenschap en universiteit." In *Abraham Kuyper, zijn Volksdeel, zijn Invloed.* C. Augustijn, J. H. Prins, and H. E. S Woldring, eds. Delft: Meinema, 61–94, 236–241; *see supra* Chapter18 for a revised and translated version.

of world-avoidance, since "not only *the church* but also *the world* belongs to God" (*LC* 125). Given this perspective, Christians may enter the world without feeling uneasy about doing so, as long as the objective is nothing other than to claim the world for the Lord and, as a mobilized force, to capture it from the powers of unbelief. The doctrine of common grace legitimizes in this way the doctrine of organizational antithesis, an antithesis that assumes visible form in this world. It leads not to a critical appreciation but to a complete depreciation of non-Christian thought.[13]

On this point Kuyper seems more readily comparable with the Church Father Augustine than with the Reformer Calvin. In *De civitate Dei*, Augustine, too, proceeded on the basis of a fundamental spiritual opposition in this world, i.e., between the "city of God" and "the earthly city." Augustine, too, sought to visualize this antithesis in the course of world history by relating it to two "groups" or two "communities" within the human race (XV, 1). To concretize these still further, he identifies the two communities with the Assyrian and Roman empires on the one hand (XVIII, 2) and Israel and the church on the other (XVIII, 47; XX, 20). It needs to be kept in mind, however, that Augustine often also emphasized that these two kingdoms are always commingled in world history and that – like wheat and tares at harvest – they will not be separated before the Last Judgment (XVIII, 47; *Enarratio in Psalmum* 52, 6) (cf. ch. 1.7). Also, evaluating the goods of the Roman Empire, Augustine sometimes relinquished the religious contradiction between the two kingdoms and followed the principle of an ontological hierarchy of higher and lower goods in keeping with neo-Platonic emanation theory. In that context, at least where various worldly matters are concerned, he no longer proceeded on the basis of a contradiction but of a "harmony" between the two states, whereupon it was possible for him, too, to arrive at a more positive appreciation of worldly cultural goods, including the philosophy and science of his time.[14]

6. Herman and Johan H. Bavinck

Kuyper's view did not go unopposed. Herman Bavinck, Professor of Dogmatics at the Free University, was as staunch a supporter of a Christian approach to science and philosophy as Kuyper was. Bavinck, too, put aside scholastic dualism, which denied the total corruption of human nature, including human reason. Yet Bavinck arrived at a much more moderate judgment of non-Christian thought than Kuyper did.

In the first place, Bavinck notes that the antithesis is a conflict of principles, not of persons or of organizations. He therefore cannot follow Kuyper in concluding from two kinds of principles to two kinds of people and two kinds of science. Bavinck calls that a *metabasis eis allo genos*, a shift to another category. For Bavinck, the kingdom of the Truth can no more be equated with those who are born again than the kingdom of Satan can be identified with those who are not born again; there is in fact much error

---

13 For my objections to this "organizational antithesis," see Klapwijk, Jacob 1980. "Dooyeweerd's Christian Philosophy: Antithesis and Critique." Translated by John Kok. *Reformed Journal* 30 (March): 20–24. I believe Kuyper had other, compelling motives for establishing Christian organizations, as I argued in Klapwijk, Jacob 1979. "Christelijke organisaties in verlegenheid." In *Christelijke Organisaties in Discussie*. Ed. Vereniging van Christelijke Studenten te Amsterdam (VCSA). 's-Gravenhage: Boekencentrum, 21–66.

14 Augustine, *De Civitate Dei* XIX, 17: "*Inter civitatem utramque concordia*" (between both cities there is harmony). See also Wytzes, Jelle 1938. "Eenige gedachten van Augustinus over den staat." PR 3: 36–38.

present in the one, much truth in the other.[15]

Assuming that there is a radical opposition of principle between belief and unbelief, the wellsprings of Christianity and paganism respectively, Bavinck asserts in the second place that this opposition is not exclusively antithetical. In *Gereformeerde Dogmatiek*, his major work, he writes that in the heathen religions "elements of truth" must be acknowledged. In fact, Christianity may be called the "fulfillment" of the heathen quest on the ground of God's general revelation (*GD* I:290–92).[16]

A different view of the antithesis brings with it a different view of contemporary philosophy! Bavinck, as I see it, somewhat more consistently than Kuyper, sees common grace as a source of light and truth, because to him God's general revelation continues to shine, despite everything, in a world estranged from him. For this reason Bavinck, like Calvin, can look upon current philosophy as a *praeclarum donum Dei*, an excellent gift of God (*GD* I:509).[17]

Bavinck adds something to this. He notes that Christianity did not destroy ancient civilization and philosophy but rather "Christianized" and "sanctified" them (*GD* I:577). The Church Fathers themselves, according to Bavinck, came to the view that the existing science "was neither to be utterly rejected nor wholly accepted."[18] It is clear that compared to a consistent Kuyperian view of the antithesis this line of thought must make new and different demands of a Christian philosophy. Specifically, given such openness to non-Christian thought, it requires that Christian philosophy never fall back into Scholasticism. Bavinck wanted to avoid such a relapse.

Herman Bavinck's standpoint was subsequently worked out in greater detail by Johan H. Bavinck, who was Professor of Christian Missions at the Free University after World War II. In *Religieus Besef en Christelijk Geloof* and other publications, J. H. Bavinck shows how ambiguous both non-Christian religions and non-Christian philosophies really are. On the basis of an extensive exegesis of biblical passages, especially Romans 1, Bavinck holds that two things are revealed in the non-Christian religions. First, one finds in them the self-manifestation and self-presentation of God (*RB* 113, 123). Paul states in Romans 1:20 that God has made known "his eternal power and Godhead" [KJV]; thus, there is knowledge of God among the peoples of the earth. Secondly however, there is also in these religions something that might be called the human suppression-mechanism. Knowledge of God is constantly suppressed and replaced (*RB* 128, 172). Paul writes of those "who hold the truth in unrighteousness" (Romans 1:25). In other words, it cannot be said that the thought of non-Christians is unmitigated apostasy or pure and unmixed idolatry; rather it is evident that in their very apostasy and idolatry there is a struggle going on in them with respect to the truth; they bear

15 On this *"metabasis"* see one of Herman Bavinck's lecture notebooks for 1896–97 as cited in Bremmer, Rolf H. 1961. *Herman Bavinck als Dogmaticus*. Kampen: Kok, 40. Here Bremmer deals extensively with Bavinck's assessment of Kuyper, A. 1893–1894. *Encyclopedie der Heilige Godgeleerdheid.* 3 vols. Kampen: Kok; 3rd ed. 1908–09, 37–45.

16 In connection with the tensions in Kuyper's position, compare the *Encyclopedie* III:444, with *LC* 134, where the antithesis is described as "two absolutely differing starting-points, which have nothing in common in their origin."

17 See also Bavinck, Herman 1921. *Verzamelde Opstellen op het Gebied van Godsdienst en Wetenschap.* Kampen: Kok, 53.

18 Bavinck, Herman 1904. *Christelijke Wetenschap.* Kampen: Kok; 3rd ed. 1929, 14.

witness to both the influence of and the resistance to the God who makes himself known to all people. Writes Bavinck:

> Perhaps people will say to me, "There is that most authentic "point of contact" after all, the "suppressed truth!" Or perhaps the charge made against me will be, "Here we go then, driven into psychology under full sail." To both objections I answer with a great round "No!" For this suppressed truth is not something of man's; it is there despite and against man's will. It is there because powerless man in his abominable immorality is capable of pushing God's truth aside, of banishing it, of putting it away from him, but he is never capable of destroying it without remnant. It is always there in his life as a threat, and it never lets go of him. (*RB* 175)

7. The Van Peursen–Dooyeweerd Discussion

Against the background of this sketch of Kuyper and the Bavincks, I add a comment on the discussions between the two Free University philosophers Cornelis A. van Peursen and Herman Dooyeweerd, portions of which were published in *Philosophia Reformata*.[19] Their arguments are of importance for us because one of the main points of difference between them is their evaluation of non-Christian philosophy. And, as far as I can see, this difference arises from the fact that where the principle of antithesis is concerned, Dooyeweerd is in the line primarily of Kuyper while Van Peursen's position is more like that of J. H. Bavinck.

Dooyeweerd and Van Peursen both want to give a positive evaluation of non-biblical thought. However, both the degree and the grounds of their appreciation differs considerably. Dooyeweerd holds that human thought and, hence, all rational and philosophical systems are subject to the principle of religious antithesis. Most theories are driven by an apostate religious motivation, a motivation which stands in "radical antithesis" (a term of Kuyper's) to the biblical groundmotive, that is to say, the all-embracing power of God's word as it is incarnated in Jesus Christ, the crucified and risen Lord (*PR* 25, 144ff.). Non-Christian philosophies can and ought to be appreciated only insofar as they appear to be confronted with undeniable "states of affairs which conform to the law-structures of creation." That is to say, in spite of conflicting religious starting points, Christian and non-Christian philosophers alike have to face the states of affairs which impinge upon every person within the structures of God's creation order (*PR* 25, 105ff., 150).

Van Peursen does not recognize such a divine creation order, nor does he recognize anything like "states of affairs" based on it. According to him the "affairs" are never "static;" to the contrary, they are related to the meaning-giving human subject and therefore move within patterns of human interpretation (*PR* 24, 162ff., 168). Where,

19 See: Van Peursen, Cornelius A. 1959. "Enkele Critische Vragen in Margine bij *A New Critique of Theoretical Thought*." PR 24: 160–68.
   Dooyeweerd, Herman 1960. "Van Peursen's Critische Vragen bij *A New Critique of Theoretical Thought*." *PR* 25: 97–150.
   Van Peursen, Cornelius A. 1961. "Antwoord aan Dooyeweerd." *PR* 26: 189–200.
   See also Van Peursen, Cornelius A. 1981. "Culture and Christian Faith." In Peter Blokhuis, Bastiaan Kee, Jacob H. Santema, and Egbert Schuurman, eds. *Wetenschap, wijsheid, filosoferen. Opstellen aangeboden aan Hendrik van Riessen bij zijn afscheid als hoogleraar in de wijsbegeerte aan de Vrije Universiteit te Amsterdam*. Assen: Van Gorcum, 32–37.

then, does Van Peursen find a ground for this appreciation of and communication with non-Christian thinkers? In separating faith and reason? That would be impossible, because both Dooyeweerd and Van Peursen are convinced of the impact of religion on human rationality. But for Van Peursen the religious antithesis is not as absolute as it is for Dooyeweerd. To Van Peursen the religious antithesis, God's No to sin, is preceded by a religious thesis, God's Yes to the whole of creation. In the line of the Bavincks, Van Peursen emphasizes the presence of God in our created world on the ground that God reveals himself to humans even within false religions and humanistic ideologies (*PR* 24, 168). Not in the general structures of a supposed creation order but in this general appeal of God to every human being can the real basis be found for a mutual appreciation and a rational communication between Christian and non-Christian scholars, as Van Peursen sees it (*PR* 24, 168).

8. Questions and Considerations

The controversy about "states of affairs" and "God's presence" raised many questions, the most crucial of which for the Reformed tradition would be whether an inevitable dilemma confronts us here.

Consider Dooyeweerd's point. Does he not deserve support when he speaks of incontrovertible states of affairs? Granted that humans are able to give a new meaning to certain matters and to re-interpret familiar events, it remains the case that the possibilities for doing so are always limited and never arbitrary. Human meaning-giving is always effected within the framework of divine meaning-stipulation. If God is the Creator, is he not likewise the final law-giver and meaning-giver of creation? "Lift up your eyes on high, and behold who hath created these things, that bringeth out their host by number: he calleth them all by names by the greatness of his might, for that he is strong in power; not one faileth" (Isaiah 40:26 [KJV]).

It is precisely at this point, I believe, that the great value of Kuyper's doctrine of common grace is to be found, too. With this doctrine Kuyper wanted to express the fact that in spite of human sin and self-will, God does not forsake the work of his hands. He upholds the world by his "creation ordinances" (*GG* I:243, 259). In his grace he is and he remains the sovereign law-giver and meaning-giver. Yet, as we have seen, Kuyper did not adequately stress that God does all this for the sake of Christ. Kuyper stated that the earth (common grace) bears the Cross (particular grace); he often did not see that in a deeper sense the reverse is true: the Cross bears the earth. Now, Dooyeweerd's contribution has been to re-formulate Kuyper's view of common grace on such a christocentric basis.[20] The doctrine of common grace can be kept unsoiled by the stubborn tradition of the two-realms theory on condition that it be anchored christocentrically alone. Only then, furthermore, is it able to offer the possibility of evaluating non-Christian thought correctly.[21]

---

20 See also Klapwijk, Jacob 1980. "The Struggle for a Christian Philosophy: Another Look at Dooyeweerd." Translated by John Kok. *Reformed Journal* 30 (Feb): 12–15. Dooyeweerd solves Kuyper's problem (a christocentric, yet non-ecclesiastically oriented view of culture) by making a sharp distinction between religion and faith. His view of culture and science, while religiously rooted in Christ, does not imply any direct tie with ecclesiastical articles of faith.

21 Any two-realm theory has to be rejected here. As I see it, it is necessary to realize that Christ and his redemptive grace are both present in the heart of man and revealed as the ground of culture. The same holds

Granted the truth of all this, the question still arises whether something else should not be taken into consideration as well. By that "something else" I mean the point urged by the Bavincks and Van Peursen: God's presence. The theme of God's presence is, as I see it, closely related to the question of the nature of all religion, including Christianity. No religion is comprehensible apart from the presence of God. Every religion has an "answer-structure." That is, religion is religion because and to the extent that it responds to an appeal from God, be it to God's revelation in his Word (special revelation) or to God's revelation in his works (general revelation). The answer that people give in religion is always one of either surrender or rebellion. Whatever the human response, there echoes in it always something of the original call of God.

> And they heard the voice of the LORD God walking in the garden in the cool of the day: and Adam and his wife hid themselves from the presence of the LORD God amongst the trees of the garden. And the Lord God called unto Adam, and said unto him, Where art thou? (Genesis 3:8,9 [KJV])

I think one has to grant Dooyeweerd that an apostate groundmotive is at work in non-Christian thought. It must be added, however, that this apostate motive also affects the mind of the Christian, who is likewise a sinner; and that the presence of this motive in no way contradicts the presence of God. Conversely, the apostate motive, too, is always religiously directed toward God in the sense that it is a self-willed cry against heaven, a suppressing and distorting of the Truth that confronts humans continually, rebellion notwithstanding.[22]

---

for common grace. Common grace is revealed not only in the world of culture and science (for example, in the moments of truth when pagan and secularized thought is able to give a convincing interpretation of incontrovertible "states of affairs") but also, and even in the first place, in the religion and heart of man. Calvin has already pointed to the awareness of divinity (*divinitatis sensus*) and sparks (*scintillae*) of the knowledge of God in the hearts of all men. Cf. John Calvin, *Institutes of the Christian Religion* I, 3, 3; 4, 1; 4, 4; 5, 1; 5, 14; and 11, 2, 12. Kuyper himself has said that God's common grace has checked the corruption of sin even in the heart of man. Cf. *GG* I:250.

22 As a consequence of this, non-Christian thought cannot simply be understood as Dooyeweerd would understand it, that is, in terms of apostate religious groundmotives such as form–matter, nature–freedom, and so forth. Similarly, there should be no talk, at least in the absence of further qualification, of a "radical antithesis" between religious groundmotives, as if there were a perfect parallelism involved in which non-Christian thought would flow from the apostate motives in a way strictly analogous to that in which Christian thought would flow from the "biblical groundmotive" of creation, fall, and redemption. The biblical witness to the enmity between "the seed of the woman" and "the seed of the serpent" (Genesis 3:15), between Christ and Satan, must in no way be diluted; yet the religious attitude of the non-believer can only be understood in terms of both. In other words, one can say that non-Christian thought is ruled by an apostate groundmotive (and one has to add that the Christian mind, too, never frees itself entirely of its influence), but this does not alter the fact that non-Christian thought ought to be examined precisely in its apostate groundmotives, in the overpowering light of the Christian groundmotive. Dooyeweerd touched on this problem himself when he said, "The biblical groundmotive in the revelation of the fall embraces and discloses them [i.e., the non-Christian groundmotives] in their true nature" (*PR* 25: 146). I agree with this, but I think the Christian groundmotive (I would rather say "the biblical Word-revelation") is much more sweeping and penetrating than Dooyeweerd suggests. The Word-revelation "discloses" not only through the revelation of the fall but also through the revelation of creation and the revelation of redemption: it makes clear that non-Christian thought is driven both by the power of sin and by God's revelation in creation (so that sayings of pagan sages and philosophers even appear in the Old and New Testaments), and that influence of God's revelation in creation is in its turn an expression of God's overpowering redeeming grace in Jesus Christ.

We must acknowledge that the Christian life is a mixed existence: Christian thought does not escape the blight of sin. We must likewise recognize that, thanks to God's grace, non-Christian existence is also a *mixtum*: on the plane of human rationality remarkable insights have been achieved, even though ultimately the full Truth always has been suppressed. This is why all pagan religions and every apostate ideology and theoretical system proves to be ambiguous and ambivalent. It would be incorrect to conclude from this that they turn out to be better than could have been expected (as Kuyper did); for the fact that the human lie is mixed with the divine Truth does not tend to weaken the lie, it just discloses its guilty, parasitic power. Even the lie feeds on the Truth. In its own way, it confirms the superior power of the Truth: "For we can do nothing against the truth, but for the truth" (2 Corinthians 13:8 [KJV]).[23]

In summary it can be said that, to render the ambivalent character of non-Christian thought comprehensible, it is not enough to appeal only to the personal presence of God, nor does it suffice to appeal exclusively to the structural order of creation. An exclusive appeal to the presence of God detached from recognition of the creation order will not do, if for no other reason than that God's personal self-revelation already presupposes a created order. That man is made for God – "Thou has made us for Thyself," said Augustine – is, after all, one of the creation ordinances (Genesis 1:26). Consciousness of the Godhead is written (*inscriptus*), yes, engraved (*insculptus*) in the hearts of all people, says Calvin.[24] Yet, the reverse one-sidedness must be rejected as well. An exclusive appeal to universal states of affairs in God's creation order does not work either, because it does not make clear why humans in their sinful nature should not consciously disregard or deny the facts or values of life, turning philosophy into a grandiose lie devoid of all truth.

Since the issue here is one of a controversy within the Calvinist tradition, it is relevant to cite Calvin's *Institutes* at this point:

> The final goal of the blessed life, moreover, rests in the knowledge of God. Lest anyone, then, be excluded from access to happiness, he not only sowed in men's mind that seed of religion (*religionis semen*) of which we have spoken but revealed himself and daily discloses himself in the whole workmanship of the universe. As a consequence, men cannot open their eyes without being compelled to see him. (I, 5, 1)

In a broader context Calvin makes clear that the possibility of philosophy, and of the sciences, too, depends in part on the unavoidable sense of "God's created order."[25]

It seems that it would be impossible to overemphasize the close coherence between God's action upon the human heart (general revelation) and his upholding of creation structures (common grace).[26] We cannot separate revelation and creation, because the Bible teaches that God reveals himself to us in and through the created works of his

---

23 See also Klapwijk, J. "Dooyeweerd's Christian Philosophy: Antithesis and Critique."

24 Calvin, *Institutes* I, 3, 1; 4, 4.

25 Calvin, *Institutes* I, 3, 3: "creationis lex;" 5, 5: "ordo a Deo prescriptus."

26 The relation between general revelation and common grace is continually discussed in the history of Reformed theology. However, its elaboration was often quite unsatisfactory. e.g., a falling back into the scholastic idea of a "*lumen naturale*," etc. The *Canons of Dort* III/IV are curious in this connection with their rejection of the Remonstrant doctrine of "common grace (through which they understand the light of nature)" in article 5. This is the only place in the Reformed confessions where the term "common grace" is mentioned *expressis verbis*.

hands. God's voice and the voice of the facts are indivisible. If the voice of God were no longer to be heard throughout the length and breadth of the world, the human mind would disintegrate and the facts, too, would fall still.[27]

9. Critical Transformation

At this point one might ask: granted that the Christian has good reasons for paying close attention to non-Christian thought and for appreciating positively greater or lesser parts of its contributions in science and philosophy, how can he avail himself of them in his own thought?

Any attempt to bring Christian faith and pagan or secularized ideas together in an all-embracing synthesis is misguided and leads astray, I believe. It cannot be correct to judge by the standard of Christian faith some concepts of modern or ancient philosophers to be true and therefore suitable for such a synthesis and to lay aside some others as untrue. Any such eclecticism, however often Christians may have applied it, proceeds on the basis of the false assumption that truth is divisible. When we proceed eclectically, we cannot do justice to the philosophers we use. We detach the conceptions from the person who advanced them. We divorce from the thinkers ideas that they have forged into a unity and that they experience or once experienced as a result of their personal struggle, as the way to deeper insight, as a window through which the light of the Truth might fall. Most importantly, eclecticism ignores what Kuyper rediscovered: the biblical antithesis between the "wisdom of this world" and the "wisdom of God" (1 Corinthians 1:18–25).

In other words, the value of non-Christian thought for the Christian cannot be done justice through a procedure of synthesizing and eclecticism. It can be done justice, as I see it, only in a process of critical *appropriation through transformation.* Let me try to be as concrete as possible by referring to a favorite theme of Augustine and other Church Fathers – Origen for example – namely, the theme of "despoliation," or plundering. The Church Fathers recalled how the children of Israel were asked to despoil the Egyptians of their cultural treasures, their silver and gold, when they left the land (Exodus 12:35, 36: ". . . and they borrowed of the Egyptians jewels of silver, and jewels of gold, and raiment. . . . And they spoiled the Egyptians"). As the Israelites made use of the treasures of Egypt, so, the Church Fathers believed, were they justified in making use of the cultural treasures of the classical world, including its philosophy.[28]

I think that in principle this despoliation theme yields a useful analogy to what can be done with non-Christian ideas and insights. Yet the Church Fathers did not always have sharply in view (a) that the Israelites were called to take the gold and the silver of Egypt and to use these valuables for the "work of the tabernacle" and the "service of the sanctuary" (Exodus 35:21; 36:1); and (b) that these treasures had to be smelted and refined before they could be used as vessels in the service of God. What I mean to say is that, thanks to God's universal creation order and to his universal self-presentation within it, the philosophies – not to mention the sciences – of the day can be viewed in certain respects as excellent gifts of the Spirit of God, and that to that extent they can be used by Christians. On two conditions:

---

27 Calvin, *Institutes* I, 3, 3.
28 See Augustine, *De doctrina christiana* II, 40, 60; cf. *Confessiones* VII, ix, 15.

(1) *Critical appropriation or integration.* Knowledge and wisdom, wherever we may find it, will have to be taken up into the service of the Lord. In other words, the purpose can never be simply to adopt the valuable insights of non-Christian thinkers or to accommodate them in some way to the content of the Christian faith. That would amount to either eclecticism or Scholasticism. No, if we think it possible to make use of the chattels of non-Christian thought – the Egyptians' silver and gold, much of it useful, some of it excrescent – then this is only permissible, I think, to the extent that we are in a position to really integrate it into a Christian, God-directed view of life.

(2) *Transformation.* The integration of non-Christian thought into the Christian view of life can never take place in the absence of far-reaching changes. The insights of philosophy and even, I think, of science in general, function in the framework of a total view of life, in a *Weltanschauung* that is religiously charged and that I would call an ideology to the extent that it is in conflict with the gospel of Jesus Christ. It is therefore necessary for the Christian thinker to take the ideas he borrows from others and smelt and refine them. At the very least, he must pry them loose from their ideological context. The Christian philosopher should engage in communication and discussion with non-Christian thinkers, and yet must always disentangle their insights from the ideological connections present in their minds and perhaps present in his or her own mind as well – the connections which lead people to resist and suppress the truth of God. Christian philosophers must take these insights and critically transform them. In short, they must take the gold that comes *from God* and consecrate it again *to God.*

When the apostle Paul spoke of non-Christian thought, he had in view, I suggest, a similar process of rejection and appropriation, of criticism and transformation: "We destroy arguments and every proud obstacle to the knowledge of God, and take every thought captive to obey Christ" (2 Corinthians 10:4–5 [NRSV]). On the basis of the Christian faith, it is simply not possible to accept in part and to reject in part either ancient, pagan philosophy or modern, secularized thought. From the Reformed perspective it is appropriate to plead for the reformation of philosophy itself. But the reformation of philosophy is never possible without communication with dissenters. Such a communication means transformation after the model of the Israelites. Thus, a program for a reformation of philosophy is at the same time a call for an on-going transformation of philosophy.

21

Common Grace or the Antithesis? Towards a Consistent Understanding of Kuyper's "Sphere Sovereignty"

Tim McConnel

Introduction

When Abraham Kuyper presented his seminal speech on "Sphere Sovereignty"[1] at the founding of the Free University of Amsterdam, he used his key phrase in two different ways. The first usage of "sphere sovereignty" referred to the different spheres or areas of life, which are free to develop within their own bounds, following their own God-given laws. These spheres, such as the family, education, the state, and the church, were derived from the structure of human life in the creational order. The second usage, later in the speech, referred to the freedom for different philosophies or "life-principles" to develop across the whole "sphere" of thought. This usage was based on the conflict Kuyper perceived between the different ideological groups within society. Was Kuyper confused and inconsistent in this presentation? Was his approach contradictory at the core? Or did this twofold development of his theme, admittedly in very different senses, reveal an underlying unity in his thought that spanned his lengthy, illustrious career?

In his excellent study on Abraham Kuyper entitled *Creating a Christian Worldview: Abraham Kuyper's Lectures on Calvinism*, Peter S. Heslam argues the following:

> It should be pointed out here that this secondary meaning of the concept of sphere-sovereignty was incompatible with the first. . . . The contention of this book is that the same confusion amounted to two usages, one creational and the other socio-ideological; that the two were irreconcilable with each other; and that this double usage is likely to have served as a stimulus to the development of *verzuiling* in Dutch society.[2]

---

1 Kuyper, Abraham 1880. *Souvereiniteit in Eigen Kring: Rede ter inwijding van de Vrije Universiteit, den 20sten October 1880 gehouden, in het Koor der Nieuwe Kerk te Amsterdam*. Amsterdam: J. H. Kruyt. This work was republished in de Gaay Fortman, W. F. ed. 1956. *Architectonische critiek: Fragmenten uit de sociaal-politieke geschriften van Dr. A. Kuyper*. Amsterdam: H. J. Paris. A slightly abridged translation by George Kamp, edited by James D. Bratt, appears as "Sphere Sovereignty" in *AK:ACR*—referenced in what follows as *SS*.

2 Heslam, Peter S. 1998. *Creating a Christian Worldview: Abraham Kuyper's Lectures on Calvinism*. Grand Rapids: Eerdmans, 160. *Verzuiling*, or "pillarization," was a practice during the earlier part of the twentieth century in the Netherlands of the ideological grouping of society, including Catholics, Calvinists, socialists, etc. Each group developed on its own such institutions as schools, newspapers, and labor unions. This is one approach to coexistence within a pluralistic society.

Heslam claims to be following Herman Dooyeweerd's critique in this problem in Kuyper.[3] William Edgar, in his review of Heslam's work, seems to agree, and if anything states it more strongly when he summarizes Heslam's thinking:

> Heslam's point is that there was confusion in Kuyper's writings between at least two notions of the spheres, one from the Creation, the other an organic social or ideological grouping. Though contradictory, the double usage is the key to the later development of *verzuiling* in Dutch society.[4]

However, as James D. Bratt points out in his introductory remarks to Kuyper's essay "Sphere Sovereignty," there seems to be a studied ambiguity in the Dutch term itself, pointing to its application in both senses, as Kuyper did within the essay.[5] The two usages do not function as an exact parallel, as the first refers to God's creation and the second to the working out of human sinfulness and redemption in society, as Heslam and Edgar note. Nevertheless, it is the contention of this paper that the two usages do not display a confusion in Kuyper's thought but an application of his tension between common grace and the antithesis, and thus demonstrate his ability to hold them in balance – something many of his followers have had trouble doing. Sphere sovereignty as a notion is distinct from common grace and the antithesis, but Kuyper's twofold exposition of it in his speech in 1880 is consistent with his later developments of these themes. As each are explained in turn below, it will become clear that the two usages are neither confused nor contradictory, but consistently fit together in Kuyper's thought.

Sphere Sovereignty

The notion of sphere sovereignty was developed early by Kuyper as the justification for his political and educational endeavors. The definitive statement of his view was given in the speech he delivered at the founding of the Free University of Amsterdam, on October 20, 1880. It was published at the same time as *Souvereiniteit in Eigen Kring*. The title translated literally is "Sovereignty in Its Own Circle." As mentioned above, Bratt suggests that the very title points to an ambiguity in Kuyper's thought and use of the term. On the one hand, the first usage of the term "circle" refers to the different spheres of human life, such as art, education, the family, the church, the slate, etc. Kuyper viewed each of these as answering directly to God as a result of creation. In this view, the differences between the spheres are ontological in nature, and each sphere displays development due to God's "common grace." On the other hand, the second usage of the term is that the various "circles" refer to those who hold differing worldviews. This second approach would divide each sphere of human life into two or more partitions. Each worldview "circle," according to Kuyper, must be given the freedom to work out its own principles in every area of life.

In this second usage, the differences are ethical and epistemological, and they express the working out of the antithesis. The first usage generally dominated Kuyper's thought regarding sphere sovereignty, but the latter usage is also clearly there, as will be shown below.

---

3   Ibid., 160.

4   Edgar, William 1998. Review of *Creating a Christian Worldview: Abraham Kuyper's Lectures on Calvinism* by Peter S. Heslam. *Westminster Theological Journal* 60: 356.

5   Introduction to "Sphere Sovereignty." In *AK:ACR* 461–462. Bratt suggests applying Heidegger's twofold division of "Being and Time" to Kuyper's two usages.

Kuyper located the origin of sphere sovereignty in the sovereignty of God, who established each of the various spheres of life:

> This perfect sovereignty of the *sinless* Messiah at the same time directly denies and challenges all absolute Sovereignty among *sinful* men on earth, and does so by dividing life into *separate spheres*, each with its own sovereignty.
>
> . . . Just as we speak of a "moral world," a "scientific world," a "business world," the "world of art," so we can more properly speak of a "sphere" of morality, of the family, of social life, each with its own *domain*. And because each comprises its own domain, each has its own Sovereign within its bounds. (*SS* 467)

Kuyper saw a multitude of divinely established, intermeshing spheres as comprising the complexity of human life. The State had a special function of protecting individuals and of defining the relationships among the various other spheres; but its role was to acknowledge the authority of other spheres, not to confer authority upon them.[6] In Kuyper's view, the only safeguard for freedom was to submit to the sovereignty of God in every area. This submission would prevent the State from claiming supreme sovereignty, which is its sinful tendency. For Kuyper, the totalitarian state was the natural outworking of the principles of the "Revolution." The followers of the "Revolution" were those who rejected revelation and replaced it with the autonomy of human thought, as typified for Kuyper by the French Revolution. This opposing principle saw the highest sovereignty as embodied in the supreme State, the final authority for all other spheres of life.

The last section of his speech, in which he focused on sphere sovereignty "As a Reformed Principle," developed the second usage of Kuyper's notion. In it he argued for the necessity of a university founded on Reformed principles that would be able to develop freely those principles. He based this argument on the subjective character of knowledge, and argued, as in his later writings on the antithesis, that the Christian principle affects every area of scholarship:

> I readily grant that if our natural sciences strictly limited themselves to weighing and measuring, the wedge of principle would not be at the door. But who would do that? What natural scientist operates without a hypothesis? Does not everyone who practices science as a *man* and not as a *measuring stick* view things through a subjective lens and always filling the unseen part of the circle according to subjective opinion? (*SS* 487–88)

The inevitable "subjective opinion" to which Kuyper refers he would later call the conflict in "worldviews." Thus, he argued that in scholarship there must be freedom for each group or circle to work out its own principle. Kuyper goes on to claim the following:

> Rather, considering that something begins from principle and that a distinct entity takes rise from a distinct principle, we shall maintain a distinct sovereignty for our own principle and for that of our opponents across the whole sphere of thought. That is to say, as from their principle and by a method appropriate to it they erect a house of knowledge that glitters but does not entice us, so we too form our principle and by its corresponding method will let our own trunk shoot up whose branches, leaves, and blossom are nourished with its own sap. (*SS* 484–85)

---

6   In the immediate application of sphere sovereignty to his historical situation, Kuyper was justifying the founding of a "Free University"; that is, one that was free from state control. Freedom to do so had just recently been granted in the Netherlands, and was one of Kuyper's early political goals. Thus, the sphere of education and scholarship was fundamentally independent of the state in Kuyper's view, and could not legitimately be made to serve state purposes of an ideological nature.

Note that while Kuyper was arguing for the right of Calvinists to establish their own educational institution on the basis of sphere sovereignty, he was also safeguarding the right of his opponents to do the same. In effect, in his development of the second usage of sphere sovereignty, Kuyper argued for a pluralism without succumbing to a notion of ethical or epistemological relativism.

As he came near to the end of this seminal speech, Kuyper sounded the cry for action in terms that recalled his emphasis on the antithesis, but especially sounded the note so dear to his Calvinist heritage, that of the sovereignty of Christ:

> How could it be otherwise? Man in his antithesis as fallen *sinner* or self-developing *natural creature* returns again as the "subject that thinks" or "the object that prompts thought" in every department, in every discipline, and with every investigator. Oh, no single piece of our mental world is to be hermetically sealed off from the rest, and there is not a square inch in the whole domain of our human existence over which Christ, who is Sovereign over *all*, does not cry: "Mine!" (*SS* 488)

These words were a call for the Christian to social and academic engagement, not withdrawal from the world. This call recognizes the sovereignty of Christ over every area of human endeavor, reflecting Kuyper's first usage of sphere sovereignty, but it also indicates the need to subject oneself to Christ in these cultural endeavors, which, in the "antithesis as fallen sinner," necessitates his second usage. It also underscores the fact that Kuyper was seeking both to confirm and to build on the Reformed heritage, to extend it in the face of the circumstances of the modern world.[7]

The Antithesis

The term *antithesis* had been popularized in nineteenth-century philosophy by Hegel's use of it. Kuyper took over the term, but gave it his own specific meaning. He also developed his notion of the antithesis in terms of a Christian worldview, as opposed to a non-Christian worldview.[8]

The classic exposition of Kuyper's notion of the antithesis occurs in his *Principles of Sacred Theology* (volume two of the *Encyclopaedie der Heilige Godgeleerdheid*).[9] He outlines

7 Spykman, Gordon J. 1976. "Sphere Sovereignty in Calvin and the Calvinist Tradition." In *Exploring the Heritage of John Calvin: Essays in Honor of John Bratt*. David E. Holwerda, ed. Grand Rapids: Baker, argues that the notion of sphere sovereignty finds its beginnings in Calvin, who left it as an undeveloped idea, and has been extended by subsequent Reformed theologians, including Kuyper and Bavinck, but also their successors, including H. Dooyeweerd. Spykman wrote, "What was left to later Calvinists was to take the germinal principle of sphere-sovereignty in Calvin, delineate it more clearly with respect to church and state, and then to extend it to the other spheres in society as one by one they came to the fore in more clearly differentiated ways: commerce, for example, arising from modem capitalism; labor unions, emerging from the Industrial Revolution; modern universities, resulting largely from the scientific explosion" (194). Spykman does a good job of addressing the historical development of the first usage of Kuyper's thought regarding sphere sovereignty, but does not deal with the second.

8 The Dutch term *wereldbeschouwing* (*Weltanschauung* in German) has no exact English equivalent, though the term "worldview" has become common since Kuyper's day. Early translators often used the cumbersome "life-and-worldview" or "life-system" when they did not want to bring over the Dutch or German term into popular discussion. The notion of the contrast between the Christian view and non-Christian view has a long pedigree in theology, dating at least as far back as Augustine's massive study on the *City of God*.

9 Kuyper, Abraham 1894. *Encyclopaedie der Heilige Godgeleerdheid*, 3 vol. Amsterdam: J. A. Wormser. Volume 1, Part 1, and Volume 2 were translated by J. Hendrik de Vries as *Principles of Sacred Theology* (*PST*).

the application of the antithesis to worldviews in his *Lectures on Calvinism*.

Kuyper began developing his notion of the antithesis in the second part of the *Principles of Sacred Theology*, entitled "The Organism of Science," specifically in his discussion of "Science Impaired by Sin."[10] Here he identified a number of ways in which sin interferes with the pursuit of any science, resulting in falsehood, mistakes, and self-deceit. "The chiefest harm," he writes,

> is the ruin, worked by sin, in those data, which were at our command, for obtaining the knowledge of God, and thus for forming the conception of the whole. Without the sense of God in the heart no one shall ever attain unto a knowledge of God, and without love, or, if you please, a holy sympathy for God, that knowledge shall never be rich in content. Every effort to prove the existence of God by so-called evidence must fail and has failed. By this we do not mean that the knowledge of God must be mystic; for as soon as this knowledge of God is to be scientifically unfolded, it must be reproduced from our thinking consciousness. But as our science in no single instance can take one forward step, except a bridge is built between the subject and the object, it cannot do so here. If thus in our sense of self there is no sense of the existence of God, and if in our spiritual existence there is no bond which draws us to God, and causes us in love to go out unto him, all science is here impossible. (*PST* 112–113)

This quote contains the basic thrust of Kuyper's notion of the antithesis. He distinguished between those who can and those who cannot obtain a true knowledge of God. There must be a spiritual bond with God in order to have knowledge of God; and not everyone has this bond. His argument also reveals his own attitude towards a traditional apologetic based on proofs for the existence of God. Kuyper simply states that they fail, and furthermore implies that the one who lacks any sense of God will simply reject such proofs.

Kuyper went on to connect this failure in the knowledge of God with failure in the knowledge of the cosmos as a whole. He argued that in order to answer basic questions about the cosmos as a whole, such as its origin and end, "in your consciousness you must step out from the cosmos, and you must have a starting-point . . . in the non-cosmos; and this is altogether impossible as long as sin confines you with your consciousness to the cosmos."[11] Kuyper found the starting point he needed in God's revelation.

What did a starting point mean for the attainment of truth? In his section on "Truth," Kuyper introduces the terms "antithesis" and "worldview" into his argument. Here he distinguishes between mere observation in the "domain of pure matter" and the "domain of the real spiritual sciences," the latter of which he thought had shown very little agreement or unity in results. He explains this fact in the following way:

> Because here the subjective factor becomes preponderant; and this subjective factor is dependent upon the antithesis between falsehood and truth; so that both the insight into the facts and the structure which one builds upon this insight must differ, and at length become, first contrary and then contradictory.
>
> The fatality of the antithesis between falsehood and truth consists in this, that every man from his point of view claims the truth for himself, and applies the epithet of "untrue" to

---

10 This is the first part of volume two in the Encyclopaedie. Kuyper used "science" (*wetenschap*) broadly, as the equivalent to the German *Wissenschaft*. For an examination of Kuyper's use of the image of "organism," see Veling, K. 1984. "Kuypers Visie op de Wetenschap als Organisme: Kanttekeningen bij een Metafoor," in *Bezield Verband*. Kampen: Van den Berg.

11 *PST* 113. This argument would seem to be applied to the materialistic scientific positivists who were beginning to gain influence in the late nineteenth century.

everything that opposes this. (*PST* 117)

According to Kuyper this conflict explains the development of opposing schools of thought:

> If this concerns a mere point of detail, it has no further results; but if this antithesis assumes a more universal and radical character, school will form itself against school, system against system, worldview against worldview, and two entirely different and mutually exclusive representations of the object, each in organic relation, will come at length to dominate whole series of subjects. From both sides it is said: "Truth is with us, and falsehood is with you." And the notion that science can settle this dispute is of course entirely vain, for we speak of two all-embracing representations of the object, both of which have been obtained as the result of very serious scientific study. (*PST* 117–118)

Note that Kuyper here connects the "antithesis" between truth and falsehood with a difference in "worldviews." He recognizes the inevitability of a subjective factor in knowledge, and thus even the desirability of dealing with that factor; yet he also insists that in a fallen world, sin prevents the possibility of a general agreement, due to that subjective factor.

Kuyper spells out both the basis and the results of the antithesis in the area of knowledge through his analysis of "The Twofold Development of Science." Beginning with the notion that there are "Two Kinds of People," he argues that the unity of the human consciousness is broken by the fact of regeneration. He concludes the following:

> We speak none too emphatically, therefore, when we speak of two kinds of people. Both are human, but one is inwardly different from the other, and consequently feels a different content rising from his consciousness; thus they face the cosmos from different points of view, and are impelled by different impulses. And the fact that there are two kinds of people occasions of necessity the fact of two kinds of human life and consciousness of life, and of two kinds of science; for which reason the idea of the unity of science, taken in its absolute sense, implies the denial of the fact of palingenesis,[12] and therefore from principle leads to the rejection of the Christian religion.[13]

For Kuyper, to deny this distinction in fact proves it, as the denial involves the rejection of the Christian religion, a rejection which is the operating principle of unregenerate humanity!

The "Two Kinds of Science" thus results directly from the two kinds of people. Kuyper clearly states that he does not mean that there are two different "representations of the cosmos" that are equally valid. Ultimately, only one can be true, and thus the other must be false. He explains the difference in this way:

> But however much they may be doing the same thing formally, their activities run in opposite directions, because they have different starting-points; and because of the difference in their

---

12 Note that Kuyper often transliterated the Greek term παλιγγενεσία (Dutch, "*palingenesie*," English, "palingenesis") rather than using the Dutch term "*wedergeboorte*" (English "regeneration"). This practice will be followed in the paper, since Kuyper's notion is somewhat different from the common evangelical usage that restricts regeneration to what Kuyper calls conversion.

13 *PST* 154. A significant aspect of Kuyper's thought is revealed in this section. He argued that the subject of scientific endeavor is, properly speaking, the general human consciousness, and not particular individual scientists. Thus the idea that there is an antithesis between the regenerate and the unregenerate consciousness takes on a greater significance than that of individuals, but sharpens the cleavage within humanity as a whole. This approach to the problem reveals the degree to which Kuyper was influenced by nineteenth century idealistic thought.

nature they apply themselves differently to this work, and view things in a different way. Because they themselves are differently constituted, they see a corresponding difference in the constitution of all things. They are not at work, therefore, on different parts of the same house, but each builds a house of his own. (*PST* 155)

Kuyper goes on to say that, while the builders of each house can recognize the "scientific character" of the other's efforts, they are bound by their own principles to reject the other's work as false.

However, Kuyper immediately mitigates this stark contrast by giving several reasons why this division has often not been apparent. First, he distinguishes between the "natural" and the "spiritual"[14] sciences. The beginnings of the former consist of observation and the operations of weighing, measuring, and counting:

> The entire domain of the more primary observation, which limits itself to weights, measures and numbers, is common to both. The entire empiric investigation of the things that are perceptible to our sense (simple or reinforced) has nothing to do with the radical difference which separates the two groups. By this we do not mean, that the natural sciences as such and in their entirety, fall outside of this difference, but only that in these sciences the differences which separate the two groups exert no influence on the beginnings of the investigation. (*PST* 157)

Thus Kuyper claims a large "common realm" that both kinds of science share, in the area of empirical observation. Regeneration does not give new sense organs or change the ones which all people share in common. He also recognizes a common realm in the "spiritual sciences" as well, using examples from history and the study of language (*PST* 159). In general, Kuyper recognizes a more "objective" area of study in all sciences, in which the fact of *palingenesis* plays no discernible role.

Kuyper also sees logic as part of the common realm of the two kinds of science. He argues that the "formal process" of thought has not been attacked by sin and thus is shared by both kinds of people. While the starting point, and therefore the conclusions, are radically different, the reasoning process remains the same. Thus, each side can understand and follow the demonstration of the other. As Kuyper puts it,

> . . . the accuracy of one another's demonstrations can be critically examined and verified, in so far at least as the result strictly depends upon the deduction made. By keeping a sharp watch upon each other, mutual service is rendered in the discovery of logical faults in each other's demonstrations, and thus in a formal way each will continually watch over the other. (*PST* 160)

He concludes that, in spite of the inevitability and irreconcilability of the divergence between the two kinds of science, there is some common task to almost every form of science and that both sides are able to give a clear account of their starting point.

Another reason for continued agreement between the two kinds of science, according to Kuyper, is the fact that palingenesis is a slow process that begins with repentance and conversion and continues to develop over a person's lifetime. The fact and effects of sin remain with the regenerate so that they continue to experience a false "unity" with the

---

14 The Dutch "*geestelijk*" (like the German "*geistig*") has no English equivalent; it can refer to either spiritual, mental, or intellectual, corresponding to the noun form "*geest*" (German "*Geist*"), which can mean spirit, mind, or intellect. The ambiguity in use can be intentional, making a translation difficult.

unregenerate in any number of areas in science.[15] However, Kuyper expected the separation of the two kinds of science to continue and to become more pronounced as the various sciences progressed. The previous unity had been only apparent. He argues the point in these terms:

> Neither the tardiness, however, of the establishment of this bifurcation of science, nor the futile effort of Conservatism to prolong its existence, can resist the continuous separation of these two kinds of science. The all-decisive question here is whether there are two points of departure. If this is not the case, then unity must be maintained by means of the stronger mastering the weaker; but if there are two points of departure, then the claim of two kinds of science in the indicated sense remains indisputably valid, entirely apart from the question whether both will succeed in developing themselves for any good result within a given time. This twofold point of departure is certainly given by palingenesis. (*PST* 167–168)

Kuyper pointed to the universities at Brussels, Louvain, Amsterdam (his own institution), and Freiburg as the places where an attempt was being made to develop science on a consistently Christian basis.

At this point in his argument, Kuyper emphasizes the subjective aspect of knowledge. In this regard, he writes the following:

> In the abstract every one concedes that the subjective assimilation of the truth concerning the object cannot be the same with all, because the investigating individuals are not as alike as drops of water, but as unlike as blades of grass and leaves on a tree. That a science should be free from the influence of the subjective factor is inconceivable, hence with the unlikeness of the individuals the influence of this factor must appear.[16]

In as much as regeneration affects human consciousness at its deepest level, and in every aspect, Kuyper regards it as the fundamental dividing point for human consciousness and hence for science.

Kuyper admits that as soon as the two kinds of science developed separate results, they would no longer acknowledge the other side as being science, but rather as being "science falsely so called." He puts it this way:

> So far, on the other hand, as the antithesis between our human personality, as it manifests itself in sinful nature and is changed by palingenesis, governs the investigation and demonstration, we stand exclusively opposed to one another, and one must call *falsehood* what the other calls *truth*. (*PST* 177)

The existence of two kinds of science does not mean, therefore, that the different sides recognize each other as valid. They may have a "formal" appreciation for the other science, but can only accept as true what is in accord with their own premises. Kuyper also explains that neither side has unity in its own development, due to the subjective factor. Rather, both kinds have experienced the development of numerous schools of thought in the various

---

15 Kuyper also noted another, historical cause for the apparent unity of the two kinds of science, in that both kinds of science for several centuries operated under an outer conformity to special revelation, although the unregenerate never assimilated its point of view.

16 *PST* 169. Kuyper went on to make reference again to the "universal human consciousness" as being the "subject" of science. "For this reason science in its absolute sense is the property of no single individual. The universal human consciousness in its richest unfoldings is and ever will be the subject of science, and individuals in their circle and age can never be anything but sharers of a small division of science in a given form and seen in a given light" (*PST* 169).

sciences. However, he does not consider this development to be necessarily negative, as this is the process by which science advances.

Kuyper's conclusion on the impact of the antithesis on knowledge is that Christian and naturalistic science not only operate with different theologies, but develop different *sciences*.

> The proposition, that in virtue of the fact of palingenesis a science develops itself by the side of the naturalistic, which, though formally allied to it, is differently disposed, and therefore different in its conclusions, and stands over against it as *Christian* science, must not be understood in a specifically theological, but in an absolutely *universal* sense. The difference between the two is not merely apparent in theological science, but in *all* the sciences, in so far as the fact of palingenesis governs the *whole* subject in *all* investigations, and hence also, the result of all these investigations as far as their data are not absolutely material. (*PST* 181)

Naturalistic science and Christian science each claim to be true whereas the other is false; they are formally similar, but operate on different premises and hence reach different conclusions. The divergence between the two is not limited to theology but extends to every area of human knowledge, inasmuch as the knowing subject is either regenerate or unregenerate.

Kuyper's division between Christian and naturalistic science is consistent with his second usage of "sphere sovereignty." Both types of science demand the freedom to be developed from their own controlling principles and should be allowed to do so.

Worldviews as an Expression of the Antithesis

Kuyper went on to develop his notion of sphere sovereignty and antithesis further into a Christian worldview. He did so especially in his initial Stone Foundation Lecture, delivered at Princeton Theological Seminary in 1898, where he urged that Calvinism be understood as a whole "life-system" that included politics, science, art, and theology.[17]

Early in the first lecture, Kuyper alludes to his Anti-Revolutionary background by raising the specter of Modernism in its fullest sense, not restricting it to the theological realm as he had earlier in his career.[18] Now he links it directly to the French Revolution:

> But, in deadly opposition to this Christian element, against the very Christian name, and against its salutiferous influence in every sphere of life, the storm of Modernism has now arisen with violent intensity. In 1789 the turning point was reached. (*LC* 10)

Thus Kuyper points to the ideology of the Revolution as being directed against Christianity. He goes on to say, "There is no doubt then that Christianity is imperiled by great and serious dangers. Two life-systems are wrestling with one another, in mortal combat" (*LC*

---

17 The 1931 edition of *LC* is more readily available than the original 1898 one published in Amsterdam. While Kuyper himself did not translate his Dutch original into English, he played an active role in editing the English translation before its publication. It is his only work that was originally published in English, although later it was published in Dutch. The six lectures are entitled: "Calvinism a Life-system," "Calvinism and Religion," "Calvinism and Politics," "Calvinism and Science," "Calvinism and Art," and "Calvinism and the Future." A recent work that gives an extensive background on Kuyper by a thorough, historically grounded exposition of his Stone Lectures is Heslam, *Creating a Christian Worldview*.

18 See Kuyper, Abraham 1906. "A Fata Morgana." *Methodist Review* 88: 185–208, 355–378. A more recent translation appears in *AK:ACR* 87–124, as "Modernism: A Fata Morgana in the Christian Domain." The original was published as *Het Modernisme, een Fata Morgana op christelijk gebied*. Amsterdam: H. de Hoogh, 1871, from a lecture delivered on 14 April 1871 in Amsterdam.

11). In a footnote, Kuyper explains his use of the term "life systems" thus:

> As Dr. James Orr . . . observes, the German technical term *Weltanschauung* has no precise
> equivalent in English. He therefore used the literal translation *view of the world*, notwithstanding
> this phrase in English is limited by associations, which connect it predominatingly with
> *physical* nature. For this reason the more explicit phrase: *life and world view* seems to be more
> preferable. My American friends, however, told me that the shorter phrase: *life system*, on the
> other side of the ocean, is often used in the same sense.[19]

At that time, the English term "worldview" had not yet come into general acceptance.
Kuyper clearly intended his use of the term "life system" to include the broadest view of
reality, which undergirds all other beliefs and actions. He expresses himself in this way:

> From the first, therefore, I have always said to myself, – "If the battle is to be fought with
> honor and with a hope of victory, then *principle* must be arrayed against *principle*; then it must
> be felt that in Modernism the vast energy of an all-embracing *life-system* assails us, then also it
> must be understood that we have to take our stand in a life-system of equally comprehensive
> and far-reaching power. And this powerful life-system is not to be invented nor formulated
> by ourselves, but is to be taken and applied as it presents itself in history. When thus taken,
> I found and confessed, and I still hold, that this manifestation of the Christian principle is
> given us in *Calvinism*." (*LC* 11–12)

While Kuyper's opening mentions just two worldviews as being in conflict, the later
parts of the chapter refer to numerous other worldviews: Romanism and Lutheranism
as other Christian worldviews, as well as Islamism and Paganism as other non-Christian
worldviews. Kuyper views Calvinism as the purest manifestation of the Christian principle,
and also considered Modernism to be the chief threat to Christianity in Europe and
America. Although recognizing a greater complexity to the world, Kuyper epitomizes the
contemporary antithesis as a battle between the systems of Modernism and Calvinism.[20]

Kuyper considers one's understanding of three key relationships as essential for a
general system of life. These include "(1) our relation *to God*, (2) our relation *to man*,
and (3) our relation to the *world*" (*LC* 19). After discussing the various ways in which
these relationships have been developed in different worldviews, Kuyper concludes that
Calvinism offers a distinct view on each of these points:

> Thus it is shown that Calvinism has a sharply-defined starting-point of its own for the

---

19 *LC* 11, fn 1. See Orr, James 1897. *The Christian View of God and the World as Centering in the Incarnation, Being the Kerr Lectures for 1890–91*. Grand Rapids: Eerdmans [1948], 3. Heslam writes of Kuyper, "Despite the existence of certain elements of this concept [i.e., worldview] in his earlier work, it was not until the Stone Lectures that he employed it in a deliberate and specific way, defining it in terms of Weltanschauung and using it to give shape to his entire body of thought" (92). Heslam goes on to attribute this change to Kuyper's encounter with James Orr's Kerr *Lectures, The Christian View of God and the World*. Heslam concludes, "The only significant difference between Orr's intention and that of Kuyper in presenting Calvinism as an independent and coherent worldview resistant to modernism, was that Orr pleaded the merits of a Christian worldview while Kuyper pleaded a specifically Calvinistic one – albeit Calvinistic in the broadest possible sense" (95)

20 At this point Kuyper did not follow the lead of Orr, who gave his taxonomy of worldviews in note B to Lecture I, Christian View, 367–370. There Orr gave one classification as 1) Phenomenalistic and Agnostic; 2) Atomistic and Materialistic; 3) Pantheistic; and 4) Theistic. He gave a second classification as 1) Scientific; 2) Philosophical; and 3) Religious. He admitted that the different types influence each other, so that in practice there are none free from outside influences. However, Orr's primary interest, like Kuyper's, was in the religious worldview, especially that of Christianity in opposition to modern worldviews.

> three fundamental relations of all human existence: viz., our relation to *God*, to *man* and to the *world*. For our relation to God: an immediate fellowship of man with the Eternal, independently of priest or church. For the relation of man *to man*: the recognition in each person of human worth, which is his by virtue of his creation after the Divine likeness, and therefore of the equality of all men before God and his magistrate. And for our relation to the *world*: the recognition that in the whole world the curse is restrained by grace, that the life of the world is to be honored in its independence, and that we must, in every domain, discover the treasures and develop the potencies hidden by God in nature and in human life. (*LC* 31)

This last relationship points us to the next aspect of Kuyper's thought, that of the doctrine of common grace, as well as back to his notion of sphere sovereignty.

In his last Stone Lecture, dealing with "Calvinism and the Future," Kuyper gave this charge to his Princeton audience:

> With such a coherent world and life-view, firmly resting on its principle and self-consistent in its splendid structure, Modernism now confronts Christianity; and against this deadly danger, ye, Christians, cannot successfully defend your sanctuary, but by placing, in opposition to all this, *a life- and world view of your own, founded as firmly on the base of your own principle, wrought out with the same clearness and glittering in an equally logical consistency.* (*LC* 189–190)

Thus Kuyper sought to respond to the challenge of Modernism by using modern means, namely the development of a consistent, self-conscious worldview based on the traditional Christian beliefs of orthodox Calvinism. His development of a "worldview" analysis had by this time replaced Kuyper's earlier second usage of the notion of "sphere sovereignty," while maintaining the same distinction between opposing systems of thought across the various spheres of human life.

Common Grace

Kuyper's notion of common grace underlay his positive, world-engaging approach to Calvinism in the Stone Lectures. He developed this notion over a period of years, 1895 to 1901, in his weekly columns in *De Heraut* (The Herald). These were later collected and published in three volumes as *De Gemeene Gratie* (Common Grace).[21] In his chapter on "The Forms of Grace," Kuyper distinguishes two basic forms: special grace, which is saving grace, and common grace, which is extended to all aspects of life. He writes:

> For this reason we must distinguish two dimensions in this manifestation of grace: 1. A saving grace, which in the end abolishes sin and completely undoes its consequences; and 2. A temporal restraining grace, which holds back and blocks the effect of sin. The former, that is saving grace, is in the. nature of the case special and restricted to God's elect. The second, common grace, is extended to the whole of our human life. (*CG* 168)

---

21 Kuyper, Abraham 1902–1904. *De Gemeene Gratie*, 3 volumes. Amsterdam: Höveker & Wormser. For background, see the introduction (*CG* 165–166) to John Vriend's translation of "Common Grace" in *AK:ACR*—referenced below as *CG*. Kuyper's doctrine of common grace has generated a great deal of controversy, including a denominational split in the 1920s, when Herman Hoeksema and others who denied the doctrine left the Christian Reformed Church to start the Protestant Reformed Church. For the debates over common grace, see Van Til, Cornelius 1972. *Common Grace and the Gospel*. Phillipsburg: Presbyterian and Reformed; this includes the text of his 1947 *Common Grace*; Ridderbos, S. J. 1949. *Rondom het Gemeene-Gratie-Probleem*. Kampen: Kok; Masselink, William 1953. *General Revelation and Common Grace*. Grand Rapids: Eerdmans; and Douma, Jochem 1966. *Algemene Genade*. Goes: Oosterbaan & Le Cointre.

For Kuyper the doctrine of common grace expresses God's gracious dealing with this fallen world in two different aspects. First, sin is restrained and the effects of sin tempered. In this sense, common grace serves a necessary, albeit negative role. God's grace holds back human rebellion, and furthermore, alleviates to a large extent the destructive results of that rebellion. This grace allows, secondly, for the possibility of human development of culture and society. All good gifts, whether employed by believers or unbelievers, are seen to come from God and to result in the glory of God. As a result, believers can enter into cooperation with unbelievers in the various cultural tasks, e.g. science and politics. As Kuyper states, "The fundamental creation ordinance given before the fall, that humans would achieve dominion over all of nature thanks to 'common grace,' is still realized after the fall" (*CG* 179). Kuyper sees God as working through common grace to restrain the effects of sin, and thereby to develop the creation through human cultural development.

For Kuyper, special grace presupposes common grace and could not function without it. While he sees a major purpose of common grace being that of preparation for the special grace given to God's elect, he definitely does not confine the purpose or operation of common grace to salvation. Rather, he puts both special grace and common grace into a doxological context, namely that all things are done to the glory of God. He goes so far as to subsume common grace under special grace in the following way:

> In that sense, then we must acknowledge that common grace is only an emanation of special grace and that all its fruit flows into special grace – provided it is understood that special grace is by no means exhausted in the salvation of the elect but has its ultimate end only in the Son's glorification of the Father's love, and so in the aggrandizement of the perfections of our God. (*CG* 170–71)

Kuyper does not see either special grace or common grace as operating on its own, but rather as being intertwined in accomplishing God's purposes. To express this relationship, he compares them to two branches of one tree. Both branches of grace are rooted in Christ:

> Does not the apostle write to the church of Colosse that the self-same Christ is simultaneously two things: the root of the life of creation as well as the root of the life of the new creation? First we read that Christ is "the first-born of all creation, for in him all things were created, in heaven and on earth," so that he is "before all things and in him all things hold together." It could hardly be stated more plainly and clearly that Christ is the root of creation and therefore of common grace, for it is common grace that prevents things from sinking into nothingness. (Does not the text say that all thing *hold together in him*?) But we immediately note in the second place that the same Christ is "the *Head of the Body* and the first-born from the dead," hence also the root of the life of the new creation or of special grace. The two things are even stated in parallel terms: he is the root of common grace, for his is *the first-born of all creation*, and simultaneously the root of special grace, for he is the *firstborn from the dead*. There is thus no doubt that common grace and special grace come most intimately connected from their origin, and this connection lies in Christ.[22]

By focusing on Christ, rather than merely on one's own salvation, the believer is relieved of the tension of relating common grace to special grace in an unbalanced way. Kuyper sees this sort of imbalance as tending toward the Anabaptist error that sharply distinguishes between the spiritual realm and the world all around. Instead, creation and

---

22 *CG* 186–187. This is from his chapter on "The Contact of Sphere and Sphere." Here the "spheres" seem to be referring to the "spheres" of grace, i.e., special and common.

redemption both belong to Christ, and redemption is of the whole world, not just human souls. He concludes his chapter on the "Two Forms of Grace" by claiming the following:

> For that reason Scripture continually points out that the *Savior* of the world is also the Creator of the world, indeed that he could become its Savior only *because* he already was its Creator. Of course, it was not the *Son of man*, not the *incarnate Word*, who created the world. All that was human in the Mediator was itself created, creaturely as it is creaturely in us. Still, Scripture repeatedly points out that he, the first-born of the dead, is also the firstborn of creation, that the Word Incarnate nevertheless always was and remained the same eternal Word who was with God and was God, of whom it is written that without that Word nothing was made that is made. Christ then is connected with *nature* because he is its Creator, and at the same time connected to *grace* because, as Re-creator, he manifested the riches of grace in the midst of that nature. (*CG* 173)

In this way Kuyper roots both common grace and special grace in Christ: common grace in Christ as Creator, special grace in Christ as Redeemer. In every aspect Christ is to be seen as Lord and Sovereign over all.

> In fact, Kuyper views the doctrine of common grace as an implication of the Reformed doctrine of the sovereignty of God. As he expresses it in his foreword to *Common Grace*. . . the doctrine of common grace proceeds directly from the Sovereignty of the Lord which is ever the root conviction of all Reformed thinking. If God is sovereign, then his Lordship *must* remain over *all* life and thinking. If God is sovereign, then his Lordship must remain over all life and cannot be closed up within church walls or Christian circles. The extra-Christian world has not been given over to Satan or to fallen humanity or to chance. God's Sovereignty is great and all-ruling also in unbaptized realms, and therefore neither Christ's work in the world nor that of God's child can be pulled back out of life. If his God works in the world, then there he must put his hand to the plow so that there too the Name of the Lord is glorified. (*CG* 166)

A major part of Kuyper's agenda in writing the lengthy series of articles on common grace for *De Heraut* was to call the Reformed community in the Netherlands to action. He completed the series as he was about to become prime minister of the Netherlands in 1900, and it was published in book form during the latter part of his term. The doctrine of common grace provided the theological justification and the spiritual motivation for Christians to be actively involved in every aspect of their culture, including politics, science, and the arts. Common grace also provided an understanding of history, from paradise to the Second Coming, as the outworking of God's sovereign plan for humanity, in cultural and scientific development, as much as in spiritual and ecclesiastical growth. All people, believers and unbelievers alike, serve God through the developments of human history.

Conclusion

Sphere sovereignty provided Kuyper with a conceptual tool for Christian action in society in its various aspects. God had created all things, and Christians were called to develop each "sphere" in accordance to its own God-given ordering and potential. Kuyper himself contributed significantly in a number of different spheres during his career. As an educator, he founded and taught at the Free University of Amsterdam. As a politician, he started the first modern political party in the Netherlands, the Anti-Revolutionary Party, and served in parliament, including four years as prime minister of the Netherlands. He spent several decades as a journalist, editing a daily paper. As a pastor, he opposed liberalism in the church of his day and was one of the leaders of an eventual split from the state church. In theology, he contributed the works surveyed above, as well as a lengthy commentary on the Heidelberg Catechism and three volumes of collected columns on the work of the Holy Spirit.

Abraham Kuyper's most enduring legacy has been in the realm of theology, and particularly in his attempt to take account of both common grace and the antithesis. The former provided a basis for unity and cooperation in the cultural task, while the latter maintained a sharp distinction and even cleavage. Kuyper held this tension in balance consistently throughout his career, as can be seen in his 1880 speech on "Sphere Sovereignty." While the doctrines of common grace and the antithesis had not yet been worked out by Kuyper at that point, their presence is felt.

Common grace, according to Kuyper, was the basis of human achievements in the different spheres of life. Progress can and has been made in each of the spheres as creation has been developed through human history. While it has clearly been tainted by sin, yet the progress has been real and will rebound to the glory of God. Kuyper's first usage of "sphere sovereignty," the different societal spheres, and common grace were both firmly rooted by Kuyper in creation, and both were seen as expressions of the sovereignty of God. To repeat his claim from *Common Grace*, "If God is sovereign then his Lordship *must* remain over *all* life and thinking" (*CG* 166). This statement clearly echoes his theme from "Sphere Sovereignty": "Oh, no single piece of our mental world is to be hermetically sealed off from the rest, and there is not a square inch in the whole domain of our human existence over which Christ, who is Sovereign over *all*, does not cry: 'Mine!'" (*SS* 488).

On the other hand, the antithesis demanded a separate development by the regenerate and unregenerate in every area. In "Sphere Sovereignty" Kuyper also argued in his second usage of the term that there must be freedom for developing scholarship in every area from the Reformed principle, in contrast to the opposing principles of his "opponents." By the time of the Stone Lectures, he had developed this analysis into a call for developing a consistent and well-thought out Christian worldview to oppose "Modernism." Kuyper never denied the accomplishments of the unregenerate, but he always saw the need for the regenerate to build consistently on their own principles.

For Kuyper, to have abandoned either of the usages of "Sphere Sovereignty" in his inaugural speech would have been to deny either the goodness of God's creation and providence or the pervasive effects of sin on humanity. This Kuyper was unwilling to do, and we would do well to emulate his example as we engage our own culture in our day.

22

Sphere Sovereignty for Kuyper and for Us

D. H. Th. Vollenhoven

A number of people have raised the question: Didn't Kuyper mean something completely different with "sphere sovereignty" than does Calvinian philosophy, and is that legitimate?

In this regard one does well to distinguish clearly between historical interpretation on the one hand and systematic clarification and deepening on the other hand.

When someone gives a different interpretation to words spoken in the past, great care must be taken not to insert into these sayings things that aren't there. Those who take this norm lightly fall into anachronisms: they get predecessors saying things they never intended. We have to keep that in mind here too.

The expression "sphere sovereignty" [literally, "sovereignty in one's own sphere"] comes, as many still know, from Dr. Abraham Kuyper. Those who want to get to know Kuyper, then, have to accurately trace what this expression meant for him as he used it. People who do this will conclude that this great thinker, also on this point, did not always express himself consistently. But what is clear is that when Kuyper uses these words, he was thinking primarily of the diversity of creation ordinances for everyday societal connections like church, state, and business enterprise.

Now it happened repeatedly that office bearers from one sector of society would infringe upon the authority of office bearers in another sector. Church and state, for instance, have gotten into each other's business more than once. But whenever these kinds of intrusions transpired, things in daily life inevitably went awry.

This sequence of events is often quite obvious and was likewise, also earlier, more than once the topic of serious reflection. The part that the conflict (c.1250) between emperor and pope played in the thomistic theme of nature and grace is a case in point.

Kuyper, too, came to reflect on these conflicts. He obviously could not accept Aquinas's solution. Kuyper was convinced that religious belief belongs to human nature and is not a *donum superadditum*. Besides that, the problem as he posed it was much less limited. It was not simply a matter of the relationship between church and state, but had to do with the mutual relationships between all societal connections. As a result, compared with the thomistic solution, Kuyper's was not only purer, but also broader. Kuyper concluded from these recurrent events that the jurisdiction God established for one sphere did not include the authority to intrude on another, if the life in both societal connections is not to be damaged when such a conflict arises.

Kuyper uses the term "sphere," then, almost exclusively to refer to societal connections.

Therein lies the limitation of this view. This shortfall can also be related to the fact that Kuyper, because he had not yet clearly distinguished sovereignty and autonomy, took these spheres to be regional in character and not modal. As a result, in 1913, for example, he was faced with a painful dilemma when Talma's "Bakers Law" legislation was being discussed.[1]

In spite of this (if you will, "double") limitation, the sound scriptural character of this perspective cannot escape those who take a close look. The diversity of these spheres is correlated with a diversity of authority. Their origin is not rooted in man's will but in the abundance of God's creation work.

The teaching of "sphere sovereignty" marked an important step forward at the time. None of our spiritual forbearers, not even Groen Van Prinsterer, showed such clear insight on this point. Groen saw the antithesis but did not follow through from there to a different analysis of reality.

This view has certainly proven tenable in the practice of everyday. In the first place, positively: the struggle here in The Netherlands for freedom of choice in education, which remained unresolved in most other places, would have never ended so quickly in a complete victory for the advocates of this freedom had Kuyper's maxim not worked to bring clarity to the many involved. But when it is lost sight of, confusion grows with leaps and bounds. The Dutch political situation after the war is an unfortunate case in point. Had more people taken Kuyper's view into account at the time, government authorities would not have repeatedly tried so hard to arrange all kinds of things about which they lacked competence, while at the same time the promotion of the government's interests for which they were officially responsible was scandalously lost sight of.

But this is just in passing. Our topic here is not the importance of Kuyper's teaching, but its limited character. More specifically, our topic is whether the advocates of Calvinian philosophy have kept this sufficiently in mind.

This question can be answered confidently in the affirmative. Indeed, from this philosophy's circle of supporters there have been a number of publications that, in addition to praising the originality and depth of Kuyper's conception, clearly and explicitly address its limited focus. Two titles would be C. Veenhof's little book on sphere sovereignty published in 1939 and J. Dengerink's PhD thesis of 1948, which was a critical, historical investigation of the sociological development of the principle of sphere sovereignty during the nineteenth and twentieth centuries.

That we are attributing the views of his pupils to Kuyper himself is, therefore, simply not the case.

But someone is bound to reply that if we, when interpreting the founder of the Free University's principle of sphere sovereignty, truly are aware that Kuyper's theory had to do primarily with what we today call "societal connections," how can we then use this notion in a much broader sense?

The question is an understandable one, and I am happy to deal with it all the more

---

1 Translator's note: A. S. Talma (1864–1916) was a pastor in the Reformed Church and member of Kuyper's Anti-Revolutionary Party. As Secretary of Labor in the Heemskerk cabinet, Talma introduced reformist legislation to prohibit working hours in bakeries between 9 PM and 6 AM. Many accused him of socialist leanings; even some of his colleagues in parliament found his ideas to be too radical. The bill was defeated, with Kuyper abstaining when the vote was taken – a humiliating and painful turn of events for Talma.

so because the answer is not difficult to come by. This shifting and broadening of the term "sphere sovereignty" is the result of elaboration.

There is nothing unique about that. It happens every day. Take the word "love," for instance. However seriously intended, on the lips of a young man and young lady who recently have taken a liking to each other, this word has a much less deep sound to it than when they use that word after many decades of being happily married. They are also very much aware of this difference. Surely no one would deny them the right to use the same word years later.

The situation is similar with the meaning of the term "sphere sovereignty" for Kuyper and for his students. That he understood less with these words than do we is obvious. But that is no reason for us to choose different words! It is just the other way around. By consciously sticking to the words he used, we want to express the thought that what we advocate is nothing more than an elaboration of what Kuyper had in mind. That is why using the same term is entirely justified.

What remains to be shown is that our view is indeed an extension of the line that Kuyper followed. To that end I want to point to a few of his thoughts that did not fall under the term "sphere sovereignty" but which with reflection proved to be very closely connected with it.

The first thing that comes to mind is the basic thought of his *Encyclopedia of Sacred Theology*, that the diversity of scientific methods is not rooted in the human mind but in the diversity of what is being investigated.

To grasp the weight of this premise, one must take stock of what was happening philosophically at the time. Kuyper lived during the era of positivism, which, like seventeenth century philosophy, overestimated mathematics and mathematical physics. Besides this similarity, however, there was a significant difference. Descartes and Leibniz had limited themselves to the sub-analytic aspects. Enlightenment and pre-Romantic thinkers as a result, with their keen interest in supra-analytic areas like history, language, social movement, art, government, ethical life, and faith, saw no chance to include these fields under "science" and therefore assigned them to the domain of practical reason. Positivism, though it shared the breadth of the Enlightenment's scope, rejected that solution. If the supra-analytic aspects do not fit the seventeenth century's notion of science, then the bounds of science have to be expanded. The thought itself was a good one. The mistake was that, in spite of broadening the scope of science, they continued to understand it mathematically, equating the latter with precision thinking. As a result, people were forced to reduce the diversity in method required by the diversity of the research to a difference in men's minds. Instead of acknowledging a manifold of areas open for investigation, they proposed a diversity of points of view from which the human mind would view reality.

To expand the range of the sciences was not a problem for Kuyper, nor was recognizing a diversity of methods. What he strongly protested against was the positivistic derivation of this diversity. The many different methods of the sciences are not rooted in the activity of the human mind, but in the richness of God's work of creation.

How Kuyper worked out this thought can indeed, after the fact, be criticized on more than one point. By latching on to the usual number of departments within the university at the time, he distinguished only five areas; on top of that, he equated "area" and "object." On both points the founders of Calvinian philosophy have had to correct their mentor.

But, here too, pointing out this shortcoming was accompanied with a thankful tribute to the validity of the basic thought. In this way, deeper reflection on Kuyper's results was simply a matter of course.

Kuyper's Calvinian sense of reality twice led him to argue for the recognition of diversity in God's works. But while he spoke of "sphere sovereignty" in the case of societal connections, he did not do so with reference to the diversity that the sciences investigate.

The difference in Kuyper's stance here was no coincidence. According to him, the connections of everyday life have to do with subjects, while research deals with objects. In addition, when he spoke of "sovereignty," he thought not only of God's sovereignty, but, influenced by romanticism, also of the authority of office bearers in the various sectors of society.

Here, too, further reflection brought light.

In the first place, equating "field of investigation" with "object" didn't seem to work. I will use the example of psychology to make that clear. Its field of investigation is the psychic or sensitive aspect of things. Is that the same thing as "sensed object"? In no way! The sensitive aspect of reality does include sensed objects, like colors, but also much much more, namely, the entire emotive, sensitive life of man and animal. In other words, it also includes what we call "psychic subjects." Hence, psychology's field of investigation includes objects, but also subjects. Indeed, the latter are even more important than the former. On the other hand, the higher, more complex areas one finds with societal connections may not be equated with subject functions. The economic arena includes more than just economic activity. Without objects – goods in this case – economic activity would even be unthinkable. And so we see that "lower" arenas include more than objects and that "higher" ones comprise more than subjects!

In like manner, the sovereignty of God had to be distinguished from the authority of office bearers. Their authority does come from God, and in fulfilling their task to positivize God's law for a particular arena they do, in their office, stand on the side of the law. But as office bearers they are also human and remain subject to the law of God, even within the arena for which they hold office, just like those over whom they are entrusted with authority.

Both changes were conscious deviations from Kuyper. On the other hand, they lay completely in line with what he had done. As Kuyper did more than once, anyone who makes a case for recognizing the riches in God's creation work cannot fail in the long run to see the diversity of object and subject. As far as the second point is concerned, things are even simpler. To the extent that people, with Kuyper, bow before the majesty of God, they will also outgrow their romantic perception of office bearers, which is still evident here and there in Kuyper.

When both changes are accepted, however, all of it, whether it's what Kuyper spoke of using "sphere sovereignty" or those arenas where he couldn't do this, all of it is subject to the law of God. This, of course, is not to deny the diversity of these areas. But this diversity, however extensive it may be, proves to be a diversity all of which is subject to the law and therefore to God, whether it functions as a subject or as an object.

That being the case, Kuyper's pupils are entirely justified in using "sphere sovereignty" even when not talking about societal connections.

The difference between "sphere sovereignty" for Kuyper and for us rests, then, on a few corrections, by means of which greater justice is done to Kuyper's deepest intention: respect for the diversity in God's work. That is why this difference should sooner be praised than censured.

These corrections were inescapable. Without them Kuyper's view would have become inflexible and his work be erased in the future. That is why I just had to continue to distinguish field of investigation and object, even when a number of theologians asked that I follow the principles of sacred theology found in Kuyper's *Encyclopedia*. That the contact between the special sciences and philosophy is beginning to bear some fruit in more than one department can be ascribed to distinctions unfortunately dismissed by some of Kuyper's students around 1930.

But let's be fair. That the theologians in particular were at the time extra careful is understandable. Innovations in 1920 and 1926 had yielded nothing but disappointment. On the other hand, they knew us. And it isn't difficult for a healthy intuition to figure out whether the critique by fellow disciples of their common mentor comes from a range of ideas that is totally foreign to his view and arbitrarily expressing scorn and jeers, or whether it is moved by the desire to preserve the valuable stem even though that might require some powerful pruning.

But enough of that. The purpose of this article and the next one is not to dig up sad stories from the past, but just the opposite: to contribute to restoring the unity in the camp of Kuyper's students. The point now is simply this: when Kuyperianism first began to unfold on a limited scale, many opponents were initially interested and convinced; as time passed it had difficulty recruiting continued support and hence needed correction on a number of points. When Calvinian philosophy introduced these necessary revisions, it did not revolutionize things but continued on in the spirit of Kuyper

23

Abraham Kuyper's Philosophy of Science

Del Ratzsch

The writings of Abraham Kuyper have had enormous influence upon Reformed thought,[1] but there are few (if any) systematic expositions in English of his views on science and its relationship to Christian belief.[2] That issue has been of perennial importance to Christians (both scientist and nonscientist), and there may well be things that we can learn from taking a close look at Kuyper. It may be that one reason for the scarcity of work on Kuyper's views specifically on science and belief is that Kuyper does not seem ever to have made explicit just what his views were. In no place that I know of does he give a formal, detailed philosophy of science. But there are bits and hints in many different places, and the pieces fit together so well that it seems as though Kuyper did have a fairly well-developed philosophy of science and that when the occasion arose he would simply borrow from it what he needed. So in what follows, I will attempt to construct the picture Kuyper would have presented had he set down his views from the period around the turn of the century in any complete fashion.[3]

1   See, e.g., Wells, D. F., ed. 1985. *Reformed Theology in North America*. Grand Rapids: Eerdmans.

2   In an article in *Philosophia Reformata* 4 (1939): 193–232, Herman Dooyeweerd discusses Kuyper's views of science; *see supra* Chapter 14. However, Dooyeweerd's primary concern there is to isolate some vestigial remains of "synthesistic" thinking in Kuyper's views rather than to lay out the formal elements and technical details of Kuyper's philosophy of science as such. Discussion both of some part of Kuyper's views on science and of Dooyeweerd's treatment of Kuyper's views can also be found in part 2 of C. Van Til, *Herman Dooyeweerd and Reformed Apologetics* (unpublished manuscript), 22ff. See also the 1993 dissertation by W. Kobes, *Sphere Sovereignty and the University* available through University Microfilms. Relevant works in Dutch include Klapwijk, J. 1987. "Abraham Kuyper over Wetenschap en Universiteit." In *Abraham Kuyper: zijn volksdeel, zijn invloed*, edited by C. Augustijn, J. H. Pruis, and H. E. S. Woldring. Delft: Meinem, 61–94; *see supra* Chapter 18 for the revised and translated version.

3   I do not know of any other discussion at a later point. Remarks he made earlier – for instance, in the October 20, 1880 "Sphere Sovereignty" speech – fit very well into the picture we get from the period around the turn of the century. See Kuyper, A. 1880. "Sphere Sovereignty." Inaugural address, Free University, October 20, 1880. Originally published as *Souvereiniteit in Eigen Kring*. Amsterdam: J. H. Kruyt, 1880. A translation of the first part of the speech is contained in *Political Order and the Plural Structure of Society*, edited by J. W. Skillen and R. McCarthy. Atlanta: Scholars Press, 1991; and a translation of the entire speech is contained in Kobes. References in the following refer to the Kobes translation and will hereafter

I am indebted to several colleagues at Calvin College for criticisms and suggestions. I wish also to thank J. van der Meer and two anonymous referees. Work on this project was supported in part by the Calvin College Faculty Development program.

Epistemology

Kuyper was a scientific realist and accepted some version of the correspondence theory of truth. Objects and processes in the material world proceed independently of man, and the scientist is to make his thought "entirely correspond" to what is objectively before him. Otherwise he is "no man of science."[4] (There is in human nature as such a drive toward that correspondence, a "thirst for knowledge," and since it is a part of human nature as such, the subject of science is "humanity as an organic whole.")[5] Since the aim of science is knowledge,[6] whatever constraints there are on knowledge will also be constraints upon science, so we must set the background for Kuyper's philosophy of science by looking at his more general epistemology.

Perception

Kuyper appears to have believed that all of our substantive knowledge of the material realm must rest upon perception (sensation). He further believed that this requires that there be an "organic relationship" between the object in question and our senses – otherwise knowledge of the object would be "utterly impossible" (*PST* 68). Given the materiality of things in the material realm, we must have physical senses in order to be in the correct relationship to that realm.

But having physical senses is not enough. In order for the reports of the senses to be delivered into the mind, the mind and the physical senses must also stand in the proper organic relationship, and there must also be an organic relationship between the mind and the object known (*PST* 216, 217). We must also have the proper mental organization to be able to take in the sensory reports or to be able to observe the world via our physical senses (*PST* 68). According to Kuyper, perception involves only "elements" – things (properties) to which simple sensations or representations correspond. The necessary components for taking representations of these elements into our thought must "appear beforehand as fundamental types in our consciousness" (*PST* 72).

So the senses must be integrally related to nature, the senses must be properly related to the mind, and the mind must be properly structured. If all of that is the case, then one can have "an apprehension, a perception and an impression of the existence and of the method of existence of the object" in question (*PST* 69). But that would not yet yield knowledge of a very high level. To reach a more complete knowledge, the elements perceived must be seen in their various relationships to each other. The "seeing" of those relationships takes place in the realm of thought, and not in the realm of perception.

Thought

For Kuyper, an aim of science is truth, and that applies to the relationships in "the world of thought" as much as to the elements in the area of perception.[7] Thus, if science

---

be cited as "Sphere Sovereignty."

4 *PST* 78. Also, "Sphere Sovereignty," especially sect. 2. Although "Sphere Sovereignty" came twenty years earlier, several of the claims made there so closely parallel Kuyper's views from around the turn of the century that I have included a number of references from it.

5 *PST* 64, 169, 182.

6 E.g., *PST* 180; "Sphere Sovereignty," sect. 2, par. 8.

7 In fact, Kuyper claims that in science "truth is sovereign" ("Sphere Sovereignty," sect. 2, par. 10).

is done correctly, "when human thought is completed it shall be like the completed organisms of these relations."[8] Here again Kuyper claims that the relations in thought of the representations of the elements and the relations in reality of the elements themselves must "entirely correspond." He further insists on the objectivity of the correspondence, claiming that it cannot be accounted for by appeal to any sort of subjectivism (*PST* 77).

If our thought can correspond to those objective relations, there must be a further structural parallel between our minds and the cosmos – and that is Kuyper's position exactly when he says that "before we become aware of these relations outside of us, the setting for them is present in our consciousness" (*PST* 11). Or again, "there must be an organic relationship between that object and our nature, between that object and our consciousness, and between that object and our world of thought (*PST* 67, 68). Thus in thought (relations) and with perceptions (elements) there is a prior, inherent fitness of our minds to the world they are to reflect. (Anthropological dualism is here important for Kuyper – mind reflects relations, body reflects elements. Both are essential to the possibility of humans doing science.)

What accounts for that fitness? What accounts for our capacity to know truth about the cosmos? The answer is that there is "thought embedded in" things and that things are ordered according to logic (*PST* 78), and that the thoughts embedded in things and the structure of logic and the capacity for thought that lies in us are all creations of God (*PST* 83). We are created after God's image as "microcosms" of the cosmos which he brought into being, and in doing science, in thinking out relations, we "think the thought over again, by which the Subject defined these relations when He called them into being."[9] Thus, there is a chain of relationships among our senses, our perceptions, our thought, God's creating, and the cosmos. The relationships and the truths about those relationships and the elements among which those relationships hold are objective features of reality, but features and truths which our thought is capable of discovering and incorporating.

Faith

That gives us a brief and general idea of Kuyper's account of the observational base of our knowledge of the material world. That basis is, according to Kuyper, in principle absolutely firm:

> Everything that is material and can consequently be counted, weighed and measured, no doubt offers us at least as far as these relations are concerned, a universally compulsory certainty, which, if observation be correct, bears an absolutely objective character. (*PST* 104)

So observations (elements) and thought (relations) both involve (at least ideally) "compulsory certainty."

Why should that be the case? It is perfectly possible that one should through observation and thought be presented with a particular conception of an object before one but have no confidence in that conception at all, just as one can read an account of some alleged object and not have any particular inclination to believe the account to be true. But with respect to our own direct observations, for instance, we do not find that to be the way it works. We are, under normal conditions, absolutely certain that, for example, there are

---

8   *PST* 77. Also in "Sphere Sovereignty," Kuyper says that "our knowledge is like a mirror in us" (sect. 2, par. 10).
9   *PST* 78, 175; "Sphere sovereignty," sect.2, par. 8, in *LC*.

tables before us. What is different in such cases? How does that epistemic certainty – that compulsory certainty – arise?

Kuyper's answer is faith. Kuyper uses "faith" to refer to a faculty – in particular, a certainty-producing faculty. Specifically, faith is an "instrument" (*PST* 131) or "that function of the soul by which it obtains certainty directly and immediately, without the aid of discursive demonstration" (*PST* 128, 129). Further, "faith is the only source of certainty, equally for what you prove definitely and conclusively by demonstration [and for what may not be so proven]" (*PST* 219), as well as the source for any "firm conviction."[10] Faith is absolutely indispensable for science. Faith is the means by which we are assured of the legitimacy of our observations, and by which our ego (the center of consciousness) (*PST* 132) believes our senses (*PST* 133). Further, faith is what undergirds reasoning and logic – the very axioms from which one begins cannot themselves be demonstrated, and thus our confidence in them rests exclusively upon faith. Consequently, "with the so-called exact sciences there is no investigation nor any conclusion conceivable except insofar as the observation in the investigation and the reasoning in the conclusion are grounded in faith."[11] Without the operation of faith, there would be no escape at all from Fichtean idealism (*PST* 133). Thus, our certainty in our observations, and the certainty that we attach to reasoning – which things alone allow us to escape idealism, and which is also a counter to skepticism – are the results of this instrument, faith.

Faith not only operates over a large territory, but it is also quite powerful. We do not, apparently, have a choice when faith operates. Faith "binds your ego to . . . axioms" (*PST* 136); it "makes you believe."[12] When it operates one is "bound to believe" and it "prevents the rise of differences of opinion" (*PST* 143). And not only does faith make us believe, it also gives us the right to believe those things on which it operates (*PST* 139).

So the ego is presented with perceptions and thoughts, and faith operates (normally) to produce certainty that the perceptions are veridical and that the thoughts reflect reality. If all goes correctly, then, one can have accurate observations, can reason correctly about observations, and can have certainty with respect to those things (and with respect to a variety of other things as well).

Data of consciousness

But that will not yet do as a basis for science in the broad sense in which Kuyper generally uses the term – i.e., an integrated whole of all of higher learning – or even for natural science in any full sense. Science has to be comprehensive – its object is roughly all that there is (at least all that we can discover of all there is).[13] If all we have is sensation and reasoning to begin with, we will never arrive at any of the principles that a comprehensive picture of even the material cosmos requires – for example that nature is "uniform and stable" (guaranteed, for Kuyper, by the unity of God's decrees) (*LC* 115, 116), that there is "something universal hidden behind the special phenomena,"[14] etc. What, then, is the

---

10 *PST* 131; see also Kuyper, A. *Gemeene Gratie*, cited in Van Til, H. R. 1959. *The Calvinist Concept of Culture*. Grand Rapids: Baker, 143, 145, 146.

11 *PST* 131; "Sphere Sovereignty," sect. 2, par. 12.

12 *PST* 183, 145, 146.

13 *PST* 65, 176; *LC* 126.

14 *LC* 131; Kuyper, A. 1893. "Pantheism's destruction of boundaries." *Methodist Review* 53 (July): 520–535

source of such principles? Kuyper's answer is that such principles are "given with our self-consciousness" (*PST* 136; *LC* 131). Logical axioms and principles concerning "self," "self-consciousness," "accuracy of the senses," "correctness of the laws of thought," etc. (*LC* 131), and "the reality of the phenomena" (*PST* 145, 146) are all given in self-consciousness. They "inhere in it . . . they are inseparable from it" (*PST* 136). Again, "whatever among men originates directly from creation is possessed of all the data for its development in human nature as such. . . . The same may be said of [all the] spheres of life" (*LC* 91). Thus the broad, foundational principles needed are simply given in consciousness (which is why Kuyper repeatedly claims that science must begin with the self-consciousness)[15] and are made compelling by the operation of faith. (There are other contents of consciousness, which I will discuss later.)

There is another important component of the givens of our consciousness: common sense. We have, says Kuyper, an "immediate affinity to that which exists outside of us" and "[feel] nature's pulse beat" (*PST* 123). This common sense, which in heightened form is wisdom, is "independent of scientific investigation and has a starting point of its own, this intuitive knowledge, founded on fixed perceptions given with our consciousness itself" (*PST* 123).

This common sense, this intuitive knowledge, seems to perform at least two functions: it provides protection against skepticism and tends to "exclude follies from the process of discursive thought, and in empirical investigations to promote the accuracy of our fact" (*PST* 124). Thus, given in our consciousness are certain "fixed perceptions" which – perhaps as part of the parallelism between our categories and conceptions and reality mentioned earlier – serve to keep our ideas and investigations from going too far off the rails.

So our senses present us with perceptions of the elements of things, thought reproduces their relations, our consciousness presents us with essential basic principles, common sense keeps us generally on track. Faith produces certainty concerning observations, the principles and a variety of other things. With this picture of Kuyper's general epistemology, we are in better position to turn more specifically to science.

Physical Science

According to Kuyper, there seems to be an ascending hierarchy through which scientific investigation passes (*LC* 115). First the scientist must determine the specific facts within the area of investigation. From there one goes to general facts (*PST* 79), and from general facts to the law which "rules over" the (general and specific) facts in question.[16] (One may then have to go on to a single principle which encompasses all the laws within one discipline. The English is ambiguous, but the Dutch seems to hint in that direction.)[17] That seems to be the route within any specific discipline. Science, however, must constitute an organic, unified whole. Thus, all the separate special sciences must be taken up together under one single principle "which is dominant over all" (*LC* 115), and then all the interrelations, results, their relation to man, to origins, etc., must be woven "into an organic whole" by

---

and (September): 762–778—Retranslated by John Vriend in: *AK:ACR* as "The Blurring of the Boundaries"—referenced below as *BB*.

15 E.g., *PST* 130, 389; *LC* 137, 138.

16 *LC* 115; *PST* 209. Possibly also "Sphere Sovereignty," sect. 2, par. 10.

17 *LC* 113; Kuyper, A. 1898. Het Calvinisme. Kampen: Kok, 99, 100.

philosophy.[18]

These final steps are both characteristic of and important for Kuyper. Kuyper believed in the ultimate unity of all things created; thus science (broad sense), which is supposed to mirror reality, must reflect that unity also. But "a basic dualism yields no system"[19] and "Thought by its very nature tends toward system" (*BB* 373). That does not mean that, for example, biology is ultimately reducible to physics, only that both are ultimately under the same ruling principle. Since the natural sciences do not contain that single ruling principle or all the relationships woven by philosophy, they are all basically incomplete (*PST* 218).

The initial steps through which Kuyper's hierarchy of investigation passes seem to be the following. First, determination of specific facts is made purely by observation – either direct or via instrumentation. (Kuyper holds that instruments are merely "reinforcement" of the senses.)[20] Such observation gives rise to justified, "compulsory certainty" along the lines laid out earlier, and thus, on Kuyper's view, presents no insurmountable difficulties. But although an essential basis for science,[21] observation is not itself scientific in nature.[22]

Of course, there are lots of different sorts of specific facts, not all of which will be relevant to a given science. Kuyper says little concerning how one picks out relevant facts for natural science, but it is likely that his position would parallel that which he takes to be the ideal concerning the same question relative to theology: one should "include as fact everything that *announced itself* as a theological phenomenon, without discrimination or choice, *not organically, but atomistically*."[23] (For Kuyper, the creation had a number of distinct, although related, domains, each having its own integral structure, governing ordinances, status and, in some sense, sovereignty. Such domains – which Kuyper called "spheres" – include the family, the state, the church, science and others.[24] Kuyper held that we know the boundaries between the spheres intuitively.) The necessity of some means of selecting out only some facts from among all those available, even in the case of natural sciences, Kuyper seemingly admits (*PST* 341), calling each respective set of facts the "fountain" of the science in question.[25]

One of the intermediate aims, remember, is to discover the laws that "rule over" the facts so selected. So what, for Kuyper, is natural law? Kuyper associates law with "the thought which governs the whole constellation of phenomena" in question (*LC* 112, 113). Those are (some of) the thoughts that we rethink in doing science. Kuyper generally describes laws with reference only to observation and data – for instance, "the law by which these data are governed" (*PST* 209). Again, "Science is born of observation only when from these phenomena, each of which by itself furnishes nothing more than a concrete and separate case, we have reached the universal law which governs all these

18 *LC* 113; *PST* 611–614.
19 *BB* 395; possibly also *LC* 113.
20 *PST* 132, 134, 154, 209.
21 *PST* 134, 137, 601.
22 *PST* 134, 135.
23 *PST* 637, 638. My emphases.
24 "Sphere Sovereignty," sect. 2, par. 10–15. See also 260–261 of the partial translation of "Sphere Sovereignty," in Skillen, and McCarthy eds. *Political Order and the Plural Structure of Society*.
25 Kuyper, A. "Modernism, a Fata Morgana in the Christian world," reprinted as chapter 2 of Hospers, G. H. 1924. *The Reformed Principle of Authority*. Grand Rapids: The Reformed Press, is a related passage. A more recent translation appears in *AK:ACR* 87–124.

observed phenomena in their changes" (*PST* 137). Again, to produce scientific results, the scientist "must *prosecute his observations and formulate what he has observed*."[26] Kuyper is most specific when he says, with reference to knowledge of law, "You have observed a certain number of cases, which observation shows you a certain constant action: *this constant action makes you surmise that this action will always be constant*."[27]

Thus, the sort of law in question seems to concern only patterns and regularities within observable phenomena – one formulates observations, surmising constancy of observed actions. Thus, what Kuyper means by "law" seems to be what would now be called "empirical law" – a phenomenal instead of a theoretical principle. Confirmation of that reading seems contained in Kuyper's further remarks in connection with the establishing of just what the various laws are. For instance, after discussing scientific tests that were testimony of other observers and other conditions, he says that "it is scientifically determined that in this group of phenomena such and such a law operates thus and so," then contrasts that case (of a law operating in a group of phenomena) with one in which one knows "the genetic operation of the cause." That contrast seems to amount to that between empirical regularity and the theoretical processes which account for it.

Kuyper does not go into great detail concerning the method by which we arrive at laws. We are confident that there are laws and that those laws can be discovered through limited observation, on the basis of the operation of faith (*PST* 139). Since we cannot make all possible relevant observations[28] we must make generalizations (*PST* 137, 138), based upon the observations we do make, since that is where we have to begin.[29] It is perhaps at the point of generalization (the "surmise" mentioned earlier) that our common sense operates to keep us on track, although in this whole process reason plays an essential (but not clearly described) role: "the principium of knowing, from which knowledge comes to us with these several groups of phenomena, is ever one and the same. It is, in a word, the natural man who by his reason draws this knowledge from his object."[30] However it works exactly, it begins with observation, involves generalization (since we cannot make all the relevant observations) and ends with statements of empirical regularities.

At this point, the question naturally arises: are there not, for Kuyper, two sciences? Indeed, is not the normalist/abnormalist division a major theme of Kuyper's?[31] But we have already followed the course of science up through the establishment of natural law without reference to any such split.

Exact science: no split

There are, indeed, two sciences according to Kuyper – but there is only one set of exact sciences, and they are common to Christian and non-Christian alike. That Kuyper holds such a view is fairly clear. Among things held in common by the two groups, Kuyper

---

26 *PST* 607. My emphasis.

27 *PST* 137–138. Emphasis mine.

28 *PST* 79, 137, 638.

29 *LC* 112, 115; *PST* 134, 209.

30 *PST* 341. Kuyper sometimes uses "natural man" to mean "unregenerate man," but it is apparent that that is not his intent in this context. Others consulted (professors John Cooper and John Bolt) are unsure of what Kuyper may have meant by this phrase on this occasion.

31 *LC* 132ff. Roughly, normalists claim that the present state of reality is its proper state – thus denying the Fall – whereas abnormalists take the present state to be a fallen, and aberrant, state.

includes:

> in the first place, everything that is commonly called science by the English, and *sciences exactes* by the French; at least so far as the exponents of those sciences hold themselves to their task, and do not make cosmological inferences or construct philosophical hypotheses. (*PST* 600)

In order to see what does or does not fall into this commonly held area, we must know (i) what Kuyper means by "exact sciences," (ii) what he means by "philosophical hypotheses," and (iii) what he means by "cosmological inferences." With respect to the first, it is fairly clear that by "exact science" Kuyper means a sort of empiricism – the mere logical summation and consequences of observation. That this is Kuyper's conception is made clear in several passages. He argues against the adequacy of the "so-called exact science" by saying that "the simple observation of what one hears, sees, tastes and handles, even with the aid of instrumental reinforcement of our senses, and under proper verification, is never anything more than the primitive point of departure of all science. . ." (*PST* 209). And when speaking of what the English and Americans call "science" and the French "*sciences exactes*," he denies "that mere empiricism in itself is ever perfect science. Even the minutest microscope, the farthest reaching telescopic investigation is nothing but perception with strengthened eyes" (*LC* 112). Kuyper also says that "So far as the *sciences exactes* rest simply on counting, weighing and measuring, they do not stand very high" (*PST* 601), and uses the phrase "clumsy detail-empiricism."[32] So by "exact science," Kuyper seems to mean observation and what immediately follows from it, or "the simple results of weight, measure and number" (*PST* 209). (That, in fact, was a fairly popular conception during Kuyper's time and afterwards.) Exact science, so construed, would thus rest upon observation, the required data of consciousness and logic. But Kuyper saw no difference in any of those three respects between believer and unbeliever. With respect to the senses, Kuyper says that it would be "unfair, for the sake of accentuating the difference, to deny the absolute character of perception by the senses" and, more specifically, that there is "no change in the senses, nor in the plastic conception of visible things" (*PST* 157) brought about in the Christian. Kuyper insists that any fact discovered by any person "has to be recorded by [the believer] also, as a fact, and as a fact that is to be incorporated as well into his [science] as in theirs" (*PST* 157). Sin may have had some effect, but those effects are, for example, that we are prone to mistakes, although those mistakes can to a large extent be overcome by cross-verification, etc. (*PST* 107). More on that later.

With respect to logic, "As far as the impulse of its law of life is concerned, the logic has not been impaired by sin" (*PST* 110). Again, "the formal process of thought has not been attacked by sin, and for this reason, palingenesis works no change in this mental task" (*PST* 159), and "there is but one logic, and not two."[33] Sin has, however, "weakened the energy of thought" (*PST* 111). Regarding the data of consciousness relevant to empirical matters, Kuyper says that "all scientific research which has things seen only as object, or which is prosecuted simply by those subjective factors which have undergone no change, remains the same for both."[34] Thus observation is not fundamentally different, there is only

---

32 Kuyper, A. 1899. *Evolutie*. Amsterdam: Höveker and Wormser. In *AK:ACR* "Evolution"—referenced below as *EV*; *EV* 429.

33 *PST* 159. Kuyper may seem to some to suggest otherwise in "Sphere Sovereignty," sect. 2, par. 16, but subsequently remarks in sect. 3 par. 19 make it clear.

34 *PST* 168. My emphasis.

a single logic, and even the subjective factors relevant to the empirical (and some others besides) are shared (*PST* 158). There are thus no essential differences between believer and nonbeliever in this whole area. Thus exact science, which rests solely on those three, should also be common to both Christian and non-Christian (*PST* 159, 601). (This commonality is evidently due to common grace.)

Kuyper in fact adopts just that position, claiming that "empiric investigation . . . has nothing to do with the radical difference which separates the two groups" (*PST* 157). Again, "Near the ground, the tree of science is one for all."[35] And in the earlier "Sphere Sovereignty," Kuyper says that on the level of weighing and measuring "the wedge of principle could not enter."[36]

Natural science: beginnings of a partial split

Although the exact sciences as defined are not involved in any split, the same cannot be said for the natural sciences. Kuyper says that:

> we do not mean that the natural sciences as such and in their entirety fall outside of this difference. . . . If it be mistakenly supposed that the natural sciences are entirely exhausted in this *first* and *lowest* part of their investigation, the entirely unjust conclusion may be reached, that these sciences, as such, fall outside of the difference. (*PST* 157)

Kuyper goes on to say that that conclusion would be "inaccurate." Given that exact science and natural science must be different, what distinguishes them? One difference seems to be that natural science is concerned with law. Kuyper says that exact science is only "transformed into science when you discover . . . a universal law, and thereby reach the thought which governs the whole constellation of phenomena. In this wise, the special sciences originate" (*LC* 112, 113). Again, "Observation itself is not science yet in its higher sense. Science is born . . . only when . . . we have reached the universal law which governs all these phenomena in their changes" (*PST* 137). Again, "Only by the discovery of the laws which exercise general rule in that which is particular does this science raise itself to its second stadium. . ." (*PST* 209). Thus it seems fairly clear that the natural or special sciences must concern themselves with law, unlike the exact sciences which are part of, but not all of, the natural sciences.

That concern with law is not, however, the only difference. Kuyper claims that one of the tests for law is that "*no one* contradicts your surmise; and *everyone* who devotes his attention to what has attracted yours, arrives at the same conclusion; and upon this (and other) ground, it is scientifically determined that . . . such and such a law operates" (*PST* 138). There is no mention here of differences between the two groups at the level of law. Again, Kuyper says that "the formulation [of a law] is the result of your investigation" (*PST* 139) and that "the difference between the science of the Normalists and Abnormalists is not founded upon any differing result of investigation" (*LC* 138). So with respect to law, everyone should agree. Thus, if law were the only thing that distinguished natural science from exact science, there would be no natural science split. And, in fact, "Aristotle knew more of the cosmos than all the Church Fathers taken together."[37] But, as already noted,

---

35 *PST* 168. See also 155, 166, and other remarks on 157.

36 "Sphere Sovereignty," sect. 3, par. 19

37 *LC* 117; "Sphere Sovereignty," sect. 3, par. 11.

Kuyper says that there is such a split.

What causes the split is that believers and unbelievers differ in the data of their consciousness,[38] and since the data of consciousness constitute the starting point of science,[39] the split develops whenever one or the other science incorporates some part or other of the data that is not shared. Exactly where that begins is unclear. On the one hand, we find that the split begins "just as soon as the investigation deserts the material basis and can no longer be constructed without the intermingling of the subjective factor,"[40] and that the split affects the "result of all these investigations as far as their data are not absolutely material" (*PST* 181). Yet, as also quoted earlier, Kuyper says that "all scientific research . . . which is prosecuted simply by these subjective factors which have undergone no change, remains the same for both" (*PST* 168). It is apparent that Kuyper is using "subjective factors" in different ways here, but I think that Kuyper's view is nonetheless clear: there need be no split when a science is dealing with purely material matters (where the appropriate contents of consciousness are shared by all), but when one goes beyond that and gets into areas where the contents of consciousness of believers and unbelievers are not the same, a split begins to develop.

It seems fairly clear, at any rate, that if one goes beyond the laws and on to origins, relations of man to nature, etc. (*PST* 209), there the split is pronounced:

> With the aid of all possible means at his command, he must prosecute his observations and formulate what he has observed. If, on the other hand, he undertakes to construct a system from his discoveries, or commits himself to hypotheses by which to interpret his observations, the leaving out of account of the factor of Revelation is equivalent to the work of one who, in the biography of his hero, ignores his correspondence or autobiography. Whatever applies, therefore, to the origin and end of things cannot be determined by the laws he has discovered . . . . (*PST* 607)

especially since the laws seem to be merely empirical laws, and since revelation (inspiration) constitutes data of consciousness only for the believer (*PST* 163, 225). And, again, commonality is lost as soon as scientists, from data, begin to "make cosmological inferences, or construct philosophical hypotheses" (*PST* 600).

Natural scientific theory: the partial split widens

A key question for determining what Kuyper means here is the second of those that arose earlier: what is intended by "philosophical hypotheses"? During and before Kuyper's time, that phrase was used to refer to almost anything that was not empirically determinable. That could include both what we would now call "philosophical hypotheses" and what we might now call "scientific theory" (i.e., theorizing involving unobserved entities and processes as opposed to scientific empirical principles). Atomic theory was labeled a philosophical hypothesis by Ernst Mach, for example, at about this period (around 1895). Mach argued that science had no business dealing with such notions, but only with the empirical or observable. Kuyper may have used that phrase in that sense. If he did so use it, then despite all the commonality up to that point, purely scientific theorizing could be involved in the split.

---

38 *LC* 132, 136, 138; *PST* 152, 154, 164, 679.

39 See again *PST* 130, 389; *LC* 137, 138.

40 *PST* 679. See also "Sphere Sovereignty," sect. 3, par. 19.

There is, perhaps, some indirect support for attributing that view to Kuyper. In *Principles of Sacred Theology* he says:

> Everything that is material and can consequently be counted, weighed, and measured . . . offers us . . . a universally compulsory certainty. . . . As soon, however, as you venture one step further in this physical domain, and from these empiric data try to obtain a construction by which to discover among these scattered data a unity of thought, the process of an idea, or the progression from a first phenomenon to a result, you have at once crossed over from the physical into the psychical, the universally compulsory certainty leaves you. . . . (*PST* 104)

Perhaps it is not clear what a "construction" of the specified sort is, but it sounds like a theoretical construct. Note that such a construction involves taking a step further in the *physical* domain. Yet it also involves a move into another domain as well, and perhaps into an area not shared by both sides, since the *universally* compulsory certainty is lost. (That leaves open, apparently, the possibility that each side may have something that has compulsory certainty for it but not for the other. Thus, compulsory certainty may not be lost, just the universality of that certainty for any particular result.)

This brings us into the area of exactly where, how and to what extent the split develops, and consequently to where it would be most helpful to have explicit positions laid out by Kuyper. Unfortunately, it is just at this point that things become less clear. In addition to the suggestive but undefined terms employed in the above quotation, Kuyper also speaks of "insight into the facts" in a variety of places,[41] as well as of the "structure which one builds upon this insight" (*PST* 608). The insight and structure differ in the two camps, but exactly what the referent is remains unclear; although there may be some connection to a common sense (*PST* 123). In any case, on these also theoretical-sounding matters a split exists.

The most explicit discussions concerning genuinely scientifically theoretical matters take place concerning evolution (in "Evolution" and "The Blurring of the Boundaries"). And here there are fairly strong suggestions that at least some *theoretical* scientific matters are *not* subject to the split. Consider: "These studies of heredity . . . [made] us aware of a much more complex existence in the most deeply hidden life of the cell than we had suspected thus far" (*EV* 427), and "Galton gave [Darwin's pangenesis theory] the death blow by his transfusion experiments with the rabbit,"[42] and "some things might throw new light on the glories of the entire cosmos in its visible phenomena and its invisible operations" (*LC* 126).

In the first two cases, reference is being made to hidden, theoretical mechanisms and entities. In the first case Kuyper is accepting scientific conclusions concerning hidden matters which have grown out of work intended to support a view which he takes to be unacceptable to Christians (I will discuss this more at a later point). In the second, he is evaluating a purely theoretical hypothesis on the basis of shared, empirical, observational data. The third passage, with its references to "invisible operations," occurs in a passage specifically on common grace. Thus, it seems fairly clear that Kuyper accepted the theoretical as legitimate science, and held that at least some theoretical principles could be held by and commonly evaluated by both believers and unbelievers.

But it is near here where splits do explicitly emerge. Kuyper distinguishes between

41 E.g., *PST* 117, 123, 160, 608.
42 *EV (Calvin Theological Journal* 31(1996): 30.

"the empirical and the theory built upon it," between "facts and the conception of the facts," between "those *facts* and the philosophizing linked to them" (*EV* 416), and between "these *facts* [and] their *explanation*" (*EV* 425). In the context it is clear that he wishes to leave room for divergence over the latter of those pairs even when there is agreement on the former. In any case, the risk of divergence will come when "inferences" are drawn (*PST* 116) or when the varying data of consciousnesses come into play in the scientific enterprise, which it sometimes does when interpretations, explanations and connected philosophies are at issue.

However, there are some theoretical agreements, even though humanity is split between believers and nonbelievers. Also, not all divergences are linked to sin (*PST* 116). Therefore, even if there were no unbelief, there would still be different schools, emphases, etc., due to the differences that there are within the consciousnesses even of Christians.[43] In fact, according to Kuyper, science proceeds by a dialectical tension (or "friction, fermentation and conflict"–*PST* 171) between different views and schools, and could not survive without it.[44] Thus, some of the differences in consciousness ("temperament, personal inclination, position in life . . . circumstances [which] cause each individual investigator to become one-sided, and make him find his strength in that one-sidedness"– *PST* 169) properly persist even among believers (*PST* 171) as do different schools of science. In fact, there is Roman Catholic science, Lutheran science and Calvinist science (*PST* 172). After all, even within Christian science, it is by "antithesis, tendencies, and schools . . . and by this process alone that science . . . advances" (*PST* 181). But there are also some data of consciousness shared by all believers and by no (consistent) nonbelievers (although that is a bit inexact).[45] Those data include the reality of God, the creation of the world, man as *sui generis*, the fall (*PST* 163), and the phenomena of personal regeneration, of its corresponding inspiration, of the final restoration of all things, of the manifestation of God's power in miracles (*PST* 225), and a consciousness of sin, certainty of faith, and the testimony of the Spirit (*LC* 136). The consciousness of nonbelievers may also contain data not found in that of believers – e.g., principles of mechanism, materialism, monism, pantheism, etc. Whenever any thing in science touches any of those (and anything related) there is a split between believing science and nonbelieving science.[46]

The difference in consciousness between believers and nonbelievers is not the only effect of sin upon science, either. Had there been no sin, science could have proceeded along the same basic lines, but the subjective data built into the scientific enterprise would have been reliable and thus their essential presence in science would not have detracted from the compulsory certainty of science (*PST* 90) as it does now (*PST* 104). In fact, the world would be an "open book" (*PST* 90), with perhaps infallible and compulsory scientific results possible (*PST* 91). But beyond that, because sin and falsehood are in the world, we make observational mistakes, are subject to self-delusion and self-deception, have an impaired imagination, are taught incorrectly, allow bodily ailments to affect our thinking, have impaired our life relationships, and have made mistakes in one part of consciousness that affect other parts (*PST* 107–09). All of these things Kuyper seems to classify under

---

43 *PST* 150, 169, 170, 608.

44 *PST* 151, 169, 170, 171, 173, 178, 179, 181.

45 *LC* 133; *PST* 163, 164.

46 *PST* 117, 118, 160, 175, 180, 181, 679, passim.

"darkening of our understanding." Sin also works through our motives (*PST* 220) and affects our nature (*PST* 110, 111). It has affected the love and "seeking sympathy" we need to understand what we study.[47] Sin has created a disharmony within each of us and has worked a "ruin" in the data needed to form a "conception of the whole" of reality (not just of the natural cosmos). This, recall, is the ultimate aim of science broadly conceived (*PST* 112), and "modifies so largely all those data with which you have to deal in the intellectual domain and in the building up of your science" (*PST* 113–14). So sin has not brought about a complete split on the theoretical level (and there would be divergences in any case) but it has had a profound general impact on the pursuit of science. But a split does emerge. How it emerges is fairly clear in such areas as the origin of all things, ends, and other topics which fall within the broader science. But how exactly does it develop within restricted natural science, which may not involve those things directly? (Remember, the natural sciences are all incomplete, simply because they do lack those things.) If one tries to project some part of natural science into a world and life view, the difficulties will become obvious – in fact, Kuyper thinks that there will even be logical difficulties in such cases (*PST* 607). But what of the restricted natural sciences?

Kuyper's discussion of evolution is where he is most explicit about such questions. In order to extract any lessons, we must first see exactly what Kuyper says about evolution. First of all, Kuyper did reject evolution as a worldview (e.g., *EV* 439). He leaves no doubt whatsoever about that. He did not, however, think that evolution as such – the development of all species out of a single progenitor – was contrary to any fundamental Christian doctrines, as evidenced by the following statement:

> Of course, it is an entirely different question . . . whether religion as such permits a spontaneous unfolding of the species in organic life from the cytode or the nuclear cell. This question must be answered affirmatively, without reservation. (*EV* 436)

Kuyper then goes on to indicate that he does not, however, think that that is the way things actually happened.[48]

Kuyper's reason for thinking that the development of all species from a single progenitor had not in feet happened was at least in part straightforwardly scientific. He argues that evolution has not been proven (*BB* 376–77), that it is "a hypothesis supported by a highly deficient process of induction" (*BB* 377), that it is "inadequate to explain the morphological differences of species" (*BB* 376), that it has been "falsely distilled" from the facts (*EV* 416), that there are no transition fossils (*EV* 416), that the artificial breeding evidence does not support speciation claims based on it (*EV* 429–30), and perhaps that it is internally inconsistent (*EV* 427). We find a somewhat different tone in his remarks, however, when he speaks of Darwin's particular theory of evolution: "Evolution-theory [is] the application of the pantheistic process to the empirical investigation of the phenomena" (*BB* 375). "In the theory of evolutionary . . . lurks the desire of the human heart to rid itself of God" (*BB* 377). "Darwin's theory [is] purely atheistic" (*BB* 377; cf. *EV* 436). The "whole theory was devised to avoid . . . the unexplained act of a creating God" (*BB* 377). It is "in Darwin's theory of evolution that [pantheism's] deposit [of a toxic slime] manifests its power" (*BB* 378). He goes on to say that Darwinian evolution is antithetical

---

47 *PST* 111; "Modernism," 31.

48 See also *Kuyper Newsletter* 1(2) (June 7, 1980); Lever, J. 1958. *Creation and Evolution.* Grand Rapids: International Publications, 228, 229.

to the Church of Christ and requires the removal of the "folly of Golgotha" (*BB* 390), that Darwin "fostered the birth of the monster that our age had long carried in its womb" (*BB* 397), that Darwin needs to be "disarmed" (*BB* 394), that Darwinian evolution is "deadly bacteria" and that it is more deadly than higher criticism or pantheism (*EV* 439). None of that is really high praise. Why does he reject Darwinian evolution so forcefully? What distinguishes it from evolution-as-such which makes it so repulsive?

Kuyper distinguishes Darwinian evolution from other possible types on the basis of its fundamental insistence upon a purely material, mechanistic, planless explanation of speciation, heredity, etc.[49] And here Kuyper thinks that Darwinian evolution fails demonstrably for scientific reasons, arguing that there can be no adequate mechanistic account of the sort Darwin would have to have of (most importantly) heredity, symmetry, the survivability of rudimentary organs, a variety of specific biological facts, the origin of life, and perhaps of variation (*EV* 427–29). Mechanistic evolution further involves an unacceptable reduction of organic to inorganic (*EV* 419), and there is no good case for thinking that mechanistic evolution is even possible, much less actual (*EV* 431). Darwinian evolution is also beset with all the problems of evolution in general referred to earlier.

"Broad" Sciences: Unbridgeable Split

Kuyper rejects Darwinian evolution on deeper grounds than scientific inadequacy. Darwinian evolution is contrary to Christianity in being anti-theistic (*EV* 436), monistic (*EV* 416), in destroying sphere boundaries (e.g., between organic and inorganic),[50] in denying man an ethical nature,[51] and in denying man's nature as in God's image (*EV* 438). Its reliance on the destruction of the weaker by the stronger is inconsistent with the idea of mercy.[52] The idea of the struggle for life is not Christian (*LC* 179), nor is the elevation of the species at the total cost of the individual (*EV* 412, 439). There is a conflict between the ideas of selection and election (*EV* 439). Darwinism can give no explanation of the material and laws it presupposes (*EV* 438).

But the most serious difficulty is that "Darwinism teaches the mechanical origin of things that excludes all plan or purpose or draft."[53] It can accommodate no shred of plan (*EV* 414). More fundamentally the selection mechanism depends on "blind natural forces" and is thus contrary to God's sovereignty (*LC* 197). Again, "The entire cosmos, instead of being the plaything of caprice and chance, obeys law and order, and . . . there exists a firm will which carries out its designs" (*LC* 114). Even apart from Christian belief, "The entire development of science in our age presupposes a cosmos which does not fall prey to the freaks of chance" (*LC* 115). In Kuyper's view, all things are subject to election and predestination concerning what they will be and (perhaps) what properties they will have as well (*LC* 197). Thus, Kuyper speaks of an "all embracing predestination (not) in the hand of a blind natural force, but in the hand of Almighty God, Sovereign Creator

49 *EV* e.g., 415, 429, 430, 438.

50 *EV* 416; *BB* 375, 378.

51 *EV* 435; "Modernism," 29.

52 Winckel, W. F. A. 1919. Summary of *Evolutie* from 1950 *Leven en Arbeid van Dr. A. Kuyper on Evolution*. Grand Rapids: Youth and Calvinism Group; Rullmnan, J. C. 1940. Summary of *Evolutie* from *Kuyper Bibliography*, vol. 3. Kampen: Kok, 197–200.

53 Lever, 229; *EV* 436, 437.

and Possessor of heaven and earth" (*LC* 197). So Kuyper sees Darwinian evolution as essentially mechanistic, materialistic, monistic and directed only by chance. One could, as noted earlier, accept a view of all species developing according to direction from a single original cell (other things being equal), but "this would never have been the Evolution of Darwinism, for then the foreordained purpose would not have been banished. . . ."[54] It is here, then, that the split emerges. Darwinian evolution was advanced as a purely scientific, purely biological explanation. Yet it was constructed along lines of mechanism and chance. Those philosophical principles are not, according to Kuyper, consistent with Christian belief, and thus that theoretical explanation has to be rejected – not merely when extended into a worldview or part of such (e.g., social Darwinism), but as a biological explanation. Those principles are part of the data of consciousness of some unbelievers, and thus can govern scientific explanation for those unbelievers. But, they cannot be part of the data of consciousness of the believer, and can have no part in faithful science, and consequently cannot figure into that science as components of explanatory principles.

We can now return to our initial question. Kuyper's view seems to be that there is no essential internal difference between the science of believers and that of unbelievers up to the level of theoretical postulates and that there is not even difference there in all cases. Observation is common, logic is common, the data of consciousness having to do with the empirical are common, laws are common, and even some theoretical explanations or interpretations are common. But it is at this level of theoretical explanation or interpretation where the potential for divergence is manifested, for it is at this level that deeper components of the data of consciousness enter science. Some of those data too may be shared, in which case there is no necessary divergence.

But some of those data are not shared, and wherever nonshared data of consciousness are woven into explanation or interpretation, the resultant science will not be common. There will be a split and, given the logical inconsistency between the diverging components of consciousness, the split will be unbridgeable. Kuyper makes that clear in a variety of places: "The sciences of each must become entirely different" (*PST* 118). "[E]very effort to understand each other will be futile in those points of the investigation in which this difference comes into play. . . . [So] soon as the lines have diverged but a little the divergency cannot be bridged over. . . . [At] this point of intersection no agreement can be reached" (*PST* 160). That "which is governed, directly or indirectly, by these premises comes to stand entirely differently to the one from what it does to the other. . . . So far . . . as the antithesis . . . manifests itself . . . we stand exclusively opposed to one another" (*PST* 176–77). "[It] is an impossibility that both should agree, and . . . every endeavor to make them agree must be doomed to failure."[55] Notice that Kuyper does not say here that the unbridgeable difference which manifests itself at this point destroys any of the earlier and lower level commonality. It is merely that once the paths split, that split cannot be papered over. And since any authentic science must be built upon the contents of one's consciousness, any compromise at this level is impossible. And the split is basically unavoidable, because science inherently tends to move always toward an ultimate principle governing the lesser principles and facts.[56] That very impulse toward a unity in broad science itself aggravates

---

54 *EV* 436; Lever, 229.

55 *LC* 138. See also "Sphere Sovereignty," sect. 3, par. 8.

56 *EV* 415.

the split because sin has caused a disruption, but the impulse to unity drives the normalist to extend his inferences right through the disruption, leading to even more aberrant results than would otherwise be the case,[57] especially since nature itself is apparently affected by the disturbance (*LC* 123). These sorts of inferences (dealing, perhaps, with origins and ends) are perhaps what Kuyper means by "cosmological inferences" – the inferences he indicates are subject to the split (see *PST* 600 quoted above). This is an area that may require further work.

With respect to the human and other sciences, the separation emerges at a much earlier point than it does in the natural sciences. The reason is that the noncommon subjective factors which create the split are much more important to those disciplines (*PST* 150, 220). In fact, one can construct a hierarchy in which the split surfaces at increasingly early stages of the disciplines' investigation and with increasing severity: "With . . . Natural Philosophy . . . least; a little more with the Medical; more strongly with the Philological; almost overwhelmingly with the Juridical; but most strongly of all with the Theological. . ." (*PST* 220). The separation is never in fact as complete as it should be in principle, however, because our regeneration is not yet complete. Were regeneration complete, says Kuyper, the separation would be absolute (*PST* 162).

But again, does Kuyper not repeatedly speak of the two sciences? What does he mean by that phrase in a context where there are large and significant chunks of commonality and where the divisions that are present while potentially in principle unbridgeable are in fact still less than absolute?

The first thing to keep in mind here is that, in Kuyper's *broad* sense of "science," a science must constitute a unified, coherent *whole*. Kuyper is insistent upon that.[58] The achieving of that unity is the last process within science (broad sense) when "Systematics [philosophy], as the queen of the sciences, comes forth from her tent to weave all the different results into one organic whole" (*LC* 113). The natural sciences, however, are only components of that larger science – they, being incomplete (*PST* 218), cannot be identified with science in the broad sense. And parts of those restricted natural sciences can be incorporated into different complete wholes (broad sciences) just as (Kuyper says) the same specific facts have to be incorporated into the theories of both believer and unbeliever (*LC* 139; *PST* 157). Thus, although there are common components, it is essentially two *distinct, complete* structures that are being raised (*PST* 156, 603), which is very different from saying that it is two *completely distinct* structures that are being raised (*PST* 168). Since the ultimate principles to which each point are incompatible with each other, even though there are common observational, factual, lawful and (partially) theoretical elements, what they are ultimately incorporated into, point to and serve may give those components a different systemic significance, but does not make them different components.[59]

That different systemic significance apparently takes its character from a fundamental difference in the differing contents of consciousness. At the deepest levels of the contents

---

57 *LC* 131 suggests this. See again note 32.

58 *PST* e.g., 117, 118, 602, 675, 676; *LC* 133, 138, 189.

59 In a coherence epistemology, it might make them different components, but Kuyper, at least during this period, was pretty explicitly committed to a correspondence epistemology – see again *PST* 77, 78, and "Sphere Sovereignty," sect. 2.

of consciousness (the "fundamental data") there is an irreconcilable split between those whose consciousness contains a recognition of the fact of sin (the abnormalists) and those whose consciousness contains the denial of sin (the normalists) (*LC* 132). Such recognition or denial at the deepest level in some way colors the whole of any structure built upon it[60] to the point that those "absolutely different starting points" will support systems that "never intersect" (*LC* 134). Evidently then, although the two sciences will share common components, even those points of sharing cannot be made congruent in any sense, despite their identity.

That different systemic significance may be what Kuyper meant in saying that "every single science is more or less connected with the antithesis of principles, and should consequently be permeated by it" (*LC* 139), and that the two sciences even give rise to "two entirely different and mutually exclusive representations of the object" (*PST* 177), and that the result of science "constantly appears to be governed by subjective influences, and is affected by the conflict between truth and falsehood which is a result of sin" (*PST* 125), despite his repeated insistence that simple scientific descriptions of objects are common, that the results of natural science as such often do not differ, and that some areas are not at all as such affected by the split.

So Kuyper's view seems to be that observation, logic, some of the relevant data of consciousness, all of empirical science, laws and some theoretical principles are all properly held in common between believers and nonbelievers. There are, however, differences in data of consciousness between believers and nonbelievers, and the types of data where the differences lie are incorporated into the special sciences at the level of explanatory theories, setting up the potential for differences in those sciences between believers and nonbelievers (and among believers as well). (Those differences emerge at an even earlier stage in the human and theological sciences.) As each group strives toward the unity and comprehensiveness characteristic of broad science, the differing contents in consciousness and the inevitable splits in the upper levels of the natural sciences as well as in the higher sciences guarantee the unbridgeable inconsistency between the two broad sciences (believing and unbelieving). Thus, the broad sciences as whole sciences will be sharply distinct, although some of the same components will appear in both.

I am still not quite sure how to reconcile these statements with Kuyper's repeated insistences of commonality, however, and have resorted to the use of "systemic significance" to gloss it over. These statements may simply represent a tension in Kuyper's position – wanting to recognize that there are no apparent differences between the observations, measurements, etc., done by a believer and an unbeliever, but at the same time wanting the profound differences between them to be so prominent as to completely "permeate" all they do. Or maybe Kuyper himself would have appealed to something like "systemic significance." In fact, in "Sphere Sovereignty," Kuyper says that various studies "take on another aspect" for the believer. It is on the heels of that statement that we find Kuyper's famous line that "there is not one part of our world of thought that can be hermetically separated from other parts."[61] Here too is an area that may require further work.

---

60 *LC* 138. See also "Sphere Sovereignty," sect. 3, par. 7, 10, 15.

61 "Sphere Sovereignty," sect. 3, par. 21.

The Primacy of Scripture

There is also another perhaps deeper theme running through Kuyper's thinking in this area: our allegiance must be to Christ in all things, and we need not expect that following the paths which it requires will always lead us to the same destinations as unbelievers. It may be that we will be called as scientists to hold to various views in the face of ridicule and in the face of our inability to justify them in terms of the secularly accepted canons of good science.[62] We have no guarantees that our methodologies inevitably and ineluctably lead to physical truth. Sometimes the sciences may seem to lead to results specifically contrary to Scripture, in which case we would have to reject those results.[63] (The creeds of the church, however, do not have that status—*PST* 174.) Many believe that although as Christians we may be called to suffer, we will not as Christian scientists be called to suffering or to rejection by the world. Kuyper may be suggesting otherwise.[64]

Kuyper's Anticipation

Looking at the foregoing summation of Kuyper's views, one is struck by the extent to which they anticipate later views. Fifty years before many Western philosophers, Kuyper had already seen that "values" and even metaphysical principles play a proper, ineradicable role in science, that there are legitimate subjective factors in science, that formal manipulation of observational data cannot carry us to science in any robust sense, that whatever generates certainty in our beliefs must (on pain of skepticism or idealism) operate at the level of our acceptance of even logical axioms and observational data and that realism levies constraints on our nature, the structure of our thought and our relation to the world.[65] All of that is thoroughly contemporary. Kuyper thus managed to avoid the sterility of positivism, even before its full development. But exactly how much anticipation to give Kuyper credit for is difficult to judge, since we are not given a detailed and complete explication of Kuyper's views during the very early years of the twentieth century. But surely what we are given provides reason to be impressed.

Conclusion

What lessons can we then learn from Kuyper? First, that with respect to data collection, uncovering of empirical regularities and at least some theoretical matters, we can work perfectly confidently with and beside unbelievers – just as most working Christian scientists in fact do. Even though various bits of human subjectivity enter into science even on that level, the subjectivity at that point can still be shared subjectivity. But as we go up the scale of disciplines and out into the further, more global theoretical reaches of each of the individual disciplines, our Christian antennae must be increasingly sensitive (just as those most keenly aware of the antithesis claim), for it is in those areas that unbelieving subjectivity can (and perhaps eventually must) make its appearance.

Truly Christian science will be indistinguishable (and properly so) from the science

---

62 Kuyper, in "Sphere Sovereignty," emphasizes just how out of step with secular academic respectability even the founding of the Free University was.

63 *PST* 175, possibly also 611.

64 That suggestion is fairly explicit in "Sphere Sovereignty," sect 3. Par. 11.

65 For summary discussion of current views in philosophy of science see Ratzsch, D. 1986. *Philosophy of Science*. Downers Grove: InterVarsity, ch. 4 and 5.

of unbelievers on the lower levels. Since Kuyper rejects coherentist conceptions of truth in the period in question,[66] the irreconcilable differences in the upper levels of theoretical science, or in "broad" science, will not infect science at its lower levels. Thus, there will be much in the work of unbelievers which the Christian can incorporate unchanged into his own science. But the believer must reject anything in the unbeliever's science which has woven into it any subjective factor which encompasses unbelief and its products – materialism, mechanism and so forth. On the other hand, not all scientific disputes are rooted in unbelief. The very progress of science is fuelled in part by the clash of variant systems and would so operate even in the absence of unbelief.

Kuyper has provided conceptual resources both for taking at face value the apparent identity of, say, Christian and non-Christian chemistry, while simultaneously recognizing the profound and perhaps unbridgeable differences between not only the "broad" sciences of believers and nonbelievers, but even between some higher level theorizing by the two groups even within science in some more restricted sense. Further technical work in the direction which Kuyper's work around the turn of the century pointed might be well rewarded.

---

66 As indicated earlier in the section entitled "Epistemology," Kuyper accepted a correspondence theory of truth, and such theories entail the denial of coherence theories.

24

Critical Reflections on
Abraham Kuyper's *Evolutie* Address

Clarence Menninga

A complete English translation of the *Evolutie* address that Abraham Kuyper delivered before the trustees of the Free University of Amsterdam in 1899 was published in the April 1996 issue of *Calvin Theological Journal*.[1] It is appropriate now to consider Kuyper's *Evolutie* address, and to provide some evaluation of his assessment of biological evolution. We do this evaluation, of course, from the vantage point of an additional century of study in science and in theology.

In his lecture, Kuyper frequently refers to Darwinian evolution theory as "evolution dogma." For some of Kuyper's contemporaries, as for some of ours, the theory of biological evolution provides a foundation stone for a godless world-and-life view properly called philosophical naturalism. In this view, the only things we know about reality, and the only things we can know about reality, are to be discovered through scientific study of the physical universe. Many adherents to philosophical naturalism think that biological evolution provides an adequate substitute for the Christian conviction that the God of the Scriptures is the Creator of all that there is. Those who place a heavy emphasis on biological evolution as a foundation for their thinking about reality subscribe to a world-and-life view that might properly be called evolutionism, which is actually a variant of philosophical naturalism. All of life, in that view, is to be accounted for in evolutionary terms, including the social, political, and moral character of human existence as well as the structures and functions of living organisms, plant and animal.

Christians reject the position of philosophical naturalism, of course. One of the barriers to fruitful discussion of biological evolution among Christians is the confusion among some of us between the philosophy of evolutionism and the scientific explanations of the history of change and development among living organisms. Later in this article I will call attention to some of Kuyper's comments about proper distinctions in our discussion of evolution.

Immediately after the publication of Darwin's *Origin of Species*, several of the adherents to philosophical naturalism applied Darwinian ideas to explain change and development in social organizations, an enterprise called social Darwinism, and to the development of social and moral characteristics of humans. The major thrust of Kuyper's

---

1   It was reprinted with slight revisions in *AK:ACR*: 405–440—referenced in what follows as *EV*.

negative criticism of evolution is directed against those applications of Darwin's theory of evolution to human affairs. Many of Kuyper's references are to works by Ernst Haeckel of Germany and Herbert Spencer of England, both of whom had taken the ideas of biological evolution as proposed by Charles Darwin and had attempted to apply them bodily to social structures and to human activities within social structures. Kuyper rejected the claims that ethics, aesthetics, and even religion could be understood as nothing more than products of evolutionary development among humans. I agree fully with Kuyper in his rejection of these misapplications of Darwinian ideas. The basic foundation for our human moral behavior is found in our responsibility toward God, our Creator, and in our God-ordained responsibility toward our fellow humans and the rest of creation. In addition, while there has been continuing change in social structures throughout history, those changes have been more the product of human intention than the results of biological pressures for survival.

For a detailed critique of social Darwinism, read the book *Vaulting Ambition* by Philip Kitcher.[2] Kitcher is convinced that change and development in plant and animal organisms over time have been the result of evolutionary processes, but he argues strongly against the legitimacy of applying those principles to behavior and social relationships among humans.

Please allow me a slight digression with regard to scientific explanations and the implications that may be drawn from them. Sometimes scientific theories are developed in a particular field of study and then are put to use in a quite different endeavor. In considering some philosophical implications of quantum mechanics in physics, the late Richard Feynman, Nobel laureate and professor of physics at California Institute of Technology, made the following statement: "As always, there are two aspects of the problem: one is the philosophical implication for physics, and the other is the extrapolation of philosophical matters to other fields. When philosophical ideas associated with science are dragged into another field, they are usually completely distorted."[3]

If a scientific explanation that has been developed in a particular field of study is to be useful in a different field of endeavor, the applicability of that explanation in the new field must be justified just as thoroughly as has presumably been done in the field in which it was first developed. This is not to say that ideas and explanations in any field should not be subjected to study by, say, philosophers, or theologians, or anyone else. But to take an idea, such as biological evolution, from the field of biology, and to apply its principles to some other area of study, such as sociology, without a careful examination of its applicability, is not legitimate endeavor. The unjustified application of biological Darwinism to social matters, therefore, is not legitimate.

There is an area of biology called animal behavior that involves the legitimate activity of drawing comparisons between animal activities and human behavior. However, it is a quite different thing to take relationships among animal behaviors and to claim that *the same* relationships and the same cause-effect explanations can be applied to human behavior. That claim would require justification by way of some broader principles that pertain to both animals and humans.

In his *Evolutie* address, Kuyper also discussed some biological matters in connection

---

2   Kitcher, Philip 1985. *Vaulting Ambition*. Cambridge: MIT Press.
3   Feynman, Richard 1963. *The Feynman Lectures on Physics*. Reading, MA: Addison-Wesley, 38-8.

with his criticisms of biological evolution. As noted in a footnote to the translation, Kuyper (as well as the rest of the academic and scientific community) was obviously unaware of the work on genetics that had been done thirty-five years earlier by Gregor Mendel. In addition, we have advanced a great deal since 1899 in our understanding of the principles of genetics; we explain the propagation of various characteristics from parents to offspring, as well as the occasional appearance of new characteristics in the offspring, on the basis of the structure and chemical behavior of DNA (deoxyribosenucleic acid) in the nucleus of the cell. Kuyper's long discourse on the failure of evolutionary theorists to account for the propagation of various characteristics from parents to offspring is no longer a valid criticism of biological evolution. Those questions and objections have all been answered by our present understanding of genetics.

Some of Kuyper's objections to biological evolution are built on a caricature of evolutionary processes rather than on a confrontation of the actual proposals of the theory (the long-used technique of building a straw man that is easily felled). For example, he portrays the theory of biological evolution as claiming that the eagle's ancestors must have started out with no wings, then developed stumps that would be useless for flying, then, finally, fully feathered wings. But that is not what the explanations of biological evolution suggest. The explanations of biological evolution suggest that the eagle's ancestors had four limbs and that the forelimbs were modified so that they might serve a *different* function – that of flying – than the forelimbs had served in the ancestor. That suggestion is very different from development of functional wings from nothing. We note here that the earliest known fossil birds had a skeletal structure that was very similar in many respects to skeletons of small dinosaurs that were living on Earth at that time in history. The study of the fossil remains of those dinosaurs provides a basis for comparing the structure and function of forelimbs in those dinosaurs with the structure and function of forelimbs in birds.

It may be that Kuyper did not know much about fossil birds and fossil dinosaurs, although reptile-like fossils were first given the name *dinosaur* in 1841, the famous Archaeopteryx bird fossil was discovered in 1861, and the relationship between birds and dinosaurs was widely discussed during the latter part of the nineteenth century. In any case, Kuyper surely should have known the claims of biological evolution in sufficient detail to avoid the caricature of evolutionary explanations. Such caricatures in Kuyper's address need not be refuted; they may simply be pointed out and recognized as caricatures.

Kuyper had serious objections to biological evolution as proposed by Charles Darwin, even when evolutionary explanations were applied strictly to the descent of present-day living organisms from different species of ancient organisms by change and development in response to natural conditions and pressures for survival. Kuyper considered Darwin's formulation of evolutionary theory to be incompatible with Christian faith in a Creator because he thought that any Christian formulation of an explanation for the rise of extant species through descent with modification from previously existing species must include the recognition of *purpose* and *plan* in the development of living organisms. Darwinian theory includes no explicit consideration of purpose or directed plan in the processes of biological evolution. Kuyper's criticism is expressed forcibly when he says that evolutionary change under God's direction "would never have been the Evolution of Darwinism, for then foreordained purpose [*Zweck*] would not have been banished but would have been all-controlling. Then the world would not have constructed itself mechanistically but God would have built it with elements He himself had prepared" (*EV* 437).

Kuyper pursues the same line of reasoning in some detailed discussion of the mechanistic character of the theory of biological evolution (*EV* 418–20). He considers Darwinism to be antithetical to the Christian doctrine of creation especially in that the scientific theory does not embody a "previously established goal toward which the development of living organisms would be impelled, either by means of an indwelling principle or through divine power working from without" (*EV* 419).

Was Kuyper correct in his judgment that the Christian doctrine of creation and the Darwinian theory of biological evolution are incompatible? With respect to Darwin's proposals for biological matters (setting aside, for now, his worldview), I think not. Is it reasonable, or even possible, for God and God's purposes in creation to be incorporated explicitly into scientific explanations as Kuyper apparently expected? I think not.

We explain the motions of the planets in the solar system on the basis of the physics of motion and gravitational force. There is not an explicit factor for God nor for God's action in the equations developed by Isaac Newton and Pierre Laplace. Nevertheless, we Christians affirm that God's purposes are part and parcel of the motions of the planets, and that it is God who brings "forth the constellations in their seasons" (Job 38:32). Or, perhaps more explicitly, we Christians recognize God as the Governor who guarantees that "As long as the earth endures, seedtime and harvest, cold and heat, summer and winter, day and night will never cease" (Genesis 8:22), while our scientific explanation of the day-night sequence and the annual cycle of the seasons is in terms of the motions of planet Earth under the influence of momentum and gravity without any explicit mention of God or God's governance. Yet, we do not think that our scientific explanation for the changing seasons is incompatible with our Christian doctrine of providence. Just different.

Similarly, our scientific understanding of the biological processes of conception and childbirth is in terms of sperm cell and egg cell, DNA, and food transport to the fetus by means of blood flow in the umbilical cord with no explicit mention of God as the Creator of every one of us. The perception of the Psalmist, on the other hand, is that "you [God] created my inmost being; you knit me together in my mother's womb" and that "my frame was not hidden from you when I was made in the secret place. When I was woven together in the depths of the earth, your eyes saw my unformed body" (Psalm 139:13, 15–16). But we do not find the scientific perspective to be incompatible with the biblical perspective, do we? Just different.

Those are only two examples; we could find hundreds more that demonstrate the same conclusion, namely, that the concepts of purpose or pre-established plan are not explicitly incorporated into scientific explanations. And there is good reason for that. Scientific explanations arise from our human efforts to explain and understand what we observe in our physical world. Scientific explanations are also tested on the basis of their consistency with our observations of our physical world. And our notions of purpose and pre-established plan do not arise from our observations of the physical world; they arise from our faith in the God who created and sustains the world in consistently ordered ways, as Abraham Kuyper himself attests in his 1898 (*LC*) lecture, "Calvinism and Science."

So, Kuyper was unjustified in his expectation that God or God's purposes in creation should find explicit expression in the Darwinian theories of biological evolution. We cannot, indeed should not, expect an explicit factor for God in any scientific theory. The absence of explicit mention of God's purpose in Darwin's scientific theory of biological evolution does not mean that the theory is *incompatible* with the Christian doctrine of creation; it means that scientific theories are an *incomplete* explanation of reality. There is more to reality than we can investigate by the methods of science, and there is more to reality than we can explain by means of our scientific theories. It is "by faith [that] we understand that the universe was formed at God's command, so that what is seen was not made out of what was visible" (Hebrews 11:3). It is by *faith* that we understand that "The Son is the radiance of God's glory and the exact representation of his being, sustaining all things by his powerful word" (Hebrews 1:3). Abraham Kuyper was looking for more from science than science could provide when he criticized Darwin's theory for not explicitly expressing purpose and pre-established plan.

There are several passages in Kuyper's address in which he calls attention to reliable information and good insights that have resulted from studies encouraged and initiated by the ideas of biological evolution. He comments that we do not deny changeableness in living organisms nor the transmission of characteristics from parent to progeny (*EV* 425). At the same time, Kuyper warns the listener (and reader) that these good results should not lead us to accept the view of philosophical naturalism, namely, the [evolutionary] "system *as system*. That system remains evil, even though in many respects good has come out of evil" (*EV* 439). Kuyper is unsatisfied with the mechanistic character of Darwinism, and he wants to see a "guiding principle" expressed explicitly in the scientific explanation of the development of living organisms over time. However, if we make the distinctions that I have recommended above, noting that we should not expect to find purpose, meaning, or guiding principles in our scientific explanations of God's world, and that, in many demonstrable cases, we Christians affirm that the processes of nature are under God's direction even though God and his activity are not explicitly incorporated into our scientific description of those processes, then I think that we Christians may accept the processes of evolution, perhaps even some form of Darwinism, as our scientific explanation of the development of living organisms without denying the Christian doctrine of creation.

Even though Kuyper rejected the evolutionary development of species by the mechanistic processes proposed by Darwin, there are passages in Kuyper's address in which he allows the conclusion that biological organisms have been brought into existence by God through the use of process. The most familiar of these has been quoted often:

> We will not force our style upon the Chief Architect of the universe. If He is to be the Architect not in name only but in reality, He will also be supreme in the choice of style. Had it thus pleased God not to create the species but to have one species emerge from another by enabling a preceding species to produce a higher following species, Creation would be no less miraculous. (*EV* 436–37)

In a footnote related to this comment, Kuyper mentions two of his contemporaries, Emil Heinrich Du Bois-Reymond and Gerardus Johannes Mulder, who had published their suggestion that God had used the processes of evolution to bring species into existence.

There is another comment in the same vein a few paragraphs later when Kuyper said:

> To this I may add that the Scriptural charter of Creation eliminates rather than commends the *dramatic* entry of new beings. Scripture states that "*the earth brought forth* herb yielding seed after its kind" and also that "*the earth brought forth* the cattle and everything that creepeth upon the earth" [Genesis 1:11, 24], not that they were *set down* upon the earth by God like

pieces upon a chessboard. (*EV* 438)

While Kuyper rejected the mechanistic views of Darwinism as a way in which God might have created living organisms, he certainly conceded that God might have used natural processes in his creating work.

Kuyper explicitly rejected the view that we sometimes call theistic evolution. He relates an example suggested in support of evolution by Haeckel, asking whether a Zulu, seeing an English armored vessel for the first time, would not think it to be some organic monster, while we know that it was mechanically constructed. Kuyper adds that Haeckel was mistaken in thinking that this example supported an undirected mechanistic view of development, since we also know that the armored vessel was constructed on the basis of a previously prepared plan. Kuyper said:

> The same difference would distinguish such an evolutionistic Creation of God from the system of the Darwinists. Evolutionistic creation presupposes a God who first prepares the plan and then omnipotently executes it; Darwinism teaches a mechanistic origin of things, which excludes all plan or specifications or purpose. (*EV* 437)

And thus Kuyper dismissed the possibility of incorporating Darwinian explanations into any Christian view.

In rejecting the notion of theistic evolution, Kuyper pointed out that the purpose that should be evident in the created world, as perceived by the Christian, should be incorporated into such a theistic explanation. Kuyper said that if the evolutionary view is to be compatible with the Christian perspective, that idea of *purpose* would not have been abandoned. Contrarily, Darwin proposed that the evolutionary changes that had occurred in plant and animal history were the result entirely of the working of natural processes. That is to say, explicit mention of God and any notion of a Creator's purposeful intention are strictly excluded from Darwinian theories of biological evolution. It seems unlikely that Kuyper would be satisfied with current forms of theistic evolution, either. None of them, as far as I can tell, has incorporated explicit mention of *God's purpose* as an integral term in the scientific explanation. In every case, as far as I can tell, the conviction of God's presence and purpose in the history of change and development of living organisms *underlies*, and, perhaps, *overarches* the scientific theory but is not an integral part of that scientific explanation. As noted earlier, God's plan and purpose are not to be found explicitly in scientific explanations, which are based on human observations of our physical world.

Kuyper advised his hearers and readers to make proper distinctions between facts that have been discovered by careful scientific investigation and philosophical ideas that have been construed on the basis of such facts (*EV* 417). I agree with Kuyper on this score. We must separate out and reject the claims of social Darwinism that have mistakenly been construed from information obtained in biological studies. We must also separate out and reject the claims of atheistic evolutionism that have mistakenly been construed from the proposals of the scientific theory of biological evolution. Kuyper failed to make this second distinction clearly, often using the word *evolution* interchangeably as dogma and as biological process, and so he rejected the idea of creation by process. The distinction, however, is valid, and we Christians may accept evolutionary processes as God's method of creating new species of living organisms. We certainly have made a similar distinction in our Christian perspective on most (all?) other scientific theories, namely, that God is active in the processes of nature even though there is not an explicit factor for God in the scientific explanation. The claim that *there is* a divinely ordained plan that is directing the processes of nature, like the claim that *there is* no divinely ordained plan and that these processes are purely mechanistic, is a presupposition or construal that arises from outside our observations of God's world, and *neither* claim appears, or can appear, as an explicit factor in properly constructed scientific explanations.

We should note here that there are other Christian scholars of the past and present who think that uniquely Christian ideas and perspectives can and should be incorporated into scientific explanations and theories explicitly. Notable among these is Professor Alvin Plantinga of the Department of Philosophy at the University of Notre Dame. See, for example, his article "Methodological Naturalism?"[4] There is not sufficient space in this article to review that issue completely, nor is this the appropriate place for a dispute on that issue. The discussion should continue; the matter is not yet resolved. I, for one, am not convinced that it is possible or fruitful to attempt to incorporate explicit terms for God or for God's activity into scientific theories of the biological evolution of plants and animals. To invoke God or God's activity into theories in sociology or psychology in some explicit way may be a different matter; that issue should be reviewed by Christians who are competent in those fields of study.

Before leaving this review of Abraham Kuyper's ideas on evolution, we should also take note of some ideas about the history of living organisms that have come to be called intelligent design theory. Those ideas have been publicized in various ways, notably in the book *Darwin's Black Box*[5] and in an article entitled "Intelligent design as a theory of information."[6] The ideas of intelligent design theory have received a great deal of attention in the Christian community. All Christians, of course, confess that the universe is the product of God's design. What is added in the ideas of Behe and Dembski is the claim that an intelligent and powerful being has brought certain structures in living organisms into existence by some kind of special action rather than through change and development by natural processes. While some Christians are finding these ideas attractive, others of us perceive these ideas as a new valiant on the old "God-of-the-gaps" proposal; when there are phenomena or structures that we do not understand completely, some Christians are inclined to jump into the gap in our knowledge hastily with the claim, "God did it!" That approach has not served us well in the past, and it is not likely to serve us well in our consideration of the history of living organisms on Earth, either.

At the present time, we have achieved some understanding of the broad outlines of the history of living organisms on Earth, but we don't have good answers to all of our questions about the details of that history. So, we keep on studying.

Kuyper was not favorably inclined toward the ideas of biological evolution as formulated by Charles Darwin. He was adamantly opposed to applying the principles of biological evolution to social structures and social behavior of humans. He thought that the mechanistic nature of the Darwinian theory of evolution was incompatible with Christian

---

4   Plantinga, Alvin 1997. "Methodological Naturalism?" *Perspectives on Science and Christian Faith* 49 (September): 143–54.

5   Behe, Michael J. 1996. *Darwin's Black Box*. New York: Free Press.

6   Dembski, William A. 1997. "Intelligent Design as a Theory of Information." *Perspectives on Science and Christian Faith* 49 (September): 180.

faith, but he left opportunity for the Christian to accept the processes of evolutionary development as an explanation for the history of living organisms on Earth, provided that God is recognized as the supreme Governor and Director of those processes.

25

A Theology of the Arts:
Kuyper's Ideas on Art and Religion

Peter S. Heslam

Kuyper's vision of the arts has been virtually neglected in scholarly study, but perhaps not without good reason.[1] When he spoke about politics, science, and religion he was dealing with areas in which he was heavily and professionally committed; when it came to the arts he spoke as an "outsider." Added to this is the fact that he occasionally made embarrassingly frank dismissals of certain forms of art, particularly in the field of the dramatic arts. From his correspondence with Jo Schaay during their five-year engagement, we learn not only that he could not dance (much to his annoyance, because Jo could) but that he tried to temper his fiancée's passion for reading novels by questioning whether it was a good use of her time – along with her attendance of concerts, the theatre and, of course, dances.[2] On top of all this we have the testimony of one of his great-grandchildren that he was not a tuneful singer.[3]

Against this background, it is striking that Kuyper's influence in the field of the arts should have been so effective and enduring: his legacy in this sphere in Great Britain will be considered towards the end of this paper.[4] It is clear, however, that Kuyper took

---

1   The only serious treatment of the Kuyperian perspective on art is that by the British theologian Jeremy Begbie in his *Voicing Creation's Praise: Toward a Theology of the Arts.* Edinburgh: T & T Clark, 1991. See my review in *Theology* 44 (1991), 388–89.

2   Puchinger, George 1987. *Abraham Kuyper: De jonge Kuyper* (1837–1867). Franeker: Wever, 65.

3   From a conversation I had with George Puchinger in 1987. Puchinger has written of Kuyper's lack of artistic gifts. See Puchinger, G. 1989. "Opwaartsche wegen: een opwekkend geneesmiddel." In *Juffrouw Ida* 15: 50–54. Kuyper's extraordinary visionary, oratory and literary talents are, however, acknowledged elsewhere in Puchinger's writings. See, for instance, Puchinger, G. and Scheps, N. 1971. *Gesprek over de onbekende Kuyper.* Kampen: Kok, 8–26; Puchinger, G. 1987. *Kuyper-herdenking 1987 (de religieuze Kuyper): vijf opstellen en lezingen van de herdenking van de honderdvijftigste geboortedag van Abraham Kuyper; 29 oktober 1987.* Kampen: Kok, 33.

4   Kuyper's influence in the field of art theory is reflected chiefly in the work of Hans Rookmaaker, Calvin Seerveld, and Nicholas Wolterstorff. See, for instance, Rookmaaker, Hans 1970. *Modern Art and the Death of a Culture.* London: IVP; Seerveld, Calvin 1962. *A Christian Critique of Art.* St. Catherines, Ontario: The Association for Reformed Scientific Studies, and 1980 (1997). *Rainbows of the Fallen World: Artistic Life and Aesthetic Task.* Toronto: Tuppence Press/ Carlisle: Paternoster; Wolterstorff, Nicholas 1980 (1997). *Art*

This paper is based on the contents of my book *Creating a Christian Worldview: Abraham Kuyper's Lectures on Calvinism.* Grand Rapids/Carlisle: Eerdmans/Paternoster, 1998.

the arts seriously and appreciated their value. He lectured at the Free University in both aesthetics and the history of Dutch literature;[5] he paid particular attention to the novel in a lengthy series of articles in *De Heraut*;[6] he published a collection of prints made of original paintings of biblical scenes, and provided a commentary;[7] he corresponded with Joseph Israels (1824–1911), a well-known artist of The Hague School;[8] and he wrote extensively on the relationship between theology and the arts, tackling the subject on two key occasions: his inauguration as Rector Magnificus of the Free University in 1888, and in his presentation of the Stone Lectures at Princeton a decade later.[9] Why, though, should Kuyper have paid much attention to this subject, especially in view of the fact that serious treatments of the arts that go beyond moral critique are rare within the history of Protestantism?[10] This paper will offer five reasons, all of which are suggested by Kuyper's actual treatment of the subject but which take his socio-cultural and intellectual context as the primary point of reference.[11]

---

in Action: Toward a Christian Aesthetic. Grand Rapids: Eerdmans/Carlisle: Paternoster. Rookmaaker's book so impressed Malcolm Muggeridge that he made it his *Observer* book of the year in 1971. Jeremy Begbie writes about this book: "No other work from the pen of a Dutch Neo-Calvinist has ever reached such wide readership as that remarkable study" (Begbie, *Voicing Creation's Praise*, 127). Begbie leaves Wolterstorff's ideas out of his analysis, on the basis that Wolterstorff's philosophy of art "strays far from the Kuyperian path" (83). This is a judgment Wolterstorff would not accept, and it leads to a regrettable omission. See Wolterstorff's review of Seerveld's *Rainbows* in *Third Way* 5 (1982), 22–23.

5   His lecture notes for these courses are kept in *Het Kuyper Archief* (The Kuyper Archive), held at the Documentatiecentrum voor het Nederlands Protestantisme (1800–heden) at the Free University, Amsterdam (portfolios LB; P2 and LG; P12). Further references to this archive will be abbreviated to KA, followed by the portfolio reference. A transcript of Kuyper's lectures in aesthetics was made by one of his students. From the notes and the transcript it is clear that the course included sections on the definition of art and beauty, on the history of art and aesthetics, and on the theory of music. Evidence of the extent to which Kuyper was well read in the history of music can be found in the published version of his rectorial address of 1893, *De verflauwing der grenzen: rede bij de overdracht van het rectoraat aan de Vrije Universiteit*, October 1892. Amsterdam: Wormser, 85–87 n. 105.

6   *De Heraut*, 1901: February 10 and 24, March 10, April 7, May 5 and 19, June 2. Kuyper had received a solid grounding in literary and linguistic studies as a student at the University of Leiden, where the great linguist Matthijs de Vries was one of his mentors. The young Kuyper was an ardent admirer of the language of Byron and of the Dutch novelist Multatuli. See Puchinger, *Abraham Kuyper*, 63.

7   Kuyper, A. n.d. [1910]. *Modern Masters as Interpreters of Holy Writ: A Series of Seventy-two Mezzogravures from the Work of Some of the Leading Modern Painters.* With an introduction by The Right Reverend Arthur Foley Winnington-Ingram, DD, Lord Bishop of London. 2 vols. London: Gresham Publishing.

8   Letters from Joseph Israels to Kuyper can be found in KA: *Brieven*, nos. 6884, 7213, 7262, 7317.

9   Kuyper, A. 1888. *Het calvinisme en de kunst: rede bij de overdracht van het rectoraat der Vrije Universiteit op 20 October 1888.* Amsterdam: Wormser; and in *LC* 142–170. Kuyper also dealt with this subject at length in the following publications under his name: *Encyclopaedie der Heilige Godgeleerdheid*, 3 vols. Amsterdam: Wormser, 1894, III, 331–338, 341–343; *De Gemeene Gratie in Wetenschap en Kunst.* Amsterdam: Höveker & Wormser, 1905; *PrRege* III:470–580. *Het calvinisme en de kunst* is the most important as far as the relationship between Calvinism and art is concerned, and for this reason it will receive more attention in this paper than the others.

10 Begbie, *Voicing Creation's Praise*, xv–xvi.

11 This contextual method of interpretation is not meant to imply that Kuyper's approach to the arts can be explained merely in terms of his particular circumstances, as if his beliefs and convictions were of no real importance. However, as present-day biblical scholars tend to agree, historical context is not everything, but it is certainly something.

The Popularization of the Arts

Kuyper was ambivalent about the current burgeoning of interest in art amongst ordinary people. On the one hand he felt that it amounted to the "almost fanatical worship of art," and encouraged the proliferation of poor-quality productions; on the other, it provided a welcome respite from the current infatuation with wealth and the intellect. Increasing materialism and rationalism had brought atrophy to the human heart, and were threatening to "reduce the life of the emotions to freezing-point." An antidote was sought in the gratification of the artistic instinct, a demand which could increasingly be met because "the finest artistic enjoyments are now brought for almost no price within the reach of an ever-widening class."[12]

It is likely that the invention of the phonograph, or gramophone, by Thomas Edison in 1877 and the mass-production of gramophone records that followed in its wake were foremost in Kuyper's mind when he wrote these words. Together they represented a major turning-point in the history of the performing arts, allowing large numbers of people to gain easy and relatively inexpensive access to the kind of music which had hitherto been patronized only by a small, wealthy minority.[13] He was not alone in his mixed assessment of the consequences of such popularization: the great nineteenth-century art critic John Ruskin wrote that "there is no limit to the good which may be effected by rightly taking advantage of the powers we now possess of placing good and lovely art within the reach of the poorest classes," but he went on to lament "the great harm [that] has been done . . . by forms of art definitely addressed to depraved tastes."[14]

Ruskin and Kuyper's concern reflects a strand of thought that was prevalent in intellectual circles in the second half of the nineteenth century, in which commentary on art and artists tended to focus on what could be considered "good taste" – true art being that which measured up to certain standards of taste. Since, however, there was disagreement on what these standards should be, no scientific study of art or artists could proceed very far, and many forms of art were not considered "true art." In 1898, Leo Tolstoy (1828–1910) went so far as to exclude from art those symphonies and paintings which appealed to the more sensual and decadent tastes, including some of the most respected works of

---

12 *LC* 142–43. In an article in *De Standaard* of August 31, 1903, Kuyper again expressed a qualified approval of the wide-scale renewal of interest in the arts, and contrasted it to the barrenness of rationalism. Now, however, he believed the latter to be on the wane: "The period of dry intellectualism lies behind us. To be practical, before everything else, was then the watchword, and every guilder spent on decoration and ornamentation was considered wasted money."

13 Kuyper is likely also to have been referring to the increased opportunities for international musical tours, brought about by improvements in rail and sea travel. It is interesting to note the way in which the November, 1898, edition of the British journal *The Musical Times* gave expression to some of the excitement and enthusiasm with which the invention of the gramophone was received: "As to the newest Edison phonograph, we can say from practical knowledge that it is a very wonderful instrument [. . .] whose use will give much pleasure and not a little amusement." Cited in Scholes, Percy A. 1955. *The Oxford Companion to Music*, 9th edition. London: Oxford University Press, 421–422.

14 Ruskin, John 1892. *Lectures on Art. Delivered before the University of Oxford in Hilary Term*, 1870, 6th ed. London: George Allen, 13. Ruskin appears to have shared with Kuyper the belief that if art was dominated by the search for fame and fortune, public taste rather than artistic genius provided the chief impulse in the production of art. See Kuyper, A. 1905. *De Gemeene Gratie in Wetenschap en Kunst.* Amsterdam: Höveker en Wormser, 73; *De Standaard*, 29 december 1883.

Wagner and Michelangelo.[15]Within this environment, artistic taste rather than religious or moral principles became the principal criterion for judging the arts – hence Kuyper's claim that art was becoming a new form of religion. It was a claim shared by his younger contemporary Max Weber (1864–1920), who wrote concerning the development of art in the nineteenth century, "Art became a cosmos of more and more consciously grasped independent values . . . taking over the function of a this-worldly salvation."[16] In the words of a more recent commentator, it became "the ultimate redemption."[17]

Kuyper's perception of art as a new form of popular religion is crucial to understanding why he gave so much attention in his works to the subject of the arts. As the leader of a social and religious movement that relied heavily on popular support, he was intensely aware of the emergence of new social and religious trends, and he took every opportunity he could to demonstrate that Calvinism provided a viable alternative for ordinary people in contemporary society. In doing so, he was not oblivious to the obstacles, and a second reason why Kuyper turned his attention to the arts was to challenge what he saw as "a deeply-rooted prejudice" that Calvinism was incapable of producing notable works of art or of contributing to art's development.[18]

Challenging a Prejudice

In his rectorial address on "Calvinism and Art," he introduced his subject by referring to a report published in Germany three years earlier, in which the author expressed his surprise that at the Free University of Amsterdam he was able to attend a lecture on aesthetics.[19] This, Kuyper pointed out, was a testimony to the fact that the idea that Calvinism and art were mutually incompatible was still alive and well, and it was in the hope of correcting this misunderstanding that he had chosen the subject of his address. The same incentive lay behind a number of his articles on art in *De Standaard*. One of the earliest of these was written in response to an article which had ridiculed Calvinism for its lack of artistic creativity, claiming that the great artists of the Dutch Golden Age were masters in spite of their Calvinism.[20]

Three points of particular pertinence can be drawn from Kuyper's treatment of the prejudice he identified. First, it appears from the concrete examples he gave that the hostility was real rather than imagined. Dismissals of Calvinism from contemporary theologians such as Albrecht Ritschl (1822–1889) certainly tended to single out its attitude towards the enjoyment of the arts as a focus of attack.[21] Second, Kuyper's discussion of the arts

---

15 See Tolstoy, Leo 1930. *What is Art?* Translated by Aylmer Maude. Oxford: Oxford University Press.

16 Weber, Max 1958. *The Rational and Social Foundations of Music*, trans. and ed. by Don Martindale, Johannes Riedel and Gertrude Neuwirth. Carbondale: South Illinois University Press, 117.

17 Peckham, Morse 1976. "Iconography and Iconology in the Arts in the Nineteenth and Twentieth Centuries" in: *Romanticism and Behavior: Collected Essays*, 2 vols. Columbia: University of South Carolina Press, 90–108 (106).

18 *LC* 144. See also *Het calvinisme en de kunst*, 5.

19 Kuyper, *Het calvinisme en de kunst*, 5. The publication to which Kuyper was referring was Gloël, J. 1885. *Hollands Kirchliches Leben. Bericht über eine im Auftrag des königlichen Domkandidatenstiftes zu Berlin unternommene Studienreise nach Holland* (Wittenberg: Herrose, 1885).

20 *De Standaard*, Aug. 27, 1873.

21 Ritschl wrote that "Calvin . . . combated everything that pertained to the gay and free joyousness of life and luxury." See Ritschl, Albrecht (1880–86). *Geschichte des Pietismus*, 3 vols. Bonn: Marcus, I, 76.

is frequently apologetic in tone and alert to the fact that this was an area that had been virtually disregarded by Calvinist theologians. He thereby unwittingly gives the impression that what he would have wanted to call a prejudice regarding Calvinism's relationship to the arts was to some extent justified. Third, given his aim of presenting Calvinism as a worldview of all-embracing proportions, it is understandable that Kuyper should have been so concerned about an opinion which held that Calvinism had no place for the arts. If his claim for Calvinism was to have any credibility, he needed to be able to demonstrate that it had sustained, and could still sustain, a positive impact in this sphere. His lecture on "Calvinism and Art," consequently, was the most crucial of all the six Stone Lectures he delivered at Princeton.

If, however, the prejudice against Calvinism's relationship to the arts was exactly that – a prejudice, having no basis in fact – then why had Calvinism failed to develop its own form of ecclesiastical art? Kuyper met the challenge of this question head on, declaring it was because Calvinism represented such an advanced form of religion. The argument with which he backed up this claim reveals another of his reasons for addressing the arts: to respond to the rise of symbolism.

The Rise of Symbolism

Both G.W.F. Hegel (1770–1831) and Eduard von Hartmann (1842–1906) had taught, Kuyper wrote, that it was only in its lower, sensual stages that religion needed the support of art. The more religion progressed towards maturity, the more it liberated itself from the bonds of art, because art is unable to express the essence of religion.[22] This theory – later reflected in the work of Karl Barth (1886–1968), who insisted that "images and symbols have no place at all in a building designed for Protestant worship" – was fundamental to Kuyper's view of the arts.[23] It also provided him with a starting point from which to assess the re-establishment of symbolist forms of worship in the church – a movement which reached its peak in England towards the end of the nineteenth century, and which had its origins in the Oxford Movement. "In her Thirty nine Articles," Kuyper wrote, "the Church of England is strictly Calvinistic, even though in her Hierarchy and Liturgy she has abandoned the straight paths, and has met with the serious results of this departure in Puseyism and Ritualism" (LC 16).

Ever since Edward Pusey (1800–1882) had joined it in 1835, the Oxford Movement had come to be associated with his name. This was reflected in the nickname "Puseyism," which had been given to the movement by those outside it and is here employed by Kuyper.[24] It was, however, John Henry Newman who laid down the theological groundwork

---

22 LC 148, cf. 67. Kuyper was evidently referring to a passage from Hegel's *Enzyklopädie der Philosophischen Wissenschaften in Grundrisse* (Berlin, 1845), which he reproduced in full in his *Het calvinisme en de kunst*, 80 (n. 91). The key sentence, for Kuyper, was the following: "Aber die schone Kunst ist nur eine Befreiungsstufe, nicht die höchste Befreiung selbst." In the Stone Lectures he rendered this in somewhat contracted form as: "beautiful art is not its [the human spirit's] highest emancipation" (LC 148). Kuyper's appeal to Von Hartmann was to his *Ästhetik*, 2 vols, II, 458, 459.

23 Barth, Karl 1965. "The Architectural Problem of Protestant places of Worship." In *Architecture in Worship: The Christian Place of Worship*, edited by André Bieler. Edinburgh/London: Oliver & Boyd, 93. The emphasis in the quotation is Barth's own. Kuyper's approach is expressed succinctly in the following sentence from the Stone Lectures: "The purely spiritual breaks through the nebula of the symbolical" (LC 147).

24 R. W. Church, an adherent of the Oxford Movement and one of its early historians, recorded in 1897 that

of its vision who insisted that the outward and visible aspects of worship should not be disregarded in favor of the inward and spiritual:

> There is no such thing as abstract religion. . . . What will the devotion of the country people be, if we strip religion of its external symbols, and bid them seek out and gaze upon the Invisible? Scripture gives us the spirit, and the Church the body, to our worship; and we may as well expect that the spirits of man might be seen by us without the intervention of their bodies, as suppose that the Object of faith can be realized in a world of sense and excitement, without the instrumentality of an outward form to arrest and fix attention, to stimulate the careless, and to encourage the desponding.[25]

Kuyper and his colleagues on the editorial board of *De Heraut* reacted to such reasoning – and its effects – with considerable alarm, and regular reports on the development of the symbolistic and ritualistic trend in the Church of England were contained within its columns.[26] One of the lectures Kuyper gave in the United States after his visit to Princeton was largely given over to a criticism of this trend. It was a trend, he declared, which was becoming "almost dominant in England, and now already in a considerable degree menaces our Calvinistic church-life."[27] Obituaries carried in *De Heraut* of some of the influential figures in this movement did, however, display a large degree of personal sympathy and respect for their causes,[28] and Kuyper never lost his admiration for traditional Anglican

---

this derogatory term was used widely on the European continent: "this nickname, partly from a greater smoothness of sound, partly from an odd suggestion of something funny in it, came more into use than others; and the terms *Puseismus, Puséisme, Puseista* found their way into German lecture-halls and Paris salons and remote convents and police offices in Italy and Sicily; indeed, in the shape of ποζεισμη it might be lighted on in a Greek newspaper" Church, R. W. (1897). *The Oxford Movement: Twelve Years, 1833–1845.* London: Macmillan, 1897, 183. In 1915 the historian S. L. Ollard wrote about the term "Puseyite": "I saw it myself in a Danish dictionary some five years ago (where it was strangely confused with "Puss" and "Pussy-cat"): Ollard, S. L. 1915. *A Short History of the Oxford Movement.* With an introduction by A. M. Allchin. Oxford: Mowbray, 48. G. W. E. Russell, one of Pusey's early biographers, retells Lady Frederick Cavendish's account of an audience she had with the Pope: "It was in the year 1867 that we paid our respects to Pope Pius IX. . . . The Pope spoke to us in French, so the word he used for Puseyite was '*Pousséiste.*' He could not pronounce the French 'u.' He said to me, '*M. Gladstone est Pousséiste, n'est ce pas?*' To which I replied, '*Oui, Saint Père, et moi aussi*' – at which he was much amused." Russell, G. W. E. (1907). *Dr. Pusey.* Oxford: Mowbray, 38, n. 1. Kuyper's use of the term "Puseyism" in his *Stone Lectures* was thus in keeping with a trend at the time and indicates his generally hostile attitude towards it. W.E. Gladstone's 1875 response to ritualism can be found in his *The Church of England and Ritualism.* London: Straham.

25 Newman, J. H. 1873. *Parochial and Plain Sermons,* 8 vols. II, 74–75; cf. IV, 176.

26 These reports appeared in *De Heraut* between Dec. 7, 1877, and Nov. 2, 1902. A report in *De Standaard* during Kuyper's visit to America commented that "ritualism was being discussed in England more than ever before" (Nov. 6, 1898).

27 Kuyper, A. 1899. *The Antithesis Between Symbolism and Revelation.* Amsterdam and Pretoria: Höveker & Wormser; Edinburgh: T&T Clark, 5. Kuyper set his entire address against the background of the ritualistic trend in England.

28 The following obituaries appeared in *De Heraut*: E. B. Pusey (Nov. 5, 1882); J. H. Newman (Sept. 21, 1890, Oct. 19, 1890); H. P. Liddon (Oct. 19, 1890). The mixture of criticism and respect is exemplified in the following passage from Newman's obituary: "Following his death both friend and foe have paid tribute to his honest character. But it is regrettable that a man of such rich gifts as Newman should have given himself to initiating a contra-reformation" (*De Heraut,* Sept. 21, 1890). A similar tone was sounded by B. B. Warfield, Kuyper's host on his visit to Princeton in 1895. In his review of the third volume of Liddon, H. P. 1894. *Life of Edward Bouverie Pusey,* 4 vols. London: Longmans, Green & Company, Warfield wrote: "Here we have a picture of a good man's unwearied and generally useful efforts to do good,

liturgy, first instilled through his reading of *The Heir of Redclyffe*, whose author, Charlotte Yonge (1823–1901), was a member of the Oxford Movement and a friend of John Keble, another of its leaders.[29]

Kuyper's chief concern was that the reintroduction of symbolism would inevitably lead to doctrinal indifference because it was rooted in pantheistic thought.[30] He illustrated such indifference by relating an encounter he had had with an Anglican clergyman who was a distinguished advocate of the symbolist movement. In conversation with him, Kuyper wrote, he had made "no secret whatsoever to me of his absolute apostasy from the Christian faith." Three days later, however, Kuyper had attended an Anglican service, only to witness the same clergyman "mounting the pulpit, solemnly reading what in the Book of Kings is written about Elijah's miracles, and thereupon leading the collects of the Book of Common Prayer." Kuyper recounted his sense of shock: "I frankly confess that I felt unable to explain such a bold contrast of personal conviction and outward performance." Later, the clergyman had explained to him that he was able to take part in Christian worship on the basis of its poetic qualities, rather than because it expressed any essential reality.[31]

Kuyper's idea that the symbolist movement was rooted in pantheism explains his preoccupation with a movement largely contained within the Anglican church. However, he considered the advances of pantheistic thought to constitute a threat to Western Christianity as a whole, and so it was only a matter of time before the pantheism already manifest in the Church of England would take firmer hold in the Calvinistic churches of The Netherlands and the United States: "there exists an undeniable affinity," he declared, "between the, as yet, feeble symbolic action in our own churches and the dark ritualistic cloud pending over Great Britain."[32] The establishment of a link between symbolism in liturgy and indifference in doctrine by assigning them a common source in pantheism suggests that it was the maintenance of doctrinal purity, rather than the fortunes of art, that was Kuyper's chief concern in his discussions of symbolism. It enabled him, in characteristic fashion, to reduce the entire issue to a clash of antithetical principles – Calvinism on the one hand against pantheism on the other.[33]

---

mingled, of course, with the evils which grew out of the nature of his religious opinions." *The Presbyterian and Reformed Review* 7 (1896), 347–350 (349).

29 For the profound effect this novel had on Kuyper's spiritual development, see Heslam, *Creating a Christian Worldview*, 31–32. Kuyper's appreciation of Anglican forms of worship is particularly apparent in his major liturgical work *Onze Eeredienst* (Kampen: Kok, 1911), where he wrote that the Church of England was "much more highly developed liturgically" than the Reformed churches of The Netherlands (492).

30 Kuyper's main objection to pantheism was that it tried to abolish the boundary between God and the world. Symbolism, similarly, sought to abolish the distinction between the infinite and the finite, the eternal and the temporal realms. See Kuyper's *The Antithesis*, 15.

31 Kuyper, *The Antithesis*, 17–18.

32 Kuyper, *The Antithesis*, 9. Kuyper's perception of pantheism was in part indebted to Constance E. Plumptre, from whose book *A General Sketch of the History of Pantheism*, 2 vols (London: Samuel Deacon 1878, 1879), II, 263, Kuyper cites the following definition of pantheism: "science among us is at its height when it interprets all orders of phenomena as differently conditioned modes of one kind of uniformity" (Kuyper, *De Verflauwing*, 18).

33 Kuyper wrote: "The principle of Symbolism and that of Calvinism are precisely the opposite of one another. An abyss is gaping between them" (Kuyper, *The Antithesis*, 21).

An Alternative Aesthetic

A fourth reason why Kuyper sought to address the arts was to provide an alternative in the field of aesthetics. He took the biblical notion of God's "glory" (*doxa*), which for him included the idea of God's radiance, perfection, splendor and divinity (*thelotes*), as the basis on which to construct a theology of art and beauty.[34] God's glory, he explained, was impressed upon all his creation, such that beauty was the shining through of God's glory in both spiritual and material things.[35] As a result of the fall, the original beauty of creation was lost, but had been restored in and through Jesus Christ: "Christ . . . is the canon and ideal of all beauty."[36] The vocation of art, therefore, was not to imitate nature, as the realists taught, but to reveal "a higher reality than is offered to us by this sinful world."[37] Art, in other words, had the prophetic function of reminding human beings of the lost beauty of paradise and of anticipating the future glory of a new heaven and a new earth.[38] For Kuyper this could only take place effectively, however, if art corresponded with "the forms and relations" exhibited in nature (*LC* 154). Thus he distanced himself not only from realism but also from idealism – the Kantian trend which understood art not as deriving its laws from nature but as standing above nature and prescribing its laws to it. Kuyper wanted his system of aesthetics to occupy a position of its own between these trends, but to be close enough to both to derive some insights from them. He claimed, in fact, that because God's glory was manifest in both spiritual and material phenomena, the antithesis between idealism and realism simply fell away. In seeking the essence of the beautiful only in the realm of the spirit or in the realm of matter, both schools sacrificed one realm of the beautiful for the other. If, however, God's glory was reflected in both material and spiritual phenomena, then true beauty could be manifest in both spheres: "A color, a tone, or a line can be beautiful in itself just as much as a character trait, a disposition, a thought or a deed."[39]

While, therefore, rejecting idealism and realism as total explanations of the function of art, Kuyper integrated a synthesis of their insights into an alternative vision that he felt was true to Calvinism's commitment to scripture.[40] He was only able to do so because of the close link he perceived between aesthetics and theology, reflected in the fact that he,

---

34 Kuyper, *Het calvinisme en de kunst*, 10–12.

35 This thought is closely akin to Kuyper's idea that all created things contain and reflect God's thoughts, an idea he often used to stimulate the pursuit of science. Kuyper contrasted this position to that of the Hegelian school which regarded beauty as the shining through of intellectual ideas. See Kuyper, *Antithesis*, II.

36 Kuyper, *Het calvinisme en de kunst*, 12. Begbie sums up Kuyper's position thus: "Beauty must therefore now be understood in the light of Jesus Christ, through whom all things were created, and in whom creation is restored to its intended beauty." Begbie, *Voicing Creation's Praise*, 97.

37 *LC* 154. Kuyper reckoned those belonging to the realist or "empiricist" school to include Helmholtz, Pfau and Semper, and those of the idealist school to include Schelling, Solger, Seising, Kostlin, Zimmerman, and Von Hartmann. That Kuyper kept abreast with new developments in aesthetics is illustrated by the fact that Yon Hartmann's work *Ästhetik*, to which Kuyper refers in his rectorial address, was published in 1888, the same year as Kuyper's address. See Kuyper, *Het calvinisme en de kunst*, 71 (nn. 61, 62).

38 Herman Bavinck also stressed the prophetic function of art; art allowed creaturely beauty to lift beholders above the conflicts of life and point them towards the glory yet to be revealed. See Bavinck, H. 1921. "Van schoonheid en schoonheidsleer," in *Verzamelde Opstellen*. Kampen: Kok, 262–280. Cf. Begbie, *Voicing Creation's Praise*, 99.

39 Kuyper, *Het calvinisme en de kunst*, 17.

40 Kuyper, *Het calvinisme en de kunst*, 18, 73 (n. 68).

as a professor of theology, considered it part of his task to teach courses in aesthetics. In a circular he distributed to new students of theology, aesthetics appeared as an integral part of the curriculum; indeed, it stipulated a good "aesthetic development" as a formal requirement for proceeding from preliminary to advanced theological studies. The reason given was that "the life of art is more closely allied to the religious life than the life of the intellect."[41]

The Cultural Impact of Calvinist Doctrine

Common grace

Kuyper also paid so much attention to the arts, finally, in order to highlight the cultural impact of Calvinist theology. Two doctrines are of particular relevance here: those of common grace and election. Restricting the enjoyment and production of art to the regenerate, Kuyper explained, would make it a product of particular grace, whereas for Calvinists both history and experience taught that the highest artistic instincts were natural gifts which flourished by virtue of common grace. It was, in fact, pagan Greece that had given to art its fundamental laws, and it was the Calvinistic commitment to common grace that had caused art to rediscover them (*LC* 160-61).

Kuyper's argument here stands in stark contrast to his insistence elsewhere that the starting point for science lay in the human consciousness, which was either regenerate or unregenerate; there is no mention of "two kinds of art" to complement his idea of "two kinds of science." A number of factors help account for this discrepancy, including, first, that as someone intimately involved in the academic world of his day, Kuyper was more closely acquainted with trends within the scientific world that were antagonistic to Christian principles than with those within the arts. This is demonstrated in his Stone Lectures, where, in contrast to his lecture on science, his lecture on art makes no mention of any artistic school constituting a threat to orthodox belief. Clearly Kuyper was familiar with contemporary discussions of aesthetics, but this discipline did not concern the production of art as such, and, as we have seen, Kuyper tended to treat it as a branch of theology rather than as a discipline of its own.

A second factor was the greater strategic importance of providing an independent alternative in the areas of politics and science than in the area of the arts. Kuyper fought persistently for the establishment of independent political and scientific institutions, believing this to be the only way the orthodox Protestants in The Netherlands could be free to organize their own lives, and to make an impact on society at large. Both the Anti-Revolutionary Party and the Free University were conceived at the end of the 1870s with this end in view. In the area of the arts, however, Kuyper made no attempt to pursue similar projects, and his first serious treatment of the subject came as much as ten years later, in 1888. He clearly felt that politics and science were of more importance than the arts when it came to effecting social change.

Third, Kuyper's ideas on the duality of science were formulated in response to the threat imposed by positivism, with its confidence in the benefits of an objective, neutral science.

---

41 Kuyper, *Methode van Studie*, published in Rullmann, J. C. 1923–40. *Kuyper-bibliographie*, 3 vols. Kampen: Kok, II, 263–65. Kuyper considered, nevertheless, that dealing with aesthetics in the theology curriculum was a temporary necessity, given that there had not yet developed any Christian aesthetics within the Faculty of Arts. See *Encyclopaedie* III:343.

In the area of the arts, however, although ideas hostile to Christianity, such as nihilism, had begun to find expression by the end of the nineteenth century, no one proposed that the arts could provide a radically new order and a means of solving all manner of problems in human society, as was thought to be the vocation of modern science.

Such reasons as these may help to explain the differences between Kuyper's thinking on the arts and on science, but they do little to help resolve what appears to be an inconsistency between the two approaches. If he intended to take a different line on art than on science, it is mystifying that he provided no explanation as to why this should be the case. In seeking to emphasize the impact of common grace, he failed to address the notion of an antithesis between the work of Christian and non-Christian artists.

Election

It was with respect to painting that Kuyper was most forthcoming as to how specific aspects of Calvinistic belief influenced artistic productions. Given the international fame of the Dutch School, it is not surprising that he should have selected the Golden Age of Dutch art during the seventeenth century to highlight the cultural significance of Calvinist theology.[42] His argument was not that the greatness of the Dutch School was due to its members being staunch Calvinists, as not all of them were; it was rather that Calvinism formed the context within which they worked, influencing their perceptions of the world they sought to represent. In this way, the doctrine of election by grace had encouraged Dutch artists to portray the hidden importance of the seemingly small and insignificant:

If a common man, to whom the world pays no special attention, is valued and even chosen by God as one of his elect, this must lead the artist also to find a motive for his artistic studies in what is common and of every-day occurrence, to pay attention to the emotions and the issues of the human heart. Thus Rembrandt's chiaroscuro embodied the reality and significance of ordinary human life.[43]

---

42 Kuyper's references to the Golden Age of Dutch art during his visit to the United States betray the kind of triumphalistic and nationalistic sentiments that were on the increase in Europe towards the end of the nineteenth century. For a discussion of these sentiments in the Dutch context see Wilterdink, Nico (1991). "The Netherlands between the Greater Powers: expressions of resistance to perceived or feared foreign cultural domination: in *Within the US Orbit: Small National Cultures vis-a-vis the United States*, ed. by Rob Kroes. Amsterdam: Free University Press, 13–31. These sentiments are reflected in particular in those comments Kuyper made which highlighted the world-wide supremacy of the Dutch School; for instance, his comment that it had produced "those wondrous art-productions which still immortalize its fame, and which have shown the way to all the nations for new conquests" (*LC* 167). See also his *Encyclopaedie*: "the same Calvinistic Holland that had censured church art saw the rise of a general human school of art which has not yet been surpassed" (III:342). Expressions of nationalistic zeal permeated the elaborate celebrations in July, 1906, of the third centenary of Rembrandt's birth, which received extensive coverage and comment in De Standaard (see, for instance, *De Standaard* of July 17, 1906).

43 *LC* 166. Kuyper also held that the doctrine of election undergirded Calvinism's championing of democracy, for which he found support in the work of George Bancroft and F.D. Maurice. He appealed to the work of Hippolyte Taine in making his point about Rembrandt's chiaroscuro. See Taine's (1869) *Philosophie de l'art dans les Pays Bas*, 2 vols. Paris: Germer Bailliere, II, 164–5. John Ruskin was far from sharing this interpretation. He wrote that in as much as artists were searchers after truth, Rembrandt belongs to the lowest class of artists who only perceive and imitate evil: "they delight in the beggary and brutality of the human race; their colour is for the most part subdued or lurid, and the greatest spaces of their pictures are occupied by darkness." See Ruskin, John 1907. *The Stones of Venice*, 3 vols. London: Routledge, II, 206 7. Despite such sharp criticism, Ruskin did acknowledge that Rembrandt's strength lay in his rendering of human character. See *Selections from the Writings of John Ruskin*. London: Blackfriars, [n.d.], 167.

It is here, Calvin Seerveld has argued, that Kuyper came to his "most decisive insight" in his ideas on art.[44] Certainly it is a perspective that points to the fact that Kuyper was alive to the possibility of art not only illustrating theology, but contributing to it, which is a possibility only now being rediscovered by contemporary theologians.[45] This suggestion is born out by his treatment of other great artists such as Shakespeare, Mozart and Beethoven. Whereas he found Beethoven's 5th and 9th symphonies made unwelcome contributions to a pantheistic theology, the same composer's *Busslied* in Opus 48 was a glorious interpretation of atonement theology:

> the entire gospel of the atonement – profound contrition followed suddenly by the purest holiest rejoicing – washes over you in waves of glorious sound . . . resounding with a hallelujah of deliverance.[46]

Perhaps somewhat surprising then, there are indications that Kuyper regarded the arts as a way of approaching theology.[47] His theology of the arts led him to catch glimpses into how theology could be done through the arts.

Kuyper's Legacy in Britain

Kuyper's influence in Britain has worked largely through his Stone Lectures. They were published within a year of their delivery in both London and Edinburgh, and after their reissue in Britain in the early 1930s, they found their way into the hands of many university and college students.[48] In the area of the arts in particular, however, it is Hans Rookmaaker (1922–1977), professor of art history at the Free University from 1965 to 1977, who was largely responsible for establishing the Kuyperian tradition in Britain. During the 1960s and 1970s Rookmaaker made a number of trips across the North Sea to address large audiences of students and academics. This short, rather chubby, pipe-smoking, whisky-swigging Dutchman, who looked to British students uncannily like the then Prime Minister Harold Wilson, invariably held his audiences in the palm of his hand, and succeeded in

---

44 Seerveld, *A Christian Critique of Art*, 50. Seerveld develops Kuyper's insight in an attempt to suggest criteria for a Christian critique of art.

45 See the sections by Graham Howes and by Jeremy Begbie on theology and the arts in Ford, David F., ed. 1997. *The Modern Theologians*. 2nd ed. Oxford: Blackwell, 669–85 and 686–99: and Chia, Roland 1996. "Theological Aesthetics or Aesthetical Theology? Some reflections on the theology of Hans Urs von Balthasar." *Scottish Journal of Theology* 49: 75–95. Howes admits that John Ruskin frequently reminded his readers that the supreme value of art was that it disclosed spiritual and ethical insights that could not be reached in any other way, and he highlights the value of Paul Tillich's proposal of "theology through the arts" (see Ford, *The Modern Theologians*, 670, 676).

46 Kuyper, *Het modernisme*, 41–42 and n. 49. See translation in *AK:ACR* 112–13 and n. 31. Kuyper's portrayal of Beethoven's fifth and ninth symphonies in terms of pantheism can be found in his *De verflauwing*, 85–87 (n. 105). For a translation of part of this footnote, see Bratt, 382 (n. 34). Kuyper goes so far as to label Beethoven "the musical apostle of pantheism: whilst acknowledging that in his final years he "returned towards a more positive Christianity."

47 The portrayal of the dignity of human life outside the ecclesiastical sphere in the works of the Dutch School also suggested, for Kuyper, the doctrine of common grace and the Calvinistic love of liberty. Kuyper claimed support for this thesis in the work of Hippolyte Taine and Moriz Carriere, two art historians who were "far from sympathizing with Calvinism" (*LC* 166). See Taine, *Philosophie de l'art*, II, 148; Carriere, M. 1873–80. *Die Kunst in Zusammenhang mit der Culturentwickelung*, 5 vols. Leipzig: Brockhaus, IV, 308.

48 Kuyper, A. 1898. *Calvinism: Six Stone Lectures*. Edinburgh/London: T&T Clark/ Simpkin, Marshall, Hamilton; Kuyper, A. 1932. *Calvinism: Being the Six Stone Lectures Given at Princeton Theological Seminary USA. With an Introductory Chapter by Rev. Henry Beets*. London: Sovereign Grace Union.

inspiring a whole generation of Christian art students with the vision of thinking about the arts, and indeed practicing the arts, from a committed Christian perspective.[49] This may not sound a very remarkable vision to seasoned Kuyperians in The Netherlands and the United States, but it came as a bit of a shock to British evangelical sensibilities of the time, which were focused on "winning souls for Christ" and were generally negative or at least suspicious towards the arts – except, of course, art that was directly illustrative of biblical truth, and useful in mission. "Why should you spend your lives evangelizing?", Rookmaaker once railed to a student audience in Oxford. "There are more important things to do in the world. I have done twenty-five years of thinking, relating biblical principles to art. You should be willing to do the same."[50] The deliberate provocation contained in such remarks were reinforced not only by Rookmaaker's transgression of the prevailing nicotine and alcohol taboos current within the Christian circles in which he moved, but through the liberties he took in illustrating his lectures with nude subjects. It was, however, provocation designed to encourage his listeners to think for themselves about what it meant to be a Christian artist. Once, during the time set aside for discussion after a lecture, he turned on one of his questioners: "I am the Pope of Christian Art History. I have the answers to your questions right here in my pocket and I am not telling you. Think for yourself!"[51]

The response from the evangelical constituency that Rookmaaker was looking for was not long in coming, aided by a new self-confidence it had recently begun to experience after its somewhat narrow-minded self-defensiveness of the post-war years. From 1968 onwards a succession of evangelical arts conferences was organized, attended by poets, dramatists, film-makers, designers and architects. Eventually these weekend events developed into larger-scale, long-term enterprises, the most significant being the Arts Centre Group, the Institute for Contemporary Christianity in London, *Third Way* magazine, and the Greenbelt Arts Festival. Since its foundation in 1974 the Greenbelt Festival has attracted thousands of participants each year and has been responsible for a number of art exhibitions and publications in the area of Christianity and the arts. It has served to challenge the stigma that evangelicals so often attached to the arts, and to facilitate a Christian appreciation of the arts in their own right.

In more recent years, and partly due to Rookmaaker's untimely death in 1977, Kuyperian influence in the area of the arts in Britain has been more diffuse, affecting groups and institutions in a partial and indirect way – such as in the case of the newly founded Leigh School of Art in Edinburgh and the Theology Through the Arts project in Cambridge. Younger evangelicals who espouse a holistic worldview are often unfamiliar with the names Rookmaaker and Kuyper, reflecting the extent to which the Kuyperian vision has become such an accepted part of evangelical spirituality that its distinctiveness is no longer apparent. It remains to be seen whether this will change in any way as a result of the stream of publications from or about the Kuyperian tradition that have recently appeared or re-appeared from the British publisher Paternoster, including two seminal

---

49 My comments on Rookmaaker are based partly on conversations I have had with British artists who attended his lectures and partly on Linette Martin's biography, Martin, L. 1979. *Hans Rookmaaker: A Biography*. London: Hodder & Stoughton.

50 Martin, *Hans Rookmaaker*, 150.

51 Martin, *Hans Rookmaaker*, 152.

books on aesthetics by Calvin Seerveld and Nicholas Wolterstorff.[52]

Conclusion

Kuyper's treatment of the arts is more about religion than about the arts *per se*. At every stage it is clear that religious and theological concerns, rather than strictly artistic ones, dominate the argument. It would, on the face of it, have offered little by way of practical guidelines to the interested artist – unlike his treatments of politics and science, which, though equally theological were aimed at stimulating specific kinds of political and scientific activity. The message is clear in Kuyper's works that Calvinism has a vocation in the realm of the arts, but it is unclear how this vocation should be fulfilled. Some guidelines can be extracted, and these will be noted below, but there is a general lack of clarity and consistency, particularly when his perspectives on art and on science are compared. The resulting ambiguity may well have contributed to the fact that, compared to the achievements of Kuyper's immediate followers in the area of science and politics, those in the production of and performance of the arts were unimpressive. By allowing what he perceived to be a prejudice against Calvinism to dominate his argument he forfeited the opportunity to present a vision for the renewal of the arts along Calvinist lines. The impression given is that once the prejudice had been removed, the struggle for the acknowledgement of Calvinism's contribution to the arts would be over. But correcting a misunderstanding is not the same as presenting a program for change.

It was, however, as a theologian, not as an artist or art critic, that Kuyper addressed the arts. His significance probably lies more in the fact that he addressed the subject, and did so in a positive and creative way, avoiding moral questions, than in what he had to say about it in detail especially in view of the tendency in Protestant circles to marginalize the arts. In fact, it is not his specific ideas on art that have been responsible for the flourishing of neo-Calvinistic discussions of art and aesthetics, but his idea of worldview and its role in shaping culture. Rookmaaker's *Modern Art and the Death of a Culture*, for example, interprets art as an expression of the worldview held by the artist.[53] Seen in this light, the leading motifs of the neo-Calvinistic school in the sphere of the arts probably owe more to Kuyper's ideas on science than to those on art, however strange this may seem.

That Kuyper was able to display a positive approach to the arts was largely due to his doctrine of common grace. The fact that he emphasized this doctrine at the expense of his notion of the antithesis is revealing of a central tension in his thought between isolation and distinctiveness on the one hand, and engagement and accommodation on the other. It was a tension he never resolved, and, as we have seen, it led to certain weaknesses in the overall coherence of his thought. It is possible, however, to extrapolate from Kuyper's arguments

---

52 Seerveld, *Rainbows for the Fallen World*; Wolterstorff, *Art in Action* (see n. 4 above). See also Seerveld, Calvin 1999. *Take Hold of God and Pull*. Carlisle: Paternoster. Paternoster is also responsible for the publication of work by the renowned Dutch Christian artist Anneke Kaai and art critic Adrienne Chaplin. See Kaai, Anneke 1992. *The Apocalypse*. Carlisle: Paternoster, and 1995. *I Believe*. Carlisle: Paternoster; and Chaplin, Adrienne and Hilary Brand 1999. *Art and the Soul: Signposts for Christian Artists*. Carlisle: Paternoster. For the work of a British art critic, published by Paternoster, that is indirectly inspired by the Kuyperian tradition, see Thistlewaite, David 1998. *The Art of God and the Religions of Art*. Carlisle: Paternoster.

53 See n. 4 above. Rookmaaker's book is the most widely distributed Christian critique of modern art in Great Britain.

the characteristics he would expect art to possess if it were to be true to Calvinism. They are listed here, along with the specific doctrines from which Kuyper derived them: free from political and ecclesiastical control (because of the doctrine of sphere-sovereignty); beautiful (because God had placed a stamp of his glory on all created things, a belief derived from the doctrine of God's sovereignty); in obedience to classical norms (because of common grace); attentive to the significance of the commonplace and the ordinary (because of the doctrine of election).

Although it apparently was not Kuyper's intention, his discussion of the relationship between theology and the arts could have provided the rudimentary criteria for a specifically Christian critique of art. It certainly provided the groundwork for a sophisticated, albeit partly Platonic, theology of beauty; and it is beauty, Hans Urs von Balthasar has argued, that is the most neglected of God's attributes in modern theology, because of the separation of aesthetics and theology.[54] But this is a neglect and a separation of which Kuyper is not guilty. On the contrary, because his overriding concern was to bring the Calvinistic worldview up to date, he was keen to show how Calvinist theology was entirely relevant to contemporary trends in the world of art. In order to do so, he tended to reduce them to their underlying principles: thus the democratization of art was a result of materialism, and symbolism in worship a product of pantheism. This illustrates the kind of culture critic Kuyper was. Although his knowledge of such trends was based on his familiarity with a broad range of primary sources, he rarely engaged in detailed analysis and criticism of them but used a considerable amount of intuition, and not a little polemical verve, to characterize them in their general lines and in their fundamental positions.

It is perhaps chiefly for this reason that Kuyper's ideas on art have been neglected in scholarly research. Hopefully, however, this paper has provided sufficient evidence that they are well worth revisiting, not least because they issue a powerful challenge to the Christian community to consider how its faith can give shape to contemporary art and how the arts can contribute to its understanding of the faith. Kuyper's ideas on art and religion go way beyond the commonly expressed attitude that the arts are theologically interesting only when they have an explicitly ecclesial function or didactic purpose. He saw that the visual arts could give theology its eyes, and music its ears. This can provide a valuable source of inspiration in contemporary culture, which is neither primarily visual, nor verbal, but audiovisual. To do theology is to respond to God in language – and Kuyper's works are a reminder that that language needs to be verbal, audible and visual, embodying both a theology of the arts, and art as an expression of theology.

---

54 Von Balthasar's theology of beauty also falls into Platonic categories. He seeks to lay the blame for the neglect of the concept of beauty on the Protestant tradition from Luther to Kierkegaard. Beauty is like a Cinderella, Von Balthasar declares, compared to the attention that is paid to her two sisters, goodness and truth; that is, to ethics and doctrine. Von Balthasar, Hans Urs 1964. *Word and Revelation.* New York: Herder & Herder, 162. See also Sherry, Patrick 1992. *Spirit and Beauty: An Introduction to Theological Aesthetics.* Oxford: Clarendon Press, 59. Roland Chia points out that Von Balthasar has based his critique mainly on the visual arts, at the expense of the aural, and therefore intangible, aesthetics of the Reformed tradition. Chia points out that both Calvinists and Anglicans could agree with Luther's words: "After theology I give music the highest place and highest honour" (cited in Frank Burch Brown, *Religious Aesthetics: A Theological Study of Making and Meaning.* London: Macmillan Press, 1990, 121); Chia, Roland 1996. "Theological Aesthetics." *Scottish Journal of Theology* 49: 77

26

Re-fashioning Faith:
The Promise of a Kuyperian Theology of Fashion

Robert Covolo

What a profuse diversity of styles and costumes, of fabrics and colors.
Abraham Kuyper

Fashion, Theology, and the Kuyperian Tradition

In the last thirty years the academic world has developed a vast literature on the subject of fashion.[1] Nearly every discipline within the humanities and social sciences has constructed a detailed dialogue on the nature and role of fashion.[2] In strong contrast, however, the field of theology has, for the most part, remained silent on the subject, a fact which is all the more conspicuous considering theology's historically critical posture towards fashion: Tertullian associated fashion with Eve's participation in original sin,[3] Barth with demonic activity.[4] Only recently has theology attempted to gain a more nuanced understanding

---

1   By fashion I am referring to the broad idea of dress. For a wonderful review of the various ways the term "fashion" has been used see: Svendsen, Lars 2006. *Fashion: A Philosophy.* Translated by John Irons. London: Reaktion, 9–20. For and excellent survey of the various theories of fashion produced in the academy see Entwistle, John 2000. *The Fashioned Body.* Malden: Blackwell, 40ff.

2   Taylor, Lou 2002. *The Study of Dress History.* New York: Manchester, 1; Davis, Fred 1992. *Fashion, Culture, and Identity.* Chicago: University of Chicago Press, 5.

3   Tertullian writes: "and do you not know that you are (each) an Eve. . . . On account of your desert, that is, death- even the Son of God had to die. And do you think about adorning yourself over and above your tunics of skins? Come, now; if from the beginning of the world the Milesians sheared sheep, and the Serians spun trees, and the Tyrians dyed, and the Phrygians embroidered with the needle, and the Babylonians with the loom, and pearls gleamed, an onyx-stones flashed; if gold itself also had already issued, with the cupidity (which accompanies it), from the ground; if the mirror, too, had license to lie so largely, Eve, expelled from paradise, already dead, would also have coveted these things, I imagine!" Tertullian, "On the Apparel of Women." In Thiessen, Gesa Elisabeth ed. 2004. *Theological Aesthetics.* Grand Rapids: Eerdmans, 57.

4   "Among these lordless powers of earth that lord it over us, we must certainly consider . . . fashion – the fashion to which man thinks he must obediently subject clothes, headgear, and hairstyle, the alternation of assurance and then of exposure first to the rather sympathetic astonishment and then to the horror and amusement of those who think they must follow the new fashion. . . . Who wants it this way? The particular industry that tirelessly makes money out of it and whose kings, we are told, reside especially in Paris? But who has made these people the kings. . . . Who inspires and directs these processes, which are not a matter of indifference to the feeling for life and all that it implies? If it is a matter of rapidly changing taste, what released spirit of the earth pulls the strings so that this fancy passes, another which is

---

of the issues that have been pressing the contemporary academy.[5] This paper is a small movement in that direction. My aim is to broaden the discussion by examining the contribution Kuyperian theology offers a theological understanding of fashion. The contention of this paper is that though the Kuyperian framework is not without problems, it provides a promising structure for a substantial analysis of the phenomenon of fashion. I will unpack this claim by examining key categories of Kuyperian theology in order to explore three issues: the value of fashion as culture making, the role of fashion in culture, and the implications of fashion as art.

Dutch theologian Abraham Kuyper (1837–1920) was a seminal thinker and father of what became known as the Kuyperian tradition. Kuyper was motivated by a desire to address the culture of his day through his Calvinist theology (as detailed by the synod of Dort). After completing his theological training at the university of Leiden and serving as a pastor, he went on to found a newspaper, a political party, a university, and then to serve as the prime minister of Holland.[6] Kuyper's activism only seemed to accelerate his keen theological development, and it was because of his reformed theology that he sought "to refashion the politics, scholarship, art, and social arrangements of his time."[7] As a result, he formed categories characterized by an unusual fecundity for exploring cultural issues. Kuyper was followed as the chair of theology at the Free University by fellow neo-Calvinist, Herman Bavinck. Bavinck, equally gifted in a number of arenas, shared many of Kuyper's concerns as he developed his theological assessment.[8] Kuyper's theological project has continued to have a significant influence, inspiring notable contemporary scholars such as Richard Mouw, Max Stackhouse, and Nicholas Wolterstorff.

The Value of Fashion as Culture Making

What value should we place on fashion? Should we see it as a necessary evil of a postlapsarian world, or part of the very fabric of the world God created? Does fashion play a starring role in the development of culture, or is it more like a parasite that feeds off the vanity and excess of egos? Is the production of fashion a legitimate calling for a Christian, or should we view it as a necessary evil at best, or worse, some form of compromise? These questions and others lead us to the issue of the value of fashion as culture making. In order to understand a Kuyperian approach to these questions, we turn to the Kuyperian categories of creation ordinances, the Fall, and common grace.

---

anxiously watched by millions comes and prevails, and then after a while it too departs?" Barth, Karl 1981. *The Christian Life: Church Dogmatics IV, 4 Lecture Fragments*. Translated by Geoffrey W. Bromiley. Grand Rapids: Eerdmans, 229.

5   For a striking example of a recent attempt to address issues drawing the attention of the contemporary academy see: Cobb, Kelton 2005. *Blackwell's Guide to Theology and Popular Culture*. Malden: Blackwell.

6   Although there are numerous treatments of his life there is (strangely) no recent comprehensive biography. The only full biography in English is by Frank Vandenberg, *Abraham Kuyper* (Grand Rapids: Eerdmans, 1960). Vandenberg's treatment is largely uncritical.

7   Bratt, James D. "Abraham Kuyper: His world and work" in *AK:ACR* 1.

8   The relationship between Kuyper and Bavinck is a complex one. Although Bavinck had much in common with Kuyper's viewpoint he was a theologian in his own right who had written his substantial four volume *Reformed Dogmatics* before he took Kuyper's place as the head of theology at the Free University. For a comparison and contrast of Kuyper and Bavinck see Klapwijk, Jacob 1986. *Bringing into Captivity Every Thought*. Lanham: University Press of America.

Creation ordinances, the Fall, and common grace

Kuyper believed that the ordinances given at creation (Genesis 1:26–31) served as a vital *loci* for developing a Christian understanding of culture. This point is underscored by Kuyper's colleague Bavinck, who wrote: "if now we comprehend the force of this subduing under the term culture, now generally used for it, we can say that culture in the broadest sense is the purpose for which God created man after his image."[9] Kuyperians believe that in the commands to fill and subdue "lies the firm and abiding foundation for a myriad of practical vocations."[10] This order, given before the Fall, holds for all of humanity as the image bearing (*imago Dei*) continuation of God's own forming and filling of creation.[11] Additionally, for the Kuyperian, the trajectory of creational development was both possible and anticipated regardless of whether or not there was a fall.[12] Kuyper asserts:

> None of it can be spared because it pleases God . . . to actualize everything he had put into this world at the time of creation, to insist on its realization, to develop it so completely that the full sum of its vital energies may enter the light of day at the consummation of the world.[13]

While the Fall did not change this fact, the ability for humanity to carry out this ordinance was, however, jeopardized. This introduces the Kuyperian doctrine of common grace. Kuyper illustrates this concept by observing that "The fundamental creation ordinance given before the fall, that humans would achieve dominion over all of nature thanks to 'common grace,' is still realized *after* the fall" (*CG* 179). In noting that death did not come in its full effect following sin, moreover, Kuyper seeks to understand how this "manifestation of grace" acts by "restraining, blocking, or redirecting the consequences" that sin should have brought (*CG* 168). Adding to its remedial effects, Kuyper characterizes common grace as having a progressive function. Kuyper elaborates:

> All that God has disclosed to us already lay stored up in the creation from the beginning. But we did not know it and did not see it, and God has used the centuries, step-by-step, to help us discover ever more, ever new things by which our human life could be enriched. (*CG* 175)[14]

This development of common grace is made possible by God's "general call" through the ordinances of creation addressed to all mankind, thus producing "a higher civilization, a

---

9   Bavinck, Herman 1956. *Our Reasonable Faith*. Grand Rapids: Eerdmans, 205.

10 Spykman, Gordon 1992. *Reformational Theology: A New Paradigm for Doing Dogmatics*. Grand Rapids: Eerdmans, 178–179; Bavinck adds that "this dominion of the earth includes not only the most ancient callings of men such as hunting and fishing, agriculture and stock-raising, but also trade and commerce, finance and credit, the exploitation of mines and mountains, and science and art." Bavinck, *Our Reasonable Faith*, 207.

11 Wolters, Albert 1985. *Creation Regained*. Grand Rapids: Eerdmans, 41.

12 Spykman, *Reformational Theology*, 182.

13 "Common Grace." In *AK:ACR* 176—referenced in what follows as *CG*.

14 Some see a repetition of Kuyper's view of common grace in the song "Miracle Drug" by Paul Hewson (a.k.a. "Bono") of the band U2. In the album *How To Dismantle An Automic Bomb* (Interscope Records, November 23, 2004), Hewson writes: "God I need your help tonight/Beneath the noise/Below the din/I hear your voice/ It's whispering/ In science and in medicine/ 'I was a stranger/ You took me in.'" One blogger notes Hewson "is calling for God's help, or for the church to listen to God's teachings. That God is even in the worlds of science and medicine, a place that the church is often fighting against. Echoing the words of Christ, 'I was a stranger/You took me in' calling the church to action." Posted on *Originality*, "U2- How To Dismantle An Atomic Bomb - Miracle Drug" http://jarcaines.blogspot.com / 2004 / 11 / u2-how-to-dismantle-atomic-bomb_17.html; Internet; accessed 11 March 2013.

richer culture, and a flowering of arts and sciences,"[15] as well as enabling Kuyper to speak in glowing terms about the cultural contributions of non-Christians.[16] Speaking of the effect Kuyper's doctrine of common grace had, James Bratt observes:

> It encouraged the redeemed to respect the good remaining in the world and to strive to augment it. Even more, it made many elements of human culture . . . not just products but means of grace, instruments whereby God restrained sin and enabled men to try to develop creation as he had originally designed. Finally, it legitimized a certain amount of cooperation between the redeemed and unbelievers on the grounds that to some extent they shared a sense of the good and therefore a common purpose.[17]

Kuyperian theology therefore developed a dynamic relationship between *common* and *special* grace. Available to all is common grace, which acts to restrain sin and promote culture, even amongst non-Christians. Available to the elect, however, is saving grace, which results ultimately in the abolition of sin (*CG* 168). While these two are not identical, they do work together. For Kuyper, special grace can be both an indirect and direct influence on common grace. Indirectly, Christian faith curbs sin, while directly it can work in culture to elevate "all that is human from its sunken state to a higher standpoint" (*CG* 199). This complementary relationship between common grace and special grace "touches at once upon the connection between *nature* and *grace*" (*CG* 173). Bavinck, echoing Kuyper, declares that "grace restores nature and raises it to its highest fulfillment, but it does not add a new, heterogeneous component to it."[18] For Kuyper, though common grace enabled the enculturation project to move forward, it did not eradicate the effects of the Fall. To hold the tension between an enduring creational design together with a pervasive influence of sin, Kuyperians have therefore made the distinction between "structure" and "direction."[19] We now turn to this important Kuyperian distinction.

---

15 Bavinck, *Our Reasonable Faith*, 409. For a trans-historical/trans-cultural broadening of the scope of Bavinck's statement see *CG* 176, where Kuyper states: "There is beside the great work of God in *special* grace also that totally other work of God in the realm of *common* grace. That work encompasses the whole life of the world, the life of Kaffirs in Africa, of Mongols in China and Japan, and of the Indians south of the Himalayas. In all previous centuries there was nothing among Egyptians and Greeks, in Babylon and Rome, nor is there anything today among the peoples of whatever continent that was or is not necessary. All of it was an indispensable part of the great work that God is doing to consummate the world's development."

16 Bavinck, *Our Reasonable Faith*, 409. For a trans-historical/trans-cultural broadening of the scope of Bavinck's statement see *CG* 176, where Kuyper states: "There is beside the great work of God in *special* grace also that totally other work of God in the realm of *common* grace. That work encompasses the whole life of the world, the life of Kaffirs in Africa, of Mongols in China and Japan, and of the Indians south of the Himalayas. In all previous centuries there was nothing among Egyptians and Greeks, in Babylon and Rome, nor is there anything today among the peoples of whatever continent that was or is not necessary. All of it was an indispensable part of the great work that God is doing to consummate the world's development."

17 Bratt, James 1984. *Dutch Calvinism in North American: A History of a Conservative Subculture*. Grand Rapids: Eerdmans, 20.

18 Bavinck adds that "grace does not serve to take man up into a supernatural order, but to liberate him from sin. Grace is not opposed to nature, but only to sin." Veenhof, Jan 2006. *Nature and Grace in Herman Bavinck*. Translated by Albert Wolters. Sioux Center: Dordt College Press, 13.

19 Wolters, *Creation Regained*, 59.

Structure and direction

Kuyper was not afraid to note that cultural developments could be used in destructive ways. In fact, it was Kuyper's own concern about the destructive developments of secularism on Dutch culture that ignited so many of his initiatives in politics, education and journalism.[20] For Kuyper, the greater the trajectory of cultural development, the greater the possibility for it to become good or evil.[21] The dynamic between a normed creation in tension with the un-norming effects of sin is clarified by the structure/direction distinction. For Kuyperians, all creational entities "whether physical, societal, [or] cultural," have a design that implies an appropriate end.[22] But with the Fall came the potential for misdirection of these good creational designs towards the wrong ends.[23] As we have seen, though, God's spirit is at work maintaining creational structure and enabling fallen humanity to see the appropriate design of creation through common grace. The Christian call is therefore to discern the work of common grace in culture and, at times, to engage in antithetical practice in support of the creational design.[24]

To summarize, Kuyperians believe culture making is ordained at creation, distorted through sin, preserved through common grace and tasked to the church through antithetical practice.

The importance of fashion as culture making

For the Kuyperian, the use of fashion for the development of culture is tacitly decreed in scripture. In other words, "God takes delight in the production of culture."[25] Kuyperians should, therefore, pay greater attention when scholars, speaking of dress, note its culture producing significance by providing "an interdependent relationship with the social institutions like religious, stratifying, political, and economic structures. It is a factor in the organization of a society, in its roles and their status . . . dress is a powerful social force, especially in unstable societies where the existing order is frequently challenged."[26] Furthermore, the importance of dress for utility, convenience, protection, modesty, shared meaning, personal dignity and shared history could all be deemed part of cultural embellishment and therefore have the stamp of divine favor.[27] Moreover, the raw potentialities of creation are a direct gift from God and include color, form, tint, shape, symbol and meaning. By engaging in the perception, shaping and enjoyment of these raw-datum, Kuyperians views the fashion designer as manifesting an aspect of the *imago dei*

---

20 Bratt, *AK:ACR* 20.

21 "So it continues and so it will continue until the very end when at last development can go no further, when all hidden powers have been discovered, released, subjected to human control, and fully harnessed. Only then can the dreadful person arise who, uniting all the threads of these various powers in a single hand, will want to possess them apart from God, direct them against God, and apply them as though he were God" (*CG* 180).

22 Wolters, Al 2007. "Some Remarks on Neocalvinism and Globalization." Paper presented at The Abraham Kuyper Consultation, Princeton, NJ, March 2007, 3.

23 Ibid.

24 Mouw, Richard 2001. *He Shines in All That's Fair.* Grand Rapids: Eerdmans, 26–27.

25 Mouw, *He Shines in All That's Fair*, 39.

26 Storm, Penny 1987. *Functions of Dress: Tool of Culture and the Individual.* Englewood Cliffs: Prentice-Hall, ix.

27 For a detailed list of the ways dress interacts with culture see Storm's *Functions of Dress*, ix.

(*LC* 157). Additionally, the "development and progress" of technological advance in such aspects as fabric design, production, durability, insulation, and breathability is implicit within the creation ordinance, possible by common grace, accelerated when in league with special grace, and able to bring about significant good.

Our sketch thus far demonstrates that the Kuyperian approach has much to offer by way of valuing fashion as a culture making activity. This should come as little surprise given that Kuyper was "opposing, among other things, the introverted attitude, the inclination toward other worldliness and suspicion of culture."[28] The Kuyperian tradition does this by accepting "human responsibility for the cultivation of the world and therefore of the shaping of culture,"[29] because:

> The tendency in devout circles to oppose that progress and perpetual development of human life was . . . misguided. It must undoubtedly be acknowledged that Christians, by refusing to participate in that development, were the reason why morally and religiously that development often took a wrong turn. Those who are in Christ must not oppose such development and progress, must not even distance themselves from it. Their calling also in this cultural realm is rather to be in the vanguard. (*CG* 175)

The misdirection of fashion

While fashion as a cultural product can therefore be shaped and engaged within a productive, biblical manner, Kuyperians do not believe fashion to be immune from taking a destructive direction. For just as dress can be used by human beings in alignment with the normative nature of the creational structure, it can also be used in a death dealing way. This assessment makes sense of the polyphonic voices within the academy that speak of the darker side of fashion. For example: some psychologists of dress warn of viewing fashion as "one means whereby an always fragmentary self is glued together into the semblance of a unified identity."[30] Other psychologists see obsession with dress as a vain attempt to close the gap between "the conscious self" and "the ideal self."[31] Such victims inevitably echo the words of fashion designer Monah Li, who said, "I have always had more faith in fashion than in God . . . I believed that the right clothes could make me perfect. I still do."[32] Gender studies warn us of the use of fashion for sexist statements and oppressive gender relationships.[33] Sociologists speak about western society's use of fashion to create individuals burdened by the oppressive task of continually re-creating self-identity among a myriad of clothing choices.[34] Meanwhile, philosophers of fashion speak of modern

---

28 Veenhof, *Nature and Grace in Herman Bavinck*, 16.

29 The Evangelical Outpost, "What is Neo-Calvinism"; http://www.evangelicaloutpost.com/archives/000561. html; Internet; accessed 15 February 2013.

30 Wilson, Elizabeth 2003. *Adorned in Dreams: Fashion and Modernity*. New Brunswick, NJ: Rutgers, 12.

31 Storm, *Functions of Dress*, 258–259.

32 Detweiler, Craig and Barry Taylor 2003. *A Matrix of Meanings: Finding God in Pop Culture*. Grand Rapids: Baker Academic, 135.

33 Wolf, Naomi 2002. *The Beauty Myth: How Images of Beauty are Used Against Women*. New York: Harper Colins; Faludi, Susan 1991. *Backlash: The Undeclared War Against American Women*. New York: Doubleday.

34 Giddens, Anthony 1991. *Modernity and Self-Identity: Self & Society in the Late Modern Age*. Stanford: Stanford University Press, 5.

fashion as one manifestation of the contemporary obsession with "the new."[35] For the Kuyperian, these critiques incisively highlight some of the many possible manifestations of the misdirection of fashion. In the words of one contemporary Kuyperian philosopher:

> . . . in response to this we are not to avert ourselves from our social condition, seeking closer union with God by means of undisturbed contemplation, for God himself is disturbed by our human condition; rather, we are to struggle to alter those structures and the dynamics behind them, so that the alienation is diminished and the realization advanced.[36]

The call to be engaged in this world, including the world of fashion, requires struggling for the appropriate ends of creational structures. Such a movement forward, however, implies an understanding of the boundaries and ends of such structures, which leads us to our next set of Kuyperian categories.

The Role of Fashion in Culture

If fashion is part of the creation's structure, what is its place in that world and what are the appropriate ends towards which it should aim? Is dress meant simply to protect one from the environment? Or is clothing the tip of a much larger iceberg that touches on every aspect of human action – psychological, social, linguistic, aesthetic?[37] How should fashion interact within other aspects of culture such as the family, state, business and art? These questions deal with the normative role of fashion within culture. To explore this we turn to Kuyper's categories of sphere sovereignty and multiformity.

Sphere sovereignty and multiformity

When Kuyper set out to explain Calvinism as an all-embracing view of life, he started with Calvin's indomitable view of the sovereignty of God.[38] True to Calvin, Kuyper thought of reality primarily in terms of the interface of creator and creation through God's decreeing word. As creator, God maintains "absolute sovereignty" from the "necessity" of a decreed world.[39] Kuyper developed his thought from the norming nature of God's decree to see every aspect of life operating according to "fixed laws."[40] God's sovereignty thus

---

35 "A fashion object does not in principle need any particular qualities apart from being new. The principle of fashion is to create an ever-increasing velocity, to make an object superfluous as fast as possible, in order to let a new one have a chance. Seen in this light, the Gap chain of clothes shops is exemplary, as it replaces its produce line every eight weeks! Fashion is irrational in the sense that it seeks change for the sake of change, not in order to 'improve' the object, for example by making it more functional. It seeks superficial changes that in reality have no other assignment than to make the object superfluous on the basis of non-essential qualities, such as the number of buttons on a suit jacket." Svendsen, *Fashion: A Philosophy*, 28.

36 Wolterstorff, Nicholas 1983. *Until Justice & Peace Embrace*. Grand Rapids: Eerdmans, 23.

37 Possibly the broadest statement for clothing ever was given by Thomas Carlyle: "Whatsoever sensibly exists, whatsoever represents spirit to spirit, is properly a clothing, a suit or raiment, put on for a season, and to be laid off. Thus in this one pregnant subject of clothes, rightly understood, is included all that men have thought, dreamed, done, and been: the whole universe and what it holds is but clothing; and the essence of all science lies in the philosophy of clothes." Thomas Carlyle, "Sartor Restartu" (London, 1833–4) as quoted in Svendsen, *Fashion: A Philosophy*, 28.

38 "God, surely, is in Himself the all-sufficient and the all-blessed. He does not need the world nor any creature in any way for His own perfection . . . . Indeed, the cause of the creation is simply and solely the free power of God, his eternal good pleasure, His absolute sovereignty." Bavinck, *Our Reasonable Faith*, 168.

39 "From the beginning, heaven and earth have been distinct." Ibid., 435.

40 Kuyper writes that "There is a domain of nature in which the Sovereign exerts power over matter according

became the basis for Kuyper's understanding of the distinct nature of the created world. Kuyper writes that "this dominating principle was . . . *the Sovereignty of the Triune God over the whole Cosmos*, in all its spheres and kingdoms, visible and invisible" (*LC* 79). Kuyper, building on this idea of various decreed spheres, elaborates:

> Call the parts of this one great machine "cogwheels," spring-driven on their own axles, or "spheres," each animated within its own spirit. The name or image is unimportant, so long as we recognize that there are in life as many spheres as there are constellations in the sky and that the circumference of each has been drawn on a fixed radius from the center of a unique principle, namely, the apostolic injunction *hekastos en toi idioi tagmati* ["each in its own order": 1 Corinthians 15:23]. Just as we speak of a "moral world," a "scientific world," a "business world," the "world of art," so we can more properly speak of a "sphere" of morality, of the family, of societal life, each with its own *domain*. And because each comprises its own domain, each has its own Sovereign within its bounds. (*SS* 467)

Kuyper's favorite phrase for speaking about the domain of each sphere is "sphere sovereignty," and he uses this foundational understanding of creaturely reality to make two important points. First, each sphere answers directly to God and is therefore irreducible, which means that no sphere "may encroach on its neighbor" (*SS* 468). Kuyper referred to such encroachment as something that comes from a "blurring of the boundaries."[41] The state must not play the part of the church nor visa-versa. Likewise, the family must not be treated like a business. This is not to say that each sphere is identical, for the state has a special relationship of guarding the mutual interaction of the various spheres with each other (*SS* 468), and, again, this guardianship is described in terms of the importance of the recognition of the inalienable sovereignty of spheres and their various boundaries.

Secondly, Kuyper believed the "most profuse diversity" exists within the created world through these various sovereign spheres,[42] in which "emerges the rich, multifaceted multiformity of human life" (*SS* 467–68). Kuyper was adamant that a poly-spherical world is "infinitely complex"; a quantitative complexity with "as many spheres as there are constellations in the sky" (*SS* 467). He also held that the complexity is qualitatively complex because of the inter-spherical asymmetrical set of roles among the spheres and the intra-spherical distinct "kindedness," which speaks of unique internal relationship "*within* these spheres" (*SS* 468). With this initial sketch of Kuyper's view of sphere sovereignty, we are in the place to explore a Kuyperian understanding of fashion's role in culture.

The place of fashion as cultural phenomenon
Kuyper never said fashion had its own sphere. If he counted it as such, however, his description of the natural integrity inherent within the various spheres of the created world would implicitly endow intrinsic complexity and dignity to the field of fashion. This resonates within the movement in the modern academy, which, rather than reducing fashion as a subset of any one discipline, has deemed fashion a focus of knowledge in its

---

to fixed laws. There is also a domain of the personal, of the household, of science, of social and ecclesiastical life, each of which obeys its own laws of life, each subject to its own chief." Abraham Kuyper, "Sphere Sovereignty." In *AK:ACR* 467—referenced further as *SS*.

41 "The Blurring of the Boundaries." In *AK:ACR* 363–402.

42 Bavinck, *Our Reasonable Faith*, 435.

own right.[43] The intra-diversity of fashion as a complex concept receives support from a variety of fashion studies which see fashion as having a unique domain in cultured existence by performing a broad range of tasks.[44] For example, on a rudimentary level, fashion serves to adapt one to the vicissitudes of the physical environment. Or, to put it in Kuyperian language, dress enables diverse cultures to be about the activity of subduing various climates outside the garden.[45] We can broaden this sense to see fashion as "a tool . . . to acclimatize and thrive in almost any environment," including cultural environments.[46] Anthropologists have noted the crucial role dress plays as a form of communication which enables cultures to move from small scale (tribal) to large scale (nation-state).[47] Therefore fashion, as a language, serves an important role in mankind's movement which "begins in a garden and ends in a city."[48] Sociologists note that, like language, dress enables us to communicate and commune with the changing social climates implicit with complex social contexts. Malcom Bernard writes, "it is suggested that social agreement on what will be worn is itself a social bond which in turn reinforces other social bonds. The unifying function of fashion and clothing serves to communicate membership of a cultural group both to those who are members of it and to those who are not."[49] A Kuyperian view of spheres would place these tasks as part of the domain of attired reality.

The Kuyperian concept of sphere boundaries also offers a paradigm for viewing movements and distortion within fashion due to sphere encroachment. If fashion is in the sphere of art then the overstepping of business into this field would result in a departure from its role. This is exactly how some in fashion studies have viewed the channeling of creativity into the commodification of fashion for a contemporary mass-market. Such overriding by the market precipitates what one author calls "the end of fashion."[50] Interestingly, Kuyper seemed to raise a similar point when addressing the role of mass production on the fashion of his day. Kuyper indicts how "changes in the fashion are dizzying indeed, but in fact that fashion is the same for all. A designer's whim in the capital of France, one hint from Paris – and before long every woman in Europe wears the

---

43 For an example of the new inter-disciplinary approach to fashion see: Damhorst, Mary, Kimberly Miller-Spillman, Susan Michelman 2005. *The Meaning of Dress*. New York: Fairchild.

44 Malcolm Barnard includes protection, modesty and concealment, immodesty and attraction, communication, individualistic expression, social worth or status, definition of social role, economic worth or status, political symbol, magico-religious condition, social rituals, and recreation. Barnard, Malcolm 1996. *Fashion as Communication*. New York: Routledge, v–vi.

45 "A primary means by which people worldwide generally adjust to changes in temperature is through change in the number of layers of clothing that are warn, in the amount of body coverage that the clothing provides, in the thickness and weave structure of the clothing, or in the fibers from which the clothing is made." Eicher, Joanne B., Sandra Lee Evenson, Hazel A. Lutz 2000. *The Visible Self: Global Perspectives on Dress, Culture, and Society*. New York: Fairchild, 154.

46 Ibid., 157.

47 In a large scale culture a "lack of familiarity between people was incentive for individuals to dress in a manner that provided information about family, status, village, occupation and wealth." Eicher, *The Visual Self*, 212.

48 Hegeman, David 1999. *Plowing in Hope: Towards a Biblical Theology of Culture*. Moscow, ID: Cannon Press, 31.

49 Bernard, *Fashion as Communication*, 59-60.

50 Agins, Teri 1999. *The End of Fashion: How Marketing Changed The Clothing Business Forever*. New York: Harper Collins.

same style of dress, has the same hairstyle, is shod with the same style of boot, is painted the same fashionable color. Year after year – better, every new season – an increasingly fitful industry diversifies its creations frivolously and without principle."[51] Speaking of the "dizzying" changes in fashion "year after year" touting "better every new season," Kuyper puts his finger on the commodification of fashion and the market's obsession with "the new" intruding on fashion. Kuyper's critique of 'the new' was prophetic since "the idea of 'the new' is relatively new." Today "practically all fashion theorists stress 'the new'" which consists of a "steady stream of 'new' objects replacing those that were 'new' but have now become 'old.'"[52] Kuyper seems to be putting his finger on the genesis of the relationship between fashion and consumption, a subject that has generated a large amount of scholarship in recent years.[53] Behind his words is a disdain for mindless consumption. This theme has been echoed by contemporary Kuyperians who view consumerism as "an extreme form of childishness."[54]

Also behind Kuyper's critique is the flattening of fashion by the fashion industry itself. The industry has taken a "totalizing" role in dictating fashion for "every female." The result is a "deadly uniformity" which leaves women "slavishly following" the same cues "regardless of geographical region or climate, figure or color, social status or financial resources. . ." (*Uniformity* 30). Kuyper's rejection of a "fascism of taste" echoes fashion theorist Adorno's belief that "fashion is the greatest danger to culture, because it apparently homogenizes and thereby makes society more totalitarian."[55] This theme is shared by street fashion in subcultures, which reject the encroachment the industry has had on tastes to the point where, "nobody has a capacity to look and decide what they feel about it [fashion] anymore. Nobody's allowed to have an opinion about it."[56]

Kuyper's idea of "encroachment" accommodates other implicit critiques of fashion's boundaries. Because the role of fashion includes a medium for social dialogue, it could be deemed a "blurring of the boundaries" for a state, religion or school to prescribe meticulous requirements for public dress.[57] This particularly fits with Kuyper's view of "worldview pluralism" and its relationship to the public square.[58] Or, in a different application, fashion, with its focus on the surface, can be criticized as an encroacher where "it is difficult to conceive of any social phenomenon whatsoever that is not influenced by

---

51 "Uniformity: The Curse of Modern Life." In *AK:ACR* 30—referenced below as *Uniformity*.

52 "Seen in this way, an emancipation lies in the new fashion, as one is liberated from the old one. The problem is that the one suppression is replaced by another, as one is immediately subject to the tyranny of the new fashion." Svendsen, *Fashion: A Philosophy*, 24.

53 The twentieth-century "American habit of buying cheap mass-produced goods for short use was a novel one. . . . If the old-fashioned shop assistants still mumbled 'I can guarantee this – it will last a lifetime' the modern comeback was, 'Then for goodness sake show me something else.'" Breward, Christopher 1995. *The Culture of Fashion*. New York: Manchester University, 107–208.

54 Goudzwaard, Bob 2001. *Globalization and the Kingdom of God*, edited by James W. Skillen. Grand Rapids: Baker, 37.

55 Svendsen, *Fashion: A Philosophy*, 109.

56 Detweiler, *A Matrix of Meanings*, 226.

57 Arthur, Linda B. ed. 1999. *Religion, Dress & The Body*. New York: Berg, 1999. For a detailed discussion of religion abusing its proper domain with dress see pages 73–94.

58 "It is important to observe that Kuyper's proposal made room for institutions of a variety of worldviews, not just the Reformed perspective." Bacote, Vincent E. 2005. *The Spirit in Public Theology: Appropriating the Legacy of Abraham Kuyper*. Grand Rapids: Baker, 62.

changes of fashion – whether it is body shape, car design, politics or art."[59] Thus the current use of "fashion" as a way of speaking about "which subjects are 'in' and which are 'out,' which approaches are 'sexy' and which are not."[60] Or, once again, fashion can overstep its boundaries such that it becomes engrafted in dictating sexual ethics. This parallels Kuyper's critique of art's infringement on sexual ethics. Kuyper writes that Calvinism's "moral seriousness has clashed with the sensualism of those who deemed no sacrifice too sacred for the Goddess of Art. All this, however, concerns only the place which art has to occupy in the sphere of life, and the boundaries of its domain."[61] These are just a few of any number of possible ways a Kuyperian could view sphere encroachment and fashion, all of which are contingent on boundaries for fashion. This leads us to a key problem for a Kuyperian theology of fashion.

Kuyper never gave a detailed taxonomy of spheres beyond broad categories such as "art," "science," "business," "ethics" (*SS* 467). This is why Kuyperians are not uniformly optimistic about the potential for developing a comprehensive taxonomy of sphere boundaries. This is not to say there could not be examples of sphere encroachment in fashion, just that there are inevitable complications when distinguishing precise boundaries,[62] such as in fashion's relationship to art. While fashion has an obvious association to this explicitly stated sphere, it seems to have a role in all of Kuyper's stated spheres. Because of its extensive role, fashion seems to manifest what Kuyperians have called "transpherical" qualities.[63] This follows from Kuyper's reticence to construct a precise metaphysic, making is difficult to pinpoint fashion's boundaries. As many Kuyperians have noted, Kuyper's aim was not to elaborate on metaphysics but to develop basic categories for theological reflection.[64] This is why some contemporary Kuyperians advise we "pay more attention to the general contours of his thought than to get caught up with his specific views about how the boundaries are to be drawn in practice."[65] Of course, it is not only Kuyperian theologians who should be skeptical about the possibility of determining the exact boundaries of what constitutes

---

59 Svendsen, *Fashion: A Philosophy*, 13.

60 Ibid. p.15; Kuyper himself, aware of the temptation to be "fashionable," defends his discussion on Calvinism and art as more than simply attempting to be "in the good graces" of the aesthetic movement of his day. *LC* 143.

61 Ibid.

62 "To be sure, Kuyper was never very precise as to what counted as a creational 'sphere' . . . It is not clear, for example, how navigation and agriculture deserve a separate status as distinct creational spheres in the same sense as science, art, commerce, industry, the family, and 'human relationships.'" Richard Mouw, 2000. "Some Reflections on Sphere Sovereignty." In Luis E. Lugo ed. *Religion, Pluralism and Public Life: Abraham Kuyper's Legacy for the Twenty-First Century*. Grand Rapids: Eerdmans, 91.

63 "Kuyper's third qualification has to do with what we might think of as transpherical patterns. His concern here can be illustrated by means of a simple example: roads. Thoroughfares are used to conduct the affairs of a multiplicity of spheres. Families pile into their vans to head for picnics. Heads of state travel to ceremonies in motorcades. Business leaders take cabs to meetings. Team players are bused to the stadium. Roads serve all the spheres, and everyone, regardless of status in a particular sphere, has an interest in the maintenance of appropriate patterns of transport. It is the task of the state to see to it that we all do our part to maintain a good road system." Ibid., 90.

64 The cosmonomic philosophy of Herman Dooyeweerd and D. H. T. Vollenhoven in Amsterdam in the mid-twentieth century attempted to rectify this lack of metaphysical precision in Kuyperian thought. See Wolters, "Some Remarks on Neocalvinism and Globalization," 2–3.

65 Mouw, *Religion, Pluralism, and the Public Life*, 100.

fashion.[66] As one philosopher cautions: "'fashion' is a notoriously difficult term to pin down, and it is extremely doubtful whether it is possible to come up with necessary and sufficient conditions for something justifiably to be called 'fashionable.'"[67] Still, the degree to which the boundaries of fashion remain difficult to pin down also determines the degree to which the Kuyperian paradigm maintains explanatory power in a given area.

Although Kuyper's theology of sphere sovereignty is not clear regarding fashion, Kuyper was clear about the multiformity his sphere sovereignty implied for the world of fashion. As previously referenced, his speech, "Uniformity: The Curse of Modern Life" gives ample evidence of Kuyper's grievance with the lack of robust diversity in contemporary dress. He states:

> In the matter of dress we see the same phenomenon. Look how, when Minerva's young manhood hold their masquerades, thousands upon thousands of people travel from villages and cities, by barge and boat, road or rail, to our university towns to feast upon the endless variety of colors and shapes. Compare this magnificent attire from times past with the stiff uniformity of the clothing worn by the thronging spectators and you will agree that here too a deadly uniformity has doused the sparkle of life. What an enormous array of forms in the days when every difference in rank or status was openly displayed in people's dress. What a profuse diversity of styles and costumes, of fabrics and colors, when everyone, from whatever district or region, guild or group, office or occupation he might be, remained recognizable by his clothing and everyone felt the urge to show in fabric and color, in the shape and elegance of their traditional costumes, who they were.
>
> . . . Still, in my opinion, there was also an element of straightforwardness in wearing your own colors so that human society in those days had an immediate warm, sociable look to it. Today, unfortunately, little of that splendor of forms has remained. By comparison with the luxuriant dress of the past, male attire in our day is flat and undistinguished. There is no fanciful form which has not been trimmed, no color combination which has not been dulled, no widening which has not been taken in, no collar which has not been shrunk, no pleat which has not been ironed out. All that is called male, of whatever vocation or title, rank or status, is clothed in the same ill-fitting, undistinguished garments. (*Uniformity* 29)

In the foreground of Kuyper's remarks are the pressures of "standardization" on modernity, while the background is filled with the "profuse diversity" of the irreducible nature of creation.

In his introduction to Kuyper's speech, James D. Bratt notes that Kuyper's "celebration of variety, diversity and multiformity echoes the medieval – and anticipates the postmodern" (*Uniformity* 19). Kuyper's praise of multiformity in fashion parallels the constant exploration within post-modern fashion to draw upon a wide range of design styles and themes.[68] It also speaks of what the post-modern theorist considers the "allegorical value" of multiformity in post-modern fashion as a way to explore concepts such as "health, beauty, morality, morality and sexuality, the nation, the economy, and location."[69]

66 Elizabeth Wilson takes notice of this in *Adorned in Dreams* (10), entertaining fashion is like all "cultural phenomena, especially of a symbolic and mythic kind, [which] are curiously resistant to being imprisoned in one . . . 'meaning.'"

67 Svendsen, *Fashion: A Philosophy*, 12.

68 "Consequently, the desire for another latest model is instantly satisfied by the cycle of fashion in postmodernity. This cycle is the desire for endless difference." Barnard, *Fashion as Communication*, 165.

69 Kroker, Arthur and Marilouise Kroker 1988. *Body Invaders: Sexuality and the Post-Modern Condition*. London: Macmillan, 64.

In addition, Kuyper's assumption that fashion itself should protest meaninglessness and be tied into an ongoing discussion about previous meanings resonates with the contemporary idea of the designer as a kind of *bricoleur*.[70]

On the other hand, the pre-modern aspect of Kuyper's appeal is apparent in his comment that fashion outside the theater is valued by reflecting design for the sake of genuine communication about a particular view of "difference in rank or status." The idea of a fixed rank or status regarding class or gender feels archaic to the postmodern worldview which so highly values ambiguity and ambivalence.[71] Kuyper's own view of the language of fashion exposes his confidence in a "relatively stable, fixed meaning," which conflicts with "more fragmentary postmodern societies." In these societies "clothes function more as open texts that can constantly acquire new meanings."[72] Concurrently, the idea of portraying the self with "straightforwardness" is in strong contrast to the hermeneutics of suspicion in much postmodern fashion theory which sees all fashion primarily playing the role of masquerade or performance.[73] Kuyper, however, gives a dignity to the development of multiformity that implicitly challenges fashion as simply a recycling of past forms.[74] To further understand Kuyper's pre-modern posture towards fashion, we need to turn to our final Kuyperian categories.

The Implications of Fashion as Art

Is fashion to be deemed full-fledged art? If so, what does that say about art, and what does that say about fashion? What role should beautification play in art and fashion? How might we judge the aesthetic qualities of fashion? These are just a few of the questions that surface when viewing fashion as art. In order to explore the theological underpinnings of a Kuyperian response, we turn to our final categories in Kuyper's views of art and beauty.

Kuyper, art, and beauty

Unlike many of his Calvinist contemporaries, Kuyper took the arts very seriously. In addition to speaking about art in his Stone Lectures, he lectured on aesthetics at the Free University and wrote extensively about art in a number of publications.[75] Kuyper had many reasons for writing about art, not the least being the broad popularization of art (i.e., theater, music) during his lifetime, about which he had mixed feelings. On the one hand, he believed that art for the masses was necessary to counteract the numbing influences of "materialism" and "rationalism"; on the other hand, Kuyper saw the potentially dreadful

---

70 The term has a wide variety of meanings. The reference here is not to the extemporaneous act of play but to a fixed set of meanings to create with; Barnard, *Fashion as Communication*, 179–182.

71 "What is the source of this uneasiness and ambiguity, this sense that clothes have a life of their own? . . . A part of this strangeness of dress is that it links the biological body to the social being, and public to private. This makes it uneasy territory, since it forces us to recognize that the human body is more than a biological entity. It is an organism in culture, a cultural artifact even, and its own boundaries are unclear." Wilson, *Adorned in Dreams*, 2.

72 Svendsen, *Fashion: A Philosophy*, 71.

73 The use of fashion to masquerade a constructed nature of identity has a long history which goes back to the Greek and Roman civilization. See Barnard, *Fashion as Communication*, 166–167.

74 Baudrillard, Jean 1993. *Symbolic Exchange and Death*. London: Sage, 88.

75 Heslam, Peter S. 1998. *Creating a Christian Worldview: Abraham Kuyper's Lectures on Calvinism*. Grand Rapids: Eerdmans, 197.

results of courting "sensual pleasures" in such a way to produce the "vulgarization of the arts" (*LC* 143). Peter Heslam associates Kuyper's comments with that of the intellectual establishment of his day. Heslam notes that "comments on art and artists tended to center around what could be considered 'good taste.'"[76] While Kuyper did not restrict what constituted as art to matters of taste, as we shall see, he did have a very concrete basis for what constituted "good taste."[77]

Kuyper's concern for art was also connected to his broader confessional apologetic of Calvinism as a "life-system." Calvinism's hostile critique of art has a long history,[78] and in his Stone Lectures Kuyper spends two-thirds of his lecture on art giving a spirited apologetic for Calvinism's apparent prejudice against the arts. Among the points he makes are the following:[79]

1. Calvin's own personal lack of enthusiasm or the embrace of Calvinism by the less artistically broad Northern European countries should not be confused with Calvinism as a system.[80]
2. It was because of Calvinism's advanced status that it was freed from expressing itself in artistic terms (*LC* 14).
3. Calvinism, rather than squelching the arts, has produced some of the most remarkable art the world has seen (*LC* 165).

Of these three the latter two are particularly problematic. His second point, which drives a wedge between religion and the use of symbols, has become the source of much criticism.[81] Even some ardent supporters of Kuyper believe his argument here, grounded in Calvin and supported by Hegel, is unconvincing. Others, like Philip Benedict, go so far as to see the distinction between symbol and religion as a form of Platonic dualism between matter and spirit.[82] His third point, which attempts to elevate Calvinism to a role of artistic fecundity, is equally untenable. To say that the Calvinist tradition should be noted for spawning the arts is a stretch indeed.[83] Yet in his attempt to argue this point, Kuyper

---

76 Heslam goes on to state that "true art being whatever measured up to certain standards of taste . . . many forms of art were not considered 'true art.' Leo Tolstoy went so far as to exclude from art those symphonies and paintings that appealed to the more sensual and decadent tastes, including some of the most respected works of Wagner and Michelangelo." Heslam, *Creating a Christian Worldview*, 200.

77 Though art could be "vulgarized" it would still be deemed art nonetheless. *LC* 143.

78 Benedict, Philip 1999. "Calvinism as a Culture?" In *Seeing Beyond the Word: The Visual Arts and the Calvinist Tradition*. Paul Corbey Finney, ed. Grand Rapids: Eerdmans, 21.

79 Not included here is Calvin's argument that suspicion of state-religion and its uniform artistic symbolism, not inflexibility, has cautioned Calvinism from developing a particular religious art-style. And his argument that Calvinism, rather than merge art and religion, was focused on freeing art to "an independent existence." *LC* 145–147.

80 *LC* 14; Regarding Calvin's own apathy towards the arts Daniel Hardy writes that "Calvin's notorious disinterest in the arts is not therefore based on a trait of character, but on twin theological premises-that the arts are not interesting to those concerned for the truth of God as known in God's Word, and that in themselves they are legitimate within strictly defined limits." Hardy, Daniel 1999. "Calvinism and the Visual Arts: A Theological Introduction." In Finney ed. *Seeing Beyond the Word*, 12.

81 Heslam, *Creating a Christian Worldview*, 208.

82 Benedict, *Seeing Beyond the Word*, 28.

83 "His [Kuyper's] desperation to paint Calvinism in glowing colors means he never seriously addresses the problem of Calvinism's frequent disparagement of the arts." Begbie, Jeremy 1991. *Voicing Creation's Praise*. Edinburgh: T&T Clark, 96.

develops a perceptive broadening of the scope of art based on the doctrine of election. Kuyper observes that

> If a common man, to whom the world pays no special attention, is valued and even chosen by God as one of His elect, this must lead the artist also to find a motive for his artistic studies in what is common and of every-day occurrence, to pay attention to the emotions and the issues of the human heart in it. . . . (*LC* 166)

Here Kuyper builds on his view of election as a basis for democracy, seeing election as bringing a democratic approach to art's subject matter.

In addition to giving an apologetic for Calvinism, Kuyper is concerned with constructing a theological basis for aesthetics, and his approach builds on Calvin's view that creation reflects the glory of God. Kuyper expands the sense of glory to include "God's radiance, perfection, splendor, and divinity."[84] This divine "beauty" shines in both "material" and "spiritual" things. Behind Kuyper's inclusion of beauty in both the "material" as well as the "spiritual" is his attempt to answer the question of "whether art should imitate nature or should transcend it" (*LC* 154). Kuyper's answers is a *via media*: Calvinism offers a way between the options of the "empiricist," whose "mere imitation" of nature seeks to reflect transcendent beauty and the "idealist," who's creative "interpretation" seeks beauty in the immanent (*LC* 154). According to Kuyper "by regarding God's glory as manifest in both spiritual and material phenomena, the antithesis between idealism and empiricism falls away."[85] Thus, the artist's role is "not merely to observe everything visible and audible, to apprehend it, and reproduce it artistically, but much more to discover in those natural forms the order of the beautiful, and, enriched by this higher knowledge, to produce a beautiful world that transcends the beautiful of nature" (*LC* 154).

Contemporary theologians friendly to Kuyper's project point out immediate problems with his theological aesthetic. First, Jeremy Begbie has noted that implicit within this approach "beauty appears to be a quality which the created world only points to and indicates, rather than actually contains or embodies,"[86] and the ideal of an other-worldly universal echoes a Platonic influence inconsistent with Kuyper's repeated appeal to the orderliness of the created world.[87] A second problem is the reduction of the artistic purpose to a particular type of action.[88] Nicholas Wolterstorff has observed: "over and over

---

84 Heslam, *Creating a Christian Worldview*, 210.

85 Heslam, *Creating a Christian Worldview*, 213

86 Begbie, *Voicing Creation's Praise*, 98.

87 Begbie's critique of Kuyper as under Hellenic influence has corroboration outside of aesthetic theory. Kuyper in *LC* (159) spoke in particular about the Greeks as glowing exemplars in the fields of aesthetics: "Aesthetic genius, if I may so call it, had been implanted by God Himself in the Greek . . ."; "Thus Calvinism was not only able, but bound, to confess that, by the grace of God, the Greeks were the primordial nation for art." *LC* 162. This distinction between the created world and the spiritual world is in tension with Kuyper's view of nature and grace. See Veenhof, *Nature and Grace in Herman Bavinck*, 13.

88 "In the real world, God is Creator of everything; the power of really producing new things is His alone, and therefore He always continues to be the creative artist. As God, He alone is the original One, we are only the bearers of His Image. Our capacity to create after Him and after what He created, can only consist in the *unreal* creations of art. So we, in our fashion, may imitate God's handiwork. We create a kind of cosmos, in our Architectural monument; to embellish nature's forms, in Sculpture; to reproduce life, animated by lines and tints, in our Painting; to transfuse the mystical spheres in our Music and in our Poetry. And all this because the beautiful is not the product of our own fantasy, nor of our subjective perception, but has an objective existence, being itself the expression of a Divine perfection." *LC* 156.

one comes across claims to the effect that such-and-such is 'the essential function of art.' 'Art is mimesis.' 'Art is self-expression.' 'Art is significant form.' All such formulae fall prey to the same dilemma. Either what is said to be characteristic of art is true of more than art. Or, if true only of art, it is not true of all art."[89] Additionally, it would be difficult to defend the restriction of the criteria of art to "beauty" or "unity in harmony" or some other standard of resplendence, even if such criteria have a long history and were often invoked in Kuyper's day.[90]

Fashion and Kuyper's view of art

Although Kuyper never stated that fashion was art, he did imply a strong association (if not identification) of the two. This is seen in a number of ways. First, Kuyper's description of pre-modern clothing as a "magnificent feast," an "enormous array of forms," "endless colors and shapes" and "luxuriant dress" extols the aesthetic resplendence of fashion as a primary quality (*Uniformity* 29). This parallels his bias of diverse expressions of beauty as an essential quality of art. Secondly, in speaking about fashion he makes immediate reference to the place of fashion in the dramatic arts, which associates fashion with an explicit type of art. Thirdly, as we have seen, Kuyper bemoans the market forces that shift the balance fashion has from art to capital. These three features signify that Kuyper thought about fashion in artistic terms and, moreover, he is not alone in this assessment. Contemporary theorists universally agree that fashion is clearly a legitimate form of art in itself.[91] This is not to say that the relationship between fashion and art is not a complex one, but that even those critical of fashion do not exclude it from being classified as art.[92] Because of Kuyper's association of fashion with art, and fashion's theorists' assumption that fashion is art, it is worth exploring the implications of Kuyper's view of art on fashion.

Kuyper's view of art has direct relevance to fashion. As we have seen, Kuyper had a guarded optimism regarding the popularization of art. Along with other artistic mediums, we can surmise Kuyper would include the "art of dress" as a source of "enjoyment" and "comfort, in this our depressed state of life" (*LC* 153). Fashion, like all the arts for Kuyper, can have an ennobling role within a culture as it excites the affections.[93] Additionally,

---

89 Wolterstorff, Nicholas 1990. *Art in Action*. Grand Rapids: Eerdmans, 8.

90 Begbie in his critique of Kuyper's focus on beauty outlines the following objections: (1.) There are many things we might call "works of art" that ostensibly are *not* beautiful. In fact, there are many examples of so-called Christian art that does not fit traditional notions of beauty. (2.) Examples of beauty such as "unity-in-diversity" moreover exist in a good many fields besides for art. (3.) This seems to assume the chief benefit of art is formal contemplation. In most works of art, "form" is only one aspect of what we value. (4.) The traditional concept of "beauty" replaces a potentially more intrinsic Christian view of beauty along the lines of the biblical narrative (creation, salvation, consummation). Begbie, *Voicing Creation's Praise*, 156.

91 Eicher, *The Visible Self*, 348.

92 For a more positive view of the relationship of fashion and art see: Macrell, Alice 2005. *Art and Fashion: The Impact of Art on Fashion and fashion on Art*. London: Batsford. Svendsen believes fashion has had a thorny relationship to standardized views of art for the following reasons: (1.) Fashion has always been embedded in the marketplace; (2.) fashion's uniqueness is related to its appearance en mass; (3.) there is hardly such a thing as critical fashion journals; (3.) fashion is in a reactive relationship to standardized art because function in fashion is too closely related to form. Svendsen concludes, "When considered as art, fashion is simply not all that fashionable." Svendsen, *Fashion: A Philosophy*, 100–106.

93 "Besides, it is but fair to concede that, threatened with atrophy by materialism and rationalism, the human heart naturally seeks an antidote against this withering process, in its artistic instinct." *LC* 143.

along with Kuyper's call for the liberation of the arts, the liberation of fashion includes freedom from any one particular personal or cultural expression. This is implicit in Kuyper's personalization of Calvin's artistic tastes, as well as his argument that Calvinism sought to free art from the state and church. It is also implicit in his reflections on the democratic connotations of the doctrine of election on artistic subject matter. Such fashion liberation fits with current dress theorists' observation that dress in democracies "tend to be more varied . . . since individuals are not subordinate to the state."[94] One might also intimate that, for Kuyper, fashion – once suitable only for kings and nobles – is rightly more available to the common man in the same way that art had become more available in Kuyper's day.[95] And just as Kuyper believed art can come in "high and low" forms, fashion can equally be enjoyed as a "higher pleasure" (couture) as well as "common sport" (street fashion) "to the glory of God."[96] Finally, because fashion (like art) sets its own discourse, we might deduce that in a Kuyperian framework fashion is not subservient to any one particular voice within the field.[97]

Kuyper's understanding of art, however, has limitations that must be updated lest they lead to a truncated view of fashion. Kuyper's strong association of "beauty" as the *sin qua non* of art is no longer defensible. In fact, Kuyper's understanding of art (and fashion) as organizing the creative "givens" to make theological statements about a transcendent world seems to be at odds with the independence he wishes to give the arts.[98] Modern theologians friendly to the Kuyperian tradition have sought to rectify this problem by offering broader views of artistic and aesthetic excellence. Nicholas Wolterstorff's understanding of art as action, for example, more adequately fits the various artistic performances found in design and dress. Speaking of art as action, Jeremy Begbie, elaborating on Wolterstorff's thesis, states that "works of art equip us for action. And the range of actions for which they equip us is very nearly as broad as the range of human action itself."[99] According to Begbie and Wolterstorff, the actual piece of clothing or outfit is aesthetically judged by its purpose "of contemplation for aesthetic delight" which may include a number of aesthetic factors.[100] To connect the aesthetic aspect of fashion to beauty or some other quality of resplendence reduces the role of fashion to adornment. As fashion theorists note, the aesthetic nature of fashion needs to fit into a broad set of tasks that dress has as it communicates not only adornment, but, also utility, modesty, symbol, role, status, class, economics, government,

94 Storm, *Functions of Dress*, 212.
95 "It is the democratizing, if you like, of a life-utterance which hitherto recommended itself by its aristocratic allurements." *LC* 142.
96 ". . . that by it we might glorify God, and ennoble human life, and drink at the fountain of higher pleasures, yea, even of common sport." *LC* 153.
97 "Art, like Science, cannot afford to tarry at her origin, but must ever develop herself more richly, at the same time purging herself of whatsoever had been falsely intermingled with the earlier plant. Only the law of her growth and life, when once discovered, must remain the fundamental law of art for ever; a law, not imposed upon her from without, but sprung from her own nature." *LC* 163.
98 Kuyper speaks of the role of the arts being "to discover in those natural forms the order of the beautiful, and, enriched by this higher knowledge, to produce a beautiful world that transcends the beautiful of nature." *LC* 154.
99 Begbie, *Voicing Creation's Praise*, 208.
100 Ibid.

religion, individual development, group dynamics, behavior, etc.[101] This means that one must look at the aesthetic work of fashion from a broad set of aesthetic purposes, not just beauty. With this updated understanding of artistic expression placed alongside Kuyper's defense of the integrity and breadth of the arts, a relatively sophisticated perspective emerges for evaluating the aesthetic nature of fashion.

Conclusion

Kuyper is most famous for saying, "there is not a square inch of the whole domain of our human existence over which Christ . . . does not cry: 'Mine!'" (*SS* 488). Implicit within this claim is an invitation to explore the various inches, not the least of which is fashion. Traditionally, theology's response to fashion has vacillated between neglect and hostility. The threadbare nature of this approach begs for a refashioning of faith; to move forward theologians must offer fresh reflection about fashion as it interacts in its various roles in art and market, as language and cultural artifact. As our study has demonstrated, Kuyper's framework provides just such a way forward through offering a nuanced understanding of fashion as culture maker, cultural phenomenon and artistic expression.[102] This is good news not only for theologians, but for Christians both inside and outside the fashion industry who are asking real questions about their faith amidst the complexities of contemporary culture.

---

101 Storm, *Functions of Dress*, iv–vii.

102 Kuyper believed that in the face of new questions due to the vicissitudes of culture fresh assessment would need to be made through recultivating the roots of Calvinist theology in the new context: "what the descendants of the Old Dutch Calvinists as well as of the Pilgrim fathers have to do, is not to copy the past, as if Calvinism were a petrifaction, but to go back to the living root of the Calvinist plant, to clean and to water it, and to so cause it to bud and to blossom once more, now fully in accordance with our actual life in these modern times, and with the demands of the times to come." *LC* 171.

27

Rehabilitating the State in America:
Abraham Kuyper's Overlooked Contribution

Timothy Sherratt

The political thought of Abraham Kuyper offers a theory of the state better suited than liberalism to critique and defend it in the contemporary climate of government downsizing. Despite its elegant formulae for the protection of individual liberties, the liberal tradition has failed to contain the American state. Theodore Lowi's juridical democracy fails to correct these deficiencies from within. By contrast, Kuyper's view of the state, grounded in his "sphere sovereignty," holds greater potential for securing public justice – a state limited enough to protect the basic liberty of persons and social institutions but energetic enough to arbitrate justice between and among those persons and institutions.

Introduction

From curing factions' mischiefs to balancing government budgets, from checking and balancing to term limits, the 1990s have witnessed a steady undercurrent of experimentation with governmental design as an alternative to personal choice in the American political tradition. But this current has been so dammed and diverted, it has become more and more a backwater. The Gingrich revolution was fascinating in many respects, not least for the tangled epistemology that cut government in the name of personal freedom but simultaneously freed government from the impact of personal choice to operate as a machine that would run of itself. The main currents of American public discourse trap the state in negative images of abusive power and inefficient bureaucracy, inviting both an older language of rights against such government and a more recent, increasingly discredited, rhetoric of entitlements to its resources and power. These images, and the scholarship that has failed to lay them to rest, create a fragmented and contradictory theory of government's role. Nowhere is this more so than in the courts where government must prove a compelling interest before it is permitted to place restrictions on fundamental rights but need only demonstrate a rational basis for expansionist social and economic programs – reasoning which has imposed considerable strain on the separation of powers. American public and scholarly discourse succeeds in being anti-statist despite the presence

The author would like to thank Father Francis Canavan SJ, Jesse Greendyk, Tracy Kuperus, Keith Pavlischek, Ashley Woodiwiss, and anonymous reviewers for their helpful comments and suggestions on earlier drafts of this essay.

of a large state apparatus. Lost in the shuffle, so to speak, is the state itself, its authority either defied or dissolved in notions of social contract and popular consent, its executive powers diluted in pluralist theory. If Theodore Lowi is right, there is not even the consolation of success to smooth over the contradictions. The American state has expanded despite the rhetoric of rights and the warnings about power, despite the separation of powers and the Bill of Rights. Its regulatory reach is pervasive, but its real authority is qualified by the practice of democratizing administration of the majority's will. Thus, liberal leaders "do not wield the authority of democratic governments with the resoluteness born of confidence in the legitimacy of their positions, the integrity of their institutions, or the justness of the programs they serve."[1] This paper will make considerable use of Lowi's well-received analysis and prescriptions; taken together, they lay important groundwork for the contribution neo-Calvinism might make to resolve the dilemma of the state in American politics and political science. The rehabilitation of the American state appears to be linked to the disentangling of the institutionalist, republican tradition from the quasi-libertarian language of rights and minimalist government. The "overlooked contribution" of the writings of Abraham Kuyper in particular, and of neo-Calvinism in general, lies in its theory of the internal design of the state, its juxtaposition of the state to personal and group liberty, its religious view of life and resulting respect for religious liberty, and its embrace of pluralism. The neo-Calvinist state is limited in function but morally purposeful, responsible for sharing authority with differentiated societal institutions and for interpreting the relationship between those institutions and the persons who occupy them. While the neo-Calvinist state is to a degree contained both by American-style checks on its authority, the principal "checks and balances" are structural arguments asserting the irreducible grounds of that authority. Finally, the scholarly orientation reflected in the neo-Calvinist conception of the state finds questions of the positive state and of church-and-state closely connected, whereas American political science has typically kept them separated.

Theodore Lowi and the State in America

Although it conforms in most respects to the received view of the evolution of the state in the United States, Lowi's treatment of the subject is noteworthy for its development over some three decades. Indeed, the received view owes much to his scholarship, which has had a profound effect on the study of American government, from public policy analysis to the presidency to the state of the discipline itself.[2] But in singling out Lowi's analysis of the American state, I am in a sense also invoking several generation's worth of scholarship seeking to mobilize effective authority and administration within and in the service of liberal democracy, what Seidelman and Harpham[3] term the "Third Tradition" in political

1   Lowri, Thomas 1979 (1969). *The End of Liberalism: The Second Republic of the United States*. 2nd ed. New York: Norton, 295.

2   The principal works are: "American Business, Public Policy, Case Studies, and Political Theory." *World Politics* 1964: 677–715; *The End of Liberalism*. New York: Norton. 1969 (1979); *The Personal President*. Ithaca: Cornell University Press, 1985; and "The State in Political Science: How We Become What We Study." *American Political Science Review* 86 (1): 1–7.

3   Seidelman, Raymond, with Edward Harpham 1985. *Disenchanted Realists: Political Science and the American Crisis*, 1884–1984. Albany: State University of New York Press.

science.[4] Lowi's contribution lies principally in his call for juridical democracy.[5] His insistence that the crisis of the republic under an uncontrolled interest-group liberalism should be met by attention to the basic internal design of the republic brings him into fruitful contact and even limited agreement with the Kuyperian view of the state. It does so in three respects. First, it applies a remedy where Kuyper had most to offer, not where he had least for Kuyper identified the state's purpose and limits by laying alongside one another the roles, or divine callings, of the state, social institutions and individuals rather than pursuing the Anglo-American emphasis on limited government as a corollary of pre-social individual rights. Second, Lowi's remedy is in some respects much clearer than Kuyper's and sheds critical light on the latter; specifically, the principles Lowi recommends for checking the positive state operate with less ambiguity than the principles one must infer to justify state intervention in a Kuyperian polity. Third, however, Lowi's remedy reveals the weaknesses inherent in the general tendency within political science to consider the issues of the welfare state separately from questions of religious liberty and, indeed, innocent of the "religious" presuppositions which guide them. Here, the integral Kuyperian approach is demonstrably superior.

The Federal Constitution of 1787 established a central government with exclusive functions in the area of foreign policy making, and with control over subsidies, tariffs, public lands disposal, patents, and coinage domestically. These domestic powers had been hewn from the much larger set of functions held by state governments, which retained almost all regulatory functions like judicial and criminal procedure laws, public health laws, and banking and credit laws.[6] Left obscure in the Constitution was the federal-state balance of power and function in respect of commerce, because while the Constitution granted Congress power to regulate inter-state commerce, it did not accompany that grant with a corresponding prohibition on the states. The early Federal state was a "patronage state," in Lowi's words. Though it was the largest institution in American society and its activities significantly influenced commercial development, investment, and productive population distribution, the Federal government in no sense coordinated a national policy – unless one credits Chief Justice Marshall with doing so. Instead, it brokered countless individual decisions and distributed its patronage in jobs and policies.

The patronage state was first supplemented by elements of a regulatory state in the late nineteenth century. At first the agitation for government regulation of industry barely touched the Federal government, but the inability of states to tackle the whole problem precipitated national legislative action.[7] Supreme Court decisions restricting the reach of early federal regulations perhaps retarded national regulatory efforts, notably the decision in *Hammer v. Dagenhart* in 1918, so the patronage state survived as the dominant form into the 1930s. Indeed, Lowi regards this as a settled matter within the discipline:

---

4   The first tradition is the institutional tradition of the Constitution, which achieved order by regulating not suppressing society's factions. The second tradition is democratic, in the spirit of Paine and the Antifederalists and also of the Populists and muckraking. Viewed from within either tradition, the other appeared in conflict with it. But the third tradition insisted on their compatibility, on the possibility of combining the two into a single political science. Seidelman and Harpham. 1985. *Disenchanted Realists.*

5   Lowri, 1969, *The End of Liberalism.*

6   Lowi, 1985. *The Personal President: Power Invested, Promise Unfulfilled.* Ithaca: Cornell University Press, 24.

7   Lowi, 1985. *The Personal President,* 42.

There is no need to document for political scientists the contention that the American state until the 1930s was virtually an oxymoron. The level of national government activity was almost as low in 1932 as it had been in 1832.[8]

The nationalization of political focus brought about by the Civil War and industrialization, by the mass media, and by social movements did, however, precipitate the emergence of a national state.

With the coming of the New Deal, the now-expanding patronage role was broadly supplemented by regulatory and redistributive functions that respectively imposed obligations directly upon citizens and set up the programs that earn the redistributive function the title of "welfare" state. These developments were supported by the Supreme Court from 1937 (*NLRB v. Jones and Laughlin Steel Corp.*) and then given wholehearted encouragement in 1942 (*Wickard v. Filburn*). In Lowi's words, if Filburn (a small farmer growing wheat for private consumption in excess of his federally allotted quota) can be reached by Congressional act, then "economic federalism is dead."[9]

For Lowi, the development and endorsement of the regulatory and welfare states constitute a revolution making the federal government responsible for citizens' wellbeing and steering popular expectations of good government away from its representativeness towards its capacity to deliver services. But crucial to the analysis is Lowi's charge that Court and Congress together perverted the framers' design for a separation-of-powers system and erected in place of the original balance a presidency equipped with unchecked, delegated powers of enormous reach. Despite the American tradition of individual rights and limited government and a rhetoric to match, America got a state that strained the definition of limited government and became the authoritative deliverer of rights as well as their natural enemy.

The new state, what Lowi terms the Second Republic of the United States, was a positive, interventionist state, centered on the executive branch; it began life having been granted unqualified validation by the Court concerning national economic power and the separation of powers; it controlled aspects of the electoral process traditionally left in private hands; it assumed these controls at the expense of the political parties; it rapidly acquired an autonomous bureaucracy; and its epistemology looked to economics rather than to law.[10] It is the breakdown of the rule of law and its replacement by bargaining that Lowi finds to be the distinguishing feature of the Second Republic and the focus of his proposals for reform.

Lowi's indictment of this American state is his familiar critique of interest-group liberalism. Liberal governments undermine popular decisions by democratizing their administration, decline to set standards, fall short of justice by failing to make policy on the basis of prior moral rule, and substitute bargaining for formal (legal) procedure. His

---

8   Lowri, 1992. "The State in Political Science: How We Become What We Study." *American Political Science Review* 86(1): 1.

9   Lowri, 50.

10 Lowri, 1992. "The State in Political Science," 2–3. Specifically, Lowi associates the Second Republic with a new emphasis on science, with statistics leading the way and flowering as the public opinion subfield. As he recognizes, developments of this kind were anticipated in the field of Constitutional law at least as early as *Lochner v. New York* (1905), in which social science asserted an independent authority distinct from the republican political science of the founders. See Kahn, Paul W. 1995. *Legitimacy and History.* New Haven: Yale University Press.

response is to call for *juridical democracy*, in its simplest form a return to predictable and accountable government under the rule of law, a form rejected by the Supreme Court at the very moment the United States embraced a federal state in earnest. Under juridical democracy, governments would have to define policy goals with precision, that is, they would have to write laws that leave minimal discretion to administrators. As Lowi had observed long before (1964), implementation of policy under loosely written laws involves not mere administrative rule-following but genuine decision-making power. Where that early work concentrated on analysis alone, *The End of Liberalism* was openly critical of the delegation of power, the broad discretion it gave bureaucracy, and the failure of the courts to contain delegation within a clear and workable principle conceived within the structural intent of the Constitution. The centerpiece of his remedy is a return to the rule of law. When in the American republic a political scientist reaches for internal solutions of this kind rather than further external checks on the scope of governmental authority, and when the solutions reached for are principles to govern the distribution of power and functions among the branches of a system of separated powers, then we can move beyond the stale rhetoric of more versus less government that has cramped public discourse for decades back towards the language of America's internal design. And that is to move back towards the republican foundations behind liberal-democracy. Here, Kuyperian approach has much to offer.

The State in the Political Theology of Abraham Kuyper

Abraham Kuyper (1837–1920) was variously a pastor, newspaper editor, parliamentarian, founder of a university, and prime minister of the Netherlands. His political thought emerges from writings over a long period and reflects all of these roles, yet McKendree Langley cautions that Kuyper was "unable to articulate a systematic Christian theory of the state."[11] In place of such a theory, Kuyper seems to have worked out the main lines of a perspective having the virtue of ongoing application in his journalistic and political work. Kuyper's approach to the state may be understood as practical, with the proviso that his practicality's hallmark is its consistency with a Calvinist confession. That confession, and with it Kuyper's political thought, begins and ends with the sovereignty of God.

The juridical state and sphere sovereignty

Kuyper defined sovereignty in juridical terms, as "authority that possesses the right and duty, and wields the power to break and punish all resistance to its will." And he appealed to the inner voice of conscience for the view that such a power can only be God's – intuitively we are to recognize limits on the exercise by human beings of this sort of power: "And does not an ineradicable conscience also speak within you, telling you that original, absolute sovereignty cannot reside in any creature, but must coincide with the majesty of God?"[12]

When human offices exercise an authority divine in its origins, they simultaneously gain legitimacy for that authority and acknowledge limitations to its exercise. Divine authority in human hands is limited authority both because its source is God and because its

---

11 Langley, McKendree R. 1984. *The Practice of Political Spirituality: Episodes from the Public Career of Abraham Kuyper*, 1879–1918. Jordan Station, Ontario: Paideia Press, 151.

12 *Sphere Sovereignty (Souvereiniteit in Eigen Kring)*. Kampen: Kok, 1930 (1880).

manifestation is multifaceted: there are sovereignties of state, society, and church. Not only does this threefold organization restrict the reach of each sphere into which it is organized, but each of these is also subject in turn to internal qualifications. Sin, the fundamentally disintegrating force in the cosmos, thwarts the realization of world-government, the polity befitting our human nature, for we are all of "one blood." Nation-states therefore do not harmonize with our human nature. Their status is temporary, artificial. Unlike some contemporary Reformed thinkers who derive the authority of the state directly from the "cultural mandate" (God's command to man in Genesis to subdue, cultivate, and replenish the created order), Kuyper wrote somewhat ambivalently on this subject.[13] In his *Lectures on Calvinism*, he argues the state may only derive authority directly from God, a strictly juridical authority that would be moot in a world without sin. Here the state is one of enumerated rather than implied powers, as Augustinian as it is traditionally Calvinist, whose authority is both justified and exhausted in response to the disintegrating effects of sin:

> When sin tears man apart, and when sin reveals itself in all manner of shame and unrighteousness, the glory of God demands that these horrors be bridled, that order return to this chaos that a compulsory force, from without, assert itself to make human society a possibility. (*LC* 82)

The true picture appears somewhat more complex, however. In his writings on the doctrines of particular and common grace, Kuyper clearly, if implicitly, embraces the cultural mandate. Particular grace is the saving grace of God; common grace reflects God's willingness to sustain the creation. The two are both related and "antithetical" – S. U. Zuidema[14] writes of them as polar in a magnetic sense, simultaneously attracting and repelling. Thus, common grace has to do with creation (nature – for Kuyper these were synonymous), particular grace with re-creation. Ipso, particular grace is superior and common grace is ultimately dependent upon it, for the creation itself is under judgment and awaits the fulfillment of God's purposes in history, purposes that cannot be reached through (fallen) nature:

> By its inner nature, [common grace] . . . aims at its own creaturely end, which as such has no real connection with the hereafter and no real connection with the mystic life of the souls that are saved.[15]

Kuyper always insisted that his was not an Anabaptist position[16] that wrote off creation and led to world-flight but one in which the very relationship of attraction and repulsion between particular and common grace clarified and underscored the distinct callings of social institutions and the church. Since the principles on which Kuyper's political theory rests invoke these callings and the requirement not to violate them, we

---

13 See, e.g., Walsh, Brian J. and J. Richard Middleton 1984. *The Transforming Vision*. Downers Grove: Inter-Varsity.

14 Zuidema, S. U. 1971. *Communication and Confrontation*. Toronto: Wedge Publishing. *See supra* Chapter 19.

15 Zuidema (69), *see supra* page 261.

16 Just as creation and regeneration are related and disconnected at the same time, so the church is not natural (creational) but supernatural (regenerational). Kuyper does not allow the church to seek to construct the kingdom of heaven on earth for this reason – an error of the radical Anabaptists in his opinion (*see* Zuidema *supra* pages 262-64.

can see that the particular/common grace distinction sharpens the role of the state. The state is an agency of common, not particular, grace. Thus its task is to sustain creation, not to redeem it. In Kuyper's biblical perspective, sustenance is not a neutral life-giving: sustaining a fallen creation is largely a matter of one act of correction after another – for unredeemed humanity abuses God's creation – and in *that* sense the state exercises an exclusively juridical authority. All the same, his position remains ambivalent, for the cultural mandate suggests elements of sustenance other than correction. Perhaps Kuyper viewed other elements as exclusively the province of God. Whether he was right to claim that the common grace juridical calling of government has "no real connection" to redemption is a major point of theology that I will not attempt to take on!

A state that exercises only a derived, creational authority and exercises that authority especially on account of sin can claim none of the traditionally liberal or democratic foundations for exercising governmental power – consent, majority rule, social contract and so forth, albeit democratic elections select a governing party. Indeed, Kuyper draws an explicit set of contrasts between the popular sovereignty of the French Revolution, which expressly rejected existing human and divine authorities in favor of popular sovereignty, and the state sovereignty of the Germans, which claimed that the state embodies the most perfect relationship between man and man, and this theory of derivative sovereignty. He commends Calvinism for its "two-fold insight" into the state's dark side (a potential despotism) and its light side (the only alternative to a "veritable hell on earth"). Kuyper's formulation rejects both popular and state sovereignty but preserves the legitimacy of the state without discounting the threat governments pose to human freedom:

> We have gratefully to receive from the hand of God, the institution of the state with its magistrates, as a means of preservation, now indeed indispensable. And on the other hand . . . we must ever watch against the danger which lurks, for our personal liberty, in the power of the State. (*LC* 81)

The Kuyperian state is grounded in and bounded by three principles: only God possesses sovereign rights because God is the nations' creator, maintainer and ruler; sin has broken down God's direct rule, thus the exercise of authority has been vested in men for a mechanical remedy; and man never possesses legitimate power over fellow man in any other way than by an authority which descends on him from the majesty of God. That this is a limited state is obvious in the first principle – no human being can claim the status of creator, maintainer and ruler of the nations, even if the task assigned to her office is to participate in sustaining the creation. The second principle appears illogical on its face: if human disobedience has broken the personal rule of God, vesting authority in humans seems to be exactly the wrong response. Kuyper resolves the apparent contradiction by reasoning that the only kind of authority reconcilable with God's sovereignty is an authority that leaves little discretion in the human hands that will exercise it – it is a "mechanical" authority. The third principle Kuyper justifies on the grounds that any right to rule over a fellow man will become the right of the strongest (*LC* 82).

To justify the broad division of divine authority into spheres, Kuyper offers two sorts of arguments. The first is to maintain, as Herman Dooyeweerd was to do later, that such a division is ontologically sound, deriving as it does from the ordinances of God. Kuyper argued that the independence of spheres was logically required to demonstrate that they have "nothing above themselves but God, and that the State cannot intrude here, and has nothing to command in their domain."[17] We have seen that Kuyper qualifies the common Calvinist justification that state authority derive from the cultural mandate by assigning it the principal task of counteracting the effects of sin. Accordingly, in his *Lectures*, Kuyper treats the state as a special kind of sphere, more mechanical than organic in character. The social spheres represent organic life; the family, for instance, is natural, innate, spontaneous, biological. Though sin intrudes into every area of life, its worst effects on the social spheres are blunted by common grace, the action of God that operates to benefit everyone, believer and non-believer alike, restraining sin and preserving the created order.

Kuyper described this central Calvinist dogma as God's intervention in the human condition to prevent the total annihilation of his own work, which would have led to a "total degeneracy of human life." Common grace arrests "the complete effectuation of sin . . . partly by breaking its power, partly by taming [man's] evil spirit, and partly by domesticating his nation or his family" (*LC* 124). Common grace, Kuyper claims, lends coherence to history, flowering both in classical thought and modern scientific knowledge. By its action, all things are shown intuitively to be worthy of investigation.

By resorting to an argument from common grace for the organic and relatively unsullied character of the social spheres and contrasting this with the mechanical character of the state, Kuyper further buttresses his conception of limited government. Given the ontological status of the social spheres, the state never confers authority upon them or grants them freedom(s) but "merely recognizes" the unique authority which descends on each directly from God.

The second argument is less pejorative in regards to the state. Kuyper finds the distinction among the social spheres and between them and the state marked by two antithetical "sovereignty credos." The unbeliever separates faith and sovereignty and vests the latter exclusively in the state, which confers, or if it is weak, allows, the social spheres to possess what freedom they enjoy. By contrast, the believer links the two, vesting human freedom in God and recognizing that the state is "marked by an authority derived from Him."[18] Yield the Christian revelation, Kuyper argues, and under whatever "hybrid theories" you hide it, Caesarism emerges:

Thus the ancient history of the world confronts us with the ignominious drama of how,

---

17 *LC* 91. The spheres in question are identified in quasi-functionalist fashion, for each links a function, its matching institutions and the requisite authority to give effect to both. Kuyper first distinguishes the social spheres from the sphere of government. The distinctions between spheres and institutions becomes somewhat blurred but the social spheres include the social, where differential personalities prevail, the corporate (universities, guilds, associations, churches), the domestic (the family, married life), and "communal autonomy." But in a use of the term that does not entirely fit with this, Art is described as a sphere where "genius is a *sovereign* power." In other uses, Commerce is a sphere, but so, too, is labor. Benevolence and philanthropy are described as a "field," and so on. Despite these inconsistencies, a view of society as differentiated by organic function and personal vocation and talent emerges quite clearly. Kuyper found little equality in the social spheres, but this did not concern him, for though "dominion is exercised everywhere . . . it is a dominion which works organically; not by virtue of a State-investiture, but from life's sovereignty itself" (*LC* 95). For example, the extraordinary competence of the mathematical genius is not a threat to society but a positive benefit. Citing approvingly "the dominion" of Aristotle, Plato, Lombard, Thomas Aquinas, Luther, Calvin, Kant and Darwin, Kuyper asserted that such is "a gift of God, possessed only by His grace. It is subject to no one and is responsible to Him alone Who has granted it this ascendancy" (*LC* 95).

18 *Sphere Sovereignty*, 7.

despite stubborn and sometimes heroic resistance, freedom within the various spheres dies out and the power of the state triumphs, turning eventually into Caesarism.

Rights and the state

Kuyper deduces the rights and liberties of social life from the same source from which the high authority of government flows, the "absolute sovereignty of God." And if rights and state authority come from the same source, "these two must therefore come to an understanding," for "both have the same sacred obligation to maintain their God-given sovereign authority and to make it subservient to the majesty of God" (*LC* 98). This juxtaposing of rights and state authority as derivative sovereignties will not allow their permanent situating in opposition to each other – even though Kuyper recognizes that the "battle of the ages" is the battle between authority and liberty – but points to a symbiosis by which the assertion of the one or the other may be obligatory for the good of all. Thus, Kuyper describes the struggle for liberty as "not only . . . permissible, but is made a duty for each individual in his own sphere. . . . The very innate thirst for liberty . . . proved itself the God-ordained means to bridle the authority [of the state] wheresoever it degenerated into despotism" (*LC* 80).

All political authority, then, whether in the hands of individual persons, social institutions, or the state, is derivative authority. Nor is the divine grant of authority unconditional; what was ordained (Romans 13) may be taken away by a God ever active in the affairs of humankind. Under certain conditions God plants his sovereignty in the people, Kuyper acknowledges, only to deny that this justifies an assertion of popular sovereignty "as was atheistically proclaimed in Paris in 1789." But, "(e)ven a Calvinist gratefully recognizes . . . the divine judgment which at that time was executed in Paris." The point he seems to make is that the right way to comprehend events like the French Revolution is through the lens of divine judgment, not the lens of natural rights; and an occasion for divine judgment does not translate into a grounds for popular sovereignty. Kuyper insists that the "desirable condition" of popular rule can be removed, or never bestowed, as a matter of divine judgment "when a nation is unfit for it, or, by its sin, has utterly forfeited the blessing" (*LC* 84). What he fails to explain is how one recognizes such a bestowal or removal of sovereignty. When is a military coup judgment, and thus legitimate in some limited fashion? When is it to be resisted without any moral self-examination on the part of the people or their democratically elected government? Can the legitimacy of the judgment be affirmed independently of Calvinist theology – a vital requirement for a pluralist polity one would think? The theological point being made is much clearer than any practical principle to be derived from it.

The requirement that all human sovereignties derive from God appears to circumscribe the state rather more than it does the individual. When Kuyper describes the sphere of government as supplying a mechanical remedy, he asserts that state authority is both justified *and exhausted* in correcting the disintegrative effects of sin. By contrast, the social spheres are organic and innate; that is, they enjoy the sustaining power of God (common grace) relatively unsullied by the debilitating effects of sin. The state is restricted by necessary deference to the "innate law of life" at work in the social spheres and by the limits of its own mandate:

The sovereignty, by the grace of God, of the government is here set aside and limited, for God's sake, by another sovereignty, which is equally divine in origin. Neither the life of science nor of art, nor of agriculture, nor of industry, nor of commerce, nor of navigation, nor of the family, nor of human relationship may be coerced to suit itself to the grace of the government. (*LC* 96)

I remarked above that the doctrine of vocations was the implicit ground on which Kuyper's political thinking rests, implicit enough at any rate to be largely unremarked in his treatment of politics in his *Lectures*. Contemporary neo-Calvinists allow the doctrine more force in their political theory. Discussing the doctrine of vocation as it appears in Calvin's *Institutes*, Hancock distinguishes the Calvinist official, a "conduit of the will of God, which he cannot possibly embody"[19] from the Aristotelian aristocrat whose virtue embodies what is good for man. For Hancock, Calvinist calling depends directly on God's sovereignty. One might be called equally to service of the state as to ministry in the church, yet "equality under God's will binds men to their respective callings; it does not liberate them as political actors."[20] Here is the mechanical character of office in an older, Calvinist guise.

Contemporary neo-Calvinists sometimes write as though vocation does indeed liberate one as a political actor, or at least lend further validity to the view that the state possesses some independence from the social spheres. Zylstra, for instance, argues that the norm of justice "requires social space for human personality. By personality I mean the human self whose calling lies in love of God and love of neighbor."[21] Zylstra lists the social spheres as valid domains for fulfilling one's vocation and includes public office along with them, without reference to the organic/mechanical distinction by which Kuyper divides them. This is misleading on account of the individualist motives it allows to attach to the performance of governmental office, which for Calvin and Kuyper is not a sphere in which to practice *creative* individuality, but obedience to the cultural mandate. Indeed, Zylstra himself recognized public office as unique, divinely established to "maintain a public realm in which the rights of persons and institutions are recognized, protected, and guaranteed."[22] On this reading, contemporary neo-Calvinism would seem to want to broaden the role of government to include a directive function along with the juridical function.[23]

A more far-reaching interpretation of Kuyper involves the marriage of sphere sovereignty with the concept of rights, which also emerges in Zylstra's writings, especially

---

19 Hancock, Ralph C. 1989. *Calvin and the Foundations of Modern Politics*. Ithaca: Cornell University Press, 68.

20 Hancock 1989, *Calvin*, 70.

21 Zylstra, Bernard J. 1982. "The Bible, Justice, and the State." In James W. Skillen, ed. *Confessing Christ and Doing Politics*. Washington, D.C.: Association for Public Justice.

22 Zylstra, Bernard J. 1991. "The United States Constitution and the Rights of Religion." In James W. Skillen and Rockne M. McCarthy, ed. Political Order and the Plural Structure of Society. Atlanta: Scholars Press, 321.

23 Zylstra's "departure" from Kuyper does appear more marked if one takes the "mechanical" view of the state prominent in the *Lectures* as the point of that departure. Conversely, the implicit embrace of the cultural mandate discussed by Zuidema in his discussion of Kuyper's views on common and particular grace may allow for such a role as an aspect of the organic, and thus changing, nature of creation itself. As I pointed out, however, and as Zuidema acknowledges, Kuyper became too preoccupied by the magnitude of the abuses of common grace, of creation's rich potential, to allow government much of a long leash in this respect.

in respect of religious liberty.[24] Such an interpretation is not without warrant given that Kuyper asserts the rights of people to control their own purses and insists that law, not the magistrate, must decide rights. But what is striking about Kuyper's treatment of rights is how sparse it is. Acknowledging that popular assemblies now protect rights, resisting the notion that any person possesses a right over any other, speculating on the need for a "corporative right of franchise," in Kuyper's treatment public justice depends to only a limited extent on individual rights. Perhaps the process of re-expressing Kuyper's political theory using conventional rights language robs it of its structural focus, turning Kuyperian political theory away from its continental center of gravity as a structural representation of state, individual, and differentiated society in the direction of an Anglo-American scheme for limiting government in the name of individual liberty. This interpretation must be treated cautiously if it seeks to identify itself as Kuyperian for Kuyper is never as individualist as he is personalist. At best it focuses on a secondary aspect of his political thought; at worst it distorts the latter's salient features.

The state as an agent of public justice

Kuyper's juridical conception of government's essential functions did not permit him to legitimize a patronage state along the lines of Lowi's model of the first federal regime. Subsidizing private activity to achieve governmental aims would have been suspect, I think. Sphere sovereignty permits the state to intervene to enable the social spheres to do what they do best, to prevent violations of individual freedoms within these spheres, and to maintain parity between spheres, but such intervention could never be for "positive state" reasons. It is hard to imagine Homestead Acts and railroad land grants emerging from a Kuyperian state in that these did not represent neutral governmental encouragement of private enterprise for its own sake. Sphere sovereignty principles restrain government in this way chiefly to check imperialism or other manifestations of Caesarism, but they may also unintentionally thwart economic development. Only if state encouragement of economic development can be interpreted as an expression of public justice could such intervention be justified.

Kuyper contemplated the rise of the positive state, especially the development of direct cash welfare programs, and sharply criticized it. Writing in 1891, he insisted that state and society each possess its own sphere. The class strife brought on by the industrial revolution elicited from him a restatement of sphere sovereignty principles, not a new venture in public policy. Such ventures, he warned, were the mistaken undertakings of social democrats and state socialists, both of whom erased the distinction between state and society and forfeited the free society ordained by God. What Kuyper objected to in the positive state was a distortion of divine ordinances epitomized by the presumption that men had to design governmental solutions to the social problem de novo. "We do not have to organize society," he maintained, "we have only to develop the germ of organization that God himself has created" (*PP* 62). Here, finally, Kuyper resorts explicitly to the cultural mandate. Man is to "preserve and cultivate" the natural world because barbarism will ensue when human society is left to nature without higher supervision. Kuyper acknowledges the general contribution of human governments to resisting barbarism while noting the unhealthy consequences of government action originating in false, that is, non-

24 Zylstra 1991, "The United States Constitution."

Christian, principles. Such governments permit the powerful to exploit the weak, or to co-opt government offices and turn government's powers against the weak. By contrast, a Calvinist government is to move cautiously in the area of social experimentation, refusing "to erect any structure except one that rests on foundations laid by God" (*PP* 58). Once again, as he was to do in more abstract terms in the Stone Lectures but here in an applied setting, Kuyper turns to the cautionary tale of social democracy and state socialism, the one allowing society to swallow the state, the other permitting the state to absorb society:

> Against both of these, we as Christians must hold that state and society each has its own sphere, its own sovereignty, and that the social question cannot be resolved rightly unless we respect this duality and thus honor state authority as clearing the way for a free society. (*PP* 58)

Although the terms and examples in which he expresses his reluctance to engage in social experimentation might mark Kuyper as a conservative pure and simple, they do lay the foundations for qualified intervention. Rejecting individualism on the basis of common human guilt and "the mystery of the reconciliation on Golgotha," Kuyper commends the "interconnected wholeness of our human society," rejects both an absolute property right as a violation of God's sovereignty and a community of possessions as a violation of the right of rule "in the context of the organic association of mankind," and identifies the problem of poverty as a clash *between* social spheres where government intervention is warranted.[25] The clash in question is, of course, the class struggle, the conflict between business and labor. Compelled by the ordinances of God to stay out of the social spheres but equally compelled to uphold justice equitably (which Kuyper extends to withstanding the physical superiority of the strong, presumably because this falsely advances a right to rule), the state must act even-handedly: "A code for business . . . calls also for a code for labor" (*PP* 64).

Coupled with cautious advice about direct cash payments to the poor or unemployed – he opposed them – Kuyper's prescription for the social crisis of his day is a strengthening of the structures of pluralism. The state and only the state is positioned to bring this about, hence the principle of intervention to restore balance among the spheres. In other respects, however, the problem of poverty lies beyond its reach, for state intervention of any other kind risks sapping the natural resilience of the poor. Instead, Kuyper appeals to individual Calvinists to "place life eternal in the foreground of both rich and poor."

In conjunction with his other writings, *The Problem of Poverty* sheds especially clear light on the Kuyperian state. Unlike its Lockian-American protagonist in its libertarian guise, it is not minimalist or morally neutral; quite the contrary, its role *vis-à-vis* individuals and social institutions is irreducibly moral, stemming as it does from the ordinances of God. Unlike the Lockian-American state in its interest-group liberal guise, it is not a positive state. Moreover, the will of the people provides precious little grounds for justifying social or economic experimentation. Its center of gravity lies in divinely ordained structures,

---

25 And warranted as much for the employer as the employee when the circumstances demanded it. When a railroad strike threatened to disrupt the national economy in 1903, Kuyper as prime minister provided strong support for the railroad company, condemning the strike as an illegitimate severance of contract. Subsequently, he introduced bills to prevent such strikes in the future, to explore criminal wrongdoing by the strikers, and to establish a State Commission to investigate the grievances of railroad personnel (Langley 1984, 91–101).

not in political goals. Henig, writing of a related Christian Democracy, remarks that it supplies "a framework for politics, not a set of objectives."[26] He might have added, "nor a rule-based approach to guiding and limiting public policy." His observation captures Kuyper's preoccupations with respect to the state well. The Kuyperian state stands over against the liberal state by virtue of the juridical calling to which it is confined and the new relationships among state, individuals, and social institutions that it formalizes. Its objectives turn out to be the protection of structures that secure public justice – an architectonic project in statecraft, not a prudential one in decision-making.

The problem of state intervention

The society which emerged from Kuyper's theological wrestling with divine and human sovereignty is a community of communities, and the state a special sphere in which divine authority is exercised to promote justice. However satisfying this juridical formulation may be structurally, it lacks an operationalized principle or set of principles that justify state intervention in a wide range of common situations. To put it somewhat crudely, differentiating state, society, and individuals is not the same thing as relating them. For example, it is well and good to argue for the protection of communities – families, schools, churches – from the coercive power of the state. But when is state intervention justified? Should parents be permitted, in the name of the state, to withhold essential medical treatment from children? What if schools inculcate hatred and undermine the state? In what body is that determination finally vested? What rules may courts reasonably develop for making these determinations?

Kuyper did not develop in detail the principles upon which state intervention must rest, apart from the equality principle discussed in *The Problem of Poverty* (see above), if we mean by principle the operationalizing of a value. The basic Kuyperian principle is, of course, for persons and offices to respect the substance and limits of their respective callings. It will be useful to refer parenthetically, therefore, to Herman Dooyeweerd, who explored the "inner nature" or basic character of the state, albeit in rather abstract terms. I am relying heavily on R. D. Henderson's work *Illuminating Law*[27] for the points that follow, a noteworthy contribution for its discussion of the dependence upon Kuyper Dooyeweerd acknowledged. Dooyeweerd agreed with Kuyper's distinction between the "organic" social spheres and the "mechanical" legal sphere, in large part because to depict the state as organic was to hinder it in its special task of doing justice. Organic views of the state lead to a form of state autonomy whereas Dooyeweerd insists that the state and its legal institutions must continually adapt themselves to development in other spheres. To render the state in anthropological or organic terms earns it loyalty derived from blood ties, which place other spheres in a subordinate position to it. And to justify a "concrete legal system (positive legality) in terms of a goal (for example, the general good or will of the people) negates its sovereignty as a distinct sphere."[28] Instead, the "mechanical" character of the state directly reflects the character of legality itself:

---

26 Henig, D. 1969, *Christian Democracy in Italy.* Kahn, Paul W. 1992. *Legitimacy and History: Self-Government in American Constitutional Theory.* New Haven: Yale University Press.

27 Henderson, R. D. 1994. *Illuminating Law: The Construction of Herman Dooyeweerd's Philosophy.* Amsterdam: Free University.

28 Henderson, *Illuminating Law*, 169.

Legality is characterized by a permanent principle, *viz*, the principle of retribution, taken in its most general and objective sense. . . . It is the essential reaction of the divine legal order against those who violate it in a way which demands punishment.[29]

The principle of retribution operates in two senses to limit the role of the state. First, it lays claim to an exclusive operation in its sphere. Thus, Dooyeweerd asserts, it is not a teleological, reform-oriented, or purposeful principle that would allow reform or deterrence to be proper considerations in law's administration. Liberal approaches to criminal justice are severely curtailed. Second, it operates in a mechanical fashion because it is constrained by the presence of ethics, a sovereignty grounded in love, from exacting revenge: "Retribution should be carried out in connection with the violation of a distinctly *legal* and not a typically ethical norm."[30] Both these modes of operation of the retribution principle take on greater significance given that Dooyeweerd considered retribution not to be the operative principle of criminal law alone, but of all good laws.[31]

If Dooyeweerd can be said to clarify neo-Calvinist principles for state intervention, it must be concluded that the result is much more continental than it is American with respect to the mechanism that secures the intervention. As the inclusion of the Bill of Rights as a condition for ratification of the Constitution nicely illustrates, Americans have not been satisfied with the argument that the structure of government alone can guarantee liberty; they have insisted on listing their liberties (with the additional qualification of Ninth Amendments) to keep government at arms' length from their consciences, their houses and effects, and their persons. And surely, for reasons that have much in common with Protestant suspicions everywhere, you cannot trust people with power. If the principle determining when government may intervene is not to appear abstractly lodged in the internal makeup of the state ("retribution is the meaning of the law sphere"), it must be situated in a discourse that treats the state as something other than the natural enemy of liberty (or the friend of the "interests" for that matter). It must be possible to have confidence in a set of values underlying such a state and such a theory of state intervention. What must come into view alongside the suspicion of people with power is the confidence that there are common human commitments holding civil society together. These are not absent from the American political tradition, as a reading of the framers makes only too plain. But from the triumph of the Federalists on, those common commitments have tended towards only nationalistic expression[32] Right across the political spectrum in the 1990s the nationalistic tendency remains: even among those countering individualism, the collective nouns deployed are marked by nationalist overtones – "family" and "community" are applied to the entire society. Neo-Calvinist discourse can help to remedy this situation by putting forward the language of differentiated society, a society of persons, families, churches, communities of various kinds, businesses, and voluntary organizations.

---

29 Henderson, *Illuminating Law*, 167.

30 Henderson, *Illuminating Law*, 168.

31 Henderson, *Illuminating Law*, 169.

32 Elshtain, Jean B. 1988, "Citizenship and Armed Civic Virtue: Some Critical Questions on the Commitment to Public Life." In *Community in America: The Challenge*. Charles H. Reynolds and Ralph V. Norman, eds. Berkeley: University of California Press, 47–55.

The Role of the State: Kuyper and Lowi Compared

Can neo-Calvinism ever compete with liberalism in application of a rule of law? In an American context, probably not. The liberal set-up of pre-social rights ranged against government authority contained by consent is pretty straightforward when it comes to working out how you attain a balance between the rights of the individual and the authority of government. Rights generally limit government. Fundamental rights impose especially strict limits. Liberalism's post-Lockian focus on external checks on government yields more accessible principles and, therefore, rules for determining when government may intervene. By contrast, the continental preference for internal checks, while expressible in structures of government is a good deal harder to express as a set of rules for resolving dilemmas. Kuyper's state will not take revenge or reform or deter by virtue of its calling, Dooyeweerd's by virtue of its structure – not because of a Bill of Rights. There is no equivalent to the relatively elegant liberal formula of fundamental right triggering strict scrutiny demanding evidence of compelling state interest – or non-fundamental rights resulting in milder standards of review permitting the legislature to satisfy the courts with only a rational basis for its laws.

But the crucial point here is that external checks are only as good as internal design. The two are mutually dependent in the American tradition. What liberal polities need to see, Lowi argues (though not in so many words), is that external checks alone are not enough. The United States got a state, positive, directive, relatively autonomous, and it got it *despite* a tradition of individual rights and limited government, despite simple rules and lucid logic! But rights themselves are flexible notions, as Glendon laments in an era dominated by the conversion of so many issues into rights talk.[33] Once the legitimating force of right could be attached to economic status, the state could become rights' principal agent. The liberal polity failed for this reason to contain the state not because it did not possess external checks but because the mechanism of external checks turned out to be only as good as definition of its component parts. The industrial revolution wrenched rights out of their largely political context as restrictions on a government assumed to be liberty's chief foe and threw the burden of protection back towards internal design. If Lowi is right, virtually no one noticed that this had happened, hence the resistance to Lowi's call to revive the rule of law to restore the internal design of the separation of powers (specifically the *Schechter* rule forbidding delegation of power from Congress to the President "without sufficiently defining the policy or criteria to guide the administrator").

Lowi is not as much interested in rolling back the positive state as he is in making liberal democracy a coherent form of government. It is actually far from clear that Lowi's juridical democracy would greatly clarify the role of the state, though it would equip it with greater authority within a more limited scope. A clearly defined rule of law would, it is true, encourage a new public philosophy, a new climate for politics and policy. By way of example, Lowi cites the *Dagenhart* decision as chilling new federal regulatory initiatives in the 1920s on the grounds that Members of Congress then assumed such national economic powers would be unconstitutional. His call for revival of the *Schechter* rule could create a similarly chastened climate in respect of delegation of powers. But isn't the point of *The End of Liberalism* the revival of liberalism? And are not the accompaniments to liberalism in America a thin atmosphere in which the rich web of civil society dissolves in the acid

33   Glendon, Mary Ann 1991. *Rights Talk: The Impoverishment of Political Discourse*. New York: Free Press.

of nominalism? We must go beyond liberalism to reclaim proper relationships between state, individual, and society, and thereby to clarify the proper functions of government.[34] Lowi's juridical democracy is juridical in a *procedural* sense only. Structurally, the building blocks of the positive, liberal state remain in place. At best, a course correction, albeit a very welcome one, would result from implementation of Lowi's procedural recommendations. Success, however, would be defined as a liberal government that *could* plan and could exercise meaningful authority, a government that could achieve the justice that democracies can best deliver – public policy reflective of public opinion within the framework of individual rights. The positive state would be reined in, not subjected to rethinking of the presuppositions on which it rests. In Seidelman and Harpham's observation, Lowi's research is a lengthy discovery that liberal hopes must be dashed because his formalist remedies for liberalism's contradictions are impossible to attain within liberalism.[35] Or to put it more bluntly, in the words of Paul Kahn, "[t]he break between contemporary [constitutional] theory and practice is a consequence of the ultimate impossibility of uniting self-government and the historical state."[36] Lowi's juridical democracy falls short, then. Because he will not transcend the liberal state, his prescriptions remain contained by its rhetoric.

Return to the State: the Role of Religious Presuppositions

Oddly enough in view of the foregoing, no one more than Lowi has grasped the extent of the interrelationship between political science and the state, and no one has expressed greater concern that the relationship has made political science flaccid and public discourse toxic.[37] The discipline has undergone in recent years a soul-searching transformation from behavioral hegemony towards a quasi-pluralism of method and ideology.[38] In that kind of atmosphere, the neo-Calvinist perspective can emerge from the marginalized obscurity[39]

---

34 See, e.g., Skillen, J. 1990. "Going Beyond Liberalism to Christian Social Philosophy." *Christian Scholar's Review* 19(3) (March): 220–230 in which the author argues that only a profound rethinking of the in- dividualistic assumptions of modern, philosophic liberalism holds any prospect of transcending those assumptions.

35 Lowri, 1985. *The Personal President*, 200–213.

36 Kahn, Paul W. 1992. *Legitimacy and History: Self-government in American Constitutional Theory*. New Haven: Yale University Press.

37 Lowi, 1992. "The State in Political Science," 3–6.

38 Almond, Gabriel A. 1988. "The Return to the State," *American Political Science Review* 82 (3); Seidelman, Raymond, with Edward Harpham 1985. *Disenchanted Realists: Political Science and the American Crisis, 1884–1984*. Albany: State University of New York Press; Ricci, David M. 1984. *The Tragedy of Political Science: Politics, Scholarship, and Democracy*. New Haven: Yale University Press; Easton, David 1981. *The Political System: An Inquiry into the State of Political Science*. Chicago: The University of Chicago Press.

39 Donald G. Tewksbury's *The Founding of American Colleges and Universities Before the Civil War*. (New York: Archon Books, 1965), classic study of American higher education showed how dominant were denominational colleges in the United States prior to the Civil war – in effect, they postponed a movement to establish "revolutionary" colleges on a Jeffersonian model for the better part of a century. The emergence of political science as a distinct discipline had to await this development (Haddow, A. 1969 [1939]. *Political Science in American Colleges and Universities, 1636–1900*. New York: Octagon Books.), but the rise of political science in the new state universities and certain private colleges then proceeded to bypass the denominational colleges altogether. When communities of faith came to political science, then, they encountered a fully formed discipline (organization, bureaucracy, body of knowledge). The collapse of evangelical academia in the United States was not only a function of this eventual supplanting by the

that has shrouded evangelical scholarship for decades. A rapprochement unthinkable in the behavioral era is now a possibility.

Despite the gulf which now appears to separate political scientists in the liberal progressive "third tradition" of Wilson, Ward, Beard, Merriam, Easton, Truman, Lowi et al., from Reformed evangelicals critical of liberalism, they share a concern for articulating a theory of the state in democratic polities.[40] As Seidelman and Harpham point out and as I have attempted to describe in reference to Lowi's *magnum opus*, the Third Tradition has met severe obstacles in its attempts to defend the administrative state against charges that it threatens the liberal tradition. Neo-Calvinist (Reformed) scholarship is equally concerned that a theory of the state be constructed, and with its emphasis on a limited (but not morally minimalist) state, structural (and confessional) pluralism, and consociational democracy, may be better placed than the Third Tradition to defend it.[41] Paradoxically, the gulf between Lowi and Kuyper, though narrowed by the conviction that one must articulate a theory of the state, widens also, for each brings radically different presuppositions to bear on the problem. If one can speak of religious presuppositions in Lowi's case, these do not transcend a Lockian view of humans as reasonable, socially-inclined utility maximizers.

Jeffersonian model, however. It resulted also from internal intellectual weakness (Marsden 1983) and from fragmentation in the Protestant community itself. Evangelicals and liberals had preserved a coalition on social and political, if not theological questions as late as World War I (Marsden 1980). Splitting first over questions of patriotism, the supposed impact of German theology on German culture, and the rise of premillennialist writings in the wartime atmosphere, they polarized decisively – and permanently – over evolution and modernism, disputes which culminated in the Scopes trial of 1925. Thereafter, fundamentalism, and by association evangelicalism more generally, was well and truly rusticated by liberal Protestantism and the secular academy. Denominational identity itself was downplayed, especially in higher education (1988, 184–195; see also Burtchaell 1991. "The Decline and Fall of the Christian College" *First Things* 12: 16–29).

40 If neo-Calvinist political inquiry does break new ground with respect to a theory of state and society, the widely noticed "return to the state" in the discipline at large does not promise to make this common ground (see Dryszek, John S. and Stephen T. Leonard 1988. "History and Discipline in Political Science." *American Political Science Review* 82(3)). For Lowi (1992), as for Almond (1988), the return to the state offers no fresh examination of the normative questions linking state, individual and society, but rather a new awareness of government as a variable. I agree. What is needed is not to make the state a variable, "but to make political science, through a new and higher level of discourse, a discipline worthy of constitutional democracy – scientific, theoretic, historical, and critical" (Lowi, 1992, 891). If there is nothing more to the movement than a course correction away from the Almond/Easton-inspired language of the political system (see Susser, Bernard 1992. *Approaches to the Study of Politics.* New York: Macmillan), then we cannot expect a convergence with the normative concerns of neo-Calvinist thought. Such, for the present, appears to be the case.

41 The superficial affinities between branches of evangelicalism and traditions in political science are as follows: reformed evangelicalism is hermeneutically sympathetic to the Institutionalist tradition – "the dominant mode of American governmental organization and political thought in the late eighteenth and nineteenth centuries"(Seidelman and Harpham, 4; see also Farr 1990 on the pre-history of political science as a form of hermeneutics). To evangelicals who trace their roots to the radical Reformation, to anabaptists and quietist sects, Radical Democracy with its built-in antipathy to structures and institutions, its spontaneity, and its suspicion of the powers that be, is inherently appealing. As for the Progressive liberal Third Tradition, it has attracted evangelical Realists in the tradition of Reinhold Niebuhr, who argue for prudence – a composite of factual knowledge and discernment – in translating biblical principles into policy. Adaptability to changing and interim circumstances is perhaps the hallmark of both the Third Tradition (one thinks of Herbert Croly's harnessing of Hamiltonian means to Jeffersonian ends) and this Christian Realist orientation.

Lowi's prescription for what ails the liberal state is not, on this account, radical, for the problems of the liberal state may not be laid at the feet of sinful man. As a result, Lowi seems willing to place all his eggs in the one basket of a return to the rule of law.

There can be no pretense that a Kuyperian attempt to reconcile America's institutionalist and radical democratic traditions would leave either intact and would simply discover a hitherto undiscovered unity between them. I have already noted that the more one pursues neo-Calvinism to its roots, the more it emerges in continental European guise in its view of state and society, in its qualified treatment of rights, in its defense of the legitimate authority of the state, an authority independent of popular consent. I am perhaps less confident than some of my neo-Calvinist colleagues that a Kuyperian interpretation of the American political tradition would point to anything less than wholesale transformation of that tradition. As I have observed elsewhere,[42] a Kuyperian approach to the American situation has some things in common with anti-federalism in its regard for a differentiated civil society built on common values. But there's the rub. The civil society reached for by anti-federalists and sought after again by neo-Calvinists, Catholics, and others with like sympathies today did not capture the American imagination nor dominate its rhetoric as does the curious mix of Madison and Locke. One may argue that American discourse generally is as satisfied as Lowi in particular with their "religious" presuppositions and has not seen the problems of liberal democracy as calling for their radical re-examination.

For precisely this reason, of course, one must be cautious about the prospect of neo-Calvinist presuppositions receiving a warm welcome in America. Short of a wholesale transformation, the Kuyperian orientation may make its most salient contribution by disentangling republicanism from the Lockian view of society in which rights are located outside the state, which is denied an independent foundation in common values or natural law. The republican tradition, even Madisonian republicanism with its accommodation of individualism and its ambiguity with respect to the public interest, is starved in the thin Lockian air. Elshtain puts it this way:

> [T]he empirical reality of American democracy, in [Tocqueville's] view, even as it frees individuals from the constraints of older, undemocratic structures and obligations, also unleashes atomism, individualism, and privatization. . . . The lure of private acquisitiveness spawns political apathy and invites democratic despotism. All social webs that once held persons intact having disintegrated, the individual finds himself isolated and impotent, exposed and unprotected. Into this power vacuum moves "the organizing force of the government," the centralized state.[43]

Elshtain's argument takes us beyond Lowi's prescription of juridical democracy to the disintegrative forces that would nullify that procedural cure. These are the forces neo-Calvinism addresses. Neo-Calvinism gives the republican tradition a second chance, so to speak. In its treatment of the state and no less in its treatment of rights, it brings that tradition back into view. It allows us to see again that the ratification of the Constitution represents continuity with republican thought at least as much as it represents disjunction

---

42 Sherratt, Timothy R. and Ronald P. Mahurin 1995. *Saints as Citizens: A Guide to Public Responsibilities for Christians.* Grand Rapids: Baker.

43 Elshtain, Jean B. 1988. "Citizenship and Armed Civic Virtue: Some Critical Questions on the Commitment to Public Life." In *Community in America: The Challenge.* Charles H. Reynolds and Ralph V. Norman, eds. Berkeley: University of California Press, 48.

and a new beginning. The religious character of Kuyper's thought is itself an aid to this end. "Kuyperian presuppositionalism," writes Marsden, "is a style of Christian thought that emphasizes that crucial to the differences that separate Christian worldviews from non-Christian ones are disagreements about pretheoretical first principles, presuppositions, first commitments, or basic beliefs."[44] Law and politics stem from these basic beliefs, irrespective of the deity that is worshiped. In this foundational sense Skillen writes that "religion . . . is inescapable for human beings."[45]

This treatment of Man as a religious being lends further clarity to the functions and limits of the Kuyperian state described above. Not only is the state seen as deriving its authority from God's ordinances (a view dependent on a *particular*, Calvinist, religious orientation), but, by extension, the state itself is also viewed from a perspective that holds all fundamental human commitments in high regard because they stem from basic beliefs. Giving these commitments their due requires sharing of authority in the interests of the general welfare; and it requires freedom for a plurality of such commitments to find expression politically. Here is an emphasis entirely missing from Lowi's analysis and prescriptions.

The contemporary neo-Calvinist perspective thus affirms that the theory of the state is interdependent with the theory of church and state, and it is critical of the separationalist approach to the latter, which still holds sway on the Supreme Court. For from the neo-Calvinist perspective, full religious freedom is not to be secured by reaffirming the freedom to worship in churches of one's choice, and it is positively affronted by walling off religion from the public square. On the contrary, the foundational character of religious commitment necessitates its recognition and protection in multiple domains: in churches and families, naturally, but also in schools and social service agencies, in and out of the public square. Rights are grounded in the religious character of humankind, for no right turns out to be as important as a broadly construed right of free exercise; or, to put it another way, the concept of free exercise takes on dimensions undreamed of by the founders protecting the cerebral, low-intensity protestantism of the "Gentlemen" of the late eighteenth Century, a religious outlook and practice presumably needing precious little protection! Among contemporary neo-Calvinists, this enlarged and nuanced view of religion has manifested itself in calls for pluralism in education, health, and welfare[46] and for a system of proportional representation to replace the present electoral system[47]

---

44 Marsden, George M. 1988. "The State of Evangelical Christian Scholarship." *Christian Scholar's Review* 17(4), 347–360.

45 Skillen, James W. 1995. *Recharging the American Experiment: Principled Pluralism for Genuine Civic Community.* Grand Rapids: Baker/Center for Public Justice, 35.

46 Monsma, Stephen 1996. *When Sacred and Secular Mix: Religious Non-Profit Organizations and Public Money.* Lanham: Rowman and Littlefield.
Carlson-Thies, Stanley W. and James W. Skillen eds. 1995. *Welfare in America: Christian Perspectives on a Policy in Crisis.* Grand Rapids: Eerdmans.
Skillen, James W. ed. 1993. *The School-Choice Controversy: What is Constitutional?* Grand Rapids: Baker Book House/Center for Public Justice.
McCarthy, Rockne M., James W. Skillen, and William A. Harper 1982. *Disestablishment a Second Time: Genuine Pluralism for American Schools.* Grand Rapids: Eerdmans.
Zylstra, Bernard J. 1991. "The United States Constitution and the Rights of Religion." In James W. Skillen and Rockne M. McCarthy, eds. *Political Order and the Plural Structure of Society.* Atlanta: Scholars Press.

47 Skillen, 1995. *Recharging the American Experiment,* 137–155, for example.

In sum, the neo-Calvinist perspective could rescue the American state from the theoretical obscurity it wallows in and the disdain in which its post-1930s manifestation is held. Should the present welfare state be comprehensively dismantled, the state's juridical functions would still need clarification of the kind neo-Calvinists can offer, for Kuyper shows us the need for justice within and between the various spheres of social life, in addition to criminal justice and a policy of national defense. Given the upsurge in ethnic and religious sensitivities and the troubled awareness of multiple cultures within the American nation-state, Kuyper's high view of religion as a way of life no less than the particular insights of his Calvinism takes on a new significance. It is hard to see how Lowi or the Third Tradition might articulate such issues distinctively.

Conclusion

From at least the Populists to the New Left, the American state either represented the people against the interests (taming them by regulation) or it sided with those interests against the people, indicting itself by "democratic" standards. The legitimacy of governmental authority rested on these mutually exclusive options, which built both statist reality and anti-statist feeling on their Lockian foundations. Where a quasi-Lockian discourse pits state and individual against each other and largely overlooks the intermediary institutions of civil society, neo-Calvinist discourse, a religious discourse on reality with a high view of religious freedom, situates the state in a three-way relationship with individuals and societal institutions which multiplies the roles and stances of the state: in partnership with the individual to protect civil rights when a family, school, club or business would deny these; in deference to churches in their exercise of ecclesiastical law with respect to church members; in retributive relationship with convicted criminals; in cooperation with faith-based social service providers, and so forth. Since a differentiated society is the locus of most citizen freedom (people live out their lives in the a web of institutional "memberships"), the integrity of these institutions emerges as a proper object of governmental concern and protection. If the larger number of relationships just described do not simplify the work of courts (as I allude to in my discussion of neo-Calvinism's articulation problems in regards to state intervention), it does foster a richer public discourse, one less circumscribed by artificial and typically reductionist treatment of people and their multifaceted relationships and obligations. One could put this another way, following Walzer[48] (1990) who observed that the truncated discourse of American politics could be viewed either as bad (invoking a highly restricted view of persons and societal relationships) or simply wrong. Neo-Calvinists may rightly maintain that the three-way relationships I have just described constitute a better description of *existing* relationships in which the American state is involved than the conventional terms for discussing the state offers – existing relationships denied visibility in law and political culture.[49] The situating of the state in relation to persons and differentiated social institutions takes us away from the nominalist

---

48 Walzer, Michael 1990. "The Communitarian Critique of Liberalism." *Political Theory*, 18: 6–23.

49 Monsma, *When Sacred and Secular Mix*, has documented highly interdependent relationships between faith based social service providers and state and federal governments – although in the solitary modern-era case addressing this relationship the Supreme Court's reasoning maintains a contorted separationist logic, requiring that the agencies not be pervasively sectarian and that the funds go for exclusively secular purposes (*Bowen v. Kendrick*, 1988).

categories of American discourse and allows the state to emerge from its hiding place behind a Lockian social contract formula, a formula which hoodwinked us into believing that popular consent dissolved the problem of political authority. With Kuyper's help, to put it simply, Christians may challenge and change public discourse. The importance of such challenges lies in the prevalence of the utilitarian, materialist and reductionist views of human life that have flourished in American political culture.

We are left with an interesting dilemma. If I am right, then the particular contribution the neo-Calvinist writings can make is to the reshaping of what Lowi, following Walter Lippmann, called the "public philosophy." But it lacks a practical, rule-based theory of state intervention to give practical effect to its biblically-based principle of fidelity to calling, a deficiency compounded by the elegant formulas of liberal democracy. It cultivates a biblical sensibility to politics but suggests only in general terms the outlines of public-legal arrangements. These features limit its appeal in the American context. Here, the features recognized as most attractive may be limited government and the priority for protecting religious liberty, but to speak of a religious view of all of life is more likely to invoke New Age than Christianity!

Circumstance, rather than theory, may situate American discourse in a reconsideration of the state, as the promises attached to government downsizing are held up to the light of actual experience. Moreover, as more is learned about the actual relationship between government and private agencies, along the lines of the work being done by Monsma[50] and the Center for Public Justice, a richer understanding of government's empirical role can emerge to replace overly simplistic separationist logic. This research points to complex, cooperative interaction between government and religious agencies, a reality that stretches the separationist dogmas of the Supreme Court and the volunteerist/limited government dogmas of conservatives to their respective limits. In that climate, the Kuyperian juxtaposition of society, persons and the state may inform the subsequent debate. For, despite the beating it has taken, the Madisonian tradition of confidence in internal design may have seen its time come again, although, curiously, its recent revival owes more to quasi-libertarians bent on shrinking the state than civic republicans willing to describe it afresh and affirm its necessary functions in democratic society.

---

50 Monsma, *When Sacred and Secular Mix.*

28

E Pluribus Unum and Faith-Based Welfare Reform: A Kuyperian Moment for the Church in God's World

James W. Skillen

Since 1996, when President Clinton signed into law a major reform of federal welfare programs, the debate about religion and government has taken a new turn. The primary reasons for this are the Charitable Choice provision in the welfare-reform law followed by President Bush's creation of a new White House Office of Faith-Based and Community Initiatives in 2001, designed to extend the implications of Charitable Choice.[1] In essence, Charitable Choice says that state governments, when cooperating with nongovernment social service organizations and using federal welfare funds, may no longer exclude religious service providers from cooperation with government due to their religious character. Nor may government demand of a religious service organization, as a condition for its cooperation, that it "secularize" its operations in order to hide or eliminate its religious character and motivation. Why has this relatively small ingredient in a massive welfare-reform policy caused such heated debate?

According to Larry Eichel, writing in *The Philadelphia Inquirer* (8 March 2001), it is because the issues involved go "right to the heart of what this nation is about." Indeed, I would contend that if the principles of Charitable Choice are implemented successfully and remain in place over time, the consequence will be a significant reordering of American pluralism, of *e pluribus unum*, with respect to both religion and the diverse institutions and organizations of society. The outcome could well be a *fourth order of pluralism* in the republic. For the controversy has everything to do with competing definitions of religion, with incompatible ideas of what defines the unity of a political community, and with different understandings of how the diverse associations and institutions of society are held together and protected in their own integrity. The controversy has to do precisely with the age-old questions of tolerance and intolerance, of exclusiveness and inclusiveness, of the relation of public religions to political authority.[2]

---

1   The Center for Public Justice has published at least 20 different books, booklets, and guides related to welfare reform and Charitable Choice, including *Charitable Choice for Welfare and Community Services: An Implementation Guide for State, Local, and Federal Officials* (2001). See the Center's website <www.cpjustice.org>. See also, most recently, Donaldson, Dave and Stanley Carlson-Thies 2003. *A Revolution of Compassion: Faith-Based Groups as Full Partners in Fighting America's Social Problems*. Grand Rapids: Baker.

2   Two books in particular help to highlight the controversy through the voices of those in contention. See Monsma, Stephen V. and J. Christopher Soper, eds. 1998. *Equal Treatment of Religion in a Pluralistic Society*. Grand Rapids: Eerdmans; and Davis, Derek and Barry Hankins, ed. 1999. *Welfare Reform and*

Historical Context

In order to understand the contemporary contention over government's relation to faith-based organizations, we need a brief sketch of the historical background. The *first order of pluralism* – as I am calling it – in the United States was established at the founding between 1776 and 1791. Before that time, the general pattern for a state or colony was some form of established or privileged religion, some kind of ecclesiastical or confessional pre-qualification for citizenship, thought to be necessary to hold the polity together. The bold move made by adding the Bill of Rights to the federal Constitution of 1787 was to declare that the new Congress would have no authority to legislate with respect to an establishment of religion or the inhibition of its free exercise. This first order of pluralism for the republic as a whole meant that each state was still free to make its own determination, without interference from Congress, about religious privilege and religious freedom. The national federation would be pluralistic, making room for a diversity of state religious establishments as each determined for itself.[3] This was not yet equal treatment for each American citizen as we have come to understand it today.

It is also important to emphasize that at the founding, state constitutions recognized as a condition for government (or took for granted in the common law) the rights of a variety of non-government institutions and associations, such as the family and the church, whose authority does not derive from government. In other words, each state's authority, as well as the federal government's authority, was constitutionally limited in competence, or, to state it negatively, was denied omnicompetence.

Now, as we know, the states either led or soon followed the federal government in disestablishing their churches, Massachusetts being the last to do so in the 1830s.[4] Those relatively quiet historical developments established what I would call the *second order of pluralism* in the United States. Each state, just like the federal government, accepted the principle that its unity – its *unum* – would be defined by something other than a common church or a congressionally authorized religion. The diversity of religions within each state would be given equal treatment. Part of what made this second order of pluralism possible was the fact that the country's population in the early nineteenth century shared a largely Christian/theistic/deistic heritage and climate of moral opinion, and many state constitutions and governments encouraged such a culture.

Note that this experiment in confessional pluralism did not aim to privatize religion. A diversity of churches, though not yet a wide range of religions, was recognized as having equal standing by virtue of the fact that none was established or given special public treatment. Yet this development occurred in large measure because a significant majority of the people shared a religiously grounded, publicly unifying ethos. Concern about how to keep the public moral cohesion strong was in fact the impetus for the establishment of common schools in the early nineteenth century, as advocated by Thomas Jefferson, Horace Mann, Benjamin Rush and others. With a common ethos no longer guaranteed by an established church, some other means was thought to be necessary to assure that

---

Faith-Based Organizations. Waco: J.M. Dawson Institute of Church-State Studies, Baylor University.

3   For a detailed study, see Witte Jr., John 2000. *Religion and The American Constitutional Experiment: Essential Rights and Liberties.* Boulder: Westview Press, 7–100. See also Lutz, Donald S. 1988. *The Origins of American Constitutionalism.* Baton Rouge: Louisiana State University Press.

4   For more on this matter of state disestablishment see Witte, *Religion*, 93–96.

all Americans would be nurtured in a common public morality.[5] Yet, it was taken for granted that the public ethos – the common public morality – was religion-friendly.

Part of the reason for the religious character of the republic, even after it had disestablished all churches, is that the Puritan ideal of establishing a "city on a hill" – a new covenant people of God – was attached to the country as a whole. The original Puritan ideal was ambiguous because the New England colonists had established a polity whose voting citizens had to be members of the Congregational Church. When too many citizens were no longer church members, the undifferentiated religious-political community could not survive. For many Christians thereafter, it was only the church that represented God's new covenant community. Yet as the colonies joined together to fight for their independence and then to form states and an independent federation, the myth of America as God's chosen nation was born. With the strong providential language of the Declaration of Independence, the founders created "a nation with the soul of a church," as G. K. Chesterton once said.

The critical moment that served to define the second order of pluralism for roughly the next 100 years occurred when Catholics began to immigrate in large numbers into New York and Massachusetts in the early 1800s. The largely Protestant majority, which was learning to live *without* established churches but *with* various types of common schools that reflected their civil-religious idea of the nation, quickly reached the conclusion that there would be no room for Catholic schools in the public commons. Consequently, public school societies were established by the Protestant majority in New York and Boston to make sure that only "nonsectarian" schools would be recognized as common schools and supported with public funds. The Catholic schools were classified as "sectarian" and granted freedom of operation only in private, paid for privately, outside the bounds of the supposedly nonsectarian public commons.[6] Pluralism for schooling and moral education now meant essentially the same as pluralism for churches, namely, freedom for sectarian diversity in private. Public unity would be maintained by nurturing children in the moral ethos of the majority in the common schools, which were recognized as part of the public sphere. White Anglo-Saxon Protestants, though only a majority, thus claimed a monopoly over government-supported schooling. These now officially established schools came to serve some of the same purposes that established churches had served earlier. They provided the moral and religious training needed by youngsters who were expected to become God-fearing citizens in the new nation.

Keep in mind that in the mid-nineteenth-century, the word "nonsectarian" did not mean non-religious or anti-religious. The common schools read the Bible, studied the Bible, said prayers, and inculcated a Protestant/theistic/deistic moral point of view. Thus, outside the churches, public religion flourished, but it was increasingly thought of as part of the nation's common moral ethos – and thus "nonsectarian" – over against Catholic "sectarianism." The word "sectarian" in this context was not primarily a reference to the Catholic church as a Christian sect, but to the Catholic community's position in

---

5   See McCarthy, Rockne M., James W. Skillen, and William A. Harper, eds. 1982. *Disestablishment a Second Time: Genuine Pluralism for American Schools*. Grand Rapids: Eerdmans, 15–52.

6   Ibid., 52–72. See Ravitch, Diane 1974. *The Great School Wars: New York City, 1805–1973*. New York: Basic Books, 3–91, and Glenn, Charles L. 1988. *The Myth of the Common School*. Amherst: University of Massachusetts Press.

the nonsectarian republic. The republic itself was taking on the character of universal (nonsectarian) civil-religious community, and citizens could choose either to be full members in good standing and enjoy free education in the common schools or to live on the fringes as tolerated sectarians. Gradually, the WASP majority lost consciousness of the religious character of its public identity and common schools. The word "religion" increasingly came to be used to refer only to churches and sectarian practices that had to be kept in private because they had no place in the established republic.

What happened was that a very religious, cultural set of WASP beliefs established the public conditions for associational or institutional freedom and unqualified citizenship in the republic. Catholics were allowed to associate freely in exclusive churches, just as Protestants were. The United States could establish pluralism for a diversity of exclusive churches because the all-inclusive identity of the republic was not tied to any ecclesiastical entity. However, by contrast, education, though once conducted in diverse ways and in a variety of nongovernment schools, would henceforth be treated chiefly as a public, governmental establishment, and the unified republic, mirrored in each state, would be upheld by the common ethos inculcated in the common schools.

There was an inconsistency or unresolved dilemma here, however. If education is a department of state and if common schooling for every child is necessary to hold the society together, why did public officials allow some citizens to opt out of the common schools? On the other hand, since public officials did grant that many independent and "sectarian" schools could remain open, why did those officials not acknowledge the fact that schooling was not necessarily (and never had been merely) a department of state? Local and state governments have, indeed, set up schools, but schools have also been established by other institutions and associations as well. Moreover, the responsibility for raising and educating minor children was then, and continues to be, acknowledged in law as the responsibility of parents. Thus, in the educational arena a considerable ambiguity arose about the relation of government to nongovernment institutions.[7] The same ambiguity, we will see, later took hold in the welfare policy arena.

If, by the middle 1800s, most Catholics had chosen to send their children to the culturally Protestant ("nonsectarian") public schools, then the education of Catholic children would have been fully supported by public funding. Of course, the Catholics would have had to agree to submit their children to schooling that was, in many ways, non-Catholic. But to the extent that Catholics insisted on using their own schools, their educational efforts were denied equal public treatment because government defined Catholic schools as "sectarian." On these terms, you can see, there was no room for *public educational pluralism* in the United States. That which had become the informal religion of the republic was quite evident in the prayers and (King James) Bible readings of the publicly established schools, but since these schools were run by states and local communities, not by churches, their religious character gradually receded from view.

---

7   Parental primacy or "principalship" in education as well as governmental primacy in education are both upheld in the law, quite incompatibly. See McCarthy, Skillen and Harper, *Disestablishment*, 103–106, 124–136; Arons, Stephen 1986. *Compelling Belief: The Culture of American Schooling.* Amherst: University of Massachusetts Press; and 2001. "Conference Proceedings: *Pierce*, Pluralism, and Partnership," a conference to commemorate the 75th Anniversary of the *Pierce* Decision. Washington, D.C.: U.S. Department of Education. The 1925 *Pierce* decision was *Pierce v. Society of the Sisters of the Holy Names of Jesus and Mary*, 268 U.S. 510 (1925).

The *third order of pluralism* took hold in the United States as the result of the further secularization of the second order and became dominant by the middle of the twentieth century. This is the pluralist order most familiar to us today. It is taken for granted in the constitutional arguments made by today's ACLU, Americans United for the Separation of Church and State, and People for the American Way. I would even venture to say that it is the framework now taken for granted by most Christians, both Protestant and Catholic, and Jews. To identify this third order, we need only look at how the words "nonsectarian" and "sectarian" are used, quite in contrast to the way they were used in the nineteenth century. The word "nonsectarian" now means "secular" or "nonreligious" and no longer corresponds to the ethos of older cultural Protestantism. The word "sectarian" now refers not only to "Catholics," but to all who are explicitly or self-professedly "religious." The underlying political structure has not changed: the supposedly nonsectarian political majority still claims the right to monopolize the public square while upholding pluralism in private for "sectarians." But the change in the connotation and denotation of the terms reflects a significantly new meaning of pluralism.

To say this is not to imply that an American civil religion has disappeared, but only that its character is now more deistic and secularized, framed more by an Enlightenment point of view than by the older Protestant consensus. Also keep in mind that it is during the time when this third order of pluralism came to dominate public opinion and the courts that the largest and greatest number of public welfare programs was established. By definition, the major federal programs to end or alleviate poverty, joblessness, drug abuse, and other poverty-inducing or poverty-aggravating problems were put forward as *secular* public programs, programs of and by government for citizens identified in their "secular" capacity. Almost all discussion of poverty and welfare since the 1960s has focused on government's actions toward secular citizens, with the consequence that most nongovernment programs of poverty relief fell from public view, despite the fact that those nongovernment services have made a huge public difference.[8] The same pattern holds in the educational arena. Public discussion of education policy and funding focuses almost entirely on "public" schools even though 12–18 percent of American children receive their publicly approved education in independent schools or at home.

Under the third pluralistic regime, one can understand why government aid to anything identified as sectarian – now including more than Catholics schools – had to be declared out of bounds. Ellen Willis makes the following profession of faith:

> I believe that a democratic polity requires a secular state: one that does not fund or otherwise sponsor religious institutions and activities; that does not display religious symbols; that outlaws discrimination based on religious belief, whether by government or by private employers, landlords or proprietors – that does, in short, guarantee freedom from as well as freedom of religion. Furthermore, a genuinely democratic society requires a secular ethos: one that does not equate morality with religion, stigmatize atheists, defer to religious interests and aims over others or make religious belief an informal qualification for public office. Of course, secularism in the latter sense is not mandated by the First Amendment. It's a matter of sensibility, not law.[9]

---

8   See especially Carlson-Thies, Stanley W. 2001. "Charitable Choice: Bringing Religion Back into American Welfare." *Journal of Policy History* 13 (1): 109–132.

9   Willis, Ellen 2001. "Freedom from Religion: What's at Stake in Faith-Based Politics." *The Nation* 19 February.

What makes Willis' language work is the unquestioned assumption that there is nothing religious or confessional about her own profession of faith. The language used counts on the reader agreeing that religion is a separable, private matter. However, if one recognizes this profession of secular faith for the faith that it is, just as one can now recognize the religious character of the nineteenth-century majority's profession of "nonsectarianism," then Willis' words have to be reinterpreted in order to be fair and nonimpositional toward people of other faiths.[10] In such a turnabout Willis would have to contend that the state should not "sponsor religious – including secularist – institutions and activities; that it not display religious – including secularist – symbols; that it outlaw discrimination based on religious – including secularist – belief . . . ; that, in short, it guarantee freedom from as well as freedom of religion – including secularism." A "genuinely democratic society" should, in other words, require a genuinely neutral ethos.[11] Such an argument points us toward the fourth order of pluralism to which I will turn in a moment, but first we must say something more about the third order of pluralism.

In a system where pluralism is assured to "sectarians" only in private, the only way an explicitly religious organization can participate in a publicly funded program is by demonstrating its willingness to function in public in a "nonsectarian" fashion. Catholic Charities, for example, has been free to serve as an extension of government's social service deliveries as long as it has agreed to act in a secular manner, which no one would mistakenly identify as Catholic.[12] These are also the terms on which Catholic schools have been able to win small amounts of public funding for *secular* aspects of schooling, such as busing, lunches, and certain textbooks. Secularizing the "nonsectarian" public square has also required the removal of prayer and Bible reading from the government-funded schools. Quite evidently, then, the third order of pluralism represents a new version of moral majoritarianism. The moral requirements for public inclusion – for equal public participation – have become those of the secular majority, no longer of the Protestant majority, and all professedly religious and sectarian moral convictions must be held and exercised privately.

The odd thing here is the way that this ideological point of view has been absorbed voluntarily by nongovernment organizations. Independent, often explicitly religious entities, have taken the reigning dualism into themselves, into their very identities. Whether as schools or as social-service organizations, they have agreed to identify their confessional commitment as a purely private matter. Agreeing to cooperate with government and its public funding then means agreeing to redefine part of themselves as an extension of the secular public. As America's religious and moral diversity kept expanding during

---

10 On the non-neutrality of every point of view, see McCarthy, Rockne M. et al. 1981. *Society, State, and Schools*. Grand Rapids: Eerdmans, 107–120, and Clouser, Roy A. 1991. *The Myth of Religious Neutrality*. Notre Dame: University of Notre Dame Press.

11 See Monsma, Stephen V. 1993. *Positive Neutrality*. Westport: Greenwood Press.

12 As Kate O'Beirne says, "Catholic Charities – one of the nation's largest social-welfare groups – contracts with government welfare agencies to deliver social services, and is scrupulously secular in dealing with its needy clients. The Salvation Army puts up a wall of separation between its social outreach – which includes a spiritual dimension – and its publicly funded programs, where Bible reading and prayer meetings are strictly forbidden." "Church (Groups) and State: The Problem with the Faith-Based Bit," *National Review*, 19 February 2001. See also Coleman, John A. 2001. "American Catholicism, Catholic Charities U.S.A., and Welfare Reform." *Journal of Policy History* 13 (1), 73–108.

the twentieth century, and as the number and kinds of nongovernment organizations continued to expand, room was made for everyone as long as everyone agreed to keep their sectarian differences outside public institutions and to conform to the secular norms of the majority in public life.

This frame of mind is evident in the writings of Amy Gutman, Dennis Thompson, James Bohman, Stephen Macedo, John Rawls, and others who say that America needs to strengthen "deliberative democracy" in the face of our growing multiculturalism. However, as Ashley Woodiwiss, quoting Chantal Mouffe, explains in a recent review article, "the proponents of deliberative democracy 'generally start by stressing what they call the "fact of pluralism" and then proceed to find procedures to deal with differences whose objective is actually to make those differences irrelevant and to relegate pluralism to the sphere of the private.'"[13] This is pluralism of the third order.

Challenges to the "Secularized" Public Square

A major public challenge to the deepening secularization of the American public square was mounted by groups such as the Moral Majority, beginning in the 1970s. These groups still breathe the air of the moral/religious ethos of second-order pluralism. Jerry Falwell, Pat Robertson, and others cannot accept that the old public consensus has dissolved, so they assume that a secular minority has illegitimately seized the monopoly privilege of the majority. The so-called New Religious Right wanted, and for the most part continues to want, to uphold pluralism in private for sectarian faiths, including freedom for atheists and secularists, but they do not want a minority secularist ethos to control the public square. They are not trying to recover the first order of pluralism, in which each state had the right to establish Christianity, and even a particular church. Charges of this sort against the Moral Majority, the Christian Coalition, and Focus on the Family by third-order pluralists are mistaken and are intended to frighten ordinary citizens. No, the resurgent conservatives simply want to reestablish the pre-secularized, nineteenth-century moral order in which the word "nonsectarian" referred to the WASP consensus that once served as the civil-religious glue of the country. For second-order pluralists the protection of religion in private goes hand in hand with public rule by those who have the same moral sensibilities as those who go to church and acknowledge God.

By contrast, for third-order pluralists the guarantee of religious freedom goes hand in hand with public secularity. The only legitimate moral majority today, in their view, is the one that works vigorously to exclude all sectarian preferences, languages, and doctrines other than its own from control of the public square. Religion, they insist, is a private matter that should be disconnected from, and left unaided by, government. The nonestablishment of religion means no entanglement with sectarian activities; the free exercise of religion means freedom in private to be as sectarian as one chooses. A secular view of public life, even if held only by a majority, should, on these terms, monopolize schooling and welfare services. But of course, People for the American Way is no less

---

13 Woodiwiss, Ashley 2001. "Democracy Agonistes." *Books and Culture* (March/April), 24. Nicholas Wolterstorff critiques this kind of liberal thinking in his discussion with Robert Audi in their book, *Religion in the Public Square: The Place of Religious Convictions in Political Debate.* Lanham: Rowman and Littlefield, 1997. See the fine review of this and several related books by Stiltner, Brian 2000. "Reassessing Religion's Place in a Liberal Democracy." *Religious Studies Review* (October): 319–325.

sectarian in the eyes of the Christian Coalition than is the Moral Majority in the eyes of Americans United for the Separation of Church and State.

One can see from this simple sketch why at one level in today's contention over the new faith-based initiatives the conflict truly is all-or-nothing, because each claimant to public moral authority and political power wants to monopolize the entire public square. The structure of the conflict is the same for Pat Robertson and Barry Lynn, the director of Americans United. Both want the majority to hold a monopoly in the public square with the right to determine who and what is sectarian. But whereas Robertson is a second-order pluralist who is willing to let secularists thrive in private where they cannot, for example, write the curricula for public school classrooms, Lynn wants a secular majority to control school curricula and define the terms of publicly funded welfare services while making room for Falwell and other fundamentalist sectarians in private quarters alone. The battle is all or nothing – a true culture war – because neither viewpoint can envision genuine *public* pluralism. The side that gains control of Congress, the courts, and the schools will claim the right to define what the entire nonsectarian republic should be.

However, as much as the media prefer a simple two-sided conflict, the contention over Charitable Choice and faith-based social policy today is actually three-sided, not two-sided. The reason is that a new and different view of pluralism has joined the fray, presenting a challenge to both second-order and third-order pluralists. The new pluralist challenge also emerged in the 1970s and 1980s and is an ingredient in both the Charitable Choice provision as well as the White House Office on Faith-Based and Community Initiatives. For this reason, the true significance of Charitable Choice cannot be grasped within the framework in which it is being contested by second- and third-order pluralists, the framework that most commentators and the media take for granted.

Peter Dobkin Hall, for example, contends that "the concerns expressed a century ago" about government's subsidizing of "sectarian institutions" differ little from those expressed in our contemporary debate. "The main difference," he says, "was that [in the late 1800s] most Protestants (especially evangelicals) opposed government subsidy because they felt that most of the money went to Catholics."[14] While it is true, as we've said, that the framework in which a "nonsectarian" majority worries about funding "sectarians" remained the same from the nineteenth century through the twentieth, Hall overlooks the significant change in the meaning of the words "nonsectarian" and "sectarian" from the 1840s to the 1940s and thus misses the important cultural shift that took place. Moreover, Hall does not see the even greater difference between the public monopoly claims voiced by both the nineteenth- and the twentieth-century majoritarians, on the one hand, and the new pluralist framework that undergirds Charitable Choice, on the other. There are, in fact, important differences among the three contenders in today's debate.

A New Pluralism

In contrast to the first three orders of pluralism in the United States, *the fourth order of pluralism* for which I am contending requires a different understanding of religion, political order, and social diversity.[15] The new pluralism starts with the understanding that

---

14 Hall, Peter Dobkin 2001. "Diminished Authority: Church, State, and Accountability." *Nonprofit Times* (March): 45.

15 For some of the background of what follows see Skillen, James W. and Rockne M. McCarthy, eds. 1991.

the religions by which people live, whether traditional or modern, whether acknowledged or unacknowledged, exert themselves in public life and not only in private quarters. The effort to force a private, "sectarian" confinement on religious ways of life is itself a form of religious imperialism. The Enlightenment's dichotomy of a secular public on the one hand and religious privacy on the other arises from a religiously deep and all-encompassing worldview. It is no more neutral or tolerant or all-inclusive than was the nineteenth century's Protestant cultural ethos. The Latin word "*saeculum*" means "of or pertaining to this age," or to this world. Until the modern era, it was taken for granted that "this world" – the secular – is connected to and dependent on God. It is true that the words "religion" and "religious" came to be associated with the Catholic Church's authority structure, church vocations, orders, worship, and the Eucharist. Even after the Protestant Reformation reaffirmed the priesthood of all believers and the importance of recognizing "vocations" in all areas of life as religious service to God, the words "religion" and "religious" continued to be used mostly to refer to church-related activities of worship, piety, and evangelism. Nevertheless, there is no basis in those traditions, or in Judaism or Islam, for thinking of the "secular" as unrelated to God or of the "religious" as belonging to the church alone or to inner personal space alone. The modern presumption that the "secular" world stands on its own, dependent on nothing beyond itself, represents a radical change in worldviews, a fundamental religious reorientation or conversion, a basic change in assumptions. There is nothing religiously neutral about a view of reality that insists on privatizing the religious and disconnecting it from a supposedly religion-free *saeculum*. Thus, from the new pluralist point of view, it is not possible to speak of the "religious" and the "secular" in modern, Enlightenment terms.

If we now reread the Constitution's First Amendment from the viewpoint of fourth-order pluralism, the religion clauses appear in a different light. The First Amendment does not call for public secularity and the privatization of religion. It does not grant to a religious majority, disguised as a nonsectarian guardian of the public square, the right to define certain confessional viewpoints as sectarian and thus ineligible for equal treatment by government. Instead, the First Amendment says that religious free exercise really must be protected in public as well as in private life and that the establishment of religion can only be avoided by treating all citizens equally and not granting the privilege of establishment to any religion or ideology. The First Amendment's non-establishment clause does not mean "no aid to religious groups"; it means no establishment of any religion or religiously equivalent worldview. If the convictions of citizens, whether Christian or secularist, whether Jewish or Muslim, guide them to serve their neighbors with drug treatment and job training programs, then government may not discriminate against any of them when it invites nongovernment organizations to cooperate with it in serving those who need drug treatment and job training.

What about Jerry Falwell's and Pat Robertson's worry that such an open and nondiscriminatory pluralism may mean government's support of what they consider to be objectionable sects? That is a worry that only makes sense from the point of view of a

---

Political Order and the Plural Structure of Society. Atlanta: Scholars Press; Carlson-Thies, Stanley W. and James W. Skillen, eds. 1996. *Welfare in America: Christian Perspectives on a Policy in Crisis.* Grand Rapids: Eerdmans; and Glenn, Charles L. 2000. *The Ambiguous Embrace: Government and Faith-Based Schools and Social Agencies.* Princeton: Princeton University Press.

second- or third-order pluralist who presumes that the country's majority should have the political authority to decide what is an objectionable religion. In the nineteenth century, it was Catholics and then Mormons who were considered to be the objectionable and dangerous sects. For third-order pluralists, the Christian Coalition is as objectionable as scientologists and black Muslims; they are all sectarians. For the new pluralism, by contrast, the principle that should hold is equal public treatment of all faiths, with none having the right, through control of government, to monopolize public policy and funding for its point of view.

This takes us to the heart of the matter regarding government's cooperation with faith-based social-service ministries and organizations. Today's secularized nonsectarians define all public welfare and social programs not only as secular but as *governmental* through and through. The implication is that anything government touches or funds, any organization it works with in social-service or education delivery, must be treated as an extension of government and its purposes. Moreover, if government and its services have already been defined as secular, then ipso facto, any organization with which government chooses to cooperate becomes a secular extension of government. In this case, not only does the secular triumph over the religious, but government overwhelms the nongovernmental.

There are two mistakes in this way of thinking and policy making. First, as we've already argued, government has no constitutional right to define its terrain as "secular" and to outlaw religion from public expression. That is a discriminatory imposition of secular sectarianism. Second, government ought not to obliterate or undermine that which is legitimately nongovernmental – the families, churches, business enterprises, and diverse nongovernment associations organized outside of government. Whenever government cooperates with nongovernment organizations, it has every obligation to recognize and protect the independent integrity of those organizations, including their confessional freedom. The relationship should be one of partnership, not co-optation and takeover. There are countless examples at local, state, and federal levels where government cooperates, whether by contract or by some other means, with organizations that have their own reason for being and for serving people.

Consider, for example, one of the most obvious religious partnerships of the federal government, namely the military chaplaincy. The military services pay the salaries and provide the commissions, uniforms, and offices for those who also, at the same time, serve as ordained clergy of their respective religious bodies. We do not presume for a moment that because the government employs and pays for the chaplains it thereby has the right to take over or incorporate the institutions that those chaplains represent. Nor do the chaplains then become a simple extension of government. The chaplaincy program gives the government no authority to require the Catholic Church to ordain women or to demand that Muslims be nondiscriminatory in their hiring practices by hiring Baptist or Presbyterian chaplains. No, the relationship is a partnership in which government and religious institutions cooperate, each fulfilling its own purpose. The integrity of each is upheld. Government does not *do* priestly and pastoral work, but it can cooperate with organizations that do.

Ambiguity has arisen in the areas of education and welfare policy because in both of these areas government has presumed to *do* education and poverty relief. One answer to this ambiguity could be offered by arguing that government ought not to set up schools and welfare agencies as a direct extension of government. Instead, it ought to partner with independent schools and agencies, providing funding and other means in an equitable, pluralist manner. Another answer is that even when government sets up its own schools and welfare agencies, it should give them no advantage or privilege that is denied to independent schools and service organizations. Thus, when government acts on its obligation to provide for the public welfare by determining that a certain class or sector of eligible citizens should receive certain services, it ought to proceed in a way that takes fully into account the organizations that are already offering such services. If it chooses to partner with such organizations, it can do justice to them and to all eligible recipients only by preserving the full integrity of all parties. Government must establish its own general qualifications, conditions, and purposes for the service it mandates or funds, but justice also requires that it not discriminate against any qualified nongovernment organization because it is religious or nongovernmental. The question of an organization's secular or nonsecular viewpoint is simply irrelevant. The proper question from government's side is whether the organizations that agree to cooperate with it can demonstrate a capability of serving those who are eligible for the service.[16] And this is where confessional pluralism is so important. Not every group will be able to serve every eligible person, nor will every eligible person want to receive his or her benefits indiscriminately from every service provider. The government's general or universal public purpose can best be fulfilled through partnership with a diversity of providers that can, in a variety of ways and from a variety of viewpoints, reach all the different kinds of eligible recipients.

Look again, by analogy, at the military chaplaincy program. Government's general public service is to provide military chaplains. Recognizing that military personnel require chaplains of different confessions, the government partners with diverse religious institutions to recruit a diverse range of chaplains in proportion to the need for them. Government does not first create a uniform public profession of faith and way of worship and then demand that, regardless of the chaplain's religion of origin, he or she put "sectarian" commitments aside and become a "nonsectarian" chaplain for everyone. What the military actually does is to demonstrate the principle that should hold true for social and welfare services. A wide variety of groups in the United States may offer drug treatment, job training, and other services in different ways and from different points of view. As long as eligible recipients are free to enter and exit the programs, and as long as no service organization has a monopoly in a territory, then government properly fulfills its general obligation by partnering with a diversity of demonstrably capable service organizations without regard to the viewpoints, philosophies, and religions of the latter.

The new pluralism directly challenges the argument by third-order pluralists that faith-based organizations which receive public funds should not be allowed to discriminate in their hiring practices. Rep. Bobby Scott (D-VA) and Barry Lynn say that an independent service-provider's right to hire in accordance with its convictions "would allow religious

---

16 I certainly agree with Hall ("Diminished Authority") that faith-based organizations should not be granted relief from health, safety, and fiduciary requirements that would apply to groups that make no religious claims for their work. But the opposite should also be true, namely, that government-owned and "secular" nonprofits should not be granted privileges denied to faith-based organizations because the latter are "religious." The question is how to remove religious (or viewpoint) discrimination while also doing justice to the integrity of every nongovernment organization and to all citizens. For more on this, see Glenn, *Ambiguous Embrace*, 99–130 and 266–296.

bigotry in hiring to be practiced with the use of federal funds."[17] The error here begins with the denial that any true partnership can exist because every participating organization becomes, by definition, an extension of government. Thus, any group that serves the needy represents the single public monopoly that stands behind those funds. On Scott and Lynn's terms, any discrimination in hiring is the same as public exclusion based on bigotry. But that is nonsense from a genuinely pluralist point of view. There is absolutely no discrimination being practiced by a Pentecostal drug-rehabilitation center when it hires a person of Pentecostal faith qualified to perform the service and refuses to hire an atheist or a Muslim, as long as atheist and Muslim drug-rehabilitation centers are free to hire whomever they want for the programs they operate. Catholic chaplains ordained exclusively by the Catholic Church are not keeping Jewish chaplains from serving those who want a Jewish chaplain, as long as the government that employs the chaplains remains fully pluralistic in its partnerships.

The second error in the Scott/Lynn argument is the presumption that the religious or ideological commitment of the people who provide welfare services is irrelevant to the "secular" service being provided. The fact is that the food, or shelter, or job training, or drug treatment being offered by many groups is offered as an act of Christian, or Muslim, or humanist charity. In which case, the hiring of staff members who share a common motivation and commitment may be integral to the job's definition, just as Catholic, or Jewish, or Lutheran faith is integral to the job of a military chaplain. Government's nondiscriminatory, general public purpose is fulfilled precisely and only by not discriminating against any group, regardless of its religious point of view, when it decides to partner with any of them. The public delivery plan is pluralistic from the start so that no one is excluded. It is the Scott/Lynn argument that represents bigotry and illegitimate exclusiveness, because their prejudgment that government should exclude explicitly religious groups from partnership with government altogether represents unjust religious discrimination from the outset. What Americans United and People for the American Way cannot see is the anti-pluralist bias of their own argument and that is because the injustice resides in their most fundamental, unquestioned assumptions.

Charitable Choice does not call for special privileges for religious groups or a special pot of money exclusively for faith-based organizations; it simply requires the halt to public discrimination against such groups. That, of course, amounts to the end of public-monopoly privileges for "secular" moral majoritarians as well as for "religious" moral majoritarians. A new order of pluralism will mean that all of America's communities will have the same legal protection to practice their religions and nonreligions freely in public and that they may do so in partnership with government in many instances. Religious freedom will no longer need to be conceived as a right that is protected only when completely disassociated from government. And this means that public Christians, along with people of every other religion, can be forthright in public life and live out their deepest convictions in the social and educational service they offer because they will be acting in accord with pluralist principles that assure the same freedom to every other group. Not only should citizens be free to worship or not worship in accord with their conscience, they should also be free to live their religions openly in public without discrimination and without opportunity to monopolize the public order for themselves. This is genuine pluralism. It is the only way

17 Quoted in the *Washington Post*, 12 March 2001.

to do justice to human beings who are at root religious creatures. This is what Christian-democratic political service is all about.

What about the worries of some religious and libertarian groups that "mixing government and charity . . . could undermine the very things that have made private charity so effective," and that "faith-based charities could find their missions shifting, their religious character lost, the very things that made them so successful destroyed," as Michael Tanner puts it?[18] First, if one presumes that whatever government touches it corrupts, then Tanner's argument holds. Further, if one assumes that no form of partnership can possibly preserve the integrity of the nongovernment organization, the argument also holds. And finally, if one presumes that faith-based efforts are, by definition, private and authentic only if they remain disconnected from government, then the argument holds.

The argument for a new pluralism, however, challenges all of these assumptions. Neither second-order nor third-order pluralism can do justice to contemporary reality and public welfare policy. The argument of Ellen Willis is the flip side of Michael Tanner's. Both make the same assumption about a dominating, demanding, secular government that leaves nothing that it touches unsecularized. And both make the same assumption that religion and charity belong in private. From the viewpoint of the new pluralism, any group or religion that conceives of itself and its purpose as entirely private should, of course, be free not to partner with government. There is nothing about Charitable Choice that says all religious social-service organizations *must* partner with government. At the same time, the government's aim should be to define the nature of its partnerships so that every religious organization, just as every cooperating organization that thinks of itself as not religious, will be fully free and responsible to maintain its own integrity and mission.

This is the context in which the new pluralism rejects the whole idea that cooperation between government and faith-based groups requires a prior determination to segregate the public's "secular" funds and services from the "sectarian" elements of the faith-based groups that cooperate in providing the service. The mistaken assumption of third-order pluralists continues to be that the "nonsectarian" secular function (which belongs in the public domain) is a religion-free zone and must be separated from the "sectarian" function or domain in any organization that chooses to partner with government. But, according to the Constitution's First Amendment, the privilege of constructing this dichotomy does not belong to government, for it does not lie in government's authority to define, prescribe, or proscribe the nature of religion.[19] There may indeed be groups like Catholic Charities that think of themselves as a two-part composite of the secular and the religious. There may be other groups that think of themselves as integrally religious or as integrally secular. None of this need concern government. Its only concern, when cooperating with nongovernment organizations, should be to make sure that the partnering organizations demonstrate the

---

18 From the executive summary of "Corrupting Charity," Briefing Paper No. 62, by Michael Tanner, The Cato Institute, Washington, D.C., 22 March 2001.

19 See Esbeck, Carl H. 2001. "Religion and the First Amendment: Some Causes of the Recent Confusion." *William and Mary Law Review* 42 (3) (March), 907–914, and Esbeck, 1998. "The Establishment Clause as a Structural Restraint on Governmental Power." *Iowa Law Review* 84 (1) (October): 1–113. For more on the First Amendment and whether there is one clause or two, see Esbeck, 2000. "Differentiating the Free Exercise and Establishment Clauses." *Journal of Church and State* 42 (Spring): 311–334; Monsma, Stephen V. 2000. "Substantive Neutrality as a Basis for Free Exercise-No Establishment Common Ground." *Journal of Church and State* 42 (Winter), 13–35.

ability to perform or provide the service. If an organization is proving that it can help drug addicts break their habits and if that is government's general public purpose in funding drug-rehabilitation services, then the philosophy or religious orientation of different nongovernment organizations is of no concern to government, as long as those eligible to receive the services are free to choose or not choose, to enter and exit, the various programs.

One way to avoid potential entanglement problems for government is for it to fund vouchers for eligible recipients so they can choose a service provider. For various government programs, from food supplements to child care to drug rehabilitation, vouchers might, indeed, be the best and most efficient means of providing funding to eligible individuals. However, from the new pluralist point of view, vouchers are not required for reasons that are peculiarly *religious*. If no group or majority is allowed to predefine the public's services as nonsectarian and thus to exclude "sectarians," then there will be no reason to give special attention to those unjustly excluded by giving vouchers for use in "sectarian" institutions. From the third-order pluralist point of view, vouchers may give the appearance of allowing individuals to make a "sectarian" choice without government being responsible for endorsing it. But government must still decide which organizations are allowed to accept and cash in the vouchers. One way or another, a counter-argument will be made either that "sectarian" organizations may not participate or that they must separate their "sectarian" part from their "nonsectarian" part in order to receive public funds for the "nonsectarian" service they offer. That entire framework must be dissolved if justice is to be done to all citizens and to all nongovernment organizations.

If the fourth order of pluralism takes hold and endures, then there will come a day when the words "nonsectarian" and "sectarian" will become as useless and obnoxious as the disparaging words that white Protestants once used to put down blacks and Catholics.[20] No one will then be able to get away with calling the public square secular, for it will finally be open to all faiths and ideologies, without an establishment or a privileged role for any of them. The new order will, for the first time, establish public and not just private pluralism and will eliminate monopoly privileges in the public square for any religious or ideological viewpoint.

---

20 See Baer, Jr., Richard A. 1990. "The Supreme Court's Discriminatory Use of the Term 'Sectarian'." *Journal of Law and Politics* 6(3) (Spring): 449–468.

29

Abraham Kuyper, South Africa, and Apartheid

George Harinck

Last year, when I was a visiting scholar at Princeton Seminary, I was asked by my friend Max Stackhouse to write a book on Abraham Kuyper (1837–1920) and apartheid. During my research I found out that since 1975 the topic of Kuyper and apartheid has been well known in the international academic world. And it is common knowledge in the English-speaking world that Abraham Kuyper is one of the fathers of apartheid. But in the Netherlands this topic is rather unknown. Is that not strange?

Dutchmen know Kuyper of course. He founded one of the ten Dutch universities, the second largest Reformed denomination in the country, one of the three most influential political parties of the last century, and he was their prime minister from 1901 until 1905. The Dutch know about apartheid too. Many Kuyperians were active in the anti-apartheid movement. Just because they were related to the white Reformed churches in South Africa, and just because the Free University was related to Potchefstroom University, the Dutch Calvinists were all the more opposed to apartheid. In the 1970s they severed their ties with white churches and white universities and started to support black churches and black universities instead. When Alan Boesak said that to the black South Africans "the God of the Reformed tradition was the God of slavery, fear, persecution, and death,"[1] the Dutch Calvinists blamed this on the Boers, not on Kuyper.

The absence of the Dutch in the international Kuyper–apartheid debate has not been noticed, but it is a missing link and it certainly influenced the course and scope of the debate. For example, the relation between Kuyper and South Africa, between his Calvinism and the Calvinism of the Boers, plays a formative role in the debate. Many South African, American, and English sources on this topic do contain some information on what Kuyper said about South Africa, but they never tell *why* and *when* he said so. Kuyper is simply considered to be a Boer with the Boers and a Calvinist with these Calvinists. But in reality he had an ambivalent relationship with South Africa and its white inhabitants, and hundreds of pages have been written about it in Dutch.

Kuyper's interest in the Boer cause had two aspects: a national and a Calvinistic one.

---

1   Boesak, Alan 1984. *Black and Reformed: Apartheid, Liberation, and the Calvinist Tradition*, edited by Leonard Sweetman. Maryknoll: Orbis, 83.

These remarks were delivered at the opening ceremony of the Abraham Kuyper Institute for Public Theology at Princeton Theological Seminary, at the Nassau Inn on February 1, 2002.

As for the national aspect, the Boers were a cognate people. The Dutch usually neglected them, but in the period of the Anglo-Boer wars, from 1880 until 1900, they changed their attitude and ardently supported the Boers against imperialistic Britain. Why this change? For a very interesting reason. The Netherlands was a small nation that feared its future as an independent nation in Europe. Germany was the rising power in the east, and England was the mighty world power at its west side. Under these conditions, the Boers functioned as an anchor of hope to the Dutch: in the Boer opposition to the British in Africa the Dutch recognized their will to survive in Europe. Kuyper was at the head of this nationwide pro-Boer movement. Petitions were offered to the British government, and streets and squares were named after famous Boer generals. But sympathy for the Boers vanished as suddenly as it had risen. When the Boers lost the war in 1902 the Dutch forgot about them, Kuyper included.

Soon after 1880 Kuyper was already disappointed by the Boers, not so much because they lost a war they never could have won, but because they were not interested in his Calvinistic ideals. According to Kuyper a true Dutchman was a true Calvinist, and in the Boers he had meant to find a true specimen of the classic God-fearing Dutchman. He even considered that the Boers might play a role in his plan to restore and renew the position of the Calvinists in church and society. But to his disappointment, the Boers were unwilling to set foot on Kuyper's stage. That is why he turned his back on them in the 1880s. His famous brochure on *The Crisis in South-Africa*, published in 1900, is more anti-British than it is pro-Boer.

Kuyper never went to South Africa, and his decision to visit the United States and Princeton in 1898 is more than accidental. He had realized that the future for Calvinism lay not in Africa, but in America. He easily left behind the nationalistic South African dimension of his Calvinism, for it was Calvinism, not nationalism that guided him. The fact that Kuyper's sympathy for the Boers was as serious as it was short, has only recently come to light in the international debate on Kuyper and apartheid. In recent years distinctions have been made between Kuyper and the South African interpretation of Kuyper, between Kuyper's neo-Calvinism and the Calvinism of the Boers. As a result the role of Kuyper in the apartheid debate is diminishing. Had the Dutch participated in the Kuyper–apartheid debate, such distinctions would have been drawn much earlier.

One possible reason the Dutch were absent from this international debate is that in the nineteenth, and for a long time in the twentieth century, race was not an issue in Dutch society. The impulse for Dutch involvement in the anti-apartheid movement was not their own experience with racial issues, but the fact that the Boers were related to them. The same was true in the nineteenth-century world of Kuyper. In his publications race is not a category. A clear example of this is that the distinction he made between white and colored people in his 1898 Stone lectures only appeared in the American edition.[2] In the Dutch edition it would have made no sense.

Race was not an issue in Kuyper's thinking. But it is clear that his publications presuppose the superiority of the white race and western civilization. Time and again he mentions the African people in a negative sense, for example in his Stone lectures – and

---

2   *LC* 197: "whether one is to be born as girl or boy, rich or poor, dull or clever, *white or colored*, or even as Abel or Cain, is the most tremendous predestination conceivable in heaven or on earth." The words in italics are missing in the Dutch edition.

his audience agreed with him. We deplore the fact that he did not unravel, but instead followed the prejudice of his time. Yet, his attitude towards race is not so monolithic that he should be considered an outright racist. Kuyper's Stone lectures do not argue for the superiority of race or civilization, but for the superiority of Christianity. It is not always easy to distinguish between the two, but it is clear that, for Kuyper, historic development is not a process determined by race. Neither is the superiority of race fixed, but can be lost by the white and gained by the yellow race – as Kuyper himself wrote. The black people that according to the exegesis of his days lived under the curse of Ham could receive the blessing of the Lord. Decisive in Kuyper's thinking on history and civilization is in the end not race or historic development, aspects that are beyond our control, but Christianity, and the human responsibility to choose for God.

According to Kuyper, "Calvinism was bound to find its utterance in the democratic interpretation of life; to proclaim the liberty of nations; and not to rest until both politically and socially every man, simply because he is man, should be recognized, respected and dealt with as a creature created after the Divine likeness" (*LC* 27). Later, Kuyperians recognized the historical limitations of Kuyper's scope and did not hesitate to add racism to the list of evils Kuyper's Calvinism must combat.

They had good reason to do so, for there is evidence that Kuyper applied his Calvinistic conviction of the equality and responsibility of man not only to the position of women or the poor, but to the position of colored people as well. In 1896 he formulated rules for church planting in the Dutch East Indies, where Kuyper's churches had their main mission field. In these rules he stated that, according to the gospel, different races and nations had to live together in one church. This unity might only be broken up in case of difference in language or confession.[3]

In 1901, the year Kuyper became prime minister of the Netherlands, he introduced an important change in Dutch colonial politics, when he introduced the so-called ethical policy. The basics of this policy were an application of his view of human equality and of the responsibility of people and races to spend their superiority in the service of God. In the program of his administration he described the responsibility of the Dutch nation towards the East-Indian peoples as guardianship, over against the realities of colonization or exploitation. The underlying idea is clear: the Netherlands was not allowed to abuse their superiority over the Dutch East Indies. I do not deny the paternalistic character of this view, but this policy marked a major advance over the nineteenth-century Dutch colonial policy of exploitation. And it shows that Kuyper was not guided by the cultural racism of his day, but by his Calvinistic creed of human equality.

This is the way the Dutch understand Abraham Kuyper. They certainly do not have the final clue to all the challenging and sometimes disturbing opinions about Kuyper, but I hope I have made clear my case, that a Dutch Kuyperian voice can add something to the international Kuyper debate and research. I am grateful that Princeton Seminary has shown a real interest in its historic Dutch connection, and I hope this Abraham Kuyper Institute for Public Theology will fuel the relationship and use its excellent location in Princeton Seminary to further the international Kuyper dialogue and outreach. I would

---

3   Adonis, J. C. 1982. *Die afgebreekte skeidsmuur weer opgehou: Die verstrengeling van die sendingsbeleid van die Nederduitste Gereformeerde Kerk in Suid-Afrika met die praktyk en ideologie van die Apartheid in historiese perspektief.* Amsterdam: Rodopi, 59.

like to congratulate Princeton on the opening of this Institute, also on behalf of the president of the Free University of Amsterdam, and I hope Max Stackhouse and his staff will succeed in making this Institute like the Aeolian harp Kuyper wrote about at the end of his last Stone lecture: its strings tuned aright, ready in the window, awaiting the breath of the Spirit.

30

Abraham Kuyper and the Cult of True Womanhood: An Analysis of *De Eerepositie der Vrouw*

Mary Stewart Van Leeuwen

1. Introduction

Abraham Kuyper's *De Eerepositie der Vrouw* ("The Woman's Position of Honor") was originally a sequence of eight articles published in 1914 in the Dutch Calvinist daily newspaper *De Standaard*.[1] I was first referred to these articles while presenting a paper on the gendered public private dichotomy during a 1990 conference at the Free University of Amsterdam.[2] Having been told that these (then untranslated) articles remain a significant source of gender traditionalist sentiment among Dutch Calvinist immigrants and their descendants in North America, I arranged during the same year to have them translated, with a view to broadening their availability among non-Dutch speakers[3] and reflecting on their significance for the future of Calvinistic thought in the decades following the "second wave" of feminism.[4]

A second reason for examining these articles comes from the fact that we have recently witnessed in South Africa the dismantling of *Apartheid*, the forty-year application of a

---

1   The present analysis relies on the second reprinting of these collected articles, *De Eerepositie der Vrouw.* Kampen: Kok, 1932, which totals approximately seventy pages of text. *De Standaard* was one of several Dutch neo-Calvinist movement newspapers. Kuyper edited this political daily, along with a religious weekly, *De Heraut*, for almost fifty years. For further background details, see Bratt, James 1984. *Dutch Calvinism in North American: A History of a Conservative Subculture.* Grand Rapids: Eerdmans, ch. 2.

2   See Van Leeuwen, Mary Stewart 1990."Should Private Morality Go Public? A Christian Feminist Evaluation." In *What Right Does Ethics Have?* Edited by Sander Griffioen. Amsterdam: VU University Press, 79–104. See also Van Leeuwen, Mary Stewart et al. 1993. *After Eden: Facing the Challenge of Gender Reconciliation.* Grand Rapids: Eerdmans, especially chapter 12 "Private Versus Public Life: A Case for De-Gendering" and chapter 13 "Family Justice and Societal Nurturance: Re-Integrating Public and Private Domains."

3   The English translation, funded jointly by the president's office of Calvin College and by Dorothy and Dale Van Hamersveld, was done by Irene Brouwer Konyndyk. Page references in this article are to the text of this translation. Thanks are also due to John Vander Stelt of Dordt College, Sioux Center, Iowa, for motivating my examination of these articles.

4   Historians commonly distinguish between two waves of modern feminism: the first beginning at the end of the eighteenth century and ending with the attainment of women's suffrage in most Western industrialized countries, and the second from the early 1960s up to the present. See Banks, Olive 1981. *Faces of Feminism: A Study of Feminism as a Social Movement.* New York: St. Martin's Press; Cott, Nancy 1987. *The Grounding of Modern Feminism.* New Haven: Yale University Press; and Tong, Rosemarie 1989. *Feminist Thought: A Comprehensive Introduction.* Boulder: Westview.

doctrine of racial separation based in no small part on a particular interpretation – most Calvinists would say a *mis*interpretation – of Kuyper's principle of "sphere sovereignty." At the root of this principle is Kuyper's concern for institutional diversity – for the freedom of societal institutions, or God-ordained "spheres" (e.g., church, marriage, family, business, politics, education, science, art) to develop as creationally intended without being overwhelmed by the state, denied in the name of individual freedom, or reduced one to another among themselves.[5] There is no evidence in Kuyper's work that racial groups (and the activities that make up their common stereotypes) constitute permanent, separate "spheres" as he used that term, although this is precisely what Afrikaner *Apartheid* theorists – many of them trained in Kuyper's thought at the Free University of Amsterdam – tried to claim during the development and hegemony of *Apartheid*.[6] By the same token, there is no reason intrinsic to the notion of sphere sovereignty for the sexes (and the activities and traits stereotypically attributed to them) to be assigned to God-ordained, largely non-overlapping domains. Yet this is what Kuyper himself seems to be arguing for in *De*

5   Among Kuyper's translated works *LC* and *PP* refer to this concept. Bratt, *Dutch Calvinism*, chapter 2, lists other Dutch sources, and notes (pp. 26–27) that "Kuyper wished each functional, occupational, and geographic unit to have independence from external imposition. . . . In such 'organic' communities he also saw an alternative to the twin demons of Revolution: atomism and collectivism. They provided an authentic sense of identity, a social location between the individual and the mass, and a source of firm but manageable discipline." Albert Wolters further defines sphere sovereignty (also called the "principle of differentiated responsibility") as the principle that "no societal institution is subordinate to any other. Persons in positions of societal responsibility are called to positivize God's ordinances directly in their own specific sphere. Their authority is delegated to them by God, not by any human authority. Consequently, they are also directly responsible to God. . . . The Christian is called to oppose all totalitarianism, whether of the state, church, or corporation, because it always signifies a transgression of God's mandated societal boundaries and an invasion into alien spheres. Perversion of God's creational design for society can occur in two ways: either through perversion of norms within a given sphere (as in cases of injustice in the state, child abuse in the family, exploitative wages in the business enterprise) or through the extension of the authority of one sphere over another." See Wolters, Albert M. 1985. *Creation Regained: Biblical basics for a reformational worldview.* Grand Rapids: Eerdmans, 82–83.

6   Much of the Calvinist critique of *Apartheid* (in English, at least) is theological and exegetical: see, e.g., DeGruchy, John W. and Charles Villa-Vincencio, eds. 1983. *Apartheid is a Heresy.* Grand Rapids: Eerdmans. Works in English on the selective use of Kuyper's thought to justify *Apartheid* include Strauss, P. J. 1995. "Abraham Kuyper, Apartheid and Reformed Churches in South Africa in Their Support of Apartheid." *Theological Forum*, 23 (March): 4–27, and Bloomberg, Charles 1989. *Christian-Nationalism and the Rise of the Afrikaner Broederbond in South Africa, 1918–1948.* Bloomington: Indiana University Press. Bloomberg, a South African Jewish liberal, wrote the following about Kuyper's views on race and class: "According to Kuyper, God created a diversity of races, colors and cultures which humans should recognize as part of reality. His views on race were conventionally conservative, although they varied to the point of self-contradiction. . . . [He] is nowhere critical of Boer racial attitudes, tacitly accepting them as part and parcel of Calvinist democracy. On the other hand, he felt that intermarriage could improve the human stock. . . . Calvinism, he believed, encouraged and provided conditions for 'the mingling of the blood'. . . . Politically, he opposed the champions of those who sought humankind's liberation both from God and monarchy, but he was not opposed to human emancipation, regarding God as a liberator. . . . [He] supported democracy (provided it was based on Calvinism) which 'condemns not merely all open slavery and systems of caste, but also all covert slavery of women and the poor' [a reference from Kuyper's *LC*]. . . . Despite an aversion to socialists (he mourned 1917 as an even bigger catastrophe for mankind than 1789) Kuyper was aware of urban poverty, criticized capitalism and proposed social reforms which, for their time, were progressive. Kuyper's legacy, while rightist-leaning, is therefore equivocal, with signs of compassion for the human condition absent in many contemporary Christian theorists" (pp. 8, 9). This interpretation of Kuyper is affirmed and developed in more detail in the Strauss article.

Eerepositie der Vrouw, although with interesting ambiguities which will be noted.

A final reason for undertaking this analysis is the tension in neo-Calvinist ethics between allegiance to a fixed creation order (or to what some people have *claimed* to be the details of a fixed creation order) and a concern for those who, in the name of that so-called creation order, continue to suffer chronic marginalization and/or injustice. Thus, one issue at stake in this analysis of *De Eerepositie der Vrouw* is the extent to which Kuyper has essentialized a limiting view of gender relations and contributed, as a result, to the perpetuation of that view among his Calvinist descendants.

2. Historical Background to *De Eerepositie der Vrouw*

In 1914, when Kuyper wrote the articles later to be assembled as *De Eerepositie der Vrouw*, he was only six years from his death, and had arguably become the "old grey lion" of the Dutch neo-Calvinist movement. From 1901 to 1905 he had been the prime minister of the Netherlands at the head of the Calvinistic Anti-Revolutionary Party. From 1905 until 1907 he spent much of his time in the Mediterranean, recovering from the last of four nervous breakdowns that he sustained during his lifetime.[7] By 1909 his Anti-Revolutionary Party was again in power, but dominated by younger members of the movement, with the result that Kuyper was appointed neither prime minister nor a cabinet member, but instead given a semi-honorific appointment in the parliamentary upper chamber.

By the time he wrote the eight articles on "The Woman's Position of Honor," Kuyper's influence – previously embodied in political, university, and editorial appointments – had become largely limited to his writing outlets.[8] He was, as well, in a more "antithetical" mood than in previous decades. Part of the genius of neo-Calvinism had been its determination to hold in fruitful tension the themes of "antithesis" (the religious, and hence institutional, gap that must distinguish Christians from the unredeemed) and "common grace" (the doctrine that God enables knowledge and virtue to flower even in persons not espousing true faith in God).[9] Kuyper's own writings on common grace first appeared as a newspaper series during the years when he was Dutch prime minister and hence charged with finding enough common ground among the various political parties – Christian and otherwise –

---

7   The other episodes occurred in 1858, when Kuyper was twenty-one years old, in 1876 when he was thirty-nine, and in 1894 when he was fifty-seven. See Bratt, James 1987. "Raging Tumults of the Soul: The Private Life of Abraham Kuyper." *Reformed Journal* 37 (November): 9–13, *see supra* Chapter 3, and "Abraham Kuyper's Public Career." *Reformed Journal* 37 (October): 9–12.

8   Kuyper's lifetime written output included over 20,000 newspaper articles (which series on women under consideration constituted only eight), scores of pamphlets and published speeches, and multivolume treatises on theology, politics, education, science, and philosophy. See Bratt, *Dutch Calvinism* for background and basic bibliography.

9   Of the doctrine of common grace, Bratt notes the following: "Common grace reconciled the doctrine of total depravity with the presence of good among the unconverted, at the same time reaffirming God's sovereignty by making that good the fruit of divine grace rather than of human effort It encouraged the redeemed to respect the good remaining in the world and to strive to augment it. Even more, it made many elements of human culture – institutions such as the law and the community, artistic and technical ability, academic disciplines, and scientific methods – not just the products but means of grace, instruments by which God restrained sin and enabled men [sic] to try to develop creation as he had originally designed. Finally, it legitimated a certain amount of cooperation between the redeemed and unbelievers on the grounds that to some extent they shared a sense of the good and therefore a common purpose." Bratt, *Dutch Calvinism*, 19–20.

to keep the nation running smoothly and justly.[10]

But in the last decade of his life – perhaps partly to rationalize his loss of national political power – he returned to the theme of antithesis: the kingdom of God in opposition to the world, and the strengthening of creational distinctions in opposition to the modernist extremes of individualistic atomism and collectivist totalism. Among the creational or "natural" distinctions needing to be proclaimed and protected by true believers, Kuyper announced, was the distinction between men and women and between their proper domains – namely, public versus private life. This is a central theme of his articles on "The Woman's Position of Honor."

3. Summary of the Content of *De Eerepositie der Vrouw*
The translated text of the eight articles in *De Eerepositie der Vrouw* runs to thirty single-spaced pages, based on the 1932 Dutch edition of seventy-six pages. It is worth noting that in the course of the text, Kuyper makes authoritative appeals to God, creation and/or Scripture no fewer than twelve times in support of his view of gender relations. He also uses essentialist-leaning phrases such as "feminine nature," "unnatural situation," "natural distinction between man and woman" (etc.) no fewer than twenty-eight times. Finally, he uses paired terms such as "physical and psychical," "bodily and spiritual" no fewer than seven times when speaking of the nature, place, and interrelationship of the sexes, suggesting that his natural theology of gender includes relatively fixed biological *and* psychological categories.

Part I of the series sets the historical and political context. Kuyper notes that women's suffrage has been accepted in principle among Dutch liberals (recall that the date is 1914), though the range of the female franchise is still a matter of debate. This way of thinking, Kuyper says, is the predictable result of three secularized, liberal assumptions, namely: (1) that the individual is the basic unit of political and social life; (2) that the adult individual should therefore be the basic voting entity (what we would today call the principle of "one person, one vote"); and (3) that the nation consists only of "the aggregate of individuals" and not an "organic national whole" (p. 3).[11] He locates the origin of the movement for

---

10 These articles were collectively republished as a three-volume treatise, *De Gemeene Gratie*. Amsterdam: Höveker and Wormser, 1902–4. Bratt, comparing Kuyper's rhetorical style to that of Martin Luther King (who built on the African-American oral preaching tradition) points out that "Kuyper's words, which come to us deceptively in scholarly tomes . . . were originally daily installments passed around among Friesian fishing families and Amsterdam bricklayers." (Bratt, "Abraham Kuyper's Public Career," 11). While affirming the doctrine of total depravity, Kuyper had great faith in the traditional and emergent folk wisdom of *de kleyne luyden* – "the little people" of the lower-middle socioeconomic strata living in the rural areas and smaller cities where Calvinism flourished. He felt that their varied yet more organic life was the creation-based antidote to the modern trend toward atomistic individualism on the one hand and state-imposed uniformity on the other. This is why he tailored his philosophical writings first for their consumption, and was accordingly rewarded with their loyalty, first in the Netherlands but also among Dutch Calvinist immigrants to North America.

11 In his use of this last phrase – and particularly the use of the term *organic* – Kuyper shows his continuing concern for sphere sovereignty: Creational norms for society demand that there be self-governing institutions that mediate between the individual and the collective, the family being one of these. It was his concern for the sphere sovereignty of the family that led Kuyper to espouse not the individual but the "household" vote – *viz.*, one vote per household "head," normally the father (even grown sons were not to vote as long as they stayed under their father's roof as single men). On this account widows – as heads of household by the force of circumstance – could also vote, but only as long as they did not remarry. Kuyper

women's suffrage in the French Revolution, and notes that it has spread not just to the Netherlands, but to Scandinavia, other parts of Europe, England, and England's overseas dominions, such as Australia and New Zealand.[12]

In Part II Kuyper distinguishes what he calls "social feminism" from the movement for women's suffrage: "One can be a rousing and convinced advocate of Feminism, and yet on principle oppose all Women's Suffrage" (p. 5). He admits that "the woman has been undervalued and oppressed for centuries" and that she is still not in control of "her future position." (p. 5). But what *is* her appropriate and ideal position? Apparently it is in marriage, the rate of which has fallen drastically in the Netherlands, particularly in the cities. The attractions of an affluent life-style have made young men delay the financial burdens of marriage (exacerbated by a similar desire for affluent living on the part of young women), and neo-Malthusian thinking has given them a high-sounding rationale for delaying, then limiting, the conception of children. This "relega[tion] to a life beyond marriage, from the man's side, by choice; from the woman's side often by force" is, in Kuyper's view "unnatural" (p. 6).[13]

By default then, the middle-class woman looks for other ways to keep occupied – in philanthropy, needlework, the arts, and especially the intellectual life.[14] However, Kuyper warns, it is precisely "this one-sided intellectual world that then breaks the harmony in the feminine nature, which, glittering in her inner emotional richness, will tolerate no supremacy of the intellect." Worse still, as her biological clock ticks relentlessly on,[15] she is at particular risk of being led astray by the women's suffrage movement. Her nature "all too

makes this point in passing in Part VI of the series.

12 Kuyper's own political party was called the Anti-Revolutionary Party in stated opposition to the human-ist, atheist, and materialist ideals of the French Revolution. Hence any movement, like feminism, seen as connected to that revolution would easily provoke opposition among his Calvinist *kleyne luyden*. Kuyper also seems to espouse an essentialist view of national (not just sexual) character here, since he holds British women particularly responsible for the spread of women's suffragism: "[I]t was the Anglo-Saxon woman who influenced the robust development of her strength of personality in every area towards women's suf-frage The theory of individualism was working [in America, Australia, and New Zealand] together with the forceful personality development in the woman of Anglo-Saxon descent. . . . When the strength of will in the Anglo-Saxon woman awakens, her power for self-control against the rising passion of the rougher element so easily escapes her." (Quotations are from p. 4).

13 Kuyper's natural-theological argument for marriage as everyone's (but especially women's) destiny rests on the point that God has so ordered the genetic lottery that roughly equal numbers of males and females are born on earth: "Now [this] equal number of men and women which the statistics (as far as they do differ from this equality the numbers are insignificant) of all countries show us, is sufficient proof that the purpose of our sex, apart from exceptions, is to have all men and all women get married" (p. 7). Although guilty of ignoring Paul's high praise for the state of singleness in the New Testament epistles (perhaps part of the ongoing Calvinist reaction against the Catholic mystique of celibacy), Kuyper does display an appreciation for sex within marriage unusual among the nineteenth-century middle class. He is as much concerned that the pursuit of material affluence will lead to an "unnatural" decrease in "desire for conjugal relations" as he is that it will lead to smaller families or no families at all (p. 6). Nor does he follow the standard Victorian line that only men find sexual intercourse pleasurable, for later on (p. 14) he chides women who love "the delight which sexual intercourse can give" but want at the same time to avoid the gestation, birthing, and nursing of children.

14 But according to Kuyper, "the less gifted and lower-class woman will probably lose herself in simply doing nothing" (p. 7).

15 In Kuyper's words, "her years of glad hope were dragging by, without bringing her the fulfillment of that hope . . ." (p. 7).

painfully masculinized," she then "forsakes the mystical heartfelt expression in which the earthshaking power of the woman lies, in order to lose [herself] in a struggle for women's rights, which, alas, can have no other result than to cause the essential superior power of the woman over the man to diminish" (pp. 7 and 8).

Thus, Kuyper concludes, the selfishness of men causes women to remain unmarried, then to sublimate their frustrations in intellectual and political causes whose "masculinizing" effect simply reinforces the likelihood that no man will choose them to live out their natural destiny in marriage.[16]

In Part III Kuyper makes both pragmatic and principled concessions to feminism. The "non-political feminism" that strives "to give the woman a part in a higher education and a more independent existence . . . to share in the progress of human knowledge, in the strength of personality, and in the freedom of position which characterizes all of life in the cultural world: this is something which deserves unqualified applause" (p. 9). Moreover, if young women must wait for marriage until they are in their thirties (or older), one can hardly criticize them for wanting "to provide the necessities of life on [their] own strength," rather than remaining an economic burden to their parents (p. 10). Working-class women thus enter the ranks of domestic servants,[17] but this is an unthinkable option for those from the middle class and the civil-servant class. These women seek refuge in wholesale, retail, and garment industry jobs, in clerical positions, and finally and most alarmingly, in intellectual and professional training at the universities.

Kuyper concedes that "the woman can lend herself to such study as well as the man" (p. 11). He even concedes that women doctors are needed to service women patients.[18] Nevertheless, he asserts, the result is still counter-normative. The woman "compete[s] for all kinds of posts and positions . . . as the rival of the man" (p. 12), but thereby ensures, even as she gains economic independence, that few men will want to marry her. Moreover, as the ranks of single women professionals grow, so grows their rivalry with each other to obtain husbands. Either way, their natural calling to domesticity remains thwarted.

In Part IV Kuyper elaborates his ideas on the essential "nature and being" of the two sexes (p. 13). Consistent with the notion that sphere sovereignty is balanced by sphere universality, he states that woman and man are "fundamental variations in the one human being," and this being the case that they can "both draw too close to each other or can become too alienated from each other" (p. 13). At this point, however, he is much more

---

16 Kuyper is aware that married women are also attracted to the message of women's suffrage, although he claims that their numbers are small (p. 9). He also has no illusions about the sexual temptations of the long-unmarried male: "[B]ecause, for no small part, many of the men who do not marry make up for what they are missing by seeking out indecent women, the chaste spinsters see themselves deprived of the bliss of children, the joy of motherhood, and along with this the happiness of marriage" (p. 7). Thus "men's lewd existence" combines with "the prevailing desire for affluence" (p. 9) to keep urban, middle-class young women unmarried. (He mentions more than once that the situation is, fortunately, not yet this bad in the villages and rural areas.)

17 And in doing so, Kuyper demonstrates with population statistics, they are the ones mostly responsible for the fact that female Amsterdammers outnumber males by 25,000, "something which, if general voting rights for the woman were adopted, would directly result in the fact that the woman would be master over the entire city area." (p. 10).

18 "There was always something repugnant about a sensitive mother of a newborn child having to surrender herself to a male doctor for treatment of all kinds of intimate discomfort, or for the delivery itself. The view of replacing this male physician with a female doctor naturally found acceptance" (p. 11).

concerned with the former of these two problems. Physical differences between the sexes – in strength, stature, voice quality, and body build – all attest to deeper psychological differences. Women – true women, that is – are characterized by *shame*, (p. 13), *reticence* (pp. 13–14: even in the throes of love they must wait for the man to take the *initiative*), *flexibility and compliance* (p. 15), and a vaguely defined "mystical power . . . which is not weaker nor less persistent but *different*. . . . [I]n the undulation of her flexible feeling she knows precisely how to arouse a current of more powerful life, than that over which the man rules with his iron will, his probing thinking, and his powerful arm" (p. 15).

Essential differences in psychology imply parallel differences in activity:

> Herein the clear idea is expressed, that woman and man cannot be considered as identical; that man and woman are fundamentally different in kind; and that whoever has the man take his place at the cradle and the woman take her place at the lectern, makes life unnatural.[19]

Not only unnatural, but unscriptural: "Life remains as God created and ordered it, and this has as result that the being and nature of the woman simply is and remains different from the nature and being of the man, and that from both basic differences, in spite of the adjustable variations, unbridgeable differences of human life result" (p. 14). Indeed, "all undervaluation or elimination of this distinction betrays a seeking to nullify God's established order by means of human will" (p. 17).

Kuyper continues to develop the theme of "natural distinctions" in Part V. He concedes that these distinctions, statistically speaking, are not of an all-or-none sort: some women are stronger – or more clever, or more resolute – than some men. But these are at best exceptions that prove the rule, and at worst so "unnatural" that they are "whole-heartedly abhorred by every right-minded person" (p. 17). The more usual distinctions of body and character, he admits, do not logically require a gendered division of labor, but the record of history points to the conclusion that, for reproductive and other reasons, women are not made for extra-domestic life:

> A fleet at sea manned with women is unthinkable. . . . An army of women could not exist for a moment over against an army of men. . . . A female firefighter would put an entire city at risk. . . . A police force made up of women would indeed cause every guarantee of the preservation of order to be lost. . . . Only men and no women serve as guides in the mountains. It is the same with hunting and plowing. (p. 19)

The conclusion, Kuyper asserts, is that there are two kinds of persons and two corresponding "life tasks," with "no similarity" between the halves of either (p. 19). His conclusion to this section is such a trenchant assertion of the normative gendering of public and private life that bears quoting in full:

> There are two *kinds of life*. A life in the family, with the relatives, with the children, which has a more *private* character, and almost completely outside of that, a different life in Councils

---

19 Kuyper's emphasis. At the end of part IV he adds that "[t]he woman has not been endowed more poorly but more richly than the man. She finds her portion in the pearls and rubies sparkling out of an eye that can spark and captivate the man; in a laugh around the lips which softens and conquers; the deepest offering of her soul, if it is pure, is irresistible. Yet if she now strips herself of this womanly nature of hers in order to buckle herself into the harness of the man and, with the coat of mail of his brain-power and his fist muscle, seeks to assure herself a place in life, then she does not *climb* but rather *sinks* as a woman, breaking the balance in which her ascendancy lay, and she ends up forever forfeiting her high position of honor" (pp. 15–16).

and States, in the navy and in the army, which has a more *public* character. These two kinds of life require clearly distinguished gifts and talents; and now it is the lesson of history, and the empirical given of today that those two kinds of gifts and talents, at least as a rule, seem to fall along the lines of the natural distinction between man and woman. The private and public life form two separate spheres, each with their own way of existing, with their own task; and each task calls for its own kind of qualities and talents. This is the harmony between life and human nature. And it is on the basis of this state of affairs, which has not been invented by us, but which God himself has imposed on us, that in public life the woman does not stand equally with the man. No more than it can be said of the man that in married life he has been called to also himself achieve in the family that which is achieved by the woman (pp. 19–20; his emphases).

In Part VI Kuyper turns from general revelation in history and experience to the special revelation of Scripture. Unlike Augustine and Aquinas, he does not argue that women were created inferior to men, nor that they become inferior by virtue of having caused the Fall of humankind (the latter was Luther's position).[20] With Calvin, he sees the sexes as being equal in both creation and redemption, as far as ultimate religious status goes. They are equal, yet different: in Genesis 2, the woman is made a helper to the man – but, to balance the equation, the man leaves father and mother to cleave to the woman. Scripture further honors the woman, despite her participation in the Fall, by making her the bearer (with help from no man) of humankind's Savior. Moreover, mothers and fathers are reverenced equally in Israel – witness for example the virtuous woman of Proverbs 31.[21]

The only qualifier that Christ adds to this creation theology, in Kuyper's analysis, is the announcement that in heaven there will be no giving or taking in marriage (Matthew 22:24). For Kuyper, this means that all the distinctions he has drawn so far between the sexes "[have] meaning only in this earthly life, and not in heavenly life. . . . [In heaven], in body and soul man and woman will be one, and nothing other than human" (p. 22). However, he adds, let no one make the mistake of the Anabaptists and some others, who think that we can cast off creational norms for family and/or church and/ or society in the meantime, just by virtue of being in the company of the redeemed. In church, no less than in family and society, women remain in different roles and in submission to men as long as earthly life lasts.[22]

Thus, Kuyper concludes in Part VII, Scripture shows that "the position of woman as willed by God, the strength, the calling and the honor of the Woman thus lies on *the*

---

20 For a detailed treatment of theological positions on gender relations throughout church history, see Reuther, Rosemary Radford 1983. *Sexism and God-Talk: Toward a Feminist Theology*. Boston: Beacon, especially chapter 4, and Borresen, Kari E., ed. 1991. *Image of God and Gender Models in Judaeo-Christian Tradition*. Oslo: Solum Forlag.

21 "But only *in the gates* did this ideal woman [of Proverbs 31] not sit. The person who sits there is not she, but her husband. She sparkles like the ruby, as it says in verse 10, but in private life, not public life" (p. 22). Generally speaking, Kuyper concludes, "in Scripture the woman stands very high." But he betrays something of a lapse into Luther's position when he adds: "So high that it is sometimes difficult for us to reconcile this with her being the cause of the Fall" (p. 21). Nor is it clear how the virtuous woman of Proverbs 31 manages to "bring home food from afar" (v. 14) "[buy] a field" and "[plant] a vineyard" (v. 16) and "[make] linen garments, [sell] them, and [deliver] girdles to the merchant" (v. 24), all without straying into the public domain.

22 With regard to male headship in the church, Kuyper makes the predictable appeal to passages such as 1 Corinthians 11, Ephesians 5, Colossians 3 and 1 Peter 3.

inside of our human life together, and she only moves to the outside, at least partly, when there is a task to be done, the completion of which causes the man to stand behind her" (p. 24).[23] Despite exceptions, women are not fitted for success in the highly visible public domain of "representative bodies, lecterns, courtroom, cabinet and high administration" (p. 24). On the whole, "woman may walk busily about in the public arena, but that . . . is not her domain. She might try to capture a certain place for herself there, and might even be partly successful, but in her rivalry with the man, she will never win a *position of honor* in that arena" (p. 24).

Nevertheless, Kuyper sees a place for women "at the fringe of public life" (p. 25). For one thing, widows who are acting heads of households should be allowed to vote – although only as long as they remain widows.[24] Moreover, there are "third domains" such as public health, child pedagogy, philanthropy, and art that are so much more "feminine" than "masculine" in character that men will rightly and happily call for female assistance in them. For example, "A men's society for mothers of newborns is unnatural, [and] only the woman is in her place in nursery schools" (p. 25).

However, even these domains are being run in a counter-normative fashion, Kuyper asserts. For really, it is only the *married* woman (the "level-headed housewife" – p. 25) who is truly suited for work in hospitals, orphanages, nursery schools and the like, because these are logical extensions of her domestic sphere. The single women, who in fact *do* staff such institutions, come ill-prepared for the work involved, whereas the conscientious housewife, who is better prepared, will ideally be too busy at home to take part! Kuyper does not go so far as to say that single women should be deprived of such tasks. He reiterates that as long as "male lechery and the dazzle of affluence cuts off marriage for a certain period of time in a broad circle of people, then forced relationships arise because of this, which necessitate explorations into otherwise forbidden terrains" (p. 26). But he sees this situation as definitely second-best: a kind of "middle terrain where [the woman] can turn up [temporarily] if necessary" (p. 25, 26). He warns that "a healthy life view requires that one not flatter such a state of need which wishes to become a habit, but resist it" (p. 27). He does not, however, offer any long-term constructive alternatives.

Part VIII is Kuyper's conclusion to the entire series of articles. He reiterates his basic points – that men and women are fundamentally different, both physically and psychically, and that these differences are correlated with fundamentally different life callings, the man to public and the woman to private life. The woman's "place of honor is most effectively maintained if she can sparkle in the private domain, and that in the public arena, for which the man is the appointed worker, she will never be able to fulfill anything but a subordinate role, in which her inferiority would soon come to light anyway" (p. 28).

Such subordinate, quasi-public roles are possible for women in public health, child pedagogy, philanthropy, and even as nurses behind military battle-lines, but the political arena, so prominently public, should be off-limits to them. Not only do population numbers "clearly prove that equality of the man and woman at the voting booth would result in the absolute defeat of the man" (p. 28), but the entire idea of universal suffrage, to Kuyper, is based on the false notion that the state exists primarily to protect individual

---

23 This qualifier might apply to his exegesis of Proverbs 31 (see note 21), but Kuyper does not make this clear when he mentions the Proverbs text.

24 See note 11.

rights, rather than the integrity of creation-based societal spheres.[25] He reiterates his support for non-political (i.e., "social") feminism: women should be the equals of men with regard to civil law and business practice, and treated justly in labor and industrial relations.[26] But in the end, for leadership in the public life of academy, politics, and marketplace "the all-disposing Creator and Master of our life did not give special gifts to women" (p. 29).

A woman can indeed influence state and society through her "delicate, tender, moral and religious strength" – but if she tries to do so at the voting booth she will lose her unique moral power. She can only "feed the religious element into public life . . . if she remains a woman, and housewife in the fullest sense of the word, and if she causes the deep tone of God glorification to resound in her husband and son" (p. 30). And having said all this, Kuyper seems certain that the common sense of his readers will triumph, for he ends the series with the following challenge:

> In your thoughts place next to each other the emancipated Hetaera of Paris, the Suffragette of England, and the still-so-lovely Housewife from the Netherlands' middle-class life, and we won't complain any more, and we won't argue any longer, but we will leave the choice to you yourself. (p. 30)[27]

4. Some Critical Reflections on *De Eerepositie der Vrouw*

Kuyper appeals to history, contemporary observation of women's and men's character and behavior, and Scripture to make his case for the assignment of each to separate spheres. Consequently, my critical analysis of the articles will also be in terms of these three categories. Before that, however, some comments on Kuyper's rhetorical style are in order.

When reading *De Eerepositie der Vrouw*, one is struck by Kuyper's frequent use of superlatives and other extreme terms, the impact (and perhaps the intent) of which is to silence opposition, at least among the believing majority who are not intellectually equipped to meet Kuyper on his own ground. This is particularly the case when such superlatives are combined with an appeal to Scripture and/or the will of God. Who, after all, would dare to challenge the will of God, especially as interpreted by such a giant of God as Kuyper? Examples include the following (and others can be found in previous quotations from the text):[28]

> [I]t is *absolutely inexplicable* to us how . . . some people do not see how the general voting right arises out of the individualistic idea of the state. (3)

> [T]he work of John Stuart Mill . . . provided very strong propaganda for *the preposterous view* [of women's voting rights]. (4)

---

25 "Always again the root ideal of the Revolution in Paris in 1789, that we only have to reckon with a product of human will in the national State life, not with an ordinance of God" (p. 29).

26 In earlier decades, as the industrial revolution gained unregulated momentum, Kuyper worked strenuously on behalf of protective labor legislation for both women and children.

27 The phrase translated as "middle-class life" (*burgerlijke leven*) needs nuancing, as it actually refers to life outside church and state – what we would today call "civil society."

28 The emphases in the quotations are my own. I have not included any of Kuyper's couple of dozen appeals to what is "natural" and "unnatural," although this kind of language also has the effect of silencing opposition. (What Christian, after all, would deliberately flout nature, when it is understood as a synonym for God's creation order?)

[T]he feminine nature, which glittering in her inner emotional richness, *will tolerate no supremacy of the intellect.* (7)

[F]rom this exception *conclusions should never be made* with regard to the general suitability of the woman for this intellectually high sport. (11)

[If] she now strips herself this womanly nature . . . she ends up *forfeiting forever* her high position of honor. (15–16)

All attempts at reducing the difference to a variation has therefore *failed in the most absolute sense* with both man and woman. (17)

A fleet at sea manned by women is *unthinkable.* . . . Night-watch and dike-watch by women is *unthinkable.*

As long as we live here on earth, the distinction between man and woman holds firm, and the rule continues that the man is the head of the woman and that the woman must be submissive to the man. (23)

Whoever submits to the authority of the Holy Scripture will therefore see all uncertainty disappear [regarding Kuyper's distinctions between man and woman]. (23)

It will *never* come to an equality of man and woman in this high sphere [of political office]. (24)

[I]n the public domain . . . she will *never* be able to fulfill anything but a subordinate role. (28)

Whoever pulverizes this authority [i.e., regarding Kuyper's view of the State's role] . . . reduces *the national order established by God* to an instrument which must serve one's own advantage. (29)

[I]t can *never be maintained* that the High authority in public life could be partly diverted from the man and carried over to the woman. (29)

Whoever is of Calvinist conviction cannot and may not judge otherwise [than that the woman's creational place is in the home]. (30)

It would be easy to dismiss these rhetorical devices as no worse than those commonly used by other popular Christian writers – then and now – who are convinced that God is on their side. But when placed in context, it must be remembered that Kuyper is addressing (among others) women who do not have the theological or philosophical literacy to challenge him. And if they seek to gain such literacy in the academy, or even raise a question in public, they are said to risk violating the creation order and condemning themselves before God. The net result is likely to be a powerful (and self-perpetuating) silencing of the people who, in the end, are the most affected by Kuyper's argument.[29]

---

29 The parallel with the religious rhetoric justifying *Apartheid* should not be missed. Consider the following, written in 1939 by Afrikaner clergyman P. J. S. De Klerk: "Equalization leads to the humiliation of both races. Mixed marriages between higher civilized Christianized nations and lower nations militate against the Word of God. . . . This is nothing less than a crime, particularly when we take note of the very clear lines of division between races in our country. The Voortrekkers constantly guarded against such admixture and because of their deed of faith the [Afrikaner] nation was conserved as a pure Christian race up to this day." (Quoted in Kinghorn, Johann 1990. "The Theology of Separate Equality: A Critical Outline of the

Historical context: the "Cult of True Womanhood"

Kuyper, of course, did not invent the gendering of the public/ private dichotomy by himself: It was a staple feature of nineteenth-century social thought, both in Europe and America.[30] Variously called "the doctrine of separate spheres," "the cult of domesticity," and "the cult of true womanhood," it arose in the wake of urbanization and industrialization, both of which broke up the long-standing unity of workplace, living place, and childrearing space (as exemplified by family farms and small family businesses). With more and more husbands working away from home in offices and factories, with women and children shielded from the need to do likewise by protective legislation and the emergence of the "family wage" for male heads of households, a revised concept of women's roles was needed.

The doctrine of separate spheres thus allocated to the woman the behavioral tasks of nurturing husband and children and maintaining the home. Her parallel ethical task, in the common parlance of the day, was to be "angel of the home," that is, to be a moral and spiritual example to other family members, but especially her husband, whose work in the rough-and-tumble public realm ever threatened to debase him. In their role as "angels of the home" women were generally held to be men's moral superiors.[31] Kuyper is too good a Calvinist in his awareness of pervasive depravity to go this far.[32] He argues rather for

---

Dutch Reformed Church's Position on *Apartheid.*" In *Christianity Amidst Apartheid: Selected Perspectives on the Church in South Africa*, edited by Marti Prozesky. London: MacMillan, 57–80 (quotation from p. 62).

30 See, e.g., Cott, Nancy F. 1977. *The Bonds of Womanhood: "Women's Sphere" in New England, 1780–1835.* New Haven: Yale University Press; Degler, Carl N. 1980. *At Odds: Women and the Family in America from the Revolution to the Present.* New York: Oxford University Press; Elshtain, Jean Bethke 1981. *Public Man, Private Woman: Women in Social and Political Thought.* Princeton: Princeton University Press; Marshall, Barbara L. 1994. *Engendering Modernity: Feminism, Social Theory, and Social Change.* Boston: Northeastern University Press; Rothman, Sheila M. 1978. *Woman's Proper Place: A History of Changing Ideals and Practices, 1870 to Present.* New York: Basic Books; Ryan, Mary P. 1992. *Women in Public: Between Banners and Ballots, 1825–1880.* Baltimore: Johns Hopkins University Press; and Vincus, Martha, ed. 1972. *Suffer and Be Still: Women in the Victorian Age.* Bloomington: Indiana University Press. Church historians dealing with the gendering of the public/private dichotomy (which has endured as a norm in conservative Christian circles up to the present) include DeBerg, Betty 1992. *Ungodly Women.* Philadelphia: Fortress Press; Hassey, Janette 1986. *No Time for Silence: Evangelical Women in Public Ministry Around the Turn of the Century.* Grand Rapids: Zondervan; and Lamberts Bendroth, Margaret 1994. *Fundamentalism and Gender, 1875 to the Present.* New Haven: Yale University Press. A sociological account of its contemporary expression can be found in Klatch, Rebecca 1987. *Women of the New Right.* Philadelphia: Temple University Press.

31 See Degler, *At Odds*, chapter 2. It is not uncommon for contemporary feminist theorists to refer to this cult of true womanhood as a form of feminism – usually "domestic" or "romantic" feminism – inasmuch as it applauds (rather than denigrates) the stereotypically feminine virtues. See, e.g., Ruether, *Sexism and God-Talk*, ch. 4, and Cott, Nancy F. 1987. *The Grounding of Modern Feminism.* New Haven: Yale University Press. Opinion in the nineteenth century (and particularly toward its end, when the women's suffrage movement gained momentum) differed as to whether women would *lose* their peculiar moral qualities if they ventured into the public realm. Kuyper appears to have held this view (see especially pp. 29–30), but other domestic feminists argued that precisely *because* women were 'morally superior' to men – e.g., in their concern for peace, their concern for children and the aged, their concern for temperance and chastity – they should be given the vote in order to do "municipal housekeeping" – an appropriately domestic metaphor for social and political reform.

32 He comes close, however, when he warns (on p. 7) that participation in the suffrage movement will "cause *the essential superior power of the woman over the man* to diminish," and, conversely, when he says (p. 15) that a "real woman" knows "precisely how to arouse a current of *more powerful* life, than that over which the man rules with his iron will, his probing thinking, and his powerful arm" (my emphases).

creationally "different but equal" moral sentiments in men and women (see especially pp. 29–30), in a way that reflects (even as it adapts to neo-Calvinist categories) the general thinking of the times.

Historians who label this "separate spheres" thinking "cultic" usually do so in order to pass negative judgment on it, for they see the "cult of true womanhood" as not only restricting the scope of women's activities but also degrading their economic status in the family relative to earlier times. This conclusion, however, may be too simple, for in bequeathing women a superior morality (or, in Kuyper's case, a "different but equal" one) many apologists for the "two spheres" doctrine did aim at elevating women's status, both materially and psychologically. Materially, by confining women's attentions to the home, they removed them from the heavy outdoor labor common to pre-industrial and also many industrial settings. And psychologically, in historian Carl Degler's words, within the home women did gain a new recognition, and in the process broke the ancient hierarchy that had assigned superiority to men in all spheres of activity Domesticity, in short, was an alternative to patriarchy, both in intention and in fact. By asserting a companionate role for women, it implicitly denied patriarchy.[33]

Kuyper seems to share this kind of thinking, believing as he does that women are "elevated" to a "position of honor" in the home, and idealizing their role there in terms of almost mystical admiration. However, when he maintains that the "separate spheres" concept has remained constant throughout history (thus supporting his view that it reflects essential, virtually nonoverlapping gender roles), he is being ahistoric. One has only to go back a few generations, when farming families were the norm, to see a very different pattern, one in which fathers, mothers, and children all work together and in which sons, from a very early age, "learn by doing" from their fathers, as daughters do from mothers. Gender roles do exist in such settings (indeed, they could hardly be absent in a pre-industrial, labor-intensive situation), but the dichotomy is nowhere near as extreme as Kuyper describes.[34]

Indeed, it is perhaps significant that Kuyper ends his series with an appeal to the "still so lovely Housewife *from the Netherlands middle-class life*" (p. 30, my emphases), for the gender roles he is describing are an urban, middle-class, industrial-society phenomenon, quite foreign even to Dutch peasant life of the nineteenth century.[35] The standard of femininity Kuyper holds up as normative was economically available only to a minority – and then often at the expense of the working-class women Kuyper describes as having flocked to the cities in search of domestic work. It was the latter who relieved wealthier urban women of their routine domestic tasks, thus freeing them up to concentrate on being "angels of the home." One can only wonder how many rural and urban working-class Calvinist women (in addition to those of the middle and upper classes who felt drawn to public life) were made to feel inadequate by Kuyper's baptizing as transculturally normative what was actually a historically recent – and for many an economically

---

33 Degler, *At Odds*, 28.

34 See, e.g., Aries, Phillipe 1962. *Centuries of Childhood.* New York: Knopf; and Rotundo, E. Anthony 1987. "Patriarchs and Participants: A Historical Perspective on Fatherhood in the United States." In *Beyond Patriarchy: Essays by Men on Pleasure, Power and Change*, edited by Michael Kaufman. Toronto: Oxford University Press, 64–80. See also Carr, Anne and Mary Stewart Van Leeuwen, eds. 1996. *Religion, Feminism and the Family.* Philadelphia: Westminster/John Knox, especially ch. 4–7.

35 But see note 27 for a qualifier regarding the term translated as "middle-class life."

unattainable – mode of existence.[36]

Psychological considerations: are women and men that different?

With regard to his psychology of gender, one can hardly hold Kuyper accountable to the standards of a discipline that was still in its infancy when he wrote *De Eerepositie der Vrouw*. However, it is worth noting both that he has a sense of what psychology will later confirm about male-female differences, and that he uses this intuition in inconsistent ways.

Kuyper is clearly aware of what psychologists nowadays call "over-lapping bell curves" in the distribution of certain traits in men and women. For instance, when we say "men are taller than women," we clearly cannot mean that all men are taller than all women; we are talking only about an average difference. There are some women who are taller than some men, and even some men who are shorter than the average woman. Indeed, it turns out that the range of heights *within* each group (male or female) is much larger than the small average difference in height *between* the two groups.[37] The same is true of the (very few) psychological traits that show consistent gender variability. For example, at this point in time in North America, young females show slightly greater verbal ability than males, and males show a slight superiority to females in certain measures of spatial ability. But as with height differences, the distributions overlap so much that the range of scores within each sex is much greater than the small average difference between them.[38]

Throughout *De Eerepositie der Vrouw*, Kuyper uses his experiential awareness of such psychological realities quite selectively. When it is convenient to his argument, he treats what are only *average* sex differences (for example, in bodily strength, in aggressiveness) as evidence for absolute, God-ordained "natural" roles for all men and all women – in effect trying to argue from "what is" (or what he claims to be so – i.e., non-overlapping distinctions in men's and women's characteristics) to "what was creationally intended." On the other hand, when honesty compels him to acknowledge the existence of overlapping distributions of those same traits, he then argues from "what is" to "what must be changed." For example, the minority of women who "walk busily about in the public arena" (p. 24)

---

36 For an elaboration of this critique, see the following chapters of Van Leeuwen et al. *After Eden*: Koch, Margaret and Van Leeuwen, Mary Stewart "Feminism and Christian Vision: Lessons from the Past" (ch. 2); and Koch, Margaret "A Cross-Cultural Critique of Western Feminism" (ch. 4).

37 This, of course, makes it quite hard to talk about "essential" differences between the sexes. However, in spite of this overlap there is continuous social pressure to make the height distinction more neatly dichotomous. Women are supposed to marry men taller than themselves, and if by chance they don't (as in the case of Prince Charles and Princess Diana) they will be pressured to find ways to make it *seem* as if the man is taller: for example, the woman will wear flat shoes, or stand a step or two lower than the man when photographs are taken. The same applies to other traits: women are supposed to marry men who are not only taller than they, but who are older, richer, smarter, and stronger, in order to preserve the illusion of greater gender dichotomy than is in fact the case. Sociologist Jessie Bernard, in *The Future of Marriage* (New York: World Publishers, 1972), invokes the power of this ideology in order to account for data showing that never-married women are disproportionately highly intelligent and mentally healthy, while never-married men are disproportionately of lower than average intelligence and adjustment: members of each of these groups will obviously find it hard to "pair off" according to the dominant gender-relations norms for husbands and wives.

38 For a review of the pertinent literature, see Basow, Susan A. 1992. *Gender Stereotypes and Roles*, 3rd ed. Pacific Grove, CA: Brooks/Cole; or Lips, Hilary 1993. *Sex and Gender*, 2nd ed. Mountain View, CA: Mayfield.

are evidence of temporary necessity at best (because men are not marrying as they should) or a willful perversion of the creation order at worst. Either way, he writes, things should be changed to restore the proper assignment of men to public and women to domestic life.

Moreover, Kuyper continues to ignore historical and cross-cultural data in his attempt to essentialize absolute psychological differences between the sexes. For example, it is simply not the case that the life of the mind is always considered a badge of masculinity. In more labor intensive societies men who sit and discuss abstractions are often those whose masculinity is suspect. Nor is it the case, historically or cross culturally, that men always do harder physical work than women. On the contrary, hegemonic males often use their power to assign most of the necessary physical work to women (and/or to non-hegemonic males of other races or castes).[39] Although Kuyper shows some awareness of cross-cultural variability (e.g., in the gendering of dress, and in what constitutes female modesty – see p. 13) his attempt to reduce these to variations on the theme of women's natural sense of shame gives too little credit to the social construction of gender.[40]

The appeal to scripture: men, women, and the order of creation

From the standpoint of the Calvinist tradition, Kuyper's argument might have endured better (at least among Calvinists) if he had avoided appealing to history and experience and simply reiterated the standard Calvinist reading of gender relations. Unlike Augustine, Aquinas, and Luther (who held that women were inferior to men either by creation, as a result of the Fall, or both) Calvin saw woman as equal to man both in creation and in redemption. As much as man, she is created in the image of God, and no more than man is she responsible for the Fall of humankind. Nevertheless, according to Calvin, women are under men's authority because God has mandated certain creation orders – based neither on human sin nor human merit but simply as a matter of divine will for the smooth running of human society.

Such a reading of gender relations has the advantage of being less likely than earlier ones to slip into misogyny – although it has the disadvantage of seeming more arbitrary. In any event, if Kuyper had simply reasserted this reading as being more or less confessional, then that presumably would be the end of the matter, at least for most Calvinists. If women are under men's God-ordained authority, and if men do not want them in the public sphere, then they will simply have to stay away. Kuyper, however, is much less concerned in *De Eerepositie der Vrouw* to demonstrate the authority of men over women

---

39 See Connell, Robert W. 1987. *Gender and Power*. Stanford: Stanford University Press; MacCormack, Carol and Strathern, Marilyn, eds. 1980. *Nature, Culture and Gender*. New York: Cambridge University Press; and Sanday, Peggy Reeves 1980. *Female Power and Male Dominance: On the Origins of Sexual Inequality*. New York: Cambridge University Press. Note, too, the conclusion of a United Nations (1980) study: "Women constitute half the world's population, perform nearly two-thirds of its work hours, receive one-tenth of the world's income, and own less than one-hundredth of the world's property." For a detailed analysis of this statement, see Jacobson, Jodi 1992. *Gender Bias: Roadblock to Sustainable Development*, Worldwatch Paper, no. 110. Washington, D.C.: Worldwatch Institute.

40   It should also be noted that as gender-role flexibility has increased, average differences in those few traits and behaviors that have distinguished males from females in the industrialized West continue to shrink. (See Basow, *Gender Stereotypes and Roles* or Lips, *Sex and Gender* for a review of the pertinent literature.) This is clear evidence for the power of nurture to affect nature. Although this says nothing about the ethical normativity of such shifts, neither does it allow for an appeal to the historical constancy of psychological and behavioral gender differences as a reason for retaining a given dichotomy in gendered behavior.

per se than to show that the gendering of the public/private dichotomy is an unchanging scriptural theme, with all that this implies for the allocation of women's and men's roles. He does not, it seems, want to use the bludgeon of male authority to get women to stay at home, but rather, to show how Scripture gives women a "position of honor" there, and to persuade them that this is both a nobler and, in the end, a happier calling for them than seeking a permanent place in the public square. This is certainly in keeping with the wider nineteenth-century rhetoric about women's calling to be "angel of the home."[41]

But does Scripture consistently support such rhetoric? Only, it seems, by forcing anachronisms onto it. The very dichotomy between public and private life means very little in traditional hunting, herding, or agricultural societies where family members all work together and rarely leave home. This was very much the norm in Old Testament times, except among the elite. And while it is probably true that Jesus' critics were scandalized by the fact that women were among the disciples following him from place to place, Jesus takes their presence (and their right to sit at his feet and learn – recall Mark 10:38–42) entirely for granted.

But what is most curious about Kuyper's selective reading of Scripture is his bypassing of the scriptural passage that is the basis for the important neo-Calvinist idea of the "cultural mandate" – the idea that God placed humankind in the world to open up the potential latent in creation, and that this mandate is in no way changed by the Fall, but if anything, strengthened by the need to *reclaim* the world for God, restoring the rightful manner of unfolding to all spheres of created life.[42] I refer, of course, to Genesis 1:26–28:

> Then God said, "Let us make humankind in our image, according to our likeness; and let them have dominion over the fish of the sea, and over the birds of the air, and over the cattle, and over all the wild animals of the earth, and over every creeping thing that creeps upon the earth."
>
> So God created humankind in his image,
> In the image of God he created them;
> Male and female he created them.
>
> God blessed them, and God said to them, "Be fruitful and multiply, and fill the earth and subdue it; and have dominion over the fish of the sea and over the birds of the air and over every living thing that moves upon the earth." (NRSV)

Two aspects of the image of God embedded in this passage are *sociability* (implied in the mandate to form families together) and *dominion*. Together they made it possible

---

41 It is of interest that, once women's suffrage was granted, there was a similar appeal to women by some Christians to abstain on principle from what was theirs by law. For example, eleven years after women's suffrage became law in America, a well-known fundamentalist leader eulogized his late wife as "a woman who could never be induced to cast a vote at the polls" See Riley, William Bell 1931. "Mrs. W. B. Riley: In Memoriam." *Christian Fundamentalist* 5 (September): 99. Kuyper's descendants in the Christian Reformed Church in North America may have been more adaptable, as they decided in their 1918 Synod (two years *before* women's suffrage came to North America) that women's suffrage in the civic arena – as distinct from women voting in church congregational meetings – was not an ecclesiastical but merely a political question. In doing so, however, they dichotomized what was earlier seen as a unified principle of male family headship – and it is not clear how much moral pressure continued on women to stay away from the voting booth. See De Moor, Henry 1986. "Equipping the Saints: A Church Political Study of the Controversies Surrounding Ecclesiastical Office in the Christian Reformed Church in North America, 1857–1982." *Th.D. Diss.* John Calvin Academy, Kampen, Netherlands, ch. 8

42 See, e.g., Wolters, *Creation Regained*, 35–41.

for the first human beings to begin responding to the cultural mandate, as summarized by God's instructions – to *both* of them – to "be fruitful and multiply, and fill the earth and subdue it." But what Kuyper has done in *De Eerepositie der Vrouw*, in the process of affirming the cult of true womanhood, is to dichotomize the cultural mandate by gender. Women, he says in effect, are made to be fruitful and multiply, while men are made to subdue to earth. And ideally these tasks should not overlap.

I think we may give Kuyper the benefit of the doubt and assume that, like many of his contemporaries, he was convinced that women's status was being elevated by the doctrine of two spheres. Moreover, one cannot expect him (or anyone else) to have predicted all the consequences of such a dichotomy, including the progressively greater intellectual and social isolation of the women so domesticated, and their progressively greater economic dependence on men – which, in a later and less sentimental era, also made them more vulnerable to domestic violence.[43] Nor could he predict the consequences of effectively reducing *parenting* to *mothering* as fathers spent more and more of their time in the public sphere and, unlike their preindustrial forebears, hardly got to know their children.[44]

It is more difficult, however, to excuse Kuyper for the absolutist language with which he lards his defense of the doctrine of two spheres – thus strongly implying that anyone who ever disagrees with him will be guilty of defying God's will.[45] This leads me to some final comments on the implications of Kuyper's series of articles for Calvinists at the close of the twentieth century.

5. The Continuing Legacy of *De Eerepositie der Vrouw*

Kuyper's insistence (and persuasive demonstration) that all of life is religious – and the

---

43   The introduction of the "family wage" for male heads of households was also a mixed blessing. On the one hand, it helped justify taking women and children away from the exploitative industrial labor into which many had been drawn in the eighteenth and nineteenth centuries (a campaign in which Kuyper himself had been active earlier in his career). On the other hand, it also helped to justify the idea that every normal adult woman *should* have a husband making a family wage, and thus that women in the waged workforce were there at best temporarily, and at worst to take jobs away from men who needed them to support their families. This in turn helped to rationalize lower wages for women than for men, even for comparable work – a situation that persists in industrial and postindustrial countries to this day. See, e.g., Van Leeuwen et al., *After Eden*, chapters 15–16.

44   The feminist school of thought arising from the psychoanalytic tradition of object-relations theory links the entrenchment of male contempt for women to the fact that young boys, lacking a readily available male role model, grow up with a much more insecure sense of gender identity than girls do, and compensate for it by denigrating women and their activities, and by trying to contain them. When women are thus contained at home to raise children largely on their own, this perpetuates the cycle. See, e.g., Chodorow, Nancy 1988. *The Reproduction of Mothering: Psychoanalysis and the Sociology of Gender*. Berkeley: University of California Press; Osherson, Samuel 1986. *Finding Our Fathers*. New York: Fawcett; and for an empirical account of parents attempting to reverse this pattern, Ehrensaft, Diane 1990. *Parenting Together: Men and Women Sharing the Care of Their Children*. Urbana: University of Illinois Press. See also Van Leeuwen, Mary Stewart 1990. *Gender and Grace: Love, Work and Parenting in a Changing World*. Downers Grove: InterVarsity, ch. 7–10.

45   James Bratt evaluates Kuyper's rhetoric as follows: "An uneasiness arises in reading [Kuyper's works], a disappointment all the keener for their having come so close to greatness. Critical genius, passionate logic, spiritual depth, social sympathy, expansive architecture, wit, satire and hope flood his pages, all encumbered with exaggeration and pomposity, cheap shots and quick generalization. Kuyper was a polemicist who little bothered to control his bias and never used two words where three would do." (See Bratt, "Abraham Kuyper's Public Career," 11).

related notions of antithesis, common grace, sphere sovereignty and the cultural mandate – makes for a very potent theological mix. It provides tools both to affirm and criticize one's own nation, culture, or discipline and suggests ways to restructure various societal activities so that they function and interact in a more balanced and just fashion.

Small wonder, then, that for generations after Kuyper's death "the Reformed would define themselves by the selections they made from his system or by their agreement or disagreement with that system as a whole." Hence also "the remarkable . . . scope of Reformed ambition among [neo-Calvinism's] enthusiastic adherents, and their passion for making deep study and bold pronouncements about almost everything on earth . . . [as they set out to] apply Calvinistic principles to every sphere of life."[46]

However, it would be less than honest not point out that Christian *women* activists and academics have historically been relegated to the fringes of the neo-Calvinist movement and continue to be to this day.[47] And one is bound to wonder just how much of Kuyper's legacy accounts for this. True, it could have been worse: Among the descendants of neo-Calvinists there has not been created a "gender *Apartheid*" of parallel stubbornness and damage to the racial *Apartheid* of South Africa.[48] But when reading *De Eerepositie der Vrouw*, one does get the impression that it was a near miss, for what is both exciting and frightening about Kuyperian thought is its thoroughly systematic character. Often described as a species of latter-day Plato, Kuyper placed great confidence in the possibility of elaborating complex thought-systems from fixed principles. Indeed, it is the intellectual sophistication and universal scope of the resulting Christian philosophy that makes it so attractive to intelligent believers frustrated by the separation of nature from grace that too often characterizes other Christian traditions.

But what if one gets some of those first principles wrong? What if one carves up the creational spheres in a mistaken way, for example by designating race or gender as a separate sphere that must be *kept* separate according to principles that are less biblical than they are reflective of a particular, culturally-specific ideology? Then it is clear that great mischief can be done, especially if the writer has both the intellectual brilliance and the community stature to invoke (however selectively) God, history, and statistics to buttress his case, as Kuyper does in *De Eerepositie der Vrouw*.

---

46 Bratt, *Dutch Calvinism*, 31–32.

47 One might try to argue that the Christian school movement has been an exception to this tendency to marginalize women. Yet here, too, women function disproportionately in the lower ranks – as mothers donating much of their time to fundraising and other auxiliary activities, as teachers – but rarely as principals or Christian college professors. For example, a survey of the *C.S.I. Bulletin* (the yearbook of the North American Christian Schools International) shows that in 1923, 19 percent of C.S.I. principals were female. By 1989, this had risen to only 20 percent. Similarly, at Calvin College in 1990 the ratio of women students to women faculty was 51:1, while the ratio of male students to male faculty was 10:1, with women faculty showing a higher turnover than men and a greater concentration in the lower teaching ranks. In both respects the college lags well behind comparable independent liberal arts colleges. (*Calvin College Gender Concerns Task Force Report* [December 1991], 8, 15, 16.)

48 There has been more damage than many have suspected, though. For example, a 1990 survey of the Christian Reformed Church in North America found that the reported prevalence of physical, sexual, and emotional abuse was within the same range as typically found in surveys of the more general North American population. Abusers were reported to be overwhelmingly adult males, and victims mainly women and children (parallel to studies of the more general population). For a detailed summary of this study, see "Report of the Committee to Study Physical, Emotional, and Sexual Abuse" *Agenda for Synod of the Christian Reformed Church in North America* (1992), 313–58.

What is both fascinating and alarming about Kuyper's articles on women is the certainty he exudes about the rightness of his analysis, and the degree to which he elaborates his convictions about the proper place of women.[49] For example, he speaks not just about the rightful parameters of gendered public and private life per se but of "fringe domains" in which women can legitimately appear, "temporary domains" in which they can appear as the lesser of two evils, and invokes a complex psychology of gender that is held up as the eternal model for Christian women and men alike. The result is a system with alarmingly totalitarian overtones, reminiscent at times of the gradations of racial purity elaborated (and relentlessly applied) both by the Nazis and by Calvinist-descended Afrikaners.[50]

To compound the tragedy, even those most damaged by this misplaced labeling of spheres may begin to support it. One of the most disturbing examples of this is the apparent indifference over the years of most Afrikaner women to the injustice of *Apartheid*. As late as 1986, Potchefstroom University political scientist Elaine Botha (one of very few women descendants of neo-Calvinism to gain international recognition) described them in the following terms:

> What is comes down to is that [Afrikaner] women are so accustomed to the idea of men taking leadership that they never learn to think for themselves. In a society so conscious of Scripture, they have been taught that this is biblical. On the whole, I don't think Afrikaner women understand the implications of *Apartheid* or think much about it. We have produced a race of women in blinders.[51]

There is, however, another possible – and more flexible – reading of Kuyper's position. South African church historian P. J. Strauss has shown that although Kuyper supported the informal *Apartheid* of his era, he saw it as a time-bound measure, aimed at the upliftment and development of native South Africans, and thus probably would not have supported the theory of closed and permanent *Apartheid* defended by his Calvinistic descendants.[52] So too, it is possible that Kuyper, in his defense of women's entry into certain quasi-domestic public institutions (education, social work, nursing) may have been expressing residual

---

49   Again, the parallel with the Afrikaner defense of racial *Apartheid* should not be missed. As late as 1970, the moderator of the Cape district's Nederduitse Gereformeerde Kerk in South Africa wrote as follows: "Our only guide is the Bible. Our policy and outlook on life are based on the Bible. We firmly believe the way we interpret it is right. We will not budge one inch from our interpretation to satisfy anyone in South Africa or abroad. The world may differ from our interpretation. This will not influence us. The world may be wrong. We are right and will continue to follow the way the Bible teaches." Quoted in de Gruchy and Villa-Vicencio, *Apartheid Is a Heresy*, 59.

50   Although the majority of Dutch Gereformeerde church members opposed the Nazis during World War II (and many risked or lost their lives working in the underground to save Jews from destruction) Kuyper's own son, Professor H. H. Kuyper, was a noted right-winger who not only supported Afrikaner nationalism and color racism but eventually became a wartime Nazi collaborator in the Netherlands. Kuyper's grandson died fighting with the German S.S. on the Russian front in World War II, and one of Kuyper's own protégées, Professor Hugo Visscher, became an advisor to the Dutch Nazi party in 1937. The design and elaboration of sphere sovereignty can thus work either toward greater justice (if the spheres are rightly understood and protected) or toward tremendous injustice (if they are wrongly set up to begin with). See especially Bloomberg, *Christian Nationalism*, chapter 1.

51   Botha, Elaine 1986. "Voices from a Troubled Land." *Christianity Today* 30 (November 21): 8 (in a special insert on South Africa). For an account of an encouraging exception see Van Leeuwen, Mary Stewart 1989. "Sticking a Needle in *Apartheid*." *Christianity Today* 33 (March 17): 13.

52   Strauss, "Abraham Kuyper, Apartheid, and Reformed Churches in South Africa in Their Support of Apartheid."

ambivalence about the absolute character of the gendered public-private dichotomy.

This possibility is strengthened by the fact that he sees no problem with women's involvement with public art and musical activities (p. 25 – although, admittedly, because he sees these as "fundamentally dealing with the more feminine side"), takes for granted their office-bearing activity as deacons in the church (pp. 23, 24, and 26), and sees no contradiction in having a Dutch female monarch for whom, in fact, "the woman's position of honor is even heightened, thanks to a quiet devotion to duty" (p. 25). Thus, it is possible (as with the development of *Apartheid)* that Kuyper's Calvinistic descendants have read him to be less flexible on the gendering of the public-private dichotomy than he actually would have been, had he survived for several more decades.

In either case, we need to consider possible antidotes to the lingering effect of Kuyper's writings (or others' interpretations of them) on women among his Calvinist descendants. Part of the solution is, of course, historical awareness; recognizing the extent to which Kuyper participated in what were in fact local patterns of thought during his time, regarding both race and gender issues. But another part is the cultivation of an empathic ear – that is, the willingness to listen to marginal groups within one's own constituency, rather than authoritatively speaking for them at every turn. In his 1987 talks to new faculty at Calvin College, philosopher Nicholas Wolterstorff put it well when he noted that in the past this Calvinist institution did its best to *assimilate* those who were not white, not Dutch-American, not Reformed, and not male. In the future, he continued, what is called for instead is *dialogue* – a genuine encounter or conversation:

> We must allow our whiteness, our Dutch-American ethnicity, our Christian Reformedness, our maleness, to become legitimate topics of conversation; and we must genuinely listen to those who find these traits odd or oppressive. I say, we must *listen* to such people, not try to talk them down. I recognize that to do this is to take a step into the unknown. One can predict the outcome of assimilation. The outcome of an encountering dialogue one cannot predict. For in dialogue, each learns from the other.[53]

Moreover, to those in his audience who were not white, Dutch-American, Reformed, or male, Wolterstorff had this to say: "Treasure what you are. Do not let us humiliate or overwhelm you. You have something precious to bring to us and to this tradition. Have the courage to keep putting before us the gift that you bear in your own person."[54]

No woman could have said it better.

---

53 Wolterstorff, Nicholas 1989. "Keeping the Faith: Talks to New Faculty at Calvin College." *Occasional Papers from Calvin College* 7 (February): 21.

54 Ibid., 21.

31

Kuyper's Legacy and Multiculturalism: Gender in his Conception of Democracy and Sphere Sovereignty

Hillie J. van de Streek

In February 1998, Princeton Theological Seminary hosted a conference to celebrate the legacy of Dutch theologian Abraham Kuyper (1837–1920). Celebration turned to criticism when one of the keynote speakers, Yale philosopher Nicholas Wolterstorff, stated that Kuyper's notions of race and gender, not to mention his extreme patriotism, were "shameful." In response to Wolterstorff and further associations of Kuyper with discrimination and oppression, Princeton conferees passed the following resolution (nearly unanimously):

> We, participants in the 1998 Kuyper Conference held at Princeton Theological Seminary, regard the legacy of Abraham Kuyper as a rich resource for Christian reflection and cultural engagement today. However, we profoundly regret the limitation and shameful distortions of the Gospel present in aspects of Kuyper's writings. In particular, we acknowledge that Kuyper's understanding of race and ethnicity, gender and sex have resulted in much pain and suffering.
>
> In prayerful dependence on God, we commit ourselves, in working with the Kuyperian legacy, to redress these wrongs, and to engage in our academic and cultural callings in the spirit of the message and ministry of reconciliation which we share in Jesus Christ (2 Corinthians 5).

Peter Schuurman, who reported about the resolution in the *Christian Courier*, concluded that the resolution would mean a great deal to those who have been hurt. "It will allow for dialogue in the future," he wrote, "and short-sighted aspects of the Kuyperian legacy will be given their proper historical place."[1] The dialogue he referred to began in the *Courier*'s same edition. Editor Bert Witvoet commented that he had never felt personally attacked by anything Kuyper had ever said or written. "Frankly," he wrote, "I am not aware of his understanding of sex, for example, but I can imagine that Kuyper was a man of his time. The distortions of the gospel present in Kuyper's writings were distortions shared by the whole Christianized Western world."[2]

In his quick historical analysis, however, Witvoet is wrong: Kuyper's perspective on gender was not shared by the whole Christianized world of his day; rather, it was highly

---

1 Schuurman, Peter 1998. "Profound regrets voiced about Kuyper's prejudices." *Christian Courier* 13 March: 2.
2 Witvoet, Bert 1998. "How profoundly do I regret Kuyper's limitations?" *Christian Courier* 13 March: 4.

debated. From about 1880 until the early 1920s, Christian circles were influenced by the so-called first feminist wave, when women in The Netherlands, as elsewhere in the western world, asked for equal access to all higher education and the labor market and demanded equal voting rights in politics and in the church. For example, in 1897 the Dutch Reformed Church began to debate the individual voting rights of women in the church and whether women could be ministers, using such passages as 1 Corinthians 14 and 1 Timothy 2. In 1902 its Synod rejected a proposal, with only ten votes against nine, that would have allowed women to become ministers, because it was considered not to be in accordance with the will of God. Twenty years later the Synod decided to give women the right to vote.[3] The debate on women as ministers in the Dutch Reformed Church was not reopened until the late 1950s and 1960s.

This paper focuses on the historical development of the Christian debate over gender issues. It continues the dialogue about Kuyper's view of gender begun at the Princeton Conference by comparing Kuyper's pluralism with late twentieth-century pluralism, now equated with multicultural- ism. In general, a pluralist society can be defined as a society consisting of several different minorities, based on certain cleavages in that society, like religion, ethnicity, politics, or social class. Kuyper had a similar view on society. In particular, his outlook was characterized by social justice and democracy, but also by the idea of sphere sovereignty, i.e., that society consists of several independent spheres of life, each with its own rights and duties. Kuyper's pluralism, however, is significantly different from present-day pluralism (or multiculturalism) in its treatment of gender. In this paper I elaborate on Kuyper's view of gender grounded in his pluralism, particularly within his conception of democracy and sphere sovereignty. I will develop the historical context referred to by Witvoet, then use this historical perspective to evaluate Kuyper's legacy, and compare his pluralism to late twentieth century multiculturalism.

Gender in Kuyper's Thought on Democracy

Dutch Orthodox Protestant ministers, rather than theologians or other scholars from abroad, were instrumental in formulating neo-Calvinist conceptions of women.[4] The neo-Calvinist approach to women's roles in society was thus generally nationalist (i.e., Dutch) in orientation. (In this it differed from the Catholic view on women developed in the same period by Pope Leo XIII, a view that had an international orientation.) Kuyper was the most influential of these Dutch pastors. After holding pastorates in several churches, Kuyper became interested in politics and engaged in political and theological controversies. He founded not only the Dutch Reformed Churches (GKN) and the Free University but also, in 1878, a neo-Calvinist political party, the Anti-Revolutionary Party (ARP).

As did Pope Leo XIII in his well-known encyclical *Rerum Novarum*, Kuyper made known his views on women in response to the social problems stemming from the Industrial Revolution. This Revolution changed people's lives significantly. Many peasants

---

3   Van de Streek, Hillie 1992. "De vrouw zwijgen in gemeente!? Een traditie van 19 eeuwen." In *Op Haar Plaats? 13 Vrouwen over hun positie in kerk en maatschappij*. Christelijk Studiecentrum ICS: Amsterdam, 55–64. The Gereformeerde Kerken in Nederland (GKN) started a discussion on women in the early 1920s shortly after Kuyper's death.

4   In this section I rely in part on Van de Streek, H. J., H.-M. Th. D. ten Napel, and R.S Zwart 1995. "Tegen de ordeningen Gods. Sekse en kiesrecht in de christelijke politiek." *Christelijke Politiek en Democratie*. SDU: Den Haag, 97–127.

emigrated from the countryside to industrial towns to become factory laborers. Working conditions there were bad. Laborers worked long days of 12 hours or more, often in less than healthy conditions. Women and children, too, worked long days to provide income for their family. Furthermore, housing was in short supply and of poor quality and there were no adequate healthcare facilities. Kuyper, Pope Leo XIII, and other so-called Christian-social reformers proposed that working days should be shortened, that the labor of women and children should be reduced, and that a man should earn an income on which he and his family could live. These ideas were inspired by the Bible. Kuyper also, on the basis of certain biblical texts, claimed that God had ordained family-life. A man had to be the head of the household and his wife was to be subject to him; a woman's proper place was in the family as wife and mother. This subordination of a woman to her husband made sense, according to Kuyper, because it imaged the subordination of the Church to Christ and of Christ to the Father (Ephesians 5).

Kuyper categorized life into two spheres: public and private. The public sphere concerned life outside the home, namely politics, science, labor, and the church. Men, Kuyper argued, possessed talents for participating in public life. Women's talents, in contrast, lay in the private sphere of life revolving around the family and the home. Hence, a woman's proper role was to raise children and perform domestic chores. By no means was a married woman to enter the political arena or the paid labor force. For Kuyper, the only acceptable activity for a woman outside the home was to serve as a volunteer in areas of social welfare, health care, and child rearing.

Kuyper elaborated on these views most extensively in *De Eerepositie der Vrouw* ("The Woman's Position of Honor"), published in 1914. (In 1906 he also published a book on *Women of the Old Testament.*) Especially his ideas from the publication from 1914 found political support in the ARP and a splinter group of this party, the Christian Historical Union (CHU).[5] These parties, along with the Catholic People's Party, were all based on Christian political thought. There were also parties based on secular political thought. Among these were the Social Democrats and several Liberal parties. Because the Christian parties were certain that they understood the mind of God concerning the nature and role of women, they labeled liberal, feminist, and socialist thought as anti-Christian and therefore dangerous. They worked hard to prevent society from developing in a secular direction.

Their first challenge arose in the first decade of the twentieth century, when the Dutch women's movement, the Liberals, and the Social Democrats began to campaign for universal suffrage. These groups argued that every individual, whether man or woman, should have the right to vote and be represented in parliament and in the provincial and municipal councils. Their stance compelled the Christian parties to formulate a stance on women as well.

From its beginning, the ARP opposed universal suffrage. They maintained, according to Kuyper's principle of sphere sovereignty, that society is organic in character and that it consists of several, rather independent spheres such as the church, family, labor unions,

---

5   In 1984, the ARP split into two parties; the old ARP headed by Kuyper, and a Christian Historical group led by Jhr. Mr A. F. de Savornin Lohman. In 1908 the Christian Historians established the Christian Historical Union (CHU). In 1980 the Catholic People's Party (KVP), ARP, and CHU merged to form the Christian Democratic Appeal (CDA).

politics, and so on. The ARP believed that the family was the nucleus of society, its most elemental sphere, and that the country would be at risk if the family was not respected and protected by legislation. Adopting universal suffrage would encourage individualism and deny the communal basis of the family. Kuyper therefore proposed that the head of the family should cast a vote for the entire household. This stance, "householder's suffrage," meant that all married men would be granted suffrage, as would all men living on their own. Kuyper asserted that the Bible clearly showed that women (and children) were not to be given the right to vote. When God declared in Genesis 2:18, "It is not good for the man to be alone. I will make a helper suitable for him," he was ordaining the subordination of women to men. It was a pre-fall, creation ordinance.

The ARP could not reach a consensus on whether a widow should have a vote as replacement of a deceased male head of the family. Most party members did not want any woman to have suffrage; they argued that, according to the Holy Bible, a woman belonged in the private, not public, domain. Kuyper, however, stressed the argument that a widow must replace her husband as head of the family, a role that carried over into the public domain. Kuyper eventually prevailed. In its renewed program of basic principles of 1916, the ARP denied women individual suffrage but allowed widows the right to vote as a logical consequence of the principle of "householder's suffrage."

The Christian Historical Union generally agreed with Kuyper and the ARP that one (male) vote per household was sufficient. Gradually, however, another view gained support. A minority of liberally-minded Christian Historians stressed that women, too, had an individual political responsibility, even though their first place of course was in the home. They claimed that no Bible text prohibited women from casting votes or taking up seats in parliament and the lower councils. Moreover, they argued, had not the Apostle Paul in Galatians 3:28 emphasized that there is neither male nor female, that all are one in Christ? Why, then, should man make a distinction where Christ did not? The CHU remained divided on this issue.

Kuyper Meets Critique: Herman Bavinck

In 1917, shortly after the renewal of the ARP's program of basic principles, an argument similar to that held in the CHU unexpectedly took root within Kuyper's party. The critique originated from Dr. Herman Bavinck, a Kuyperian theologian with nearly as renowned a reputation as Kuyper. Bavinck publicly disagreed with Kuyper over whether the subordination of women to men was creationally ordained. He focused on Genesis 1:27 – not Genesis 2:18 – as the basis for a biblical perspective on gender: "So God created man in his own image, in the image of God he created him; male and female he created them." Bavinck inferred from this verse that God ordained man and woman to be equal and asserted that this pre-fall creation ordinance must guide all aspects of life. He concluded that since the Bible did not directly reject women's voting rights, the ARP's decision on the matter could take into account non-biblical factors such as the modernization of society and the changing roles of women. Even with the Bible in hand, Bavinck said that he could agree wholeheartedly with universal suffrage. He commented further that he expected female participants to enrich politics by adding new, "female" insights.[6]

---

6   Bavinck, Herman 1916. First Chamber of the States General. In Kan, J. B. 1916. *Handelingen over de Herziening de Grondwet* III. 's-Gravenhage, 102–105.

Kuyper was furious. In *De Standaard*, the neo-Calvinist daily newspaper, he openly accused Bavinck of being a traitor of the ARP's basic principles. Kuyper reinterpreted one by one each Bible text Bavinck had mentioned in order to show that Bavinck was wrong. The angry editor ultimately concluded that the Bible did not contain a single passage from which the suffrage of women could be argued or justified and that Bavinck had been too much impressed by recent developments in society. Indeed, Kuyper argued, society was changing, but that did not mean that neo-Calvinists had to accept a situation that was deeply sinful in God's eyes. Claiming the correct theological analysis of the Bible, Kuyper rejected Bavinck's theological exegesis.[7] Bavinck reacted by publishing a monograph in 1918, *De Vrouw in de hedendaagsche maatschappij* (The Woman in Contemporary Society), a work of nearly 200 pages explaining his views. Any response Kuyper might have given was prevented by the illness that led to his death in 1920.

While Kuyper and Bavinck were debating the issue of gender roles, the Dutch government presented two bills concerning suffrage. In 1917 the Second Chamber debated whether to give women the right to stand for elections. The ARP unanimously stuck to the principle of householder's suffrage and opposed the legislation, but the CHU was still divided (although its majority preferred householder's suffrage). Because of this Christian dissension, not enough votes were mustered to prevent passage of the legislation on women's representation. Two years later the Chamber discussed giving women suffrage. Again the ARP was unanimously opposed and the CHU divided. Although Christian, the large Catholic caucus voted unanimously in favor of the bill for political reasons. The Liberals and Social-Democrats were also in favor, so the bill granting women suffrage was written in the Statute Book.

Although they did not enthusiastically encourage women to become politically involved, the Christian Historians and the Catholics grudgingly accepted universal suffrage. According to the ARP, however, revolution and godlessness had triumphed. Kuyper's party held onto the idea of householder's suffrage and continued to fiercely oppose the political involvement of women. In 1920 its members established a commission to advise the party whether it was scriptural to allow women to be nominated as candidates for parliamentary or the provincial and municipal councils. Within a year the commission reported that God had relegated women to a non-political domain and that they should not participate in politics. Subsequently, the ARP continued to refrain from nominating women. Only in 1953 did the heirs of Kuyper recall this decision. In 1963 the first Anti- Revolutionary woman took a seat in the Second Chamber.

From 1917 on, a Christian minority criticized Kuyper's understanding of women and supported Bavinck's interpretation of Scripture. Among Bavinck's supporters were J. Th. de Visser and J. C. Sikkel, both Kuyperian theologians, and C. Smeenk, a politician. A small, highly educated group of neo-Calvinist women was also inspired by Bavinck's arguments: among them A. M. Lindeboom-de Jong, a minister's wife; A. C. Diepenhorst-de Gaay Fortman, married to P. A. Diepenhorst, professor of Law at the Free University and Minister in several coalition-governments; the young teacher and journalist G. H. J. van der Molen, later to become professor of International Law at the Free University; and Johanna Breevoort, a writer. Although these women had once supported the concept of

---

7   Kuyper, Abraham 1916. "Het vrouwenkiesrecht voor Gods Woord." I, II, III *De Standard* 19, 20, and 21 June.

householder's suffrage, the majority decision of Parliament in 1919 caused them to rethink and be influenced by Bavinck's comments. They began to argue that women were wrongly withheld from societal positions for which some of them were exceptionally gifted. Their protests soon ceased, however, when they realized they would meet few or no supporters within the ARP. Although Bavinck's perspective remained a minority viewpoint within the ARP after his death in 1921, the voices of his supporters were not heard until after the second World War. Even after his death in 1920 Kuyper was surrounded by such a sacred glow of memory that serious criticism was prevented for the next thirty years.

What is Kuyper's Legacy?

Let me interject at this point that we have met here some people who to a certain extent might have been subjected to "pain and suffering," as the Princeton resolution put it, as a result of the controversy within the ARP about the right understanding of sex and gender: the neo-Calvinist women who started to protest the Kuyper-led decision of the ARP. These women were scarcely taken seriously. They were not Kuyperian theologians, so who were they to criticize Kuyper's views? In response, the women pointed to Bavinck, the only one on equal footing with Kuyper who presented an alternative still founded on more general, agreed-upon Kuyperian theology. These women felt ostracized by the ARP-decision to refrain from nominating women. From their weak protests, it becomes clear that they must have felt offended and humiliated by their party.

The question, however, is whether Kuyper is to be blamed for the "pain and suffering" of the women and whether the ostracism of women merits such a strong statement. Perhaps the issue was not what the Bible said but the character of the ARP itself. As indicated by the continual discussions within the ARP in the early 1920s, perhaps Kuyper's followers were simply too conservative to admit women into the public domain, regardless of what Kuyperian theology said about it. Furthermore, both Kuyper and Bavinck died shortly before the ARP began to discuss the gender issue in real depth. Even in the last years before their deaths they were physically unable to provide further guidance. Shortly before his death, Kuyper was asked for advice by H. Colijn, his successor as chair of the ARP. Colijn, struggling to hear Kuyper's labored speech, thought he heard Kuyper say that he had changed his mind concerning the right of women to be elected representatives. After all, he reasoned, the ARP believed the rule of a female monarch, Queen Wilhelmina (1898–1948), to be faithful to the Holy Scriptures. The ARP did not take into account this remark of a weak and failing 83-year-old man; rather, its leaders decided to support Kuyper as represented by his earlier thought and described most extensively in his "The Woman's Position of Honor" (1914). Bavinck's 1918 analysis of the issue was also put aside. Kuyper was canonized until the 1950s, at which time new theological research gave preference to Bavinck.[8]

Meanwhile, a younger generation of neo-Calvinist women was fighting to be accepted in the political realm. Among them were F. T. Diemer-Lindeboom, daughter of A. M. Lindeboom-de Jong who had a PhD in law and was married to a leading Kuyperian, and (again) G. H. J. van der Molen. In 1949 Lindeboom wrote a book, *Man en Vrouw in het*

---

8   *Rapport van de antirevolutionaire commissie inzake de verkiesbaarheid van der vrouw*, 1949. ARP: Den Haag z.j. [1952]); Hommes, N. J. 1951. *De Vrouw in de Kerk, Nieuwtestamentische Perspectieven*. Franeker; Huls, G. 1951. *De Dienst der Vrouw in de Kerk*. Baarn: Bosch en Keuning.

Volle Leven, in which she evaluated the 1921 decision of the ARP that women should not participate in politics. Lindeboom showed respect and understanding for Kuyper, Colijn, and other antirevolutionary leaders. She drew the conclusion, however, that traditionalism and conservatism rather than a thorough study of the Bible had been the main reasons for their decision to deny women the right to stand for elections. When the Bible is read from a Christocentric viewpoint, stressing texts from the New Testament and the meaning of Christ's resurrection, the opposite conclusion can be drawn. Men and women are each other's companion in every field of life, each gifted with personal talents. She stressed that there were antirevolutionary women gifted with political talents who felt a burning desire to spend all their energy and strength to work in politics as a servant for the Lord. She lamented that the ARP had closed that realm to women.

G. H. J. van der Molen was a woman to whom Lindeboom could have been referring. At the end of her life, in the 1950s, she was appointed professor in Law of the Nations at the Vrije Universiteit. She was interested in politics too, but the party, her party to which she belonged by conviction, had locked her out. She could not even stand for elections. In 1953 she spoke at the ARP meeting at which the decision of 1921 was undone. With tears in her eyes she told the audience she had been waiting for this decision for 32 years. During all these years her love for the ARP had not died, in spite of its position on women in politics. She rejoiced in the fact that the ARP had changed on this issue.

As a result of both theological study and female activism, the ARP in 1953 recalled the decision of 1921. Many women felt as if, after more than 30 years, justice had prevailed. From their point of view, one of the "shameful distortions of the Gospel present in aspects of Kuyper's writing" had been done away with. From their viewpoint, the words "pain and suffering" would not be too strong to qualify the struggles they endured within the party.

The Princeton Resolution with which we began does not clarify whose "pain and suffering" we are talking about or when it occurred. In the past? Today? For example, given what we have covered it becomes clear that talking about the pain of some of the ARP-women also means that we have to speak about the pain of other antirevolutionary party members in the 1950s. How many were there who considered Kuyper's exegesis to be truly biblical and therefore rejected Bavinck's views as not in accord with the Bible? A coin has two sides. More questions can be raised. Is Kuyper to blame for conclusions his heirs drew from his thought? In discussing the legacy of Kuyper, the Princeton Resolution fails to acknowledge many things.

We have seen that Kuyper's conception of democracy was highly gendered. Except for widows, women did not have the right to take part in the political democratic decision-making process. Men participated in politics as family representatives, as bearers of the (God-given) "rights of the family"; thus even the individual rights of men were tempered by responsibility to the family. We can conclude that Kuyper's pluralism is a pluralism without individual rights, certainly those of women. Kuyper fiercely rejected the French Revolution's goal to protect the individual rights of citizens, for individualism went counter to God's ordinances. Sovereignty belonged not to individual people but to God alone as Creator; humans in humble community were responsible to God and his commands.

Gender in Kuyperian Thought on Sphere Sovereignty

To consider the Kuyperian perspective on gender within the principle of sphere sovereignty, we focus briefly on the political debate over the right of married women to work outside the home.[9] This debate aroused strong feelings among Kuyperians between 1905 and 1960. A preliminary question was, which sphere should decide the issue: the state or the family (i.e., a man and his wife)? The heirs of Kuyper did not consider the option that individual women be allowed to make the decision for themselves.

In the early 1910s, Kuyper gave the task of developing a platform on this issue to E. J. Beumer, a high school teacher and future parliamentarian. Beumer concluded that the state should be allowed to decide whether married women could work, because moral values were at stake.[10] In his eyes, women's entrance into the (modern, industrial) labor force was a negative development in the national morality. Adding it to the list of feminism, equality demands, and universal suffrage, Beumer claimed that women working outside the home presented one more danger to the family. To safeguard the family as the Christian foundation of society, the internal structure of the family had to be strengthened. According to the ARP's interpretation of Scripture, this implied that the woman should leave her job and return home to fulfill her proper role as wife and mother; the man must financially support his whole family. First stated in the ARP's election manifesto of 1922, the party aimed to restrict women's work outside the home. The ARP was supported by the conservative Catholic party, the RKSP, whose Catholic basis had led it to a similar policy.

In 1924 the Christian cabinet proposed a bill to limit the work of married women in government. This bill honored the goals of the Catholic and neo-Calvinist parties; it also helped the cabinet, struggling in an economic recession, to cut its administrative expenditures. The three Christian parties warmly welcomed the bill and voted unanimously in favor. The secular Social Democrats and Liberals, on the other hand, argued that the government had no right to interfere in the personal life of individuals or restrict the freedom of women. In a move to protect the equal rights of men and women, these parties united in a veto, but their minority position could not prevent the legislation from being passed. This marked the first successful step of the Christian parties to shape a gendered society corresponding to their religious ideas.

A Christian cabinet continued to preside in government, but the idea of restricting women in the labor force gained more support among the secular parties as the economic crisis deepened in 1929 and male unemployment increased. In the early 1930s a bill was passed so that, beginning in 1934, women were honorably dismissed from their teaching positions on the day they got married; their jobs were given to unemployed male teachers. Later the ARP, CHU, and RKSP united to pass another bill: on January 1, 1937, all married female teachers were dismissed. (Liberal and Social Democrats argued that this bill was unnecessary because they claimed that hardly any married women teachers remained after 1934.) Stimulated by increasing unemployment rates and convinced that they were acting upon Christian principles, the religious parties continued to fight for further legislation. They wanted to limit women's presence in the labor force to specific "female" jobs in areas of social welfare, health care, housework, and child-rearing. In 1935 a Christian-Liberal cabinet proposed a bill that allowed women to be excluded from office

9   For this part of my paper I rely on the fifth chapter of my PhD thesis on "Gender and Christian politics in the Netherlands, 1890–1960."

10 Beumer, E. J. 1910. *Het voorgestelde ontslag van vrouwelijke Rijksambtenaren en onderwijzeressen*. Utrecht: Ruys.

work, predominantly viewed as "male" work. This bill was not passed, because it turned out to be impossible to give a clear definition of which work was intended.

After the general elections of 1937, which were won by the RKSP and the ARP, the Catholics initiated a family politics. The newly formed Christian cabinet appointed the Catholic C. P. M. Romme as Minister of Social Affairs. The day after his inauguration he proposed a bill to discharge all married women from their jobs, except for housekeepers and domestic servants. Since the economic tide had turned for the better, Romme's proposal was motivated not by economic reasons but by the desire to give public voice to Catholic principles. The RKSP and the ARP welcomed the bill with enthusiasm, but the women's movement and employers' organizations offered strong opposition. The women's movement as well as the secular parties objected to the unequal treatment of women. Employers objected because women were cheap laborers (earning far less than men); farmers particularly feared that they would lose women workers essential during harvest time. Surprisingly, the CHU also opposed the bill. They agreed with Romme regarding the role of women in society, but they envisioned the economic problems that would arise if all women were denied work. They feared the crops would not be harvested in time and shopkeepers would get into financial trouble if they had to do away with the (unpaid) help of their wives and daughters. Another problem was how to police the bill across the nation. That would take too many law enforcement officials!

The CHU joined forces with the opposition, thereby denying the RKSP and the ARP a majority. Romme had to recall his proposal. After the Second World War, the Christian parties lost their strong position as the Social Democrats gained power. Also, a shortage of laborers relaxed earlier policies restricting women from working outside the home.

It was not until after the war that Kuyperians began to question the right of the state in this issue: should not the family – or even the woman herself – decide whether a woman should work? Until the late 1940s, Kuyperians did not consider the individual rights of women. They did not consider that a woman's rights might be violated by restricting her role by law to that of housewife and mother. They argued rather that laws of this kind liberated women from carrying a double burden – work in the home and work in society – and enabled them to dedicate themselves fully to the family where they truly belonged. Only after the United Nations Declaration of Human Rights was signed in 1948 did Kuyperians openly begin to recognize the weaknesses of their previous position.

Taking Kuyper's conceptions of sphere sovereignty and women's role in society as starting points, his followers had developed a labor-policy by which women were given a fixed role in society, namely that of housewife and mother in the family. Part of the policy was that it was the state that gave women their clearly defined role. Women were not allowed the individual freedom to choose their own roles, except within the limited sphere of the family. But things began to change and after 1950 the case for individual rights and equal treatment of men and women gained strength.

Kuyper's Pluralism and Present-day Multiculturalism

We have discussed Kuyper's influence on the gender debate in the Netherlands. Now we turn to a comparison of his pluralism with late twentieth-century multiculturalism. Based on Kuyper's conception of gender roles, we can make three distinctions.

First, Kuyper assigned men and women to different spheres, that is, men to the public sphere and women to the private.[11] Modern multiculturalism, on the contrary, rejects such assignments. It emphasizes instead such aspects as equality and proportional representation, or affirmative action, to guarantee that the voices of "minorities" are heard in the dominant societal groups.[12] It strives not to assign people to different spheres but rather to integrate and represent all people in all areas of society without obliterating their individual identities.

Second, Kuyper rejected the concept of individual political rights for men and women alike. According to the principle of householder's suffrage, political rights were given to the family as a whole. Men were required to represent their households and as such they were given political voice. Women, except widows, were not allowed to speak up for themselves or for the family in the public domain. In contrast, individual rights form the basis for present-day multiculturalism. Equal treatment regardless of gender and sex or of race and ethnicity has become a sacred value. Ever since the Declaration of Human Rights was signed by the United Nations in 1948, the momentum has changed into the direction of a positive appreciation of individual rights.

Third, in certain circumstances, as the Christian labor-policy of the 1920s and 1930s indicates, Kuyper's followers believed that it was within their neo-Calvinist convictions to make use of the state as a (God given) instrument to remodel family life into the direction Kuyper thought to be in accordance with the Bible. So, the state confined married women to their believed-appropriate sphere, forbidding them to enter the labor market.

Compared with multiculturalism this would mean that the state could impose certain political measures upon certain groups of people in society on the basis of religious arguments. Unlike the in 1930s, few people in today's secularized Dutch society would accept this political platform.

The above points demonstrate why Kuyper's pluralism cannot be equated with multiculturalism. Kuyper's ideal pluralist society would have looked quite different from an ideal multicultural society of the late twentieth century. It is difficult to say, however, whether it is good or bad that Kuyper's pluralism differs from multiculturalism. We have to take into account the time period and the societal structures in which Kuyper came to his thought and that are quite different from our individualistic postmodern era. Kuyper formulated a response to the societal problems of his days. Present-day society has to deal with aspects Kuyper could not even think of, for example, issues of equal rights, race and ethnicity, and gender and sex. Thus, in the first place, Kuyper has to be evaluated as a historical person who was a child of his days. There are certain central elements in Kuyper's thinking, however, that can make a positive contribution in current debates. Most important of these, as I see it, is his positive evaluation of a society that consists of minorities of whatever kind or structure. Kuyper not only was able to justify the existence of each of these but also to show their contribution towards a society in which social justice and mutual respect prevail. Kuyper's positive, pluralist view on society has kept its value. This constructive way of thinking can be helpful in answering the difficult questions of our multicultural society today.

---

11 Van Leeuwen, Mary Stewart 1998. Kuyper conference, Princeton, NJ, February 1998.

12 An example of this is the clamor that arose in the Dutch mass media and among feminists when the orthodox-Calvinist political party of the SGP in 1993 denied women the right to party membership on neo-Calvinist theological grounds.

A Bibliography of Works On/About Abraham Kuyper

Steve Bishop

1890s

Vanden Berge, Ebenezer 1898. "Dr. A. Kuyper." *Banner of Truth* 33 (October): 60.

de Savornin Lohman, Witsius H. 1898. "Dr. Abraham Kuyper." *The Presbyterian and Reformed Review* 9(36).

Minton, Henry Colin 1898. "Review of Kuyper's *Encyclopedia of Sacred Theology.*" *The Presbyterian and Reformed Review* 10: 677–685.

Hulst, John B. 1899. "Dr. Abraham Kuyper." *Banner of Truth* 34 (December): 86–87.

Warfield, Benjamin B. 1899. "Introductory note." In Kuyper, A. *Encyclopedia of Sacred Theology, Its Principles.* London: Hodder and Stoughton.

1900s

Warfield, Benjamin B. 1900. "Introductory note." In Kuyper, A. *The Work of the Holy Spirit.* Funk and Wagnalls.

Darling, Timothy G. 1901. "Review of *The Work of the Holy Spirit.*" *The Presbyterian and Reformed Review* 12: 499–506.

Beets, Henry 1902. "Dr. Abraham Kuyper; his life and principles [Parts 1–3]." *Banner of Truth* 36 (May): 170–174; (June): 186–188; (July): 10–13.

Beets, Henry 1904. "Dr. Abraham Kuyper." *Banner of Truth* 39: 65–68.

Beets, Henry 1907. "Dr. Abraham Kuyper." *Banner* 42 (October): 520–521.

1920s

Beets, Henry 1920. "Dr. Abraham Kuyper [Parts 1–3]." *Banner* 55 (January): 53; (December): 730–731; 746–748.

Beets, Henry 1921. The Calvinism of Dr. A. Kuyper – two publications of loving tribute to Dr. A. Kuyper. [Parts 1–4]." *Banner* 56 (February): 69, 100–101; (March): 164–165; (April): 229.

Tanis, Edward J. 1921. "An appreciation of Dr. A. Kuyper." *Banner* 56 (January): 9.

Van Lonkhuyzen, Jan 1921. Abraham Kuyper – a modern Calvinist." *The Princeton Theological Review* 19(1): 131–147.

Beets, Henry 1925. "Dr. A. Kuyper as seen through German and American eyes." *Banner of Truth* 39 (February): 26.

1930s

Kolfhaus, Wilhelm 1930. "The significance of Dr. Abraham Kuyper for Reformed theology." *The Evangelical Quarterly* 2: 302–312.

Sherda, Zacharias J. 1930. "Kuyper's Calvinism. Parts 1–3." *Banner* 65 (February): 28; (March): 225; (March): 249.

Kromminga, Diedrich Hinrich 1937. "Dr. Abraham Kuyper, Sr." *Banner* 72: 1012–1015.

Hendrik de Vries, John 1931. "Biographical note." In Kuyper, A. *Lectures on Calvinism.* Grand Rapids: Eerdmans, i–vii.

Bouma, Clarence 1937. "The centenary of Abraham Kuyper's birth, and honoring the memory of Kuyper." *Calvin Forum* 3: 51–52.

Bouma, Clarence 1937. "Abraham Kuyper: kingdom warrior and kingdom builder." *The Banner* 72: 1013–1014.

Berkhof, Louis 1937. "Dr. Kuyper and the revival of Calvinistic doctrine." *Calvin Forum* 3 (December): 104–106.

Kuiper, Henry J. 1937. "How Abraham Kuyper influenced our churches in America." *Banner* 72 (November): 966.

Kuiper, Henry J. 1937. "My acquaintance with Kuyper." *Banner* 72 (October): 966.

Noteboom, J. W. 1937. "Kuyper's significance for Christian politics." *Calvin Forum* 3: 88–90.

Tanis, Edward J. 1937. "Abraham Kuyper, Christian statesman." *Calvin Forum* 3 (October): 53–56.

Tanis, Edward J. 1937. "Kuyper's centenary." *Banner* 72 (December): 2.

Vanden Berg, Frank 1937. "Dr. Abraham Kuyper." *Young Calvinist* 18 (November): 3–5.

Van Til, Cornelius 1937. "Reflections on Dr. A Kuyper." *Banner* 72 (December): 1187.

Volbeda, Samuel 1937. "Dr. Abraham Kuyper as a churchman." *Calvin Forum* 3 (November): 85–88.

Vogel, Leroy 1937. "The political party of Abraham Kuyper." *Calvin Forum* 3 (October): 58–60.

Kuyper, L. J. 1939. *The Doctrine of Sin in the Old Testament with Special Consideration Given to the Position of Reformed Theologians in the Netherlands viz. A. Kuyper, H. Bavinck, G. Ch. Aalders.* New York: Union Theological Seminary.

1940s

Vanden Berg, Frank 1940. "The seven cities of Dr. Kuyper." *Christian Home and School* 19 (November): 9–10.

Van Til, Cornelius 1947. "Abraham Kuyper's doctrine of common grace." *Common Grace and the Gospel.* Nutley: Presbyterian and Reformed.

Van der Kroef, Justus M. 1948. "Abraham Kuyper and the rise of neo-Calvinism in the Netherlands." *Church History* 17(4): 316–334.

1950s

Jellema, Dirk W. 1950. "Abraham Kuyper: forgotten radical?" *Calvin Forum* 15 (April): 211.

Jellema, Dirk W. 1950. "Kuyper and the crisis of the West." *Banner* 85 (February): 156–157.

Rullmann, J. C. 1950. *Abraham Kuyper on Evolution.* Grand Rapids: Youth and Calvinism Group.

Stob, George 1950. "Abraham Kuyper on evolution [book review]." *Banner* 85 (September): 1075.

Rooy, Sidney H. 1956. "Kuyper vs. Warfield: an historical approach to the nature of apologetics." *STM Thesis,* Union Theological Seminary.

Jellema, Dirk W. 1957. "Abraham Kuyper's attack on liberalism." *Review of Politics* 19(4).

Jellema, Dirk W. 1958. "Kuyper's visit to America in 1898." *Michigan History* 42: 227–236.

Kuiper, Henry J. 1959. "Abraham Kuyper on inspiration. Parts 1–3." *Banner* 94 (8 May): 9; (29 May): 9; (12 June): 9.

Kuiper, Henry J. 1959. "Kuyper on the criticism of scripture." *Banner* 94 (19 June): 9.

Van Til, Henry R. 1959. "Abraham Kuyper: theologian of common grace." In *The Calvinistic Concept of Culture.* Nutley, Presbyterian and Reformed, ch. 8.

1960

Kuyper, Catherine M. E. 1960. "Abraham Kuyper: his early life and conversion." *International Reformed Bulletin* 3 (April 1960): 19–25. Also in *Calvin Forum* (1950) 16(4): 64–67.

Vanden Berg, F. 1960. *Abraham Kuyper.* Grand Rapids: Eerdmans.

1961

Hoekema, A. A. 1961. "Kuyper, Bavinck and infallibility." *Reformed Journal* 11: 18–22.

Witt, Cornelius 1961. "Abraham Kuyper." *Banner* 96 (May): 14.

1962

Runia, K. 1962. "Dr. Kuyper on . . . the outpouring of the Holy Spirit at Pentecost and later on." *Trowel and Sword* (May).

1965

Jellema, Dirk W. 1965. "Abraham Kuyper's answer to 'liberalism.'" *Reformed Journal* 15 (May/June): 10–14.

1966

De Jong, Peter 1966. "Kuyper on the American church scene." *Torch and Trumpet* 16 (September): 14–15.

1967

Ambler, Rex. 1967. "The Christian mind of Abraham Kuyper." In *Profitable for Doctrine and Reproof*. London: Puritan and Reformed Studies Conference.

1968

Mennega, Aaldert 1968. "Abraham Kuyper and evolutionism." *Banner* 103: 10.

1969

Vander Stelt, John C. 1969. "Christian Social action and sphere sovereignty." National Congress of the Christian Action Foundation, Dordt College (July).

1970

Faber, J. 1970. "The incarnation of the word." Translated by R. Koat first published in Dutch as "Kuyper over de Vleeswording des Woords." *The Canadian Reformed Magazine* 19 (December): 5–9.

1971

Langley, McKendree R. 1971. "Abraham Kuyper 1830–1875: How Kuyper broke the stronghold of humanism in Dutch politics, and the Christian principles of thoughtful action that lead him to do it." *Vanguard* (May/ June): 7–10, 22.
Mennega, Aaldert 1971. "Science, evolution, and Abraham Kuyper." *Outlook* 21 (September): 23–24.

1972

De Jong, Peter 1972. "The Bible and church doctrine." *The Outlook* 22: 8–9.
Star, Ring 1972. "Appeals to Kuyper for a literal Genesis." *Banner* 107 (March): 20.
Skillen, James W. 1972. "The political theory of the Dutch statesman, Abraham Kuyper (1837–1920)." *Master's Thesis*. Department of Political Science, Duke University.
Westra, John 1972. "Confessional political parties in the Netherlands, 1813–1949." *PhD Thesis*. University of Michigan.
Zuidema, S. U. 1972. "Common grace and Christian action in Abraham Kuyper." In *Communication and Confrontation*. Toronto: Wedge, 52–105.

1973

De Gaay Fortman, W. F. 1973. "Kuyper and the social problem." *Perspective Newsletter* 7: 12–15.
De Jong, Peter Y. 1973. "Comments on criticism of Dr. A. Kuyper." *Outlook* 23 (June): 10–11.
Nichols, Anthony H. 1973. "Abraham Kuyper: a summons to Christian vision in education." *Journal of Christian Education*, 16 (October): 78–94.
Vander Stelt, John 1973. "Kuyper's semi-mystical conception." *Philosophia Reformata* 38: 178–190.

1974

Zwaanstra, Henry 1974. "Abraham Kuyper's conception of the church." *Calvin Theological Journal* 9(2): 149–181.

1975

Fernhout, Harry 1975. "Man, faith, and religion in Bavinck, Kuyper, and Dooyeweerd." *M Phil Thesis*. Institute for Christian Studies.
Nichols, Anthony H. 1975. "The educational doctrines of Abraham Kuyper: an evaluation." *Journal of Christian Education* 18: 26–37.

1976

Lloyd Jones, D. Martyn 1976. "The French Revolution and after." *The Christian and the State in Revolutionary Times.* London: Westminster Conference, ch 6.

1978

Fernhout, Harry 1978. "Man, faith and religion in Bavinck, Kuyper and Dooyeweerd (I)–(III)." *Journal of Christian Scholarship.*

Vander Werff, Pieter H. 1978. "Kuyper no evolutionist." *Banner* 113 (August): 23–24.

1979

Langley, McKendree R. 1979. "The political spirituality of Abraham Kuyper." *International Reformed Bulletin* 76: 4ff.

Vander Werff, Pieter H. 1979. "Dr. Abraham Kuyper and evolutionism." *Banner* 114 (February): 23–24.

1980

Kuyper Newsletter 1(1) (January) 1980.
    Spykman, Gordon 1980. "A Kuyper logo." 2–3.
    McCarthy, Rockne J. 1980. "The Kuyperian tradition and mediating structures." 3–4.
    Mouw, Richard J. 1980. "Kuyper and South Africa." 6–7.
    Spykman, Gordon 1980. "Kuyper on political cartooning." 4–6.

Kuyper Newsletter 1(2) (June) 1980.
    Mouw, Richard 1980. "Our readership." 1–2.
    Spykman, Gordon 1980. "Flashbacks." 2–3.
    Jansen, John F. 1980. "A Kuyper vignette." 3–4.
    Brinks, Herb 1980. "Abraham Kuyper: it might have been." 4–5.
    Skillen, James W. 1980. "Kuyper on covenant and politics." 5–6.
    Jellema, Dirk W. 1980. "Martyn Lloyd Jones on Kuyper." 6–7.
    Jellema, Dirk W. 1980. "Evolutionism." 7.
    Jellema, Dirk W. 1980. "Bibliographical notes." 7–8.

Kuyper Newsletter 1(3) (December) 1980.
    Mouw, Richard J. 1980. "One hundred years of Kuyper's ARP." 1.
    Spykman, Gordon 1980. "The sly cartoon." 2–3.
    Voskuil, Louis J. 1980. "A note on Emile Boutmy." 3–4.
    Vander Weele, Steve J. 1980. "Kuyper's devotional works an overview." 4–5.
    McCarthy, Rockne J. 1980. "Kenneth McRae on societal pluralism." 5–6.
    McCarthy, Rockne J. 1980. "Sphere sovereignty – strategy or ideal?" 6.
    Jellema, Dirk J. 1980. "Bibliographical notes on materials in English." 7.

Lee, Francis Nigel 1980. "Abraham Kuyper and the rebirth of knowledge." The 1980 Commencement address Graham Bible College.

1981

De Jong, James A. 1981. "Henricus Beuker and *De Vrije Kerk* on Abraham Kuyper and the Free University." In *Building the House: Essays on Christian Education*, edited by James A. De Jong and Louis Y. Van Dyke. Sioux Center: Dordt College Press, 27–45.

Kuyper Newsletter 2(1) (April) 1981.
    Jellema, Dirk J. 1981. "Kuyper and Pierre Van Paasen." 1–2.
    Vander Weele, Steve J. 1981. "Encyclopedia of Sacred Theology." 3–4.
    McCarthy, Rockne J. 1981. "Kuyper and South Africa."4–5.
    Jellema, Dirk J. 1981. "Notes and queries." 5–6.

Jellema, Dirk J. 1981. "Bibliographical notes on materials in English." 6–7.

Kuyper Newsletter 2(2) (Winter) 1980–81
> Bolt, John 1981. "Kuyper and Herman Bavinck (1)." 1–2.
> Brinks, Herb 1981. "Kuyper in Michigan." 2–3.
> Spykman, Gordon 1981. "Fido with his bone." 4–5.
> De Jong, James 1981. "Henricus Beuker and Kuyper." 5.
> Carpenter, Joel 1981. "On Kuyper as evangelical leader." 6.
> Jellema, Dirk J. 1981. "Notes and queries." 6–7.
> Jellema, Dirk J. 1981. "Bibliographical notes on materials in English." 7.

Langley, McKendree R. 1981. "Creation and sphere sovereignty in historical perspective." *Pro Rege* 9: 12–22.
Seel, David John, Jr. 1981. "Critical comparison of Abraham Kuyper's and Klaas Schilder's views on the basis of Christian cultural responsibility." *Salt: Official Student Publication of Covenant Theological Seminary* 9(2) (Spring): 20–29.
Van Til, Nick 1981. "Calvinism and art (1)." *Pro Rege* 9(3): 10–20.

1982

Gaffin, Richard B. 1982. "Old Amsterdam and inerrancy." *Westminster Theological Journal* 44(2): 251–289.
Dooyeweerd, Herman 1982. "Dooyeweerd commemorates Kuyper." *Anakainosis* 5(1).
Monsma, Timothy Martin 1982. "Kuyper and Orange City." *Banner* 117 (June): 2, 4.
Van Schouwen, Cornelius J. 1982. "A. Kuyper on headship." *Outlook* 32: 24.

1983

Hexham, Irving 1983. "Christian politics according to Abraham Kuyper." *Crux* 11(1) (March): 2–7.
Vander Goot, Henry 1983. "Portraits of Kuyper." *Christian Renewal*, 1 (April): 2.

1984

Deenick, J. W. 1984. "Christocracy in Kuyper and Schilder (the theory and the practice of it)." *Reformed Theological Review* 43: 42–50.
Gousmett, Chris 1984. "Bavinck and Kuyper on creation and miracle." *Anakainosis* 7(1/2): 1–19.
Hexham, Irving 1984. "Abraham Kuyper." In *Evangelical Dictionary of Theology*, edited by Walter A. Ewell. Carlisle/Grand Rapids: Paternoster/Baker, 616.
Langley, McKendree R. 1984. *The Practice of Spirituality: Episodes in the Public Career of Abraham Kuyper*. Ontario: Paideia.
Tangelder, Johan D. 1984. "Abraham Kuyper (1837–1920) – the antithesis theologian." *Christian Renewal* 3 (November): 8.

1985

Praamsma, Louis 1985. *Let Christ be King: Reflections on the Life and Times of Abraham Kuyper*. Ontario: Paideia.

1986

De Jong, James A. 1986. "Abraham Kuyper's edition of the *Institutes*." *Calvin Theological Journal* 21(2): 231–232.
De Jong, Peter 1986. "1886 – a year to remember." *Mid-America Journal of Theology* 2: 7–52.
Praamsma, Louis 1986. "A great enterprise." *Christian Renewal* 5 (October).
Vander Hart, Mark D. 1986. "Abraham Kuyper and the theonomy debate." *Mid-America Journal of Theology* 2(1): 63–77.
Vander Kam, Henry 1986. "Some comments on Kuyper and common grace." *Mid-America Journal of Theology* 2(1): 53–62.

1987

Bratt, James D. 1987. "Abraham Kuyper's public career." *The Reformed Journal* 37(10): 9–12.

Bratt, James D. 1987. "Raging tumults of soul: the private life of Abraham Kuyper." *The Reformed Journal* 37(11): 9–13.

Bratt, James 1987. "Kuyper's legacy in North America." In *Abraham Kuyper: Zijn Volksdeel, Zijn Invloed*, edited by C. Augustijn, et al. Delft: Meinema.

Bratt, James D. 1987. "Abraham Kuyper: 150th birthday anniversary." *Origins* 5(2): 23–27.

Ericson, Edward E. 1987. "Abraham Kuyper: cultural critic." *Calvin Theological Journal* 22(2): 210–227.

De Jong, Peter Y. 1987. "1837– 1987: reflections on the 150th anniversary of the birth of Dr. Abraham Kuyper." *Mid-America Journal of Theology* 3(2): 196–217.

De Jong Peter Y. 1987. "Abraham Kuyper on Russia and the "Filioque" clause." *Mid-America Journal of Theology* 4(1): 54–82.

Pronk, C. 1987. "F. M. Ten Hoor: defender of Secession principles against Abraham Kuyper's Doleantie views." *Master of Theology Thesis*. Grand Rapids: Calvin Theological Seminary.

Schoffer, I. 1987. "Abraham Kuyper and the Jews." In *Veelvormig verleden: Zeventien studies in de vaderlandse geschiedenis*. Amsterdam: De Bataafsche Leeuw, 159–170.

Wintle, Michael J. 1987. *Pillars of Piety: Religion in the Netherlands in the Nineteenth Century, 1813–1901*, Hull: Hull University Press.

1988

Durand, J. 1988. "Church and State in South Africa: Karl Barth vs. Abraham Kuyper." In *On Reading Karl Barth in South Africa*, edited by C. Villa-Vicencio. Grand Rapids: Eerdmans, 121–138.

Morbey, Michael M. 1988. "Kuyper, Dooyeweerd, and the reformational vision: theosophy reformed." *Nuances* (online Journal now discontinued, 1988, 1995), online at <http://www.members.shaw.ca/aevum/Theosophy.pdf>

Hexham, Irving 1988. "Abraham Kuyper." In *New Dictionary of Theology*, edited by S. B. Ferguson and D. F. Wright. Leicester: IVP, 374–375.

Reformed Ecumenical Council's Theological Forum: "Abraham Kuyper: his international influence" 16(2) (June 1988):

  Velema, Willem Hendrik 1988. "Abraham Kuyper – born 150 years ago: a study in strengths and pitfalls." 9–14.

  Skillen, James 1988. "Kuyper was on time and ahead of his time: an essay on religion as a way of life and societal differentiation." 15–19.

  Smit, Kobus 1988. "Kuyper and African theology." 20–28.

  De Moor, Henry 1988. "Kuyper's imprints on the Christian Reformed Church in North America."

  Langley, McKendree 1988. "A sketch of Abraham Kuyper's life."

  Schrotenboer, Paul G. 1988. "Abraham Kuyper: his international influence."

  Van Dyke, Harry 1988. "Kuyper in post-war Canada: an interim inventory." 34–40.

1989

Begbie, Jeremy 1989. "Creation, Christ, and culture in Dutch neo-Calvinism." In *Christ in Our Place*, edited by Trevor A. Hart and Daniel P. Thirnell. Allison, PA: Pickwick Publications, 113–132.

Heslam, Peter 1989. "The Christianisation of the East Indies: the ideas of Abraham Kuyper on Dutch colonial policy." *Reflection: An International Reformed Review of Missiology* 2: 13–17.

1991

Begbie, Jeremy 1991. "Kuyper and Bavinck: art, beauty and the sovereignty of God." In *Voicing Creation's Praise*. Edinburgh: T & T Clark, ch 2.

Boer, Jan H. 1991. "Introduction." In *You Can Do Greater Things: Demons, Miracles, Healing and Science.* Translated by Jan H. Boer. Nigeria: Institute of Church and Society/ Northern Area Office (Christian Council of Nigeria).

Bratt, James D. 1991. "American culture and society: a century of Dutch–American assessment." In *The Dutch in North-America: Their Immigration and Cultural Continuity*, edited by Rob Kroes and Henk-Otto Neuschafer. Amsterdam: VU University Press, 369–390.

Godfrey, W. Robert 1991. "Kuyper and materialism." *Outlook* 41 (July/August): 17–18.

Heslam, Peter 1991. "The politics of Abraham Kuyper in historical perspective." *Christianity and History* 8: 9–12.

Klapwijk, J. 1991. "Antithesis and common grace." In *Bringing into Captivity Every Thought*, edited by J. Klapwijk, S. Griffioen and G. Groenewoud. Lanham: University Press of America, ch. 8, 169–90.

1992

Bratt, James 1992. "Kuyper, Abraham." In *The Encyclopedia of the Reformed Faith*, edited by D. K. McKim. Westminster/ John Knox Press.

Campbell-Jack, Walter Campbell 1992. "Grace without Christ? The doctrine of common grace in Dutch-American neo-Calvinism." *PhD Thesis*. University of Edinburgh.

Henderson, Roger D. 1992. "How Abraham Kuyper became a Kuyperian." *Christian Scholar's Review* 22: 22–35. [Reprinted in *Christianity and Society* 12(4) (2002); and in Kuyper, A. 2011. *The Problem of Poverty*. Sioux Center: Dordt College Press, Appendix.]

Monsma, Stephen 1992. "A transforming vision of life." *Modern Reformation* 1(4).

Ratzsch, Del 1992. "Abraham Kuyper's philosophy of science." *Calvin Theological Journal* 27: 277–303.

Rogers, R. E. L. 1992. *The Incarnation of the Antithesis: An introduction to the Educational Thought and Practice of Abraham Kuyper*. Durham: Pentland Press.

Strauss, Gideon 1992. "Abraham Kuyper – Christian cultural activist." *Many to Many* 2: 91ff.

1993

Kobes, Wayne A. 1993. "Sphere sovereignty and the university: theological foundations of Abraham Kuyper's view of the university and its role in society." *PhD Thesis*. Florida State University.

Heslam, Peter S. 1993. "Abraham Kuyper's lectures on Calvinism: an historical study." *D. Phil.* Oxford University.

Hiemstra, John L. 1993. "The role of worldviews in the politics of accommodation: a case study of Dutch broadcasting policy, 1919–1930." *PhD Thesis*. University of Calgary.

1994

McGoldrick, James Edward 1994. "Every Inch for Christ: Abraham Kuyper on the reform of the church." *Reformation & Revival Journal* Fall, 91–99.

1995

Chaplin, Jonathan P. 1995. "Abraham Kuyper." In *New Dictionary of Christian Ethics and Pastoral Theology*, edited by D. J. Atkinson and D. H. Field. Leicester: IVP.

Godfrey, W. Robert 1995. "Kuyper and politics." *Outlook* 45(2): 5–7.

Langley, McKendree R. 1995. "Emancipation and apologetics: the formation of Abraham Kuyper's Anti-Revolutionary Party in the Netherlands, 1872–1880." *PhD Thesis*. Westminster Theological Seminary.

Pronk, Cornelius 1995. "Neo-Calvinism." *Reformed Theological Journal* (November).

Strauss, Piet J. 1995. "Abraham Kuyper, apartheid and the Reformed Churches in South Africa." *Reformed Ecumenical Council Theological Forum* 23(1): 4–27.

1996

Bolt, John A. 1996. "Legacy of Abraham Kuyper." *Calvin Theological Journal* 31(1).

Bratt, James D. 1996. "In the shadow of Mt Kuyper: a survey of the field." *Calvin Theological Journal* 31(1): 51–66.

Bratt, James D. 1996. "The Dutch Neo-Calvinist tradition." In *Theological Education in Protestant Traditions*, edited by R. Albert Mohler, Jr., and D.G. Hart. Grand Rapids: Baker.

Bratt, James D. 1996. "Cross, crown, and Kuyper's legacy: response to Mark Noll." In *Adding Cross to Crown: The Political Significance of Christ's Passion*, edited by Luis E. Lugo. Grand Rapids: Baker.

Bratt, James D. 1996. "Abraham Kuyper, American history, and the tensions of Neo-Calvinism." In *Sharing the Reformed Tradition: The Dutch–North American Exchange, 1846–1996*, edited by George Harinck and Hans Krabbendam. Amsterdam: VU Uitgeverij.

Harnick, George and Krabbendam, Hans (editors). 1996. *Sharing the Reformed Tradition: The Dutch–North American Exchange, 1846–1996*. VU Studies on Protestant History.

Lugo, Luis E. 1996. *Adding Cross to Crown: The Political Significance of Christ's Passion*. Grand Rapids: Baker Books.

Petcher, Donald N. 1996. "What does it mean to be Kuyperian?" Covenant College address.

Tangelder, Johan D. 1996. "Review of *Incarnation of the Antithesis*." *Calvin Theological Journal* 31: 621–622.

Van Leeuwen, Mary Stuart. 1996. "Abraham Kuyper and the cult of true womanhood: an analysis of *De Eerepositie der Vrouw*." *Calvin Theological Journal* 31(1): 97–124.

1997

Bacote, Vincent 1997. "Called back to stewardship: recovering and developing Kuyper's cosmic pneumatology." *Journal for Christian Theological Research* 2(3).

Bratt, James D. 1997. "Abraham Kuyper, J. Gresham Machen, and the dynamics of Reformed anti-modernism." *Journal of Presbyterian History* 75(4) (Winter): 247–58.

Cromartie, Michael 1997. "*Nearer Unto God* – briefly noted." *First Things* (December).

1998

Calvin Theological Journal. 1998. 33(2)

   Bolt, John A. 1998. "Abraham Kuyper in context." 275–276.

   Harinck, George 1998. "Give us an American Abraham Kuyper: Dutch Calvinist reformed responses to the founding of the Westminster Theological Seminary in Philadelphia." 299–319.

   Haas, Gene. 1998. "Kuyper's legacy for Christian ethics." 320–349.

   Van Dyke, Harry 1998. "How Abraham Kuyper became a Christian Democrat." 420–435.

   Menninga, Clarence. 1998. "Critical reflections of Abraham Kuyper's *Evolutie* address." 435–443.

   Mouw, Richard J. 1998. "The seminary, the church, and the academy." 457–468.

   Van Dyke, Harry 1998. "Review of Bratt *Centennial Reader*." 490–493.

   Van Dyke, Harry 1998. "Review of Heslam *Creating a Christian Worldview*." 503–508.

Bolt, John 1998. "Abraham Kuyper and the Holland–America line of liberty." *Journals of Markets & Morality* 1 (1).

Dunahoo, Charles 1998. "Creating a Christian world view [book review]." *Outlook* 48: 9.

De Vries, John H. 1998. "Abraham Kuyper 1837–1920." *Christian Renewal* 16 (January): 14–16.

Edgar, William 1998. "Review of Heslam *Creating a Christian Worldview*." *Westminster Theological Journal* 60: 38.

Engelsma, David J. (editor). 1998. *Standard Bearer* 75(2)

   Hanko, Herman C. 1998. "Abraham Kuyper: a short biography."

   Cammenga, Ronald L. 1998. "The Doleantie."

   Dykstra, Russell J. 1998. "Abraham Kuyper and the union of 1892."

   Kamps, Marvin 1998. "The Son of God eternally our mediator."

   Terpstra, Charles J. 1998. "Abraham Kuyper, developer and promoter of common grace."

   Laning, James L. 1998. "Do we hold to Kuyper's view of presupposed regeneration?"

   Koole, Kenneth 1998. "Dr. Abraham Kuyper, politician: a critique."

   Engelsma, David 1998. "'Father Abraham': or, the indebtedness of the Protestant Reformed Churches to Abraham Kuyper."

   Engelsma, David 1998. "Review of Heslam *Creating a Christian Worldview*."

Hall, David W. 1998. "Review of Bratt's and Heslam's books on Abraham Kuyper." *Journals of Markets & Morality* 1(2).

Heslam, Peter S. 1998. "The meeting of the wellsprings: Kuyper and Warfield at Princeton." *Many-to-Many* 25 (Dec): 16–18.

Heslam, Peter S. 1998. *Creating a Christian Worldview: Abraham Kuyper's Lectures on Calvinism*. Grand Rapids:

Eerdmans.

Heslam, Peter S. 1998. "Faith and reason, Kuyper, Warfield and the shaping of the Evangelical mind." *Anvil* 15(4): 299–313.

Langley, McKendree R. 1998. "Looking back with Kuyper. [Part 1–3]." *Christian Renewal* 16 (January): 14–15; (February): 14–15.

Langley, McKendree R. 1998. "Kuyper legacy takes a beating at Princeton conference." *Christian Renewal*, 16 (April): 6.

Langley, McKendree R. 1998. "Kuyper's growing perspective. [Part 1 of 2]." *Christian Renewal* 17 (September): 14.

Lazarus, Stephen 1998. "Review: Kuyper's gift to modern Christians" [review of Heslam]. *Public Justice Report* (4th Quarter); also in *Many-to-Many* 28 (December 1998).

Maynard, Roy 1998. "Amsterdam unraveled." *Christian Renewal* 17 (December): 12–13.

Mouw, Richard J. 1998. "Abraham Kuyper: a man for this season." *Christianity Today* 42(12): 86–87.

Puchinger, G. 1998. *Abraham Kuyper, His Early Journey of Faith*, edited by George Harinck. Amsterdam.

Stockwell, Clinton 1998. "Abraham Kuyper and welfare reform: A reformed political perspective." *Pro Rege* 27: 1–15.

Strauss, Gideon 1998. "Not winking at the fierce licentiousness of kings: a personal response to Abraham's Kuyper's Stone Lectures on Calvinism and Politics." *Many-to-Many* 28 (December): 24–26.

Strauss, Gideon 1998. "*Creating a Christian Worldview*: Abraham Kuyper's Lectures on Calvinism." *Many-to-Many* 28 (December): 33–35.

Strauss, Gideon 1998. "Abraham Kuyper: *A Centennial Reader*." *Many-to-Many* 28 (December): 36.

Smit, Harvey Albert 1998. "Abraham Kuyper revisited." *Banner* 133 (June): 29.

Thomas, Geoffrey 1998. "Abraham Kuyper belittled in Princeton: The 1898 Stone lectures dismissed in the 1998 commemoration." *Banner of Truth* (Aug/Sept): 42–43.

Van de Streek, Hillie J. 1998. "Kuyper's legacy and multiculturalism: gender in his conception of democracy and sphere sovereignty." *Pro Rege* 27(1): 16–24.

Van der Walt, B. J. 1998. "Kuyper's philosophy of society." *Many-to-Many* 28 (December): 19–21, 40–41.

Van Dyke, Harry. 1998. "Abraham Kuyper 23 October–8 November 1920." *Many-to-Many* 28 (December): 7–8.

Van Dyke, Harry 1998. "Abraham Kuyper: heir of anti-revolutionary tradition." Paper presented at International conference "Christianity and Culture: The Heritage of Abraham Kuyper on Different Continents" held on 9–11 June, 1998. Free University, Amsterdam.

Venema, Cornelius, P. 1998–99. "Abraham Kuyper – his life and legacy. [Parts 1–6]." *Outlook* (Sept): 3–8; (Oct): 18–23; (Nov): 18–23; (Dec): 13–17; 1999 (Jan): 15–19; (Feb): 17–21.

1999

Bolt, John 1999. "Whose liberty? Which religion? Acton and Kuyper." *Religion & Liberty* 9(1).

Chung, Kwang-Duk 1999. *Ecclesiology and Social Ethics. A Comparative Study of the Social and Ethical Life of the Church in the views of Abraham Kuyper and Stanley Hauerwas*. Kampen: Van den Berg.

Godfrey, Robert W. 1999. "Neither individualism nor statism: Kuyper on Christian concern for laborers." *Modern Reformation* 8(3): 21–24.

Heslam, Peter S. 1999. "Architects of evangelical intellectual thought: Abraham Kuyper and Benjamin Warfield." *Themelios* 24(2) (Feb): 3–20.

Kamps, Marvin 1998. "The Son of God eternally our mediator (contd.)." *Standard Bearer* 75(3).

Knight, J. 1999. "Common grace according to Herman Bavinck and Abraham Kuyper." *Stromata* 40(2): 24–25

Langley, McKendree R. 1999. "Abraham Kuyper: a Christian worldview." *New Horizons* 20: 20–21.

Miller, Glenn T. 1999. "Review of Heslam Creating a Christian Worldview." *Church History* 68(2)(June): 479–481.

Miller, Glenn T. 1999. "Review of Bratt *Centennial Reader*." *Church History* 68(2)(June): 481.

Peck, John 1999. "Reviews of Heslam and Bratt." *Christianity and Society* 9(3): 28–29.

Sherratt, Timothy 1999. "Rehabilitating the State in America: Kuyper's overlooked contribution." *Christian Scholar's Review* 29(2): 323–346.

Strauss, D. F. M. 1999. "The viability of Kuyper's idea of Christian scholarship." *Journal for Christian Scholarship* (1–2): 125–139.

Strauss, Gideon 1999. "Not winking at the fierce licentiousness of kings: a personal response to Abraham's Kuyper's Stone Lectures on Calvinism and Politics." *The Big Picture* 1(2): 24–26; 2(3): 10–13.

Van der Kooi, Cees and de Bruijn, Jan (editors) 1999. *Kuyper Reconsidered. Aspects of his life and Work.* Amsterdam, VU Uitgeverij.

    Part I: Kuyper from a cultural historical point of view

        Heslam, Peter S. 1999. "A theology of the arts: Kuyper's ideas on art and religion."

        Bolt, J. 1999. "Abraham Kuyper as poet: another look at Kuyper's critique of the Enlightenment."

        De Bruijn, J. 1999. "Abraham Kuyper as a romantic."

        Bratt, James D. 1999. "Abraham Kuyper: Puritan, Victorian, modern."

        Kuiper, D. Th. 1999. "Groen and Kuyper on the racial issue."

    Part II: Kuyper's theology

        Van Egmond, A. 1999. "Kuyper's dogmatic theology."

        Van der Kooi, C. 1999. "A theology of culture: a critical appraisal of Kuyper's doctrine of common grace."

        Van der Schee, Willem 1999. "Kuyper's Archimedes' point."

        Brinkman, Martien E. 1999. "Kuyper's concept of the pluriformity of the church."

        Van Keulen, Dirk 1999. "The internal tension in Kuyper's doctrine of organic inspiration of scripture."

        Smit, Kobus. 1999. "Horse cheese has never been made: on the anthropology of Kuyper."

    Part III: Kuyper from a philosophical perspective

        Van Woudenberg, Rene 1999. "Abraham Kuyper on faith and science."

        Van den Brink, Gijsbert 1999. "Was Kuyper a Reformed epistemologist?"

        Inagaki, Hisakazu 1999. "Comparative study of the Kuyperian Palingenesis. The transcendent and human ego in Japanese thought."

    Part IV: Kuyper and pluralistic society

        Son Bong, Ho 1999. "Relevance of sphere sovereignty to Korean society."

        Wolterstorff, Nicholas 1999. "Abraham's Kuyper's model of a democratic polity for societies with a religiously diverse citizenry."

        Woldring, Henk E. S. 1999. "Kuyper's formal and comprehensive conceptions of democracy."

        Strauss, P. J. 1999. "Abraham Kuyper and pro-apartheid theologians in South Africa: the former misused by the latter?"

        Van der Walt, B. J. 1999. "Christian religion and society: the heritage of Abraham Kuyper for (South) Africa."

        Sturm, Johan and Miedema, Siebren 1999. "Kuyper's educational legacy: schooling for a pluralist society."

        Zondergeld, Gjalt R. 1999. "Against the uniformness of modern life! The influence of Kuyper's thought about a pluralist society on the Frisian language movement."

    Part V: Historiographical perspectives

        Adonis, J. C. 1999. "The role of Abraham Kuyper in South Africa: a critical historical evaluation."

        Harinck, George 1999. "A triumphal procession? The reception of Kuyper in the USA (1900–1940)."

        Hans-Martien ten Napel 1999. "The post-war ARP and Kuyper's legacy."

        Van Klinken, G. J. 1999. "Abraham Kuyper and the 'Jewish question.'"

        Vree, J. 1999. "More Pierson and Mesmer, and less Pietje Baltus. Kuyper's ideas on church, state, society and culture during the first years of his ministry (1863–1966)."

Witte, Jr., John 1999. "The biography and biology of liberty: Abraham Kuyper and the American experiment." *Koers* 64(2–3): 173ff.

2000

Bolt, John 2000. "Common grace, theonomy and civic good: the temptation of Calvinist politics (Reflections on the Third Point of the CRC Kalamazoo Synod, 1924)." *Calvin Theological Journal* 35(2): 205–237.

Faber, Riemer 2000. "Abraham Kuyper: two Reformers, and the church." *Christian Renewal* 19 (October): 18–19.

Harinck, George 2000. "Geerhardus Vos as introducer of Kuyper in America." In Hans Krabbendam and

Larry J. Wagenaar, *The Dutch–American Experience: Essays in Honor of Robert P. Swierenga*. Amsterdam, 242–262.

Kim, Juan Ok 2000. "The relevance of Abraham Kuyper's doctrine of sphere sovereignty for the Korean Presbyterian Church." *MTh dissertation*. Grand Rapids: Calvin Theological Seminary.

Lugo, Louis E. (editor). 2000. *Religion, Pluralism and Public Life, Abraham Kuyper's Legacy for the Twenty-First Century*. Grand Rapids: Eerdmans.

> Bratt, James D. 2000. "Abraham Kuyper: puritan, Victorian, modern."
> Heslam, Peter S. 2000. "The meeting of the wellsprings: Kuyper and Warfield at Princeton."
> de Bruijn, Jan 2000. "Calvinism and Romanticism: Abraham Kuyper as a Calvinist politician."
> Van Leeuwen, Mary Stewart "The carrot and the stick: Kuyper on gender, family, and class."
> Mouw, Richard J. 2000. "Some reflections on sphere sovereignty."
> Welker, Michael 2000. "Is theology in public discourse possible outside communities of faith?"
> Harris, Harriett 2000. "A diamond in the dark: Kuyper's doctrine of scripture."
> Bolt, John 2000. "Abraham Kuyper, Leo XIII, Walter Rauschenbusch, and the search for an American public theology."
> Woldring, Henk E. S. 2000. "Multiform responsibility and the revitalization of civil society."
> Storkey, Elaine 2000. "Sphere sovereignty and the Anglo–American tradition."
> Sigmund, Paul E. 2000. "Subsidiarity, solidarity, and liberation: alternative approaches in Catholic social thought."
> Botha, M. Elaine 2000. "Prospects for a Christian social philosophy in a shrinking world."
> Witte, John Jr. 2000. "The biography and the biology of liberty: Abraham Kuyper and the American experiment."
> Paris, Peter J. 2000. "The African and African–American understanding of our common humanity: a critique of Abraham Kuyper's anthropology."
> Abrams, Elliott 2000. "Living in Christendom: Jews and modern democracy."
> Thangaraj, M. Thomas 2000. " The clash of world religions in the emerging global society."
> Elazar, Daniel J. 2000. "Extending the covenant: federalism and constitutionalism in a global era."
> Goudzwaard, Bob 2000. "Globalization, regionalization, and sphere sovereignty."
> Botman, H. Russel 2000. "The legacy of Abraham Kuyper for Southern Africa."
> Skillen, James W. 2000. "Why Kuyper now?"

McGoldrick, James E. 2000. *God's Renaissance Man: Abraham Kuyper*. Darlington: Evangelical Press.

McCarthy, Mark 2000. "Kuyper and Bulgakov: Christian involvement in worldly affairs." *Contact: Newsletter of the International Association for the Promotion of Christian Higher Education* (Feb) Academic insert.

Tangler, John D. 2000. "Review of Lugo (editor). (2000)" <http://www.reformedreflections.ca/biography/abraham-kuypers-legacy.pdf>

Van Leeuwen, Mary Stewart 2000. "The signs of Kuyper's times." In *Women and the Future of the Family* (4th Kuyper Lecture 1998), edited by James W. Skillen and Michelle N. Voll. Grand Rapids: Baker.

Vree, Japser 2000. "The editions of John à Lasco's works, especially the *Opera Omnia* edition by Abraham Kuyper, in their historical context." *Dutch Review of Church History* 80(3): 309–26.

2001

Bolt, John 2001. *A Free Church, A Holy Nation*. Eerdmans: Grand Rapids.

Bolt, John 2001. "The 'culture war' in perspective: lessons from the career of Abraham Kuyper. The Witherspoon lecture [available online: http://www. frc.org/get.cfm?i-WT01G1

Harinck, George 2001. "Henry Dosker, between Albertus C. Van Raalte and Abraham Kuyper." *Origins, Historical Magazine of the Archives, Calvin College and Calvin Theological Seminary* 19(2): 34–41.

Hoekzema, Ray 2001. "Abraham Kuyper's legacy" [Review of Lugo]. *Trowel and Sword* (May).

Kamps, M. 2001. "Translator's introduction." In Kuyper, A. *Particular Grace: A Defense of God's Sovereignty in Salvation*, Grandville, MI: Reformed Free Publishing Association, vii–xx.

Kamps, M. 2001. "Appendix: Abraham Kuyper's distinction between grace and *gratie*." In Kuyper, A. *Particular Grace: A Defense of God's Sovereignty in Salvation*, Grandville, MI: Reformed Free Publishing Association, 353–356.

Kloosterman, Nelson D. 2001. "Review of Lugo, Luis E. *Religion, Pluralism, and Public Life: Abraham Kuyper's*

Legacy for the Twenty-First Century." *Mid-America Journal of Theology* 12.

Kuntz, J. J. 2001. "Kuyper's cartoonist." *Christian Renewal* 19 (March).

Langley, McKendree R. 2001. "Civil War: Kuyper's crusade for Christian schools 1869–1880." *Christian Renewal* 20 (September): 14–15.

Naugle, David. 2001. "The Lordship of Christ over all of life: an introduction to the thought of Abraham Kuyper." Paper presented at Dallas Baptist University 2 February 2001.

Skillen, James. 2001. "*E pluribus unum* and faith-based welfare reform: a Kuyperian moment for the church in God's world." *The Princeton Seminary Bulletin* 22(3): 285–305.

Stockwell, Clinton 2001. "Abraham Kuyper, common grace and the diversity of God's creation" Presentation to faculty and students of Dordt College March 12. Available online: http://chicagosemester.org/about/staff/articles_and_essays_clinton_stockwell/abraham_kuyper_common_grace_and_the_diversity_of_gods_creation

Van Geest, Fred 2001. "Review of Bolt." *Pro Rege* 29(4): 31–32.

Vorster, J. M. 2001. "Kuyper and apartheids theology in South Africa – another perspective." *Studia Historiae Ecclesiasticae* 27(2): 56–73.

Westendorp, John 2001. "Abraham Kuyper – A Centennial Anthology" review of Bratt. 1998): *Trowel and Sword.*

No author given. 2001. A Free Church, A Holy Nation: Abraham Kuyper's American Public Theology (Book review – Briefly noted). *First Things: A Monthly Journal of Religion & Public Life* (Oct) (116): 69.

2002

Proceedings of "A Century of Christian Social Teaching: The Legacy of Leo XIII and Abraham Kuyper." *Journal of Markets & Morality* 5(1) (Spring).

    Bolt, John 2002. "Calvinism, Catholicism, and the American experiment: what is the question?"

    Bratt, James D. 2002. "Passionate about the poor: the social attitudes of Abraham Kuyper."

    Goudzwaard, Bob 2002. "A response to Michael Novak's 'Human dignity, personal liberty.'"

    Griffioen, Sander 2002. "After Civil Religion."

    Hall, David W. 2002. "A response to Johan D. van der Vyver's 'The jurisprudential legacy of Abraham Kuyper and Leo XIII.'"

    Harinck, George 2002. "A historian's comment on the use of Abraham Kuyper's idea of sphere sovereignty."

    Heslam, Peter S. 2002. "Prophet of a third way: the shape of Kuyper's socio-political vision."

    Kennedy, James C. 2002. "The problem of Kuyper's legacy: the crisis of the Anti-Revolutionary Party in post-war Holland."

    Koyzis, David T. 2002. "Differentiated responsibility and the challenge of religious diversity."

    Noll, Mark A. 2002. "A century of Christian social teaching: the Legacy of Leo XII and Abraham Kuyper."

    Novak, Michael 2002. "Human dignity, personal liberty: themes from Abraham Kuyper and Leo XII."

    Van der Vyver, Johan D. 2002. "The jurisprudential legacy of Abraham Kuyper and Leo XIII."

    Wolterstorff, Nicholas 2002. "A response to Michael Novak's 'Human dignity, personal liberty.'"

Bacote, Vincent 2002. "The role of the Holy Spirit in creation and history with special reference to Abraham Kuyper." *Thesis Drew University.*

Berends, Bill 2002. "Abraham Kuyper and politics." *Trowel and Sword* (August).

Harinck, George 2002. "Abraham Kuyper, South Africa, and apartheid." Speech at the opening ceremony of the Abraham Kuyper Institute for Public Theology at Princeton Theological Seminary, *The Princeton Seminary Bulletin* 23(2): 184–187.

McConnel Timothy I. 2002. "Common grace or the antithesis? Toward a consistent understanding of Kuyper's 'sphere sovereignty.'" *Pro Rege* 31(1): 1–13.

Noll, Mark A. 2002. "Pope Leo XII and Abraham Kuyper." *Public Justice Report.*

Skillen, James 2002. "Review of John Bolt, *A Free Church, a Holy Nation: Abraham Kuyper's American Public Theology.*" *Calvin Theological Journal* 37(1): 135–138.

Spoul, R. C. Jr. and Ligonier Ministries 2002. "Abraham Kuyper: a man for all spheres." *Tabletalk* (October)
Sproul, R. C. 2002. "A free and lasting legacy: right now counts forever."

Beeke, Joel 2002. "Taking Every Thought Captive."
Pulliam, Russ 2002. "Setting a standard."
Hall, David 2002. "Life of the party."
Strevel, Chris 2002. "'Not one square inc. . . . ': A pastor's perspective."
Sproul Jr., R. C. 2002. "Unto the Lord: Coram Deo."
Bailey, Greg 2002. "Lectures on Calvinism: Tolle lege."
Wilson, Douglas 2002. "Courage and Kuyper: the cultural mind."

Van Drunen, David 2002. "Review of Bolt *A Free Church*." *Modern Reformation* 11(6).
Venema, Cornelius P. 2002. "Review of Bolt *A Free Church, A Holy Nation*." *Mid-America Journal of Theology* 13: 181–182.
Vollenhoven, Dirk H. Th. 2002. "Sphere sovereignty for Kuyper and for us." Translated by John H. Kok. In *Philosophy as Responsibility: A Celebration of Hendrik Hart's Contribution to the Discipline*, edited by Ronald A. Kuipers and Janet Catherina Wesselius. Lanham: University Press of America.
Woods, Oliver 2002. "Abraham Kuyper: God's renaissance man." *The Christian Statesman* (July/August).

2003

Anderson, Clifford B. 2003. "A canopy of grace: common and particular grace in Abraham Kuyper's theology of science." *The Princeton Seminary Bulletin* 24(1): 122–144.
Bacote, Vincent 2003. "Common grace and 'spiritual' stewardship: guidance for development?" *Princeton Seminary Bulletin* 24(1): 84–93.
Friesen, J. Glenn 2003. "The mystical Dooyeweerd once again: Kuyper's use of Franz von Baader." *Ars Disputandi* 3.
Harinck, George 2003. "Dinner speech at Second Kuyper Consultation on "Theology and economic life: exploring hidden links." Princeton Theological Seminary.
Pennings, Ray 2003. "Kuyper's sphere sovereignty and modern economic institutions." *Comment* (January).

2004

Bacote, Vincent 2004. "Gifts from father Abraham." *Comment* 22: 3 (April).
Balkenende, Jan Peter 2004. "Solid values for a better future." *The Princeton Seminary Bulletin* 25(2): 143–52.
Baskwell, Patrick 2004. "Kuyper and apartheid: a revisiting." *HTS Teologiese Studies/ Theological Studies* 64(2): 1269ff.
Beeke, Joel R. 2004. "The life and vision of Abraham Kuyper." *Christianity and Society* 14(1): 24–31.
Koekkoek, A. K. 2004. "Review of Luis E. Lugo (editor) *Religion, Pluralism, and Public Life.*" *Philosophia Reformata* 69(1): 102–104.
Lee, Francis Nigel 2004. "Abraham Kuyper and Islam." *Christianity and Society* 14(3): 9–12.
Lucas, Sean Michael 2004. "Southern-Fried Kuyper? Robert Lewis Dabney, Abraham Kuyper, and the limitations of public theology." *Westminster Theological Journal* 66(1): 179–201.
Perry, John 2004. "The weight of community: Alasdair MacIntyre, Abraham Kuyper, and the problem of public theology in a liberal society." *Calvin Theological Journal* 39(2): 303–331.
Schaap, James Calvin 2004. "A writing exercise in identity: Abraham Kuyper's 'To be near unto God.'" In *Celebrating the Vision: The Reformed Perspective of Dordt College*, edited by John Kok. Sioux Center: Dordt College Press, 39–45.
Sewell, Keith 2004. "Calvin and the stars, Kuyper and the fossils: some historiographical reflections." In *Celebrating the Vision: The Reformed Perspective of Dordt College*, edited by John Kok. Sioux Center: Dordt College Press, 265–283.
Vree, Jasper 2004. "The Marnix-Vereeniging: Abraham Kuyper's first national organisation (1868–89)." *Nederlands Archief voor Kerkgeschiedenis/ Dutch Review of Church History* 84(1–4): 388–475.
Wolterstorff, Nicholas. 2004. "Abraham Kuyper on Christian learning." In *Educating for Shalom: Essays on Christian Higher Education*. Grand Rapids: Eerdmans, 199–225.

2005

Bacote, Vincent 2005. *The Spirit in Public Theology: Appropriating the Legacy of Abraham Kuyper*. Grand Rapids: Baker Academic.

Bacote, Vincent 2005. "A neo-Kuyperian assist to the emergent Church." Paper presented at Covenant College.

Harinck, George 2005. "Abraham Kuyper's historical understanding and Reformed historiography." *Fides et Historia* 37 (Winter/Spring): 71–82.

Harman, Allan M. 2005. "Review of Kuyper's *Particular Grace*." *Reformed Theological Review*, 64(2): 99–100.

Harman, Allan M. 2005. "Review of Bolt's A *Free Church, A Holy Nation*." *Reformed Theological Review* 64(2): 99–100.

Lee, Francis Nigel 2005. 'The cross and the crescent – Abraham Kuyper: Islam revived." *The Counsel of Chalcedon* 3: 3–8.

Moore, T. M. 2005. "Abraham Kuyper and the Christian Cultural Consensus." *Reformation & Revival* 14(4): 57–79.

Van Til, Kent 2005. "Abraham Kuyper and Michael Walzer: the justice of the spheres." *Calvin Theological Journal* 40(2): 267–289.

Vree, Jasper and Zwaan, Johan (editors). 2005. *Abraham Kuyper's Commentatio (1860): The Young Kuyper about Calvin, a Lasco, and the Church*. Vol. 1: *Introduction, Annotations, Bibliography , and Indices*. Vol. 2: *Commentatio*. Brill's Series in Church History, 24. Leiden: Brill.

2006

Ables, Travis E. 2006. "Review of Bacote." *Reviews in Religion & Theology* 13(3): 376–379.

Anderson, Clifford Blake 2006. "Neocalvinis. . . . Abraham Kuyper? Maybe." *Comment* June: 53–57.

Bolt, John 2006. "Abraham Kuyper and the search for an evangelical public theology." In *Evangelicals in the Public Square: Four formative voices on political thought and action*, edited by J. Budziszewski. Grand Rapids: Eerdmans, 141–161.

Budziszewski, J. 2006. "Four shapers of evangelical political though." In *Evangelicals in the Public Square: Four formative voices on political thought and action*, edited by J. Budziszewski. Grand Rapids: Eerdmans, 55–72.

Carson-Thies, Stanley 2006. "Abraham Kuyper in the White House?: Why Dordt isn't so far from Washington, DC." *Pro Rege* 34(3): 11–17.

Chan, Alan L. 2006. "Review of *The Spirit in Public Theology: Appropriating the Legacy of Abraham Kuyper*." *Journal of Church & State* 48(2): 470.

Heslam, Peter 2006. "Abraham Kuyper." *New Dictionary of Apologetics*, edited by Campbell Campbell-Jack and Gavin J. McGrath. Leicester: IVP, 389–390.

Naylor, Wendy Fish 2006. "Abraham Kuyper and the emergence of neo-calvinist pluralism in the Dutch school struggle." *Doctoral dissertation*. University of Chicago.

Tuyl, Carl D. 2006. "Abraham Kuyper's Life of Faith." *Banner* 141 (January): 38.

Kloosterman, Nelson 2006. "Review of Vree and Zwaan (2005)." *Mid-America Journal of Theology* 17: 275–377.

Van Dyke, Harry 2006. "Kuyper the politician." Outline for a lecture in the Ethics class of Professor Max Stackhouse. Princeton Theological Seminary.

Wolterstorff, Nicholas 2006. "Abraham Kuyper." In *The Teachings of Modern Christianity: On Law, Politics, and Human Nature*, edited by John Witte Jr. and Frank Alexander. New York: Columbia University Press.

2007

Bratt, James. D. 2007. "Abraham Kuyper's Calvinism: society, economics, and empire in the late nineteenth century." In *Calvin Rediscovered: The Impact of His Social and Economic Thought*, edited by Edward Dommen and James Bratt. Westminster/ John Knox Press.

Bratt, James D. 2007. "Review of: *Abraham Kuyper's Commentatio (1860): The Young Kuyper about Calvin, a Lasco, and the Church*." *Church History and Religious Culture* 87(1): 130–132.

Dekker, Gerrard and Harnick, George 2007. "The position of the Church as institute in society: a comparison between Bonhoeffer and Kuyper." *The Princeton Seminary Bulletin* 28(1): 86–98.

Jeynes, W. H. and Naylor, Wendy 2007. "Government involvement in religious education: perspectives from Abraham Kuyper on school choice." *Religion & Education* 34(1): 76–97.

Kim, Ha Yong 2007. "The relevance of Abraham Kuyper's understanding of liberty as an antidote to authoritarianism in the Korean Protestant churches." *ThM*. Calvin Theological Seminary.

Moore, T. M. 2007. "Foundations for Christian cultural consensus." In *Cultural Matters: A Call for Cultural*

Consensus on Christian Cultural Engagement. Grand Rapids: Brazos, ch. 4.

Mouw, Richard J. 2007. "Mine! Kuyper for a new century." *Comment* 38(2): 58–64.

Mouw, Richard J. 2007. "Culture, church, and civil society: Kuyper for a new century." *The Princeton Seminary Bulletin* 28(1): 48–63.

Mouw, Richard J. 2007. "The postmodern maze: Abraham Kuyper reminds us that only Christ can bring wholeness to our fragmented age." *Christian History and Biography* 94: 36–38.

Van Drunen D. 2007. "Abraham Kuyper and the Reformed natural law and two kingdoms traditions." *Calvin Theological Journal* 42: 283–307.

2008

Anderson, Owen 2008. *Reason and Worldviews: Warfield, Kuyper, Van Til and Plantinga on the Clarity of General Revelation and Function of Apologetics.* Toronto: University Press of America.

Bacote, Vincent 2008. "Abraham Kuyper's rhetorical public theology with implications for faith and learning." *Christian Scholar's Review* 37(4): 407–425.

Beach, Mark J. 2008. "Abraham Kuyper, Herman Bavinck, and The Conclusions of Utrecht 1905." *Mid-America Journal of Theology* 19: 11–68.

Beer, R. 2008. "The Anti-Revolutionary vanguard: the padre cadre of the Anti-Revolutionary Party in the Netherlands, 1869–1888." *MPhil* History. Leiden University.

Bolt, John 2008. "A Kuyperian reflects on father Abraham and the 'Religious right.'" *Perspectives* (June/July).

Crowe, Don 2008. "Salt and light illustrated in history: Abraham Kuyper" *The Counsel of Chalcedon* 4: 8–11, 26–32.

Gaffin, Richard B. 2008. *God's Word in Servant Form: Abraham Kuyper and Herman Bavinck and the Doctrine of Scripture.* Reformed Academic Press.

Henderson, Roger 2008. "Kuyper's inch." *Pro Rege* 36(3): 12–14.

Harinck, George 2008. "Twin sisters with a changing character: how neo-Calvinists dealt with the modern discrepancy between Bible and natural sciences." *Nature and Scripture in the Abrahamic Religions: 1700–Present, Volume 2*, edited by Jitse M. Van Der Meer and Scott Mandelbrot. Leiden: Brill.

McGoldrick, James Edward 2008. "Claiming every inch: the worldview of Abraham Kuyper." In *A Christian Worldview.* Taylors, SC: Presbyterian Press.

Molendijk, Arie L. 2008. "Neo-Calvinist culture Protestantism. Abraham Kuyper's *Stone Lectures.*" *Church History and Religious Culture* 88: 235–250.

Molendijk, Arie L. 2008. "'Mine': The Rhetorics of Abraham Kuyper." *Journal for the History of Modern Theology/ Zeitschrift für Neuere Theologiegeschichte* 15(2): 248–262.

Van Til Kent A. 2008. "Not too much sovereignty for economics, please: Abraham Kuyper and mainstream economics." *Perspectives* (November).

Van Til Kent A. 2008. "Subsidiarity and sphere-sovereignty: a match made i. . . . ?." *Theological Studies* 69(3): 610–

Visser, Rob P. W. 2008. "Dutch Calvinists and Darwinism 1900–1960." *Nature and Scripture in the Abrahamic Religions: 1700–Present, Volume 2*, edited by Jitse M. Van Der Meer and Scott Mandelbrot. Leiden: Brill.

Wood, John Halsey, Jr. 2008. "Church, sacrament, and society: Abraham Kuyper's early baptismal theology, 1859–1874." *Journal of Reformed Theology* 2(3): 275–296.

2009

Bolt, John 2009. "All of life is worship? Abraham Kuyper and the neo-Kuyperians." In Kuyper, A. *Our Worship* (Calvin Institute of Christian Worship). Translated by Harry Boonstra. Grand Rapids: Eerdmans.

Boonstra, Harry 2009. "Introduction." In Kuyper, A. *Our Worship* (Calvin Institute of Christian Worship). Translated by Harry Boonstra. Grand Rapids: Eerdmans.

Covolo, Robert S. 2009. "Re-fashioning faith: the promise of a Kuyperian theology of fashion." *Cultural Encounters* 5(2): 41–62.

Engelsma, David J. (editor) 2009. *Always Reforming: Continuation of the Sixteenth-Century Reformation.* Jenison, MI: Reformed Free Publishing Association.

Hommes, J. 2009. "A Response to: 'The Kuyperian Vision for culture: what it is, and how is it doing?'" http://blog.cityreformed.org/.

McIlhenny R. 2009. "A Third-way reformed approach to Christ and culture: appropriating Kuyperian Neo-calvinism and the two kingdoms perspective." *Mid-America Journal of Theology* 20: 75–94.

Palmer, T. P. 2009. "The two-kingdom doctrine. A comparative study of Martin Luther and Abraham Kuyper." *Pro Rege* 37(3): 13–25.

Rouwendal Pieter L. 2009. "The Reformed dogmatics of Kersten compared with those of his older contemporaries, Abraham Kuyper and Herman Bavinck." *Puritan Reformed Journal* 1(2).

Snoke, David 2009. "The Kuyperian vision for culture: what is it, and how is it doing?" http://blog. cityreformed.org.

Spinks, Bryan D. 2009. "Abraham Kuyper on baptismal belief and practice." In Kuyper, A. *Our Worship* (Calvin Institute of Christian Worship). Translated by Harry Boonstra. Grand Rapids: Eerdmans.

Wainwright, Geoffrey 2009. "Abraham Kuyper: pioneering liturgist, Reformed dogmatician, Dutch aesthetician." In Abraham Kuyper, *Our Worship* (Calvin Institute of Christian Worship) translated by Harry Boonstra. Grand Rapids: Eerdmans.

Wolterstorff, Nicholas 2009. "Reflections on Kuyper's *Our Worship*." In Abraham Kuyper, *Our Worship* (Calvin Institute of Christian Worship) translated by Harry Boonstra. Grand Rapids: Eerdmans.

2010

Boer, Jan H. 2010. "Preface." In Kuyper, Abraham. *The Mystery of Islam*. Translated by Jan H. Boer. Christian Classics Ethereal Library.

Chen, Paul H. S. 2010. "Interest group politics within Kuyper's sphere sovereignty." Western Political Science Association 2010 Annual Meeting Paper.

Cooke, Clay 2010. "Kuyper the mystic: public piety and private life." *Comment*: 24–31.

Faber, Riemer 2010. "Abraham Kuyper's *Commentatio* (1860): The Young Kuyper about Calvin, Lasco, and the Church. Vol. 1: Introduction, Annotations, Bibliography, and Indices / Abraham Kuyper's "Commentatio" (1860): The Young Kuyper about Calvin, Lasco." [book review]." *Sixteenth Century Journal* Spring 41(1): 181.

Graham, Gordon (editor). 2010. *Kuyper Center Review 1. Politics, Religion and Sphere Sovereignty*. Grand Rapids: Eerdmans.
   Graham, Gordon 2010. "Editorial."
   O'Donovan, Oliver 2010. "Reflections on pluralism."
   Chaplin, Jonathan 2010. "The concept of 'civil society' and Christian social pluralism."
   Bratt, James 2010. "Sphere sovereignty among Kuyper's other political theories."
   Graham, Gordon 2010. "Kuyper and contemporary political philosophy."
   De Moor, Michael 2010. "Sphere sovereignty and the possibility of political friendship."
   Wood, John Halsey 2010. "Kuyper, covenant and secular society."
   Harinck, George 2010. "Neo-Calvinism and the welfare state."
   Foster, James 2010. "Sphere sovereignty: A reluctant friend of civil unions."
   Bowlin, James 2010. "Kuyper, tolerance and the virtues."
   De Vries, Rimmer 2010. "Kuyper on Islam."

Van der Kooi, Cornelis 2010. "The concept of culture in Abraham Kuyper, Herman Bavinck, and Karl Barth." In *Crossroad Discourses between Christianity and Culture*, edited by Jerald D. Gort, Henry Jansen, and Wessel Stoker. Amsterdam: Rodopi, 37–51.

Van Drunen, David 2010. "Calvin, Kuyper, and 'Christian Culture.'" In *Always Reformed: Essays in Honor of W. Robert Godfrey*, edited by R. Scott Clark and Joel E. Kim. Escondido: Westminster Seminary California.

Vos, David 2010. *Servants of the Kingdom: Professionalization among Ministers of the Nineteenth-Century Netherlands Reformed Church (Brill's Series in Church History)*. Leiden: Brill.

Wood, John Halsey, Jr. 2010. "Going Dutch in the modern age: Abraham Kuyper's struggle for a free church in the nineteenth-century Netherlands." *PhD Dissertation*. [To be published by Oxford University Press, 2013.]

2011

Baruch, Jeffrey A. 2011. "Abraham Kuyper's Calvinism and politics." *Journal of Christian Legal Thought*

(Spring): 9–10.

Bacote, Vincent 2011. "Introduction." In Kuyper, A. *Wisdom & Wonder: Common Grace in Science & Art.* Translated by Nelson Kloosterman. Grand Rapids: Christian's Library Press.

Bacote, Vincent 2011. "Considering a legacy." *Capital Commentary* (October).

Bowlin, John (editor). 2011. *The Kuyper Center Review: 2 Revelation and Common Grace.* Grand Rapids: Eerdmans.

Part I: Philosophy and revelation

Veenhof, Jan 2011. "Revelation and grace in Herman Bavinck."

Graham, Gordon 2011. "Bavinck, Nietzsche, and secularization."

Harinck, George 2011. "Why was Bavinck in need of a philosophy of revelation?"

Van den Belt, Henk 2011. "An alternative approach to apologetics."

Hocking, Jeffrey S. 2011. "The promise of Herman Bavinck's doctrine of revelation: theology beyond dogmatism and relativism."

Stanley, Jon 2011. "Restoration and renewal: the nature of grace in the theology of Herman Bavinck."

Eglinton, James 2011. "To be or to become – that is the question: locating the actualistic in Bavinck's ontology."

Mattson, Brian G. 2011. "Bavinck's 'revelation and the future': a centennial retrospective."

Part II: Common grace and common word

Batnitzky, Leora 2011. "Love and law: some thoughts on Judaism and Calvinism."

Emon, Anver M. 2011. "Sharia and the (em)brace of difference: from theology to law to identity politics."

Kaltwasser, Cambria Janae 2011. "Assessing the Christological foundation of Kuyper's doctrine of common grace."

Van Keulen, Dirk 2011. "From talking about to speaking with: the Reformed Churches in the Netherlands and Islam."

Dumler-Winckler, Emily 2011. "Common grace: a distinctive resource for 'A common word'."

Willson, Cory 2011. "*Simul Humanitas et Peccator*: the Talmud's contribution to a Dutch Reformed notion of the Imago Dei."

Eglinton, James 2011. "How many Herman Bavincks? *De Gemeene Genade* and the 'two Bavincks' hypothesis."

Harmon, Andrew M. 2011. "Common grace and pagan virtue: is Kuyperian tolerance possible?"

Covolo, Robert 2011. "Advancing a neo-Calvinist pneumatology of religions: the role of recent Yongian contributions."

Conradie, (editor) Ernst M. 2011. *Creation and Salvation: Dialogue of Abraham Kuyper's Legacy for Contemporary Ecotheology*, Leiden, Brill.

Conradie, Ernst. M. 2011. "Part 1: Abraham Kuyper's legacy for contemporary ecotheology: Some reflections from within the South African context."

1. Introduction: "How are they telling the story?"

2. Revisiting the reception of Kuyper in South Africa

3. General and special revelation: Kuyper, Bavinck and beyond

4. Creation and salvation: revisiting Kuyper's notion of common grace

5. Conclusion: Kuyper's significance for ecotheology and the need for further reflection on creation and salvation

Part 2: An Intercontinental dialogue

Anderson, Clifford 2011. "Kuyper in the civil sphere."

Bacote, Vincent 2011. "A response and a strategy."

Engdahl, Hans 2011. "Abraham Kuyper and F. J. M. Potgieter: Some Swedish-Lutheran perspectives."

Van Keulen, Dirk 2011. "Leads for ecotheology in Arnold A. van Ruler's work."

Van der Kooi, Kees 2011. "*Gratia non tollit naturam, sed perficit.*"

Myers, Benjamin 2011. "'Through him all things were made': creation, redemption, election."

Van Rooi, Leslie 2011. "The legacy of Abraham Kuyper and its impact on the theology and ecclesial identity of the URCSA: A church historical overview."

Thomas, Günter 2011. "Why reanimate a dead concept? Observations on promises and prospects of 'natural theology.'"

Conradie, Ernst M. 2011. "Rejoinder: Kuyper's significance for ecotheology and the need for further reflection on creation and salvation."

Edgar, William 2011. "The future of kuyperian answers." *Capital Commentary* (December).

Edgar, William and Oliphant, K. Scott (editors). 2011. "Abraham Kuyper." In *Christian Apologetics: A primary Source Reader (Vol. 2, From 1500)*. Crossway, ch. 13.

Harinck, George 2011. "Foreword: Being Public: On Abraham Kuyper and his publications." In Kuipers, Tjitze. 2011. *Abraham Kuyper: An Annotated Bibliography 1857–2010*. Leiden: Brill.

Kaemingk, Matthew (curator). 2011. *Comment* (July).

　　Mouw, Richard 2011. "Kuyper for Christians."

　　Bennett, Kyle David 2011. "Taking the game a little more seriously."

　　Liou, Jeff 2011. "Neither salad bowl, nor melting pot."

　　Yang, Edward 2011. "Art: a gift of God."

　　Whitney, William 2011. "'Pray more' is not counselling."

　　Kaemingk, Matthew 2011. "Faith, work, and beards: why Abraham Kuyper thinks we need all three."

　　Covolo, Bob 2011. "How Abraham Kuyper saved my GPA (Or, why college ministries need Kuyper)."

　　Willson, Cory 2011. "Learning proper manners for the religious roundtable: Kuyper and convicted civility."

　　Cooke, Clay 2011. "Evangelicalism and Neocalvinism: friends or enemies?"

Kuipers, Tjitze 2011. *Abraham Kuyper: An Annotated Bibliography 1857–2010*. Leiden: Brill.

Kuyper, A. 2011. *Wisdom and Wonder: Common Grace in Science & Art*, edited by Jordan J. Ballor and Stephen J. Grabill, translated by Nelson D. Kloosterman. Grand Rapids: Christian's Library Press.

Molendijk, Arie L. 2011. "'A Squeezed out lemon peel.' Abraham Kuyper on modernism." *Church History and Religious Culture* 91(3–4): 397–412.

Mouw, Richard J. 2011. *Abraham Kuyper: A Short and Personal Introduction*. Grand Rapids: Eerdmans.

Mouw, Richard J. 2011. *The Challenges of Cultural Discipleship: Essays in the Line of Abraham Kuyper*. Grand Rapids: Eerdmans.

Price, Timothy Shaun. 2011. "Abraham Kuyper and Herman Bavinck on the subject of education as seen in two public addresses." *The Bavinck Review* 2.

Van Dyke, Harry 2011. "Abraham Kuyper and the continuing social question" *Journal of Markets & Morality* 14(2): 641–646.

Wood, John Halsey, Jr. 2011. "Review of *Abraham Kuyper: A Short and Personal Introduction* by Richard Mouw." *Journal of Markets & Morality* 14(2): 587.

Wood, John Halsey, Jr. 2011. "Making Calvin modern: form and freedom in Abraham Kuyper's free church ecclesiology." In *John Calvin's Ecclesiology: Ecumenical Perspectives*, edited by Gerard Mannion and Eddy Van Der Borght. Continuum Press, ch 9.

2012

Bacote, Vincent 2012. "Abraham Kuyper." In *Cambridge Dictionary of Christian Theology*, edited by David Fergusson, Karen Kilby, and Iain Torrance. Cambridge: Cambridge University Press.

Bishop, Steve 2012. "Review of E. M. Conradie (editor) *Creation and Salvation*." *Philosophia Reformata* 77(1): 83–84.

McIlhenny, Ryan C., ed. 2012. *Kingdoms Apart: Engaging the Two Kingdoms Perspective*. Phillipsburg: Presbyterian & Reformed.

　　Skillen James W. 2012. "Foreword."

　　McIlhenny, Ryan C. 2012. "Introduction: In defense of neo-Calvinism."

　　Venema, Cornel 2012. "The restoration of all things to proper order: an assessment of the 'Two Kingdoms/natural law' interpretation of Calvin's public Theology."

　　Haas, Gene 2012. "Calvin, natural law, and the Two Kingdoms."

　　Kloosterman, Nelson "Natural law and the Two Kingdoms in the thought of Herman Bavinck."

　　De Graaf, S. G. 2012. [Translated with Foreword by Nelson Kloosterman] "Christ and the magistrate" and "Church and state."

Scheuers, Timothy R. 2012. "Dual citizenship, dual ethic? Evaluating the Two Kingdoms perspective on the Christian in culture."

Wood, John Halsey, Jr. 2012. "Theologian of the revolution: Abraham Kuyper's radical proposal for church and state."

Parler, Branson 2012. "Two cities or Two Kingdoms? The importance of the ultimate in Reformed social thought."

Swanson, Scott A. 2012. "How does 'Thy kingdom come' before the End? Theology of the present and future kingdom in the book of Revelation."

Lief, Jason 2012. "Eschatology, creation, and practical reason: A reformational interpretation of the Two Kingdoms perspective."

McIlhenny, Ryan C. 2012. "Christian witness as redeemed culture."

Naylor, Wendy 2012. "School choice and religious liberty in the Netherlands: reconsidering the Dutch school struggle and the Influence of Abraham Kuyper in its resolution." In *International Handbooks of Protestant Education* International Handbooks of Religion and Education, Volume 6, Part 2, ch 12, 245–274.

O'Donnell III, Laurence R. 2012. "Review of *Abraham Kuyper: A Short and Personal Introduction* by Richard J. Mouw." *Calvin Theological Journal* 47(1): 162–63.

Summers, Stephanie 2012. "Review of Mouw *Abraham Kuyper.*" *PRISM Magazine* (Jan/Feb) 19(1): 44.

Van Vliet, Jan 2012. "Abraham Kuyper's *Wisdom and Wonder.* a review essay." *Pro Rege* 41(1) (September): 16-23.

Venema, Cornelis P. 2012. "One kingdom or two? An evaluation of the 'two kingdoms' doctrine as an alternative to neo-Calvinism." *Mid-America Journal of Theology* 23: 75–128.

Alphabetical List for the Bibliography

Ables, Travis E. (2006)
Abrams, Elliott (2000)
Adonis, J. C. (1999)
Ambler, Rex (1967)
Anderson, C. B. (2003)
Anderson, C. B. (2006)
Anderson, C. B. (2011)
Anderson, Owen (2008)
Bacote, Vincent (1997)
Bacote, Vincent (2002)
Bacote, Vincent (2003)
Bacote, Vincent (2004)
Bacote, Vincent (2005)
Bacote, Vincent (2005)
Bacote, Vincent (2008)
Bacote, Vincent (2011)
Bacote, Vincent (2011)
Bacote, Vincent (2012)
Bailey, Greg (2002)
Balkenende, Jan P. (2004)
Baruch, Jeffrey A. (2011)
Baskwell, Patrick (2004)
Batnitzky, Leora (2011)
Beach, Mark (2008)
Beeke, Joel (2002)
Beeke, Joel R. (2004)
Beer, R. (2008)
Beets, Henry (1902)
Beets, Henry (1904)
Beets, Henry (1907)
Beets, Henry (1920)
Beets, Henry (1920)
Beets, Henry (1920)
Beets, Henry (1921)
Beets, Henry (1921)
Beets, Henry (1925)
Begbie, Jeremy (1989)
Begbie, Jeremy (1991)
Bennett, Kyle D. (2011)
Berends, Bill (2002)
Berkhof, Louis (1937)
Bishop, Steve (2012)
Boer, J. (1991)
Boer, J. (2010)
Bolt, J. (1999)
Bolt, John (1981)
Bolt, John (1996)
Bolt, John (1998)
Bolt, John (1999)
Bolt, John (1998)
Bolt, John (2000)
Bolt, John (2000)

Bolt, John (2001)
Bolt, John (2001)
Bolt, John (2002)
Bolt, John (2006)
Bolt, John (2008)
Bolt, John (2009)
Boonstra, Harry (2009)
Botha, M. Elaine (2000)
Botman, Russell H. (2000)
Bouma, Clarence (1937)
Bouma, Clarence (1937)
Bowlin, James (2011)
Bowlin, John (2011)
Bratt, James D. (1987)
Bratt, James D. (1987)
Bratt, James D. (1987)
Bratt, James D. (1987)
Bratt, James D. (1991)
Bratt, James D. (1992)
Bratt, James D. (1996)
Bratt, James D. (1996)
Bratt, James D. (1996)
Bratt, James D. (1996)
Bratt, James D. (1997)
Bratt, James D. (1999)
Bratt, James D. (2000)
Bratt, James D. (2002)
Bratt, James D. (2007)
Bratt, James D. (2007)
Bratt, James D. (2010)
Brinkman, M. E. (1999)
Brinks, Herb (1980)
Brinks, Herb (1981)
Budziszewski, J. (2006)
Campbell-Jack, W. C. (1992)
Cammenga, R. L. (1998)
Carpenter, Joel (1981)
Carson-Thies, S. (2006)
Chan, A. L. (2006)
Chaplin, Jonathan (1995)
Chaplin, Jonathan (2010)
Chen, Paul (2010)
Chung, S. K. (2010)
Conradie, Ernst (2011)
Conradie, Ernst (2011)
Conradie, Ernst (ed.) (2011)
Cooke, Clay (2010)
Cooke, Clay (2011)
Covolo, Bob (2011)
Covolo, Robert S. (2009)
Covolo, Robert S. (2011)
Crowe, Don (2008)

Darling, Timothy G. (1901)
De Bruijn, J. (1999)
De Bruijn, Jan (200)
De Graaf, S. G. (2012)
De Gaay Fortman, W. F. (1973)
De Jong Peter Y. (1987)
De Jong, James (1981)
De Jong, James A. (1986)
De Jong, James A. (1981)
De Jong, Peter (1966)
De Jong, Peter (1972)
De Jong, Peter (1986)
De Jong, Peter Y. (1973)
De Jong, Peter Y. (1987)
De Moor, Henry (1988)
De Savornin Lohman, Witsius H.
   (1898)
De Vries, John H. (1998)
Deenick, J. W. (1984)
Dekker, Gerrard and George
   Harnick. (2007)
DeMoor, Michael (2010)
DeVries, Rimmer (2011)
Dooyeweerd, H. (1982)
Duk, Kwang (1999)
Dumler-Winckler, E. (2011)
Dunahoo, C. (1998)
Durand, J. (1988)
Dykstra, Russell J. (1998)
Edgar, William (1998)
Edgar, W. (2011)
Edgar, W. and Oliphant, K. S.
   (eds) (2011)
Eglinton, James (2011)
Eglinton, James (2011)
Elazar, Daniel J. (2000)
Emon, Anver M. (2011)
Engdahl, Hans (2011)
Engelsma, David (1998)
Engelsma, David J. (1998)
Engelsma, David (ed.) (1998)
Engelsma, David (ed.) (2009)
Ericson, Edward E. (1987)
Faber, J. (1970)
Faber, Riemer (2000)
Fernhout, Harry (1975)
Fernhout, Harry (1978)
Foster, James (2010)
Friesen, J. Glenn (2003)
Gaffin, Richard B. (1982)
Gaffin, Richard B. (2008)
Godfrey, W. R. (1991)

Godfrey, W. R. (1995)
Goudzwaard, B. (2000)
Goudzwaard, B. (2002)
Gousmett, C. (1984)
Graham, Gordon (2010)
Graham, Gordon (2010)
Graham, Gordon (2011)
Griffioen, Sander (2002)
Haas, Gene (1998)
Haas, Gene (2012)
Hall, David W. (1998)
Hall, David W. (2002)
Hall, David (2002)
Hanko, Herman C. (1998)
Hans-Martien ten Napel (1999)
Harinck, George (1998)
Harinck, George (1999)
Harinck, George (2000)
Harinck, George (2001)
Harinck, George (2002)
Harinck, George (2002)
Harinck, George (2003)
Harinck, George (2005)
Harinck, George (2008)
Harinck, George (2010)
Harinck, George (2011)
Harnick, G. and Krabbendam, H. (eds) (1996)
Harman, Allan M. (2005)
Harman, Allan M. (2005)
Harmon, Andrew M. (2011)
Harris, Harriett (2000)
Henderson, R. D. (1992)
Henderson, R. D. (2008)
Hendrik de Vries, J. (1931)
Heslam, Peter S. (1989)
Heslam, Peter S. (1991)
Heslam, Peter S. (1993)
Heslam, Peter S. (1998)
Heslam, Peter S. (1998)
Heslam, Peter S. (1999)
Heslam, Peter S. (1999)
Heslam, Peter S. (2000)
Heslam, Peter S. (2002)
Heslam, Peter S. (2006)
Hexham, Irving (1983)
Hexham, Irving (1984)
Hexham, Irving (1988)
Hiemstra, J. L. (1993)
Hocking, Jeffrey S. (2011)
Hoekema, A. A. (1961)
Hoekzema, Ray (2001)
Hommes, J. (2009)
Hulst, John B. (1899)
Inagaki, Hisakazu (1999)

Jansen, John F. (1980)
Jellema, Dirk J. (1980)
Jellema, Dirk J. (1981)
Jellema, Dirk J. (1981)
Jellema, Dirk J. (1981)
Jellema, Dirk J. (1981)
Jellema, Dirk J. (1981)
Jellema, Dirk W. (1950)
Jellema, Dirk W. (1950)
Jellema, Dirk W. (1957)
Jellema, Dirk W. (1958)
Jellema, Dirk W. (1965)
Jellema, Dirk W. (1980)
Jellema, Dirk W. (1980)
Jellema, Dirk W. (1980)
Jeynes, W. H. and Naylor, W. (2007)
Kaemingk, M. (2011)
Kaemingk, M. (ed.) (2011)
Kaltwasser, Janae (2011)
Kamps, Marvin (1998)
Kennedy, James C. (2002)
Kooi, C. (2010)
Kim, Ha Yong (2007)
Kim, Juan Ok (2000)
Klapwijk, J. (1991)
Kloosterman, N. (2001)
Kloosterman, N. (2012)
Knight, I. (1999)
Kobes, Wayne A. (1993)
Koekkoek, A. K. (2004)
Kolfhaus, Wilhelm (1930)
Koole, Kenneth (1998)
Koyzis, David T. (2002)
Kromminga, D. H. (1937)
Kuiper, D. Th. (1999)
Kuiper, Henry J. (1937)
Kuiper, Henry J. (1937)
Kuiper, Henry J. (1959)
Kuiper, Henry J. (1959)
Kuiper, Henry J. (1959)
Kuiper, Henry J. (1959)
Kuipers, Tjitze (2011)
Kuyper, L. J. (1939)
Kuntz, J. J. (2001)
Kuyper, A. (2011)
Kuyper, C. M. E. (1960)
Langley, M. R. (1971)
Langley, M. R. (1979)
Langley, M. R. (1979)
Langley, M. R. (1981)
Langley, M. R. (1988)
Langley, M. R. (1999)
Langley, M. R. (1984)
Langley, M. R. (1995)

Langley, M. R. (1998)
Langley, M. R. (1998)
Langley, M. R. (1998)
Langley, M. R. (2001)
Laning, James L. (1998)
Lazarus, S. (1998)
Lee, Francis Nigel (1980)
Lee, Francis Nigel (2004)
Lee, Francis Nigel (2005)
Lief, Jason (2012)
Liou, Jeff (2011)
Lloyd Jones, D. M. (1976)
Lucas, Sean M. (2004)
Lugo, Louis E. (1996)
Lugo, Louis E. (2000)
Mattson, Brian G. (2011)
Maynard, Roy (1998)
McCarthy, Mark (2000)
McCarthy, R. J. (1980)
McCarthy, R. J. (1980)
McCarthy, R. J. (1980)
McCarthy, R. J. (1981)
McConnel Timothy I. (2002)
McGoldrick, J. E. (1994)
McGoldrick, J. E. (2000)
McGoldrick, J. E. (2008)
McIlhenny R. (2009)
McIlhenny, Ryan C. (2012)
Mennega, Aaldert (1968)
Mennega, Aaldert (1971)
Menninga, Clarence (1998)
Miller, Glenn T. (1999)
Miller, Glenn T. (1999)
Minton, Henry Colin (1898)
Molendijk, Arie L. (2008)
Molendijk, Arie L. (2008)
Molendijk, Arie L. (2011)
Monsma, S. (1992)
Monsma, T. M. (1982)
Moore, T. M. (2005)
Moore, T. M. (2007)
Morbey, Michael M. (1988)
Mouw, Richard J. (1980)
Mouw, Richard J. (1998)
Mouw, Richard J. (1980)
Mouw, Richard J. (1980)
Mouw, Richard J. (1998)
Mouw, Richard J. (2000)
Mouw, Richard J. (2007)
Mouw, Richard J. (2007)
Mouw, Richard J. (2007)
Mouw, Richard J. (2011)
Mouw, Richard J. (2011)
Mouw, Richard J. (2011)
Myers, Benjamin (2011)

Naugle, David (2001)
Naylor, Wendy F. (2006)
Naylor, Wendy F. (2012)
Nichols, Anthony H. (1973)
Nichols, Anthony H. (1975)
Noll, Mark A. (2002)
Noll, Mark A. (2002)
Noteboom, J. W. (1937)
Novak, Michael (2002)
O'Donovan, Oliver (2010)
Palmer, T. P. (2009)
Palmer, Timothy P. (2008)
Paris, Peter J. (2000)
Parler, Branson (2012)
Peck, John (1999)
Pennings, Ray (2003)
Perry, John (2004)
Petcher, Donald N. (1996)
Praamsma, Louis (1985)
Praamsma, Louis (1986)
Price, Timothy S. (2011)
Pronk, C. (1987)
Pronk, C. (1995)
Puchinger, G. (1998)
Pulliam, Russ (2002)
Ratzsch, Del (1992)
Rogers, R. E. L. (1992)
Rooy, Sidney H. (1956)
Rouwendal, P. L. (2009)
Rullmann, J. C. (1950)
Runia, K. (1962)
Schaap, James C. (2004)
Scheuers, Timothy R. (2012)
Schoffer, I. (1987)
Schrotenboer, Paul G. (1988)
Seel, D. J. Jr. (1981)
Sewell, Keith. (2004)
Sherda, Z. J. (1930)
Sherda, Z. J. (1930)
Sherda, Z. J. (1930)
Sherratt, Timothy (1999)
Sigmund, Paul (2000)
Skillen, James (1988)
Skillen, James (2001)
Skillen, James. (2002)
Skillen, James W. (1972)
Skillen, James W. (1980)
Skillen, James W. (2000)
Skillen, James W. (2012)
Smit, Harvey Albert (1998)
Smit, Kobus (1988)
Smit, Kobus (1999)
Snoke, David (2009)
Son Bong, H. (1999)
Spinks, B. (2009)

Spykman, G. (1980)
Spykman, G. (1980)
Spykman, G. (1980)
Spykman, G. (1980)
Spykman, G. (1981)
Sproul, R. C. (2002)
Sproul Jr., R. C. (2002)
Stanley, Jon (2011)
Star, Ring (972)
Stob, George (1950)
Stockwell, Clinton (1998)
Stockwell, Clinton (2001)
Storkey, Paul E. (2000)
Strauss, D. F. M. (1999)
Strauss, Gideon (1998)
Strauss, Gideon (1998)
Strauss, Gideon (1998)
Strauss, Gideon (1999)
Strauss, P. J. (1999)
Strauss, Piet J. (1995)
Strevel, Chris (2002)
Sturm, Johan and Miedema, Siebren (1999)
Summers, S. (2012)
Swanson, Scott A. (2012)
Tangelder, J. D. (1984)
Tangelder, J. D. (1996)
Tangelder, J. D. (2000)
Tanis, Edward J. (1921)
Tanis, Edward J. (1937)
Tanis, Edward J. (1937)
Terpstra, Charles J. (1998)
Thangaraj, Thomas M. (2000)
Thomas, Geoffrey (1998)
Thomas, Günter (2011)
Tuyl, Carl D. (2006)
Van de Streek, Hillie J. (1998)
Van den Belt, Henk (2010)
Van den Belt, Henk (2011)
Van den Brink, Gijsbert (1999)
Van der Kooi, C. (1999)
Van der Kooi, Cees and de Bruijn, Jan (eds) (1999)
Van der Kooi, Kees (2011)
Van der Kroef, Justus M. (1948)
Van der Schee, Willem (1999)
Van der Vyver, Johan D. (2002)
Van der Walt, B. J. (1998)
Van der Walt, B. J. (1999)
Van Dyke, Harry (1988)
Van Dyke, Harry (1998)
Van Dyke, Harry (1998)
Van Dyke, Harry (1998)
Van Dyke, Harry (1998)
Van Dyke, Harry (1998)
Van Dyke, Harry (1998)

Van Dyke, Harry (2006)
Van Dyke, Harry (2011)
Van Egmond, A. (1999)
Van Geest, Fred (2001)
Van Keulen, Dirk (1999)
Van Keulen, Dirk (2011)
Van Keulen, Dirk (2011)
Van Klinken, G. J. (1999)
Van Leeuwen, M. S. (1996)
Van Leeuwen, M. S. (2000)
Van Leeuwen, M. S. (2000)
Van Lonkhuyzen, J. (1921)
Van Rooi, Leslie (2011)
Van Schouwen, C. J. (1982)
Van Til, Cornelius (1947)
Van Til, Cornelius (1937)
Van Til, Kent (2005)
Van Til Kent A. (2008)
Van Til, Henry R. (1959)
Van Til, Nick (1981)
Van Woudenberg, R. (1999)
Vanden Berg, F. (1937)
Vanden Berg, F. (1940)
Vanden Berg, F. (1960)
Vanden Berge, E. (1898)
Vander Goot, Henry (1983)
Vander Hart, M. D. (1986)
Vander Kam, Henry (1986)
Vander Stelt, John (1969)
Vander Stelt, John (1973)
Vander Weele, S. J. (1980)
Vander Weele, S. J. (1981)
Vander Werff, P. H. (1978)
Vander Werff, P. H. (1979)
Van Drunen D. (2002)
Van Drunen D. (2007)
Van Drunen, D. (2010)
Veenhof, Jan (2011)
Velema, Willem H. (1988)
Venema, C. P. (1999)
Venema, C. P. (1999)
Venema, C. P. (2002)
Venema, C. P. (1998)
Venema, C. P. (1999)
Venema, C. P. (2000)
Venema, C. P. (2012)
Venema, C. P. (2012)
Visser, Rob (2008)
Vogel, L. (1937)
Volbeda, Samuel (1937)
Vollenhoven, D. H. Th. (2002)
Vorster, J. M. (2001)
Vos, D. (2001)
Voskuil, Louis J. (1980)
Vree, J. (1999)

Vree, J. (2000)
Vree, J. (2004)
Vree, J. and Zwaan, J. (eds)
    (2005)
Wainwright, G. (2009)
Warfield, B. B. (1899)
Warfield, B. B. (1900)
Welker, Michael (2000)
Westendorp, John (2001)
Westra, John (1972)
Whitney, William (2011)
Willson, Cory (2011)

Willson, Cory (2011)
Wilson, Douglas (2002)
Wintle, Michael J. (1987)
Witt, Cornelius (1961)
Witte, John Jr. (2000)
Witte, John Jr. (1999)
Woldring, Henk E. S. (2000)
Woldring, Henk E.S. (1999)
Wolterstorff, N. (1999)
Wolterstorff, N. (2002)
Wolterstorff, N. (2004)
Wolterstorff, N. (2006)

Wolterstorff, N. (2009)
Wood, John Halsey Jr. (2008)
Wood, John Halsey Jr. (2010)
Wood, John Halsey Jr. (2011)
Wood, John Halsey Jr. (2011)
Wood, John Halsey Jr. (2012)
Woods, Oliver (2002)
Yang, Edward (2011)
Zondergeld, Gjalt R. (1999)
Zuidema, S. U. (1972)
Zwaanstra, Henry (1974)

Contributors

Vincent Bacote is Associate Professor of Theology and the Director of the Center for Applied Christian Ethics at Wheaton College in Wheaton, IL. He is author of *The Spirit in Public Theology: Appropriating the Legacy of Abraham Kuyper* (2005)

Steve Bishop maintains the neo-Calvinist website www.allofliferedeemed.co.uk, and lectures at the City of Bristol College, Bristol, UK. He is the co-author of *The Earth is the Lord's* (1990). Steve thanks Richard Russell and Mark Roques for first introducing him to Abraham Kuyper.

James D. Bratt is Professor of History at Calvin College and coeditor of *Perspectives: A Journal of Reformed Thought and* author of *Abraham Kuyper: Modern Calvinist, Christian Democrat* (2013).

Robert S. Covolo is a doctoral student in theology and culture at Fuller Theological Seminary.

Herman Dooyeweerd (1894–1977) was one of the pioneers of the school of "the philosophy of the cosmonomic principle." He was Professor of Law at the VU University Amsterdam.

Edward E. Ericson, Jr. is emeritus Professor of English at Calvin College. He is co-author of *The Soul and Barbed Wire: An Introduction to Solzhenitsyn* (2008).

Chris Gousmett is Corporate Information Manager at Hutt City Council, New Zealand. He has a PhD in Patristic theology from the University of Otago, New Zealand.

George Harinck is Professor of History at the VU University Amsterdam and Theological University Kampen, Director of the Archives and Documentation Center of the Reformed Churches, Kampen, and of the Historical Documentation Center for Dutch Protestantism at the VU University Amsterdam.

Roger D. Henderson is an independent researcher based in the Netherlands.

Peter S. Heslam is Director of Transforming Business, a multi-disciplinary research and development project on enterprise solutions to poverty at Cambridge University. He is author of *Creating a Christian Worldview* (1988).

John H. Kok is Professor of Philosophy, Dean for Research and Scholarship, and the Director of the Andreas Center for Reformed Scholarship and Service at Dordt College.

Jacob Klapwijk is emeritus Professor of Modern and Systematic Philosophy at the VU Amsterdam.

Catherine M. E. Kuyper (1876–1955) was the daughter of Abraham Kuyper.

McKendree R. Langley (1945–2005) lectured at Westminster Theological Seminary in Philadelphia. He is the author of *The Practice of Political Spirituality* (1984).

Timothy I. McConnel was Assistant Professor of Theology at Dordt College from 2001–2004.

James Edward McGoldrick is retired Professor of History from Cedarville University and currently teaches part-time in the Greenville Presbyterian Theological Seminary Dr. McGoldrick is ordained in the Presbyterian Church in America and is author of *God's Renaissance Man* (2000).

Clarence Menninga was the first Professor of Geology at Calvin College, Grand Rapids, USA.

Timothy P. Palmer is Professor of Theology at the Theological College of Northern Nigeria (TCNN), Bukuru, Nigeria.

Del Ratzsch is Professor of Philosophy, Calvin College, Grand Rapids, USA.

Timothy Sherratt is Professor of Political Science, Gordon College, Wenham, USA.

James Skillen is the former President of the Center for Public Justice and is author of numerous books on politics.

Daniël F. M. Strauss is a research associate in Philosophy at the University of the Free State. He was the first director of the Dooyeweerd Center for Christian Philosophy.

Hillie J. van de Streek is Director of the Center for Reformational Philosophy, Amersfoort, The Netherlands. She is also secretary general of the EPP Women, Brussels, European Union.

Harry Van Dyke is Professor Emeritus in History at Redeemer University College in Ancaster, Ontario, and Director of the Dooyeweerd Center for Christian Philosophy.

Mary Stewart Van Leeuwen is Professor of Philosophy and Department Chair at Eastern University, St Davids, Pennsylvania.

Cornelius P. Venema is President of the Mid-America Reformed Seminary, Dyer, Indiana.

D. H. Th. Vollenhoven (1892–1978) was Professor of Philosophy at the VU University, Amsterdam.

Michael R. Wagenman is the Christian Reformed Chaplain and Director of the Kuyper Centre for Emerging Scholars at the University of Western Ontario.

S. U. Zuidema (1906–1975) was a Professor of Philosophy at the VU University, Amsterdam.

CPSIA information can be obtained
at www.ICGtesting.com
Printed in the USA
FFOW031707040413
1068FF

9 780932 914965